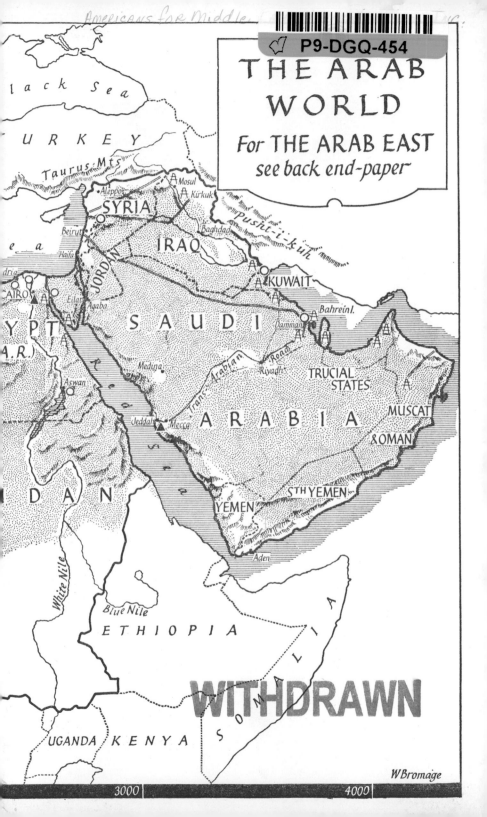

EGYPT

The Crucible

By the same author

NEW WORLD ARISING:
A Journey through the New Nations
of South-East Asia

ENGLAND IS RICH

THE NEW LOOK:
A Social History
of the Forties and Fifties
in Britain

EGYPT

The Crucible

THE UNFINISHED REVOLUTION
IN THE ARAB WORLD

Harry Hopkins

*Illustrated with Maps
and Photographs*

Houghton Mifflin Company Boston

To My Wife

A well-known Conservative statesman in conversation with me once gave utterance to an opinion which involves the *ne plus ultra* of anti-conservative principles. 'The East,' he said, 'is languishing for want of a Revolution.' This statement is true; for the violent changes . . . which Oriental history has frequently recorded have generally been the result not of revolution but of palace intrigue.

Earl of Cromer
Modern Egypt (1908)

CONTENTS

MAPS

LIST OF ILLUSTRATIONS

PICTURE CREDITS

AND ACKNOWLEDGEMENTS

Farouk and Nahas Pasha, the Revolution Command Council,
Nasser, Neguib and Dulles, and Nasser, Khruschev, Aref and
Sallal: *Keystone Press Agency*. Nasser as student, Mahmoud
Yunis, Dr Stino, Dr Sidky, Mohamed Hassenein Heikal, Ali
Sayed Ali, Ahmed Fahim, Anwar Salama, and Khaled Mohieddin: *Al Ahram* (Cairo). Om Kolthoum: *L'Orient* (Beirut). The
remainder of the pictures are by the author, with the exception
of the portraits of Sidky Soleiman, Sayed Marei and Dr Kaissouny, the photograph of the National Assembly, the 'Pillars'
cartoon and the scene from *The Tree Climber*. The author
wishes to express his thanks to the Egyptian Embassy, London,
the State Information Department, and the newspapers *Al
Ahram*, *Akhbar El Yom*, and *L'Orient* for help in assembling
the illustrations.

INTRODUCTION

THE DISTORTING LENS

In recent years relations between the West—at least as represented by America and Britain—and the Arab world have ranged from the bad to the calamitous, reaching their nadir in the summer months of 1967 when, with communications almost totally cut, the Arabs vilified much of the West, and the West applauded the Israelis' battering of the Arabs in a manner which suggested that anti-Semitism, denied its former outlet, had quickly found a substitute.

And yet the new régime which seized power in Egypt in 1952, and which was to open a new chapter in the relations of the Arabs and the West, had been well disposed towards the Americans and had made its peace with the British. The Americans commended themselves to it by their anti-colonialism, by their educational efforts in the Middle East over many years, by their famous 'know-how', and while the British were inevitably tarred with the Imperialist brush here too there were many solid and long-standing relationships which might have been expected to bear fruit now that the Occupation was being wound up at last.

What then went wrong?

A great many things went wrong, but not the least of them was that so many people in Britain and America were quite certain they knew what they were. The single answer was 'the machinations of Nasser.' It was comprehensive, emotionally satisfying, and conclusive, and for well over a decade a very large part of the news from the Middle East was formed in this mould. If the material proved intractable it tended to be discarded or to be tucked away obscurely. In this way the striking achievements of the Egyptian Revolution have gone largely unrecorded; a crucial historical development, the emergence of a new sort of society in the Middle East, has hardly been noticed. It was not 'news' as Middle Eastern news was conceived.

Furthermore, the British public, as the popular saying goes 'did not want to know.'

Some of the reasons for this will emerge in the course of this book; but the distorting lens through which we view the Arab world is complex and many-faceted. Some of its elements are as old as the Crusades; some are very new. For more than a century and a half the West has been in the habit of seeing the Middle East as the arena of Great Power conflict, the juncture of Spheres of Influence. In the world of newly independent Arab states it still finds it hard to see peoples for pacts and bases. Again, the script of Arabic is beautiful, but, to the West, opaque; the Islamic idiom with its high emotional charge requires not so much to be translated as, like electricity, to be transformed for consumption in the prosaic and alien West. In times past a long line of French and British Arabists opened for us a small breach in this high Arabic wall. But today the very brilliance of these men obscures as much as illuminates. For those in the Burton-Doughty-Philby tradition may lovingly interpret the wisdom of the desert sheikh, but are likely to have little but contempt for the politically-minded trade-unionist clerk; it would be interesting to know what the fastidious 'Lawrence of Arabia' would have made of Gamal Abdel Nasser.

In the 1950s in Britain there were, of course, more obvious reasons for a highly jaundiced view of the Arab world. The extraordinary speed with which the edifice of Empire had collapsed had left many bewildered, resentful, or simply unbelieving. It was 'Suez' which tore away the last shreds of illusion, stripping Britain naked to the world—and it was Nasser who (it seemed) had encompassed Suez, and who now, with intolerable haste and effrontery, was seeking to step into Britain's shoes in the Middle East. In the same period, the Americans, newly come to global responsibility, and eager to welcome the Arabs into 'the Free World,' experienced in Egypt the full shock of that rude ingratitude to which the old Imperialists had long been inured, if scarcely reconciled.

The mortification of peoples who suffered these experiences was not to be assuaged by impersonal explanations in terms of major movements in the tides of world history. A scapegoat was needed—and one was ready to hand in the person of Gamal Abdel Nasser. In the West he was built up into a tower-

ing 'Dictator' figure of such supernatural malignancy that almost every unwelcome event over the vast area of the Arab
world—and even beyond it—was without hesitation attributed
to a 'Nasser Plot.' Nasser was seen as creating, for his own
power-seeking purposes, almost unaided, the vast revolutionary
movement sweeping the Arab world, rather than as express-
ing or canalising it.

Established governments rarely welcome foreign revolutions, unless they happen to serve their interests. Yet, in the
West, in the normal way, idealistic revolutionary régimes have
generally been able to count on some friendly liberals, ready to
join with them in saluting their new dawn. For the Egyptian
Revolution even this source has largely failed. The sympathies
of those who might have been expected to back Arab Socialism in its attack on Levantine capitalism and Islamic obscurantism had been pre-empted in this region of the world by
the pioneering socialism of the early Zionists and the admirable practical Utopianism of the kibbutz. The British Labour
Party, in particular, had old links with the Zionist Labour
Party, and readily accepted its view of Israelis as 'the progressive social forces' ranged against feudal, backward and
reactionary Arabs.

Of all the elements in the multiple distorting lens it has been
this, the Zionist element, which has most dangerously nar-
rowed the field of vision. For it is the peculiar nature of the
Arab and Zionist 'cases' that they form opposite faces of a
single coin : if one is visible, the other is eclipsed. Seen through
Zionist eyes Israel is the tiny outpost of civilisation and tolerance, besieged by fanatic and politically-exploited hordes intent on her destruction. Seen through Arab eyes, Israel becomes
a 'bridgehead' in which builds up an ever-growing force of
invaders, lavishly financed from the West, and liable, at any
moment, to erupt again. As the Arabs see it the Zionists, in
seeking to establish a *Jewish* state in their midst are 'racists';
as the Jews see it, the Arabs are 'racists' for resisting them.
According to the Jews, they have no alternative but to fight
for their existence; according to the Palestinians they have no
alternative but to fight for their existence. To the Jews, the
Arab-Israeli war of 1956 was a continuation of the 'War of
Independence'; to the Arabs, it is 'the Tripartite Aggression.'

The Israelis tell you incessantly that they only wish to live at peace with their neighbours, but the Arabs tell you incessantly that 'Zionism is aggression in itself.'

Since 1948 when Britain resigned the Mandate, and with it, her responsibility for the Palestine Arabs, it is the Zionist side of the coin which has generally been uppermost in America and Britain alike. And the reason for this is not that both cases have been carefully considered and a verdict arrived at. The Arab case in its modern form has largely gone by default, whereas the Zionist case has been tirelessly propagated in the West for half a century by one of the most extensive, entrenched and sophisticated organisations of persuasion the world has ever seen. Furthermore, in a world living still in the long shadow of the Nazi gas chambers, accusations of 'anti-Semitism,' freely employed, have understandably proved effective in silencing any thorough-going criticism of Israeli conduct. The result has been that the Western world in the 'sixties has been continuously reminded of Arab rhetoric about the 'elimination' of Israel, a holy war and so on, but has remained largely unaware of that Israeli 'expansionism' which is the other side of the coin of 'eliminationism'—even though this expansionism is a matter of simple, consistent and recent historical fact.

The concern of this book is Egypt and the Arab revolution, but it is a misfortune of the Western writer on this subject today that he cannot proceed without at least attempting to open a line of sight through the tangled undergrowth of the Arab-Israeli affair. For unless he does so—and even if he does so—the reader's whole approach to the people and developments described is likely to be violently prejudiced. It is vital that what might be called the grammar of the Arab-Israeli imbroglio should be understood at the outset. Fortunately, it is by no means as obscure as it is sometimes made out to be.

'Land,' writes Walter Schwarz, in his careful study, *The Arabs in Israel*, 'was what the Palestine war was about. In the Zionist idea return to the land was synonymous with return to Israel. . . . It was equally precious to the Arabs.' In 1947, after complaining of the Mandatory Power's restrictions on land sales to Jews, Mr David Ben Gurion told the United Nations Special Committee on Palestine that 'the Arabs own

94 per cent of the land, the Jews only 6 per cent.' This was an overall average, and as such a little misleading; but even in the Palestine sub-district of greatest Jewish ownership, around Tel Aviv, Jewish land-ownership only reached 39 per cent. The great bulk of the land was owned by Arabs, and, in 1947, most of it was worked by its proprietors in small holdings. Four-fifths of the land of Israel as established within the 1948-9 borders—and two-thirds of the cultivated area—consisted of former Arab lands.

They are Arab no longer. Yet this land was never transferred by any international treaty or agreement. It was not, in general, sold by its Arab owners. It was, as the Israeli term goes, 'abandoned.' But even those 140,000 Arabs who did not flee from Israel and 'abandon' their land lost something like half their land by one form of expropriation or another.

The United Nations Partition Plan, passed by the General Assembly after a two-month debate in November 1947, and the only legal basis for the state of Israel, did not provide for transfer either of population or of land; on the contrary, it insisted on fundamental laws for the protection of the large minorities, one point specifically dealing with the protection of property. It provided for a Jewish state of 5,500 square miles (compared with the 8,000 which emerged from the 1948-9 war) with a Jewish population of around 500,000 and an Arab population of around 400,000, interlocked in economic union with the Arab state which was to have had Jerusalem—as an enclave under U.N. trusteeship—at its centre. It gave the Arab state a strip of the northern coast from Acre and of the southern coast from what is now the new Israeli port of Ashdod southwards.

It is true that the Arabs rejected this plan outright, whereas the Jews accepted it. We can only guess at the Zionist motives in accepting it, but it is hard to see how their leaders could ever have accepted the implied restrictions on that absolute Jewish sovereignty—what Mr Ben Gurion called 'the sovereign power of the Hebrews'—on which they have so often and ardently insisted. The matter was never fully put to the test, because when the new state came into being in May the Arab states in effect declared war on it, invaded, from three sides, and were defeated.

The Arab case has suffered heavily ever since from the impression created by this ineffectual action. For the notion, now common in the West, that the Arabs, the primary-aggressors, thus launched the Arab-Jewish hostilities is true only in the most limited sense. What they did was to make official and governmental—and somewhat extend—a war which had long been raging, and which was the reality determining everything else, including the United Nations partition decision.

In the full perspective—which is essential—this war is most truly seen as what Israel's Prime Minister, Mr Levi Eshkol, recently called 'the Battle of Numbers.' It was a long battle, sometimes silent, often frenzied and bloody, always bitter and continuing, but it gained its objective: it converted the 84,000 Palestinian Jews of 1922 (11 per cent of Palestine's population) into the 650,000 (or 35 per cent) in 1948—a number sufficient to gain sovereign control of most of Palestine, there to create the Jewish State. It was a process of escalation, extending over almost half a century, unique in history, patient, controlled, indomitable. It may be said to have been launched—and its method marked out—with the careful selection of the equivocal phrase 'national home for the Jewish people,' an acceptable screen behind which determined preparations for the Jewish State could go ahead.[1] From the first the Jewish authorities in Palestine, in fact, acted like—in the Zionist phrase—'the state-on-the-way'; and from the first the Arabs resisted them and the Jewish waves of immigration which they saw as invasion.[2] Whether the approach of the Zionists was that of the gradualist colonisers, with the slogan 'donum after donum, goat after goat,' or of the militants with the slogan 'In blood and fire did Judea fall, and in blood and fire will Judea rise again,' to the Palestinian Arabs—not unaware of the somewhat sweeping

---

[1] Actually adopted in 1897, its originator explaining 'It was equivocal, but we all knew what it meant' (Christopher Sykes, *Crossroads to Israel*, London, 1965). Weizmann wished for '*the* national home' in the Balfour Note: it was reduced to 'a national home' because of opposition by anti-Zionist Anglo-Jewry, notably the Cabinet Minister, Edwin Montagu.

[2] An agreement between Dr Weizmann (for the Zionists) and Feisal, signed in 1919, provided for Jewish immigration into Palestine and settlement on the land. But it was strictly conditional on the Arabs obtaining their 'independence as demanded,' i.e. this Zion would have been within the context of an independent Arab Greater Syria. The failure to achieve this obviously transformed the situation and nullified the agreement.

promise of the Lord in Genesis XV—the threat appeared very
much the same. Nor was this remarkable when Arab fellahin
found themselves evicted from land a few big Arab landowners
sold to the Jews, nor when the leases of the new great proprietor, the Jewish National Fund, dedicated to gaining land 'as the
perpetual and inalienable property of the Jewish people,' stated
that no non-Jewish labour might be employed; nor when the
great Jewish trade union federation, Histadruth, a prime source
of employment, did not accept Arab members.[3]

The Arab Palestinians resisted the advance of the Zionist
state-within-a-state by every means they knew. But on every
count save numbers, they were hopelessly outclassed. The
British, striving to reconcile the irreconcilable—or at least
ambivalent—undertakings of the Balfourian Mandate, sought
by Jewish immigration quotas, and in other ways, to hold
the communal balance, to frustrate a Zionist take-over. But
Governments and High Commissioners came and went; what
did not change was the Zionist will to victory, powerfully
reinforced from the 1930s by Hitler's persecution of German
Jewry. In the event, the Arabs had the desperate experience
of looking on, in furious and bloody impotence, while British
power held the ring, and step by step over a quarter of a
century their worst expectations were confirmed. But while
British power had effectively prevented Palestinian self-determination in the 1920s, it had nevertheless served as a certain
protection for the weakness of the Arabs. Much battered by
both sides, the British Mandatory had, in effect, refereed the
'war of numbers.' But by 1945 even that dubious protection
was about to be withdrawn.

This final, triumphant, phase of the Zionist struggle to
realise a Jewish State in Palestine really opens with the British
White Paper of 1939 which set a final term to Jewish immigration, after which entry was to be so regulated as to keep
the Jewish population around its existing level of one-third
of the total population. After twenty years of equivocation,
this was the 'final' showdown : 'a national home for the Jewish
people' did not, after all, mean (as Churchill had solemnly

[3] Histadruth's policy was not changed until 1953, when Arabs were permitted to join—but with separate Arab labour exchanges. Full membership
did not come until 1960.

assured the Arabs in 1921 it did not mean) a Jewish State; the Balfour Declaration's reservation that 'nothing shall be done which may prejudice the civil and religious rights of the existing non-Jewish communities' apparently still retained some meaning. The fact that the White Paper had been wrung from the British Government by the Arab rebellion in Palestine and the approach of war with Germany did not lessen its validity. Palestine is a small and 'exceedingly poor' (UNSCOP) country and, academic arguments about absorptive capacity notwithstanding, it was obvious that an unlimited Jewish influx—which was what the Zionists required—backed by all the resources of world Jewry, would end in the dispossession of the Arab peasantry. A Jewish tragedy in Germany could in no wise justify an Arab tragedy in Palestine—except to those practising the Nazi variety of moral arithmetic.

The Zionists, however, treated the White Paper as an act of war by Britain, and only refrained from immediately proceeding on this assumption because of the existence of the other war, with Nazi Germany. Massive illegal immigration was, however, at once set on foot. The secret arming of Haganah, the Jewish Defence Force, had been going on for years against just such a moment. In 1942 a Zionist conference, meeting at the Biltmore Hotel in New York, passed unopposed, at the urging of Mr Ben Gurion, a resolution demanding that 'the gates of Palestine be opened, that the Jewish Agency be vested with control of immigration . . . and that Palestine be established as a Jewish Commonwealth.' From 1943 Irgun Tsvai Leumi, the Jewish terror organisation, resumed its acts of outrage (the Stern Gang had never stopped them) temporarily suspended on the outbreak of the German war, and by the summer of 1947, greatly increased in numbers and prestige, had thoroughly undermined law and order in Palestine. In October 1945 Ben Gurion had himself sent a secret cable to the leaders of Haganah instructing them to take the offensive against the British Mandatory, to set up Jewish settlements in forbidden zones, to step up illegal immigration yet further, to sabotage and attack police and military installations. 'Since the beginning of 1945,' ran the British memorandum to the United Nations in July 1947, 'the Jewish community has implicitly claimed this right of political terrorism and has been supported by an organised commission of lawlessness, murder and sabotage, their contention being that, whatever other interests might be served, nothing should be allowed to stand in the way of the Jewish State.'

By November, 1947, when the members of the U.N. General Assembly voted on the Partition Plan, they faced a situation in which British control in Palestine was manifestly collapsing, and in which the outstanding fact was Jewish organised, armed power. Some delegates explained that they voted for Partition not so much from any sense of justice as in recognition of a *fait accompli,* choosing the least evil. Their vote recognised, in effect, the Zionist victory in the long 'war of numbers.' But to the Arabs it seemed that a verdict gained by force must be overthrown by force. On the very day of the vote, Arab bands attacked some Jewish travellers, killing several. The Arabs declared a three-day strike; fighting between Arabs and Jews flared up in many places. In Cairo, the sheikhs of El Azhar called for a *jihad;* the Arab League declared that the U.N. vote 'violates the rights of nations to self-determination . . . people who are strangers to Palestine, coming from different parts of the world, are taking away from the Arabs by all means in their power Arab lands and sources of existence.' Early in 1948 a few thousand Arab irregulars from Syria and Iraq entered north Palestine; to the south a band of Muslim Brethren from Egypt raided and ambushed; the racial war of reprisal and counter-reprisal was resumed. But now the British were no longer a primary target; they no longer controlled the contest; they were leaving. The determining factor now was that the Zionists, so long the 'state-within-a-state,' were organised; the Arabs were not. Well before the Arab states launched their invasion in May, the Zionist forces had taken over a string of Arab towns and villages, some in Israel-to-be, some in the new Arab-state-to-be, and scores of thousands of Arabs, often suitably encouraged, were in flight.

As a result the Zionists had by 1949 achieved an Israel over 40 per cent larger than provided for by the U.N. plan, containing most of the best land in Palestine, all the ports, and the modern city of Jerusalem. Did Israel, rejoicing at this good fortune, thereupon set out to make a serious effort to conciliate and reassure the confused, embittered, and utterly defeated

Arabs? Did she now fulfil the role of the 'little country only desiring to be allowed to live at peace with her neighbours?'

The reader seeking an honest answer really need look no further than the collected speeches of David Ben Gurion, the creator of modern Israel, and the archetypal Zionist. The proclamation of the state of Israel began 'By virtue of our natural and historic rights,' and only after that continued 'and by the resolution of the General Assembly'; and at an early date Mr Ben Gurion, the author of the proclamation, is to be found congratulating himself on not having specified in it any defined frontiers for the new state. In the 1952 Government Year Book, he writes: 'I add now that it [the State] has been established in only a portion of the Land of Israel. Some are hesitant at the restoration of our historical frontiers, fixed and set from the beginning of time, but even they will hardly deny the anomaly of the new lines. . . .'

Always a basic element in political Zionism, this appeal to 'historic rights,' resumed after an effective lapse of well over two thousand years, seems to have grown rather than diminished with the years. In 1956, Ben Gurion, who described Sinai as 'the cradle of the race,' is to be found telling the Knesset that one of Israel's objectives in the Sinai campaign was 'to free part of the fatherland which is still in foreign hands.' Eleven years later, after the advance of 1967, we find the Socialist Minister of Labour, Mr Yigal Allon, declaring that the Golan Heights in Syria (although over the Jordan) are 'no less a part of Israel than Hebron and Nablus [in Jordan West Bank] for did not Jephthah rule there?'; we find General Dayan insisting that 'people abroad must realise . . . that the mountain range west of the Jordan [and in Jordan] lies at the heart of Jewish history,' and Premier Levi Eshkol insisting that the world must likewise understand the historical reasons why Israel must possess Jerusalem.

Language of this kind can scarcely convince the Arabs of peaceful intentions. In the meantime that 'Ingathering of the Exiles' which is 'the cardinal aim of our state' (Ben Gurion) has been pushed ahead with such vigour that the Jewish population of Israel more than trebled in the twenty years after 1947 —the newcomers moving into the places vacated by the Arabs. This 'dynamism' is rightly saluted as an essential part of the

Zionist process. On 9 June 1967, on the very morrow of the
Arab defeat, with streams of Arab refugees once again in
flight, this time across the Jordan, we find the Israeli Ambassador in London publicly calling for another million Jews to go
to Israel. Other Israeli spokesmen did not limit themselves to
so modest a figure. On June 11, 1968, Mr Levi Eshkol appealed
once again to Jews everywhere to help Israel 'win the battle of
numbers.'

Spiritual messianism is one thing; messianism translated into
political and territorial terms in a country as poor and small
as Palestine—in the sensitive heart of the Arab world—is something manifestly very different. For by its nature it can acknowledge no limits.

This is written not to attack Zionism, but merely in the hope
of being able to rectify a little the more persistent distortions
of the lens through which we have lately been in the habit of
seeing the Arab world. For is it really self-evident that of the
two alternative stereotypes for Israel we are offered—'the
beleaguered outpost' and the 'invasion bridgehead'—the 'beleaguered outpost' contains all the truth?

Yet this is the side of the coin which has been uppermost,
and the result has been much comment of an extraordinary
moral obliquity which has deepened Arab despair and desperation. It is, for instance, repeatedly argued—often in the same
breath—that the desire of the Jews to 'return' from thousands
of miles away to a land their ancestors—or symbolic ancestors
(although in fact today requiring the stimulation of a massive
—occupied more than two thousand years ago is mandatory
propaganda machine) while the desire of poor Palestinian
peasants to go back to their farms a few miles away which
their families have often cultivated for hundreds of years and
from which they fled only recently is somehow artificial, and
would hardly exist were it not sustained for wicked political
purposes.

The only inference to be drawn from such double standards
—and it would be easy to multiply instances—is that Arabs
are not people. The massive indifference displayed by the
West in the long aftermath of the 1967 war strongly suggests
that such a notion is indeed entertained.

In September 1968 the American Presidential candidate, Mr

Richard Nixon, said that the balance of military power in the Middle East should be kept tipped in Israel's favour against the combined power of all the Arab nations. At this time, as a result of her pre-emptive strike of June 1967 and the over-whelming technical superiority then demonstrated, Israel was in occupation of large areas of Egypt, Jordan and Syria. The barren hillsides of Jordan were littered with the tents of 300,000 new refugees whom Israel again refused to allow to return to their land and homes. In defiance of repeated resolu-tions by both the U.N. General Assembly and the Security Council, Israel had officially annexed all Jerusalem. Ten months after the Security Council had unanimously passed its resolu-tion requiring, among other things, Israel's withdrawal from the occupied lands, she had not accepted the resolution and was merely demanding direct negotiations with the defeated Arabs. America, explained Mr Nixon, 'supports Israel because we believe in the self-determination of nations . . . we oppose aggression in every form . . . and because her example offers a long-range hope to the Middle East.'

Similar views were expressed by other Presidential candi-dates. Yet how oddly they must have read to any Arab. But with the distorting lens in position the Arab world that is visible has little or no relation to the Arab world seen by the ninety million non-Jewish people who happen to live there. With the lens in position the vast constructive efforts that have been made by, for instance, Egypt to meet the formid-able challenge of poverty and over-population—efforts gravely set back by the Israeli attack—become wholly invisible. Whereas millions of enthusiastic words are lavished on Israel's very costly 'miracles in the desert,' Egypt's tremend-ous efforts—and achievements—in desert reclamation, if noticed at all, are most likely to figure as *folies de grandeur*. And so on.

It may be, however, that we are now approaching a new phase. Both Arab and Zionist revolutions have had their apoca-lyptic moments and have emerged, so to speak, in the hard workaday world on the other side. Having all but completed their long withdrawals, the old Imperialist powers may at last be able to approach the peoples of the Arab world on a some-what more normal footing. And between the Super-Powers, the

U.S.A. and the U.S.S.R. whose ideological and power struggle has formed yet another facet of the distorting lens, there is also at least a measure of *détente.*

It may be that a moment of historic opportunity is approaching when it will be possible for the West at last to come to terms with the Arab world. But it can only be with the new Arab world, not with the 'romantic' old one; only with the Arab world that is, and will be, not with that the West would like it to be. We need to be ready for this moment; we need to discard our old distorting lenses, however formed, and take a new, long look. It is, of course, entirely possible that in this exercise we shall receive no assistance from the Arabs—who have distorting lenses, also very complex, of their own. That need not deter us. It has been pointed out—from the East to the West—that it is both wiser and more practicable to remove the beam from one's own eye before going on to work on the mote in one's neighbour's.

The aim of this book is to offer the ordinary reader in the Western street some of the material to begin such a reappraisal. It seeks to present an intelligible picture of the confused and tumultuous movement of people and ideas which—with Egypt as its epicentre—is today transforming the Arab world. Since only thus will it be possible to make sense of it, the picture will on occasion be presented from the Arab point of view. This does not imply, of course, that this view is wholly endorsed. Self-absorption, the single view, is to be expected of young revolutions and emergent nations; but in old, developed, and world-ranging ones, it is both inexcusable and disastrous.

The concern of this book is the years of transition, the years in which the keys of the Arab world's future were being formed. The political game of 'ins' and 'outs' is played with as much zest (if with slightly different methods) in the East as in the West, although in both the same faces have a way of recurring. But the importance of the figures in the book is as representatives—of their moment in history, of their class, region, ideology, and rôle in the grand processes of change of which they are a part. Since these processes of change are still under way, it would be vain to attempt a definitive view. Thus, no attempt is made to 'revise,' say, the Egyptian euphoria of 1964 in the light of the dismay of mid-1967, or of any other, transitory, moment in history. This is, rather, a stage-by-stage account of a long and complicated human journey, in unfamiliar country. We can trace its beginnings, chart the directions taken, read the signposts ahead—but we cannot know the end. In other words, if the account begins as History, it shortly changes into something less grand, but more exciting, history-in-the-making, taking on the overlapping perspectives, the multiple, interlocking planes, of a Braque painting. For the author, as for the painter, it is nevertheless perhaps permissible to hope that under scrutiny a certain solidity may emerge.

Note: Diacritical marks have been omitted from transliterations of Arabic names, and the forms most recognisable to the general reader preferred.

PART ONE

THE LAST FLOOD

I do not know why I always imagine that in this region in which we live there is a rôle wandering aimlessly about seeking an actor to play it. I do not know why this rôle, tired of roaming about in this vast region, should at last settle down, weary and worn out, on our frontiers, beckoning us to move, to dress up for it, and to perform it, since there is nobody else who can do so.

—Gamal Abdel Nasser, *The Philosophy of the Revolution*, Cairo, 1954

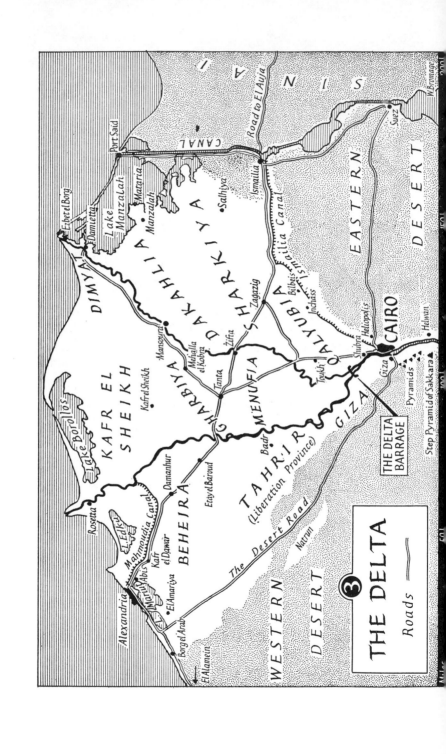

THE DELTA

Roads ═══

I

THE VIEW FROM ASWAN

Men, women and children of Egypt: the miracle has been wrought. You have built the Dam.

—Gamal Abdel Nasser, 14 May 1965

In Upper Egypt these days the wonders of the ancient world and the wonders of our modern age rub shoulders. From the steps of the Kalabsha Temple, its huge stone blocks transported forty miles downstream and painstakingly re-erected high and dry on a lofty spur above the Nile, tourists can now look out over the listless waters of Lake Nasser, the man-made sea that stretches back between the granite for more than three hundred miles, far into the Sudan. The kingdom of Nubia lies lost beneath it. As the waters rise and swell behind the Dam the old Nubian villages crumble and moulder, the decorated plates—souvenirs of service in Cairo—once bravely embedded in their walls slip deeper into the Nile silt. Twice already in this century some of those villages have moved higher on their cliff-sides at successive British heightenings of the old Aswan Dam; now *Sadd el-Aali*, Egypt's own, claims all: behind it the waters close over millenia of human history.

Southward from the Kalabsha Temple the scene is desolate, warming to primeval life only in the evenings when the dark whalebacks of the granite boulders flush rose-red in the setting sun. But northwards the scene springs to life—although at this height the sound that trickles up is muffled and diffused. A thick wedge of sand lies athwart the river. It is *Sadd el-Aali*, the High Dam. From this distance it looks absurdly simple, an anti-climax. But descend the road that winds steeply down to the site and you are enveloped in a very different sort of solitude; you are lost in the organised, earth-shaking chaos of a great civil engineering project. Monstrous dump trucks, belching black smoke, charge endlessly along the serpentine roads, some loaded with granite rocks, others with sand. The roaring procession has continued for more than five years: for the

appetite of *Sadd el-Aali* is huge. The earth lies raw and torn
and the great boulders throw out heat like ovens. There is, in
the scene under this stabbing sun, more than a hint of Genesis
Chapter One.

And that is as it should be, for it is not only the landscape
of Nubia that is being re-made here; the High Dam re-moulds
the geography of Egypt also, breaking a pattern of Nature that
has shaped and confined the life of the Nile Valley for thousands of years.

For if vastly bountiful, the Nile is also extreme. Its flow
fluctuates greatly not only over the months, but also between
years. Its discharge in spring averages a twentieth of that in
the summer months of Flood. A year of 'high Nile' might mean
disastrous inundation; a year of 'low Nile'—when less than
half the seasonal flow comes down from the Ethiopian mountains—deepened the people's impoverishment.

For more than a century in modern times successive barrages and dams have been directed towards disciplining the
Nile. But even after the completion of the second heightening
of the Aswan Dam in 1933, on the average two-fifths of the
Nile's flow still escaped in the Flood, unused, to the sea. Now,
with the High Dam, this rock-and-earth stopper in the granite
neck of the Nile Valley, eight hundred miles from the Mediterranean, this time-honoured process of harnessing the Nile
enters a new stage. The reservoir it creates, Lake Nasser, is vast
enough to store water not merely over the twelve-month, but
down the years.

Egypt is delivered at last from the bondage of the 'lean years'
and the 'fat years.' With the water saved one and a quarter
million acres of land can be added to the six million cultivated
before the High Dam; a further 900,000 acres will produce
three crops a year instead of only one or two, and more valuable crops, such as rice and sugar-cane, can be grown. In a
country so close-penned by desert these are spectacular gains,
but what really offers hope of a breakout is the fact that henceforth the 'gift of the Nile' will be not merely fertilising water,
but power; the great river, on its way to the fields, will generate in the High Dam power station ten thousand million
kwh of cheap electricity a year, trebling Egypt's 1964 power
supply, already multiplied by the opening of the country's

first hydro-electric station beside the old Aswan Dam in 1960.

The quickening touch of the High Dam can be felt through-out the length and breadth of Valley and Delta. But it is no-where more dramatically evident than in Aswan itself, the little 'frontier' town beside the first cataract, which is now the power house of the New Egypt, the anteroom of an in-dustrial revolution. Dr Hilmy, who came up here in 1955 to open up the iron-ore mines, recalls that when he and his staff went to work in the early morning they were continually being stopped by the police who were convinced they must be burglars. 'I used to call it "the Dead City",' he said. It was a place living on its memories of the great days of Thomas Cook, of wintering Edwardian valetudinarians and gentle lady water-colourists in solar topees. For Egyptian officials, it was the limbo to which the Cairo 'Ins' of the moment were accustomed to banish the incompetent—or inconvenient.

Now Aswan works around the clock: out by the Dam the desert blazes with light through the night. In five years, since the work on the Dam seriously started in 1960, the population has grown from 30,000 to 150,000. Attracted by the high pay, workers have been drawn here from every part of Egypt; one Delta factory sent up a sightseeing party only to find to its chagrin that it did not return. By the end of 1962 there were 12,000 labourers at the dam site, together with 1,200 Egyptian technicians and 300 engineers; by 1964, when the first phase of the work was completed, and President Nasser and Khruschev pressed the button that turned the Nile from its course, the number of site workers had grown to 35,000. A large part of the town is new: smart new tourist hotels and air-conditioned workers' flat-blocks are everywhere. Suddenly, this remote little place is in the middle of the contemporary world: tourists and technologists rub shoulders on its Nile Corniche.

A party of American tourists, disembarking from King Farouk's old yacht, the *Khassed Kheir*, now tied up at the bank, passes a group of Russians, waiting at a bus-stop lettered in Cyrillic. The Russian husbands look so solid, so uncompromisingly proletarian and out of place in this exotic setting, that one's heart goes out to them. The families have been on a shopping expedition and now wait for the bus that will take them to their apartment blocks in 'Sahara City' on the other side of the Dam.

The High Dam Authority buses are grey-green and carry an electric flash symbol. They share the streets with the blue buses of the State tourist organisation, the buses of the Iron Mines company, the grey buses of KIMA which run out to yet another of Aswan's self-contained, air-conditioned technological kingdoms—a welfare world of apartment blocks (57 piastres[1] monthly for 3 rooms), free clubs, cinemas, swimming pool. In other ways, too, KIMA, which is the chemical fertiliser plant, offers a stimulating foretaste of the New Egypt that starts from Aswan. Using French, German and British equipment and the power output of four of the nine turbines of the new hydro-electric station on the old Dam, it conjures from water, air and local limestone one million poundsworth of ammonium nitrate a month to feed the fields of Egypt. With the High Dam's power fully tapped, it will almost double this.

Probably the Russians have been shopping at Omar Effendi, Aswan's smart new (1963) four-storey department store, complete with espresso bars, self-service grocery and roof-top café from which flies Omar Effendi's houseflag with the three interlocked circles of Co-operation—one of the most familiar symbols of this new Egypt. In fact, however, this is not a co-operative, but a branch of a Government-owned store chain and the apple of the eye of Egypt's American-educated Minister of Supply, Dr Kamel Ramzy Stino.[2] Dr Stino would undoubtedly view with benevolent approval the two ladies, heavily shrouded in the black draperies of Upper Egypt, who are currently gazing excitedly at Omar Effendi's window display of kitchen equipment while a protective husband or brother hovers behind. In the flow of Arabic one catches the word 'grille.' The ladies are clearly eager apprentices to Egypt's incipient consumer society, and, although the display may be a trifle wooden, the cornucopia that awaits them on the four

[1] About 11 shillings, post-British-devaluation. There are 100 piastres to the Egyptian pound, and at the official rate of exchange £1·04 sterling equals £E1. The Egyptian pound is, however, worth very much less than this on the free, or black, market.

[2] From 1959 to September 1966. In October 1968 he was elected to the Arab Socialist Union's ten-member Higher Executive Committee.

floors within is—for Upper Egypt—astonishing enough. It ranges from Egyptian-made television sets (there is a service in Aswan) to Czechoslovak pottery, from Hungarian Trappist cheese to the alarm clocks, toy dolphins and hockey knee-pads of the People's Republic of China. But it is in the Book Department that the Russians come into their own with row after row of translations from the Russian, from the *Diseases of the Ear, Nose and Throat* to the *Life of Tolstoy* or a well-illustrated primer from the 'Soviet Children's Library' boldly entitled *What is Good and What is Bad*:

> If a boy is clean and neat,
> Washes every day,
> He's a lad we love to meet—
> He is good, we say.

A block away on the Corniche stands another instalment of the new Egyptian Way of Life, a striking white building built around a courtyard with ornamental water. Inspired by a Yugoslav model, it is the Palace of Culture, the first in Egypt and the progenitor of a good many others. It is both excellently equipped and well used. Despite the glass-and-neon gloss, ordinary workers and fellahin go in and out as if the place belonged to them. Both the cinema hall and the rows of chairs in front of the television are full. There is a children's reading room, an adult library of 10,000 volumes (including many translations of British and American authors as well as techni-cal works) and two foreign-language teaching rooms. In the music rooms on the ground floor a group of Nubians—workers at KIMA and on the High Dam—are rehearsing 'folklorique' song-and-dance to the music of *hud* and *tambour*. They are lithe, natural dancers, obviously in their element. The first song is modern. Composed by a High Dam telephone operator who is at the rehearsal, it is 'about the High Dam and the benefits it will bring.' The second number, traditional, with a refrain and a handclap, is, I was told, 'about a lover who wishes to leave all other people and go with his love outside.'

All indeed was sweetness and light until, going out, one passed the fine girls' secondary school and observed, painted on its white wall. a giant soldier's jackboot, stamping on the

Star of David hemmed in by the flags of all the Arab nations.

Aswan is something of a showplace; its themes are the chosen themes. Yet an engineering undertaking as vast and ramified as the High Dam has its own brisk logic, reshaping life around it. A ponderous and grossly inflated bureaucracy was—and is—one of the most deep-seated of the plagues of Egypt. It is an endemic defect of Oriental societies which Westernisation merely enriched, adding, in Egypt, the ever-circulating file to the ever-full divan,[3] and, considerably later, the permissible Coca-Cola to the ritual Turkish coffee, sweet, unsugared, or *masbood*. Thus, at the beginning, bureaucratic rigidity and centralisation—in Russia as well as Egypt—bogged down the High Dam project. But the stakes were high : failure to complete on schedule would wreck the Revolution's national plan. The man who got the project moving, Mr Sidky Suleiman, made Minister for the High Dam in 1962, could scarcely be accused of bureaucratic remoteness. He lived and worked for much of the time almost literally on top of the job in a tall office block erected on a waste of sand on the West Bank of the Nile, overlooking the Dam. The green baize door to his room was about his only concession to Departmental tradi-tion : beyond it the Minister sat in his shirt-sleeves, surrounded by plans and blueprints, a quiet man, utterly matter-of-fact, without pretension. He is, in fact, a soldier, a former lieuten-ant-colonel in that Engineering Corps which was to prove a major source of strength to the régime, bridging over the gaps events opened up and keeping the Revolution a going concern.

Brought down from Aswan to Cairo to take over the Prime Ministership in 1966, Sidky Suleiman is, indeed, in some ways typical of that small but growing body of men who are mak-ing the New Egypt. Lower-middle-class in origins, with roots in rural Egypt, he also personifies two other critical features of the revolutionary régime in its early days—the army mystique or freemasonry and the army technician's approach. Born in the Delta village where his father had a few feddans

---

[3] The capacious article of furniture which, eternally crowded with sup-pliants, lines every Ministerial anteroom. By derivation, and in old Oriental use, *divan* means 'council' or 'council-chamber.' Literally translated, the Egyptian office Arabic for 'Are you busy?' is still 'Are you full?'

of land, he found a modern career in the army and was director of a military factory when the Revolution came. Although he took no part in it, he knew Nasser well, and in 1954 was recruited to the National Production Council which the Junta had almost immediately established. They had very quickly seized on the High Dam scheme, which had been unsuccessfully hawked around the Ministries since 1948 by its originator, an Egyptian-born Greek agriculturalist named Daninos. Sidky Suleiman participated in the meetings of the committee of international hydrological experts summoned to pronounce on the scheme. Later he was to step in as chief of the State Nasr Company for Export and Import; and again, as Manager of the Economic Development Organisation.

'Yes,' said Sidky Suleiman, eyes shining, 'that was a very interesting time. There were many problems and we learned much.' But he remained reticent, almost shy—very unlike the normal exuberant Egyptian. And in this, too, he seemed to resemble a lot of the régime's best army work-horses, particularly the engineers among them, self-contained professionals, quietly getting on with the job that had been assigned to them. These are the men Egypt needs, but it is not, as yet, over-burdened with them.

The brave themes of Aswan culminate in the High Dam, *Sadd el-Aali*, the shining star of innumerable popular songs, focus of pilgrimage for endless parties of workers—trips financed on factory profit-sharing—from all over Egypt. Few modern structures have attracted to themselves such a weight of symbolism as this great dyke of rock and sand. Not only was it the keystone of the Revolution's grand design for a new Egypt, but it also celebrated that revolution's hardly less unique moment of world triumph. For it was Dulles's deliberately punitive withdrawal of the American High Dam loan in an attempt to dictate Egyptian foreign policy that precipitated the nationalisation of the Suez Canal, which revitalised the Arab Revolution, allied it to the Asian Revolution and 'Third World,' and demonstrated that the famous 'vacuum in the Middle East,' which had been pre-occupying the Great Powers since the decay of the Ottoman Empire, might conceivably yet be filled by the people who lived there. To *Sadd el-*

Aali's pilgrims, the liberation promised was not only economic but also spiritual; it was not the Nile alone that had been diverted here, but also the ignoble course of history.

In early 1953, when the High Dam was first seriously planned, the Arab World was still in essentials a world which Miss Gertrude Bell or any of that great camel-riding generation of British Arabists would have had little difficulty in recognising. In Amman, young King Hussein, lately returned from Harrow and Sandhurst, had acceded to the throne of a Jordan where the *Pax Britannica* was paternally maintained by Glubb Pasha, the Arab Legion and the British subsidy. In Baghdad, Hussein's uncle, the Regent, Crown Prince Abdul Illah, and the perennial Nuri es-Said managed a sheikhly Parliament with the adeptness of long practice; restored to their palace by the British Forces after the uprising of 1940, the position of the Iraqi Hashemites still rested ultimately on the 'invisible' buttress of the British Embassy and the R.A.F. at Habbaniya. Less pretentiously, the Hashemite's tribal enemy, old Ibn Saud, still travelled his primitive kingdom, flinging bagsful of gold to loyal tribesmen. Of late multiplying oil millions had made it more difficult for him to discipline his own prodigious princely brood, and if the thief's hand was still struck off, Aramco doctors might now be permitted to anaesthetise and dress the stump. No such 'progress' had, however, yet broken in on Yemen, a medieval theocracy, isolated from the outer world, a whimsical tyranny doubtfully tempered by assassination. The Gulf remained the preserve of the British Political Officers, encouraging 'enlightened' sheikhs, rebuking—and, if necessary, deposing—'bad' ones.

The vast Arab West was still 'French North-West Africa.' In Morocco, the disobedient nationalist sultan, Mohamed V, had just been exiled; Algeria was—and looked—a Department of France; and Tunisia's Neo-Destour[4] leader, Bourguiba, was still in exile. French was the official language. In Cairo, a young Algerian rebel named Ben Bella, lately escaped from prison at Blida, had recently made the acquaintance of a compatriot, a teacher and former student of the Cairo mosque-university of

---

[4] The Neo Destour ('New Constitution') Party—the Tunisian national organisation which took over the fight for Tunisian rights from the more traditionalist Old Destour in the mid-thirties.

El Azhar, Houari Boumedienne. Libya had been born on 24 December 1951 under U.N. auspices but—still oil-less, and clearly a premature infant—could not survive without her British subsidy, Anglo-American bases, and the services of numerous foreign experts.

Only in Syria and Egypt were there breaks in the familiar pattern, and to many observers these seemed slight enough. But the French had gone from Syria at long last and, the Army variously participating, young ideological parties were challenging the traditional networks of the sheikhly families, merchant families and sectarian clans. In Egypt the young officers had exiled the King, and made, they said, a revolution. Yet the tutelary spirits of Cromer, Kitchener and Lloyd were still in residence. The British Embassy, it was true, did not disapprove of General Neguib's young reformers; but when the energetic new Minister for Municipal Affairs, Wing-Commander Abdel Latif el Baghdadi, seeking to give the Cairo masses a little more light and air, proposed to extend the Nile Corniche, he was brought up short by the high wall of the British Embassy garden which came right down to the river. When he applied for a slice of the garden, he was told to take his Corniche around the back. His plans had to wait until the following year when the régime inserted a special clause in the Anglo-Egyptian (Canal Zone Evacuation) Treaty by which British Forces finally withdrew from Egyptian soil.

By 1964, when the High Dam had progressed far enough for the Nile to be diverted at Aswan, the Arab world was a world transformed. From the Ocean to the Gulf every Arab country had attained its independence. In the room of the old Imperialist occupiers, the two global powers, the U.S.A. and the U.S.S.R.—their zeal sharpened by the Chinese—competed with aid for Arab attention and favours. It was a world in ferment, thrust about by violent and continuous pressures, both internal and external, ideological as well as material. Three 'traditional' monarchs had succumbed; three remained —but even Kuwait in the patriarchal Gulf now had a National Assembly and manhood suffrage. The precarious survival of the frontiers which Gertrude Bell and her colleagues had lovingly drawn across the desert in 1919 could no longer conceal the reality of an Arab Revolution in full spate.

The difficulty of many in the West was to determine what the 'Arab Revolution' was, for few large-scale socio-political movements have been compounded from so many diverse, even dissonant, elements, or have so bafflingly telescoped the centuries. Here was secular French Revolutionary nationalism washing against Islamic *revanche* that harked back to the Crusades, long smouldering revolt against colonial land-theft as in Algeria and Morocco, and against alien domination, as in Egypt and Syria, tribal *jihad* against the flaunting impious town, townee aspirations for Constitutions and Cabinets, the call for Wilsonian 'self-determination,' and the yearning for the womb, the great Islamic *Umma*, the community of Believers. Here was nostalgia for the Great Arab Past, desperation over the Arab present, and limitless hope for the Great Arab Future.

It was a potent, if confusing, mixture, and in the 1950s the emphasis within it moved in a way which made it more potent —and possibly more confusing—still. To the Rights of the Arab Nation were added the Rights of the Arab Man, and, more perilously yet, of Arab men—and these were now rapidly clothed in such startling modern forms as social insurance, trade unions, land reform, co-operatives, worker co-partnership. There was a compulsive new watchword 'Socialism,' coupled with 'Science,' and this, displacing the old watchword 'Constitution,' was revealed as the key that would unlock the Arab Future.

The change began to take shape after the officers' coup in Egypt in 1952. By 1956, with some external assistance, this revolution within a revolution had discovered its prophet and was rapidly to gain definition and impetus; by the 1960s the immemorial Nile Valley scene bore its unmistakable marks.

As he makes his way from Dimyat in the far north of the Delta to the New Nubia—from Lake Manzalah on the Mediterranean to Lake Nasser—the traveller becomes familiar with the ubiquitous rural health units, the morning's crop of patients waiting in their verandahs; with the new secondary schools, with the grey water-towers taking clean water to the villages, with the grouped white buildings of the 'combined service units,' the storage depots of the agricultural Co-operative organisation, the chunky workers' flat-blocks which signal the approach of a town.

But it is up here by the First Cataract in this Nile Valley *Ultima Thule* that the primeval Egypt and the new are most dramatically married. Twenty miles or so south of Aswan the bleak mountain wall on the east of the valley recedes a mile or two, leaving a low plateau of good soil which had hitherto lain barren because it was too high to receive, by natural flow, the waters of the Nile. This is the New Nubia. Now powerful pumps were being installed which, driven by High Dam electricity, could lift the High Dam's bonus of water.

Already in 1965 the water gleamed in the long dark furrows of newly ploughed earth that stretched back to the mountain, and much of the land had borne its first crop of barley. Buses sped along miles of new asphalt roads traversing what was lately desert, linking the thirty-three new villages, each with its white-domed mosque, its club with fluted white façade, its school, its Nubian-style guest house, its market hall, its rows of shops.

In thus transplanting these 50,000 primitive people, of three separate tribes, whose old villages are lost beneath Lake Nasser, the Egyptian planners, architects, social scientists, were at pains to preserve Nubian tradition and custom—even to the extent of reproducing here the old order of the villages in relation to the Nile, and of neighbours and shopkeepers within each village.

The first principle gave rise to some ironic reversals of fortune. Kalabsha, the most wretched of the old villages, clamped in its granite Nile gorge, became, in the New Nubia, the most prosperous, already in 1965 under a heavy crop of sugar cane while other villages would have to live on doles for months while they awaited the arrival of power and water. The New Ballana was one of the villages that waited. We sat there in the courtyard of the eighty-four-year-old Omda,[5] drinking tea and nibbling the dried dates brought down from the Old Ballana, while Sheikh Maker Ismail, the Nubian deputy in Egypt's National Assembly, complained that the new houses lacked 'izzat,' that is, dignity. It was perhaps a predictable complaint

[5] The headman or mayor of a village.

since the sheikh, a rich date merchant, had occupied a 'palace' of forty rooms in the Old Ballana and now found himself reduced by the new Egyptian egalitarianism to four (as provided for the largest families)—in a house in a row at that.

The sheikh declined to be drawn on the future. 'If you come back in five years I will tell you,' he said sagely. But he did praise the skill with which this great migration down the Nile —of animals as well as people—had been carried through by the Egyptians. 'Much progress has been made,' he said. 'More in the last ten years in Egypt than in a hundred years before. The great thing is the better future for our children. If we went on as in the past we should always remain a nation of servants and porters, below other peoples.' Perhaps indeed some sort of verdict was already implied in the return of some thousands of Nubians from Lower Egypt (where they enjoy comparative wealth as the aristocracy of service) to rejoin their families in a Nubia now capable of sustaining them.[6]

Although the Nubians captured the headlines, many such migrations to new lands and new lives were under way in this Egypt of the 'sixties. From Menufiya province in the Delta, the landless had gone to eight new villages and more than six thousand farms rescued from the reedy bed of Lake Mariut, behind Alexandria; from overcrowded Sohag they migrated to the expanding oases of 'The New Valley'; from the poor villages of Dakahliya to the strange new world of Liberation Province, carved from the Western Desert.

All over Egypt, on the fringes of Valley and Delta, fleets of earth-movers cavorted and roared; armies of labourers plied mattock and basket. Wherever, in the Valley, the hills recede far enough and soil survey gives a chance, new land is being whittled from the desert. Thousands of acres are reclaimed from Lake Manzalah, to be distributed in five-feddan[7] lots; two bites are being taken from the marshes of Lake Borollos; a small bite from Lake Edku. But it is on the western and eastern edges of the Delta itself that the greater part of the million and more new acres the High Dam will water are being won from the desert.

[6] According to the Egyptian authorities, by 1965 a total of 46,000 Nubians had made application to return home.
[7] One feddan equals 1·038 acres.

None of this, in itself, is new. This indeed is how Egypt was made. 'Under a good administration, the Nile gains on the desert; under a bad one, the desert gains on the Nile,' remarked the observant Bonaparte. The High Dam and the vast scheme of which it is the cornerstone are in a sense merely the logical culmination of the great process which began when the first Pharaoh built the Left Bank of the Nile to protect his new capital at Memphis, or Amenemhat III constructed a dam at the Second Cataract which is now beneath Lake Nasser.

But hitherto, the more closely men controlled the Nile, the more closely they were themselves controlled by it, the more firmly imprisoned within that tremendous natural process. On the shore of Elephanta Island, by the First Cataract, an ancient Nilometer still bears eloquent witness. A series of stone steps, set in a well in the Nile bank, it is covered in level marks and inscriptions in hieroglyphics, in Greek and Roman capitals and in Arabic. There is a Greek inscription which records the height of the Flood in A.D. 100 in the reign of the Emperor Trajan.

This is the process which Nasser's Egypt now brings to its logical culmination. And, paradoxically, to do that today is also to break out of it. The year 1966 saw the last flood. For the first time since recorded history began, the annual deposit of silt will no longer fall upon the land—for the High Dam is a dam without sluice-gates. Instead, with an almost poetic appropriateness, the electric power generated by the Nile's flow will transmute the local air and local limestone into chemical fertiliser. The back-breaking toil of cleaning out the silt-clogged canals each winter will abate;[8] equally, the age-old material for bricks will no longer be to hand. As the high-tension towers hint as they stride off across the desert, the consequences of breaking such a pattern, in such a country, are endless, and do not lack drama. The cheap electricity they carry will drive the pumps, light the mud villages, make possible the industrialisation of a country hitherto lacking in other sources of power.

[8] But silt-free water may set intricate new problems for Egyptian hydrologists (who are working on them at the Barrage Laboratory) by scouring deeply the nearer sections of canal and river-bed and depositing the scourings lower down their courses.

But the pattern being broken is not only the technological pattern. For the Egyptian Revolution is a peculiarly contemporary revolution in the closeness with which technological advance and socio-political revolution are harnessed together. As elsewhere it seems likely to prove an uneasy partnership, posing vast questions about the ends of human life in the twentieth century.

2

EGYPTIANS AND ARABS:
A REDISCOVERED DESTINY

Arab, noun : Native of Arabia,

—Concise Oxford Dictionary

All are Arabs who are Arab in their language, culture and loyalty . . . I am an Arab and I believe that the Arabs constitute one nation.

—Pledge, First Arab Students Congress, Brussels, 1938

As the Arabs have their excellencies, so have they, like other nations, their defects and vices. Their own writers acknowledge that they have a natural disposition to war, bloodshed, cruelty, and rapine, being so much addicted to bear malice that they scarce ever forget an old grudge; which vindictive temper some physicians say is occasioned by their frequent feeding on camel's flesh.

—George Sale : 'Preliminary Discourse' to his translation of The Koran, 1734

The symbolism of the High Dam is not exhausted by its evocation of the new Arab revolution; it celebrates a point of culmination in the complex relationship between Egypt and the rest of the Arab world stretching across the thirteen centuries since, under the second Caliph, nine years after the death of the Prophet, the army of Ibn al-As Amr took Alexandria for Islam. It is a relationship which, like that of Britain and Continental Europe, has waxed and waned exceedingly, and yet remained critical and fundamental. It is a double counterpoint, composed by geography as well as politics, which the High Dam at Aswan is well placed to illuminate.

Gateway through which the wealth of Africa flowed down to the Mediterranean—and which now transmits the energy of an African river—Aswan, beside the First Cataract, is an ancient junction of caravan routes across the Libyan and Eastern deserts. It pivots two continents. Westwards from the

Nile bank at the Dam the desert sweeps away, three thousand miles, to the Anti-Atlas and the Atlantic. Eastwards, where the rocks and sand are streaked with the dust of iron ore (which the ancient Egyptians used for colour and the modern use for steel-making), a stony wilderness tilts upwards to the Red Sea mountains and continues through Medina, the birthplace of Islam (almost on Aswan's latitude), running on in a great arc across the wastes of Arabia, twelve hundred miles to the Euphrates and the Tigris and the high mountain walls of Persia and Turkey.

This is the 'Arab Fatherland,' homeland of 'the Arab Nation' of a million perorations. A certain mysticism is perhaps permissible—for this is a region unique and strange. Physically close to Europe, culturally and economically linked with it over centuries, the Mediterranean's other shore, littered with the ruins of Greece and Rome, it has yet remained a world apart. The facts of geography impose its difference upon it. Its ninety million inhabitants are, even now, inhabitants of islands set in a vast ocean of sand, rock and scrub. The islands may be large or small: a few river valleys, the coastal fringes, the city-states grown up where caravan routes meet, the oases, the upland steppe and the mountain slopes where rain uncertainly falls. Even in the days of jet-flight, a great Arab city like Fez or Aleppo, with a rich tradition of art and science and trade, may possess a reality, a vitality, an assurance rarely met with in the more theoretical nation-state of which it is a part. And in the mountains, Atlas and Anti-Atlas, Lebanon and Anti-Lebanon and the mountains of northern Syria and Iraq, the racial remnants, the imperfectly Arabised, the devotees of various Eastern mysteries—Berber and Kurd, Maronite, Druse and Yezidi—still pursue their clannish interests, cement their own alliances and make their own richly varied contribution to the ferment of 'the Arab Revolution.'

Today this attenuated world is bridged by pipelines and airlines and tourist buses, as earlier it was linked by the movements of merchant caravans and Bedouin tribes. But then—as now—its true cement was not material; its true cement was Islam. It was indeed itself largely the creation of the first Arab Revolution—the revolution of Mohamed, which energised the Arabs, conferred on them an identity, the sense of possessing a sacred language, and the omnipotence of God's Chosen. The Koranic Law and code of life, the *Sharia*, and the simple yet demanding disciplines of daily prayer, of the Fast and the Pilgrimage, harnessed the restlessness of the tribes and bound them with the towns in a *Pax Islamica*. Between A.D. 622 and 750 quite small Arab armies, gathering recruits as they went, carried the green banners of Islam from Persia to Spain as the Omayyed Empire, with its Caliph in Damascus, rose on the wreckage of Byzantium. In Toledo sword steel was damascened and in Cordoba the Great Mosque echoed the horseshoe arches, the double-tiered arcades, of the Mosque of the Omayyads in Damascus, and Arabic was the written language of the learned from Spain to Turkestan, an area greater than had been dominated by Greek or Latin.

Arab Islam implied unity, but, in the event, Arab unity was fleeting. Long before the Great Mosque in Cordoba was completed in A.D. 787, the universal Arab Golden Age was ended. Abd Er Rahman, the mosque-builder of Cordoba, was in fact a refugee—the only Omayyad to escape the massacre of his family contrived by the ambitious clan of Abbas who had removed the Caliphate to Baghdad. It was but the first of many such shifts in the centre of power. For the Koran which provided a community of faith and a durable social code did not furnish political forms adequate to an empire—or even so much as a firm law of succession. Since the murder of Othman, the third successor to the Prophet, followed by the reprisal killing of the fourth Caliph, Ali, the problem of political continuity has notoriously remained unsolved; it has been calculated that between Othman in 656 and King Feisal II and Abdul Illah in 1958, almost nine in ten of all Muslim rulers have died by violence while in office.

Under the ever more shadowy suzerainty of Baghdad, numerous local dynasties, large and small, rose and declined. Some able or ambitious leader, perhaps wrapped in the mantle of sherifdom, or founding some militant mystic brotherhood, would sweep quickly over vast expanses. But the wave would in due time spend itself, or be overtaken by another. In the early tenth century, the heretic Fatamids[1] got a hold among

[1] So named because they claimed descent from Mohamed's daughter, Fatima, and her husband, the murdered fourth Caliph, Ali.

the Tunisian Berbers, and, their leader taking the title of *El Mahdi*,[2] extended their sway to the Atlantic. By 969 they had taken Egypt from the Abbasid Caliphs of Baghdad, building a fine new Cairo, *El Kahira* ('the Victorious') near the old Roman-Byzantine 'Babylon' on the Nile and the 'Fustat' (tent) of the first Muslim conqueror, Ibn al-As Amr. But as they pushed their rule southwards to Nubia and north-eastwards towards Aleppo, the Fatamid rulers lost the Arab West: another militant sect had arisen and was carving out vast domains. Without the close texture and economic disciplines of Europe, the Arab world was to remain locked in the patterns of raid and ambush, of Mahdism and *jihad* and tribal feud, of perpetual conspiracy and dissimulation and 'my house against thy house' which have characterised it from the earliest days of Islam to our own times.

In this shifting, oceanic, universe there was one island of permanence: in the long deep cleft of the Nile Valley the Egyptian fellahin, their feet in the water and their hands in the mud, continued to pursue with little change the way of life they had followed since the days of the Pharaohs. Waves of invasion passed over them; Persians, Greeks, Romans, Byzantines might despise and in their various ways misuse them, but in the end it was the conquerors who were eclipsed, the fellahin who remained.

Egypt's conversion to Islam under the second Caliph, Omar, was swift and on the whole benign. To the monophysite Copts the simple 'no-god-but-God' of the Koran came as something of a relief from the heresy-hunting, hair-splitting Byzantine theologians of Alexandria. Within the harsh unity of the Nile Valley, which had earlier worshipped the Pharaonic Sun-God, the singleness of God required no urging and to turn to Mecca instead of Jerusalem was small hardship. Within a century, the Nile Valley was won for Arabic, that new and potent *lingua franca*, a blessing which would henceforth bind it to the wide world which shared it. But the continuity of the Valley's life remained unbroken. The fellahin continued—and

[2] The Right-Guided One, a persistent tradition of something like a Second Coming—in this case, of Ali's son Mohamed, who had disappeared but was reputed by some never to have died.

continue—to guide their days by the ancient Coptic calendar which derives from the Nile flow; they continued, as they continue, to celebrate feasts that pre-date both Islam and Christianity, like Sham-el-Nessim ('Smelling the Breeze') which hails the spring; and in the recesses of Upper Egypt the Muslim fellahin remained indistinguishable from their unconverted Coptic neighbours save for the small blue cross tattooed on the latter's wrists.

Here and there, clans of Arab invaders continued to hold themselves apart, wrapped in the pride of descent from the Prophet. But for the most part these newcomers, too, were absorbed in due time into the rich green-and-brown Coptic tapestry of the Nile Valley. The Arab arrogance, sharpened by the desert, was tempered and mellowed by the earthy humanity of the long-suffering fellahin. It was a relationship of mutual and far-reaching benefit. For if the Egyptian 'islanders' were made free of the vast commercial and intellectual realms of Arab empire, Arab Islam found in the Nile Valley a redoubt into which it could withdraw, gathering strength before issuing to repel some new and yet more menacing attack. Thus Salah el-Din, builder of Cairo's Citadel, vanquished the all-conquering Crusaders; thus the Mameluke Beybars in 1260 led out the *levée-en-masse* which, at Ain Jalut near the Palestine border, saved the Islamic West from the Mongol hordes which erased Baghdad from the world map for centuries.

With Salah el-Din, a Kurd, self-proclaimed Sultan in Cairo, in 1171, Arab rule in Egypt ceased—but Islam and Arabs and Arabic remained, adding their durability to the durability of the Nile Valley. Egypt, which had escaped the Mongols, fell in 1517 to the Turks.

Faced by some national shortcoming, it is the habit of politically-minded Arabs to lay the blame fairly and squarely on the Turks who, by the mid-16th century, had taken possession of 'the Arab world' from Baghdad to Algiers. But although often deplorable, four centuries of Ottoman rule did impose on this vast and fragmented area a ramshackle—Islamic—unity, a rough yet common fabric, a focus, however hazy, in the Sultan-Caliph in Constantinople—and from this, in the fullness of time, it was possible for an Arab identity to re-emerge.

It was, ironically, from the infidel West that deliverance came. For the Imperialism of Sword and Book, of Pasha and Tribute, was no match for the Imperialism of railways, stock markets and the 'civilising mission'—although the two long continued a bizarre, but mutually convenient, tacit collaboration. In 1830 the French—the last Europeans to abandon the Crusades and now the first officially to return—landed troops at Algiers, and gave rise to the Arab World's first 'modern' anti-West revolt, the uprising of young Abdel Kader, the son of a *marabout*, or holy man. In 1881 French 'protection' was extended to the Bey of Tunis; a year later the British landed troops at Alexandria in what was unquestionably still the territory of the Ottoman Empire for the strictly temporary task of restoring order after Colonel Arabi's revolt. In 1907, after the secret agreement between France and Britain ('a free hand in the Arab West for a free hand in Egypt'), Marshal Lyautey began the 'pacification' of Morocco which was not to be completed until the 1930s.

Since the British were at pains to sustain the elaborate pretence of Turkish suzerainty in Egypt, and since it was still largely unchallenged in Syria, Iraq and almost all Arabia, the 'Arab world' remained in a sense real enough. Right up to the outbreak of the First World War, it continued to be possible for an Arab to travel without let or hindrance from Baghdad to Aswan.

The Turks performed one further service for the Arabs: they encouraged them by their example in the secular nationalism of the West, unconfused by Islamic yearnings. The 'Young Turks' duly inspired in the Syrian Province the 'Young Arabs'—Christian now as well as Muslim—and then, in the logic of their Ottomanising nationalism, repressed them.

But if it was the Turks who thus watered the seeds of the Arab Nation with the blood of the martyrs, it was the Western Powers, with their long trail of broken promises, their multiple betrayal, who endowed the Arab cause with its characteristic aura of despair and desperation.

The story is all too familiar, yet even now retains a certain poignancy. For a brief moment in 1918, when Feisal's horsemen, entering Damascus ahead of Allenby, raised the Arab standard over the old capital of the Omayyads, it seemed to

politically conscious Arabs that their dream was at last about
to be realised and that soon a renascent Arab Nation, comprising the old Turkish Arab provinces, would stretch from the
Euphrates to the Hedjaz. For was not this the natural sequel to
the Ottoman defeat in which the Arab armies had played a
critical rôle—the just reward which the British had led the
Grand Sherif in Mecca to expect in return for Arab entry into
the war?

Disillusionment was swift. The French hauled down the
Arab standard in Beirut, and when the elected Syrian National
Congress rejected all foreign tutelage, marched on Damascus.
With a small regular force and a crowd of shouting volunteers,
the young Syrian 'Minister of War'—he was twenty-five—
marched out to repel the French Army. He was killed and his
forces decimated. The British took over the direct administration of Palestine in which, it was now admitted, the Balfour
Note had pledged a National Home to the Jews. And if the
Balfour Declaration itself was guarded, Balfour himself, at the
Peace Conference in 1919, hardly bothered to be. 'In Palestine,'
he minuted for the Cabinet, 'we do not propose even to go
through the form of consulting the inhabitants. . . . Zionism
is of far profounder import than the desires and prejudices of
the 700,000 Arabs who now inhabit the ancient land.'

With President Wilson's call for 'self-determination' still
echoing about the world, the Mandatory Powers presently
proceeded to rule across the vast expanses of the Arab East
that network of pseudo-national frontiers which were to
contribute so richly to the region's multiple frustrations. The
French, hereditary protectors of 'the Mountain,' the refuge-
home of the Maronite Christians behind Beirut, now carved
out of Syria a Greater Lebanon calculated to leave Christians
and Muslims in impotent and precarious equilibrium. The
British, drawing the frontiers of Palestine and Iraq, decided
to recognise the ambitious Emir Abdullah's partial *fait
accompli*, and create, by the way, yet another 'nation,' Transjordan. Both mandatories proceeded to replace the dilapidated,
if comfortable, old Turkish political furnishings in their own
favoured styles—Republicanism, the Deuxième Bureau, and
the *mission civilitrice* on one side, hereditary monarchy,
parliamentary ritual, boarding schools for the élite on the

other.

Although outside Palestine there was no organised land settlement by foreigners, by 1922 the Arab lands of the Middle East had thus been as thoroughly partitioned as the Arab lands of North Africa.

But if 'divide-and-rule' had rarely been more smartly demonstrated, it has to be admitted that few peoples can have been more temptingly divisible than the Arabs at this time. The alacrity with which the leaders of the Revolt in the Desert became competitive collaborators with the 'Imperialist betrayers' suggests that even had Feisal and his National Congress been left undisturbed in Damascus, the Arab Nation would have eluded them. The Hashemite Family claims were in the main to tribal fealty and Muslim respect for descendants of the Prophet. And even in 1920, even if reclothed, somewhat unconvincingly, as 'constitutional monarchy,' these were rapidly wasting assets, particularly among Syrian townsmen. Still more poetry than programme, Arab nationalism was the victim of its central dilemma: that Islam which gave the Arabs identity and historical dignity could not give them— indeed seemed specifically to deny them—the basis of the modern nation-state. Nor in the Arab East had either geography or economic development come to their aid; it was still clan against clan, sect against sect, chief against chief, brother against brother in an endless flux of alliances and enmities which parliamentary forms could not yet bind even into that single web of conflict from which a nation may grow.

In the vast expanse of the Arab World, only the Nile Valley afforded the raw material of a nation-state: a homogeneous population within compact frontiers—and what a frontier was the desert!—a web of towns and villages, a rising middle class, technical as well as administrative, sprung lately from the soil whose unique character and intricate cultivation bound all together in a durable common culture.

Under the Ottomans, geography had continued to confer upon Egypt a certain independence, even if only of Mameluke anarchy.[3] And at the end of the 18th century the country had

[3] Mameluke signifies in Arabic 'bought men'—and the Mamelukes were in origin youths imported mainly from the Caucasus and trained to form

once more been set apart: in 1798, many years before similar stirrings elsewhere in the Arab world, Egypt was abruptly awakened from her Oriental torpor by the invasion of Bonaparte and the French Revolutionary army. The twin messages of Science and Liberty emblazoned on that army's banners were not understood, but Mohamed Ali, Egypt's tyrant of genius, had at once begun to rehearse the first of them; and in doing so, he performed for Egyptians the inestimable service —in Cromer's phrase—of 'amputating their country from the decaying body of the Ottoman Empire.'

The Bonapartian message of Nationalism and Liberty disappeared from view, but like a stream that goes underground, did so only to bubble up to the surface again in due time, coloured now by the local soil. From the 1880s onwards there developed in Egypt a nationalistic movement that was earthier and more solid than the Mazzinian flights of the young Syrian and Lebanese intellectuals. It was so because it was not merely 'nationalist,' but also *national*, giving expression to the emotions of a people long submerged, but at last becoming aware of itself and finding its voice. The point is made if, in the year 1920, one looks from Colonel Lawrence's protégé, Feisal, just expelled from Damascus, the Muslim aristocrat, subtle and sinuous, yet alone, accepting, in the end, inglorious compromise, to the Egyptian leader, Saad Zaghloul, once Cromer's protégé, but now founder of a national party, the Wafd, a westernised lawyer, yet also the son of a well-to-do fellah, earthy, roughly humorous, totally commanding the Egyptian crowd, and merely strengthened by his two deportations.

Soon after the end of the war (when, with Turkey's defeat, Egypt became in name as well as fact a British Protectorate), Zaghloul had appeared at the head of a delegation (*wafd*) at the British Residency in Cairo to demand independence for

the élite of the Egyptian Sultan's army. From 1252 they took over Egypt for themselves, boisterously and incessantly fighting over the division of the spoils, each Mameluke chief having his own private Mameluke army. Even after the Turkish conquest in 1517 they soon regained effective control, using the Turkish governor as a figurehead, and they continued to plague Egypt until Mohamed Ali rid the country of them in 1811 by the celebrated expedient of inviting 470 of their leaders to a banquet at the Citadel and slaughtering the lot.

Egypt (with a British alliance). When the High Commissioner had declared himself powerless to grant this, Zaghloul asked to lead the delegation to London. The request was transmitted —and rejected. The then Egyptian Prime Minister took it up, supported by the British High Commissioner. But the answer was still a refusal. The British Foreign Office was then in charge of Lord Curzon, who described Zaghloul and his colleagues as 'men of doubtful standing and antecedents who had organised a disloyal movement.'

When Zaghloul was arrested and deported, all Egypt rose in revolt. A new High Commissioner, Lord Allenby, insisted on his release. He returned to a hero's welcome. But, still unwilling to compromise, he was deported again, this time to Aden and the Seychelles.[4] The Wafd under Zaghloul in the 'twenties *was* the Egyptian people in much the same way as Congress under Gandhi's leadership in the 'thirties was India. Few nationalist parties have had a more rousing beginning than the Wafd—and not many have dragged out a more miserable end.

The very intensity of these experiences further cut off Egypt from the wider Arab world whose 'desert' and 'tribal' characteristics had been further underlined by the British sponsorship in Transjordan and Iraq of the Hashemite family of the Hedjaz, hereditary keepers of the Holy Places of Arabia. 'Our problem is an Egyptian problem, not an Arab problem,' Saad Zaghloul firmly told the Arab delegation at the Peace Conference in 1919. And through the 'twenties and 'thirties the politicians of Egypt remained absorbed in their national cause and personal ambitions; its intellectuals looked to Paris and Rome and London rather than to Damascus or Baghdad. Although their nationalism had its roots in Islam and, in its natal days, had shared the agonies and ecstasies of the nationalists of neighbouring Arab lands, the word 'Arab' had not yet acquired those political overtones which were later to make it so potent and universal a shibboleth.

But the Second World War forcibly demonstrated once again the physical indivisibility of the Arab world. From the

---

[4] A first-hand account appears in *Old Men Forget*, the autobiography (1955) of Mr Duff-Cooper, at the relevant time working in the Egyptian Department of the Foreign Office.

great Nile Valley base Allied armies flowed east and west and north. Europe was saved in the North African desert. And, for Egyptians, 1945 re-created, superficially, the situation of 1918: nominally 'independent,' in fact as strenuously 'protected' as ever, they were embarked again on the fight for self-determination that had been in progress intermittently since the 1880s— embarked, however, in a changed Arab world that was now to change yet more.

Two events recalled the Egyptians to their Arab destiny— and their history, as we have seen, does permit the word 'recalled.' The first event was the birth of the League of Arab States at Alexandria in 1944; the second, the vote in the United Nations General Assembly on 29 November 1947 which partitioned Palestine to create the Jewish state of Israel.

The midwife at the Arab League's birth was Britain. In May 1941 the Foreign Secretary, Anthony Eden, had made a speech offering British support for any widely accepted Arab move to achieve 'a greater degree of unity.' It was an ideal to which British Arabists had frequently paid lip-service, but Rommel's presence at the Egyptian frontier, and the Rashid Ali revolt in Iraq suggested that, in Britain's own interests, more might now be required. Thus encouraged, the Prime Minister of Iraq, Nuri es-Said, put forward a plan for an initial combination of a Greater Syria and Iraq, to which other Arab states might accede in due course. But when the seven Arab states, with an observer for Palestine, met at Alexandria, what emerged was a wider and looser association in which the central rôle —and the key secretary-generalship—went to Egypt. The British promoted this development, seeing in Egypt a solid foundation for the post-war Arab world-to-be, and a familiar and convenient channel by which British influence could be projected over the whole region, guiding it to stability and prosperity.

The Arab League was soon to illuminate the disunities of the Arab world more effectively than its unity: nevertheless, this in itself was a move towards greater realism. Unquestionably, the birth of the League is a landmark in modern Arab history. It gave material form, in the phrase of the Lebanese, Emile Bustani, to 'an Arab super-ego.' It formally acknowledged Egypt's place as the keystone of the Arab arch. 'Egypt saw herself as the natural leader of the Arab world, and the Arab world saw Egypt as its natural leader.'[5]

The second event, the creation by force of the state of Israel in 1948, effectively prevented any Egyptian withdrawal from this new pan-Arab rôle.

Even in the later 'thirties, the relentless advance of the Zionists towards that Jewish state which was for most of them the only meaningful interpretation of Balfour's 'national home' of the Jewish People in Palestine, had called forth a volume of pan-Arab protest loud enough to be heard in the Nile Valley. In 1938 Egyptian senators and deputies had staged in Cairo a pan-Arab Congress for the Defence of Palestine. In common with other Arab countries Egypt had attended the abortive Palestine Round Table Conference in London in 1939. Nasser himself has related how, as a schoolboy in Egypt, 'the first elements of Arab consciousness began to filter into my mind' when 'I went out with my fellow students on strike on 2 November every year as a protest against the Balfour Declaration whereby Britain gave the Jews a national home usurped from its legal owners.'

After the Second World War the success of the Jewish terror groups, the vast, highly organised illegal immigration of Jewish refugees into Palestine, were among the earliest signs of the collapse of British Imperial power in the Middle East. For the Arabs, the British retreat under American Zionist pressure from the White Paper of 1939 (which set a final limit to Jewish immigration and rejected partition and a Jewish state) vividly foreshadowed the abdication that was to follow. The British refusal to enforce—or co-operate in enforcing—the United Nations Palestine partition plan of 1947, and the precipitate departure of the British Forces, leaving the proposed frontiers undemarcated, created a power vacuum into which the largest Muslim, Arabic-speaking state of the region must, willy-nilly, be drawn.

In the perspective of history, few wars appear more inevitable than the Arab-Zionist war of 1948-49, given the equivocal promises of 1917. But, through it, Egypt and her Arab neighbours gained a powerful bond, the 'Arab bond' of common humiliation, betrayal and defeat. The Palestine Arabs, fleeing

[5] Emile Bustani, *Marche Arabesque*, London, 1961.

their homes before the tide of war, streamed toward Egypt as well as towards Transjordan, Syria and Lebanon. And by an accident of the Cease-Fire situation, Egypt gained a new physical link with the Arab East, a strange and angry appendix —the Gaza Strip. A young Egyptian officer, Major Gamal Abdel Nasser, returning from the lost war to Cairo, noted that he was going back 'with the whole region (the Arab East) in my mind, one complete whole' for the first time.

It was to prove a momentous discovery.

3

THE CRUCIBLE

There is no country in the world where the government controls more closely, by means of the Nile, the life of the people.

—Napoleon Bonaparte in Egypt, 1799

The paddle wheel is the great conqueror . . . I think an allegory might be made showing how much stronger commerce is than chivalry and finishing with a grand image of Mohamet's crescent being extinguished by Fulton's boiler.

—W. M. Thackeray, *Cornhill to Cairo*, 1844

The triumphal arch squad was hard at work again on the Aswan Corniche; from the back of their lorry the inevitable face, ten times larger than life, the temples now flecked with white, beamed out *in serio*.

The young accountant from the newly-built hotel on Elephanta Island followed my glance. 'We love Gamal Abdel Nasser very much,' he said quietly. 'He is our spirit. . . .'

Few men in recent times have gained such moral ascendancy over a nation as had Gamal Abdel Nasser over Egypt in the ten years following 1956. When he made a speech his ideas were taken up, echoed and re-echoed on a million lips in a way no mere propaganda machine alone could ensure. Dicta from earlier orations sanctified public utterance like verses from the Koran. Nasser lives modestly, eschewing pomp as far as a Head of State can. Western headline writers to the contrary, he behaves most of the time in a markedly undramatic fashion.[1] Yet Egyptians, who, in general, are cynical about

[1] Compare, for instance, the Presidential style of Bourguiba in Tunisia, always the 'good Arab leader' in the Western Press, who 'proceeded to embroider on the pageantry traditionally associated with the Bey's office,' 'built or restored at least two presidential palaces' on a lavish scale, and spent 12m. dollars—one-eighth of Tunisia's annual Budget—to make his home-town of Monastir a summer capital, and 'incidentally to build his own Mausoleum there.' C. H. Moore, *Tunisia Since Independence* (University of California Press 1965). In 1961 the well-known Tunisian periodical *Jeune Afrique* pointedly praised Nasser's austere way of life.

politicians, and doubt other leaders of the régime, commonly reposed in Nasser an implicit trust which, in 1967, was to prove strong enough even to carry him through national military disaster. The managing director of a large state enterprise assured me that Nasser personally vetted every directorial appointment to Egypt's hundreds of nationalised companies. 'But how can he possibly *know* about so many men?' I asked. 'Ah, he knows—he has his ways.' In Cairo's busy Ataba Square where the pavement merchants outside the G.P.O. display a glossy gallery of the Arab World's current heroes, there are gilt-framed portraits of Nasser which, as one walks by, change by some optical device to reveal the Arab characters for the name of God.

No case, on the face of it, might seem to lend more support to the 'great man' approach to history. Yet if Nasser has made history on the grand scale he has also, superlatively, been made by it. The more one studies the rise of Nasser and Nasserism, the more one immerses oneself in Egyptian history, the more one is overtaken by a sense of inevitability, of long historical processes slowly working themselves out, of events determined by a unique and overmastering environment.

Inhabited Egypt has the quality of a lucid, compelling diagram. Seen from the outside, from the desert, the Delta rises like a low green wall; southwards, from its apex, the Valley's escarpments rule other sharp enclosing lines of limestone, sandstone, finally granite. Within this hard-edged outline, like a long-necked laboratory flask with its base on the Mediterranean, the elements have almost magical simplicity : the Nile, immensely powerful, eternal, bearing down prodigious volumes of water gathered over its 4,000-mile course, yet without a single tributary in Egypt; the annual Flood with its vast burden of fertilising silt, which from Pharaonic times to 1967 has built up the Delta, lying yards deep on the Valley floor; the unremitting sun; the cool North wind; the near rainlessness of Upper Egypt: a man living in Luxor said that it had not rained since his birth thirty-five years ago.

Above all, the extraordinary regularity of the process in which these elements are combined gives to the Nile Valley almost the pulse and rhythm of a living organism. In Mesopotamia the Flood was capricious and often accompanied by storms; in Egypt, although it came later in the year, its annual cycle was so regular as to inspire the first scientific calendar. And the days have a rhythm as strongly marked as the year: the cold dawn, the warming sun, the sun that strikes blindingly out of a metallic sky, the oven of the afternoons, and, rising after nightfall like a blessed miracle, the cool North wind off the Mediterranean, breezing revivingly along the Nile —save on the March-May days of the *Khamseen* when the wind swings round and for fifty (*khamseen*) days may blow bitingly off the desert.

Such rhythms in Nature induce responding rhythms in Man. The Nile Flood, at once watering and fertilising, created each year an excellent seedbed and the winter sun germinated the seed and ripened the harvest and when it was gathered the hotter summer sun fissured and aerated the earth. By 5000 B.C. the Egyptians were growing barley and emmer wheat; by 3000 B.C. they were breaking the sun-hardened mud with shallow wooden ploughs; one of the earliest representations of a Pharaoh shows him, mattock in hand, ceremonially cutting an irrigation canal.

The major hydraulic works of the Pharaohs apart, the system employed for making use of the Nile's rise—and it was to survive into the 1960s—was that now known as 'basin irrigation.' Earth banks divided the valley floor into vast rectangles into which the water was run by opening sluices at the height of the Flood in August or September. For from forty to sixty days the valley disappeared under a sheet of water in which the villages, built on higher ground, floated like islands. And then, the Nile having fallen enough, the sluices were re-opened and the water allowed to drain off, leaving hardly a puddle behind—for in centuries of slowly dropping its silt the Flood had graded the land to perfection. It was ready to produce its bounty.

The Nile shaped the people. Its control demanded detailed social organisation and, finally, unified government. It nurtured a technology whose science might be much mixed with priestcraft and magic, but was also basic. Techniques of measurement and calculation, of surgery and shipbuilding, of written communication and building, both in brick and stone, were developed to meet the insistent demands of that clear-cut and challenging environment. The Nile, whose marshy borders provided the papyrus reed for writing material, also bore the great blocks of limestone and sandstone from the valley's enclosing cliffs to form architecture's first colonnades—again of natural inspiration, with columns bearing palm-leaf and lotus capitals.

Yet the Nile by the very rigidity of its discipline could also hypnotise and stultify. Tradition and ritual were elevated into a way of life, the unending mechanical repetition of the figures on the walls of the temples and tombs. The walls of a tomb at Thebes of 1250 B.C. show the *shaduf*, the long sweep and bucket designed to raise water from river or canal to the fields. It is a handy device and, counter-weighted with a ball of mud, is used to this day. But it is vastly laborious—to irrigate a quarter-acre with it takes one day. Yet despite this, the next advance in irrigation machinery had to wait 1,500 years—for the Greeks who brought in the *tambour* or Archimedes' screw (a long cylinder with an internal spiral, originally used to bale out warships) and the *sakia*, a water-wheel turned through wooden cogs by ox-power.

Fortunately, the Nile, a magnificent highway into the heart of Africa, also made possible such periodic renewal from beyond the Valley. The steady North wind, filling lateen sails, drove the ships up to the First Cataract at Aswan; the current bore them down again. During the two centuries of Arab Fatamid rule the commerce of the Mediterranean and Indian Ocean converged on Egypt. Gold coming down from the Sudan primed the Egyptian economy and the ships of Venice and other Italian trading republics came to Alexandria, bringing timber in exchange for Egyptian carpets, porcelain and paper and other luxury goods from further East.

But in an insecure and shifting Arab world prosperity founded on expanding trade and industry could not endure. By the 16th century Mameluke violence and the opening of the ship route via the Cape had caused the West to turn away from the old overland trade routes to the East. The industrial revolution came to Western Europe—and Egypt receded from view beneath the baroque squalors and splendours of the Ottoman Empire. But the Nile—and the isthmus of Suez—continued to extend a bland and silent invitation which an expanding Europe could not, it was certain, ignore for ever.

When the Italian Consul, on 1 July 1798, reported to Murad Bey, the Chief Mameluke in Cairo, that Napoleon Bonaparte and his army had landed at Alexandria, Murad at once replied that the Franks were mere 'donkey boys'; let them be given a few pence and told to go—he had no wish to hurt them. For Murad history had stopped at the Crusades; but the subsequent slaughter of the magnificently anachronistic Mameluke horsemen, as they charged waving their jewelled scimitars and pistols at the French artillery and infantry squares, bridged the intervening five hundred-odd years with speed.

It was the first, briskest and grandest example of the *mission civilitrice*. Declaring that he had come to emancipate the Egyptians, Bonaparte was equipped with a stock of tricolour cockades, a printing press, and the famous mission of 165 savants, a living encyclopaedia. Beheading five or six people daily in the streets of Cairo in the interests of order, he installed his experts in the 'Institut d'Egypte' (where any Muslim would be helped to satisfy his curiosity about Science), appointed French provincial commissioners to supervise a new hierarchy of Coptic tax-collectors, and summoned the first representative assembly in the East, carefully including representatives of Cairo's illustrious mosque-university, El Azhar, a well as of the merchants, fellahin, village headmen, Bedouin tribes. A self-declared admirer of Islam, Bonaparte gave a dinner to learned sheikhs and other notables at which each place was marked by a copy of the Koran on one side and Tom Paine's 'Rights of Man' on the other—a remarkable anticipation of contemporary synthesising themes.

Meanwhile the savants were giving a brilliant display of revolutionary zeal. A languages school was set up, a French-Egyptian dictionary got under way; Pharaonic Egypt was being rediscovered and described. While the engineers surveyed the route for a canal across the isthmus of Suez and designed dams for the Nile, the architects planned new boulevards—and sewers—for Cairo, and the musicians studied Arab music. A census and an accurate map were projected and the geologists surveyed the desert for minerals. The doctors, appalled at Cairo's solitary hospital, whose beds were of stone, drew up plans for a 400-bed installation with central pharmacy and medical school.

After Nelson's victory of the Nile few of these plans had any chance of coming to fruition. Within two years the French were gone; but the processes of change they so dramatically set on foot were still working themselves out more than a century later. For although the Egyptians might find Bonaparte's notion of a representative assembly baffling, the infidel blatancies of the French citizen army roused them to revolt in a way the outrages of their Mameluke and Turkish brothers-in-Islam could never have done. It was from these years that the Egyptian nationalist movement was to derive its first martyrs.

Watching the perturbed sheikhs hurrying hither and thither, carrying arms, the French Consul, Drovetti, wrote that a Frenchman in Cairo just then was reminded of the early days of the French Revolution. And the parallel perhaps had more point than met the eye—for when, from the five years of turmoil that followed Bonaparte's departure, a new ruler arose in Egypt, he was duly installed on his Pasha's throne by the acclaim of 'the People', rallied by Omar Makram, a leading sheikh at El Azhar. Although the new ruler, Mohamed Ali, like his predecessors for centuries past, was a non-Egyptian, he nevertheless thus gained a certain 'national' character—soon to be confirmed by his triumphant repulse of the British landing force sent to restore the Mamelukes and the Turks.

Nor did it matter greatly that Mohamed Ali had contrived his own acclaim—as indeed he contrived most things—for he was a new type of Oriental ruler, uniquely determined and equipped to propel this medieval country into the 19th century. A Turk from the small Aegean tobacco port of Kavalla, nephew of the local governor, an officer in the gendarmerie and a dealer in tobacco, Mohamed Ali had arrived in Egypt with the Albanian contingent of the Ottoman forces sent to drive the French from the Nile Valley. He was a strange mixture of East and West. He was Oriental in his deviousness, in his dissimulation, and the ruthlessness with which he employed massacre, poison, bribe and bastinado; he was Greek in his questing intelligence, his adaptability, his lively appreciation of science as the key to Western progress. The first set of qualities enabled him to emerge victorious from the years of anarchy in which French, English, Turks, Albanians, Mamelukes and other factions struggled bloodily for the control of the Nile Valley; the second prompted him to import from the West a number of remarkable foreign experts—Linant de Bellefonds, a Belgian engineer who became his irrigation expert, Michel Jumel, a Swiss textile manager, the French doctor, Clôt Bey, who organised a medical school and midwifery service, Colonel Sève, the Napoleonic veteran who modernised his army, R. M. Galloway, a London industrialist who built at Bulaq, the river-port of Cairo, an eight-furnace foundry capable of making looms, spinning machines and even steam engines.

The Pasha boasted of having been born on the same day as Napoleon Bonaparte and set out to emulate his hero. He set up technical departments of State—a divan of education, and of commerce, a directorate of the arsenal and dockyard to make weapons, ropes and warships, and the first printing press in the Turkish Empire, working in Arabic, Turkish and Persian. By 1825 there were ten cotton mills; a glass factory was started in Alexandria, and, in 1830, Egypt's first sugar refinery. In 1826 the first state 'mission' of twenty-five young Egyptians travelled to France for education—the forerunners of hundreds of others. Several state primary schools were set up in every province, sending pupils on to a preparatory school in Alexandria, to another in Cairo, and, finally, to an Egyptian Polytechnique. It was the first western pattern of schools in the Orient. Mohamed Ali personally dragooned reluctant parents, footing the bills for food, clothes and books.

The land was surveyed and tenancies registered—again a radical innovation. But as the costs mounted—of modernisation, of expansion into Syria and the Sudan, of expeditions on behalf of the Sultan-Caliph against the rebellious Wahhabis in Arabia and Greeks in Crete—the Pasha took more and more land into his personal proprietorship. He had already monopolised most of the new industry, and by 1836 two-fifths of Egypt's imports and nine-tenths of her exports were in his hands. But at least he kept the country out of pawn to the foreign moneylenders and merchants who were now pouring into Alexandria as the new steamships opened up a quick Mediterranean route to the East. When the British organised a Transit Company to take passengers and goods from Cairo to Suez for transhipment via the Red Sea, Mohamed Ali, recognising its importance to Egypt, took it over.

The principle of hereditary succession by primogeniture which he finally succeeded in establishing gave Egypt some continuity of government; it would have been too much to expect it to ensure continuity of statesmanship and wisdom as well. Mohamed Ali's obscurantist successor, Abbas, dismissed most of his foreign experts and shut down his schools. In truth, before Mohamed Ali died many of his factories had fallen into decay. Although by 1838 he had invested no less than £12 million sterling in industrial enterprises which employed 30,000-40,000 workers, his aspirations were in advance of his resources. Oxen power, used in default of coal, jerked the machinery and broke it; press-ganged fellahin let it rust. Prompted by Britain, the Sultan in Constantinople at last asserted himself to enforce the 'Capitulation' treaties, and, forcing open Egypt's door to foreigners and European manufactures, completed the destruction.

Nevertheless, this extraordinary man—illiterate until a Negress in his harem taught him to write at the age of forty-seven, and then a correspondent of J. S. Mill—did Egypt a great service. Subduing Muslim fanaticism and protecting Christians, he laid the foundations of a modern technical middle class a century before similar developments in any other part of the Near East. In particular, he made three major innovations which were to shape the Egyptian society of the future. He formed an army from Egyptian fellahin. He turned the country over to the cultivation of a new variety of fine cotton. And, in order to make the latter possible, he broke away from the irrigation methods of the Pharaohs to construct a system of 'perennial' irrigation, which in the fullness of time was to turn Egypt into a vast and intricate soil-and-water machine.

The fellahin army was in fact a desperate last resort. As the history of the Turkish Empire so liberally demonstrates, mercenary soldiers are capricious and dangerous—and none more so than the Albanians on whose scimitars Mohamed Ali had ridden to power. But when the Sudan was conquered to provide as a substitute a more biddable black army, the wretched Sudanese conscripts, brought down to Egypt, died off in droves.

It was then that the French consul, Drovetti, suggested to Mohamed Ali the 'outlandish' notion of recruiting the Egyptian fellahin. This counsel of despair was adopted. The village headmen marked down their victims; Colonel Sève, now converted to Islam under the name of Suleiman Pasha, drilled them; and the resultant New Model army emerged creditably enough from its baptism of fire in Syria. Its officers were Turks, Circassians (the families of former Mamelukes), Europeans, and a few Americans. Its soldiers were those too wretchedly poor to be able to buy their way out, neither fleet enough to escape the recruiters, nor resolute enough to maim themselves (as many did) before the manacles were clamped upon them. Yet, hideous caricature of a citizen army as this was, it nevertheless constituted a national body of a sort that had not before existed. It gathered together the disinherited from the hidden villages of Egypt. And in the 1850s it got its first sprinkling of 'native officers'— among them a certain Ahmed Arabi, son of an eight-feddan fellah, and, thanks to the patronage of the military-minded Sultan Said, a colonel at twenty-two.

Even today Egyptian eyes light up when the name of Arabi is uttered. And this is as it should be, for, despite its confusion of motive, the army revolt that centred around Colonel Ahmed Arabi at the end of the 'seventies marks the beginning of the emergence of the Egyptian people from their long dark night of bondage.

Reporting on the state of Egypt for the benefit of Lord Palmerston in 1840, the British Member of Parliament, Sir John Bowring, commented on the extraordinary influence enjoyed there by the Turkish upper class. 'They are few, but they tyrannise; the Arabs are many, but they obey.' Forty years later, it was the continuing dominance of Turkish and Circassian officers in the Egyptian army which caused Arabi and two fellow colonels to dispatch (in January, 1881) their famous petition of protest to the Prime Minister. When, by way of reply, the three 'native officers' were arrested, and put on trial, their troops marched to the court-chamber, wrecked it, and freed their colonels. They then marched on to the Khedival Palace and successfully demanded the dismissal of the Minister of War.

The worm had turned. As in India, in 1857, long accumulating resentments of a subjugated people had found a focus in the army; in Egypt they had also found a colonel to give them voice. Yet 'Arabi the Egyptian,' as he proudly called himself, was no mere malcontent. Sir Auckland Colvin, the British Controller of Egyptian Finances (under the European Debt Commissioners) who was certainly no radical, describes an interview with him. A liberated slave, Arabi gravely assured Colvin, was a freer man than a free-born Arab in Egypt. The most ignorant Turk was preferred to the best of the Egyptians. 'He then went on at great length to explain that men came of one common stock, and had equal rights of personal liberty and security. The development of the theme . . . was curious in its naïve treatment, but it evidently was the outcome of the speaker's laboured thoughts. . . . Arabi, who spoke with great moderation, calmness and conciliation, is a sincere and resolute, but not a practical, man.'

Colvin's last point was to be amply borne out as, between 1879 and 1881, what had begun as a protest against manifest injustice drifted into mutiny, and by September of the latter year had been propelled by fear of reprisals into open rebellion. On 9 September 1881, suspecting from troop movements that a blow against his group was impending, Arabi and his regiment, 2,500 men with eighteen guns, marched on the Abdin Palace. The scene enacted then in the great square outside is a set-piece of Egyptian history books: the mutinous troops drawn up around the square, Arabi and a number of officers and men in the middle, and, advancing towards them, the Khedive with the British Controller, Sir Auckland Colvin, at his side. According to Colvin: 'Arabi Bey approached on horseback, and the Viceroy (Khedive)[2] called out to him to dismount. He did so, and came forward with several others, and a guard with fixed bayonets, and saluted. I said to the Viceroy: "Now is your moment." He replied, "We are between four fires." I said, "Have courage." He took counsel of a native officer on his left, and repeated to me, "What can I do? We are between four fires. We shall be killed."'

[2] In 1867, Ismail, the fifth 'Viceroy' in the line of Mohamed Ali, and as such nominally subject to Ottoman authority, had succeeded in acquiring at great cost from the Sultan the archaic but grandiloquent title of Khedive, together with the grant of its descent by primogeniture.

Arabi's will prevailed. The Khedive dismissed his Ministers, and appointed a new Chief Minister, approved by Arabi, who later himself took office as Minister of War. But Arabi's triumph was short-lived. As ever, the nominal suzerainty of the Ottoman Sultan in Constantinople added further confusion to an already richly confused situation, which was getting increasingly out of control. Ten months later, in July 1882, the British Fleet bombarded the Arabists in Alexandria, and by September, a British army of occupation had routed Arabi's troops at Tel el Kebir. But although now to be overlaid by so much else, the scene in the Abdin Palace Square remained etched on Egyptian memories, and the triangular confrontation of forces so dramatically demonstrated on that famous day was to be resumed, remaining unresolved for a further seventy years.

With Arabi's exile the rôle of the Egyptian army in this contest passed into other hands. Possibly Arabi was hampered by his lack of schooling. But precisely because his nationalism was instinctive it readily communicated itself to other Egyptians of similar social origins but great intellectual resources. Most notable among these was Mohamed Abdu, son of a fellah of Beheira Province, and one of the most unusual Koranic scholars ever to graduate from Cairo's 1,000 year old mosque-university, El Azhar. Abdu's self-appointed mission to reform Islam, rejecting sterile scholasticism and superstition alike in order to interpret the Koran in the light of science, gave Egyptian nationalism another point of departure, enabling it to put down another tap-root as deep as that nurtured by the fellah colonels. And in 1881 Sheikh Mohamed Abdu, Colonel Ahmed Arabi, and their mutual friend, Wilfred Scawen Blunt, the English poet, Arabist, former diplomat and dedicated anti-Imperialist, together drew up a document entitled 'The Programme of the National Party of Egypt.'

In retrospect, Egyptian nationalism may be seen to have emerged, as much as to have been consciously created. But this is to anticipate. For its emergence was a consequence not only of Mohamed Ali's fellahin army, but also of another of that extraordinary man's innovations—the propagation of the 'Jumel' variety of cotton.

7 MAY 1951: King Farouk and Wafd leader, Nahas Pasha, at a Palace party to celebrate the King's marriage to Narriman Sadck. *Below* **18 JUNE, 1953**: the Revolution Command Council photographed after the proclamation of a Republic. *L to R: seated* Abdel Latif Baghdadi, Nasser, Neguib, Abdel Hakim Amer, Salah Salem, Anwarel Sadat *standing* Hussein El Shafei, Khaled Mohieddin, Gamal Salem, Kamal Eddin Hussein, Hassan Ibrahim, Zakaria Mohieddin.

Beni Mor, the Nasser family
village in Upper Egypt,
photographed by the author in
1965. Nasser's father left here
for Alexandria where his first
son, Gamal, was born—here
seen as a schoolboy (1928 an
30), nationalist student (1935
and *bottom left* as a Cairo
undergraduate reading Law.
Two uncles remained fellahin
Beni Mor.

Although a mediocre sort of cotton had grown in Egypt for centuries, it was not until 1820 that Lewis Alexis Jumel paid his historic visit to the Cairo home of Maho Bey, a former governor of Sennar on the Blue Nile. Invited to inspect his host's garden, he found growing there, as an ornamental shrub, a cotton plant whose fibres were of extraordinary length and fineness. His professional interest was aroused. He reported his find to Mohamed Ali, who promptly assigned a few acres for the plant's propagation. By 1822 the first sample bales had been despatched to Lancashire and Europe. The reports were good. Second only to the American Sea Island variety, which grew only in small quantities, 'Jumel' commanded a premium of 50 per cent over the old local Egyptian cottons.

It was the perfect marriage of land and product—for by reason of its deep alluvium, its dry air, hot sun, liberal supplies of Nile water, and, above all, its phenomenal climatic regularity, Egypt was uniquely suited to the cultivation of fine long-staple cotton. In the cool airs of the Egyptian night the cotton bolls developed with an evenness and a sureness no other country could rival: each twenty-four hours another cycle of cellulose grew around the fibre.

The social, economic and political consequences of Jumel's discovery were tremendous. The age-old primitive valley of the Nile became geared to the looms of Lancashire at the moment when Lancashire was becoming the roaring heart of a new industrial age. In an Alexandria which Mohamed Ali had restored and linked by canal to the Nile, rich European Levantine merchant dynasties were founded on cotton. The Peels, the Benachis, the Plantas, the Carvers, the Toriels, built their vast warehouses and set up their hydraulic baling presses, and an endless stream of sweating horses bringing the cotton from the canal boats or taking it to the ships plunged about on the stone setts of the cotton port of Minet El Bassal. It was the classic demonstration of the miraculous virtues of Cobdenism and Free Trade; the mutual enrichment of the nations from specialisation according to the natural endowment of each. For many years—until yesterday—four-fifths of Egypt's exports were cotton. They sustained a population that quadrupled in the 19th century.

It is possible, however, that the benefits were more obvious

to some than to others. The cotton plant is enormously exacting of labour—sowing, thinning, hoeing, irrigating, worm-
hunting, picking, sorting. Mohamed Ali instructed the fellahin
to have large families in order to cope with the cotton. 'Let
the mudirs and nazirs (officials) take care of agriculture,' ran
his order of 1824, 'or they will be buried in a common trench.'
The discipline of the Nile was now darkened by the tyranny
of the cotton plant; the fellah shared the servitude—as he also
shared the fortitude and rueful humour—of the Lancashire
millhand.

Since cotton was a leading counter in world commerce
Egypt was inevitably drawn into the orbit of international
capitalism in its exuberant 19th-century heyday. The powerful but regular rhythm of the Nile which had shaped the
country's life for many centuries was now overlaid by the
ticker-tape excitements of world stock and commodity
markets. The history of Egypt became a history of boom and
slump. In the first great boom set off by the American Civil
War the price of cotton quadrupled between 1861 and 1862.
Foreigners of all sorts, from Parisian bankers to Syrian pedlars,
began to flock to the new Klondyke on the Nile, many bearing
out Cromer's remark that 'whatever national defects they may
have possessed in their country of origin' were to be 'enhanced
when on arrival in Egypt they had to deal with a people who
were ignorant, credulous and improvident and therefore easily
despoiled.' When an acre of cotton was worth £1,000, money
fructified wonderfully in the pockets of those who already had
it, or could borrow some. Egypt became a casino in which the
counters were land, and the Khedive Ismail, whose private
cotton income reached one million pounds annually, was
among the most excited players. Quickly learning the secrets
of high finance, he issued Government Bonds with abandon—
and dealt in them as speculators drove their prices higher. On
this foundation arose Ismail's new 'Parisian' Cairo, with its
boulevards, its Opera House, its road to the Pyramids—and
its Bourse.

But the Khedive's financial education was not yet concluded.
As he bought yet more farms and plundered the fellahin, the
European merchant bankers and a hundred adventurers in turn
plundered Ismail, who knew no distinction between public

and private finance, and kept no books worth the name. At his accession in 1863 the public debt was £3·3 millions; by 1876 it had become £81 millions, and Ismail was desperately borrowing at interest rates of 30 per cent.

The goose being now plainly voided of golden eggs, the foreign bondholders prepared to foreclose.

'My country,' said poor Ismail, 'is no longer in Africa; we are today a part of Europe.' By a supreme irony this famous boast occurs in a speech addressed to the European Debt Commissioners, by which Ismail, dispossessed of vast plantations, accepts an annual dole, a modest 'Civil List.' Less than a year later, on 26 June 1879, deposed by the Sultan-Caliph in Constantinople at the nod of the bond-holding Powers, he was on his way into exile in that Europe he so admired, and the British were preparing to move in to supplement the Napoleonic lessons on Science and Liberty with a protracted course in book-keeping and administration.

He left behind his twenty-six-year-old son Tewfik, to inherit a kingdom in pawn (and soon under foreign military occupation), and to confront, as the new Khedive, Egyptian army officers whose humiliations had been sharpened by cuts in pay occasioned by an empty Treasury. Predictably, their animosity against the Turks henceforth embraced Europeans also.

A slump rarely sweeps away all that a boom has conjured up. Ismail's boom left behind a new, ever-expanding Cairo, ugly and ill-planned, yet the undoubted metropolis of the Near East, a vulgar and vigorous Levantine society—probably the most genuinely international in the world outside the Americas—and that new hinge of continents, the Suez Canal.

And the cotton plant, while it might corrupt and enslave, was also a powerful educator. Its cultivation demanded agricultural expertise—hence the young men Mohamed Ali sent to Europe for training were followed by many others. Yield figures and price premiums infallibly indicated the successful student. New varieties of cotton were at first developed from hybrids spotted by 'prospectors': thus the classic high-yielding 'Ashmouni,' discovered in 1860 and still being grown in Upper Egypt; thus the wondrous, long-staple 'Sakel,' named after a Greek, Sakellarides, who found it in a seed cotton sample in

1904. But from 1905 a Government plant-breeding station took over the critical rôle of developing varieties, and the whole present elaborate system of fibre classification, crop-sampling and test-spinning began to evolve.

The cotton plant wove science and technology into the very fabric of the country. It gave a critical rôle not only to the plant geneticist, and the agronomist, and the agricultural economist, but also to the irrigation engineer. Turning Egypt into a vast cotton plantation called for immense irrigation works. Under Mohamed Ali 400,000 fellahin were conscripted to dig hundreds of miles of new 'summer' canals. Ismail continued these Herculean labours, digging the massive 200-mile Ibrahamia Canal which taps the Nile above Assiut to water the whole of the west side of Middle Egypt. In order to take their water by gravity from the Nile at its low season, the 'summer' canals had to be dug very deep, and this in turn created the problem of raising the water to field level. Mohamed Ali boasted of having installed 38,000 *sakias* or water-wheels, bringing 100,000 acres into cultivation. But the labour of lifting the water remained formidable, and the possibilities of the new system of perennial irrigation appeared limited—until Mohamed Ali's irrigation expert, Linant de Bellefonds, advanced a plan for a great masonry barrage across the Nile at the apex of the Delta, raising the head of water high enough to permit free flow from the canals to the fields.

Work on the river bed started in 1833, and Mohamed Ali's last public act was to lay the foundation stone for the structure. But the barrage was to prove a long, hard lesson in the disciplines of hydraulic engineering. Mishaps were endless. It was not until the 'eighties, half a century after the launching of the scheme by the masterful but impetuous Pasha, that the Delta Barrage, repaired and re-designed by irrigation engineers from British India, at last delivered its full bounty. But then the effect was to increase the area under perennial irrigation by almost half.

The powerful process of technological logic which had led to the pioneer barrage continued to operate. In 1902 the first Aswan Dam initiated 'annual storage,' holding back part of the late autumn flood water for release the following spring. It was complemented by the Assiut Barrage, feeding the summer canals of Middle Egypt, and the Zifta Barrage, pushing out the margins of cultivation in the Eastern Delta. Under the pressure of soaring population, the machinery for the fuller utilisation of the Nile's water was steadily developed and refined. There followed the Esna Barrage in 1906, the Nag Hammadi Barrage in 1928, two heightenings of the Aswan Dam, quintupling its reservoir, and—completing the circle embarked upon a century earlier—a new and higher Delta Barrage alongside Mohamed Ali's. By 1960, when the High Dam got under way, the two million acres under cultivation (i.e. irrigated) in 1813 had become 6·3 millions.

The great barrages, with their scores of sluice-gates and the roads along their tops, are impressive features of the Egyptian scene. But they are merely the high points of a vast and intricate system of canals, weirs, branch canals, sluices and 'distributories,' drains and irrigation ditches that penetrate and spread over the country like the veins, arteries, capillaries and excretory organs of the human body. To keep this functioning calls for the daily attentions of two thousand irrigation engineers and two thousand civil engineers, organised in fifteen 'Circles'—or subsidiary circulatory systems. Supplying more than a quarter million acres, the Ismailia Circle, for instance, controls more than 1,250 miles of canals, with 1,070 bridges, 280 'head regulators' (distributing sluices) and 230 'tail escapes' from which the used water runs away into 600 miles of drains.

It is a system of total interdependence: as in the human body, a change in any part may produce a whole train of changes elsewhere. As the irrigation system was extended, the natural water table of the Delta rose and, in order to prevent damage from water-logging and salination, a complementary system of deep drains had to be developed. In the far north of the Delta a chain of generating stations and power lines was erected to drive the huge pumps which lift the water from the main drainage canals and push it into the coastal lagoons—Mariut, Borollos, Manzalah—and thence into the sea.

Thus the strong and challenging partnership of Man and Nature which had characterised the Valley almost from the earliest days grew ever closer and more intricate. It was still, in the last resort, Nature which dictated pace and rhythm, dominated by the age-old rhythm of the Flood. Yet Egypt had become that paradoxical thing, a natural machine, and a machine, after the introduction of Jumel Cotton, often as sensationally productive as the machines of the West. If Egypt had missed the Industrial Revolution, she nevertheless thus early acquired a cadre of native agricultural and irrigation engineers and a fund of technical experience on which she could later build. Scientific experimentalism had been embedded in the heart of an Islamic world constructed in the faith that all truth had been finally revealed more than a thousand years before.

By the time the fourth member of the Mohammed Ali Dynasty, the Sultan Said—French-educated and a friend of de Lesseps—had opened the first leaky version of the Delta Barrage in 1861, this old Islamic society had been challenged in many other ways. And by 1879, when Said's successor, Ismail, was despatched bankrupt into exile on the royal yacht *Mahroussa*, there had been assembled in the crucible of the Nile Valley nearly all those elements which were to determine the character of a world-changing event more than two generations later—the Egyptian Revolution of 1952. They had, in the main, their origin outside the Nile Valley, but they were there to be fused with an older element—the oldest of all and the least regarded—the unique and durable character of the Egyptian people themselves.

4

THE EGYPTIANS IN EGYPT

For seven thousand years we have been united as a people living in a slice of desert—if you go outside, you die.
—Soleiman Husayan, Rector of the University of Assiut to author, 1965

A storehouse of corn and riches and blessings of every kind. . . .
—General Ibn el-As Amr, Leader of the Muslim army taking Egypt, A.D. 640

Affability is a general characteristic of Egyptians of all classes.
—*The Manners and Customs of Modern Egyptians* by Edward Lane, 1836

If Egypt's future now pivots on the High Dam in Aswan, its heart still lies at 'the Barrage' where Mohamed Ali's masonry, bizarrely equipped with towers and castellations by his military-minded son, Said, reconstructed by the British, still straddles the twin branches of the Nile just before their confluence at the Delta's apex. In the Barrage Gardens the trees grow taller, the grass is springier, the birds sing sweeter, than anywhere else in Egypt, and on feast days—which are many —the picnickers from Cairo stroll or sit about on the grass in groups, nibbling nutcakes and catching perhaps a fleeting glimpse of that Paradise of cool groves and limpid streams and doe-eyed houris which the Koran holds out as the just reward of the True Believer.

Thrice a day a boat is rowed out into mid-Nile here to measure the speed of the current so that the water released down the canals can be accurately gauged. Warehousemen of water for the Delta, the Barrage engineers meet the calls of the agricultural year: water in February for the cotton-sowing, more water in mid-April for the rice, water in late July for the cotton flowering. . . .

A broad Nile barge, high-pyramided with earthenware drinking vessels from Kena in Upper Egypt, waits at a lock gate. For another 150 miles or so the Rosetta arm and the Damietta arm pursue their separate and devious courses to the sea, the one making its exit by the half-million palm trees and labyrinthine alleys of Rosetta, the other by the old shipbuilding slipways and fishing boats of Ezbet el Borg. Down there, Egypt has a luminosity and a feeling of space and release such as are to be encountered nowhere else in this over-emphatic, hard-beset land. And west and east of the Nile mouths stretches the string of coastal lagoons, Mariut, Idku, Borollos and the vast shimmering expanse of Lake Manzalah, criss-crossed by hundreds of skiff-like fishing boats, and offering a five-hour diesel-ship passage to Port Said.

West and east of the Nile arms, the canals above the Barrage —the Beheira, the Menufia, the Tewfikia, the Ismailia—thrust back the desert and define the Delta. A triangle of fertility only 150 miles or so wide on its base along the lakes—from the desert's edge just west of Alexandria to the desert's edge short of the Suez Canal—ninety miles along the central bisecting line to its apex near the Barrage, the Delta is the home of fifteen million people, living on the most productive and one of the most humanly congested soils in the world.[1]

The land, piled up down the centuries, is high near the Nile and the old watercourses. One soon grows accustomed to the sight of white lateen sails, billowing in line across the fields like processions of majestic ghosts. One is never far from water or from sails in the Delta. The roads themselves have been built on river or canal banks and, looking down, as from a grandstand, one sees the people moving along on other, lesser banks, of sub-canals and irrigation ditches and drains, strung out in lines like a classical frieze, hauling along the lumbering buffalo or urging ahead laden donkeys or riding them, legs merrily bouncing, as they thread the intricate network of bunds and paths that links the half-hidden mud-brown villages.

---

[1] With a rural population density calculated (for 1950) at 542 per square kilometre of cultivated land in Egypt (rising to 1,700 for some districts around Cairo), the most congested agricultural settlement in the world outside Japan and one or two small areas in the Far East.

It is only briefly that one may see the soil naked and fallow. Even in January the 'agricultural road' from Alexandria to Cairo passes across an unbroken carpet of green, the silver-green of the beans, the fruity green of young barley and wheat, the fantastic vividness of berseem or Egyptian clover. And in a month or two the whole scene will be changed, yet still as crowded, still as luxuriant. It was not hard to understand that Iraqi business-man who, seeing the Delta for the first time, exclaimed: 'In Iraq our peasants are lazy!'

Up to their knees in slime, a gang of labourers is down in a distributory canal at the roadside, shovelling out the silt on to glistening black piles. January, when the flow of the water is halted, is the season for the enormous labour (which the High Dam, passing little silt, will much reduce) of cleaning out the canals and ditches. For centuries the Nile mud, mixed with the straw of beans or berseem, has provided the bricks of the villages. As the affluent societies may now be graded by the volume of their discarded packagings, the 'under-developed' may be assessed by the totality of their consumption. Last year's old corn stalks and cotton plants, carefully brought back from the stripped fields, are piled high on the village rooftops and, with the neatly stacked dung-cakes, keep the cooking fires burning. In this economy there is no room for waste. The gamoose (or buffalo), feeding on the berseem, moves on tight tether at the field corner.

Fifteen miles south of the Barrage, up-river, the Nile leaves the world of mud-brick and flickering oil lamps to traverse the vast steel and concrete jungle of modern Cairo, a city of over four million people, incomparably the biggest in Africa and the Arab world. But even here the Nile contrives to dominate; the obvious source, it seems, of the city's rude vitality and thrust. On summer evenings it visibly becomes its lungs, as people of all classes pour from the baking streets to enjoy the cool night airs along that Corniche which, with its stone benches and Flame of the Forest trees, became an early symbol of the 'Free Officers'' energy and aspirations. Until 1966 the arrival of the Flood was an event almost as marked in Cairo as in the villages; when the Flood reached the city in August the whole character of the place changed. The air became heavy and humid. Water seeped into the basements, and the telephone service, formerly merely appalling, was liable in the vicinity of the river to all-but-complete collapse.

To the south and east the desert lays siege to the city, driving in a deep salient almost to the Nile bank between the Old Cairo of the Romans and the Coptic potters and the newer Cairo of the Fatamids, of Mohamed Ali, of the Arab League and the Nile Hilton. And then, from the massive yellow limestone shoulder of the Mokattam Hills, the city's harsh backdrop, the Valley stretches down like the skinny arm of some lank Nubian in a Cairo café. It is rarely more than twelve miles wide, often a mere three. Sometimes its confining cliffs loom on one side, sometimes on the other. At Minia the escarpment is table-topped, its exposed strata as straight as a layer-cake, leaving only a ledge of green, half a mile deep, on the eastern bank; but by the time Assiut is reached the desert has retreated once more to the East, to form the fertile palm-studded salient in which lies Nasser's paternal village, Beni Morr.

With the arrival of Kena, nearly 400 miles from Cairo, the cliff, bleaker and higher now, presses in sharply again on the east; the town's main street is thickly carpeted in fine desert sand. The herds of camels being driven down the Valley from the Sudan to provide meat for Cairo appear out of moving clouds of dust. There is dust everywhere, a diabolical powder that sifts through tightly shut windows and penetrates the very fabric of one's clothes. Winter here is brief; by March one will be fleeing from the blows of the sun.

And yet, although he may often catch a glimpse of it on either side, the traveller is scarcely conscious of the desert's nearness. He is totally enclosed in the richness, the sensuousness, of the Nile Valley scene—the golden walls of wheat, the rank corn, the lush berseem, the bulging bales of cotton piled outside the gin, the great eucalyptus trees by the roadsides. The same scenes of life repeat themselves endlessly from the Nile's mouth at Rosetta to the First Cataract at Aswan—the line of village women, bending to wash clothes or pots and pans at the canal edge; the rococo dove-cotes fashioned of mud; the row of white mounds made by discarded *galabiyas* piled on the brown earth, as, beyond, their owners, stripped to vest and shorts, work the soil with their mattocks; the swaying mountains of old corn-stalks or palm-leaves, advancing slowly down the road, all but enveloping the camels or donkeys beneath them; the man, feet in water, churning the *tambour*, whose slanting timbers glisten in the sun; the youth at some field corner, cutting fresh berseem with a sickle—an everlasting task since this mainstay of the village economy grows six crops in as many months.

It is, above all, a landscape *alive* with people. Stop anywhere in it, miles it may seem from any habitation. You believe yourself utterly alone. Yet, in a moment, your solitude will be broken. There is a student down there, conning his textbook under a palm-tree; a man comes plodding down the road driving on a gamoose; or a horde of children swarm out of nowhere, one or two of the boldest trying out the universal twin sentences of school English: 'What is your name? Where have you come from?'

As one travels southward, the basic Egyptian scene remains, but its accentuation changes. There are church towers as well as mosque domes among the palm trees—for this is the aboriginal Egypt, and many Coptic families have hung on here, still faithful to St Mark who converted them to Christianity six hundred years before Islam reached Egypt. The houses, made of fired brick in the far north where it rains in winter, of mud beyond, are of fired brick again in the old areas of basin irrigation, and the palm trees around the villages rise from round plinths of root and soil about which the Flood once swirled. The dusky red brick, sometimes patterned or balustraded at the cornice, and the gently moving palms impart a faintly lyrical note to the villages of Upper Egypt that is altogether absent from the mud heaps of the Delta. Yet there is no softness in this landscape, rather a strange theatrical quality. The long flowery dresses and white muslin kerchiefs that grace the women of the Delta now give way to hooded black robes falling in deep folds about the body, so that the women, moving through the lush greenness, resemble figures of classical tragedy. And the men, statuesque giants with curling mustachios, magnificently clothed in broad blue-and-white-striped *galabiyas*, march along with long staves in their hands—the Pharaonic symbol of authority, familiar from the Tombs. The *sakias* groan and whine, a distant steam pump poops shrilly like some exotic bird, and the gamoose, Africa strong in his nostrils now, becomes shaggier, tuskier and hoarser, and drags along the small boy who attends him.

Skins grow darker as bodies grow lither. Egypt spans the human pigmentation chart from the 'whites' of the Mediterranean coast to the blacks and dark browns of Nubia. They say that around Damietta there are blue-eyed people who descend from King Louis IX of France, held prisoner there in the Ninth Crusade. I looked for them in vain, yet the old story has its point. For the Nile Valley is a classic melting-pot. Although the devout Egyptian is apt to claim a great-grandsire out of Arabia rather as an American traces an ancestor on the *Mayflower*, General Amr's army of invasion contained a mere 15,000 men, and most of those reputed Yemenites. Egypt had been, and was to be for centuries, a participant in the restless world of the Eastern Mediterranean, bringing Greek mercenaries and traders, Roman soldiers, Venetian merchants and sailors, Phoenicians and Syrians (who figure in the tomb paintings), Maltese (whose islands were within Islam for over two hundred years), Armenians, Jews, and many whose origins were too complex to put a name to.

Like most human melting-pots, the Egyptian melting-pot has been capricious in its working. The Nile Valley village, with its jealously guarded limits of family and quarter, sanctified for the last thirteen hundred years by Islam, must have constituted a pretty insoluble lump, preserving an ancient Nile Valley stock of African-Asian origin. Yet, even here, slavery, concubinage and the press-gang had their effect. And higher up the social scale, intermixing was freer. The Mameluke and Turkish ruling castes imported a lusty mongrelism, and, until very recent times, Egyptians, rising in the world, took to themselves Turkish or Circassian wives. By the end of the 19th century, the phrase 'Turco-Egyptian' recognised a formidable reality—but one in which the emphasis was increasingly on the Egyptian base of the amalgam.

For what the genetic melting-pot could not dissolve, the Nile Valley assimilated. While the newcomer to Egypt will be struck by the great diversity of face and figure in the streets, he will also, after a time, be fascinated by the emergence of

certain uniquely Egyptian types; the rangy, oval-faced fellah
of the Delta; the square-shouldered, bull-chested, bullet-headed
man-about-town, impeccably dressed and balancing on neat
well-polished shoes; the busy, dapper little men who seem to
be specially bred as under-secretaries in the Ministries; the
statuesque six-foot-plus fellah of Upper Egypt with his incised
features and rock-like dignity; the gentler, rounder, middle
class Sa'idi or Southerner, a soft, bubbling, 'happy one.'

Yet diverse as these types are, from the grave, turbanned
divine hugging to his breast some Koranic truth arrived at by
ijtihad or striving, to the young couples exchanging amorous
glances over their *Bombe Atomique* or *Comtesse Marie* ice
creams in Groppi's, all are linked by an invisible bond, a deep
and strong 'Egyptian-ness' which is as unmistakable, in its own
way, as Englishness or Frenchness.

It has been the fate of the Egyptians, as a people, to live
in the long shadow cast by their own awesome past. They
emerged from it briefly in the late 1830s when Edward Lane
published his famous pioneer description of the *Modern
Egyptians*, but were quickly lost to view again beneath the
polyglot clamour of the Ismailian Levant and the massive dis-
dain of the British occupiers. Rarely can a nation of thirty
millions, with so distinctive a character and history, occupying a strategically critical area of the globe—and one so close
to Europe—have been less known.

Although not, in fact, hard to know, the Egyptians are,
nevertheless, a people whose characteristics are not readily
fitted into any single set of pigeon-holes. Some aspects—the
more obvious—clearly owe a good deal more to Africa than
Asia. There is, for instance, a ready clubbability,[2] a collective
gusto, and a sort of steam-roller-in-gear assertiveness that is
far removed from either the 'subtlety' of the Levantine or the
aristocratic dignity of the archetypal Arab sheikh. Put four or
five grave middle-aged Egyptians together in a motor-car and
they are soon like boys out of school, roaring with laughter at
each other's sallies. They will gossip half the night with unflag-

---

[2] Literally as well as metaphorically. For instance, in the small provincial
town Sohag, I found clubs for engineers, agriculturalists, doctors, social
workers, police, young Muslims, young Christians, a Family Aid Club, and
a General Club—in addition to numerous ladies' societies.

ging zest. On Friday and Saturday nights Cairo resounds with the slap of palm on palm as Egyptian greets Egyptian on the overflowing, male-packed pavements.

But behind the bonhomie and the belly-laughter there is a basic moral seriousness of the sort many in the West have forgotten. If the Egyptians are the least fanatic, they probably also constitute the most solid Muslim community in the Middle East. In smart Cairo shop-windows, the record sleeves of Elvis Presley and of the great Koranic chanter, Sheikh Mohamed Rifaat, are displayed together—but the sheikh far outsells Elvis. Charging into the frantic traffic, a Cairo taxi-driver tunes his transistor to the poignant, stylised, endless chant of the Koran. Even here the familiar verses still solace or elevate like wine; they strike to the heart as when the Prophet first uttered them, God's revelation to his chosen people. This is the gift of the Arabs to Egypt, and it is a possession which the humble share with the high-and-mighty: at the new mosque of Omar Makram in the westernised heart of Cairo, bread-hawkers, arriving with their baskets, well-to-do bureaucrats, arriving in sleek cars, all sorts and conditions of men, stand together in orderly rows, performing the *rakkas* of the evening prayer, silent and dignified and one in the brotherhood of Islam.

They say—as they have been saying for years[3]—that Ramadan, the great fasting month, is not what it was: in these impious days people actually dare to be seen smoking on the streets. Yet it remains a unique act of collective discipline in a world not notable for that quality, as well as an intensification and stirring-up of life and the physical organism—as anyone can testify who has walked Egyptian streets as the sunset cannon sounds and suddenly every doorway and every shop and every café is full of people zestfully breaking the day's fast.

And the fast is followed by the feasts, which, unlike our bored commercialised festivals of the West, are both genuine explosions of popular rejoicing and renewals of a still meaningful tradition. Even ostensibly westernised families purchase, cost what it may—and it makes a disastrous hole in many purses—the obligatory sheep at *Kourban Bairam* for slaughter

[3] e.g. Gertrude Bell in Baghdad in 1921: 'I wonder how long the fast will hold Islam.'

in their kitchens ('blood all over the place, it's terrible, really') by the perambulant butcher, and the fellahin bring their families into town, all dressed in bright new clothes, filling the backs of the flat carts like the sudden arrival of spring.

Fast and feast—and the Copts have their own and share some with the Muslims—impart their strong rhythm to the year. The pilgrimage, too, remains a major reality; many scrape and save for years to receive its absolution. Egyptians, with characteristic generosity, are in the habit of hailing old people familiarly as 'Hag' (Egyptian Arabic for 'Hadji,' the honorific of one who has been to Mecca).

It is true that when they leave their villages for the Big City, the young, these days, very often cease to go to the mosque or to perform the prescribed prayers. But they cannot put off their religion as easily as they can abandon its exacting observances. For Islam is embedded in the language, in social custom, in the law, in the whole culture. Modern psychology, with its labyrinthine equivocations which have so deeply affected the morality of the West, has here made astonishingly little impact, and for both Muslims and Copts alike the world of the Nile Valley remains a world with purpose, a world of Good and Evil, of things permissible and things forbidden—and no word has a more scarifying finality than the word 'haram' on Arab lips. To be called an 'irreligious man' is damning, while the notion of deliberate atheism appears positively bizarre.

In this last respect the Russians are a source of much genuine puzzlement. A highly westernised Egyptian whose official duties brought him into contact with the Russians told me of one baffling encounter when he had refused an offer of vodka, explaining that his religion did not permit this.

'Religion!' laughed the Russian. 'In the Soviet Union we do not encourage such superstitions. . . .'

'A moment,' said my friend. 'Remember you will not always be as young and as strong as you now are. One day you will be old and you will need help and you will wonder about the meaning of it all . . . in what, then, will you believe?'

'In the Leningrad Technological Institute,' replied the Russian, without a second's hesitation.

My Egyptian friend shook his head. Non-communication was complete.

Egyptians of all degree are powerfully bound together by the reality of their common roots in the soil. The odds are that your engineer, your determinedly *nouvelle vague* intellectual, factory manager, professor or bureaucrat, still has a feddan or two of land in the family village, or his brother does or his uncle—or he sold it only yesterday. The odds are that in his Cairo apartment he still has *fool* (much-boiled beans) for breakfast and indeed considers this the only real breakfast in the world (although he may use olive oil for his beans whereas the poor villager makes do with cotton-seed oil). For all its chrome and neon, Cairo is one great congeries of villages, with the copper pots of *fool* for ever on the boil outside the little cafés, the hens clucking on the roofs of tall apartment blocks, and people wandering obliviously in the paths of cars and buses whose drivers seek to blast a way for the vehicles with their klaxons. Crowded shoulder to shoulder in *L'Américaine*, those well-dressed men-about-town wolf chocolate cakes by the plateful. But even with only a piastre or two in the pocket hearty peasant appetites can be satisfied—for Cairo's streets teem with eatables on barrows and stalls—the roasting corn-cobs in summer and the sweet potatoes in winter, the gaudy *kushri* wagons with their piled rice-lentils-and-fried-onion and macaroni, the carts with their yellow mountains of *thermes*, soaked in water and served in screws of newspaper—the same lupin peas the Pharaohs knew.

Perhaps this homespun village background explains why, although the forms of courtesy are important everywhere in the Orient, with the Egyptians there is a certain laboriousness about them, the eternal *Marhaba! Marhaba!* (Welcome!), the dutiful and endless *Tfaddel* (if you please). And yet, at any moment, the heavy formalism, easily degenerating into pomposity, may be scattered to the winds by that genuine sense of fun, that boyish merriment, which is never far below the surface in Egypt.

Watch a Cairo policeman trying to instil traffic discipline into pedestrians at a traffic-lights crossing. The people edge forward against the red light. First one advances a foot, then another. The policeman scowls, waves his stick. The crowd falls back, then, hope reviving, begins to edge forward again. The light is still red, but there is no traffic. The policeman holds up an imperious hand. By this time, only nine feet of road remain unencroached upon. The light is still unquestionably red. The policeman holds his ground. The creeping advance continues. Now only three feet are left, a ragged edge. The policeman is looking nasty. The crowd is becoming angry. Suddenly, someone points to 'the three feet remaining and makes some witticism. The whole menacing situation dissolves abruptly into laughter. The policeman grins as only an Egyptian can grin. *Malish!*—'Not to worry!'

Even so, the forms must be respected: a man's dignity is his most precious possession. That, perhaps, is the Ottoman legacy. My taxi-driver, going through the lights, stops fifty yards on and waves his apologies to the policeman. 'Oh, *malish!*' says the policeman—what is an odd light between brothers? Yet, a few days later, another taximan, neglecting to apologise, was called 'a donkey' by the policeman—and a minor riot resulted, with one death and several hospital cases, immobilising a Cairo main street for two hours, and requiring a public statement from the Ministry of the Interior.

So '*Malish!*' remains the great solvent, the built-in Egyptian stabiliser, and a major source of strength, as well as weakness. For it is not necessarily, as impatient Europeans see it, merely an expression of indolent indifference (although it may often be) but also of comprehensive charity. Egyptians in adversity have an un-Arab ability to crack a rueful joke against themselves—and carry on regardless. 'Malish!' encompasses the group and Egyptians, from Cabinet Ministers to sheikhs of El Azhar, seem to move and have their being by groups. But it can be disconcerting to the Westerner to experience the speed with which, no longer plugged into that communal electricity, exuberance can give way to abysmal finger-joint-cracking boredom, that inertia in which *Malish* is complemented by the blankly conclusive *Mafish*—'There isn't any.'

And yet, easy-going as they are, the Egyptians can show a plodding, dogged methodicalness, and a devotion to the schematic that sometimes seems almost Germanic. Your Egyptian bureaucrat—and not only bureaucrat—is never so happy or unstoppable as when ticking off the stages and steps of some grand design—I, II, III and i, ii, iii, *a*, *b*, and *c*—preferably while drawing an organisational diagram of it. Perhaps that is the Pharaonic heritage.

There is, in fact, a touch of the Gargantuan about this unique people, both in their faults and virtues. And this is true even physically, for where else will one see so many giants, hear more reverberant voices—or listen to more zestful, unabashed boasting? From May each year the windows of Tsarikis, the popular Greek café on Cairo's Suleiman Pasha (Talaat Harb) street, are lined with huge round water-melons, sombrely glossy in their thick dark-green skins—and it always seemed to me that there was some mysterious affinity between them and the Egyptians who are to be seen, for weeks on end, with knives and forks poised joyfully over the succulent slices. Both at least draw a rude strength from the soil and the sun of Africa, and the waters of the Nile.

Of the more recent conquerors and occupiers of the Nile Valley—the Arabs, the Turks, the French, the British—the mark left by the British on Egyptian character and culture has perhaps been the least (although their occupation did result in a widespread command of the English language, as well as the French, which greatly strengthened the bond with the West). It is evident that, in some respects, the British and Egyptian characters are antithetical—which may go some way to account for the persistent refusal of the British to take the Egyptians seriously, much less concede their historic rôle in the Eastern Mediterranean. Yet one characteristic the Egyptians did share with the people an ironic fate placed over them: both possessed the inborn conservatism—and the complementary smugness—of islanders. The Ancient Egyptians, depicting 'the four races of mankind' upon the Tombs, neatly categorised their own as 'Mankind'; and even today the Nile Valley is so much larger than life that, while one is within it, it is very apt to seem the whole world. 'How do you irrigate your fields in England?' a fellah asked me. 'From the river or from the canal?' And an Egyptian doctor of medicine assured me that only in Egypt did medical students dissect human bodies.

Yet, ever since Napoleon's arrival, Nile Valley insularism has been shaken by bouts of claustrophobia and doubt. For these, however, the geography of Egypt can offer relief. If to the fellahin enclosed within this narrow world, the Nile is 'El Bahr'—the sea, it is not Egypt's only sea. If at one extremity of the country the Nile disappears into the recesses of Africa, at the other it is flooded with Mediterranean light.

Modern Alexandria is not, in truth, a particularly attractive city, yet Egyptian voices lift as they pronounce its name. *Iskanderia* is always an exclamation with them. For Alexandria offers escape from the closed worlds both of Islam and the Nile Valley; it completes—with the pull of Europe—the three-poled field of force within which modern Egypt lives; for the Egyptian intellectual, in recent times, it has symbolised an eager—rather dogged—aspiration to a Gallic universality.

And, in fact, Alexandria, though hardly less humanly congested, does possess an urbanity that Cairo, for all Ismail's boulevards, can never have. One breathes more freely there. An Egyptian said to me: 'If I have an enemy and I meet him in Alexandria, I cannot be his enemy. In Cairo it is different. . . .' So, despite post-war Egypt's Arabism, the long love affair with Alexandria goes on and the country is full of the sound of Alexandrians congratulating each other on belonging to 'the most civilised city in Egypt.' Yet it is a matter of historical fact that the Arabs abandoned Alexandria: by the time of Bonaparte's arrival all that was left of the former 'Queen of Cities' was a ramshackle village of four thousand inhabitants. It was Mohamed Ali who, abetted by the cotton plant and Europe, re-created Alexandria, restoring to the Nile Valley that tension between East and West which energised him, had once energised Egypt, and would do so again.

It is interesting to note that Gamal Abdel Nasser, whose paternal family hails from Upper Egypt, maternally was of Alexandria and was born and bred there.

PART TWO
THE NAIVE REVOLUTION

In a serious collapse of a system . . . a small but well-orga-
nised and disciplined group is inevitably able to take authority
in its hands.

> —Milovan Djilas, *The New Class* (1957)

We went to the men of ideas for counsel and we went to the
men of experience for guidance, but unfortunately we did
not find much of either.

> —Gamal Abdel Nasser, *The Philosophy
> of the Revolution* (1954)

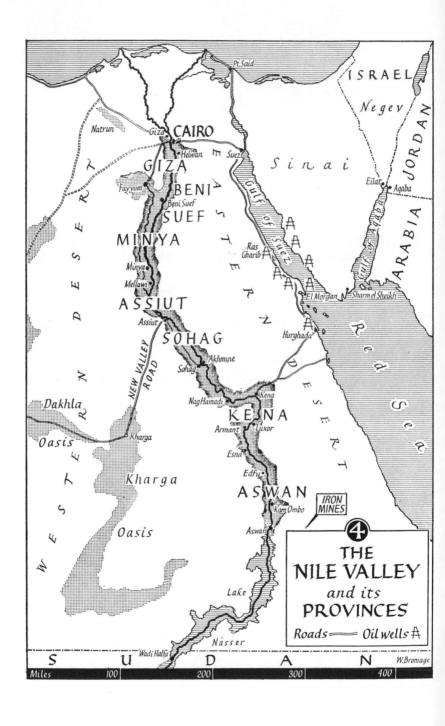

ISRAEL

Negev

JORDAN

ARABIA

Pt. Said

Natrun

Giza CAIRO

GIZA

Helwan Suez

Sinai

BENI

Fayyum

Beni Suef

SUEF

MINYA

Minya

Mellawi

Ras
Gharib

Gulf of Suez

Eilat Aqaba

El Morgan Sharm el Sheikh

ASSIUT

Assiut

Hurghada

SOHAG

Akhmine

Sohag

Nag Hamadi

KENA

Kena

Armant Luxor

Esna

Edfu

ASWAN

Kom Ombo

Aswan

Dakhla

Oasis

Kharga

Kharga

NEW VALLEY ROAD

WESTERN

DESERT

EASTERN

DESERT

Red Sea

IRON
MINES

④

THE
NILE VALLEY
and its
PROVINCES

Roads ═══ Oil wells ⚓

Lake

Nasser

Oasis

S   U   D   A   N   W. Bromage

| Miles | 100 | 200 | 300 | 400 |

5

THE FREE OFFICERS TAKE OVER

No régime ever fell more easily . . . Three days was enough
to throw down a dynasty which had occupied the throne for
one hundred and fifty years and its fall was greeted with
universal approbation.

—Anwar el Sadat, *Revolt on the Nile*

On Tuesday 22 July 1952 Lieutenant-Colonel Anwar el Sadat,
then stationed at Rafah, near the Israeli frontier, received a
telephone call from a fellow-officer, Lieutenant-Colonel Gamal
Adbel Nasser, which brought him hurrying back to Cairo. He
reached his home about 5 p.m. but, finding no message for
him there, decided to take his children to a nearby open-air
cinema. When he got back he found that Nasser had called in
his absence, leaving a note. The note read: 'It happens tonight.
Rendezvous at Abdul Hakim's at 11 p.m.'

'My heart leapt,' el Sadat wrote later. 'I tore off my civilian
clothes and flung on my military uniform. In five minutes I
was at the wheel of my car. But the rendezvous, when I got
there, was deserted. The operation had already begun.'

The date of the coup had already been brought forward
because of a warning that something was suspected: hence
the hurried call to el Sadat. But now, with zero hour set for
1 a.m. on July 23, a brother of one of the 'Free Officers' organising the revolt, had got wind of the plan and tipped off GHQ.
An emergency meeting of senior officers was known to be
gathering. It was clear that every moment counted.

Nasser and his right-hand man, Major Abdel Hakim Amer,
immediately rushed off in Nasser's small Morris to try to contact their forces. But halfway to the Almazah military air base
they ran into an army convoy. A glimpse of the Commander
of the 2nd Regiment in the first car and of his deputy in the
second seemed to confirm their worst fears. Nasser and Amer
found themselves surrounded by five young officers with
tommy guns who ordered them to put their hands up. It was

an anxious moment; but it was fleeting. A few seconds later one of the Free Officers, Lieutenant-Colonel Yussef Sadik, jumped out of the third car and hailed Nasser and Amer with delight. He had taken prisoner both his commanding officer and his second-in-command and, with eighty men, which was all his battalion could then muster in Cairo, had moved off—an hour too early.

His error proved providential. With these eighty men, GHQ was surrounded and stormed. Anwar el Sadat, hearing the stutter of machine-gun fire, and catching up with the action at last, tried to enter the headquarters building. But he had forgotten the coup password and the rebels' sentry would not let him pass. Inside, the Chief of Staff, General Hussein Farid, made a feeble gesture of resistance, firing three shots from his revolver into the ceiling. But although the building was full of officers, it was captured with the loss of only two soldiers.

Meanwhile, in the early hours, General Neguib, whose name had been linked with the Free Officers although he had, in fact, taken no personal part in the coup, was receiving a worried telephone call from the Minister of the Interior, who was at his summer residence in Alexandria. 'Your boys have started something. . . . I appeal to you as a soldier and a patriot to put a stop to it.' Neguib professed ignorance. But at 7 a.m. the General's message to the people of Egypt was read over the radio by Anwar el Sadat. It announced that the Army, formerly led by 'fools, traitors and incompetents' was now in the hands of 'men in whose ability, integrity and patriotism you can have complete confidence.'

Few *coups d'état* have been more liberally documented, and although the many accounts of the participants differ bewilderingly in details, from all of them, taken together, a fair enough picture emerges in which two main—conflicting—impressions stand out. The first is the extremely homespun character of the coup, with that strange 'typically Egyptian' mixture of total casualness and heavy melodrama, of earnestness and conviviality, of grandiose paper structures that transcend feeble reality, and all those restless, complex, apparently random, group interactions which somehow in the end miraculously produce a result.

The second impression is that this time, behind the arabesques of plot and counter-plot, there quietly moved a steady, driving will and purpose. Despite all the mishaps and near-disasters of the night of 22 July and earlier, the plan was pushed through. The affair was in fact well organised. The ten officers who were privy to the final plan covered all the vital elements. Soon after GHQ had been taken the tanks of the cavalry officers, Lieutenant-Colonel Hussein el Shafei and Major Khaled Mohieddin, took up their positions in key points in Cairo. The security squads of Lieutenant-Colonel Zakaria Mohieddin—a colleague of Nasser and Amer at the Staff College where he lectured on Intelligence work—rounded up remaining hostile police and army commanders. The planes of Wing-Commander Abdel Latif el Baghdadi and Squadron-Leader Hassan Ibrahim flew over the city.

On the 25th a column of tanks moved down to Alexandria where the King was and invested both the Ras el Tin and the Montazah palaces. At noon next day Farouk meekly signed the instrument of abdication tendered to him; at 6 p.m. he boarded the royal yacht *Mahroussa* to leave Egypt for ever. Punctiliously Egyptian to the last, three of the Free Officers—Neguib, Hussein el Shafei and Wing-Commander Gamal Salem—went on board to bid the King farewell, and an Egyptian destroyer fired the regulation salute of twenty-one guns as the ship sailed from the harbour.

Few coups which have had consequences so momentous have been conducted more quietly or bloodlessly. But it was perhaps in the final choice of the moment that Nasser's qualities of patient watchfulness and singleness of purpose were best displayed. In the ten years or so during which he had been involved in the confused fraternisations, aspirations and resentments since dignified with the name of the 'Free Officers Movement' he had resisted many hare-brained schemes urged by more impulsive comrades—for blowing-up the British Embassy, assassinating an Egyptian Cabinet, linking up with the advancing German army during the war, intervention in force in the Canal Zone—to name but a few. A variety of fanatic organisations had held out offers of alliance, and had been side-stepped. Beyond a certain stage only more-or-less open propaganda could advance the Free Officers' cause. It was fortunate that they were not the only plotters in an army where 'secret societies' and seditious leaflets were in fact endemic; but it was due to more than good fortune that they consistently had the best alibis. Lt.-Col. Nasser had a quick brain and a cool head. Once, on the insistence of the King, Nasser was severely cross-examined by the Prime Minister in the presence of the Chief of Staff. His house was searched. But he went back, un-charged, to his post as a teacher at the Staff College—the ideal location for the careful selection of Free Officer recruits. In January 1950, Nasser was elected Chairman of the Free Officers' first Executive Committee; but from 1951 onwards attention was diverted to the widely respected General Neguib whom the conspirators had brought in both for cover and as a senior figurehead.

By December 1951 the Free Officers felt strong enough openly to challenge Farouk's incessant and capricious inter-ference[1] in the army, which he regarded in the Oriental tradi-tion as his praetorian guard—and which was, indeed, the basis of his arbitrary power. They put up their own candidates against the King's nominees for the committee of the Officers' Club. At the last minute, Army Command stepped in and can-celled the election meeting. It was held just the same. Five hundred officers met in the Club's General Assembly and elected Neguib their President by a large majority; of the fifteen Committee members elected, five were known Free Officers, the rest at least sympathisers. It was the first public confronta-tion, and it might perhaps be noted in passing that the contest was an electoral one.

Until this time it was at least possible that some other con-spiratorial group might have launched the Revolution; but from December 1951 the Free Officers were identified and com-mitted; if they did not act, the King would.

The point was promptly underlined in a 'secret tract' headed 'The Army says NO to Farouk'—the beginning of a new cas-cade of mutinous print. In December and mid-January there

[1] For instance, it is said that when Farouk's chauffeur, an ex-army sergeant, reported to his master that he had been reprimanded for lounging, while waiting for him in the Officers' Club, Farouk characteristically gave him a commission and later made him a colonel. Similarly, a former prison director who had not held an army rank higher than 2nd lieutenant was made Commander-in-Chief; and Farouk's brother-in-law, a totally unqualified 'honorary Colonel,' was forced on the Government as Minister of War.

were violent student demonstrations against the King. All universities and many high schools were shut down. The Government was increasingly unsure of itself. The war boom was over, and industry had been standing off workers—although the national income per capita was still stuck around 1913 level. The guerilla war against the British in the Canal Zone fed the rising tide of violence and despair. Demoralisation deepened almost daily. On 26 January 1952 the burning of Cairo starkly revealed its true extent, setting the stage for the coup which came five months later.

Again, the timing was excellent. The King and Government were away at the summer headquarters in Alexandria. The weather was torrid: much too hot for watchfulness. Martial law and a curfew, imposed after the Cairo fire, were still in force, simplifying the rebel officers' movements. But the truly decisive factors were not the physical ones. On that fateful round of the conspirators in his little Morris car on the night of 22 July, Nasser called at the home of Lieutenant-Colonel Sarwat Okasha. His parting words to him were: 'Don't imagine you're at the cinema, Sarwat. We have ninety-nine chances out of a hundred of success.'

It was true. Despite the grandiloquence of cells, sections and committees there do not appear to have been more than a hundred Free Officers.[2] But if relatively few in the Army had been willing to risk their jobs, equally by mid-1952 few possessed either the inclination or the will to resist the coup. It was the same with the nation at large. Even in 1964, people still recalled those 'last days' with something of a shudder: 'It was terrible, you know.' In Egypt a would-be 'brilliant' society had been stripped of its pretensions and was at the end of its tether. The reins of power fell from palsied fingers into the only hands still firm enough to grip them, backed by the only organisation still representative, coherent and disciplined enough for the formidable tasks that lay ahead.

[2] The ardent Anwar el Sadat writes that in 1947/8 there were over a thousand Free Officers. Hussein el Shafei told the author that, through the years, there were 'rarely less than a hundred underground'; Khaled Mohieddin told another interviewer ninety; Nasser himself told an Egyptian Committee in 1958 that the Free Officers in 1952 did not exceed a hundred. In addition to the fogs generated by conspiracy, one is up against a certain Oriental nonchalance about figures

In retrospect the July coup appears as logical and as inevitable as the High Dam, the dénouement towards which the high drama of the Nile Valley had for more than a century—through so many turbulent scenes—been advancing.

It had, indeed, as we have seen, been rehearsed seventy years earlier, with an uncanny faithfulness (but some transpositions of sequence and rôle, as in a dream). On that other 26 July —in 1879—another profligate ruler of Egypt, the Khedive Ismail, the grandfather of Farouk, had also sailed away into exile on the *Mahroussa* to a salute of naval guns, leaving chaos behind him. And another aggrieved and earnest colonel of fellah origins had led another army secret society in patriotic mutiny. It is true that Ismail was, in effect, removed by the foreign creditors, and Arabi was checkmated by Gladstone. It was also true that by 1952 the third party in the confrontation of September 1881 on the Abdin Palace Square, Great Britain, had moved a little off-stage, and was no longer prepared to intervene in quite the old masterful way. But the social and economic forces which had produced the rehearsal of 1879-81 were essentially the same as those which, further developed, achieved the finished drama of 1952.

If doom took its time in coming, this extraordinary society was a society that was doom-laden almost from the start. On the day on which the Viceroy Said agreed to his plan for a Suez Canal, Ferdinand de Lesseps espied over the desert 'a rainbow of the most brilliant colours with its two ends plunged from east to west,' and had no hesitation in pronouncing this a clear omen of the happy 'union of Occident and Orient' that was to follow. In the event, however, the rainbow's purity soon tarnished; the union was often to be of the worst of both worlds.

Nowhere was this more depressingly demonstrated than in the Western-style parliamentary constitution which followed the grant of so-called 'Home Rule' by Britain in 1923. Drawn up by a commission of Egyptian lawyers who took Belgium as their model, it managed to give full play both to the caprice and malice of the Oriental despot and to the factiousness and pompous hypocrisies of Western parliamentary party politics. To have induced in a sovereign of the Mohamed Ali dynasty the frame of mind appropriate to a constitutional monarch must in any event have been difficult. When the Constitution allowed the King not only to appoint two-fifths of the Senate (which had a high income qualification), but also to dismiss Ministers and Governments at will, it became not so much difficult as impossible. The consequence was that for thirty years Egyptians lived within a political squirrel's cage in which first King Fuad, then King Farouk, each with his own *chef de cabinet* and private policy, struggled for the control of the country with the great Wafdist popular leaders, first Zaghloul and then Nahas, while the British, who held the real power, tenaciously retained the rôle of self-interested umpire, stepping in whenever British interests were affected. It was a system which might well have been designed to produce total demoralisation, and in due course it produced it.

But it was not only the delights of becoming 'Your Excellency,' not only the fact that sycophancy was an older habit of mind in Egypt than patriotism, that undermined the simple grass-roots nationalism evoked by Arabi and Mohamed Abdu. An old Islamic society whose Koranic law forbade usury and honoured brotherhood was scarcely to be transformed into a modern nation by being exposed to the full force of the world money game at its most hectic. And in few places in the world did men amass great fortunes more swiftly and easily than in the bloated Cairo which for so many was now Egypt. Between 1904 and 1907—to quote a participant—'a veritable rain of gold descended upon Egypt.' The Belgian Baron Empain, later creator of Heliopolis, bought 5,000 acres of desert on the city's edge at £1 for 4,000 square metres and soon afterwards sold it at £1 for half a metre. He was only one of many thus fabulously enriched. This was a society in which everything had its price—titles, votes, wives, Ministerial posts, spontaneous demonstrations (10 piastres a head), villages, murder. Both Fuad and Farouk found the sale of the titles of pasha and bey a ready source of cash, influence and land. Those who were thus honoured now included Egyptians as well as Levantines and Turks. But though the new pashas might on occasion wear *galabiyas*, pour forth the rhetoric of nationalism, and finance the Wafd, they were no kinder to the fellahin than their predecessors. They backed the Wafd because it secured their positions and kept both rural taxes and rural wages low.

In 1921 Saad Zaghloul had corrected an English friend who referred to the Wafd as 'the nationalist party.'[3] The Wafd, said Zaghloul, was no mere party; it was the Egyptian Nation. At that time there had been some substance in the claim. Zaghloul had taken part in Arabi's revolt (and had been detained in 1882 by the British), and his originality as an Egyptian politician was that, unlike the stiff Turco-Egyptian ruling caste who dominated the government party, and unlike some westernised liberals, he addressed himself not merely to the 'Notables,' not merely to the intellectual élite, but to all, to the 'dregs of the towns,' to the ignorant of the villages, to the students—to the People.

Thus beyond its undeviating 'Egypt for the Egyptians' stand which was the Wafd's *raison d'être*, there had sometimes seemed to lurk the germ of social revolution. The Wafd had, after all, been launched on the wave of unrest that followed the war and in the 1919 troubles the fellahin, having attacked the offices of the 'foreign' government, would sometimes go on to the Big House of the estate-owner pasha. Local republics were proclaimed in some small towns and some Zaghloul spokesmen in rural areas were said to be promising 'the land for the people.'[3] Whether that was true or not, in the first elections held under the new constitution in 1924, the Wafd carried all before it. In its ranks, bearing out Zaghloul's claim, a new sort of Egyptian appeared on the parliamentary stage, teachers, village *omdas*, young lawyers, obscure sheikhs. . . .

However, under the 'reserved powers' and under the Constitution, the British authority and the King between them— the one fearing the Wafd's 'extreme' nationalism, the other its latent radicalism—successfully frustrated the national party's evolution during what should have been its formative years. Finally, in 1936, under Nahas Pasha, the party of no compromise accepted the compromise of the new Anglo-Egyptian Treaty (offering ultimate retirement of the British Army to the Canal Zone); two years later, the Wafd split. Egypt had

[3] Memorandum on Egypt, 1921, prepared for the British Foreign Office, by Harry Boyle, Cromer's former Oriental Secretary, reprinted in *Boyle of Cairo* by Clara Boyle (Kendal, 1965).

become the land *par excellence* of the professional politician, of the *business* of politics. The nationalist diatribe remained, however, the easiest means of trumping one's rivals and, as the new pashas discovered, the surest cloak for the political consolidation of class interests. Few societies more thoroughly demonstrated the truth of Dr Johnson's adage about patriotism being the last refuge of a scoundrel.

But if the Second World War brought the usual boom and the usual reinforcement of the *nouveau riche* society, it also brought a series of shocks which revealed to Egyptians the depths to which their government had fallen.

The first of these shocks occurred in 1942 when the British Ambassador took armoured cars to the Abdin Palace, and under their guns and the drawn revolvers of his military escort, delivered to the King of Egypt an ultimatum. Either dismiss your (pro-German) Prime Minister, Lord Killearn told Farouk, and install Nahas Pasha and the Wafd—or abdicate forthwith. Farouk did as he was told. And the Wafd, that great national party, eagerly took office—before issuing an outraged protest against the British intervention. Both King and Wafd were thus utterly discredited at one blow. The two great institutions of modern Egypt's political life, both loudly claiming to represent the people, were shown to represent no one but themselves.

The second moment of truth came in 1948 when Britain precipitately withdrew from the Palestine Mandate. Farouk ringingly announced that the Egyptian armed forces would proceed forthwith to the rescue of the Palestinian Arabs. Vainglorious news bulletins could not conceal the fiasco that followed.

The third humiliation lay in the continuing failure to bring about the unconditional evacuation of the British. Independence had now been freely accorded to India and other lesser subject nations. In 1946 British troops had marched out of Cairo itself and in a ceremony on Mohamed Ali's birthday, King Farouk had triumphantly hoisted the Egyptian flag above the Citadel. Yet in spite of a high degree of westernisation, in spite of two generations of struggle by one of the oldest nationalist movements in Afro-Asia, Egypt still found herself in 1952 an occupied country, unwilling host in the Canal Zone to four times the number of British troops allowed there under the Anglo-Egyptian Treaty of 1936.

Of this national impotence King Farouk had now become all too apt a symbol. When, in 1936, he had returned from the Woolwich Military Academy to ascend the throne, the nation had been filled with new hope since, unlike his sombre Turkish-speaking father, Farouk might be considered one of themselves, a true Egyptian. Alas! the slim and handsome youth who fifteen years earlier had publicly dedicated his life 'to the service of the People' was by 1952 a gross figure of burlesque, a curious and pathetic blend of Western playboy and Oriental potentate in decay, speeding endlessly in his scarlet automobiles from palace to palace and 'rest house' to 'rest house,' lecherous, devious and greedy, consumed by malice and jealousy and preyed upon by flatterers and panders eager to satisfy each puerile whim. Concubinage is a traditional feature of Oriental monarchy, but the womanising of this prince whom the sheikhs of El Azhar had pronounced a direct descendant of the Prophet was conducted under the arc-lights of the world's press on the stage of 'café society.' The Egyptians are not a squeamish people, but Farouk shamed them. The grotesque double divorce he contrived, in which the Shah of Persia divorced Farouk's sister Fawzia while Farouk simultaneously divorced his own long-suffering Farida, deeply offended many; his later picking-up of a new Queen, the sixteen-year-old Narriman, in a jeweller's shop while she was trying on another man's engagement ring, did little to restore self-esteem.

Certainly the clash between the 'two Egypts,' between the old Nile Valley world of Good and Evil, of things permissible and things forbidden, and the Levantine world was no new one. But stark as it was, the distance between village and Bourse, and the presence of the Occupying Power, had hitherto enabled it to continue. But now the distance was narrowing —and the Occupier was about to depart. The battle of values, underlined in the decay of the Wafd, was moving towards a climax.

Between 1945 and 1950 the most respected Egyptian writer, Taha Hussein, published no fewer than seven books dealing with social injustice, political corruption and exploitation.

The council of the co-operative of Robh Shandied—Etay El Baroud Land
Reform Area—in session. The fellah chairman, Mohamed Tewfik El Kady,
makes a point over the Minute Book. This picture was taken in 1955 by
the author who revisited the co-operative in 1964 and 1965. By that time
the village (below) had acquired a concrete Club house with television.
(Chapters 6 and 17)

Two universal devices of rural Egypt, both thousands of years old. *Above* The *norag,* or threshing sled, pulled by a pair of gamoose—here ridden in Robh Shandied by one Ahmed Shaban (Chapter 6). *Below* Two fellahin lift irrigation water onto their fields with a *tambour* or Archimedes screw. But by 1965 at Robh Shandied the *norag* was being pulled by one of the co-operative's six tractors.

Anger now lent a sharper edge to the rising social protest; in 1952, the people could echo their nationalist poet of the 'eighties: 'O Egyptians, there is disgrace all round. Awake! Awake!'

As Western-style parliamentarianism appeared increasingly bankrupt and the Wafd degenerated into a mere spoils organisation, people, seeking some outlet for their sense of outrage and frustration, turned to older themes. The cry of 'Islam-in-danger!' which had rallied the Street against Bonaparte as it had against the Frankish Crusaders, was heard again, and proved potent still. The Muslim Brotherhood now grew astonishingly. Founded by a schoolteacher named Hassan el Banna in the Canal Zone town of Ismailia in 1928—and inspired, ironically, by the example of the local Y.M.C.A.—the Brotherhood was fundamentalist, authoritarian, profoundly anti-Western. It sought a return to the ideal Islamic society ruled according to the laws laid down in the Koran. But its message was resonant enough and its leader was inspired and eloquent enough to have something to offer to the serious-minded, the desperate, the deprived or merely disappointed of all classes. It could nourish both the narrowest traditionalist and the wildest radical, and in these post-war years it attained a membership variously estimated at from half a million to two million. Certainly, it was a mass movement as no other then was: at the universities in the early 'fifties almost a third of all students were believed to belong to it.

If it was the Free Officers who took over the task of reconstruction, it was the Muslim Brethren who lit the fuse that ignited the demolition charge under the old society. And, in retrospect, this appears predictable enough, for before the intrusion of Western parliamentarianism the religious sheikhs, sometimes the sons of fellahin freely educated at the mosque-university of El Azhar, had been the only leaders of the people. Azharites had long been in the van of the national struggle; the philosophical father of Egyptian nationalism, Sheikh Mohamed Abdu, had been one of them. But whereas Abdu had sought to demonstrate the rationality of the Koran and the Prophet's teaching, thus opening a door to the West, and to science, Hassan el Banna turned his face firmly towards Islam's heroic past, proposing to restore the Caliphate and requiring his followers to take an oath of obedience to himself, the Supreme Guide, in the words formerly used for the Caliph of Islam.

The history of every westernising Muslim country shows how deep-rooted such atavism can be, and Egypt in mid-twentieth century again underlined the point. And since historically Islam is a militant creed which was carried across Africa at the point of the sword it was not surprising that, in 1939, the Muslim Brotherhood developed a 'secret arm,' trained to use guns and explosives. In the late 'forties a series of bomb outrages in cinemas, big stores and newspaper offices announced its disapproval of Western 'immorality.' The Brotherhood was to the fore in sending fanatic volunteers to fight the Jews in Palestine or to infiltrate into the Canal Zone where an undeclared war against the British occupation forces had been raging since October 1951, when the Wafd ministry had repudiated the Anglo-Egyptian Treaty of 1936. Not that the Brethren confined their chastenings to infidels: as in the early days of Islam, murder again became a political instrument.[4] Two prime ministers, a High Court judge, a governor of Cairo, the city's chief of police were amongst those who died violently for having incurred the Brotherhood's displeasure.

And certainly in these last years the Muslim Brethren did not lack material for righteous indignation. The Arms Graft Scandal of 1949 in which the King and his motley entourage were rumoured to be involved was succeeded in 1950 by the Great Cotton Scandal, in which cornering operations during the Korean War boom almost priced Egyptian cotton out of the world's markets. 'A Cairo lady made £8,000 last week speculating on the cotton market,' reported *Akhbar El Yom*, Cairo's biggest and brightest weekly, and every reader duly filled in the name of Madame Nahas, the ambitious and rich young wife of old Nahas, the erstwhile Tribune of the People.

[4] The very word 'assassin' is of Islamic provenance—the name of an earlier brotherhood dedicated to the removal of additional schismatic errors in the already schismatic Fatamid Caliphate of the 11th century. They continued the good work until overrun by the Mongols in 1265.

Violence bred violence. Hassan el Banna was himself assassinated in 1949, allegedly on Farouk's nod, by the so-called 'Iron Guard' of Palace thugs. But the desperation he had deepened in this unfanatic but much-tried people was not so easily abated. Governments went on attempting to repress the Muslim Brethren at one moment, and at the next, seeking to enlist their support against political rivals. In the last six months before the coup Egypt ran through five governments; and at the centre of the web of intrigue which grew daily more impenetrable and self-defeating sat the gross, hysteric King, despatching prime ministers, famous names in Egypt's history, with capricious pencilled notes on scraps of paper, delivered by members of his famous 'kitchen cabinet,' the colonel-chauffeur, the Sudanese valet, the butler. . . .

The difficulty is not to see why the coup came but why it was so long in coming. The answer, easily overlooked, lies in the continuing military establishment of the British in Egypt. And this not merely in the sense of physical obstruction— although there was that, too—but also because the presence of the old Master Power was subtly inhibiting, continuing to foster a feeling of non-responsibility and an atmosphere of unreality; the British provided a universal scapegoat and a hollow unity-in-face-of-the-Imperialist-oppressor which concealed how deeply and how fatally the nation was flawed.

But by 1952, after the British scuttle, first from Palestine, then from Abadan, it was becoming very evident that the Occupying Power was a hollow figure also. In the Canal Zone Egyptian labour was withdrawn, and hit-and-run raids against the 80,000 British troops stepped up again. True, General Erskine, in riposte, masterfully expelled the local inhabitants from an area of Ismailia, and, on 25 January bombarded into submission eight hundred Egyptian auxiliary police beleaguered in their barracks in the town after they had rejected a two-hour ultimatum to give up their arms. But next day the auxiliary police of the Cairo region were on strike, marching to link up with the angrily demonstrating students, and when the capital was set on fire, and its great department stores, cinemas, hotels and banks went up in flames, the police did not intervene against the incendiaries or halt the looting mob.

The historically-minded—and in the sense of folk memory

few in this region are not—might catch in the red glow of
Cairo on Black Saturday, 1952, the reflected fires of Arabist
Alexandria, set alight under the threat of the British naval
guns in 1882. And on both occasions one must look further
for an explanation than the facile 'Eastern mob violence.' An
Oriental society, gropingly seeking its way ahead in a changed
world, struggling to adjust under the ever-mounting impact of
the West, had been driven into a corner, and, finding itself
trapped, had turned from baffled reason to primordial instinct.
Both in Alexandria in 1882, and in Cairo in 1952, Europeans
living among this normally kindly people were savagely murdered, dying martyrs to the pride and power and, above all,
to the material success, of the West.

Both in 1882 and in 1952 there were complicated—and in-
conclusive—inquiries into the responsibility for the holocaust.
In the smouldering ruins of Cairo in 1952 it was alleged that
the King had delayed action to put responsibility on the ruling
Wafd and thus wreck it; that the Wafd had plotted the fire
in order to finish off the King; and that the British had engineered the whole sequence of events in order to blacken
Egyptian nationalism in the eyes of the world.

The trails of clues and suspicions crossed, re-crossed, and
finally petered out. It hardly mattered. What mattered was
that no one had bothered either to stop the incendiaries or to
stamp out the flames—not even the British.

It was Egypt for the Egyptians—at last.

The only question was: just who—and where—were the
'Egyptians'? The Officers, who had assumed the answer self-
evident, were to find the question troublesome.

In his political testament, *The Philosophy of the Revolution*
an extraordinary blend of flashing insight and touching naïveté
—Nasser has written of his dismay at the utter lack of immediate public response to the officers' coup. 'This was the
most cruel shock I ever felt in my life. . . . I thought the
whole nation was standing on tiptoe, ready for action, and
that it awaited but the storming of the walls by the vanguard
for it to rush through. . . .'

The Officers' first proclamations were, in fact, in terms of a
purge of 'selfish and corrupt elements' after which, its duty

done, the army would return to barracks, leaving the regenerate nation at last able to fulfil its destiny. This, it is true, is the classic apologia of the ambitious soldier, and some of Nasser's political enemies have represented it as merely a manoeuvre, a deep-laid plot for seizing personal power. But this tells us rather more about the old politicos than it does about Nasser, whose dedication is the ultimate explanation of his power to command his brother officers. The contradictions of these first weeks and months are evidence of political naïveté rather than of Machiavellianism. The Officers, who thought in terms of the French (rather than the Russian) Revolution, saw their coup as a sort of storming of the Bastille, a notion in which they were encouraged by the fact that Egypt's abortive revolutions of 1882 and 1919 had indeed been accompanied by mass uprisings. What they forgot was that, unlike the 'bullet-proof' Arabi, *El Wahid*, 'the One and Only,' unlike that great demagogue, Saad Zaghloul, *they* had done nothing to rouse the masses; they had not even sought to stir their own soldiers, who marched merely because their Colonels ordered them to. There was, in fact, a deep, but unrealised, conflict between the Populist sentiment which prompted them to insist on inserting 'by the Will of the People' in Farouk's abdication document and their professional and Muslim conservative instincts. It is doubtful whether it was *merely* tactical considerations that prompted them to install the fifty-one-year-old General Neguib at the head of their movement, or to call in, the moment they had achieved power, an orthodox professional Prime Minister, Ali Maher. One of their earliest acts as a régime was to rush a military tribunal to try the Kafr el Dawar textile workers who, crying 'Long live the People's Revolution!' had seized a number of mill buildings and fired others. The Tribunal hanged two alleged Communist ringleaders and gaoled twenty workers.

The Free Officers' movement had in truth been largely nurtured on professional grievances: like Arabi's movement, it was, in origin, as much mutiny as revolt. When we first hear of a 'secret society' among the Men of 1952 it is among a group of young officers, just out of Military Academy and posted to Mankabad in Upper Egypt in 1939. They include Nasser, Anwar el Sadat and Zakaria Mohieddin and they com-

plain plaintively of the malice and sycophancy of their commanders 'forever seeking to humiliate us' (i.e. the Egyptians)
while unashamedly courting the British. One particular bane
of their young lives they called 'the Sultan' because he had 'the
arrogance of a conquering Turk'—a strange echo, across sixty
years, of Arabi's petition accusing the Minister of War of
treating the Egyptian officers 'as if they were his enemies, or
as if God had sent him to venge his wrath on the Egyptians.'

Again, in 1942, when the tiny nucleus begins to grow, it is
the humiliation of the army by the rough, tank-backed British
ultimatum to the King which is the starting point. General
Neguib, not yet linked with the Free Officers, sent a letter of
resignation to King Farouk at this time. And, what finally
turned the Free Officers' secret society into a movement was
their dismay and bewilderment at the Egyptian army's defeat
by Israel in 1948. Neguib, seriously wounded in Palestine, was
called to their attention at this time; Nasser, gaining his first
experience of war, distinguished himself by holding out to the
end in the Faluja salient, henceforth to enjoy a place in the
legend of the movement. The Syrian troops returning to
Damascus from the Israel débâcle made the first of Syria's
many post-war coups; the officers returning to Egypt prepared
for one, establishing a new organisation, with a membership
fund and an executive committee of ten, which, with very few
changes, became the Revolutionary Command Council of 1952.
One of the Free Officers, Major Kamel Eddin Hussein, quoted
the dying remark of a comrade killed in the Palestine fighting:
'Remember, the real battle is not here, but back in Egypt,' and
this struck a chord in his hearers—for if the thing nearest their
hearts was the plight of the army, the plight of the army also
reflected the plight of the nation of which it had now become
the microcosm and symbol.

The failure to produce any detailed statement of aims before
1952 has been explained by Nasser in terms of the need to
avoid division in the Free Officers' councils. In reality, save for
the odd Communist and one or two of the more dedicated
Muslim Brethren among them, such ideas as they had seem
to have been frequently inflammatory, but rarely well-defined.
Their common '-ism' was Nationalism, and while this remained

unfulfilled because of the continuing presence of British troops on Egyptian soil, anything beyond could have little reality— except that, with the British, most of the officers, more hazily but hardly less resentfully, coupled another occupying force— that of the 'Turkish' Royal House and all the grotesque, parasitic Levantine apparatus that went with it. For the name 'Free Officers' was not wholly rhetorical: their passionate preoccupation was to get rid of this crippling incubus. It was this urge that united them; until the British and the Royal House had been disposed of the future hardly existed.

This was true even of Nasser, who was certainly one of the most politically evolved and articulate among them. He was born (in Alexandria in 1918) with, so to speak, the banner of Egyptian nationalism flying over his cradle; when he was two years old, his father's brother, who lived with the family, was gaoled by the British for subversion. Since his mother died when he was eight and his father was frequently moved about the country on his Post Office duties, student politics became the focus of his boyhood. In 1935 we find him, a schoolboy of seventeen, writing bitterly to a school friend: 'We are back again in the time of Cromer'; that year he put in so much time at political meetings that he spent only forty-five days at school and was almost expelled.

In the Middle East at this time, the 'revolutions' of Mussolini and Hitler were arousing sympathetic echoes. They had an obvious appeal for frustrated Arab youth, impatient with the complacency of the old politicians. They accorded well with both the rhetorical and metaphysical possibilities of the Arabic language and with vague yearnings to recreate the glories of the first Arab Empire. In Syria, a teacher named Antun Saada founded the *Parti Populaire Syrien* which transcended the narrow old politics of interest-group and clan to espouse the heady notion of a greater Syrian Nation, mystically rendered as 'The Land.' In Beirut, a Maronite pharmacist launched the *Phalanges Libanaises*, looking to a union of 'Phoenicians' everywhere, and arousing an aggressive Christian communalism to disturb the delicate, elaborately contrived balance of the Lebanon. And in Egypt, Ahmed Hussein, an eager young lawyer—one of how many!—started *Misr El Fatat* (Young Egypt), envisioning a restored Arab Empire, industrialisation, and the corporate state on the Italian plan, which last would provide 'the only true democracy,' to be distinguished from the parliamentary plutocracies prevailing elsewhere.

Nasser, who had already tried the Wafd's Blue Shirt Youth Movement and found it wanting, was for a time a member of Ahmed Hussein's para-military Green Shirts, and in one of their many violent demonstrations acquired the three-inch scar which he still carries on his forehead, getting his name into a newspaper report and on to police records. It was because of this last that his application to enter the Military Academy was at first turned down.

After the war, with both Rome and Berlin in eclipse, the agile Ahmed Hussein renamed his movement 'The Egyptian Socialist and Democratic Party,' advocating a Russian alliance and nationalisation; and now, when it strengthened his hand, he would work with the Muslim Brethren or the Communists, or both. Much repressed, foreign in its origins, chronically splintered, the Egyptian Communist movement had gained a new lease of life in the war and postwar years, and its influence, through various national fronts and the small Left-wing of the Wafd, was greater than its growing, but still small, numbers would suggest. The Egyptian Marxist writer, Hassan Riad, indeed goes so far as to claim that in Egypt at this time it was the influence of the Communists, with their stress on a social programme, 'which radicalised political life, polarised the ideologies, put the traditional in question, and pushed to its limits the work of the first generation of the intelligentsia.'[5] Certainly for a young Egyptian cocooned in Islam, and isolated in the Nile Valley, the clinical Marxist analysis could strike with the force of revelation. One such was Khaled Mohieddin, the youngest of the Free Officers, a tank corps major who had been seconded from the army to read for a degree in Cairo University's Faculty of Commerce. An amiable but earnest young man, Khaled Mohieddin was to introduce his friend, Gamel Abdel Nasser, to such people as Dr Rashed Barawi, a university lecturer who had translated *Das Kapital* into Arabic, and to a young Communist lawyer, Judge Ahmed Fuad, who lent him the works of Harold Laski, Nehru and Aneurin Bevan—a trio of almost Arab loquacity.

[5] *L'Égypte Nassérienne* (Paris, 1964).

Since Egypt's intellectuals were apt to be literary and dilet-
tante, these left-wingers were among the few who possessed
a working analysis of modern society with some grasp of
sociology and economics. Inevitably, they had a rôle to play as
the Free Officers groped towards a programme. In 1949—as
hand mimeograph gives place after a whip-round to roneo—
we find them assisting in drafting Free Officers' circulars which
now include references to 'social justice,' 'monopoly capitalism'
and 'feudalism,' as well as to the army corruption and imperialism which remain their main burden.

The Leftward swing of most of Europe—and Russia's in-
vincibility—also had its effect. From 1943 onwards British
broadcasts in Arabic had made much play with Britain's new
Beveridge Plan of social security, and the German radio had
promised the fellahin a New Order. At least one experienced
observer of the Egyptian scene commented in 1945 on the 'very
marked spread of socialist sentiment among the petty bourgeoisie and intelligentsia,' and judged this a factor that 'might
have to be reckoned with.' But until 1954 at least, it was frustrated nationalism that made the pace in Egypt, and to this
Communism, an alien, atheist creed, had little to offer—yet.
The Muslim Brethren, on the other hand, had much. They had
a good many members among the Free Officers, a few on their
Executive Council. On a number of occasions, both before and
after the coup, Nasser tried to come to an understanding with
the Brotherhood's leaders.[6] But it was a forlorn hope: revolutions so different in spirit could not mix or marry; they could
only devour each other.

It was a steamy ideological *bouillabaisse*, bringing together
ingredients from Mecca, Moscow, the London School of Economics and Mussolini's Rome, in the much-reheated stock of
Egyptian nationalism. But the Free Officers were to leave their
mark on the history of the Middle East not for what they
thought, but for how they *felt*, and for who—and what—they
were.

[6] The régime's early Cabinets had a former Muslim Brother as Minister
of Wakfs—and a former leader of 'Young Egypt' Fathi Radwan, as Minister
of National Guidance. The Muslim Brethren were at one stage offered three
Cabinet posts—but they demanded the right to veto any legislation felt to
be 'un-Islamic.'

Some were clever, and others were not; some were devout and others were not; but with few exceptions they were serious-minded young men who believed in God, believed in Egypt, and wished to be able to believe in themselves. They were the sort of Egyptians foreigners rarely met. They were not, as an over-eager public relations department at first presented them, all-but-hornyhanded sons of the soil. But they were certainly grandsons of the soil, product of the Egyptian village and of that rural middling class from which many of Egypt's great leaders have sprung. Unlike some earlier leaders, however, they had risen, not so much *out* of this class as *with* it as, multiplying and expanding via secondary schools, trade schools and new commercial opportunities, it grew out from the five- or ten-acre patrimony and became more ramified, diversified and urbanised.

Nasser's own history vividly illustrates the theme. His father, Abdel Nasser Hussein, was born the son of a fairly well-to-do fellah in the village of Beni Morr which lies among its palm trees near the East bank of the Nile, a couple of miles from Assiut. It was a fortunate location because the soil was good, there were no big landlords such as dominated the countryside to the north and south, and Assiut, having many Copts, had attracted the attentions of the American Baptist Mission which set up schools there at a time when schools were, in general, non-existent in Upper Egypt. From the one-room *kuttab* of Beni Morr, where the local sheikh taught the village boys to recite the Koran by heart, Abdel Nasser Hussein was thus able to go on to a western-style primary school in Assiut. And though his father finally took him away because he had to read the Christian Bible, this was not before he had collected the all-important certificate that was a passport to a Government job, and out of the wilderness of Upper Egypt.

We next find Abdel Nasser Hussein stationed in Alexandria, a clerk in the postal service, having made a 'good marriage' to the daughter of a local coal merchant and canal boat transport contractor—who also hailed from Upper Egypt. By the time his first son, Gamal, was born, he had risen to District Postmaster and the family lived in a four-room 'villa' in a suburban street. It was a humble enough place, yet, with its shutters and tiny garden, a far cry indeed from the mud houses of Beni

Morr, straggling along that long, dusty lane, full of ruts and chickens and children and buffaloes and laden donkeys and women bringing water. One of Abdel Nasser Hussein's brothers had also escaped from the village to become an official in the Ministry of Wakfs;[7] another, though remaining in the Assiut area, became a coal dealer.

A family album photograph of this time shows Gamal, his father, 'nationalist' uncle, and three younger brothers. All are staring stiffly ahead, father in a well-pressed striped suit, uncle displaying a neatly pointed pocket handkerchief, and all, down to the youngest, impeccably tarbushed. Yet two uncles remained—and remain—fellahin, still occupying the family's two-storey brick house near the centre of the village. From the seventy feddans owned by the grandfather, Khalil Sultan, who felt rich enough to build a private mosque, the patrimony has now sunk to eleven acres—a familiar theme in Egypt, although by the standards of the Nile Valley the income from eleven acres still constitutes comparative wealth.

The soil and water of Beni Morr had at least proved rich enough to confer on the first-born of Abdel Nasser Hussein the freedom of the big city and the freedom of the mind. Because of his mother's death and his father's remarriage, Gamal spent periods living with his uncle, or with his maternal relations in Cairo and Alexandria, as well as with his father. He attended in all no less than nine different schools, yet managed to pass the necessary examinations, and in fact spent one term reading Law at Cairo University before he got into the Military College. When he reached the rank of major, he duly married a girl from a well-to-do Persian-Egyptian family which had prospered in the carpet trade. In 1952 two of his brothers were school teachers.

It is interesting to note how closely in essentials such a typical Egyptian case history of 'social mobility' resembles its British or American counterparts—save for the strength of the family's continuing links with the land and the village. And

[7] A *Wakf* is an Islamic trust based on entailed estate, a device formerly widely employed in Arab countries, partly because it circumvents the rigid Koranic law of inheritance. In addition to supervising Wakfs, the Ministry looks after Islamic affairs, welfare and education, and in Egypt today has a critical rôle in the plans for the modernisation of Islam. (See Part V.)

the other Free Officers' leaders had roughly similar stories. Some were richer, few poorer than the Nassers. The father of Hussein el Shafei, the cavalry colonel, inherited 18 feddans in the Delta from *his* father, but left it to his mother and went instead to college to become the Municipal Engineer of Tanta; two brothers were agricultural engineers, one a civil engineer. Anwar el Sadat's father was a ten-feddan fellah, a brother a tractor agent. The Mohieddin cousins were comparatively well-off since the family holding was at Kafr el Shukr on the Damietta branch of the Nile, an area long famed for the rich yields of its orchards and grape-vines. Nasser's bosom companion of Military Academy days, Abdel Hakim Amer, also came from a more well-to-do family which, collectively, owned a good deal of land in Minya Province.

Most of them were around the same age, majors and colonels in their mid-thirties at the time of the coup. And this was no accident: they were the 'Class of '37' when the threat from Italian aggression in Abyssinia forced not only the conclusion of the Anglo-Egyptian Treaty of 1936 (which declared the British military occupation, in principle, at an end) but also the urgent expansion of the Egyptian Army, and, more particularly, of its officer corps. With the nationalist Wafd returned to power, the annual intake of the Military Academy now rose from a hundred a year to almost a thousand. The process which Mohamed Ali started when in 1825 he press-ganged the fellahin into his *Nizam Gedid* (New Army), set up schools and technical colleges, and sent young Egyptians to study in Europe, was at last working itself out. The Sultan Said had commissioned the first Egyptian officers; Ismail allowed them to rise to the rank of Colonel; Tewfik made one, Arabi, his Minister of War. After its failed revolution of 1881 the British had disbanded the old Egyptian army, and created a new one which under its British Sirdar long wandered in Imperial limbo. But now the heirs of Mohamed Ali's fellahin were at last coming into their own. The Egyptian Army in 1937 began to appear a promising career for the lower-middle-class boy: if one pursued the Law, Nasser's school friends are reported to have calculated, one might, by the age of forty, be a *Maître*; in the army one could, with luck, by that time be a General.

'The Army,' wrote the historian C. V. Wedgwood of Crom-well's New Model Army (which had also overthrown a king), 'was a very fair cross-section of the younger generation of Englishmen, drawn from all parts of the land, from labourers, tradesmen, yeomen and gentry; it was a much more repre-sentative body of the English people than any Parliament that had ever met. . . .'

What was true of England in 1648 was also true of Egypt in 1952. Certainly, the officers into whose hands supreme power fell that summer had little in common with the rich, ostentatiously cosmopolitan upper class, the café society of Cairo, which considered them ignorant and uncouth, just as they, in turn, felt this largely self-appointed aristocracy to be alien and undignified. As the profound appeal of the Muslim Brotherhood suggested, there could be little doubt which reaction was the more representative of the people at large.

For the Western veneer remained thin. In his *Modern Egypt*, Cromer points out that, even if the British had not intervened, Arabi's revolution was foredoomed to failure because the social elements necessary to modern government just did not exist in Egypt. The mass of the fellahin were 'sunk in ignorance,' the village small proprietors were not much better, the Coptic minority was handicapped by religion, and the necessary lead could only come from the 'small but most influential' class, the *Ulema* (Koranic scholars) of El Azhar—and would certainly be reactionary.

The British, who came to Egypt primarily as bailiffs and debt-collectors,[8] had done much for administration and irriga-tion, but little to remedy the glaring educational deficiencies. Despite the brave example of Mohamed Ali, as late as 1913 there were only 2,500 students in government secondary schools. The sole text-book of the people was the Koran, got by heart in the village *kuttabs* under the rod of the local sheikh;[9] and for the poor Muslim youth the accepted road to

[8] Cromer's own first post in Egypt, when he was Sir Evelyn Baring, was that of English Commissioner to the Commission of the Debt. This was in 1877, five years before the British occupation.

[9] A classic personal account of the character of such an education is contained in Taha Hussein's autobiography, *An Egyptian Childhood* (Rout-ledge, 1932).

advancement lay through the gateway of El Azhar, where he could seat himself beneath some pillar in those many-pillared halls, at the feet of whichever sheikh he could induce to teach him.

It was an honoured road, but a highly defective one. El Azhar, 'the Splendid,' was an older foundation than any university in Europe, and had once been advanced in science, mathematics and medicine as well as Koranic studies. But the scientific spirit had been lost in the wreck of the Crusades; and while, in medieval Europe, the Schoolmen sought to harmonise theology and logic, engaging in continuous philosophic debate, in the Arab East the *Ulema* abandoned themselves to the elaboration of verbalistic footnotes to their sacred text. A generation after Darwin, *filosouf* ('*philosophe*' in the sense of the free enquirer) remained for them the term of ultimate reproach.

Thus, although with the help of the sympathetic Cromer, the would-be reformer, Sheikh Mohamed Abdu, reached the position of Grand Mufti of Egypt, and there issued a number of modernising *fetwa* (rulings), his ultimate success, in his lifetime, was little greater than that of his friend, Colonel Arabi. The ironic result of his attempt to return to the essence of the Prophet's teaching was a yet more inflexible fundamentalism. El Azhar resisted his attempts to drag it into the modern world. The sheikhs bent before the winds of change, but they did not break, and a large part of the country drowsed on under the hypnotic drone of Koranic rote.

And yet through all this, experience of the West had been hammering home the point which Mohamed Ali, rehearsing Bonaparte, had seized on over a century earlier. For the 'missions' of young Egyptians had continued to be sent by the Government to Europe for education. In addition, wealthy parents were now sending their sons abroad at their own expense, particularly to France, while foreign schools—American, French, British, Italian, Greek—multiplied in Egypt. Nor had the legacy of Mohamed Ali been wholly dissipated: in 1892 when Lord Milner wrote his *England in Egypt*, there were eight specialised colleges—for agriculturalists, for doctors, lawyers, engineers, teachers, skilled craftsmen; and sixteen years later intellectuals of the Umma Party, through public subscription, laid the foundations of Egypt's first secular university.

Thus by 1952 it was certainly no longer possible to say of the Officers' revolt, as Cromer had said of Arabi's, that the necessary elements of modern government did not exist. Yet, because the development of the educational system had so perfectly reflected the dichotomy of East and West, there was the hardly lesser peril of a split society: an Islamic mass, existing in a closed system, looking to the past, and a secularising English- or French-speaking minority, looking westwards.

Revolution, in short, was no longer premature; it was over-due. And though the social schism extended far beyond the educational system it was one which the army, both by its history and training, was now uniquely fitted to bridge. Re-flecting the belated growth of state secondary education be-tween the wars, its officers were, on the one hand, anchored to the Egypt of the villages and Islam; yet, on the other, after a world war so largely determined by technology, profession-ally committed to science and Western innovation. As repre-sentatives of the emergent nation, they had other practical advantages over the religious sheikhs, the students, the lawyers and writers who had intermittently made their voices heard in the past: they had some sense of organisation and dis-cipline; and although their various specialisations might put a distance between them and their men which had not existed for Colonel Arabi, they themselves were still unsophisticated enough to be able to identify with the fellahin soldiers. Even in the late 'thirties, a conscript who could raise £E20 could still buy himself out, and thus the ranks of the army were made up of the very poorest. 'We had before our eyes the poverty of the people,' said Hussein el Shafei. 'We felt it more and more through the army. . . .'

They were thus bound together by their social origins, by their common disgust, by the mystique of their increasingly technical profession, by the shared excitements and humilia-tions of 1942, and 1948 and 1951—and now, finally, by the climactic perils of 'the Great Night' of 22 June 1952. They were 'brothers.' This, a potent sentiment in Islam—and perhaps also now a growing consciousness of being somehow 'new men'—was their great strength. Decisions in those early days were collective decisions, taken in the council of officers after debate and show of hands. The arguments might go on half the night, with much earnest speaking of minds. 'What was most significant,' Nasser wrote later, 'was the feeling deep down in our consciousness that this was our duty. . . .'

For an Englishman, there is in the story of these days many an echo, bizarre but insistent, of Oliver Cromwell, and his 'plain, russet-coated captains' from the shires. That army, too, put in its Remonstrances before desperation and anger drove it to act. It, too, had its argumentative council of officers. Cromwell, trying to govern, had to wrestle with his Levellers and Fifth Monarchy Men and Presbyterians, just as Nasser would have to contend with the Communists and Muslim Brethren and the old Wafdists—and was to deal with them with a similar adroitness. Cromwell's officers were much exercised as to how to deal with that 'Grand Delinquent,' their King; so were Nasser's. And if Farouk went to Capri, whereas Charles went to the block, the Egyptian monarchy was by comparison a frail and alien thing. Even so, through most of the night of 25 July, in Cairo and Alexandria, the committee of officers debated the fate of Farouk. The firebrand Gamal Salem insisted that justice demanded his trial and execution. A veteran nationalist officer, of an older generation, consulted, observed cryptically: 'a head does not interest me until it is cut off.' But the coup so far had been bloodless and there were more pressing tasks than a grand trial of Farouk. It is said that Nasser had read *Tale of Two Cities* and had been impressed by the moral: that blood begets blood. According to Neguib's account, Nasser concluded his remarks with some eloquence: 'Let us spare Farouk and send him into exile. History will sentence him to death.'

By 6 a.m., when a vote was taken, the majority of the committee were for sending the King away.

Having seized power to free Egypt, as they declared, from a corrupt *ancien régime* and the unregenerate political system it manipulated, the first act of the Officers was to seek out one of that system's veteran practitioners, the seventy-year-old Ali Maher, a professional prime minister and former *chef de cabinet* of Farouk, to ask him to form a government. Probably

they felt he was the best they could do. Known to be personally honest, and admired for his stand against the British
Embassy during the war, Ali Maher had set up the Ministry of
Social Affairs, and has even been claimed to be 'the first
Egyptian premier seriously to think of introducing social reforms.'[10] He remained, nevertheless, very much the old-style
political magnate.

On the very evening of the day they seized power, the Army
announced parliamentary elections for the following October.
Yet behind this deferential observation of the time-honoured
parliamentary rituals, there was from the first a determined
social radicalism. Having sent Farouk packing and released all
political detainees except Communists, the Officers' next act
was to abolish the titles of 'Pasha' and 'Bey' (First-class and
Second-class), those alien Turkish ranks by which sycophancy
had been erected into a system of government—and which
Turkey herself had thrown out with the fez some thirty years
earlier.

'Henceforth you will no longer refer to me as Ali Maher
Pasha,' the Prime Minister informed the people. 'I shall be just
plain Ali Maher.' Coming from him it is possible that they
found this lacking in conviction, yet as early as the night of
23 June the Army had called for new 'laws to raise the standard of the people,' and, more significantly, had observed that
'foremost among such laws' must be one for the limitation of
land ownership. The abolition of 'pashadom' and land reform
were inextricably linked, and in this matter the Officers' social
instincts and life experience guided their choice of priorities
more surely than any amount of ideological sophistication
could have done.

Meanwhile, in order that parliamentary democracy could
make a clean new start, the old political parties were invited
to purge themselves of their 'bad elements' and a code of conduct, on the observance of which their registration would depend, was drawn up. If political integrity could be secured by
regulation, these new regulations were well devised. Every
party was required to outline its aims and a specific programme. President and officers were to be elected by secret

[10] J. Heyworth Dunne: *Religious and Political Trends in Modern Egypt*,
Washington, 1950.

ballot for a term not exceeding three years, and must not be directors of firms receiving government contracts, nor otherwise exploit parliamentary office for personal profit. Party funds were to be deposited in a named bank and accounted for in detail to the general assembly of the party. A party was not to be permitted henceforth to own land, except that on which its offices stood. And so on.

No fewer than fifteen parties applied for registration. But it was soon evident that the 'new leaf' turned over by the Wafd bore a remarkable resemblance to its badly blotted old one. Its veteran leader, Nahas Pasha, the heir of Zaghloul, had hurried back from Switzerland on the morrow of the coup, to resume, as he thought, the leadership of the liberated nation. Having split his own party in the 'thirties by demanding a pledge of unconditional obedience from members, he was scarcely likely now to knuckle under to these callow young men in officers' caps. In reality, neither he, nor his right-hand man and Party Secretary-General, the great landowner, Serag ed Din, at all fitted into any 'reformed' political picture.

But the Officers did not face such political realities until, so to speak, their noses were rubbed into them. In the photographs taken at this time they wear the gratified, but slightly embarrassed expressions of schoolboys who have just been made prefects. 'A lot of people,' Neguib wrote later, 'concluded we didn't know what we were doing. We did. But we didn't know how to do it.'

With the army 'clean-up,' however, they were on home ground. By the end of September, 450 *ancien régime* officers had been retired. Anti-graft committees went to work in the Ministries; and in a year, eight hundred bureaucrats were, for one reason or another, retired. Other committees investigated large-scale tax-evasion and the arms and cotton market scandals. The Government was brought back to Cairo from its Alexandria summer quarters. Ministers, it was announced, would not use their official limousines but would henceforth travel by bus. Newspapers printed pictures of the Officers at their desks in the Ministries, working late, eating the *fool* sandwiches of the people.

If some Cairo sophisticates found such gestures naïve, they also found with some astonishment that they were seriously meant: these young Puritans could not be bought—and that, in Egypt, was in itself a phenomenon of some moment. (And even six years later, when 'Egyptianisation' following Suez had multiplied opportunities, although—to quote a veteran British observer—'there were complaints of the return of corruption to government departments, of favouritism of young officers . . . there was no suggestion that the ruling group was corrupt.' In 1965 another experienced observer of the Middle Eastern scene was still able to comment: 'There can be no doubt that at the highest level the standard of economic morality is very much higher than it was before the Revolution. . . . The net gain to the country of the public's confidence that ten per cent of every foreign loan is not going into the pockets of government officials is immense.'[11])

Meantime the political education of the Officers continued: their chosen Prime Minister, for all that he might be 'plain Ali Maher now,' was showing a marked lack of enthusiasm for their central Land Reform proposal. This was scarcely unpredictable. For although since the 1940s Egyptian intellectuals and academics had increasingly pointed to the grotesque maldistribution of land-ownership as the key to Egypt's basic problems, the old political parties, if they could agree on nothing else, had been at one in their disinclination to remove the sources of their funds and power. Four times the Officers had discussed their land-reform proposals with the Wafd leaders, and on each occasion had been stymied. The politicians suggested a progressive land tax instead. This, they explained, would benefit the Treasury. 'We said,' reported Nasser, 'that we did not want money for the Treasury, we wanted to liberate the individual. But they could not understand what we meant. . . .'[12]

The Land Reform Law proposed (and later executed) was, in fact, very far from penal. The American-sponsored Land Reform in post-war Japan had set the maximum holding at $7\frac{1}{2}$ acres; in less intensively farmed Yugoslavia the limit was fixed at 50 acres. The Egyptian law of 1952, by contrast, allowed

[11] First quotation: Tom Little, *Modern Egypt*, London, 1967. Second quotation: Peter Mansfield, *Nasser's Egypt*, London, 1965.
[12] In Report to Preparatory Committee of National Congress of Popular Powers, 1962.

the landowner to keep 200 feddans (208 acres) and also to give a further 100 feddans to two children. And in Egypt 200 feddans may yield £6,000 a year—without including the income from the 3 per cent redeemable Government Bonds given in compensation[13] for the excess land (which the owners could, in addition, themselves sell off in lots of 5 feddans or less to farmers possessing ten feddans or less).

Despite this moderation, the Prime Minister, Ali Maher, continued to drag his feet before the Land Reform Law. It would be quite ruinous, it was now being said, to the country's agricultural output. A deep Islamic conservatism touching questions of property did nothing to help the reform. Even the 'radical' Muslim Brotherhood was divided on it: although Hassan El Banna had ruled that no man—on the authority of the Tradition—should possess more land than he himself could cultivate, the new Supreme Guide, a lawyer, would only agree with reluctance to placing a 500-feddan limit on holdings.

But the Officers' reaction, when it came to the point, was a professional one: make an appreciation of the situation; call in the appropriate technical specialists. They had for some time been sitting in with various academic and other experts who formed a rough-and-ready Brains Trust. Two Left-wing academics, Ahmed Fuad and Rashed Barawi, sketched out the Land Reform Law. The impatient aviator, Gamel Salem, studied the subject while recuperating from an illness in hospital. An agricultural specialist of much experience, Sayed Marei, was brought in to work out details and execute the scheme.

Meanwhile, reconstruction was proceeding over a wider field. A National Production Council was set up and, alongside it, a Supreme Council for the Social Services. Ideas were plentiful. Long-shelved plans were taken out of their pigeon-holes in the Ministries and dusted off.[14] By the end of the year, six months after the coup, the first rough outline of a national plan had begun to emerge.

But the Officers' political education continued to prove both more difficult and more eventful than their economic education. In order to give the old parties a fuller opportunity to

---

[13] At a price equal to about half the former, inflated market value.
[14] For instance, feasibility studies for steel, fertiliser and other industries had been commissioned by the Ministry of Commerce in the late 1940s.

'purify themselves,' the parliamentary elections had been set back to February. But the Wafd remained unco-operative. It was becoming obvious that the anticipated political regeneration would not, after all, be spontaneous. In early September, the irreconcilability of the Officers' social aims and the old political system at last forced a decision. Ali Maher was dismissed and General Neguib made Prime Minister. Four months later, all political parties were dissolved for the transitional period now considered necessary for the establishment of 'sound democratic and constitutional rule.'

On 9 September, just two days after the Army's formal take-over, Law 178, the Land Reform Law was enacted by decree.

The Army had broken with the old régime, in the end, on the critical issue. In forty-seven days, what began as a coup had become a revolution.

6

EXIT PASHA, ENTER TECHNOCRAT

The difference between a landless and a landed peasant is the difference between a two-footed animal and a man.
—General Mohamed Neguib, *Egypt's Destiny*, 1955

The limiting of private property is a delicate matter that would be likely to promote class war.
—President of the Liberal Constitutional Party, 1952

If the 1952 Land Reform was 'the Land to the People,' it was not very much land to a comparatively small number of people. The area liable to expropriation, 565,000 feddans, was less than one-tenth of Egypt's cultivated land, and it was to pass from less than two thousand owners to 170,000 families. That this, nevertheless, amounted to a revolution, a political revolution signalling a social—and ultimately an economic—revolution, was due to the peculiar importance of land ownership as the keystone of the extraordinary structure of Egyptian Pashadom.

In European or American terms the pashas' big estates were not, in fact, particularly big; but in the narrow, overpopulated Nile Valley, with its abject poverty and fecund soil, they represented overwhelming wealth and power which the familiar statistic—that 0.1 per cent of landowners held 20 per cent of Egypt's cultivated area—cannot adequately convey. Nor were the pashas an hereditary caste or even, as elsewhere in the Arab world, former tribal chiefs—with exceptions like the Lamlums, originally sheikhs of a Cyrenaican Bedouin tribe that came to rest on the western edge of the Nile Valley and in 1952 owned 2,000 acres in Minya. The 'tradition' of the Egyptian pasha was, in fact, that of the self-made man—although the forms of self-help favoured would rarely have secured them inclusion in the works of Horatio Alger. Some received their land in payment for their tax-gathering efforts; others had been Turkish or Circassian officers in Mohamed Ali's army. Of the mighty Badrawi-Ashur family, who owned 18,000 acres in Gharbiya and were next in point of acreage to Farouk

(130,000 acres), legend picturesquely had it that the first
Badrawi had been a poor fisherman who found favour in the
eyes of one of the women of Mohamed Ali's harem. Another
'old' family, the Sultans, with 2,000 acres in Minya and a name
to conjure with, had risen from humble origins through some
service to the Khedive Ismail. But most of the pashas were
more recently made: they were just men who had grown rich
in cotton booms, by canny land speculation, by squeezing their
fellahin and by multiple middleman profits, and had bought
up State domain, or added holding to holding. Some were village *omdas* who had used their position. A few were foreigners,
Lebanese like the Lutfallahs and Sursocks, Greeks like the
Gianaclis and Pierrekos who owned 7,000 acres in Beheira, or
Levantine merchants of origins too complex to put a name to.

The Greeks had started a wine industry. Some land companies had reclaimed tracts of semi-desert. But such enterprise
was not characteristic of the Egyptian pasha. The purpose of
land was its possession. Given possession, a fine superstructure
of loans could be erected in the best Khedival style (eight
members of the Royal Family owed £800,000 to the *Crédit
Foncier* in 1952), then more land amassed and more money
spun, the whole astonishingly inflating into that Egyptian
'palace culture' which carried into the mid-twentieth century
its peculiar combination of the barbaric splendours of the
Mamelukes and the social pretensions of the Second Empire.
Overpowering display was its object, most conspicuously
achieved in the small towns of Upper Egypt where the baroque
balconies and balustraded and statue-lined roofs of the pashas'
'palaces' still rise above the humble dwellings of the people
like wedding cakes among halfpenny buns. In Minya and
Assiut, Corinthian pillars and 'Scots Baronial' towers are enriched by Coptic spirals, rampant lions and bulbous domes. In
Kena, stone eagles soar from roof-cornices in competitive flight;
and in the middle of the little town of Mellawi, beside the
Ibrahamia Canal, the pillared palace of Neguib Abdel Pasha
with its double 'Fontainebleu' staircase and garden tower now
stares in disbelief at the plain white walls of the new 'People's
Club.'

Although 'feudalists' is now the received term for Egypt's
ex-pashas—and some indeed had what amounted to private

armies—'feudal' dues were unmatched by feudal responsibilities. In general, the pashas shared the distaste felt by both the Bedouin and the Ottomans for the muddy occupations of the fellahin. Such things they left to their bailiffs; or they sub-let their lands to others, who sub-let to others, who sub-let to others, with profit for all but the 'ignorant' creature at the bottom of the pyramid.[1] It was, in fact, both easier and more profitable to exploit the fellahin than the land.

'It is the unfitness of the Pasha class to fulfil the functions naturally appertaining to them,' reported Lord Milner in 1892, 'which constitutes one of the chief obstacles to the realisation of the ideal of a self-governed Egypt. Nor is there much sign of a desire on their part to overcome their besetting sins.'

The accuracy of this observation was still evident more than half a century later. Western parliamentarianism had merely prolonged these anachronistic arrangements by decking them out in the striped trousers of respectability. The 1923 Constitution, crowning Egypt's 'independence,' specifically guaranteed the inviolability of property, and the presence of big landowners in *every* parliamentary party ensured it. A glance through any 'Who's Who' of these years shows that most landed families had a member of parliament in their ranks, and some sported a pair, one senator and one deputy. The Wafd in the 'thirties was financially supported by the country's two largest landowners, Mohamed Badrawi-Ashur and Prince Yussef Kemal; later its secretary-general was the great landowner, Fuad Serag ed Din; and even Nahas himself had married into one of the greatest landowning houses. It was thus hardly remarkable that the land tax remained at a derisory level and was widely evaded, or that land reform bills, introduced in 1945 and 1950 were rejected. It was the Wafd's habit at election times to address its famous radicalism to the towns; in the rural areas its landowner supporters could be safely left to deliver the vote. Thus in 1942 it legalised trade unions of industrial workers, but any organisation of agricultural

---

[1] Of course, there were a few exceptions. Gabriel Saab, a Lebanese agronomist who himself farmed in the Delta, put the number of large farms in whose achievement their owners 'took a certain pride' at not more than one hundred. 'Investment for agricultural development,' he summed up, 'was exceptional.'

workers remained illegal. It would, it was explained, endanger the very fabric of society.

Nor did Egypt's increasing industrialisation produce, as had happened in England, an effective counterpoise to the landed interest. On the contrary, Egyptian merchants and industrialists, such as they were, sank their profits into the land, much as their Western counterparts might have put them into securities or a bank. Alexandrian cotton men like the mill-owner Faraghly Pasha or the boss of the biggest cotton export house, Ali Amin Yehia, bought large tracts of land in the north Delta; so did Yussef Sednaoui Pasha, chairman of one of Egypt's leading department-store chains. Even so 'modern' a business tycoon as the Glasgow-educated engineer-contractor, Ahmed Abboud Pasha, acquired a 5,000-acre estate near Luxor, with two adjoining 'palaces,' one for himself, and a second built as a wedding present to his daughter and 'furnished throughout by Waring and Gillow, of Oxford Street, London.' And the smaller men in this supremely *arriviste* society, the successful professionals, doctors, pharmacists, engineers, hastened to provide themselves with similar evidence, if not of Pasha, at least of Bey, status.

But if on the narrow stage of the Nile Valley these developments took on the sharpness and grossness of a Gillray caricature, they were by no means confined to it. Over most of the Arab world westernisation and its concomitant parliamentarianism had similarly buttressed Pashadom and extended Sheikhocracy, as tribal chiefs exchanged camel for car, responsible council of elders for irresponsible political party, and, legally or illegally, took the tribal lands as their personal estate. It was a world more than ever divided into lords and helots, Magnates and Mob, mocking the old Islamic—and tribal—ideals of community and brotherhood.

In 1938 the Egyptian writer, Tewfik el Hakim, wrote of Democracy as 'a group of hungry, bare-footed men, paying a monthly salary of forty pounds to another group composed of wealthy men.' But the mood was of bitter, fatalistic acceptance. Some Muslim Brethren or Young Egypt rally might on occasion raise a cry for land reform, but it was merely one demagogic gesture among many. On the land itself anger might smoulder, but was impotent. In 1951 there were land riots at

Hama in Syria, an area of great landowners and wretched peasant share-croppers, which had elected an activist Socialist deputy, Akram Hourani (himself son of a local landowner). There was trouble, too, on some Egyptian estates. But though radical ideas might trickle through, a Pasha was a Pasha : one greater than he might overturn him and take his place, but the notion of orderly systematic redistribution of the land in the name of social justice seemed to belong to the world of poetry and legend rather than reality.

Thus the effect of the Egyptian Land Reform, the first in the Arab world, could not be measured by acreage statistics. The important thing about it was its assurance and relatively clear-cut character, its methodicalness, its manifest—and on the whole successful—effort to recognise both due legal process and the claims of social justice. As in France in 1789 and, in other ways, in Britain in 1832 and 1911, it opened a breach in the great forbidding dyke of the 'natural order.' It was a small breach, but in Egypt itself it was immediately consolidated and enlarged. After dealing with the arrangements for land redistribution, the Land Reform Law itself went on to fix maximum rents for *all* agricultural land (seven times the land tax, in effect a reduction of around 40 per cent); to require written tenancy agreements, with a minimum tenure of three years; to forbid the renting of land to non-cultivators; to permit farm workers to organise trade unions; and to provide for a minimum agricultural wage to be set annually by a joint Ministerial committee of landholders and labourers.

The despised petty fellah, even the labourer, had been unmistakably proclaimed to be an individual possessing legal status and human rights. It was a novel idea and would take time to percolate. But it was also a potent one.

Thus the twenty-two delegates from the Ministry of Agriculture who, at 3 a.m. on 26 October 1952, left Cairo for the various regions of Egypt, each carrying a list of land to be requisitioned and a cheque on the National Bank for £50 for necessary expenses (all a routine-bound Ministry of Finance would allow), can certainly claim a niche in Middle Eastern history. They found that irrigation pumps had inexplicably 'broken down.' They were besieged by fellahin whose supply of seeds and fertilisers had been cut off by their landlords. But if the pashas did not submit with good grace, they submitted. A few weeks earlier, emulating the style of his Bedouin ancestors, the twenty-four-year-old Adli Lamlum had galloped into 'his' village of Maghagha with thirty-five armed horsemen and had threatened death to any villager imprudent enough to accept any of his Lord's 'surplus' land. But when he returned next day, soldiers and police were waiting and he was taken off to gaol.

The point was taken. But such violence was untypical. On the whole the revolution in the countryside was conducted in a very Egyptian, almost family, way. Fearing trouble in Gharbiya, where there had lately been rioting and some punitive burning of houses on the estates of the Badrawi-Ashur, the army leaders sent tanks to Mansoura. But Sayed Marei, the agriculturalist placed in charge of the land reform, persuaded the officers to withdraw them. 'I felt very strongly that the real army on our side was the army of the farmers. So I went down there and I stayed ten days and I met no resistance. The Badrawis were very keen on their palace. The head of the family wanted to keep it—and to keep his telephone number (which was One or something). They were anxious to show that they were still important. I said we wanted land, not palaces, and I arranged for him to keep his telephone number. Then I arranged to build 100 new houses for the fellahin as a practical example of the true concerns of the revolution.

'The houses—and the palace—are still there.'

The régime could afford a certain generosity in that it was already provided with a very adequate 'Enemy of the People.' Numbering 370 persons in all, the Royal Family with its ten princes, twenty-seven princesses, and its forty-eight members of the nobility, owned around 190,000 acres—more than one-third of the total due for expropriation. For them there was to be no compensation in 3 per cent redeemable bonds, no 200-feddan allocation. In November 1953, the royal property was declared forfeit to the people, its assets, calculated at £75 millions, being applied to the land reform administration, to social welfare projects and to the improvement of Cairo. The poetic justice of these arrangements was vividly illustrated in the serial 'revelations' in the newspapers and in the public trials which turned the spotlight on Farouk's motley entourage—the 'sinister' Sudanese valet; the Italian electrician-secretary-procurer; Elias Andraus, the Levantine business agent; Karim Thabet Pasha, the Lebanese press adviser; 'Brigadier' Mohamed Helmy Hussein, the much-promoted sergeant-chauffeur. Thrown open to the public, the royal palaces—eleven in number, not to mention the many 'rest houses'—could safely be left to bear corroborative witness to the disastrous extravagance—not to mention taste—of the ' "Albanian" dynasty of Mohamed Ali.' In the royal apartments the tear-off calendars with their unctuous portraits of Farouk were left eloquently halted at 26 June 1952.

Yet, if no heads rolled, much legal ink was spilled. Elaborate evasions of the land reform law were to keep the courts busy for years, and the concession permitting landowners to sell off their 'surplus' themselves in five-feddan plots was so badly abused and resulted in such destructive fragmentation that it had to be rescinded.[2] None of this, however, prevented the monumental task of redistributing and reorganising the land from going steadily ahead.

Whatever the motives of those who had advanced it, the argument that the division of the big estates would lead to a disastrous fall in production had not been unreasonable. Such, notoriously, had been the first result of land reform in a good many countries whose agricultural régimes were much less complex than Egypt's. And yet, paradoxically, it was the very intricacy of Egyptian agriculture that ensured the success of the land reform. As on earlier occasions in the Nile Valley, the challenge was sharp enough to compel a decisive response.

The necessary elements were already to hand: the traditional skills and the endurance of the fellahin; the expertise of seven thousand graduate agriculturalists, members of an established Egyptian profession which had been emerging, first from the College of Agriculture, then from the university, since the 'nineties; and, not least, although so far least developed, the device of the agricultural co-operative which the nationalist leader, Omar Lutfi, had brought from Ireland

[2] But not before 145,000 feddans had been sold off in this way by the owners.

and England in the early years of the century. The first law on co-operatives had been passed as long ago as 1923, and in 1952 about a thousand societies were in being. But, as with so much else in Egypt, the pashas had in effect taken them over, using them to get cheap credit for their estates, while the small fellah—and tenant—who really needed the co-operative's aid was either crowded out or ineligible—although sometimes a landowner or village *omda* would pass on a loan to a tenant at a vastly enhanced rate of interest. Nor had the government troubled to equip the societies with the necessary trained staff.

With the 'feudal' incubus removed, it became possible to combine these ingredients in an effective way. The chosen instrument—which had its elements of paradox—might be roughly described as the 'compulsory, supervised, co-operative farm colony.' But it is by no means as forbidding as it sounds. Built around the irrigation network, it is a complex—and a uniquely Egyptian arrangement.

As a condition of his land grant, each new peasant-proprietor was required to join one of the newly formed local land reform co-operatives. To each local co-operative, the Land Reform Authority appointed an agricultural graduate as adviser and organiser—since the logic both of the irrigation system and the Egyptian crop rotation demand that the area should be planned overall. Yet the principle of private ownership was scrupulously maintained. Each man watched and worked his own feddans and profited by his own labour at the harvests. Each of the local co-operatives was formally administered by a council elected from the farmers, but with the agricultural engineer sitting in, and was linked, through the 'Area' organisation with its professional director, to the other local land reform co-operatives, and supplied with the services of accountants, mechanics, veterinaries and so on. Peripatetic inspectors maintained contact between the Areas—which were finally to number forty-three in all—and the Land Reform Authority in Cairo.

The scheme was self-supporting. The new owners (who could not, however, sell their land) were to pay the averaged compensation cost back to the government in instalments to be spread over thirty years, with 3 per cent interest and

15 per cent administrative costs added. They would naturally buy their seeds and fertilisers through the co-operative organisation and could use it for marketing their crops.[3] The Agricultural Credit Bank was now allowed to lend on the security of growing crops as well as on land—thus delivering the fellahin from the rural moneylenders and merchants who commonly charged 30-50 per cent—and even over 100 per cent—interest per annum.

In any country the realisation of such a scheme would impose a severe test both of organising power and technical capacity. In Egypt, in addition, the architects of the land reform had to deal with a largely illiterate, intensely suspicious, population. But Nasser—whose ability to pick key men has not been the least of his qualities—found exactly the right man to head the project in Sayed Marei, an agricultural graduate who was himself a practising farmer, famed for his citrus orchards in Sharkiya province, and one of those robust Egyptian individualists whose energy and 'attack' is in such remarkable contrast to the inertia of the country's vast bureaucracy. In 1945, as a member of parliament, Marei had introduced a bill to limit agricultural rents without success. Now, co-opted to the Higher Committee for Agrarian Reform, he was successively made Manager of the Land Reform Authority, Manager of the Agricultural Credit Bank and, finally, Minister of Agriculture.

Under Marei the immense, and immensely complicated, task was tackled with a steady professionalism. Distribution was not begun until the area concerned had been thoroughly surveyed and re-planned. The new co-operatives had to be organised and likely fellah secretaries located. Sometimes a big estate was divided between several co-operatives, sometimes the new co-operative's area was larger than any single old estate. The agriculturalist supervisors had to be trained too, for, as Marei says, 'a first-class agricultural engineer is not necessarily a good co-operative supervisor: he needs to know how to get on with the fellahin also'—in itself a novel idea for many.

As the weeks went by and the invasion of agriculturalists and irrigation engineers continued, there was trouble from the fellahin. 'They didn't believe we'd ever distribute,' said

[3] For later developments here, see Chapter 15.

Marei. 'They thought we were going to take their land away. . . .' Nevertheless, by September 1954, one year after the Land Reform decree had been signed, the first 100,000 feddans had been distributed.

Dusty jeeps and lorries filled the courtyard formerly occupied by the King's fleet of scarlet limousines: a wing of the Abdin Palace had become the headquarters of the Land Reform Authority. It was from here, early one morning in late May 1955, that I set out with a young agriculturalist named Aziz Kadry on my first visit to the land reform area of Etay el Baroud.[4]

As ever early in the morning, the roads into Cairo were full of carts piled high with luxuriant vegetables. But as the city receded and the green of the Delta closed in around us, the loads on the flat-bottomed carts changed to loads of fellahin, their families and labourers, sitting, elbow to elbow, around the edges, legs dangling, on their way to the fields. The wheat had just been harvested, and all along the road, at intervals, at the edge of the fields, the oxen, one eye covered, trod in stately circles, drawing over the wheaten floor the *norag*, or threshing chair, a cumbrous wooden throne, with rough knives below its sledge, on which the fellah rides, long whip in hand, urging on the plodding ox. It is a device as old as the Pharaohs.

Yet for all his conservatism the mind of the fellah is sharp enough when it suits him. Sometimes our car ran over a carpet of grain, spread thinly across the road. The tyres picked it up, hurled it against the underside of the wings, and flung it—threshed—to the side of the road, where the fellahin waited to shovel it into sacks.

'You see,' laughed Aziz Kadry, 'that's our latest invention for threshing—and it costs absolutely nothing!'

Kadry was a 'special projects' man: it was his job to travel around the Land Reform villages, promoting a variety of self-help schemes—in-calf buffalo supplied on instalment payments, bees, buffalo insurance at six piastres a month, improved breeds of poultry made by crossing the tough, but scrawny, native Fayyumi and Denderah fowls with buxom

---

[4] Chapter 17 deals with follow-up visits in 1964 and 1965, and with subsequent developments in the co-operative system.

Rhode Islands. . . .

But it hadn't, he said, been easy. At first the fellahin had been very suspicious. He would go to a village and offer free chicks in return for four eggs from each when the pullet came to laying. And there would be no takers. The farmers' experience had not prepared them for such services from their Lords and Masters. They were sure it must be a trap. Only when Kadry actually turned up with a lorry full of chicks did they respond. The whole outlook of the village, he said, began to change. (Although not quite enough, it seemed, for when the time came, many peasants were loth to deliver the agreed four eggs.)

To reach Etay el Baroud ('the Place of the Gunpowder') from Cairo one crosses first the Damietta, then the Rosetta, branch of the Nile. Rather more than halfway to Alexandria on a branch of the Beheira Canal, it is an average enough Egyptian *markaz* (district) town—a few dusty, hole-and-corner shops, a twice-weekly market that squats in the unpaved street, a swing-bridge over the canal, opening twice a day to let the boats through, a level crossing and a railway station.

The headquarters of the Land Reform Area lie a little way beyond the town in a large stone mansion in a palm-lined garden, in the days of its royal owners modestly known as 'the Rest House.' Occupying the former estates of Prince Wahid ed-Din and of Princess Shivecar, the Turkish first wife of King Fuad, the land reform area here comprised 16,000 acres, 23,000 people, eleven villages—and eleven co-operative societies, with 4,000 fellahin members.

Inside the Rest House, ornate high-backed chairs still stood stiffly around the rooms and corridors like so many vacant thrones. But now the walls were covered with surveyors' maps, intricate jigsaws of plots and rotation zones, irrigation channels, villages, drains. The area of each co-operative was generally divided, overall, into three long parallel strips, each tinted a different colour. This, it was explained, was to facilitate the Delta's three-rotation system, which keeps the land almost continuously under crops. The land reform law provides that each man's holding (though it may be only two acres) shall be in three pieces, not more than half a kilometre apart, one piece in each rotation area. When the soil chemists and irrigation engineers had been over the ground and had worked out the intricate patterns determining the plot boundaries, a social survey decided each family's allotment, rising to a maximum of five feddans for those with many children.

Within the categories, a spin of the coin decided who got which particular plot. 'Of course,' said the *Mandoub* (agent), 'not everyone is satisfied at once. But if there are complaints we look into them and perhaps make some adjustment. In the end, it all settles down.'

This sort of overall planning means that, despite the small plots and the many irrigation channels, tractor cultivation is practicable—which means that one can plough deeper than is possible with only a gamoose and wooden plough, one can get the seeds in earlier (particularly vital with cotton), and one can spare the animals to give much-needed milk and meat. The division into three strips is dictated by the fertility-preserving triennial crop rotation and also by the law which intermittently, but for a good many years, has compelled Egypt's farmers to limit cotton cultivation to not more than one-third of their land, while putting not *less* than one-third under wheat for home consumption.

All in all, with his crops so largely dictated, the diet of his 'free' chicks prescribed by the veterinary unit, his cotton land ploughed by the co-operative tractor (for which he pays a fee), forbidden to sell or divide his holding, and in debt to the co-operative, the new landowners' freedom appeared much circumscribed. Was his lot, then, so different from that of a peasant on a collective farm in a Communist country?

It was essentially different. To the stranger's eye the great expanse of wheat or maize stretching away before him may appear totally anonymous. But the fellah member of a land reform co-operative sees it differently. He knows the exact location of the iron markers that indicate the edges of his plot. He knows the plot is registered in his name at the local land office; he holds the title deeds. The fact of its possession is at the centre of his life. In common with all his fellow members he has a personal account book in which is entered his indebtedness to the society for loans, raw materials, services. and his deliveries of crops, prices received, instalments repaid on his holding and so on. His margin of manoeuvre may seem pathetically small, yet he can do well or ill—and this book will tell the story. He has, metaphorically as well as literally, a stake in the country.

We went out into the fields. Great clouds of dust billowed out behind the car. Young cotton plants, six or eight inches high, patterned the earth. They had been planted by the women in February, eight or nine seeds popped into each hole. After five weeks they are thinned down to three plants a hole; finally to two. The economy of the Delta village revolves around cotton. Traditionally, it supplies the fellah with his meagre cash income; the rest of his farming activities feed himself, his family and two or three animals. When the cotton is coming up, no more berseem (clover) can be grown since it offers a breeding ground to the bollworm, and so, through the long summer, there is little food for the animals save straw and the green leaves from the maize. And then for two months or more, 'the season of the pests,' the whole country lives under the threat of disaster, and all through the Delta the cotton fields bob with rows of children's heads as they comb through the plants—and, sometimes, a fluttering red flag warns that the worm has been found.

At the side of the road, a couple of fellahin sat with the water up to their thighs, churning the long sloping *tambour*, propelling a stream of water from the irrigation channel into the furrows on their land. But now, a hundred yards away, a diesel engine chugged, and dark brown spurts of water came gushing from a newly drilled artesian well. A series of wells were being sunk on the estate in order to turn some 4,000 acres over to rice—an increasingly valuable cash and export crop in Egypt.

We came to one of the villages—the usual forlorn mud heap, half-submerged under its rooftop burden of corn-straw and old cotton plants. At the end of a long straggling 'street' a fellah was threshing his wheat. A golden wall of grain encircled him like a fortification as he rode majestically around on the *norag*, flicking with a rope whip at his two plodding buffaloes. When he saw us he yelled at the buffaloes, jumped off his throne, and rushing over to the *Mandoub*, directed at him a voluble flow of Arabic in which the word *roz* recurred many times.

'He's asking for rice,' explained the Mandoub. 'He wants to know when *he* is going to get the water for rice. I've told him not to worry, he'll get it sure enough. But he's very impatient. Everywhere I go they're asking for rice.'

The farmer watched us intently, searching our faces for a clue. He was a tall, upstanding fellow, lithe and alert, with a face burned a dull brick-red by the sun. Through an interpreter I was able to talk to him for a while. His name was Ahmed Shaban and he was married with six young children. He had been a tenant on the old estate, paying £E40 a feddan for four feddans. Now he had only three, but he *owned* them, and was paying for them at the rate of £E15 a feddan, spread over thirty years, with an extra £E2 an acre for his irrigation water.[5] He explained with some satisfaction that he'd cleared all that off from last year's cotton alone. And there was still this feddan of wheat—which would take him five days to thresh: not to mention his broad beans and his berseem. So with a feddan less than before, he was already better off— and he'd be better off still, he added, with a side-glance at the *Mandoub*, when he got that water he'd been promised for his *roz*.

But the *Mandoub* was not his only recourse. In common with his neighbours he elected representatives from his land-section to the local co-operative committee. As it happened, the committee of the village of Robh Shandied was meeting that morning in a room in what had been the royal stables. Aziz Kadry took me in.

The committee men sat around a long trestle table. They were wearing dark, thick *galabiyas*—although the temperature was 100 degrees Fahrenheit—and the white skullcaps called *takias*, except for one rather older member, who wore a red tarbush. The society's agricultural engineer sat at one end of the table with the district inspector of co-operatives next to him, and the village chairman and secretary, a spry gnome of a man with a wide mischievous grin, sat in the middle of one side in front of the open minute book.

It was their ninth meeting: the co-operative had been in

---

[5] Saab estimates the *average* fall in payments on Land Reform holdings compared with pre-Revolution rents at 33-40 per cent.

being only six months. But they set about the agenda with a
will. There was the question of finding more storage space for
the threshed wheat; preparations for the annual campaign
against the cotton worm; and the matter of the number of
members willing to try the new hybrid maize which the agriculturalist swore would yield two or three times as much as
the old variety. I asked the agriculturalist later what would
happen if the committee took the bit between its teeth and
ignored his advice. He said that if their proposal were against
the law, or if they were demanding a bigger loan than he
thought they needed, he would refer the issue to the Board
in Cairo. They would give a ruling.

It can never be very easy for impoverished peasants, receiving money, to invest it rather than spend it. Earlier attempts
at rural co-operation in Egypt had foundered on this rock,
and detailed control of credits was now considered fundamental in the new structure. And this tended to give the
agriculturalist what must sometimes have been a rather
awkward dual rôle of technical adviser to the co-operative's
members and also accountant and debt-collector. Yet this was
clearly no stooge assembly. These were men who had strong
opinions on matters in which they had much experience. They
did not hesitate to make them heard. Indeed, they manifestly
enjoyed making them heard. The argument grew noisier. The
little chairman bounded excitedly from side to side, waving
his ruler, his spectacles gleaming. His name was Mohamed
Tewfik el Kady, and he had eight children, and, in consequence, five acres. The law states that the committee secretary
must be literate—but it would have been impracticable to
demand this of the rest of the committee. Out of the fifteen
here, only five had been to primary school and another had
taught himself to read and write. The rest signed the Minutes
with their thumbprints.

But however primitive the conditions of their lives, Egyptian
fellahin often have a darting intelligence, and, when the mood
takes them, a lively wit. The little chairman was full of merry
sallies. There were great cackles of laughter in the stables.

Aziz Kadry watched the proceedings benevolently. 'You
know, five years ago, before the Revolution, you could hardly
have approached a farmer. They always suspected you—even

us, their fellow Egyptians. . . .'

'Yes, yes,' exclaimed the co-operative inspector, 'at first, when we started, and they found a gentleman would come and sit down with them and talk with them, they were astonished. Now, as you see, they are getting used to it.'

It was true, he said, that not all co-operatives were like this one. 'Some places are difficult. People are always quarrelling. You can't live with them at all! With such people it seems we shall just have to go trying until, somehow, we make them calm.'

In Upper Egypt, in particular, the architects of the land reform faced a challenge sharper than they had generally met in the Delta. In part, this was because of the remoteness and primitive character of the Upper Nile Valley, so narrow that a single landowner might own everything for many miles on end, in part it was because of the technical requirements of the dominating crop.

As one travels southwards up the Nile Valley, it is in Minya that the eye is first delighted by the swaying, golden-tipped stands of cane, the nostrils first assaulted by the heavy sour-sweet breath of the sugar factories. But it is not until another two hundred miles have passed and one enters the province of Kena that the rank walls of cane close in on all sides, and from January to May each year the cane rules over the life of the Valley as cotton does from June to October in the Delta. Every day then is full of the splinter-and-crash of cane—as it falls under the harvesters' sickles, as it drops from the camels' backs beside the estate-railway tracks, as it topples from the labourers' backs on to the waggons.

The harvest, geared to the appetite of the factories, lasts five months; every evening, as the shadows lengthen, the long trains of loaded cane click-clatter along miles of narrow-gauge track through the valley. As the men hack their way into the stands, the women chop off the green leaves, and the boys bear them away on donkeys. Poor stuff—but it will feed the family camel, the donkey, perhaps even the gamoose—for with so much of the soil taken up by sugar cane, there is little room for clover. Unlike cotton, the cane stays in the ground three years, sprouting up again under that ferocious sun within a week or two of the cutting.

The sugar estates were vast and, for Egypt, highly capital-ised undertakings, with big steam pumps, professional man-agement and heavy tractors—for before planting cane you must plough deep and plough twice. Some of the great land-owners parcelled out their sugar estates to operating con-tractors, who hired labourers at three piastres (6d) a day.

It was not a type of agriculture that appeared suitable for smallholders, even when organised in the land reform co-opera-tives. And indeed at first the Land Reform Authority merely retained the estates in state ownership, letting them out to share-croppers. Yet if any part of Egypt stood in need of social revolution, clearly it was this. It was a challenge the Land Reformers could not ignore. So they went ahead and distributed the sugar estates in the usual two- to five-feddan plots, and they set up their co-operatives.

If the villages of the Delta suffered from long neglect, those of Upper Egypt had dwelt in oblivion. The road southwards up the Valley is tenuous, meandering from bank to bank, rough and rocky, attuned to the bullock-cart age. Even as late as 1965 a car journey from Cairo to Aswan was a hazardous adventure. Outside one or two tourist spots, reached by air, strangers are rare, and hotels primitive or non-existent.

At Nag Hamadi the Nile swings eastwards to describe in the desert the shape of a sickle, and the road changes sides, cross-ing from the west to the east bank of the river, suspended like an afterthought from the sides of the railway bridge. But despite the bridge, the barrage, the sugar factory, Nag Hamadi remained just a big sprawling village with a long unpaved and rutted main street, along which hordes of small boys pursued my car, kicking up the dust, and shrieking 'Alemani! Alemani!' —'German! German!'

But if the memory of what Cromer liked to call 'the English-man' were evidently somewhat faded, there were other ghosts abroad here which might not be so readily laid. The palace of Prince Yussef Kemal, who owned 16,000 acres in these parts, lies along the Nile Bank in its formal gardens of cypresses and ornamental cacti with miradors upon the river. Again, a palace had been turned into a Land Reform headquarters. Behind the

high double doors, desks were stacked high with agriculturalists' returns, *galabiya*-ed fellahin came and went, and book-
keepers laboured over co-operatives' accounts.

But in the 'Islamic-style' Guest House in the gardens (with
electric lift), the Prince's solar topees were still hanging on the
hooks, his golf-clubs and lances mouldering in a cupboard.
The young agricultural engineer who now lodged upstairs,
fingered the lances, speculating on what the Prince, a celebrated big-game man, might have hunted. The 'Islamic' stained-
glass window cast a melancholy light on the big sofa, still
depressed, it seemed, with the Prince's figure. 'There he sat,'
said the young man, 'like Haroun el Rashed. And you know,
he was only here for one month a year. . . .'

Yet, one month or one year, 'feudalist' or His Exalted High-
ness, more than a decade after the Prince's latest and final
departure, the incubus of an older and more durable Occupation than the British still lay upon the Valley.

For all that, the land reformers had not been intimidated.
If Nag Hamadi is the point of the sickle the Nile outlines in
the desert, Armant on the West bank is where the blade joins
the handle. Here the 5,000-acre sugar plantation of Ahmed
Abboud joined hands with the King's 4,000 acres and Prince
Yussef Kemal's 6,000 acres and the sugar-cane acres of a
wealthy Copt. All had been put together to form a land-reform
co-operative region containing 16,000 acres, fifty villages,
eleven agricultural co-operatives, and something like 2,000 new
smallholder families.

Now the sugar-cane harvesting is run on communal lines,
the families teaming together; but the holdings remain individual, and as each stand of cane is cut, it is loaded on to a
railway-waggon which carries chalked on its side the name
of the particular smallholder—who is paid by the factory
according to the quantity and quality of *his* crop. And this
policy has worked. With the new farmer's zeal excited by
possession of his own land and the improved seeds and techniques supplied by the co-operative organisation, sugar-cane
yields have risen from seventeen tons an acre in this area to
forty-five tons, and, finally, fifty tons. A typical fellah with
two acres under cane (net profit £E60 an acre) and two under
cotton, who before the Revolution had often worked for seven

piastres or much less a day, experienced a great change of fortune. If the Delta land reform farmers' incomes increased by 50 per cent on pre-Land Reform levels, the Upper Egypt land reform farmers' incomes doubled.

But the leeway to be made up in this part of Egypt cannot be made up wholly in terms of money. Centuries of subjugation, stretching back to the Pharaohs, have left their impress on the soil here. As I had in the Delta, I asked the chief agriculturalist, the *Mandoub*, what would happen if a farmer did not follow his advice. He did not hesitate.

'I will not plough his land! I will not give him water! We must have organisation—that is our business. If you leave the farmer alone, he will just plant something to eat and he will have no money.' He tapped his head. 'You know, he has not the organisation.'

Smoke drifted across the charred fields. They burn the stubble after the cane is cut, to warm and fertilise the earth and help the breakthrough of new shoots. Three miles away to the west the sandstone cliff marked the end of the cane— and the end of the Valley.

'Yes, yes,' said the young agricultural engineer of one of the co-operatives, 'first I discuss. We discuss. If they agree, okay. If they don't, I go ahead anyway. After all, it is for their good.'

I believed him. For these Egyptian agriculturalists are a remarkable lot of men. Many have passed half their lives in the isolation of the villages; they are almost a special race of Egyptian, men of few words—yet ready to quote yields and costs at the drop of a hat—self-contained, quietly competent— even dedicated—men, conscious as few Egyptians can be of working within an honourable tradition which is both profoundly Egyptian and yet contemporary.

The chief agriculturalist here at Armant had worked out a method of growing broad beans—the true 'staff of life' in Egypt—amongst the young cane, thus snatching an extra crop. He displayed his thousand experimental acres of beans-and-cane with pride. 'In the whole world,' he said, only half-joking, 'you will not see beans like those!' For the fellahin it would mean an extra £E20 net profit per acre.

A little further along the estate road we came to a field of beans where the furrows were not getting enough water. The agriculturalist called the young fellah working there over to his car and talked to him like a father.

The young fellah listened respectfully. 'Hadr' Bey,' he said timidly, at intervals. 'Hadr' Bey!' 'It will be done, Sir . . . it will be done, Bey!'

Materially, the land reform quickly established itself. Although it is, of course, easy for any armchair critic, enjoying the benefits of hindsight and endowed with unlimited but hypothetical energy, to point to a variety of weaknesses, the fact remains that the equitable distribution and complex socio-agricultural organisation of these vast areas, all over Egypt, with no general loss of production, and the fitting of them, within the space of a few years, into a nation-wide co-operative structure—in the face of rural inertia, mass illiteracy and appalling poverty—must, by any standard, rank as a notable achievement.

Politically, the implications of the Land Reform system seemed less certain—to the Westerner, at least. Was it really 'the Land for the People'—or, once again, 'the People for the Land'? Was the absentee Pasha merely to be replaced by the all-too-present Technocrat—in what would finally amount to little more than an elaborate modern version of the Orient's old 'palace revolution'? Or could the Egyptian fellah, through this system, realise his full human stature?

The question was vital, but in Egypt it was also premature. Many co-operative officials realised that paternalism was not 'co-operation.' One whose work took him to hundreds of village co-operatives said of the fellahin 'members': 'Year after year we are trying to raise the level of their interest—to lead them to independence so that they will not just wait for things to be done for them.' The difficulty was not so much to discipline the fellah as to arouse him—for his passivity and non-commitment were ingrained by many centuries of bitter experience. 'He was examined with the rod' was, we are told, a standard administrative phrase in the New Kingdom (c.1580-720 B.C.); it was also a practice faithfully continued into the still recent past. It was thus all too easy for agricultural managers to revert to the traditional minatory stance and for the fellah to fall back on those talents for deceit and opportunism which had been so long the condition of his survival.

That this did not happen more than it did was perhaps a tribute to Egyptian good humour and basic fellow feeling. For although the co-operative system has its sanctions, in the radical and egalitarian form here adopted it depends to a high degree on mutual trust and honesty. After 1957, with the organisational stage terminating, the point was emphasised by an attempt to switch the emphasis from managerialism to that of the local, regional and national co-operative committees, with democratic election at all levels.

The co-operative ideal can have faced few sterner challenges than that which today confronts it in the Nile Valley, where it is being invited to repair the ravages of history and restore the wholeness of a nation.

7

THE SKELETON AT THE TABLE

The problem was to get Egypt out of the Middle Ages, to turn it from a semi-feudal country into a modern, ordered, viable state, while at the same time respecting the customs of the people.

—Anwar el Sadat, *Revolt on the Nile*, 1957

. . . poor as a needle which clothes others but remains itself unclad.

—Fellah saying

The new smallholders on the distributed estates were by no means the only beneficiaries of the 1952 agrarian reform. As a result of the rent and tenure laws, the incomes of tenants and sharecroppers rose by at least a quarter, according to an independent estimate. But it was a rise from often abysmally low levels, which were not thereby rendered much less abysmal. In 1956 a third of all Egypt's land-holding fellahin worked holdings of less than one feddan—often a mere sliver of soil.[1] Land here is commonly reckoned in *kirats*—24ths of a feddan. On such fragments of land a fellah cannot hope to sustain his family: he must also hire out his—and their— labour to others. But a substantial part of the rural population dependent on agriculture, perhaps 1½ million *families*, has no land at all.

The architects of the land reform calculated the size of individual holdings on the distributed estates to give the fellah and his family an income 10 per cent above bare subsistence— which in Egypt is bare indeed. Even so, these land-reform peasant-proprietors in their co-operative colonies quickly be-

[1] In 1956 the total number of land-holders, whether tenants or owners, was estimated at 1,254,000, of whom 405,000 held less than one feddan. These 405,000 *holdings* had, however, in aggregate over two million 'registered proprietors,' many of whom worked in town, and let off their sliver of land. In 1960 the total rural population was 16,120,000, the number actively 'employed in agriculture' 4·4 millions. (*Economic Bulletin*, National Bank of Egypt, quoted Hansen & Marzouk, *Development and Economic Policy in the U.A.R.*; U.A.R. Statistical Handbook.)

came something of a new privileged class in the eyes of their fellows. Sometimes, landless labourers from all around flocked into the new land-reform regions, eager to pick up crumbs from the newly enriched tables. True, under the new agrarian law even the labourer benefited, for a minimum rural daily wage had been fixed, 18 piastres for men, and 10 piastres for women.[2] But although this was at least a third above former levels, achievement fell short of promise: the actual rise in pay of male agricultural workers between 1953 and 1956 was officially estimated at 10 per cent. In so heavily over-populated a countryside, where the hunger both for work and for land was endemic, it was easier to enact such laws than to enforce them.

The Nile Valley, indeed, was like some harshly illuminated working model of the Rev. Thomas Malthus's magic thesis that population increases in geometric progression, while food supply increases merely in arithmetic progression. With each successive raising of the old Aswan Dam, each new round of desert reclamation, the population had leapt ahead, devouring the increase in production. Between 1897 and 1949 the cultivated area grew by 14 per cent and the 'crop area' by over a third;[3] but the population doubled. In 1896, the 'crop area' per head (of total population) had been over four-fifths of a feddan; by 1947 it had dropped to under half a feddan. The proportion of the landless and the minuscule landholders rose steeply.

These are classic figures in Egypt. Before 1952 they had been the skeleton at Cairo's perpetual feast, heightening the note of hysteria that sometimes broke through the smart chatter. In 1953 they were the skeleton at the council table of the officers and their apprentice planners. Nasser told a foreign Ambassador at this time that it was these figures that kept him awake at night. But that, at least, was progress.

It has been Egypt's fate to provide vivid illustration not only of Malthus, but also of Marx. In many countries the development of modern capitalism and the market economy, while it

[2] One pound of local white cheese costs 14 piastres; a plate of *fool* (boiled broad beans) 2 piastres in a café; a packet of 18 cigarettes 12-15 piastres (1965 prices).
[3] The distinction, a characteristically Egyptian one, is between the area under cultivation ('cultivated area') and the number of times an area is cropped per year ('crop area').

caused grave hardship, also spread money fairly widely around. In Egypt, however, particularly outside the towns, this was not so. With sixteen million people living on the land, two-thirds of the cultivated area was owned by less than 162,000 persons. The great State expenditures on new barrages and irrigation canals thus mainly made the rich richer. To the weight of population pressing on the scarce soil was added the weight of speculative winnings seeking safe lodgment. Leases were very short and insecure. The land was a market commodity in constant flux—indeed almost *the* market commodity. Between 1940 and 1950 cash rents rose nearly five times, the cost of living three times, and in 1945 it was calculated that an average farm acre sold for the equivalent of an Egyptian farm worker's wages for twenty years.

In 1951, after three years' research in five Delta villages, a Rockefeller Foundation team reported that, whether considered by income, housing, nutrition, sanitation, health, or education, the state of the peasants of Egypt was worse than in any other country, including China and India, in which they had conducted investigations. In 1950, only 3 per cent of the intake of the Egyptian army was accepted as fit without treatment.[4] Ninety per cent of villagers suffered from either bilharzia or ancyclostomiasis (hookworm) or both. Malaria, tuberculosis and syphilis were rife. Because they ate maize rather than wheaten bread, many suffered from pellagra. But the most depressing, because the most visible, evidence of neglect lay in the appalling prevalence of eye diseases. Egypt is hard on the eyes: Bonaparte's soldiers went down with ophthalmia in frightening numbers. But given prompt attention such troubles are readily cured. As Egypt's legions of the one-eyed, the bleary-eyed, the bloodshot-eyed, the squint-eyed and the blind liberally testified, this attention was not forthcoming. Even in 1955 a doctor at the Mehalla textile mills told me that 80 per cent of applicants for work were rejected on medical grounds, mainly eye troubles.

It is something of a mystery how, with these multiple afflictions, the Egyptian fellah continues to display the remarkable vitality that he does. Is it, perhaps, a testimony to the beneficence of the Egyptian sun, or to the virtues of his diet of

[4] Information, Adel Taher, Under-Secretary, Ministry of Youth, 1965.

broad beans, onions and white cheese? Or is it merely a tribute to the potency of the much-boiled, heavily sugared black tea to which the fellahin have turned in recent times—much, perhaps, as the English poor turned to cheap gin in the 18th century?

It could, of course, be a demonstration of the Darwinian principle of the survival of the toughest: in 1952 two-thirds of all recorded deaths were of children under five; and the official infant mortality rate was a much understated 136 per thousand (compared with 29 in Britain).

This, then, was the true face of that 'Egyptian nation' of which two generations of middle-class nationalists had boasted. This was the raw material from which the 'New Egypt' the revolution had announced must be fashioned.

Yet, in one way, the task facing the new régime was a little simpler than appeared: most of the necessary measures had long been known, even prepared. What had been lacking had been the will and firmness of purpose to carry them through. Compulsory free primary education between the ages of six and twelve had even been written into the 1923 Constitution; yet in 1952, almost a generation later, three-quarters of the Egyptian people were still illiterate. In 1950 the Wafd had made secondary education free; but only 45 per cent of the children were, in fact, in schools of any sort. Politicians, who sent their own children to private schools and foreign schools, were not unduly worried by the urgency of the task.

Again, a Five Year Plan for transport and irrigation had been drawn up in 1935; but neither it nor its successor in 1945 had been implemented. In 1952 there were a few rural health centres and, again, plenty of plans. But 85 per cent of the villages of Egypt had no drinking water other than that they took out of the Nile or canals. Of Egypt's 4,500 doctors, three-quarters were in Cairo, Alexandria and one or two other major towns. Of the 1,400 Government doctors, only 600 served in the countryside, and many of these were preoccupied with building private practices on the side. In this money-oriented land, medicine had long been viewed primarily as the road to riches.

Now, given impetus by the revolution, a large primary-school building drive was got under way: between 1953 and 1961 the number of children in primary schools doubled; it is expected that by 1970, all the 6- to 12-year-olds will be at school. In its 1954 Budget the new régime allocated about £15 million to health projects. £5,500,000 was earmarked for the project of taking piped pure water to the villages of Egypt. The grey concrete water towers and the small white health centres began their march across the countryside. In 1965 a few hundred villages were still waiting for their clean water supply. But they knew that they would get it, for like the Edwardian English, the Egyptians as a nation had now discovered 'the "condition of the people" question.'

But while such innovations were beneficial, the heart of the problem of rural rehabilitation lay in the character of the Egyptian villages themselves. Huddled in the smallest possible area (since land was costly and money-producing), the mud-brick hovels—devoid in the Delta of a single touch of decoration or splash of colour—seem almost part of the earth itself. 'In the villages they do not even know a pair of scissors,' reported Bonaparte in 1798. 'For furniture they have only a straw mat and two or three earthenware pots.' More than a century and a half later that is still largely true. People work, eat, are born, make love, die, on the earth. The bed is a raised earth platform, the *mastaba*. Smoke from the women's cooking fire of straw blackens the interior—there are no chimneys. Until very recently—and in many places still—the fellahins' only substantial purchases from outside were tea, sugar, kerosene and cigarettes. For the rest the village has been meagrely self-sufficient, its four or five families occupying the same quarters generation after generation, traditionally inter-marrying, a shut-in world, repelling outsiders as the flesh repels a splinter, or festers around it.

The rebuilding of Egypt's 4,300 villages would seem to be a first condition of true social progress—the necessary prelude to bridging the gulf between rural and urban Egypt, and fashioning a single society. But the slenderness of Egyptian resources forbids it. In the Land Reform projects all funds were at first concentrated on the soil and machinery. As Sayed Marei saw it, from increased agricultural production village improvement might eventually be financed; if human welfare was put first, the whole land-reform structure might collapse into bankruptcy.

Egypt abounds in such bitter choices; they are of the very fabric of the Nile Valley. But in this case an ingenious, if partial, answer to the dilemma lay to hand. In 1939 the Egyptian Government, responding to the climate of the times, had set up a Social Welfare Ministry with a special 'Fellah Department.' The director of this department, Dr Ahmed Hussein (later Ambassador in Washington at the time of the High Dam negotiations) evolved a plan for what he called 'social units.' Since it was not possible either to rebuild the villages or for an outsider to live in such places, one would erect outside them a local centre serving several villages, where representatives of the Ministries of Social Welfare, Health and Agriculture, leaving Cairo and departmentalism behind, would get to grips with village problems on the spot. Each centre was to have its doctor, nurses, agriculturalist-social worker and cottage industry expert. It would be a social centre for the villages, and, with its elected fellahin committees and council, would provide a nucleus for the growth of local democracy and self-help.

The first six centres were set up in 1943; by 1952 there were 136 of them.

The new régime now developed this basic design, adding a fifteen-bed hospital, full-time agriculturalist, and a primary school. It rechristened the result 'the Combined Centre,' and announced that it would build 864 of them, covering the entire country at the rate of one centre for every 15,000 people. It was a concept characteristic of these New-Old Egyptians, and it was executed with a plodding methodicalness.

'See! the fellahin playing games!' exclaimed a triumphant 'social adviser' as two youths in *galabiyas* batted a ping-pong ball about in the club room of a rural Combined Centre. The astonishment was a trifle synthetic—for by this time the centres were a familiar feature of the Egyptian scene. They are fairly standard in accommodation and equipment: a meeting hall and club room, a primary school and kindergarten, a clinic with well-stocked dispensary, pathological laboratory and small hospital, a library and 'museum,' and, often, rooms for training in cottage industries—carpet-weaving, cabinet-making, or blacksmith's work—like the making of iron-framed oil lamps to light the villages at night. Grouped around a public garden, the buildings are completed by four or five houses for the married officials and apartments for the others. With cooks and labourers, the staff of a centre numbers between twenty and sixty.

Presiding over this design for a better world, like some testimony of social interdependence, is the professional triumvirate of agriculturalist, social worker and doctor.

With his demonstration acre the agriculturalist persuades the villagers to use improved seeds, to discard ancient mud beehives for modern types, to rear his plump poultry instead of the village 'runners,' as the vernacular expression vividly has it. A few centres have milk processing depots, collecting from ten miles around, cutting out both the middleman's large profit and the canal water for which milk, in Egypt, despite repeated fines for adulteration, has long exhibited an irresistible attraction.

Meanwhile, the agriculturalist's colleague, the social worker, attacks on a somewhat wider front. It is his duty to arrange for the election of the various fellahin committees of the centre—including one for 'conciliation,' a new approach to the land squabble and the village blood feud. He might conduct a detailed survey of all families to determine how many members are fully employed, and how the income of the others could be increased. In the afternoons the school may become the scene of adult literacy classes or of sewing classes for the women, with sewing machines supplied on hire purchase, and a ready market for their output through the centres' national organisation.

But the busiest of the three—and perhaps also the nearest to the heart of the matter—is the doctor. Aided by his nurses, he tries to persuade the village women to come into his hospital to have their babies, thus getting them away from the dust and from such time-honoured traditions as not washing the child for seven days after birth. The verandah outside his office is rarely empty. Each summer, the eye troubles proliferate; all the year round the villagers pass through the laboratory to be checked for the presence of bilharzia and other parasites. Bilharzia has become a cliché of books about Egypt. But it is impossible to ignore it: its monstrously fecund larvae, circulating from the irrigation canals to the veins and organs of the people and back to the canals again, seem almost as much a part of the Nile Valley as the rains of Ethiopia, passing down to the sea in the Flood, evaporating and finally returning, to fall again.

Eggs of the bilharzia parasite have been found in the bladders of Egyptian mummies, but it was not until 1851 that a German doctor in Cairo, Dr Theodor Bilharz, identified the worm in the stomach—and not until 1911 that the carrier water-snail was detected. And even now, although bilharzia detection and treatment has been raised almost to the level of a national industry, it remains a holding operation rather than a victory. 'Actually, bilharzia is our problem,' said a young doctor in a combined centre that had been opened at Salah, near Sohag, in 1954. Sixty-two per cent of his villagers still had it, a proportion that rose to 85 per cent in the schoolchildren and youths because of their habit of swimming in the canals in the long torrid summers. Many, said the doctor, were cured and re-infected nine or ten times over.

It was true that of the eight villages served by this particular centre, only one had at that time received its promised pure water supply. But even in the villages that had, the taps were in the village itself; when the men worked in the fields they drank from the canal, bathed in the canal, turned the *tambour* for hours with their legs in the water.

'Couldn't they wear gum boots?'

'Yes, but for the *catachouc* he must pay at least £E2 . . . and he takes twenty-five piastres a day.'

Another doctor, a Copt, who had been elected President of his centre's council at Ballaks in the Delta, said to me: 'Ninety per cent of our medical problems are really social problems.' The doctors are as much educators as healers. In the centres' museums, models horrifically illuminate the bizarre life-cycle of the bilharzia parasite: the fork-tailed larvae abandoning the snail incubator, swimming, for as much as three days, seeking, in their myriads, a human host; boring into his skin, shedding tail as they do so; travelling on through the tissues, homing to the portal vein where they reside and mate before

migrating once more through the body to the bladder which
the female pierces to lay her eggs within, restarting the cycle.
   *Use a latrine, wash only in fresh water, don't drink from
the canals*, the posters appeal. But the village is a fortress
against change. The men from the cities try to persuade the
villagers to give up their habit of piling the year's kindling—
the cotton plants, the maize stalks, the wheat straw—high on
their house roofs, because as a consequence the villages are
regularly swept by disastrous fires. In vain! Even in the new
brick-built settlements of the Abis reclamation area near Alexandria the houses are rapidly disappearing under the age-old
roof-top burden, and the 'model' villages take on the characteristic 'Egyptian village' look of fecklessness and squalor.
   Herodotus, passing this way in the 5th century B.C. recorded
in his *Histories*: 'In other countries the dwellings of men are
separated from those of beasts; in Egypt man and beast dwell
together.' Twenty-three-and-a-half centuries later the problems
of the animals-inside-the-house was still the despair of rural
improvers. For in this hot climate the steamy presence of the
fellah's gamoose, his cow, his donkey, under his own roof,
separated from his family by only a decrepit door, if that, is
fraught with hazards to health. But the centres' workers have
long since abandoned this particular unequal struggle. Nothing, they will tell you, can separate the Egyptian fellah from
his beasts. He regards them as personal friends, almost as
members of his family. His gamoose, in particular, that strong,
lumbering, larger-than-life, so-very-Egyptian creature, is the
centre around which his intimate economy revolves. If it eats
three times as much as the Egyptian cow, it provides him with
oceans of fatty milk (which the cow, poor thing, doesn't) and
a useful income therefrom. It pulls his plough, keeps his family
in soft white cheese, and—Allah forbid!—should it die, its
liver is highly esteemed and capacious. For many a poor fellah
it is both his capital and his income, and therefore he keeps
it always by him, guarding it jealously against envious enemies.
   And every villager knows that envy is a force to be reckoned with. Social researchers have reported a persisting belief
that should a woman from outside the family see a cow or
gamoose being milked, the animal may dry up. Belief in the
Evil Eye lingers. In a new-built village house—itself a rarity—

I noticed on an interior wall, in green paint, a motto from the Koran, and, in yellow henna, the impress of an open hand, its five fingers spread—a defence against the Evil Eye. Lorries commonly carry on their bumpers a painted device against this lurking threat.

In such a context a quite small change ranks as a major break-through. When the first two villages in the Abis reclamation project were constructed (under joint U.S. Point Four[5]—Egyptian management), the prudent planners, knowing what they were up against, put the animals inside the houses. But from the third village onwards, they built a row of animal sheds behind the houses—only fifteen yards behind, but firmly outside. Uneasiness lingered, even so. One fellah complained that because of this alien innovation his cow had perished. In calf, it needed his attention in the night—and the guards would not let him in.

Such, indeed, is Egypt.

Nevertheless, the Combined Centres plod on. By 1960 250 had been built and were at work; seven years later the total of combined centres and social centres exceeded 500, and with the addition of over a thousand separate 'health units,' most of the country was at last brought within reach of fundamental social services. Development was at first hampered by a shortage of doctors and social workers willing to exile themselves in this rural desolation. But this was before Suez had brought to the revolution a new dynamic and philosophy.[6] And clearly nothing short of genuine dedication will do here. For as the Director of the Fellah Department[7] said to me in 1955: 'You may have the finest buildings in the world and have no effect whatsoever if you haven't the right workers in them. You may have hardly any buildings at all and work miracles—if you have workers of the right sort there.'

Such institutions as the Combined Centres decently veiled

[5] The programme of technical and financial aid to under-developed countries announced by President Truman as the Fourth Point of his 1949 Inaugural Address. More recently, after a number of changes of style, this has been the rôle of the American A.I.D.—Agency for International Development.

[6] For later developments, see Chapter 16.

[7] The Fellah Department has since been absorbed in the general expansion of the social services.

the skeleton at Egypt's table, but they did not remove it. The Malthusian vicious circle was perhaps robbed of a little of its desperation, but it was not broken; on the contrary, and in classic fashion, it was tightened. For the agriculturalists and the doctors on the centres' teams, working in close alliance, were also, at another level, working at odds. As fast as the one profession increased income and food supply, the other, promoting longer life, saving babies, consumed the gain. The doctors, it was true, now possessed in birth-control devices the means to break the circle. But in these earlier years of Egypt's revolution, as of China's, the public advocacy of population limitation was apt to look too much like a denial of the New Dawn. It also affronted deep instincts, flying in the face of a whole rural philosophy of life. Most fellahin had six children or more: a large family gave assurance both of status and virility. Many found the notion of contraception 'against religion.' When the centres' doctors broached it, the fellahin were greatly puzzled. 'But how will you feed more children?' a doctor would ask. 'God will provide,' the fellah would instantly respond. One often pregnant wife pointed to another woman who, having just given birth, was receiving free welfare foods. 'Why, then, if you don't want me to have any more babies, do you *reward* her?' she demanded with indignation.

The sheikhs of El Azhar were invoked and duly pronounced that the Koran nowhere forbade family planning. Nevertheless, Nasser himself did not come out publicly for a birth-control policy until 1963. Yet in this, as in other respects, the all-too-lucid arithmetic of the Nile Valley generates its own powerful logic. The relentless progression of population— 1900: 10 millions; 1927: 14 millions; 1947: 19 millions; 1960: 26 millions; 1970: 32 millions—makes it clear that merely to hold the present impoverished standard of life must require unceasing effort; to advance it to a decent level demands a Herculean programme and a major breakthrough.

If presented with dramatic clarity, the situation of Egypt was in many ways the classic situation of the under-developed country. Yet Egypt was better equipped than many to work through to a solution. For many years she has possessed both a technical and an administrative middle class in which East and West joined hands. Indeed, the vicious circle within which she was enclosed was, in some respects, a tribute to the skills of that class in the exploitation of the Nile—and a continuation and extension of that long process compellingly indicated the way ahead. The land must be made to yield more: that was vertical expansion. More land must be created: that was horizontal expansion. But although such measures would gain time, they were not infinitely extensible. The only ultimate solution lay in that industrialisation which had enabled Japan, a country as humanly congested as Egypt and with hardly more natural resources, to sustain a soaring population at the highest standard of living in Asia.

The difficulty was that such a programme called for simultaneous large advances on so many fronts—political, social, economic—all intricately interdependent. Failure on one could bring failure on all. Industrial advance was dependent on the agricultural advance to finance and underpin it. Both were dependent on water, water for reclamation of the desert and for more and better crops, water for electric power; all began and ended—still—with the Nile.

Three months after taking power, the revolutionary régime had accepted a design for a hydro-electric station on the old Aswan Dam. It was, astonishingly, the first time this source of power had been used in Egypt, yet the scheme had been hawked about since the 'twenties by Adrian Daninos, the same Greek agriculturalist who, in 1948, put forward another, much vaster, plan for 'over-century' water storage in a gigantic reservoir in the Nile gorge. By the end of November 1952, the new régime was inviting preliminary tenders from a German consortium for that scheme, too. Although still little more than a hope, the High Dam captured and stimulated the imagination, and quickly became the keystone of an ambitious agricultural and industrial development programme. By early 1953, the new National Production Council, given its own development budget, was considering tenders for Egypt's first integrated steelworks, designed to utilise the country's still untapped iron-ore deposits; in addition, new oil prospecting licences were being negotiated with foreign companies.

But it was evident that plans of this sort must take years to mature. A revolution cannot wait. What the Egyptian Revolution now needed was some bracing, visible, and immediate response which appeared equal to the scale of the challenge.

It received it in 1954 from a thirty-six year-old Army Service Corps major named Magdy Hassenein.

8

VISION IN THE SAND

Come through the Desert to Tahrir Province
You will find homes, and hospitals, and schools,
A new society and a new life. . . .
—Song of the children of Tahrir Province

The response was at once traditional and revolutionary. The endless struggle of the Desert and the Sown which is the fabric of Arab history has been nowhere more dramatically illustrated than along the edges of the Nile Valley and Delta. But what the régime was proposing now—in the name of the Revolution and its hurriedly improvised organisation, the Liberation Rally—was not merely encroachment on the desert, but its conquest, not merely to steal a few acres here and a few there, down the years, but to carve from it, systematically and in cold blood, a whole new province of Egypt, at least 600,000 acres—and later twice that—with a new provincial capital, eighteen district towns, thirty-six large villages and 216 settlers' hamlets. The project's author and prophet, Magdy Hassenein, described it, unblinkingly, as 'the creation of a youthful, co-ordinated and coherent Egyptian society with its peculiar individuality, aims, ability, to serve as a model of what the Revolution intends for this noble nation.'

Major Magdy Hassenein had been one of the Free Officers, not a member of their executive council, but a zealous distributor of their tracts. He was, at this time, a plumpish, square-headed, heavy-chested man whose quiet voice belied his more Napoleonic pronouncements and his immense Egyptian ebullience. Two stuffed desert wolves which he himself had shot symbolically guarded either side of the entrance to the Province's Cairo Headquarters where I found him one evening in an office on the fourth floor, sitting at a long table strewn with plans.

More plans covered the walls. 'My experts are trying to find the best forms for our new villages,' he said. 'They have

many ideas. I have everything here—agriculturalists, irrigation
men, engineers, town-planners . . . it is one of the best set-
ups in the world.' He had, he explained, been a soldier in the
Desert for eight years. 'I felt something could be done with
the desert. I made a plan. Gamal [Nasser] encouraged me. But
the National Production Council and the Ministries were
against it. They said it wouldn't work. So we had a meeting
before the Council of the Revolution—myself and all my
experts on one side of the room, the National Production Council and the Ministries on the other. It went on for six hours.
Gamal asked us many questions. In the end they decided for
us. And Gamal is a wonderful man—once he's made up his
mind for a thing, he's all behind you!'

And so, in October 1953, with the revolution still not much
more than one year old, Major Magdy Hassenein had led a
small military convoy out of Cairo, westwards across the Nile,
and finally off all roads, to pitch the first tents in the middle
of an empty expanse of desert.

'You know, it was like the—what do you call them?—the
Mormons in America. *This is the place!* You know what they
achieved. It will be so with us also.'

The place had in fact been selected with some care. Fifty
miles or so down-river from Cairo the Western Desert bites
in to within a kilometre or two of the Rosetta arm of the Nile.
Here it borders one of the most overpopulated provinces of
Egypt, Menufiya, also famed for the industry and skill of its
farmers. And here the new province was to begin, a great
oblong eighteen miles wide and seventy miles long, stretching
north and west through the desert to the shores of Lake
Mariut on Alexandria's doorstep. It would be bounded on
the east by the Beheira and Nubariyah canals, carrying the
water of the Nile, and by the Cairo-Alexandria railway. On its
western side it would be crossed by the Cairo-Alexandria
Desert Road. Thus it could be readily fed with both water and
goods.

The good communications and, even more, the midway position between Cairo and Alexandria were important because
the notion of breaking free from the domination of Cairo and
establishing industries as well as farms loomed large in Liberation Province ideology. Instead of merely patching away at

those mouldering villages, held fast in the grip of custom and superstition and disease, one would start again in the clean air of the desert to build the Egypt that ought to have been.

With this in mind Magdy Hassenein had expended much thought and care on the selection of the province's future settlers. 'I want a well-built man—and a well-built woman, too. I believe in the value of music and sports. Sixty per cent should know some musical instrument. The rest we will teach. Because a fellah who can appreciate music is more evolved, is capable of much. Every house will have electricity and running water and sanitation—and you haven't got that even in England or America. So our chemists will be fine chemists and our engineers good engineers and we shall have the best agricultural community in the world. And Egypt will lead again in civilisation as she did in the past.'

Neither the Rev. Malthus nor questions about the limitations of Nile water supply gave this prophet of the New Egypt pause. 'Yes, Egypt is 29/30ths desert—but we can make that desert one of the greenest parts of the Earth. We shall use atomic energy and distil sea-water. We shall learn more about the soil. We shall discover and tap underground water. In the Qattara Depression I shall build my power-station and it will generate 3,000 million kilowatt-hours on the sea-water that will pour down.[1] I have the plans ready now!

'What you will see now in Tahrir Province is merely a bridgehead, a pilot scheme for the first 34,000 acres. But we shall go ahead. This very night the Council of the Revolution is meeting to discuss giving me another £E3,000,000. So far, we've had £E2¾ millions allocated—and we've spent about two millions.'

The Desert Road from Cairo to Alexandria was oppressive in its monotony, a thin black ribbon running ruler-straight across featureless sand. Time slowed down when one travelled along it, with only, far over to the east, a faint green line where the Delta began for the eye to rest upon.

The oil-drum markers sped by. Sand drifted thinly over the

[1] An old, and apparently practicable, scheme originally advanced by a British official, Dr John Ball, in 1911 and since the revolution elaborated by West German engineers.

tarmac. After an hour or so a road went off to the right and we turned on to it. Grey specks in the distance turned out to be camels, nibbling lackadaisically at a few patches of sparse scrub. We left the road then and ran over the sand, the driver keeping to the crests of the long waves in which it lay.

The desert enveloped us.

And then, suddenly, there were a couple of men sitting under a red-and-green striped umbrella, stuck in the sand. They sat there, in the middle of nothingness, poring over a sheet of paper. Five hundred yards beyond, a bulldozer cavorted in a great cloud of dust. All at once, a concrete road appeared and led off across the desert.

Our wheels hummed over it. In a few minutes a water-tower and the white minaret of a mosque came into view. We had, it seemed, arrived in Om Saber—the first village of Liberation Province. It was a spruce little town. There was an open-air cinema, with a modernistic façade, concrete administrative offices, a canteen. Casuarina and eucalyptus saplings lined the wide streets and there were red-and-yellow Coca-Cola kiosks at the corners. The small central square had a monument with the Republic's Saladin eagle in relief and an Eternal Flame. When Om Saber was started, they said with some pride, the eternal flame had been oil; now it was electric—supplied with current from their own generating station.

But the streets were deserted. It was Friday noon and the entire population was at prayer. They formed a solid square on the ground in front of the neat new mosque, rising and kneeling and prostrating themselves in unison as the imam led them through the cycle of prayer.

A brisk middle-aged man in a red tarbush hurried up to greet us. He was, it appeared, the Director of Cleanliness, a former army colonel. The colonel took us along to the office of the irrigation engineer, a bright-eyed bubbling little man named Mahmoud Shetta, who at once bundled us into a jeep and whisked us off on a tour of the Province—as so far established.

The long lines of green—beans and spinach and water-melons and potatoes and cucumbers—ran away across the sand as far as the eye could see. It was a fantastic sight: the marrows under their sheaf-like straw covers to protect them from the sun; the vast fields of strawberries which were being gathered and sent off daily to the Cairo markets; the neat pattern made by the young orange saplings and the acres of young banana trees, sticking out of the sand like stubble from an unshaven cheek.

A newly made canal, the Liberation Canal, runs alongside the road, and from this a network of concrete-lined conduits leads the Nile water across the new 'fields' while at intervals wells, worked by electric pumps, supplement the flow. Mahmoud Shetta happily murmured Egyptian irrigation incantations . . . 'four-and-four' . . .'eight-and-four'—that is, eight days water for the land and four days rest. It was a liberal allowance, but the desert sand needs four times as much water as the black soil. Given that water, given fertiliser, given perhaps a ration of the clay taken from the canals, it would grow abundant cash crops.

Like the other engineers and agriculturalists and the five thousand labourers, craftsmen and tractor-drivers on the project, Mahmoud Shetta was living a camp existence, cut off from family and town. When this area's district town, Badr, was built, the authorities would provide houses there for the Province's technicians. But that was at least two years off. 'Malish!' the little engineer said cheerfully as the jeep flew along beside the canal. 'We have patience. We shall live a long time. Mohamed said "Work as if you would live for ever; pray as if you would die tomorrow."'

We passed the neat, low houses of a half-finished village, Omar Shaheen, where labourers worked over moulding machines making low-cost, hollow (and therefore heat-insulated) bricks from a mix of sand and cement. A mile or two further on, bulldozers and excavators were pushing the road and the canal on into the desert, and here was another village, Omar Makram, in the earliest—water tower and electricity sub-station—stage.

The Province's first village, Om Saber, was named for an Egyptian woman who met her death in the Canal Zone troubles. The next, Omar Shaheen, was the name of an undergraduate, also a Canal Zone 'martyr' and, in the phrase of Magdy Hassenein, who had trained Canal Zone guerrillas, 'one of my boys.' But by the time the third village was on the drawing board in 1954 the Anglo-Egyptian accord for the evacuation of the Zone had been signed. Omar Makram is a national hero of the revolt against the French and the Turks in the time of Mohamed Ali. Every village, every street, they said, was to be named after some Egyptian patriot—'to show that the Egyptians too know how to fight for their country.'

In a sense it might be said that the whole fantastic project was dedicated to the demonstration of this proposition. It was a point of particular pride with Magdy Hassenein that no foreign experts were employed.

In other ways, too, Liberation Province made a conscious break with Egyptian tradition, displaying an Ataturk-like radicalism of approach, but the radicalism perhaps of a more sophisticated Ataturk who had, shall we say, majored in town-planning and social psychology at some American Western university. Thus, the villages were designed with amenity and a new pattern of life in view, not merely brute necessity. Council House, mosque and primary school were set around lawns and gardens. The houses themselves, each with its small front garden, were constructed in U-shaped blocks, front doors opening on a public square, back doors on a service road to the fields. Communal cattle sheds, poultry houses, a village oven and storehouse lay to one side. Electricity and piped water were taken inside the house—an elementary enough idea, but given the traditional Egyptian notion of the fellahin, revolutionary indeed. (In the new villages of the Abis reclamation area, electricity cables run past the houses to light the streets, but inside the traditional oil lamps gutter.)

At the village of Omar Shaheen the new settlers were still in process of moving in. We chose a red door in a row of houses of grey desert-made brick, and we knocked. It was opened by a lean young man in a grey tunic shirt and Panama-type hat. His name, he said, was Mohamed Abdel Fattah and he had come here from the village of Beit el-Arab in Menufiya province. He invited us inside.

There was a chintz-covered sofa against a wall in the small living room and flowers in a vase on the table, which was covered with patterned oilcloth. One of the remaining two rooms had a double bed; the other, a double-decker iron bunk for the children. There was a bathroom with a flush toilet and shower. Cooking was by kerosene.

Mohamed Abdel Fattah invited us to be seated on his chintz sofa, whence we could admire the two pictures on the wall—a photographic study of the Pyramids and another of the Citadel in Cairo. As in the pre-war Italian colonisation schemes in Libya, the new settlers, on arrival, moved into houses which were completely furnished down to the pots and pans and—in the case of Liberation Province—down even to the clothes in the wardrobe which Abdel Fattah now flung open to reveal his wife's new red-chequered 'Western-style' frock—the female half of the Province's 'reformed' costume, and the complement to his own drill trousers, tunic shirt and hat. The clothes of Egypt's New Man and New Woman were run off to the Province's mass order, and the settlers bought them, like their houses and furniture, on the instalment plan—ten piastres a month for the shirt, Abdel Fattah informed us.

At the sight of the wardrobe's riches, Mahmoud Shetta, the irrigation engineer, could hardly contain his enthusiasm. Of Abdel Fattah's innermost thoughts it was more difficult to be sure. He was young and presumably resilient, but all the same his recent experiences may have been a little puzzling. When, back in his crowded Delta village, the appeal for volunteers for the new province had gone out, over a thousand had responded, but only 250 had been chosen. The new settlers had to be between twenty-four and thirty years old, married, but with not more than three children. Each family had to pass a medical examination. Abdel Fattah then had to sit at a desk and take various tests devised by the Province's social psychologists.

And now, having come through all this, here he was, on his chintz-covered sofa, with his View of the Pyramids, and outside, beyond his empty scrap of garden, the strange crops growing in the limitless sand. Did he pine, sometimes, one wondered, for the enclosure, the muddy squalor, the thronged luxuriance, of the Delta? At least there was plenty to keep him busy. For the first six months, he and his family would be on probation, working the new land for a wage. Then they would be allotted their five feddans. But Abdel Fattah would still go on attending the training courses, while his wife would be advised by the village's social worker on the mysteries of the new housekeeping—when she was not tending the chickens in her back yard or milking the cows of the village herd. Each village had its crèche as well as its primary school, so that the youngest New Egyptians would not roll in the dust and dirt in the usual fashion. They would also, thanks to Magdy Hassenein's ideas about music, early learn to perform in their own drum, pipe and tambourine band!

As in the Land Reform areas, each village was formally run by an elected committee of settlers. But the stress here was no longer so much on peasant proprietorship as on common cultivation and planning. Although the word 'collective' was still carefully avoided, there was something of the commune here —each family's five feddans was seen as a share in the common enterprise and in the herd of cattle. This was in part dictated by the nature of the land and crops. The plan was to put something like two-thirds of the area under citrus, mangoes and other fruit unsuited a small-scale cultivation and, in fact, to be cultivated by agricultural graduates on behalf of the State.

The stress on cattle farming was of potentially major importance to a country which must import much of its meat and whose milk supply is inadequate. In the traditional Egyptian agriculture, pivoted on cotton, there has been little scope for cattle, and the native 'Damietta cow,' a curious spindly creature, in any case gives little milk. In Liberation Province she was being crossed with imported Friesians and Herefords, and the herds grazed over the five-year berseem grown in the reclamation process, thus enriching both the desert and the Egyptian economy.

Liberation Province could not be completed without the water the High Dam would provide, and at this time the High Dam was neither financed nor started. It had become, however, an article of revolutionary faith. Liberation Province was to be the proof of that faith. Work began in December 1953, and by July of the following year fifteen miles of canals and conduits had been completed and 3,000 acres of desert were under reclamation. It was, said Nasser, on his first visit, conclusive evidence that Egypt was beginning to rid herself of the painful past and its poisonous dregs—egoism, enmity and corruption. 'How much I would have liked to see among us today some of those who lack decision and strong will. They would have seen for themselves that with patience, tolerance, and perseverance the sons of this land can work miracles.'

Sceptics remained in plenty to whom Liberation Province still seemed more mirage than miracle. Foreign experts, down-to-earth men, were understandably made uneasy by Magdy Hassenein's fervent Utopianism. There was eager talk of fabulous sums draining away into those bottomless sands. But however much the particular figures might be in dispute, it was hardly deniable that by European standards reclamation costs were low. Bricks for the buildings, liners for the water channels, were made on the spot. Labour was cheap. According to the official figures the cost of reclaiming an acre of land in Holland was £4,000, in Britain £800; in Liberation Province it was between £200 and £300, including housing, roads, canals, pumps, schools and hospitals. In any case, how does one calculate the 'economic' price of tolerable living conditions, more food, and an increased area of cultivation for a nation which must have these things or perish? The economists will justifiably reply that it is a question of relative yields on scarce capital resources, and particularly of the speed of the return—and the story of Liberation Province was indeed sharply to illuminate the cruel and everlasting contest in Egypt between short-term necessities and long-term goals. But nations do not—and could not—live in the perfect, airless world of academic economists, and the vision of Liberation Province, conjured up at a critical moment, served its turn.

On the official map of Egypt the long green oblong of the new province with its eighteen district towns was already marked in. Small wonder foreign observers smiled cynically! But at least Mahmoud Shetta, our irrigation engineer guide, had no doubts. He was the living embodiment of the Province Spirit. 'A day will come when everything will be found here,' he cried. 'Milk from the cattle. Leather to make our shoes. We shall have factories and make our cloth. Oh, this is a revolutionary project and we make a revolution here! By 1990, it will be Paradise!

'We can plant, water, level, thirty acres a day. And when the High Dam is finished we will do 100 acres a day. . . . See

History made—and in the making. **16 MAY 1953:** Lieut-Colonel Nasser, John Foster Dulles, and General Neguib at a Cairo dinner in the U.S. Secretary of State's honour. Nasser explained Arab suspicions of military pacts and foreign bases. But Dulles persisted, and, **15 MAY 1964,** the central figure at the High Dam—Nile Diversion—ceremony was not, as it might have been, the President of the U.S., but Nikita Khruschev. On Khruschev's left, Presidents Aref of Iraq and Sallal of Yemen.

Modernity and Tradition in Cairo. *Above* The massive Radio and TV Building on the Nile Corniche, seen from the Gezirah (island).
Below A student enters the mosque-university of El Azhar, at the foot of whose pillars learned sheikhs have taught for a thousand years.

the lorries, full of vegetables already going away, every day, to Cairo. Ah, you won't believe? But you will *see*. Come back in a year. . . . Come back in six months! I should take from you a paper that you will come back and see.'

As it happened, I did go back and see, not indeed after six months, but after ten years. And what I saw was certainly no mirage. Coming in once again from two hours travelling through the emptiness of the Desert Road it seemed much more like a miracle. The eucalyptus trees I had seen as saplings, drooping at the roadsides, were thirty feet high, and so were the cypresses grown as windbreaks. The little gardens in front of the village houses were luxuriant jungles, maize and aubergines and bananas, softening the hard lines. The Nile water was being eked out from 150 wells, and in the canals that flowed from each of the 150 pump-houses swam 5,000 dazzlingly white Chinese ducks—three-quarters of a million all told—with brightly coloured Disney-esque duckhouses on the banks. As one travelled about the 300 miles of internal roads one was buoyed by a strange feeling of escape, of having come to a brand new land of wide horizons and infinite promise, and when a big herd of white-faced Herefords came trotting down the road in a cloud of dust, it almost seemed that the land might be Texas!

One hundred thousand acres were under reclamation and of this, 60,000 were under cultivation. It was anticipated that in 1970 the extra water coming from the High Dam would bring the total up to a quarter-million acres. There were now nine villages, and the supply of Egyptian patriots and martyrs was still holding up. There was a village called Ahmed Arabi, another called Mustafa Kemal, another Salah el-Din, and then several named after Egyptian officers who lost their lives in the Yemen. And the first 'district town,' Badr (the place of the Prophet's critical victory), was also an undeniable fact, with a five-storey administration block, staff houses, a large Club with tennis-courts, a swimming pool-to-be and a forty-four-bedroom hotel, to which the inhabitants ironically referred as 'the Tahrir Hilton.'

The population of the province (in 1965) was now 30,000. But these were mostly labourers, tractor-drivers, builders and so on—for the colonisation by five-feddan settlers had not gone according to schedule. Our friend, Mohamed Abdul Fattah, was still there, however, with five children and two cows, clearing £E160 a year from his maize, groundnuts, and vegetables, after repayments on the land and house and without allowing for his milk, cheese and eggs. But then Mohamed Abdel Fattah, as someone said, had been 'one of the brave ones.' He'd seen through the hard years before the tree windbreaks had grown, when the sandstorms had cruelly blasted the growing crops. Not all had: about a third of the first settlers had given up, overwhelmed by the strangeness of it all, chilled by the desert night, unable to believe that crops would ever grow in this sand. So, after ten years, only 4,000 acres had been distributed, 800 families settled. But now the trees were tall and the land smiled and the first generation of settlers was putting down roots. The process of distribution was being resumed.

The Utopian phase was over. The more grandiose industrialising ideas had been dropped. The vegetable canning plant remained and was working, but the shoe factory had been removed to the Delta. The more Owenite exercises seemed to have petered out, although in the village nurseries the settlers' children banged their tambourines and blew their whistles and sang the Province song with as much zest as ever. In the Council House of Omar Shaheen the photographs on the walls showed, among many other things, the social workers, marching and doing their morning gymnastics. 'Do they still?' I enquired.

'No—most of them are married now. They do their gymnastics at home.'

Three members of the village co-operative council rushed to greet us and were, I noticed, clad in unregenerate *galabiyas* instead of the Province's costume of slacks and tunic.

'Yes,' admitted the young agriculturalist, who had charge of 25,000 acres. 'But they must wear their uniform this afternoon.' This, it should perhaps be explained, is a rather special Egyptian-English use of the word 'must' in which the categorical imperative becomes handily self-fulfilling. It is what one says after a third party is two hours late for an appointment: 'He must come now.'

The sad truth was that the Province had lost its prophet. In 1957, Magdy Hassenein had come under heavy attack in the newly elected National Assembly for over-spending on the project and carefree accountancy. His drive and somewhat Napoleonic stance had made him jealous enemies. An investigating committee of Ministers was duly appointed. It cleared Magdy Hassenein of corruption. But he was broken. Liberation Province was handed over to the Ministry of Agriculture. Orthodoxy had triumphed, as orthodoxy will.

But in the Club building at Badr I was glad to see that if one wall of the lounge carried the usual picture of Nasser, the other had a portrait of Magdy Hassenein. So he had not become wholly an unperson.[2] Liberation Province at least acknowledged its founder. 'Yes,' nodded the young agriculturalist, who had worked here since coming out of college eleven years ago, 'he was a big one, all right.'

And if orthodoxy had triumphed, it was an orthodoxy so vastly enlarged as hardly to be worthy of the name. The stirring theme of conquering the desert, of breaking the age-old grip of the Nile Valley, has become a central theme in Egypt's design for the future. If mistakes were made in Liberation Province it is well for Egypt that at least she had men who dared to make them. Lessons were learned as they probably could have been in no other way. In Egypt, desert reclamation, land reclamation, becomes more than ever a science, with many specialists and a large body of professional practitioners. And today, in the New Valley[3] and elsewhere, these men will tell you: 'Liberation Province was our first school. Magdy Hassenein was a real pioneer—he began with nothing.'

[2] Magdy Hassenein was in 1963 elected a Deputy for the Kasr el-Nil district of Cairo in the National Assembly.
[3] See Chapter 17.

PART THREE

CRUCIBLE UNDER HEAT

In every revolution there are two phases. First the men lead the revolution; then the revolution leads the men.

—Anwar el Sadat, *Revolt on the Nile*

Every great life is born of the meeting of a great character and a great hazard.

—André Maurois, *Life of Marshal Lyautey*

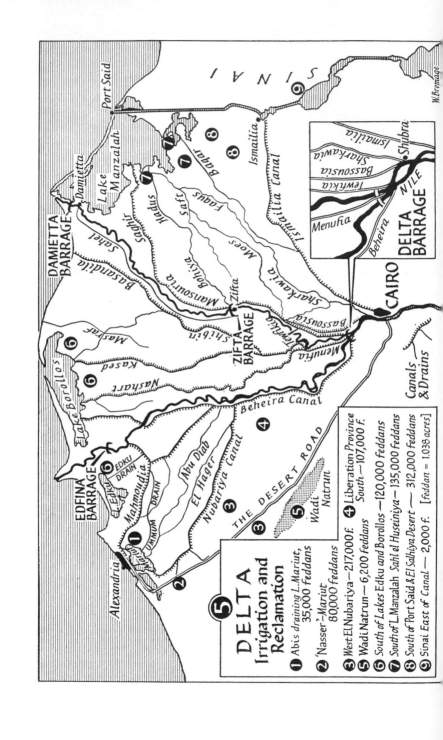

DELTA
Irrigation and Reclamation

① Abis draining L.Mariut, 35,000 Feddans
② 'Nasser'-Mariut 80,000 Feddans
③ West El Nubariya — 217,000 F.
④ Liberation Province South — 107,000 F.
⑤ Wadi Natrun — 6,200 Feddans
⑥ South of Lakes Edku and Borollos — 120,000 Feddans
⑦ South of L. Manzalah Sahl el Huseiniya — 135,000 Feddans
⑧ South of Port Said & El Salhiya Desert — 312,000 Feddans
⑨ Sinai East of Canal — 2,000 F. [feddan = 1,038 acres]

Canals & Drains

W. Bromage

DELTA BARRAGE

CAIRO

Shubra

Ismailia

Tewfikia

Bassousia

Sharkawia

NILE

Menufia

Beheira

ZIFTA BARRAGE

DAMIETTA BARRAGE

EDFINA BARRAGE

Alexandria

Port Said

Ismailia

SINAI

Lake Manzalah

Damietta

Sahel

Saghir

Hadus

Saft

Faqus

Bahr

Moes

Mansouria

Bahiya

Shtibin

Basandila

Masraf

Kased

Nashart

Beheira Canal

Nubariya Canal

El Hager

Abu Diab

Lake Borollos

Mahmoudia

EDKU DRAIN

UMMUM DRAIN

Wadi Natrun

THE DESERT ROAD

Menufia

Tewfikia

Bassousia

Zifta

9

BEHOLD THE MAN!

'Believe me, Mr Black, don't underestimate these poor people.
There is a hidden power in them—they lack only one
thing. . . .'
'What's that?'
'An idol—a man who personifies their character and their
aspirations and who is for them the symbol of the Ideal.'
—Tewfik el Hakim, *The Soul Regained* (1927)

The revolution might be of the people and for the people, but
it certainly was not, in 1953, yet *by* the people. The Officers'
régime was still paying the price of having succeeded to
power largely by default. It had never been part of a mass
movement in the way the Wafd had been under the British
repression of the 'twenties; it had received no real baptism of
fire. Most middle-class people, asked about those June days of
1952, respond in the same terms: 'We were *relieved.*' That
they might play any part other than that of spectators hardly
seems to have occurred to them, and as the resounding silence
that followed the *coup* was broken by the old professional
politicians hurrying back to reclaim the cleared stage, they
relapsed easily enough into the traditional Oriental posture
of the Ruled, waiting on events with wary, non-committed
eye.
To take the place of the proscribed parties, the régime,
early in 1953, set up the Liberation Rally which Nasser, in an
interview with *Al Ahram*, described as not a party, but an
organisation to reunite a split nation and rebuild Egyptian
society through the participation of committed individuals. It
was a theme to which he was often to return and which was
indeed central to his political thinking. But such organisations
must be forged from the national experience; they cannot be
fabricated by slogans, songs and tricolours. In 1953 it was too
early, and in the wreckage of the old political parties, the
Liberation Rally looked like the familiar old circus of paid

cheer-leaders and banner-wavers. Its preoccupations were, in fact, urgently defensive.

So the problem remained: since the middle classes, which the régime in part reflected, had failed to respond, where could it turn for active support? Presumably—and vitally—to the armed forces which had fathered it, and which had duly received an increase in pay. Possibly, but hardly probably, to the fellahin who, although beneficiaries, were suspicious by nature, ignorant and isolated. The Left-wing intelligentsia, on the other hand, was often set apart from the régime by temperament and background, and many of its members regarded the soldiery with a distaste and suspicion which was reciprocated. They, and the—often French-educated—professional class to which they often belonged, represented the secular, westernising trend shared with the upper class. The Muslim Brotherhood represented the opposite pole. The military régime, falling—like most of the lower middle class—somewhere between, with its head, so to speak, in the West, but its feet on the native soil, groped to bring the split society together. But the Communists, like the Muslim Brethren, were mainly concerned to recapture a revolution that had somehow got away from them.

There remained another small group whose political potentialities, as yet little recognised, were not without promise: by 1952 enough Egyptians had deserted the *tambour* and the gamoose for the bus and the time-clock to give Egypt the nearest approach to an industrial proletariat in the Arab world. Over 650,000 people worked in industry, but of these only about 250,000 worked in factories with more than ten men. Transport and building took another 300,000, and every year the tentacles of the Big City, and of such large expanding concerns as the Misr Textile group, reached out into the villages and drew in more.

These workers, as Lenin observed of Russia's in 1917, were still too few and too diversified to be truly class-conscious; but they did have a degree of 'trade-union awareness.' For trade unions, started at first by 'European' workers, had existed in Egypt since the 'nineties, although they had remained for the most part poor, pathetically fragmented, and often the playthings of their political patrons. In one or two foreign-run modern concerns like Cairo passenger transport or Shell Petroleum, however—and the transport and oil workers were aristocrats of Egyptian labour—there were substantial, organised unions. Strikes were common and gained respectability as patriotic resistance to the imperialist exploiter. But although a few Egyptian worker union leaders had emerged, and there had been one or two frustrated attempts at federation, the trade unions had remained mainly a police matter in Egypt where a strange blend of the philosophies of Constantinople, New Delhi and Cobdenite Manchester had prevailed since the suppression of the Islamic craft guilds in the 1880s.

Yet repression had alternated with an increasingly 'modern' paternalism. In 1931 an International Labour Office mission had been invited to Egypt to survey conditions and plan a Labour Code; even so, it was not until the Second World War that the Egyptian Government officially acknowledged the trade unions' legal status. An Act of 1942 then invalidated employment contracts which forbade union membership and provided for the unions' registration with a tutelary Labour Department; two years later another Act made provision for overtime, holidays, minimum wages, cost-of-living allowance, free medical services, canteens and so on; and in 1948 a framework of compulsory conciliation and arbitration was established.

This series of Acts, which was almost the last service of the Wafd to Egypt, gave the Officers' régime a base on which to build, and this they had both the modernity of outlook and human sympathy to do. They gave substance to the paper structure by three notable advances. They provided that a factory, once three-fifths organised, should become a union shop with automatic check-off of union dues by the management. They explicitly permitted a confederation of all trade unions. And they provided for the hitherto forbidden unionisation of the poorest, and by far the most numerous, class of workers—the agricultural labourers.[1] By 1955 union membership had reached 373,000, over thrice the 1952 figure; by 1962 it was put at 1¼ millions.

[1] This inevitably proved difficult to realise. For sequel see Chapters 17 and 19.

If the régime remained the umpire, its interventions in disputes were now generally directed towards strengthening the unions. The Labour Courts were empowered to award compensation for wrongful dismissal, with reinstatement if for trade union activity. Joint conciliation machinery was extended to most industries. Political activity by the unions remained illegal, but this, as before, was interpreted to mean activity *against* the régime: the Liberation Rally had its own Trade Union Department.

Yet any hope that organised labour could at once provide solid support for the revolution seemed certain to be disappointed. For the deep fissures of Egyptian society extended through its lower levels. Not only was there the great gap of status and way of life between the white-collar clerk and even the relatively skilled factory worker, but a yet more formidable gulf yawned between either and the mass of under-employed rural labourers, drifting hopefully citywards. For all its new-found modernity of appearance, the rising structure of Egyptian trade-unionism was built on weak foundations.

For the rest, on the heady demagogic level to which the Egyptian electorate was accustomed, the régime had little enough to offer. The Land Reform enacted, the 'social revolution' appeared to be turning into that rather chilling thing, 'the managerial revolution.' The Officers' 'Six Principles' had included the 'destruction of Imperialism'; yet the régime had surrendered Egypt's historic claim to 'the unity of the Nile Valley' (i.e. to the Sudan) in order to re-open evacuation talks with the British. They had stressed the 'suppression of the Domination of Capital,' yet, in order to encourage investment, the régime had cut the profits tax, eased restrictions on foreign capital,[2] and, typically, farmed out the Cairo bus routes to a number of private operators. Simultaneously, the régime's orthodox finance minister had embarked on a course of budget-balancing and retrenchment.

As revolutionary slogans gave way to the tackling of necessary tasks, there was a real danger that people would turn from these rather awkward, anonymous young officers, and

---

[2] For instance, the requirement that foreign companies should have 51 per cent Egyptian capital was changed to 49 per cent, and the repatriation of profits was made easier.

look again to the practised performers who had so divertingly occupied the political stage for years. Hence, in September 1953, again following the model of the French Revolution, the Officers set up a 'Revolutionary Tribunal,' which proceeded to try a number of ex-Ministers on charges ranging from being rung up by the British Ambassador to corruption on the grandest scale. It remained, however, a mild, very Egyptian 'Terror' in which exemplary sentences were uttered amid suitable blood-curdling rhetoric only to be soon afterwards quietly commuted or suspended. It contrasted oddly with the ruthlessness with which Ataturk had exterminated his rivals and former friends all over Turkey in that earlier modernising officers' revolution now often—and misleadingly—compared with Egypt's. Yet it served its purpose: 'people saw that it was not right, so they no longer approached the old political parties.'[3]

Far more serious was the threat to the revolution-in-office from the rival revolutionaries of the Islamic Right and Marxist Left, particularly since the Muslim Brotherhood was now prepared to work with the Communists in a common attack on the régime's pro-Western proclivities, exemplified by its negotiations for a settlement with Britain.

The danger from this strange alliance was the greater in that the Free Officers' own councils contained representatives of both parties to it. The Communists might be few, but they were dedicated, articulate, tactically adept; and the Muslim Brotherhood had demonstrated a formidable ability to tap mass emotion. At Cairo University, students demonstrating for the Muslim Brotherhood clashed savagely with students demonstrating for the Liberation Rally. At Alexandria, too, the students marched, calling for a break with the British and parliamentary elections. Muslim Brothers, including some army officers, now began to join the Communists in goal. As a 'religious movement' the Brethren had been exempted from the 1953 order proscribing political parties; but now, in mid-January 1954, the régime, at Nasser's urging, finally accepted the challenge, dissolved the Brethren, and proclaimed a State

[3] The exact words of a member of the Revolutionary Command Council, Hussein el Shafei, to the author—and nicely indicative of Egyptian political psychology at this time, and indeed, later.

of Emergency.

Egypt was thus launched on one of the most decisive years of her modern history, a year of turmoil which was to split the army and bring the nation to the brink of civil war. That the revolution nevertheless survived was due more than anything to the particular qualities of the two officers around whom the struggle polarised, the titular and the real leader of the coup of 1952, Mohamed Neguib and Gamal Abdel Nasser. Both were men of good-will, yet men fatally divided by the gulf between the generations—and worlds—to which they belonged.

'How easy to speak to people's instincts—and how difficult to address their minds!' Nasser noted in this year 1954. It was a thought liberally evoked by Egypt's modern political history, yet hardly one likely to trouble such sophisticated demagogues as Sukarno or Nkrumah or Bourguiba and, if it did, even less likely to be puritanically committed to public print. Yet the fact was that—however sharp his tactical skills and political intuitions—this austere and rather shy—rather 'un-Egyptian' —young man did not at this time find it easy to speak to people *en masse* at all. He was, in his way, an intellectual, much more at home on paper or in argument with his cronies than on the public platform, where he was apt to lecture his bored audience in stiff and formal Arabic. The slogan chosen for the Liberation Rally—'Union, Discipline, Work'—was a soldier's slogan, reflecting the rather nervous approach of a professional staff officer to that sovereignty of the people which the revolution conscientiously proclaimed.

It seems improbable, therefore, that the revolution could have survived until 1954 without the ballasting and emollient qualities of General Mohamed Neguib. The young officers had certainly chosen well when they selected this older man as their figurehead and symbol. With his earthy humour, his gruff, folksy utterances, Neguib was ideally suited to the classic Egyptian rôle of 'Father of the People,' and he played it all over the Delta, effectively and to heartwarming applause. Other officers diligently toured and expounded the revolution's aims, but it was Neguib who lent the words conviction, who 'put the show across.'

But Neguib also possessed the very Egyptian defects of these very Egyptian virtues. His good nature and his desire to be all things to all men made him an easy tool for the revolution's many enemies. He could turn with fatal facility from jollying along the impatient fellahin to back-slapping with the ex-pashas in their prison camps. His garrulity, stimulated by flattery, led him to make many rash promises. Educated at Gordon College in Khartoum in a simpler and more leisurely age, and possessing to the full the loving conservatism of the Nile Valley-dweller, Neguib was increasingly perturbed at the radicalism of the young Free Officers who either out-voted or ignored him. Like Cromwell's chosen figurehead, General Lord Fairfax, he had dragged his feet before the abolition of the monarchy which took place eleven months after the coup, in June 1953,[4] although not unwilling to accept the Presidency when the deed was done. Nor had he any stomach for the 'show trials' of the Old Régime politicians. It was not wise, he complained, to subject the nation to such shocks. Most embarrassing of all for the Officers' Council was Neguib's habit of harping in public on a return to parliamentary life after the elections which he had pledged at the revolution's outset.

This indeed was the régime's Achilles' heel. It was not that the Constitution had not, in the past, been suspended or flouted, and for years at a time. Censorship, confiscation of newspapers, rule by martial law, arbitrary arrest by several varieties of political police, simple murder, had been far from unknown. For all that Egypt's multitudinous lawyers might now speak sonorously of constitutional liberties, *habeas corpus* did not really run there.[5] The difficulty, however, was that all this had been characterised as the Corrupt Past—which the revolution was pledged to sweep away. Thus, liberal intellectuals, as well as the merely self-interested, might well now respond with some bitterness to the cry of 'military dictatorship!' which the Communists assiduously put about.

Since it was by this time evident to all realists in the régime

[4] Farouk's baby son, Ahmed Fuad, had succeeded, under a Regency Council, after Farouk's abdication.

[5] For instance, in the 'free' pre-Nasser years 1948-50, the number of political prisoners was 3,000, according to Walter Z. Laqueur, *Communism and Nationalism in the Middle East* (1956).

that a return to the party contest now must be a return to anarchy, it was becoming clear that a showdown with Neguib could not be much longer delayed. Neguib himself was moving towards it. Instead of talking with the old avuncular affection of 'his boys,' he was complaining to foreign diplomats about 'these young hotheads' who were 'making mistake after mistake.' He found it intolerable, he explained in his autobiography, that he, both President and Prime Minister, should possess only one vote in the Officers' Council where decisions went by show of hands and a major was as good as a general twenty years his senior. It was all the more galling in that the argument that so often prevailed was that of the Deputy Prime Minister, Colonel Gamal Abdel Nasser. 'I suggested,' Neguib wrote, 'that he allow me to run things for a few years until he had acquired the experience necessary to succeed me.'

It was Neguib, in fact, who made the first open move in the struggle that was now to develop between the two men. It came in the form of a letter, addressed to the Revolutionary Command Council on 23 February 1954, resigning all his posts —'for reasons you will excuse me from mentioning here.' Faced by this double-edged offering, the Council embarked upon one of the stormiest of its all-night debates. On the one hand, Neguib's going promised blessed relief; on the other, as Nasser is said to have objected, the timing was wrong; Neguib, half-Sudanese, was just about to go to Khartoum to celebrate the achievement of Egyptian-Sudanese unity. It was decided to defer an answer.

Next day, as more support from army partisans came in, the Revolution Command Council met again, and after another night sitting, at 3 a.m. grasped the nettle: the Presidency was declared vacant, Neguib ('a would-be dictator, playing a double game,' explained Major Saleh Salem) was placed under house arrest. Gamal Abdel Nasser became Prime Minister.

In the wave of shock that followed, the Muslim Brotherhood demonstrated, a protest delegation flew down from the Sudan—and the first open split in the army appeared. It appeared, predictably perhaps, in the cavalry, which had played a vital part in the coup but which, being the only fashionable corps, contained a higher proportion of well-to-do officers than the rest. Yet once again what the pro-Neguib revolt mainly indicated was the inchoateness and political naïveté of the Officers' movement, for its principal instigator was no man of the Right, but of the far Left, an early member of the Officers' Council and a close friend of Nasser.

The most bookish of the revolution's makers, an economics graduate and a conscientious student of the Prophet Marx, Khaled Mohieddin was, despite his nickname of 'the Red Major,' far from being a tough hard-line professional Communist. In this he was perhaps not untypical of much of the growing Egyptian Left whose Communism was idealistic and 'in the head,' almost a natural development of that ardent call for democracy by the first generation of liberal intellectuals. In any event, by 1954 Khaled Mohieddin's Marxism, his Left Book Club-ish ardour and his admiration for Russia had caused him to feel betrayed by the plodding orthodoxy of the revolution-in-office with its unimaginative commitment to the West and to Western capitalism. The Communist line against the 'military dictatorship' and in favour of an immediate return to parliamentary life thus found in him a ready advocate.

If Khaled himself was probably harmless enough, the tanks of the regiment he was seeking to use were another matter. Thus when, two days after Neguib's resignation-dismissal, news reached the Officers' Council of a mutinous meeting in the cavalry's Abbasiya Barracks, an emissary was at once despatched to patch things up. He failed. Around midnight, Hussein el Shafei, a cavalry colonel and like Khaled Mohieddin also a member of the Officers' Council, telephoned from the meeting to ask for Nasser's presence. Nasser went at once —unarmed and without a bodyguard. For two hours he stood alone in front of a hundred or more excited cavalry officers, struggling to convince them that in demanding an immediate return to parliamentary government they were demanding a step that must inevitably lose the revolution. They rounded on him angrily: it was he, Nasser, who was destroying the revolution, not they. Power had gone to his head. Nasser recognised the familiar phrases of his friend Khaled Mohieddin, that prolific writer of tracts, echoing and re-echoing. Finally, at 3 a.m., borne down by these continual accusations and depressed by the total failure, as it seemed to him, to understand the realities of the situation, he gave in. He would go. Let Khaled take over the Prime Minister's post and Neguib return to the Presidency.

But the bulk of the activist officers were in fact still behind Nasser and the Revolution Council. Artillery officers ringed the cavalry barracks with guns and carried off Neguib as hostage. The cavalry retorted by training their guns on Army Headquarters. The sort of bloodshed and civil war less fortunate Arab nations-in-revolution were to see in plenty was, in the event, averted by Nasser's endurance and by the devotion both to the army and to Nasser of its young commander-in-chief, Abdel Hakim Amer. But the immediate price was the triumphant return of Neguib as both President and Prime Minister—amid public rejoicings.

With the easy-going Neguib re-installed, Egyptians felt that they could once again sit back and relax and enjoy life as they loved to. Colonel Nasser was still known to relatively few of the public.[6] Fewer still warmed to him.

Their relief was to prove premature, however.

Nasser's withdrawal had in effect been strategic. And if his immediate reactions had been intuitive, he was now, as on later occasions, better prepared than appeared. In June 1953 he had insisted, over the protests of General Neguib, on the promotion of his close friend of Military Academy days, Abdel Hakim Amer, from Colonel to Commander-in-Chief. He himself had secured the key post of Minister of the Interior, and had continued to hold it even after relinquishing the premiership. It was thus now a simple matter to transfer or retire dissident officers, to move reliable men into the key positions, and to take advantage of Neguib's absence in the Sudan to arrest several hundred counter-revolutionaries.

The intricacy of the manoeuvres that followed inevitably attracts the adjective 'Oriental,' and yet the British reader may again catch in this succession of subtle shifts and persuasions and abrupt actions, executed with a toughness of will and total assurance in the justice of the Cause, the faint echoes of

---

[6] As late as February 1954, *The Times* of London was still finding it necessary to explain in its reports from Egypt that 'Colonel Nasser, who is 35, is a member of General Neguib's Revolution Council.'

Cromwell, compelling reluctant men to do what had to be done.

Behind a façade of brotherly unity regained, the protagonists were in fact drawing apart, marshalling their forces. Neguib was busily consulting the old political personalities, preparing for the promised June elections of what he now pointedly called 'the parliamentary republic of Egypt.' The lifting of the press censorship had raised the political temperature considerably. In the Wafdist newspaper, *Al Misri*, the millionaire proprietors, the brothers Fath, kept up a withering fire against the 'military dictatorship' in general and Gamal Abdel Nasser in particular. The Supreme Guide of the Muslim Brethren called for a *jihad* against the British with whom the régime was again preparing to negotiate.

The Revolution Council readied the army, the Liberation Rally, its companion National Guard and—their new allies— the trade unions. The indignation of the Officers mounted when they heard that Neguib had been ringing up old Nahas, addressing him as 'Pasha.'

With the stage thus harshly illuminated, his enemies overconfident, his supporters alerted, Nasser was ready for his counter-stroke, for the production—and one can almost use the word in its theatrical sense—of that storming of the Bastille, that March on Versailles, so mortifyingly absent at the revolution's outset.

The opening move was an abrupt announcement on 25 March that after the June election the Revolution Council would abdicate. The Officers would put no candidates in the field; they would simply return to barracks. The old political parties would be restored and all detainees, including the Muslim Brethren, would be released. The revolution, in short, was over.

Neguib's ultimatum—the resignation letter of February— was thus neatly trumped by Nasser's ultimatum-resignation of March : 'the People' were to be forced—and assisted—to decide between the revolution and the counter-revolution. They were to be taught that the days of comfortable noninvolvement were over.

Although Nasser had drawn up the announcement, General Neguib, as President of the Revolution Council, had signed it, proving, as a Council spokesman now blandly pointed out, that he was 'the tool of subversive elements' who wished to throw the country back into the hands of 'the old gang of dishonest politicians.' The Bar Association and the Press Syndicate (which included proprietors as well as journalists) now obligingly underlined this point by passing resolutions calling for the quashing of the verdicts of the Revolutionary Tribunal.

The battle lines were drawn, the enemy's position revealed; the campaign could begin. From a number of hurriedly sum-moned meetings of various formations of the army came a flood of demands that the revolution should continue; that those who were not loyal to it should be expelled. The Libera-tion Rally with its red-white-black tricolour came out into the streets. Members of its youth movement dashed about in army lorries, shouting slogans. The National Guard, with its women's contingent, was brought into Cairo from the outlying districts and marched about.

The number of demonstrators was not vast and their efforts may well have lacked conviction. What finally transformed the situation was the strike of the Transport Workers' Union, immobilising the capital's trams, buses and suburban railways. The idle drivers and conductors demonstrated for the revolu-tion. It was further announced that the Egyptian Fleet had put to sea and would not return to Alexandria harbour until assured the revolution would go on.

The strike now spread quickly to the main-line railways with 220,000 railwaymen out, to the textile industry, and, becoming a general strike, to government offices, banks, cinemas, petrol stations, stores, taxis. Some union leaders started Gandhi-style fasts. They called, with a confusion perhaps more apparent than real, for a boycott of the forthcoming elections and for a popular national assembly to support the Revolution Council. By 29 March, Egypt had been brought to a standstill. In the strangely quiet, immobilised streets of Cairo rival bands of demonstrators clashed. 'Down with the Dictator Neguib!' 'Down with the Dictator Nasser!' The police held meetings and recorded their refusal to co-operate in running a parlia-mentary election.

There were echoes here of that 'Black Saturday' of January 1952 when Cairo burned—except that now the army was from the first in control behind the scenes. Having given the Egyptian public a vivid preview of the abyss into which a premature return to party politics might plunge it, and having also, in some measure, alerted the revolution's beneficiaries to what they stood to lose, the Revolution Council now reversed itself. It announced that since the feeling of the country that the revolution should continue had been manifested in a manner that admitted of no doubt, parliamentary elections would be postponed for a transitional period of three years.

In his book *L'Affaire Nasser*, Ahmed Abul Fath, the Wafdist editor of *Al Misri*, asserts, as he did in his newspaper at the time, that the régime ingeniously selected for its counterstroke the day on which the transport union was due to come out over a wage-claim anyway, and merely, so to speak, took their strike over. But in the light of the most widespread union-organised strikes since the great days of Zaghoulist revolt in the 'twenties, this claim looks decidedly hollow. Quick eye as the union leaders might have for a good bandwaggon, they had in fact sound reasons for jumping on this one. They had been offered a unique opportunity to demonstrate the trade unions' and the workers' potential. They used it to good effect and it is certainly not without reason that a visitor to the Transport Workers' Federation headquarters in Cairo today may be shown a page of neat Arabic script in their Visitors' Book—Nasser's personal thanks for their efforts in those critical days. For the régime's recognition did not end there: by April, 1954, the unions were officially discussing a Confederation. They were not to achieve it for another three years, but already in these turbulent days at the end of March, the centre of gravity in this almost grotesquely bourgeois society seemed to have shifted at least a little.

Having identified and aligned its friends, the régime, still prudently retaining Neguib in the Presidency, was able to proceed rapidly to the suppression of its now unmasked enemies. Thirty-five *ancien-régime* Ministers were deprived of their political rights for ten years and debarred from serving on any professional or business association. The Press Union was re-organised and the Wafdist newspaper *Al Misri* at last shut down. The universities were purged and a Revolution Council Officer, Kamel Eddin Hussein, was made Minister of

Education. Fifteen junior cavalry officers, 'friends of Major Khaled Mohieddin,' were put on trial for conspiracy, but Khaled himself was merely despatched on a 'study mission' to Europe.

The Muslim Brotherhood remained a threat, particularly after July when Nasser initialled the Anglo-Egyptian Agreement for the evacuation of the Canal Zone. On the innumerable occasions between 1887 and 1952 on which the question of Britain's retirement from Egypt had been raised, talks had always broken down on the British insistence on the right to return, when and if judged (by Britain) 'necessary.' In the interests of Egypt's urgent domestic needs, Nasser had now broken through this pattern and accepted a 'right to return.' It was limited to seven years and it only applied if an Arab nation or Turkey were attacked, but that was enough : screaming against Nasser's 'betrayal,' the Muslim Brotherhood organised mass demonstrations in which five people were killed and many injured. Neguib, they said, had condemned the Agreement. Was it not now quite evident that Nasser was the 'tool of Western Imperialism,' the 'Gamal-Abd-Dulles' of the Communist leaflets?

So fanatic and conspiratorial an organisation long wedded to methods of violence, given enough rope, could, however, be trusted eventually to hang itself. In October, an illiterate tinsmith, acting on orders from the Brotherhood, emptied a revolver at Nasser as he spoke from the balcony of the Alexandria Bourse. Like another attempt to be made on a somewhat larger scale two years later, this attempt to destroy Nasser merely increased his stature; the would-be assassin's bullets amounted to a public consecration of the work he had set himself to do for Egypt. And in the wave of shock that followed —the third to roll over Egypt in ten months—the régime was at last able to silence this powerful but essentially reactionary force. Four thousand Brethren were imprisoned; arms caches were seized; and after a trial during which it was alleged that 150 key army officers had been on the Brotherhood's execution list, six Brethren, including the tinsmith, were hanged.

At last Nasser was safely able to dispense with Neguib. On 14 November 1954, two leading members of the Revolution

Council, Abdel Hakim Amer and Wing-Commander Hassan Ibrahim, called at the Presidency and took Neguib to a villa in a village near Cairo where he was to live under surveillance. His services to the revolution, if so largely unconscious, had been great. For more than two years, his broad grin, his large humanity, had reassured foreign powers and given his young colleagues a breathing space in which to initiate a social revolution, to outline ambitious economic plans, to identify, isolate and disarm their enemies with a minimum of that violence which history shows to be the great devourer of revolutions. Above all, he had provided the time and the occasion for the elementary political education of what he had once been pleased to call his 'boys.' It was no small service; but by the end of 1954 it was completed, and General Mohamed Neguib, a broken man, stumbled from the stage of history.

Neguib was a tragi-comic figure in what, in recent times, has been a land of tragi-comedy. But these were new times—and new men. These argumentative tank officers, these impatient wing-commanders, these thoughtful young men of the Class of '37 who had now inherited Egypt seemed different. But just how—and how far—were they different? In the testing months just concluded not all had acquitted themselves with equal credit; but one, Gamal Abdel Nasser, had emerged as an instinctive tactician, a man of quick political intuitions and great strength of will, driven by a sense of mission which increasingly compelled recognition.

In the councils of the revolution the debate continued. Votes were taken, and the majority prevailed. But in that brotherhood of revolutionary arms, Nasser was now the elder brother, the source of preferment, the final umpire of disputes, the first exponent of the revolution's Truth. From time to time a blundering or over-assertive comrade might be banished from the circle; but later, repenting after a heart-to-heart chat with Gamal, he might well be re-admitted—as happened to several officers twice and even thrice; or a more deeply errant comrade like Khaled Mohieddin might be sent abroad for a period of reflection. A few would resign finally after some bitter dispute, placed perhaps for a time under house arrest, politically unpersoned, the once prestigious name no more heard in the land. And yet the rebel, on investigation, would probably be found to have been comfortably pensioned and to be still on friendly terms with the rest of the club. It was a group cohesion of a kind rare among the makers of revolutions and perhaps rarer still among Arabs, yet very much of the Nile Valley, and perhaps the greatest source of the Egyptian Revolution's practical strength.[7]

In such a context it becomes less easy to see Nasser's struggle with Neguib purely as a struggle for personal power. If its other bases are not always clear, Nasser, too, was undergoing a political education in which the logic and implications of the naïve revolution of 1952 only gradually revealed themselves. In the turmoil of 1954 some old forms and notions were discarded; there was a groping towards new social alignments (but little more). If in Egypt some of the ingredients of a new sort of Middle Eastern society were now assembled in the crucible, a catalyst was needed before the reaction could proceed.

The catalyst was in fact already present. It had long been intermittently active; it had accelerated the coalescence of the Free Officers' movement; it had hardened the will to revolution—and now it was to trigger an extraordinary series of reactions which would carry the revolution far beyond the confines of the Nile Valley.

The catalyst was political Zionism, lately realised in the state of Israel. For Zionism embodied a principle which was wholly at variance with the manner in which the life of the Middle East had for centuries been organised.

The political habit of Arab Islam has been inclusivist. The

[7] There were, of course, exceptions to this loyalty to the group, the most notable, in the original executive committee of ten, being the airman Abdel Moneim Raouf, a fanatic Muslim Brother, who was implicated in the Nasser assassination attempt and fled. Of the participants in 'the Great Night' of 23 June 1952, Col Shawky, as an ally of Neguib, and Col Yussef Saddik, as a Communist, received long prison sentences, in effect house arrest. But even in 1968, after Israel's pre-emptive strike had taken its toll, among those elected to the Arab Socialist Union's eight-member Executive Committee were Anwar el Sadat, Hussein el Shafei, and Ali Sabri, while Khaled Mohieddin was a candidate. Zakaria Mohieddin had lately been in office, Sarwat Okasha was Minister of Culture, Sidky Suleiman was Minister of Power, and Mahmoud Yunes was in office until March. In October 1968 the funeral of Nasser's father was attended by two former—resigned—Vice-Presidents, Abdel Latif el Baghdady and Hassan Ibrahim.

extent of the Arab world today is in large part a tribute to the success with which the Muslims gathered within their on the whole tolerant embrace the rich assortment of sects, tribes, communities—Christian and Jewish and pagan as well as Muslim—found behind the eastern and southern shores of the Mediterranean. And today, however mystical it may seem to the West, the ideal of 'Arab Unity' reflects a similar urge to comprehensiveness; modern Arab nationalism is, in principle, both unsectarian and non-racial: all are 'Arabs' who inhabit the region and own a loyalty to it. Thus in recent times a large influx of Armenian refugees could be readily absorbed in Syria and Lebanon, both states which in their different ways testify to the breadth of Arabism's spectrum.

Zionism, on the contrary, exists to give territorial nation-state form to a single religion. And although the Jews are not a race, in modern times to be a Jew one must be born a Jew, and thus a Zionist state is, in essence, exclusivist.[8] Within it, by definition, Jews *qua* Jews have an over-riding claim, a principle which Israel in 1950 enshrined in the organic Law of Return, conferring on the twelve million Jews of the world the automatic right to become resident citizens of Israel. The Jerusalem to which they would 'return' was, however, the *Jewish* city, not the historic meeting place of the Middle Eastern world, sacred to three great religions.

Zionism thus appeared to require not only the redrawing of the map of the Arab East, but the re-shaping of its philosophy, culture and political organisation. Implanted in the heart of the Arab world in 1948, the state of Israel thus constituted a catalyst of remarkable insolubility and very great power.

But if Zionism furnished the catalyst, the fusing heat that speeded and intensified the series of reactions was generated by two Super-Powers of 'East' and 'West.' In May 1948 President Truman had recognised Israel within minutes of its creation (while simultaneously in the United Nations debate the State Department spokesman was recommending trusteeship for all Palestine). But Soviet Russia had not been far behind. And as the century-old Russian drive towards the warm waters of the Mediterranean was resumed, so was the Western

[8] This point, which is of critical importance for both present and future of the Middle East, is further developed in Chapter 23.

effort to exclude her. But it was resumed in a changed world. For the Western Imperial Powers were no longer in confident occupation of the area. Both they, and their successor, the United States, had to work from the outside, by devious means —by loans, technical aid, local defence pacts, popular propaganda, diplomatic persuasion, veiled threat. . . .

When applied to proud Arab states, headily conscious of their new-found independence, these were instruments that required great tact in use.

It was not, unfortunately, to be forthcoming.

10

NILE INTO TIGRIS

Under the old régime Baghdad Radio played a gramophone
record of a song about postmen to mock at his (Nasser's)
having had a postman as a father. Under the Republic the
President of the Court trying some former radio announcers
was careful to point out that the Court realised that this was
a matter for pride.

—*Revolution in Iraq*, by Caractacus, 1959

Opinions are stronger than armies.

—Lord Palmerston, Parliamentary Debates, 1849

The British began to evacuate Egypt in mid-August 1954, and
by mid-June of 1956 the last British soldier had sailed from
Port Said. An occupation which for three-quarters of a century
had nourished and frustrated Egyptian nationalism, morbidly
dominating the minds and consuming the energies of the young
and of many of the country's best men, was at last an end.
More than that, for the first time since the Pharaohs Egypt
was again ruled by Egyptians, and free to find her own way.

It should have been an exhilarating thought. Yet to Egyptians—and to Arabs in general—whose experiences had bred
in them a deep scepticism about the promises of the Western
Powers, it even now seemed lacking in conviction. If the
Imperialists had consented to go, were they not ostentatiously
leaving by the front door merely to sneak in again by the
back? In 1955 strong Anglo-American pressure on Egypt to
join a military pact linking Pakistan, Turkey and other Arab
countries with NATO and thus tying economic aid to both
political and military alignment, seemed to give a remarkably
prompt and familiar answer.

It was less than four years since the Wafd government had
resentfully rejected British demands that Egypt should join
a Middle Eastern Defence Organisation. The British, however,
continued to see the Middle East in paternal terms of 'loyalty'

to (and from) one's 'friends' (who frequently figured in *The Times* leaders in these years, but were notably harder to detect on the ground). Having begun more hopefully, with a largely clean slate, American policy had also by 1955 become hardly less remote from the psychological realities of the Arab East. Pronouncing neutralism 'immoral,' Mr John Foster Dulles had made his own stern division of the globe into the 'House of Peace' and the 'House of War,' but his classification had little in common with that long familiar to Islam. Most Arabs found the threat of 'international Communism' insubstantial beside the *fact* of occupation of Arab lands by an Israel which, in their eyes, was the creation and base of that very Western Imperialism which now sought their alliance. The fall of Dien Bien Phu in 1954 appeared merely the liberation of one more subjugated Asian nation.

Meeting John Foster Dulles during his trip to Cairo in the spring of 1953, Nasser had tried to explain to him the basis of the Arab distaste for what the Americans themselves had not so long ago called 'foreign entanglements.' He had suggested that the real Communist danger in the Arab East lay in internal subversion and that the true antidote to this was satisfied nationalism and social reform. But, once again in the Middle East, preoccupation with bases and power strategy prevented proper weight being given to such increasingly critical considerations. As Dien Bien Phu fell, as stalemate descended in Korea, and the French National Assembly rejected the European Defence Community, the American Secretary of State's determination that the Arabs should be saved from themselves redoubled.

But what in the end clinched Nasser's suspicions of Western motives was the fact that the seat of the proposed new military Pact was to be Baghdad, and its Arab sponsor Iraq's Anglophile Prime Minister, Nuri es-Said. At the moment when the Egyptian Revolution had at last overcome its own *ancien régime*, Western diplomacy thus ensured that the revolutionary conflict was widened and renewed and carried far beyond the Nile Valley, in the confrontation of worlds and generations so perfectly symbolised in the personal histories of Gamal Abdel Nasser and Nuri es-Said.

If their enmity was perhaps as predestined as the historic

rivalry of their two cities, the old leader of Baghdad and the new one of Cairo had nevertheless certain things in common. They were both professional soldiers and owed their emergence to that fact. They were both intuitive politicians of great skill and enduring will-power. Both were Arab nationalists. But here the differences crowd in—for Nasser's nationalism was of a very different sort from Nuri's.

Nuri es-Said, 'the Pasha' for a generation in Iraq, had been a devoted and skilful servant of the country's Hashemite dynasty ever since, in 1919, he had assisted at the installation of this former ruling house of the Hedjaz in his native Baghdad. Born in 1888, son of a minor official in the Ottoman service, he had passed via the local military school and the Turkish Military College to the Staff College at Istanbul. He had fought in the Turkish army in the Balkan wars against a rebel Bulgaria and had served in Iraq as officer-in-charge of tax-collecting forays against the tribes. He was a member of the *Ahad*, the secret pact of Arab officers in the Ottoman army pledged to secure autonomy for the Arab lands within a dual Turk-Arab Empire on the Austro-Hungarian model.[1] But the chauvinism of the young Turks—who would not even admit Arabic as an official language—drove the officers to more radical thinking; and when the Turks took to hanging Iraqi 'rebels,' Nuri seized the opportunity of the First World War (when he was a prisoner in India) to transfer his allegiance to the British. He first moves into modern history in a railway carriage in the company of a British officer, *en route* for Suez, sitting rather uncomfortably on a bag of gold intended to heighten the ardour for the Allied, and Arab, cause of the Sherif of Mecca, Husein, and his tribesmen of the Hedjaz. Thence Nuri went on to campaign with Lawrence in the Desert Revolt, and his name figures many times in the *Seven Pillars*, generally as the reliable professional (which he was to remain to the end). Lawrence has an affectionate anecdote of the ever resourceful Nuri merrily scaring the Bedouin troops off the captured tinned meats he himself so appreciated with loud shouts of 'Pig's bones!'

[1] The other main secret society, '*Al Fatat*,' the Young Arabs, was more Mazzinian in tone and demanded self-government. In 1914 the *Ahad* and *Al Fatat* joined forces.

By the 1950s this world of pashas, sheikhs and tribesmen, and the basic attitudes that went with it, had long been as discreetly clothed in Western parliamentary forms as had Nuri himself in suits by Savile Row. But his ways of thinking remained Ottoman. It did not occur to him, until in the end he was forced to it, to appeal to 'the People'; such a procedure must be at best undignified, at worst ridiculous. In the Ottoman tradition of baksheesh and nepotism he continued to manipulate the tribes, but now through sheikhs who travelled in limousines and had town houses and who, in return for political support, had been transformed into large private landowners. But the Western-style national army which Nuri, as its first Chief-of-Staff, had done much to create, was not to be so easily managed as the Western-style parliament and the 'ninety families.' In 1936—the year in which Nasser and his friends were applying for admission to the Egyptian Military Academy—officers of the Iraq Army and Royal Iraqi Air Force staged their first major military coup. Nuri, then Foreign Minister, saved his life by fleeing to the British Embassy.

In a country as inchoate and primitive as Iraq the motivations and genesis of such coups are inevitably complex; but the force that incubated them and swept them along was the same smouldering resentment against alien domination that had been the explosive charge in Arabi's mutiny-on-the-Nile—which has some claim to be regarded as the first of a long line of revolts by Arab 'national' armies.

In April 1941, in the third of Iraq's failed revolutions, this time engineered by four Iraqi Generals and aided by the Germans, Nuri es-Said again sought safety with the British and was flown out by the R.A.F. After a two-month interregnum the British army brought back the Royal House to the capital from which it had fled. It thus scarcely needed the propinquity of Communism on Iraq's Eastern frontiers to confirm Nuri in his long-standing conviction that wisdom for the Arabs must continue to lie in alliance with the West, and, more particularly, with his old friends the British.

Inevitably, so decadent a system, which had forfeited the dignity and accountability of the old tribalism without substituting the social responsibility of true parliamentary democracy, aroused the disgust of a large part of the educated younger generation. Their protests went unheeded. Iraq, despite her oil wealth, was still a relatively remote and primitive country which had never wholly recovered from the destruction of her irrigation system by the Mongol invaders in the 13th century. For four-and-a-half centuries—until the First World War—she had mouldered under Ottoman rule. There were still regions where fellahin in debt to their landlords (as most inevitably were) could not legally move, and were in effect serfs. Even in 1955 the entire cultivated area was owned by only 4 per cent of the population.

Nevertheless, even in such a world, news travels, and none more swiftly than news of revolution. After the announcement of the Egyptian Land Reform in 1952 there were riots among the wretched sharecroppers of the Amara marshes of the Tigris. True, Nuri, reading the signs of the times, had in 1950 set up a Development Board to receive 75 per cent of Iraq's large and rising oil revenues to expend on public works. But it was late. The time had gone by when even so immense a bag of gold could in itself prove effective. The British civil servant, Lord Salter, called in to report on the work of the Development Board in 1954, found it necessary to point out that in a country of such small population vast engineering projects—dams-and-water—had only a limited relation to the immediate basic need—which had to do with human rather than material resources. 'The people,' wrote Salter, 'may well have an ultimate power which is altogether out of proportion to their present representation in Parliament. . . . It is the contrast between immediate and potential political power that constitutes the danger.'

These were to prove prophetic words.

The Rising Tide

In 1954 Nuri was obliged to suppress all the opposition parties, gaoling their more active members. Young and educated Iraqis now looked at Nasser's 'New Egypt' and they looked at Nuri's Iraq, and they were angry and ashamed. Nor need their glance be confined to Egypt. In neighbouring Syria, three successive coups by the new national army (the French having left in April, 1946) had disrupted the cosy old pattern in which power had been shared between the great merchant families and landed clans—though increasingly challenged by the emergent ideological parties, including now the Baath Socialist Party. Iraq's sister Hashemite kingdom of Transjordan —now Jordan—had also been transformed by the influx, as a result of the violent creation of Israel, of a large body of politically conscious Palestinians who, in all, now made up 60 per cent of the population. In the schism between the Palestinian 'West Bank' (of the Jordan) and the traditionalist Bedouin East Bank, this small and highly artificial state now neatly—and nerve-rackingly—epitomised the discontinuity between the Arab Past and the Arab Present and Future. But the displaced Palestinians, who were among the most energetic and modern-minded of Arabs, were by no means confined to Jordan. As engineers, administrators, teachers, skilled workers of many kinds, they were now scattered about the Arab world in a new and subversive Diaspora that stretched from Persian Gulf sheikhdoms like Kuwait to the Senussi realm of Libya.

Westwards again, the tide of revolution was rising. By 1954 the Arabs of all the three territories of French North-West Africa had definitively rejected the 'privilege' of assimilation and were engaged in throwing it back in the teeth of the donors. And on 1 November 1954, in the Aurès Mountains of Eastern Algeria, nine young men had launched a ruthless armed insurrection that was to last for seven years and cost one million Algerian lives. Here, too, a new generation, with a new scale of values, was about to take over.

With a confused revolutionary situation thus in existence from Rabat to Damascus—and indeed in Baghdad itself—Nuri es-Said seized with professional confidence the lifeline now thrown by Providence and the West to sustain, as he robustly saw it, the Natural Order and the Hashemite Monarchy against the inroads of Communism, Nasser, and the perennial follies of youth. To him, the Baghdad Pact was the obvious sequel to the British departure from their bases at Habbaniya and Basra in May 1955. To the Egyptians, with few exceptions indeed, and to young and politically conscious Arabs everywhere, it looked like a Holy Alliance designed to repress the gathering Arab Revolution and to maintain that fatal old *status quo* in which Arab feudalism made common cause with Western Imperialism. If perhaps confused and faint—and certainly inaudible to most Europeans—the echoes of early 19th-century Europe, in the aftertow of the French Revolution, are unmistakable. Jordan, in particular, like some bizarre German principality, was torn apart in 1955 by the efforts of the Turks and the British (who tactlessly sent the Chief of the Imperial General Staff, General Templer) to get a nervous and reluctant government to join the Baghdad Pact. It became necessary to use the Bedouin East Bank, through an Arab Legion commanded by Englishmen, to repress the 'progressive' Palestinians of the West Bank.

In such circumstances, all eyes naturally turned to Egypt, which had lately overthrown an alien monarchy, and redistributed its land in the name of social justice. 'Whenever Nasser's picture appeared at the cinema,' reports a chagrined Colonel Peter Young, of the Arab Legion in Jordan, 'the audience would clap. His picture was often carried in demonstrations.'[2] In riposte to Baghdad, Egypt and Syria prepared to link in a wholly Arab Defence Pact, establishing a joint command, and vast numbers of eager listeners to Cairo Radio's 'Voice of the Arabs' received their fill of revolutionary rhetoric denouncing Imperialism's Arab lackeys.

The Egyptian Revolution was now reaching out, still somewhat tentatively, towards the wider, ill-defined Arab Revolution. They would draw strength from each other. Yet it was not easy for a country like Egypt, which most people, including its own inhabitants, still thought of as small and poor, to advance beyond largely verbal gestures. Egypt's leaders might lend an ear to such champions of non-alignment as Nehru and Tito, both of whom visited Egypt in February 1955, but much as Egyptians might feel betrayed, a connection with the West which had been growing since the days of Mohamed Ali and which was deeply woven into the fabric of the country's cultural and economic life could not lightly be broken. The very makers of the revolution, the army officers, were British-trained and English-speaking. In the autumn of 1954, even as Nasser was denouncing 'Dollar Imperialism,' he was arranging

[2] Peter Young, in *Bedouin Command* (1956), gives a vivid inside picture of these days, all the more telling for coming from a writer with the conventional British anti-Nasser attitudes.

with the United States, the American-dominated World Bank, and Britain to finance the High Dam, and announcing the results of U.S. 'Point Four' studies of Egypt's industrial potential.

In 1954, the Ismailian umbilical cord still linked Egypt to the West. But within two years it was to be severed by a series of dramatic events which followed each other with bewildering rapidity.

For the Arab world they would open a new era, and for Europe close an old one.

'A Crucial Event'

This sequence of events, forming a chain of cause and effect which was finally to encompass a large part of the world, was inaugurated on 17 February 1955, when that veteran warrior and prophet of Zion, David Ben Gurion, abruptly emerged from his 'retirement' on a kibbutz in the Negev to take over Israel's Ministry of Defence. Eleven days later three Israeli army detachments crossed Israel's southern border and struck at the Egyptian-controlled Gaza Strip, storming an Egyptian military camp, ambushing a troop carrier, blowing up buildings, and leaving behind them, when they withdrew, thirty-eight Egyptian and Palestinian dead and thirty-one wounded.

Technically, the Gaza Raid was far from being an innovation. It was fully in accordance with Israel's longstanding policy of reprisal—since 1949 directed against the Palestinian marauders who infiltrated across the armistice line to sabotage or to avenge, to recover some bit of their property, or merely to graze their sheep on their old village lands from which the demarcation line now often separated them. Such incursions imposed a strain on Israel's border areas, and, over the years, added up to serious loss of life; but until this time they had been in general sporadic, amateur, and, given the impossible unfenced border—in fact, a cease-fire line—to a large extent inevitable. The Israeli reprisals, by contrast, were official army punitive expeditions, designed to shock, to 'teach the Arabs a lesson,' and, as General Dayan, the Israeli Chief-of-Staff pointed out, they had to take place at night since otherwise they would have all too clearly ranked as war. Israeli reprisal policy had, nevertheless, been strongly condemned in United

he first major effort
desert reclamation,
beration Province
so had large social
ns. *Right*
ohamed Abdul
ttah, a new settler
home, 1955.
elow 1965—view
om the Club in the
ovince's chief
wn, Badr. Ten
ars ago there was
thing here but
nd.

ot: Nile water is
plemented by
ping from wells. In
water channels that
nd from the pump-
ses are kept
dreds of
sands of ducks.
apter 8)

For more than a century cotton has shaped the life of Egypt. *Above* Village children comb through the cotton plants for signs of worm during the 'season of the pests'. *Below* In the great cotton warehouses of Alexandria women blend to order the broken bales from the villages by hurling handfuls of cotton into the air, a unique Egyptian process known as *farfara*. (Chapters 6 and 17)

Nations resolutions, most notably in October 1953, after the destruction of the Jordan village of Kibya in which the Mixed Armistice Commission had stigmatised the 'cold-blooded murder' by the Israeli military of sixty-six villagers, including women and children.

But earlier reprisal raids had been directed in the main against Jordan and Syria. The Gaza Raid was the first serious assault on Egyptian-held territory in the six years since the Cease-Fire, and it was launched against the Egyptian army. Its challenge was unmistakable.

Until this time Nasser had been restrained in his public statements on Israel. General Burns, chief of the United Nations Truce Supervision Organisation, had found him on the whole co-operative in reducing border tension, living up to his assurance, of November 1954, that he 'wanted no trouble.' True, despite the Security Council's 1951 condemnation, the Arab blockade of Israel still extended to shipping in the Suez Canal and Gulf of Aqaba, as it had since 1949—and the war of words continued in the ether. But in private talks with foreigners, Nasser was still prepared to agree that there could be, and must be, a peace settlement with Israel. Nor did it stop there. According to the Israeli editor and Knesset member, Uri Avnery,[3] in 1954 Nasser asked the Indian Ambassador in Cairo to arrange a secret meeting with the Israeli Prime Minister, Moshe Sharett. (Negotiations dragged and the Gaza Raid supervened.) There were other go-betweens around this time: Dom Mintoff, the Malta Labour leader, and a British M.P., Maurice Orbach, who carried a personal letter from Nasser to Sharett. Nasser's *Philosophy of the Revolution*, published in 1954, contained no summons to arms against Israel; and even after the Gaza Raid and the successful Russian arms deal, Nasser, in November 1955, publicly welcomed Sir Anthony Eden's Guildhall call for Arab-Israeli negotiations—a courageous abandonment of the sacrosanct Arab position that Israel's existence could not be recognised.[4]

[3] In *Israel Without Zionism* (1968).
[4] Eden's proposal—for a compromise between the Israeli frontiers of the U.N. Partition Plan and the frontiers established by the war—was stillborn because of the Israeli outcry (which had also greeted Count Bernadotte) against the mere idea that any conquered territory whatever should be given up.

The widespread idea that Nasser worked up hatred of Israel for his own demagogic ends cannot, in fact, survive a moment's examination. Had he been the rabble-rouser that Zionist propagandists say he was, the situation in Palestine in 1954 and 1955 would have furnished almost unlimited opportunities. Now totalling almost a million,[5] the Palestinian refugees had for six years been eking out a miserable existence, herded in a sort of Arab Pale around the borders of Israel. How many had been forced from their homes in 1948 by Jewish terror tactics, how many simply fled before the tide of war, was a question much argued, but largely irrelevant. None had in any true sense abandoned their homes and lands. Yet they were not permitted to return.[6] Gazetted as 'Abandoned,' their ancestral lands were transferred to the Jewish National Fund, and in due course settled with Jewish immigrants. Four-fifths of the land of Israel, half the citrus groves, almost all the olives, and about a quarter of the houses and other buildings were 'abandoned' Arab property.

Each year the United Nations General Assembly had solemnly re-affirmed its 1948 vote that the refugees wishing to return and live at peace should be allowed to do so. Once, in 1949, Israel, under pressure, had agreed to re-admit 100,000— with the pre-condition of an Arab-Israeli peace treaty. But the obvious fact was that the return of all the Arabs was inconsistent with the maintenance of the Jewish State. In the Israel of the 1947 Partition Plan they would have constituted more than 40 per cent of the population; in the Greater Israel of 1949—40 per cent greater—they would have made up 60 per cent. Their exodus, as Dr Weizmann gratefully observed, was a 'miracle'—and for Israel a very necessary one.

One does not spurn miracles. By 1954, Greater Israel was being planted with Jewish settlements, strategically placed to

---

[5] The original number 1948-9 seems to have been around 650,000 but to this now had to be added births over six years. In addition, there were the so-called 'economic refugees' like the 85,000 Palestinian residents of the Gaza area—whose livelihood had been in what now became Israel.

[6] There is an uncanny—and rather horrifying—parallel here with the manner in which the Jews themselves were in the 1880s expelled from much of the Russian countryside. 'If a Jew left, for any reason, the place of his domicile, he could be stopped on his way back and declared an attempted "new" settler (i.e. prohibited)'—James Parkes, *A History of the Jewish People.*

ensure the whole area's irrevocable Jewishness. Thus, many of the 120,000 Arabs who had remained in Israel were now turned off their lands so that they could be 'developed' for Jewish immigrants; Arab *Wakf* (religious trust) land was also taken over, and, in the Negev, the Bedouins were either expelled or reduced to a fraction of their former acreage.[7]

The process of expropriation was necessarily accompanied by a 'dynamic' Israeli defence policy. In the words of Ben Gurion: 'We had to make them (the Arabs) understand that the presence of the Jews in Palestine was not a feeble or fleeting factor, but a decisive one, a historical reality that could not be annulled.' The effect of these endeavours was duly noted on the spot during the period June 1949 to October 1954 by Commander E. H. Hutchison, the American Chairman of the U.N.'s Israel-Jordan Mixed Armistice Commission. 'Few if any of Israel's offers of peace,' he writes, 'were matched by deeds that would invite co-operation . . . Israel led by a good margin in serious violations of the border and armistice agreements.'[8] In particular, the Israelis strenuously sought to assert their sovereignty over the Demilitarised Zones designed in the armistice agreements to provide a buffer between the sides. In the autumn of 1953, after killing a number of Bedouins and their cattle, they established a kibbutz in the El Auja Demilitarised Zone near the Gaza Strip border—wholly desert, yet a key junction of routes into Sinai. The *kibbutz* was, in fact, a military camp. A 'flagrant violation' of the Armistice Agreement was duly condemned by the Mixed Armistice Commission, which after further incidents in 1954, found the settlement to be 'organised as a unit of the Israeli Armed Forces.'

[7] For details see George Schwarz: *The Arabs in Israel*. When compensation was offered to Israel's Arabs after expulsion from their land it was at 1950 prices, although the Israeli pound had since greatly depreciated. But very many refused to be paid for what they conceived to be stolen. See also D. Peretz: *Israel & the Palestine Arabs* (Washington, 1958).

[8] *Violent Truce* (London, 1956). Commander Hutchison says that he started his duties with a 'pro-Israeli' bias. Disbelieving readers are recommended to study the works of other United Nations observers on the spot, e.g. of General Burns (a Canadian) and General Carl von Horn (a Swede). Burns' Danish predecessor, General Bennike, as a consequence of his reports, was in effect declared *persona non grata* by the Israelis and his resignation forced.

The challenge to the new régime in Egypt in all this is obvious. But the revolution, although conducted by the military, had brought neither sabre-rattling nor major military build-up. The officers were preoccupied by the vast political and economic tasks that confronted them at home. And— until the spring of 1955—the wastes of Sinai had effectively insulated Egyptians from the starker aspects of the Palestine tragedy.

Before the United Nations tribunal, the Israelis justified the Gaza Raid, as they justified all their reprisal attacks, by the statistics of border infiltration, which they claimed had been mounting. The evidence of the United Nations observers on the spot did not, however, bear their claims out: the Raid was condemned.[9] In fact, it was not the belligerence of the Egyptian régime that had prompted the Gaza expedition so much as that régime's constructive character which had made possible closer relations with the West. In the summer of 1954 the Israeli Prime Minister described the forthcoming British departure from the Canal Zone as 'the abandonment of Israel to her fate.' And not only was the protective screen of British troops being withdrawn, but the United States, Israel's chief sponsor, was also signing an economic aid agreement with the Egyptians. In a speech in April, Mr Henry Byroade, U.S. Assistant Secretary of State, had called on Israel to cease her 'conqueror behaviour' and to end her assumption that violence was the only policy understood by her neighbours.

Blockaded for six years, her insecure frontiers surrounded by implacably hostile Arab populations sworn to regain the conquered Arab lands, Israel's situation in face of the success of the Egyptian revolution was at this time, in the words of Ben Gurion's biographer, Michel Bar-Zohar, 'graver . . . than at any time since the war of independence . . . her very existence in the balance. The creative impulse had petered out and the honeymoon with the outside world was over.'

Israel—at least if she was to remain the dynamic Jewish State of the Zionist vision—had little choice but to challenge the rival revolution—and this she now did.

---

[9] Cf. General Burns, Chief U.N.T.S.O., on the Israeli complaints in November: 'The facts did not indicate that the frequency and severity of the incidents really amounted to a critical situation.'

In September 1954, for the first time since the 1948-9 war, she sent an Israeli ship, the *Bat Galim*, to pass through the Suez Canal. Predictably, it was arrested, its cargo held, its crew gaoled. But the manoeuvre failed. 'The Great Powers,' complained Mr Walter Eytan, Director-General of the Israeli Foreign Office, 'appeared to be less vexed with Egypt for this violation of Israel's rights than with Israel for provoking it.'

A few weeks after the *Bat Galim* fiasco, by what the Israeli government were cryptically to describe as 'a security mishap,' eleven Israeli agents were arrested in Egypt in the process of placing bombs to destroy British and American installations in Alexandria and Cairo.[10] The intention seems to have been to embroil the Egyptians with the West—and the outcome was a little more successful than the *Bat Galim* affair in that much indignation was directed against the Egyptians for putting the Israeli agents on trial, and executing two of them. But the ring around Israel remained unbroken. Stalemate again threatened, and stalemate was the one condition that Israel could not tolerate.

The stage was set for the re-emergence of Ben Gurion, and for the Gaza Raid.

Nasser Looks Eastwards

General Burns has described the Gaza Raid as 'a crucial event' which 'set the trend which continued until Israel invaded Sinai in October 1956'—and had he been writing later he might have added June 1967. Nasser has said that for him it 'rang the alarm bell.' With Ben Gurion now publicly speculating on how long what he called 'this one-sided war' could be allowed to continue, Nasser became more sharply aware of the implications of the Arabs' insistence on a continuing state of war with Israel. With the 1948-9 débâcle in mind, he looked to Egypt's defences and found them wanting. Unlike Israel, Egypt had no free supply of American dollars with which to go shopping for arms wherever they could be bought. Egyptian emissaries tried long and hard to secure arms

---

[10] Generally disbelieved at the time, this squalid operation later became the material of that notorious Israel political scandal, 'The Lavon Affair'— Mr Pinhas Lavon being Minister of Defence at the time.

supplies in the U.S.A., in Britain and in France, but with small success. The British and Americans required military align-ment through the Baghdad Pact, or otherwise. The French saw Cairo as the base and supplier of the Algerian rebels and, since Nasser refused to give assurances on this point, they cemented an alliance with Israel, thereby once again confirming the Arabs in their conviction that Zionism was another of the faces of Imperialism. Despite the basic condition of the British-French-American tripartite guarantee of existing Arab-Israeli frontiers—which was that the parties would seek to prevent an arms build-up on either side—France was proving increasingly receptive to the approaches of Israel's arms-seeking emissaries.

According to Michel Bar-Zohar, who was given access to Ben Gurion's diaries and private papers, Shimon Peres, Director-General of Israel's Ministry of Defence, met the French Deputy Premier, Paul Reynaud, in France in 1954 and had talks with the heads of Nord Aviation, where he asked for Mystère fighters—vastly superior to anything the Arab states then possessed. 'At the end of 1954 Peres had signed an agreement with Catroux, Minister for Air in Mendès-France's Govern-ment, which covered the purchase of arms, aircraft, guns, tanks and radar equipment.' Meanwhile, General Dayan, also visiting Paris, had talks with General Guillaume, with whom he discussed the Arabs as 'our common enemy.'

Soon after the Gaza Raid, Ben Gurion sent a personal letter to the new French Minister of Defence, General Koenig. Peres followed in person 'and then things began to move.' Peres, Dayan, and Israel's Air Force Commander met various French Ministers and officials, and the Prime Minister 'showed much goodwill.' Owing to frequent French Ministerial changes, and some foot-dragging by the French Foreign Office, the agree-ment to supply Mystères was not actually signed until Novem-ber 1955. But in view of this long-drawn clandestine activity, Nasser's statements that he had wind of the deal, and that this lent urgency to his search for arms, must be treated with a respect not accorded at the time.

But although the new Russian Ambassador in Cairo in 1954 had lined up with the Arabs against Israel and the Baghdad Pact, holding out the prospect of economic aid and arms 'without strings,'[11] it is notable that even after the Gaza Raid

Egypt was still looking to the West for assistance. Nasser and his fellow officers manifestly preferred the Devil they did know to the Devil they didn't. Egypt's Communists had always so far been the first of the régime's political enemies into gaol and the last out, and 'atheist, subversive' Communism had been singled out for exposure in denunciatory books from the Department of National Guidance.

But at this point another outside event intruded: the first Afro-Asian Conference opened at Bandung, in Java, on 18 April 1955. Nasser, flying to join the heads of the twenty-nine nations—representing more than half the world's population —and not a single 'white' skin among them—was travelling out of the Middle East for the first time. With the laurels of Egypt's deliverance from the 'colonial yoke' still fresh upon him, he found himself ranged beside such historic leaders of the Asian Revolution as Nehru, Sukarno, U Nu of Burma, Chou en-Lai. His stature—physical perhaps as well as moral —ensured for him a prominent place among these classic crusaders of—and for—the 'Third World.' Most significantly for the immediate future, Nasser got on well with Chou en-Lai —a Communist, it is true, but a Communist of Confucian charm—who tactfully offered to buy some of Egypt's cotton crop.

Quite suddenly, horizons were opening out astonishingly for Egypt. Nasser came home to a hero's welcome. 'Hail champion of Africa and Asia!' read the crowding banners, with their flanking pictures of Chou, Nehru and Nasser. And the acclaim was well based—for not only was this the first Egyptian to lead a truly independent Egypt, but now—the man and the moment being well met—he had also become the first Egyptian leader to have moved into the centre of the world stage.

Perspectives changed. The Arabs no longer seemed so isolated and alone; and there was another Devil to eclipse the Devil of Communism: that 'Neo-Colonialism' smelled out and proclaimed at Bandung as a rallying-cry for the Third World of resolute 'non-alignment.' Since traditional Lancashire and

[11] According to Tom Little (*Egypt*, London, 1958), the Russian Ambassador, Daniel Solod, after earlier offering arms to the Arab Collective Security Pact, made a formal arms offer to Egypt in January 1955.

French markets for Egypt's cotton had fallen off badly with the contraction of their textile industries, no time was lost in taking up the Chinese offer to buy cotton—which also opened up the markets of Russia, Hungary, Czechoslovakia and Rumania. With a third of their cotton going to the Communist bloc, a third to the West, and a third to uncommitted countries, Egyptians claimed to have underwritten their economic independence.

At Bandung Nasser had sounded Chou en-Lai on the possibility of arms for Egypt from China. Back in Cairo, in May, he received Chou's roundabout response—a reiterated offer of arms, in quantity now, from Russia. Yet despite mounting tension, with almost daily firing incidents now along the Gaza Strip border where—to quote General Burns—'the Israeli forces flaunted their patrols along the demarcation line as if to challenge the garrison,' Nasser still, in June, made one last appeal to the United States and Britain, indicating now that if they wouldn't supply him with arms on politically acceptable terms, he would buy from Russia. The warning was ignored; the negotiations with Russia went ahead.

In June too Nasser proposed to Burns the physical separation of the Israeli and Egyptian forces by a demilitarised zone of one kilometre on each side of the border; he was also prepared to accept Burns' proposal for joint Israeli-Arab patrols. The Israelis, however, favoured neither of these approaches, and some riposte to their military challenge had now become politically inescapable. That summer, the Nasser régime began to organise and equip the bands of *feydayin* (literally, 'self-sacrificers'), generally Palestinian refugees, sent into Israel to ambush, mine and kill. Promptly—in the process of escalation now established—this produced the Israeli reprisal—the raid on the Khan Yunis police post in the Gaza Strip on 31 August in which thirty-six Egyptians and Palestinians were killed.

Four weeks later, on 27 September 1955, Nasser publicly announced his acceptance of the Russian arms offer. The arms shipment was large and impressively modern, including MiG fighters, Stalin tanks and Ilyushin jet bombers, to be accompanied by 380 Russian and Czech technicians and trainers.[12]

---

[12] While this was the first Soviet penetration into the strategically critical area of the Nile Valley, it was not the first Soviet entry into the Near

For the moment, it established technical arms superiority over Israel. It completed the demolition of the tripartite arms restraint and changed the scale of armament in the Middle East. But it was not such calculations which accounted for the great outburst of rejoicing with which the 'Czech' arms deal was greeted all over the Arab world. It was not even the satisfaction of having scored over Israel—with an enhanced prospect of expunging that affront to Arab pride. These things no doubt contributed, but the real cause of the rejoicing was that, by daring to deal with the Russians, Nasser had, almost overnight, shattered the moral proprietorship which the British, French and Americans had so long, and so anachronistically, exercised over the whole region.

The Arab East—so it seemed to the Arabs—had been given back to its people. The Syrian, Lebanese and Jordanian Chambers of Deputies met and sent resolutions of congratulation to Nasser. Even Nuri in Baghdad, whose whole world had been destroyed and whose fate was now sealed, in prudence despatched to Cairo his telegram of felicitation.

For although Nasser at Bandung had in a sense picked up the torch of the Asian Revolution, positive neutralism, for Arabs, had older roots. The first revolution of Islam had asserted a claim to a special identity, to constitute a whole independent world, and this was a claim which the Arab revolution of our times instinctively echoed. Well before Bandung, Syria had refused American Point Four aid, roundly denouncing 'foreign entanglements.' But it had been Nasser who had inherited the place and the moment—transitory, but potent—where the rising tides of Asian and Arab and, soon, African, nationalism met the ebb tide of Western Imperialism, and it was he who would finally know how to use it. The men had led the revolution; now the revolution was about to lead the men.

Birthright Regained

It would no doubt have been over-optimistic to have

East. Thus, Turkey in the 'thirties had been lent economic and material aid by the Russians who built the textile mills at Kayseri and equipped them with Soviet machinery. The Imam of Yemen had also received Russian aid in the 'thirties.

expected that the Americans, even with their comparatively recent experience of the joys of overthrowing colonial yokes, would have understood these emotional reactions. Certainly there is nothing to suggest that John Foster Dulles dwelt long on either the Boston Tea Party or the Monroe Doctrine of positive neutralism (1823) before despatching an envoy to Nasser with a note of protest against the Russian arms deal. But when Dulles' envoy was kept waiting an hour and a half in Nasser's outer office and returned without delivering the Note—an incident which Nasser duly used to point the moral in a public speech—the Arab cup of joy overflowed. It seemed that the incredible was happening: the years of humiliation before the moral arrogance and material superiority of the West had at last begun to be repaid.

With this ringing rejection of the old paternalisms, the battle between the old and new Arab worlds was fairly joined. In Jordan the conflict of West and East banks now appeared within the Arab Legion itself, where a Young Officers' secret society, on the Egyptian model, plotted against the British command. Nor did the young King himself, despite an education at Harrow and Sandhurst, remain unaffected by these powerful emotional currents. In March, his Arab pride hurt by a London magazine article which suggested that the British commander and architect of the Arab Legion was the real ruler of Jordan, he abruptly expelled Glubb Pasha—the last of a long and splendid line of British Arabists. The Yemen and Saudi Arabia, as well as Jordan, now joined Syria and Egypt in military agreements. None could swim against this tide.

There was a strange theatricality, an uncanny symmetry and symbolic quality, in this whole developing drama of Imperialism's last days in the Arab East. Mr Dulles, in particular, seemed to experience a compulsion to play the 'neo-colonialist' rôle exactly as it might have been written for him at Bandung. On 18 June 1955, just five days after the last British soldier had sailed from the Canal Zone, he abruptly announced the withdrawal of the promised American loan to finance the High Dam, the symbol of the Egyptian revolution's mission, and the keystone of its grand design for the New Egypt. The only reason given—Egypt's mounting financial commitment—convinced no one, since the World Bank, which had spent months studying the project and was putting up the lion's share of the package credit,[13] was ready to go ahead. The American Secretary of State had invited the Egyptian President to stand on his carpet—and now he had snatched it from under his feet. It hardly needed the British echo of the Americana rejection[14] to convince all Arabs that Egypt was, in fact, being publicly punished for her independence in dealing with the Russians, and—worse—recognising Red China.

The neo-colonialist *démarche* duly produced, six weeks later, the ringing neo-Arab riposte. The Suez Canal Company was nationalised: the revenues of the Canal, instead of draining away to the West, would finance the High Dam.

For the ex-colonial world this was an act of poetic justice on the grandest and most satisfying scale. For few more effective symbols of 'Imperialist exploitation' existed anywhere in the world than the Suez Canal and the international, if Egyptian-registered, company that controlled it. Although in labour, money, and land, Egypt had furnished three-quarters of the Canal's cost, and Western financiers and governments had been prodigiously enriched, until the mid-1930s Egypt had got nothing back in dividends, profits or fees—and then little enough.[15] To economic subjection had been added personal

---

[13] The World Bank was to provide 200 million dollars, the U.S. 55 million and Britain 15 million. But the withdrawal of one partner meant the collapse of the entire deal.

[14] According to the veteran British diplomatic correspondent, W. N. Ewer, basing himself on a talk at the Foreign Office at the time, Britain had resolved as long ago as the early Spring (when Nasser refused to adhere to what the Foreign Office referred to as 'the good-behaviour clause') to 'let the High Dam project "run into the sands." ' The Eden Memoirs, though employing more devious language, confirm this. Britain's 'friends' in Iraq, they explain, had been complaining about British aid to Nasser.

[15] An annual rent of £E300,000; by 1949 nationalist pressure had brought the payment up to 7 per cent of the annual net revenue. The fact that the extravagance and folly of Ismail made him so easy a victim for European financiers and that he had been forced by his financial plight to sell 'Egypt's' Canal shares did not, of course, make these long resented and notorious facts any easier for Egyptians to accept, or remove the considerable tarnish from de Lesseps' East-West rainbow. Particularly since Britain, having fought the Canal project from the start for strategic reasons, at the last moment acquired from the bankrupt Khedive 44 per cent of the shares for £4m. which by 1955 had reached a market value of £37m. with an annual dividend yield (in 1954-55) of almost £3m.

humiliation. Few Egyptians were employed except in very subordinate posts; the first Egyptian pilot did not appear until 1947, and then only under heavy Government pressure. A well-educated Egyptian who had applied for a post there as a young man said: 'As soon as they knew you were Egyptian, you were out. They would take the lowest sort of Maltese or Greek rather than an Egyptian, no matter how well qualified.' After a lapse of many years the memory of the manner of that rejection still rankled. And even in 1956, after Britain's withdrawal, the Canal Zone—though an integral part of Egypt, with three important towns—had remained, anachronistically, to a significant extent a French enclave.

It was thus hardly remarkable that so masterful and symbolically timed a takeover of this rich and powerful foreign 'state-within-a-state' should provoke an explosion of joy which united all classes in Egypt. And not only Egypt—for as the 'Imperialists' froze Egypt's sterling, franc and dollar assets, threatened force and international law in the same breath, and sought to prevent Egypt from exercising that sovereignty over the Canal itself which was indisputably hers,[16] the thunder—and occasional lightning—of applause swept the entire Arab world from Gulf to Atlantic. When, shortly after the Canal nationalisation, Nasser, accompanied by President Kuwatly of Syria, landed at Riyadh Airport, he was greeted—according to an eye-witness, King Saud's Swiss-American steward, José Arnold—by 'the greatest crowd in the history of the city. . . .' thousands of whom, 'screaming wildly, broke through the guard lines and converged on the plane. . . . An even greater throng, hysterically chanting and clapping, lined the road into Riyadh, and police and soldiers had to use clubs and fire shots to clear a pathway for the car.' King Saud, reported his steward, was much perturbed by these popular manifestations. His advisers sat up late considering how they might be counteracted. Meanwhile, in the sheikhdom of Kuwait, the students formed Suez Clubs and collected £2

---

[16] 'The Suez Canal . . . is an integral part of Egypt'—Art. XVIII Anglo-Egyptian Evacuation Agreement, 1954. What the Company held was an operating concession, granted in 1888, expiring in 1968, not the ditch itself. Most land on the Canal's banks was excluded in 1864 by a ruling of the French Emperor, Napoleon III, brought in to arbitrate between Khedive and Company. In 1956, fair compensation was offered—and paid.

million for the support of Nasser. The authorities soon closed the clubs down. The ideas they celebrated were less easily extinguished.

The Meaning of Nasserism

The ideas? For a time Gamal Abdel Nasser now became over a large area of the world a figure as magical and universal as Mahatma Gandhi had been in the inter-war years. Indeed, in this 'two-camp' world with its war-stricken old Imperial Powers, 'Nasserism' made a sharper impact on the course of history than Gandhi's mobilised 'soul-force' ever had. Yet to define its ideas, and even more to explain their curious potency, was not easy.

Obviously the Arab World hailed Nasser as the new Saladin because his interpretation of Arab nationalism had been sensationally successful. His defiance of the West had repaid in kind a million collective and individual humiliations. On the most atavistic level—and memories in these parts run deep— he had avenged the Crusades and all subsequent spoliations of Islam. On a more sophisticated political level, he had filled, symbolically at least, the famous 'vacuum' which the Great Powers professed to find threatening the Middle East. 'Nasserism' meant to the Arabs that they had taken back their fate into their own hands, and they had no doubt of this because they had not yet learned that in the modern world there are few nations indeed which are not dependent.

But to see Nasserism as merely triumphant nationalism and 'positive neutralism' is to miss its inner and enduring source of strength. For if Nasserism breathed new life into the 'Arab Revolution,' it was not the old aristocratic-romantic Arabism of Feisal in Damascus in 1919. If it proclaimed the equality of nations, it also protested implicitly the Equality of Man. For the Egyptian Revolution had been the first true revolution in the Middle East. Hitherto there had been innumerable palace revolutions and, more rarely, the partial nationalist revolution. But even Ataturk had not displaced the landlord class. The strength of the Egyptian Revolution of 1952 was that its leaders understood that one could not have a nationalist revolution without a nation—and, in the conditions of the Levant, one could not realise, and release, the spirit of a nation without political and social revolution. In the world of Islam the message of human brotherhood and human dignity was scarcely new. But it lacked political forms appropriate to the 20th century. In search for them, the progenitors of the Egyptian Revolution had gone to other sources than the Koran. But the monolithic traditionalism of Islam had slowed and stifled the search.[17] Only now, more than one hundred and fifty years after Napoleon Bonaparte brought it to Egypt, did the message of the French Revolution, gathering strength in the Nile Valley, at last burst over the Middle East and slowly penetrate to its remotest corners.

Thus, for many thousands of the young and eager all over the Arab World, the Egyptian take-over of the Suez Canal was in a sense—though few would have drawn the parallel or even stopped to analyse their confused emotions—their Fall of the Bastille. The delirious message carried by radio across the vast desert spaces was a message of fulfilment for themselves, both as members of an Arab nation and as human individuals. It meant that that grotesque Turco-Bedouin world of tribalism-gone-bad, of massively entrenched privilege cloaked in liberal Western dress, of landed sheikhs and usurious pashas and nepotist *mudirs* and lick-spittle *omdas*, that grand conspiracy of the 'haves' against the 'have-nots,' supported by the Great Powers in the name of stability (and private interest), was at last in full retreat. It meant that the day of what had once been rather patronisingly called 'the Young Effendis'—for so many years hailed as the hope of the Arab world—was dawning at last. But the term now seemed quaint, for that world of lower-middle-class aspiration had been growing mightily.

[17] The ideas of the French Revolution also inspired the nationalist movements of India and Latin America, but there made an impact notably quicker and more vivid. The Indian Brahmin who, in 1828, founded the famous *Bramo Samaj* to effect a synthesis of Hinduism and Western science and liberalism, had made his first journey to Europe only a few years after Mohamed Ali despatched thence his first mission of young Egyptians. But in India the new ideas were soon acclimatised, and it was almost half a century before they produced a 'back-to-the-Vedas' reaction in the *Arya Samaj*, which, even so, was not obscurantist. There are, of course, many reasons for this difference in receptivity and timing, but the major one probably derives from the monolithic strength—the institutionalised traditionalism—of Islam.

Yet despite its increasing breadth, despite the teachers, engineers, oilfield technicians, managers, foremen, administrators, students, and all the eager aspirants crowding in on its fringes, it had lacked the means to articulate its confused, half-formed, but passionately felt ideas and aspirations. The Egyptian Revolution and Gamal Abdel Nasser had provided the means. The 'Young Effendis' had now spoken with the not-ineffective voice of the young majors of the new national armies—and on occasion claimed to speak with the voice of the common man.

This was the heart of the battle now joined between the old world of Nuri and the new world of Nasser, a battle of values already familiar and fought over—if not perhaps quite fought out—in Europe, between the right of birth and the claims of merit, between the Courtly and the Populist, the power of wealth and the needs of human beings, the equality of man and the inequality of men. 'The Mob'—as normal a part of life and politics of the 20th-century Middle East as it had been in 18th-century England—that base, venal, dumbly howling mob that existed to be used and consumed, was on the way to becoming 'the People.'[18] As the latest U.S.I.S. Library burned to the ground or a British Embassy was pillaged, the difference might appear somewhat academic—yet in this matter the theory was important, for history has shown it to possess a strange dynamism of its own.

The Last Act

The almost theatrical symmetry, the odd air of inevitability which had dogged this historic sequence of events, did not desert it in its thunderous last act: the eight-day 'Suez War.'

Few wars have been so confused in their beginnings and so lame in their endings—and yet so clarifying and so full of that history-made symbolism that makes history. Staged under United Nations arc-lights, in an arena created by the equal and opposite thrusts of two Super-Powers, the event almost at once turned into a morality drama in which the imperial

---

[18] In terms of British political development it was the transition, perhaps, from the Gordon Riots of 1780 to Gladstone's 'disturbing' appeal to *hoi polloi* in his Midlothian Campaign of 1879. The Gallup Poll, mercifully perhaps, has still to arrive in the Arab world!

chapter heralded by the British naval bombardment of Arabi's Alexandria in 1882 was condignly concluded at the other side of the Delta seventy-four years later.[19] For the watching millions of the Third World, the prompt halting of what in Arab history now figures as 'the Tripartite Aggression,' and the public humiliation of the Franco-British partners, bestowed the accolade of history on Nasserism. It constituted the ultimate demonstration in that long and bitter series of demonstrations of the hollowness of 'European' imperialist pretensions that had begun with Japan's defeat of Imperial Russia in 1905, had continued through the British débâcle at Singapore in 1940, and seemed now, at Suez, in 1956, more than ever conclusive because a crucial weapon was that which the Third World had made its own: moral force.

Tom Little, then the Middle East correspondent of the London *Observer*, who saw Nasser in mid-October 1956 and pointed out to him the overwhelming power ranged against him by the Anglo-French, received the reply: 'But I don't intend to fight them. I intend to stand back and wait for world opinion to save me.' In the event this—or something very like it—was what happened. 'Realists' will, of course, insist that what stopped the Anglo-French-Israeli invasion designed to 'topple Nasser' was the flight from Sterling, the cutting of Middle East oil supplies, the American refusal of credits, the Soviet threat, or simply British irresolution in attack. Certainly some of these things furnished the frame in which it was possible for world opinion to act. But ultimately it was the moral indignation of millions, all over the world, powerfully focused through global mass-communications with the aid of the United Nations, which was decisive. At Westminster the British House of Commons was suspended in an uproar of a sort hardly heard for a generation. The basically moral issue of 'Suez' split the British with a violence and bitterness rare in England's history. And the revulsion and anger of many in Britain was swollen by the sense of outrage in the Commonwealth. 'In the middle of the twentieth century,' wrote the

[19] While it was the French who at the last moment withdrew from the Egyptian Expedition of 1882 (to which they had earlier been committed), it was the British who withdrew from the Suez action in 1956 when the French would have persisted.

leading Pakistan newspaper, *Dawn*, 'enlightened countries like Britain and France have suddenly turned the clock back hundreds of years . . . and decided to act as self-chartered libertines of the gun and bomb.'[20]

Anthony Nutting, the British Minister of State who resigned over Suez, has testified how deeply the censure of the Commonwealth and the United States was felt by Prime Minister Eden, and how 'gravely anxious' he was about Britain's isolation in the United Nations. The causes of the British irresolution were not technical but moral: one day after the paratroops' landings at Port Said the British called a halt.

Suez has a claim to be considered the first war in modern history to be stopped in its tracks by the force of world opinion. It may be argued that Nasser was merely benefiting from an accident or lucky gamble. But it seems more likely that this man, so very much of his time and place, intuitively understood what was neglected by more sophisticated politicians, the power and character of the ideas at work in the world of the 1950s, and this, and his nerve in mobilising them in the construction of a sort of global morality drama of unprecedented dimensions should ensure for him, if nothing else does, a place in history.

The British had lost faith in their 'mission'; the Arabs had regained faith in theirs. For a brief dream-like moment the Suez Canal, that famous 'jugular vein' of Empire, pulsed wildly with the rising hopes of the disinherited of the Third World. On a visit to London at the time of the Canal's seizure, the former Regent of Iraq, the King's uncle, the Crown Prince Abdul Illah, had told Colonel Gerald de Gaury that unless the British Army intervened and toppled Nasser 'within a few weeks' it would be 'too late.' He recommended the restoration of the Egyptian Royal House since 'after long thought it was his considered opinion' that monarchy was the best for the East. But it was indeed 'too late'—within twenty months, Nuri, Prince Abdul Illah, the young King Feisal, and the whole quaintly anachronistic Anglo-Hashemite apparatus were to be engulfed in the aftertow of the great wave of populist emotion that swept across the Arab world after 'Suez.'

In the brother Hashemite kingdom of Jordan, Hussein—of

[20] *The Commonwealth and Suez*, London, 1964.

the new generation and therefore more sensitive to its ideas—
survived by himself assuming the revolutionary rôle, kicking
out Glubb, riding the tide. He was thus able, in April 1957, to
call in again the loyal Bedouin of the Arab Legion to save him,
by a quick counter-coup, from the Leftish Government brought
in by the free elections of 1956. He then broke again with
Egypt, availing himself of the protection of the British army
in the months of turmoil in 1958. At the same time King Saud,
confronted by a greater threat to his patrimony, at last
abandoned his family's old feud and made common cause with
the Hashemites.

But if the revolution halted, and old frontiers and forms
continued over much of the Middle East, this was not mainly
because of any such kingly resistance. It halted because the
ideological conflict of the Arab world was caught up in the
larger, global, ideological and power conflict of American
Capitalism and the 'International Communism' of the Eisenhower Doctrine. Under this new crusaders' banner the British
were able to drop their paratroops into Jordan and the American Fifth Fleet to land its Marines in Lebanon to 'maintain
the *status quo*' so painfully and expensively constructed between 1919 and 1949.

Yet it had been a near enough thing. Baghdad, the storm
anchor of the 'stabilising' military alliance, keystone of the
famous 'upper tier' of bastion states, had been violently swept
away. The easy-going, shabby old Middle East of the old-
fashioned Arabists and romantics, with its counterpoint of
dignity and obsequiousness, was passing and would not return.
Immensely powerful social forces had been released which
must end by re-shaping life in this critical area to the east
and south of the inland sea.

The West, unfortunately, continued to see this vast movement of ideas almost wholly in simple terms of conspiracy and
subversion—the 'machinations of Nasser.' The plotting
Egyptian military attaché, the Egyptian schoolteacher busily
undermining his Arab host-state, the incitements of Cairo
Radio, formed the staple of newspaper comment on the Middle
East. It was a dismal failure of imagination—and information
—which was to falsify Britain's relations with this vast area
through these critical years. Certainly, there was conspiracy

and subversion in plenty; they have been part of the Arab way of life since the days of the Prophet and earlier. Into the great golden sump of Beirut flowed rivers of bribe money from Egypt, from Iraq, from Saudi Arabia, and—for such objects as arms or buying favourable mention in the scores of venal newspapers—from France, Britain and the United States. But the real question was not whether there was Egyptian 'subversion,' but why that 'subversion' was so uniquely successful.

The answer, as has been suggested, was not far to seek. In the afterglow of the Canal nationalisation, those Egyptian teachers hardly needed to *preach* sedition. Nor was it only the volume—or invective—of Cairo Radio which caused it to be heeded, but the fact that it gave expression in popular idiom to a message so many of its listeners had long been waiting to hear; it went over the heads of Rulers, sheikhs, pashas, muftis, mudirs, omdas, and all their manifold Excellencies, and directly addressed the man in the bazaar and the fellah in the village. It was a unique—a revelatory—moment in Arab history. Such moments cannot last. In a few years the worm of sectarian and local prides and jealousies would again eat into the bud of the Arab Revolution, and Egyptian emissaries in other Arab lands would take on more dubious aspects. Nevertheless, in a few short years the clock of history in this critical region of the world had been turned forward, and would not be put back.

Nations, like people, are notably more perceptive about others when their material interests are not at stake. Thus in 1849 the British Foreign Minister, Lord Palmerston, was able to assure Members of Parliament that 'ideas are stronger than armies.' His reflection was prompted by watching—from the security of a powerful and industrially dominant Britain— the frantic efforts of the Holy Alliance to repress the forces which the French Revolution had released in Europe. In 1956, however, another British Prime Minister, Sir Anthony Eden, watching a not dissimilar upheaval—from the wreckage of an Empire—was confident that the situation could be briskly restored by a military 'fire-brigade.'

The fire, however, was not put out.

II

SUEZ SOLVENT

Nasser is a man of considerable, but immature, intelligence
. . . [who] lacks training and experience in many of the
things he is .dealing with.

—Sir Robert Menzies, Prime Minister of Australia, 1956

What I like about this young man (Nasser) is that he is always
willing to learn.

—Jawaharlal Nehru, Prime Minister of India, 1953

The French Revolution, starting out from the Rights of Man,
exploded into nationalism of a new and catalytic kind that
was to reshape Europe: the Arab Revolution, more than a
century later, was proceeding, so to speak, in the reverse direction, from nationalism to the Rights of Man. But in Egypt, the
epicentre of that revolution, the practical problem of clothing
those rights—and the less practical problem of defining them
—still remained unsolved. Founded on rural Egypt, the revolution, by 1956, seemed in some danger of halting there. Its
inexperienced leaders appeared to be losing their way in the
maze of obstacles confronting their programme of economic
reconstruction. 'Suez' renewed the revolution's impetus—and
it did so just in time. It heartened and challenged the Egyptian
people. It gave Egypt a central rôle in an Arab world which,
achieving a greater solidarity than ever before, had demonstrated both the possibilities of the Arab oil weapon, and the
futility of the imperialist gunboat. Most important of all,
'Suez' severed with one stroke the Levantine knot in which
Egyptian urban society and the Egyptian economy had for
more than a century been bound.

Suez created many problems, but it solved more. It removed
the immediate problem of mustering adequate political support for the revolutionary régime. With bombs and shells falling on Egyptian soil, even the régime's enemies rallied around,
and the young felt the stirrings of a patriotism which trans-

cended the old excitements both of nationalism and political faction. In battered Port Said the students shifted rubble with their hands, clearing space for the new Port Said of 'popular' flat-blocks that rose from ruins. These, too, were the months in which Nasser overcame his inhibitions sufficiently to play the rôle of popular revolutionary leader: in his Canal nationalising speech he put aside for the first time his lecturing manner, and broke, at the climax, into that vernacular Egyptian-Arabic idiom the crowds loved to hear. And if he remained for the most part the earnest teacher, rather than the demagogue, events had now confirmed him in the larger rôle; the fellahin began to speak with pride and proprietorship of the Ra'is (President).

In mid-1956, the régime had formally civilianised itself. At Cabinet level the civilian technocratic element—the ex-professors and the doctors, the Ph.D.s from Harvard, the London School of Economics, the Sorbonne—had in fact had an important rôle from the early days. Now these Ministers moved into somewhat greater prominence and the officers either discarded rank and uniform, or returned to the army. Although the realities of internal power remained little changed, it had become possible by mid-1957 to hold the first national elections since the coup under a new constitution with an American-type Presidential executive and a single political organisation, the National Union, to which all candidates for the National Assembly had to belong. Although an over-zealous officers' committee (theoretically 'National Union')[1] rejected 40 per cent of the numerous candidates offering themselves, there were still many lively contests in which a thousand candidates contested 350 seats, and second ballots were needed in two-thirds of the constituencies. Among others, the former judge, Ahmed Fuad, Nasser's celebrated Leftist adviser, was defeated—by a woman schoolteacher, one of the two women deputies who were elected, the first in Egyptian history.

In the four crowded years since the coup the revolutionary

[1] Having only just been invented, the National Union was in fact not yet organised at this time and the arrangements were improvised. Meanwhile the requirement of a £E50 deposit—an unimaginative carry-over from the old system—in effect largely excluded workers and small fellahin.

régime had displayed a sense of mission, a sustained purpose, not before seen in any Egyptian or Arab government. But if the officers' own social instincts had guided them in breaking the impasse on the land reform, those instincts could do little to realise their ambitious plans for industrialisation and urban social justice. Here they had almost everything to learn. In 1956 the new factories—the industrial foundation necessary to break out of the Malthusian vicious circle—still remained largely on paper.

The régime had sought to fulfil its industrialisation plan by appealing to foreign capital and to the material interests of the rich pasha class it had lately removed from the political power. An early basic theory was that the land reform would itself serve these ends by freeing large amounts of private wealth, previously sunk in the land, and diverting them into industrial enterprise. The most 'socialist' form, at this time, was the mixed company; for the pioneer integrated iron and steel works at Helwan, private investors were invited to subscribe £E3½ million of the capital, while the State put up £E5 million, and the German designers, Demag, £E2 million.

Because of its special glamour, the steel share issue was, in fact, fully subscribed. The idea of a transfer of personal capital from the land into industry was not altogether outlandish: something of the sort had happened in modernising Japan. But if there were reasons in the unique history and structure of Japan why such a thing could spectacularly happen there, equally there were reasons in the unique history and structure of Egypt (quite apart from the alarms of the 1952-4 political revolution) why any practicable policy of inducements must fall far short of the country's need.

If backward, the economy of Japan was at least national. The economy of Egypt was colonial; but it was not *merely* colonial (which might have permitted relatively straightforward control or transfer): it was Colonial-Levantine, the product of the curious but fecund union of Constantinople and Manchester. Its origin lay in the venerable device known as 'the Capitulations' by which the Ottoman Sultans contrived to enjoy some of the advantages of Western trade and enterprise without suffering contaminating contact with such ungentlemanly pursuits. The Chinese Emperors, in a similar situation, restricted extraterritoriality to the minute areas in which they penned the Foreign Barbarians. The Sultan-Caliphs' solution was less tidy. They would freely admit the businessmen of various foreign nations, but they would not 'see' them. Thus, the infidels paid no taxes, were subject to no regulations, and were policed, if at all, by their own consuls only. Naturally, the Capitulation treaties often provided for an 'open door' to the manufactures of the West (it was this provision which had wrecked the native infant Egyptian industries of Mohamed Ali).

The prospects of profit held out by such a licensed free-for-all were nowhere more mouth-watering than in Egypt where they had been enlarged under the British administration by the necessary modicum of order. And although, as an administrator, Lord Cromer might deplore the conscientious maintenance (until 1914) of the legal fiction of Turkish suzerainty over Egypt, in fact the Capitulatory system chimed well with the Manchester religion of Free Trade and the doctrine of a natural economic hierarchy of nations—in which Egypt's rôle was clearly seen to be that of Lancashire's cotton plantation and market. If, for revenue purposes, an import duty was imposed on foreign manufactures entering Egypt, it had to be balanced by excise duties on parallel domestic production. The consequence was that although Egypt had woven cotton for thousands of years, and now grew cotton in such excellence and abundance, until 1930 only 1 per cent of Egypt's cotton crop was spun in Egypt; and even in 1938, the proportion had only reached 5 per cent.

It was not, in fact, until 1930 that Egypt was able to break out of this archaic frame to the extent of minor protection for her own industries; and it was 1937 before the demolition of the Capitulations (which Turkey herself had abolished in 1923) was begun. The last relic of the system, the Mixed Courts, did not disappear until 1949.

The result was that in 1952 the new régime had inherited an Egypt formed in a curiously distorted economic pattern over which it could exercise little control. The revolution might eclipse the pashas in rural Egypt, but the pashas and beys and effendis of the city appeared indestructible, men of origins infinitely diverse, yet all born again in the golden

baptism of the Nile, and, in 1956, still to be encountered gazing complacently out of the crowded pages of *Le Mondain
Egyptien* (a Who's Who to which admission was, characteristically, by application form plus £2 subscription) for all the
world as if the word 'revolution' had never been uttered.
Foreign banks and insurance companies and merchant houses
dominated the scene; until 1951 there was not even the sem-
blance of an Egyptian Central Bank with the key governmental function of controlling the volume of credit. Such an
exercise would indeed have seemed almost an impertinence
in a society so long dedicated, without distinction of nationality, to all the swifter and more intangible processes by which
money fructifies in the pockets of those who already possess
it.

Historically, this towering but narrow-based structure of
wealth began in the commercial canyons of Alexandria, paved
with white gold and walled by foreign brokerage houses, but
Cairo continued the process of levitation with its glittering
department stores raised by French and Swiss Jews and agile
Lebanese, and the smaller but solid pharmacies and photographic stores of the Armenians and the cafés and groceries
of the Greeks. Lebanese like the Lutfallahs, Syrians like the
Chourbagis, even British concerns like Bradford Dyers, had a
large part in the growing textile industry. In this more modern
and constructive way, the most enterprising entrepreneurs
were probably the Greeks and the Jews. The Greeks gave Egypt
a wine industry, a fine worsted factory; the first steel made in
Egypt (from scrap) was made in 1949 at the Alexandria Copper
Works, founded in 1936 by Sigmund Hirsch, a German Jew.

Such men as these did Egypt, technically, good service, yet,
foreigners in a foreign-dominated economy, they also made
her all the less mistress of her own house. When Egyptians
entered the business picture, as they increasingly did, it was
often in a mere comprador rôle—as intermediaries or figure-
heads. Ex-Ministers, pashas, high civil servants were handy
and looked well on the foreign boards. Farouk himself had a
large stake in Pepsi-Cola (which from the company's point of
view usefully resulted in the Grand Mufti's *fetwa* declaring
that cola drinks contained nothing contrary to the Koran).
These 'business' Egyptians were in fact a stage army. Some

held as many as forty directorships. A check in 1948-9 revealed that less than a third of the directors of 'Egyptian' joint stock companies were Muslim Egyptians; it was estimated that only 4 per cent of the entire Egyptian middle class (then put at 6 per cent of the population) were businessmen. The Stock Exchange was wholly dominated by foreigners and minorities; the share capital of the central bank, the National Bank of Egypt, was mainly held by non-Egyptians; the tall new buildings of Cairo belonged to international insurance companies, just as the satellite town of Heliopolis belonged to a Belgian real estate company, and Alexandria's Smouha City to a cotton magnate of British nationality and Palestine Jewish origin. In such a setting, now blending the gregariousness of the old Levant and the internationalism of modern capitalism, nationality indeed seemed almost irrelevant.

It was either a fantastic anachronism—or before its time. Either way, the novice Egyptian planner, nibbling his *Glace Horreya* (Independence ice-cream) in Groppi's (Swiss-owned) restaurant, or sipping his coffee on the Semiramis verandah (like all major—and most minor—hotels, foreign-owned) might be forgiven if he experienced a certain desperation as he contemplated the disproportion between the scale and urgency of his task and the means available to him to accomplish it. The national plan required the development of consumer industries to replace the many often simple articles formerly imported; and with the aid of the foreign exchange thus conserved, it proposed the extension of Egypt's heavy industrial base, utilising local raw materials and developing the metal-using industries. With an initial home market of perhaps two million consumers, the first activity—short of the granting of private, highly protected monopolies—was rarely likely to produce the sort of return on capital that would tempt a Levantine businessman; dividends from the second would be even slower to appear. In 1955, according to the Federation of Egyptian Industries, of the £E55 millions released from the land by the agrarian reform, only £E6 millions found its way into industry. The rest went to feed a luxury apartment building boom in Cairo and Alexandria.

Cul-de-sac

The régime had to work with what it had. With business-men sitting on its committees, the National Production Council planned a variety of projects—a paper factory, a tyre factory, a car-battery factory, a fertiliser plant—in co-operation with both Egyptian and foreign private enterprise.

Predictably prominent among the personalities involved at this stage was the celebrated Ahmed Abboud Pasha, probably the only Egyptian who really rated the title of 'Captain of Industry.' Graduated as a civil engineer in Glasgow, married to a Scotswoman, Abboud had made money in railway construction in the Middle East, had bought into Egypt's French-owned sugar refineries, and had gone on, via technical expertise, financial acumen, hard work and the friendship of the Palace, to build an industrial and financial empire which included the Khedival Steamship Line and the Suez fertiliser plant, a chemicals company, textile mills, hotels, an insurance company, merchant houses. Many Egyptians admired his drive and enterprise. Many, too, admired his toughness: for he was a hire-and-fire Boss in the old industrial tradition that still survived in the Orient—a Pasha as well as a manager—exacting subservience, making inordinate profits, and paying his labourers the lowest possible wage.

If it was inevitable that the régime should seek to work out its plans through such as Abboud (it planned a paper factory project with him), it was equally inevitable that such a marriage could not last. Not only did Abboud belong essentially to the unconfined, non-national world of Levantine finance, but the small protected market of the Nile Valley and the Oriental tradition alike tended to monopoly—and the absolutism that goes with it. Abboud was, in fact, a text-book example of that 'control of capital over the system of government,' which the revolutionary régime was pledged, by a third of its Six Principles, to eradicate. He sought to impose his own prices for domestic sugar and fertiliser; unbiddable, he refused to pay the Government's scheduled cost-of-living allowance to his workers. In mid-1956, a long battle of wits ended with the sequestration of Abboud's sugar and associated distillery interests—officially for having tax arrears of £E5 millions and failing to hold shareholders' meetings. The Government thereupon took up a 51 per cent holding in the reorganised, but still capitalist, joint stock company.

The régime was now embarked on a course in which it was seeking to tame and harness, in Roosevelt's phrase, its 'Economic Royalists.' A law compelling the retirement of directors at sixty obliquely succeeded in removing a large batch of holders of multiple directorships, thus theoretically weakening their economic power. But even if the bit could be got between the horse's teeth, it was still not possible to force it to gallop as required. The régime, in short, was headed for that impasse which normally confronts would-be revolutionaries who attempt to realise their new world through the employment of the incumbents of the old one.

Talaat Harb's Signpost

Fortunately, Abboud's was not by this time the only Egyptian industrial 'tradition.' The beginnings of a way out of the Levantine impasse had already been charted. In 1920 a well-to-do Egyptian of Turkish parentage, named Talaat Harb, had founded the Misr Bank with the avowed nationalist aim of mobilising Egyptian savings to establish a purely Egyptian industry. Its initial capital was only £E80,000, but seven years later—still the only wholly Egyptian bank in the country—it was able to launch its first project—the Misr Spinning and Weaving Company in the old textile town of Mehalla el Kobra in mid-Delta. Many difficulties had to be surmounted, and the new mill did not start production until 1931 —with second-hand machinery from Lancashire. But from there Misr Bank went on to father a shipping line, a hotel company, a printing works, an airline and, in 1934, the biggest and best-equipped film studios in Egypt.

Its most notable foundation was less tangible: a progressive and modern industrial tradition. In the Misr textile establishments the old Islamic paternalism was married to 20th-century welfare and professionalised management. In order to transform the fellahin into steady, time-clock-punching industrial workers the Misr Company built a works village at Mehalla, added medical services, hospital, clubs, vast canteens, swimming baths, stadia—the whole, significantly, enclosed within a white wall. Promising young graduates were recruited for managerial posts and sent to France, Britain and the U.S.A. for long periods of study and training. They were then moved around the Misr textile group—and despatched on yet more overseas study tours. There was emphasis on the latest techniques and machines, and latterly, on scientific quality control.

By 1955 there were twenty-seven Misr companies in various fields with a paid-up capital of £E20 millions. The Misr textile companies produced half the nation's rapidly expanding textile output, and were now widening their range. In 1944, ploughing back their wartime profits, they had opened the second unit of a new 'fine-counts' complex at Kafr el Dawar, and in 1947, under American tutelage, the first rayon plant in the Arab world. By this time, the large managerial corps was almost wholly Egyptian, forming a notable addition to the older body of agricultural and irrigation engineers who were among the nation's earlier assets.

The revolutionary régime certainly had good reason to rename a central street in Cairo after Talaat Harb. Yet if the Misr companies had provided an outline of the industrial structural foundation it needed, the Misr Bank's financing approach, still depending largely on private capital, was no longer adequate to either the scale or the character of the country's need—even when supplemented by the Industrial Bank (51 per cent Government-owned) in 1949 and by the Revolution's own foundation, the Republic Bank. For, numerous as were Egypt's commercial banks, and massive as were the concentrations of wealth of some of their depositors, they were little concerned with financing industrial development. To break out of the tightening Malthusian circle, and have any prospect of achieving a decent standard of living for the majority of her people, Egypt needed to invest a minimum of £E100 million a year (in fact, double this was to be attained in the '60s). Yet up to 1955 even the best years had not produced investment in excess of eight millions.

The Misr Group's methods had blazed a trail, but were now plainly inadequate for opening it up with the necessary speed. For the Misr Bank was no 'people's bank'; at directorate level it was the old, small, immensely wealthy club of upper-class magnates, Levantine cotton families, and a few millionaire industrialists like Abboud with their close links with foreign capital (now heavily involved in a few of the Group's leading companies). And although the Nasser régime had planted its men on the Misr Bank's controlling Board (including the Marxist Ahmed Fuad), the limitations of this Fabian approach to planning were becoming daily more apparent. Egypt had undergone a political revolution, and rural Egypt was undergoing a social revolution; what was needed now if the plan of industrial reconstruction was not to be stillborn was an economic revolution. Yet even if this had been fully appreciated in the spring of 1956, in this Levantine, hydra-headed commercial society it was hard to see how such a revolution could be brought about.

The Alchemy of Suez

History shows war—even an eight-day 'Suez Crisis' war—to be the greatest revolutionary of them all. In accordance with normal practice, the large and crucial British, French and Jewish assets in Egypt were sequestered at the start of the hostilities. Enemy aliens, British, French and many Jews —who had rarely been Zionists but were now Zionism's tragic victims—were deported, including the staffs of the French and British schools which had constituted a sort of British-model public-school system for the wealthier classes.

The war having thus started—as nothing else could—the process of melting the levantine amalgam which was the Egyptian economy, it became possible in mid-January 1957 to issue the Egyptianisation decrees directing that *all* foreign banks, insurance companies and sales agencies should be transferred to Egyptian shareholders and directors within the next five years. A month later a further decree required Arabic to be used in all business records and documents—and the departure of the Greeks, Italians and other foreign residents grew apace. Many had lived in Egypt most of their lives, but had never taken out Egyptian citizenship.

Set up in January 1957, the Economic Development Organisation, now not only supervised those concerns in which the Egyptian Government had taken up a large shareholding, but also took under its wing the companies sequestered and Egyptianised as a result of Suez. The resulting public organisation, which was somewhat on the lines of Italy's Institute for Industrial Reconstruction, could now proceed to digest, direct and rationalise development over the whole range. The General Manager was an army engineer, Sidky Suleiman, later to be Minister of the High Dam, later still Prime Minister; and other officers, civilianised, were brought in to try to fill the many managerial gaps that had now appeared. It is obvious that the chaos must have been considerable, but the final result was that the Egyptian Government gained control over a large area of the economy. By 1960 the Economic Organisation's investment totalled £E20 millions and its affiliated firms produced one-third of the output of industry.

Thus if, in the short term, the Suez war and the longer economic siege which accompanied it cost Egypt dear, endangering her vital cotton trade[2] and setting back her industrialisation programme by denuding her of hard currency, on a longer view the service rendered was inestimable. The Suez war found a Levantine urban society and economy, unaccountable and long dedicated to the pursuit of the quick turn, and it transmuted it into a national economy, shaky and vestigial in many respects, yet with the necessary foundations now beginning to emerge, cleared of the worst of the debris. The national emergency not only made it politically possible to maintain price controls, the rationing of basic necessities and so on, but it also put the Egyptian people on its mettle. With the eyes of the world upon them, they were challenged to accept new responsibilities in many areas. They grew by doing so.

The Canal itself—which the British had told the world would collapse into chaos under Egyptian control—had at first to be kept in operation with a pilot force much less than half normal strength—with forty-seven Greeks and twenty-eight Egyptians. The former Canal Company had restricted Egyptian pilots to vessels of 16,000 tons or less—and experienced

---

[2] As a result of Suez, almost 70 per cent of Egypt's cotton exports were going to Communist countries by 1958, in return for a far less flexible range of barter goods than could be obtained in wider international dealings. It took some years to get back to an open world market.

Egyptian operating staff was no less scarce. They worked long hours, put their hands to every job, rushed about the Canal, slept on camp beds in their offices. 'It was like a battle, really,' one of them recalled, with some pride.

Again, Nasser had picked the right man to direct the job, another engineer officer—Colonel Mahmoud Younis, with whom he had once shared an office when both had been tutors at the Staff College. A graduate engineer, a quiet, competent man, who had already served on the National Production Council, on the Petroleum Authority, and in the Ministry of Industry, Younis was an outstanding member of the revolution's 'new class' and he set out to make this key institution, the Suez Canal Authority, the brightest monument to the new Egyptian managerialism.

At the Canal's southern extremity the Egyptian employees of the Shell Oil Company's Suez Refinery faced a hardly less strenuous challenge. After the Canal Company, Shell—Anglo-Egyptian Oilfields—was probably the most important foreign concern in Egypt. Its approach, though, was progressive, and science-based. As one Egyptian put it: 'If in the Canal Company we were kept fifteen degrees below the salt, in Shell it might be only one or two degrees.' The company ran an employee development department for bringing on local executives, and a well-equipped craft-training school. Two of its employees, a sales manager and a fitter (both union officials) became Ministers in Nasser's Government.

Like the Misr Group, like the Canal Company, the Anglo-Egyptian Oil Company offered an excellent industrial foundation on which to build, and the Suez war, with the hurried departure of the British staff, amounted to an urgent invitation to get on with it. With many difficulties and much improvisation they did get on with it; the tankers continued to bring in their oil cargoes from the small Red Sea fields and from Sinai; output in due course resumed its upward climb, and the Egyptians were able to claim that their oil industry, which had been the earliest in the Arab world, was also the first to be Arab-run.

Through the years of travail that followed both the Canal with its mounting traffic and revenues, and the oil industry, which, under the control of the General Petroleum Organisation founded in 1956, had arranged numerous exploration agreements with foreign oil companies, continued to underpin the developing economy and to offer solid hope for the future. By 1961, over half the Canal's 230 pilots were Egyptians; by 1965, two-thirds, and almost the whole of the administrative and operating staff. In 1964, a 112,000-ton tanker, the *Manhattan*, passed through the deepened Canal, a single trip that earned Egypt £E27,000 in hard currency for dues. In the ten years after the take-over the tonnage of ships passing through the Canal doubled, revenue rising year by year. At Port Saïd, deep-water quays and new shipbuilding yards were constructed; at Ismailia, the Authority's new thirteen-storey office block and a fine hydraulics research centre arose on the shores of Lake Timsah, towering over the verandahed French Colonial-style buildings as if to symbolise the triumph of nationalism which was now, paradoxically, also the triumph of inter-national technocracy.

This still lay a little way in the future, but at the end of 1957 Dr Aziz Sidky, head of the newly formed Ministry of Industry, announced Egypt's first Five Year Industrialisation Plan. A former university teacher, graduate of Oregon State University and Harvard, an engineer and town-planner, the energetic Dr Sidky was another of Nasser's discoveries. His plan proposed to raise industry's contribution to the national income from 11 per cent to 19 per cent with an investment of £E300 million. Flying to Moscow, General Abdel Hakim Amer negotiated a £E61 million credit; the West Germans, East Germans and Japanese provided others; and Dr Sidky set up an Organisation for Industrialisation to get on with the job.

There was another not unimportant service which 'Suez' had performed for Egypt. In his book about Russia, Laurens van der Post makes the comment that a nation cannot be con-sidered mature until it can debunk its own myths. But it is equally true that it cannot *be* a nation until it has adequate myths to debunk. Hitherto the national myths of modern Egyptians, a people submerged for centuries, had been myths of defiance and defeat—Omar Makram, a sheikh against Napoleon; Arabi on his white horse, a stirring image, but an Arabi, also, alas, in flight from Tel el Kebir; Zaghloul, whisper-

ing on his death-bed 'There is no hope,' a sepulchral echo on
a million lips. But now, in 1956, there had been born a potent
myth of global dimensions, the myth of the Imperialist Goliath
felled by an Egyptian David, the champion of the Arabs, at
Port Said. It was true that the new army had not on the whole
emerged well from the overwhelming attacks launched on
several fronts against Egypt. Vast amounts of military equipment had been lost; many officers had been dismissed with
ignominy. But in Port Said students and mere children, furnished with rifles by the enterprising Russian Consul, had
fought in the streets; and presently, the Cause having prevailed,
Victory Day could be added to Republic Day and Evacuation
Day in the lengthening litany of national occasion. Henceforward every school had its fresco of arms defiantly upraised
in the burning ruins of Port Said; every factory or office wall-
newspaper contained its ritual salute to the Martyrs of Port
Said.

If in the development of the revolution the phase of improvisation was still far from being over, at least by late 1957,
thanks to the Suez intervention, the logic of the situation was
beginning to emerge. Although the major finance for the High
Dam was still not settled, five miles south of Aswan they had
begun to blast the first roads in the granite. The pioneering
National Production Council of 1952 now finally gave way
to the professional National Planning Commission. From
almost no control over the economy, the Government was,
almost despite itself, moving towards total control and was
beginning to forge the necessary instruments. A new Constitution, an elected National Assembly, and the nucleus of a
national political organisation were in being.

Under the Constitution, the President was nominated by
the Assembly, then elected by nation-wide plebiscite; he could
veto acts of the Assembly, which, in turn, could overturn his
veto by a two-thirds majority vote. And although no contest
of this bracing variety was remotely likely, this first post-
Revolution Assembly had, nevertheless, once or twice taken
the bit between its teeth—as, for instance, when it forced an
inquiry into the extravagances in Liberation Province. An
earnest of democratic intentions had been given, but it was

evident to all in 1957 that events were moving too swiftly to allow much margin for leisurely debate; in the event, the Union with Syria was to cut short the life of Egypt's first Republican Assembly within the year.

The new Constitution set out in its Preamble the Six Goals of the Revolution. It was a ritual echo of the six principles of the Free Officers' leaflets, but the goals were no more clearly defined than before. 'The establishment of a sound democratic society'—that presumably was implied in the Constitution itself and in the National Assembly that had followed. The Land Reform (reaffirmed in Article 12) had certainly been a long step towards the 'extinction of feudalism.' And Article 16 advocated co-operative organisation. Otherwise, save for a clause postulating free schooling and social insurance, there was little to show how 'the establishment of Social Justice' or 'the eradication of the control of capitalistic influences over Government' were to be secured.

Such answers as were beginning to take shape were emerging under the pressure of events from the logic of the situation, rather than from any revolutionary doctrine. It was the régime's need for allies against the counter-revolution that had encouraged it to institutionalise the trade unions and enhance labour's status; the conflict with Abboud had clarified the implications of the 'control of capital' in a country such as Egypt; 'the eradication of all aspects of imperialism' had been memorably speeded by the riposte to Nuri and to Dulles.

But the sequel of the Anglo-French-Israeli 'Suez' attack of 1956 had been the 'Egyptianisation' of the businesses concerned, not their socialisation, much less socialism. Dr Kaissouni, the LSE-trained Finance Minister, had appealed to Egyptian investors to take up shares in the sequestered or Egyptianising foreign companies. Only when they failed to do so in sufficient number was it accepted that this was still a cul-de-sac, and that the State would have to step in.

On his return from Bandung in April 1955 Nasser had spoken of the Revolution as aiming 'at creating a Socialist society without class distinction.' But although the word 'socialism' was now occasionally heard, there are few signs that more was intended than the contemporary 'anti-colonial' costume

for the Rights of Man. In its first five years the Egyptian Revolution had lost some of its naïveté, but it still lacked an
economic system and a unifying ideology. At the end of 1957
Nasser's public anticipation of a 'socialist, democratic and co-
operative society' shows him still groping towards one. But
for its full emergence the revolution would again have to wait
upon the events it had set in train. As the Americans stepped
into the gap left by the eclipse of Britain and France, 1958
had brought no diminution in the external political pressures, no cooling down. If 'Suez' had made possible the economic re-possession of Egypt by Egyptians, the union with Syria
was to bring Egypt to the full espousal of Arab Socialism.

12

ORONTES INTO NILE

Syria is a battleground. Owing to its geographical position it is an area where for centuries the dialectic of the Near East and the West has been fought out in ideas and arms.

—Robin Fedden, *Syria* (1946)

I know that the stab of an enemy may wound the body but will not wound the heart. But the stab of a friend tears the heart more than it tears the body. I know this because I have felt it.

—Gamal Abdel Nasser on the Syrian defection from the U.A.R.

In March 1958 Gamal Abdel Nasser, President-Elect of the new-born United Arab Republic of Egypt and Syria, addressed a vast wildly cheering crowd from a balcony in Damascus: 'As I see my brothers from Lebanon standing side by side with their brothers from the region of Syria and Egypt, I feel I am witnessing the return of matters to their normal course. The artificial boundaries that have been put up by Imperialism between the Arab countries cannot estrange us.' A few days earlier Nasser had telegraphed his congratulations to King Feisal II on the conclusion of the federation of the Hashemite kingdoms of Iraq and Jordan, 'a blessed step towards greater unity.' The Crown Prince of Yemen had hurried to sign a pact of confederation with the new-born United Arab Republic, and the veteran Syrian national leader, President Shukri el Kuwatly, had expressed his belief that not only Iraq and Jordan, but also Saudi Arabia, Libya and Tunisia and Algeria would shortly be joining the U.A.R. to complete at last that splendid, long dreamed-of edifice, 'the Arab Nation.'

The sixty-seven-year-old Shukri el Kuwatly—although more lately the Saudi family's agent in Syria—had been a leading member of *Al Fatat*, the conspiratorial Young Arab society founded by seven Muslim students in Paris in 1911. He had been a member of Feisal I's first Arab Government in that bleak Arab dawn in Damascus in 1919. He had been imprisoned both by the Turks and by the French who succeeded them. He may well have believed what he said. But although to Arab ears the rhetoric had its own self-sufficient poetic truth, the reality was sadly otherwise. For history, a great joker in these parts, had played no more bitter joke than this: the long-awaited Arab unions, when at last they came, were unions of desperation in a collapsing universe, a line-up of hostile camps in an Arab confrontation, first prematurely forced, then distorted and halted, by the alien, global cold war. For the immense pressures generated in the Arab world by Suez had been heightened in its sequel, as the Americans, rushing into the 'vacuum' supposedly left by the Anglo-French withdrawal, pressed on the Arab capitals the Eisenhower Doctrine with its offer of military aid and funds to all who would take the pledge to resist the encroachments of 'International Communism.'

At the end of 1956 the Americans had officially registered concern at the extent of Soviet arms shipments to Syria, now ruled by a 'progressive front'—an unstable alliance of radical officers, middle-class socialists, and old-time politicians. The Syrians replied, truly, that this did not indicate adherence to Communism, but was merely an aspect of Arab independence and 'positive neutralism.' But to the Americans developments in Syria now appeared vivid confirmation of what President Eisenhower in his New Year 1957 Message to Congress called Russia's 'announced purpose of Communising the world.'

Few Arabs saw it that way; the only leaders in the Arab East who unequivocally accepted the Eisenhower Doctrine's offers were the 'reactionary' Nuri es-Said in Iraq, and Camille Chamoun, the Christian President of the Lebanon, who had already imperilled his country's delicate East-West, Muslim-Christian equilibrium by refusing to break with France and Britain after Suez. However, in June Mr Ben Gurion announced Israel's adherence to the Doctrine, later writing to Dulles to urge 'strong measures to root out the danger' from the Syrian 'base for International Communism.' 'This,' Ben Gurion warned Dulles, 'might well be the last chance.'

In the post-Suez climate it was perhaps hardly surprising that to millions of Arabs the Eisenhower Doctrine increasingly looked like one more Western attempt to destroy the Arab

Revolution, now renewed, radicalised, and centred on Cairo—
the Arab capital that was omitted from the tour of the American President's Doctrine-promoting envoy. This impression
was strengthened in August when the American Assistant
Secretary of State arrived in Istanbul for a meeting with the
Kings of Iraq and Jordan and the Prime Minister of Turkey.
But for the Americans their own interpretation of events
seemed confirmed, too, when in the same month the Syrian
Minister, Khalid al-Azm, returned from Moscow with long-term
credits for industrial development; when a pro-Communist
Syrian Chief of Staff was appointed; and three American diplomats were expelled from Syria, accused (not without reason)
of conspiring with Opposition Syrians to overthrow the
régime. On Cairo Radio in September Nasser declared his
complete support for Syria, whose 'only sin' was that 'she did
not dance to the American tune.' In October, as a gesture of
solidarity, he sent a token Egyptian force to Latakia; Mr Ben
Gurion sent his Foreign Minister, Mrs Golda Meir, to meet
Dulles in Washington.

The general Arab view of America's efforts to 'stabilise the
Middle East' might, as President Eisenhower was to complain,
be 'an upside-down picture.' But this was the way it appeared
in the Arab world—and it was both confused and threatening.
In this atmosphere it was not difficult for NATO manoeuvres
in Turkey that autumn to be seen as 'hostile Turkish troop
concentrations' poised for the imminent invasion of Syria. In
the latter part of October Syria was swept by panic. Army
leave was cancelled. Arms were handed out to 'the people's
resistance movement.' Outside Aleppo and Damascus, Ministers
led the citizenry in digging trenches—although from which
direction the attack was to come remained obscure. From the
Israelis? The Russians? The Turks? The Americans? Or from
the plotting Hashemites next door, aided by those conservative Syrian politicians who saw salvation in terms of union
with Iraq?

All seemed highly possible to *some* Syrians—and it was in
this peculiarly Syrian atmosphere of mingled panic and exalta-
tion that the union with Egypt was hastily conceived and
consummated. But whatever the motivation of that union, its
proclamation in February 1958 brought the Egyptian Revolu-

tion and all it now stood for into the very heart of the Arab East, and into physical contiguity with Lebanon, Jordan and Iraq. Early effects were the defensive, retaliatory union of the Hashemite monarchies of Jordan and Iraq, and, in May, the Muslim uprising in the Lebanon which the excessive eagerness of President Chamoun's embrace of the West had long threatened. In Lebanon some hundreds were killed in street battles, but the traditional neutrality of the Lebanese army saved the state; in Iraq, however, a regiment posted to Jordan halted on its way through Baghdad to overthrow the monarchical government, and, as in Egypt in 1952—and for similar reasons—none raised a hand to save it. But in contrast to the Cairo coup, which left the apparatus of government largely intact and disturbed Egypt's basic continuity remarkably little, the Baghdad revolt was bloody and destructive. As the revolution moved beyond the tolerant Nile Valley—the land of *malish!* —its cost was visibly rising.

The Eisenhower Doctrine had been duly invoked by President Chamoun. Fifty warships of the U.S. Sixth Fleet had stood off the Lebanon coast as the Marines landed. British paratroops had dropped on Jordan. But if, here, the old frontiers had held, anyone who thought the *status quo* truly restored was deluded. By harshly illuminating the division between the old and new forces at work in the Arab world, the Eisenhower Doctrine had accelerated and rendered more anarchic a revolution it had been designed to contain.

Although the new Iraq Republican Constitution promptly declared Iraq 'an integral part of the Arab nation,' the revolution there was to remain, like the country, peripheral. The Nile had—briefly—flowed into the Tigris, but the Tigris held its remote and wilder course. But the union of the two Mediterranean Arab lands, Egypt and Syria, in the turbulent three and a half years which it lasted, began a dialogue, set in motion a train of action and reaction, which was to have a profound effect on the character of the Egyptian Revolution and on the future of the Arab world. If the Nile flowed into the Orontes, the Orontes flowed back into the Nile.

The link-up of the two countries was by no means so outlandish as it seemed to those Westerners—and they were the majority—whose maps of the Middle East began in 1920—or, worse, in 1949 with the state of Israel athwart the historic land route between Cairo and Damascus. A longer perspective would have shown the 'United Arab Republic' as only one more chapter in a long relationship—of mutual irritation and mutual benefit—stretching down the centuries into remote antiquity. The north-eastern coastal strip—by which the armies of Islam passed from Syria to conquer Egypt—forms the natural hinge linking the Nile Valley in North Africa and the Arab East, and on at least eight occasions Syria and Egypt have been formally united. On the last of these, between 1831 and 1840, under the rule of Mohammed Ali's son, Ibrahim, the modernisation of Syria may be said to have begun. Ottoman stagnation was replaced by brisker government, 'Christians and Jews were treated as equals of Muslims (as in Egypt), trade and agriculture were promoted, government schools founded, Westernising influences welcomed.'[1]

Although this union also ended in Syrian revolt, some of its fruits were, in a curious way, gathered half a century later when the young Arab nationalists of Beirut,[2] persecuted by the Turks, took refuge in Egypt where Turkish sovereignty was merely nominal. The highly developed Egyptian press of today owes much to the early journalistic enterprise of these Syrians and Lebanese. For the agile Syrian, particularly the Syrian Christian, the noblest prospect in Syria—to paraphrase Dr Johnson—was the road to Cairo, where because of their more modern education (the effect of the activity of French, American, and other missionary schools), and greater flexibility, the British found them so useful in the Administration that in 1890, despite strong Egyptian protests, they enacted a law allowing the Syrian fifteen years resident in Egypt to be admitted to the public service on the same terms as Egyptians.

In an ideal world, the union of the two countries in the 1950s would have made a good deal of sense, for though so

[1] Professor Wayne S. Vucinich : *The Ottoman Empire* (1965).
[2] Beirut was at this time the chief town of one of the three *vilayets* (provinces) of Ottoman Syria; Lebanon was the tiny autonomous enclave of Maronite-populated Mount Lebanon under a Christian Governor and Western Powers protection since 1860, and much smaller than present-day Lebanon. Thus the term 'Syrian' should here be read in the comprehensive sense and taken to include many who would today be 'Lebanese.'

vastly different, they were also in many ways complementary. Egypt, with twenty-seven million people, was chronically short of land and wheat; Syria, with a mere four and a half millions, had twenty times as much arable land per head of farm population and a fast-growing grain surplus. Egypt had a substantial technological class, particularly agriculturalists; Syria had few —in 1953 only one trained research agronomist, and not a single Faculty of Agriculture. Egyptians have durability, but tend to be ponderous and over-schematic (of European peoples they most resemble the Germans—but Bavarians, not Prussians!). The more sensitive, quicker-witted, but humourless and over-excitable Syrians could—in theory—supply a useful leavening, much as the Celts do for the English, while the joint ship would sail better for the Egyptian ballast. Egypt's great strength is a stability which comes from her basic cultural cohesion; Syria's curse is her extreme volatility, the ceaseless fission of her many worlds. A generation earlier, T. E. Lawrence, out of bitter experience, had written: 'Only by the intrusion of a factor founded on some outward power of non-Syrian basis can the dissident tendencies of the sects and peoples of Syria be reined in sufficiently to prevent destructive anarchy.'

Until 1946, the French had provided that outward power. With their departure the 'national front' linking family and clan and sect, feudal and commercial interest, city and city in the common resistance to the Occupier quickly disintegrated. 1949 saw no fewer than three military coups in Damascus. The new Syrian national army, now attracting politically-conscious secondary-school graduates, became a forcing-house both of political ambition and of those heady ideologies which seem to draw some special nutrient from Syrian soil. As the *Parti Populaire Syrien* of the 'thirties with its 'Great Syria' aspirations was followed in the 'forties by the Baath Socialist Party, with its hardly less apocalyptic vision of One Arab Nation, Syria acquired in the 1954 elections the first Communist parliamentary deputy in the entire Arab world—in the person of an able Kurd named Khaled Bakdash.

By 1957, the traditionalist upper-class which had sought Arab Unity (and Syrian security) in union with Iraq were counter-balanced by younger, Leftist elements who found these things—*plus* modernity and 'progress'—in union with Nasser's new, triumphant and now avowedly 'socialist' Egypt. These mounting internal tensions were heightened in classic fashion as the global powers to East and West confronted each other across the Syrian Desert in a power conflict which echoed on a different, but no less strident, note the struggle of Nasser and Nuri. The American intervention had strengthened the hitherto weak Syrian Communist party, so that the 'liberal' Baath socialists now felt under threat from both sides.

New Year 1958 found the Syrian delirium at its height. As plot was piled on plot, and rumour succeeded rumour, Syria seemed to tremble on the verge of disintegration. To those on the Left unattracted to Russia, Nasser's Egypt seemed to offer the best—perhaps the only—hope for the future. A number of Syrian army officers had prepared the way. Now, at the end of January, like some masterful parent, General Afifi al Bizri, Syria's Leftist Chief of Staff, loaded the Syrian Cabinet on to a plane and flew them to Cairo in order to make sure that the rather hesitant betrothal of recent weeks should be succeeded without delay by the unquestionable bonds of matrimony.

But if, this time, it was the Syrians who had chosen the 'outward power' that was to save them from themselves, this was, in the circumstances, to prove a dubious advantage. For although there was already theoretically in being a joint military command under the Arab Defence Pact of 1955—and there had been earlier talk of federation—any true voluntary union of Syria and Egypt would clearly have required a lengthy period of preparation. It was too late now for that; however grandly named, this was in fact a rescue operation.

There seems little doubt that Nasser recognised the dangers; but in practice he had little choice. The best he could do was to try to safeguard himself, to try to pinion the drowning man's flailing arms. If, as the Syrian socialists—for their own advancement—insisted, it must be a full merger, then it should be on Nasser's terms: the Syrian army must retire from politics, and the feverish contest of the Syrian political factions must cease. In the event there were four Vice-Presidents, equally divided between the two countries, now the 'Northern' and 'Southern' Regions; but the U.A.R. President appointed the

Cabinet and, initially, both central and regional legislatures. In February the Syrian parties were officially dissolved, to be replaced in due course by an Egyptian-style 'National Union' organisation to which the Syrian people were to elect representatives on a nation-wide basis.

These over-schematic arrangements, in due course, killed whatever chances the union might have had. But these, in truth, were slender—for the project was riddled with confusions and contradictions from the start, many of them springing from the character and pretensions of its principal Syrian protagonists, the Baath Socialists.

The Baath (Rebirth) Socialist Party, which was to be the source of much ferment in the Arab East, had been founded in the early 'forties by two Sorbonne-educated Syrian teachers on the staff of the Damascus *lycée*, the one Muslim by birth, the other a Christian and former Communist. Baath Socialism was the curious, very Syrian, offspring of a marriage of Marxism, Christianity, and residual Islam, a heady mixture of Gallic intellectualism and Arab poetry and metaphysics. While it ardently espoused socialism and democracy, its potent core lay in an apocalyptic vision of Arab Unity, a mystic and immaculate rebirth of 'the Arab Nation with its Eternal Mission' (its slogan) which would give rise to that moral regeneration indispensable to the creation of the Socialist society.

Superficially, in their programmes, Baathism and Nasserism had much in common and the Baath leaders could thus both envy, and, as the senior Arab Socialists, claim proprietary rights in, Nasser's triumph. But both in origin and spirit, the movements were widely different, accurately reflecting the contrasting characters of the nations which gave them birth. For whereas the Syrians had been true cosmopolitans ever since Juvenal complained that the Orontes ran slickly into the Tiber, the well-polished shoes on the Cairo boulevards contained the feet of Nile Valley peasants. The Egyptian officers, starting out with a few simple actions, strong native instincts, and a formidable practical problem, had reached their subsequent programme empirically, under the pressure of events. The Syrian Baath leaders, by contrast, had started out by producing an ideology, embracing it with such fervour that they could scarcely bear to descend to practical details of ground organisation and realisation. At their best (in 1954) they never gained more than 10 per cent of the seats in the Syrian parliament; yet their appeal to the intellectual young, to the students, to the young army officers, was powerful and extended far beyond the confines of Syria to inflame youthful imaginations in Iraq, Jordan, Lebanon and Egypt itself. Ali Abu Nuwar, the Jordanian officer who engineered the dismissal of Glubb, was a Baathist.

By 1958, it is true, the two movements, the Egyptian revolution and the would-be Syrian-Arab revolution, were in a sense approaching each other—though from opposite directions. Nasser was becoming more urgently aware of the need for an ideology to frame and explain what had happened in Egypt; the Baathists were groping for the power to realise—or at least sustain—their ideology. Nasser appeared to have the power and organisation, and Michel Aflaq, the Baath's founder-philosopher, publicly hinted that the Baath in return would be happy to supply him with the ideological basis in which he was unfortunately deficient.

It was the beginning of one of those tortuous and obsessive relationships between schools of the Left which seem to play a critical rôle in the making of most revolutions. And unfortunately for the future of the 'United Arab Republic,' the contradictions were not only ideological. In the normal way it might have been expected that Nasser would have relied on the Baath to carry through in Syria the joint socialist policies; and the party was in fact given key Ministries in the U.A.R. Cabinet. But the strength of the Baath lay in the Syrian army which it had set out to infiltrate, not in the country. When the time came for the 'basic' National Union elections (in mid-1959)—free and by secret ballot in accordance with the democratic principle the Baath itself professed—the Baath party was able to secure only 250 from over 9,000 seats. The traditionalist—and practical—politicians did much better.

The Baath Ministers, including their U.A.R. Vice-President, the veteran socialist, Akram Hourani, had in fact anticipated this débâcle by resigning en bloc six months earlier. They had suffered the inevitable fate of politicians of the Apocalypse result was that the practical burden of carrying through the when called upon to cope with a workaday situation. But the socialist revolution in Syria fell, not on its Syrian champions, but more and more on the Egyptians themselves. Twenty thousand Egyptian administrators and specialists of various kinds carried through the Land Reform in the Orontes Valley and the Damascus *Ghuta*, instituted the 'Arabisation' of the Syrian banks and insurance companies on the Egyptian post-Suez model, introduced a progressive income tax (which in Egypt had by 1957 reached 80 per cent on incomes over £10,000), and installed exchange controls in the interests of the new 'Northern Region' (i.e. Syrian) economic plan.

But unfortunately for them, the Egyptians were no longer dealing with the docile inhabitants of the Nile Valley but with a truly redoubtable native merchant class whose wits had been sharpened over the centuries, not only in the bazaars of Aleppo and Damascus, but in the markets of the world. A few of their number had lately brought something of a boom to much of Syria by employing their funds in large-scale tractorised grain-growing operations in the North-East.

It now fell to the amiable Field Marshal Abdel Hakim Amer, whom Nasser had appointed chief co-ordinator and trouble-shooter for the 'Northern Region,' to explain to this sophisticated fraternity which constituted the economic heart of Syria that United Arab Republic socialism not only bore them no ill-will, but actually cherished the *non-exploiting* capitalist prepared to serve his nation through the Syrian Development Plan, just then issuing from the new Technical Bureau. The merchants protested their patriotism, declared their faith in the necessity of planning—and moved their funds to banks in Beirut.

In fact, the economic problems of Syria lacked both the desperation and inflexibility of those of Egypt and plainly required different emphases; the inability of the Egyptians to perceive this, and their ponderous professorial assumptions of superiority, slowly but surely lost them allies. Radical Syrian army officers who favoured land reform and socialist measures were embittered by their exclusion from politics and by the setting of Egyptian officers over them. Egyptian exports to Syria quadrupled, but Syria's to Egypt only doubled: the Communists—those still out of gaol—denounced the union as typical 'expansionism of Egypt's new ruling class.' And although in the U.A.R. National Assembly, duly called, Syrian representation (200 Syrians as opposed to 400 Egyptians) greatly exceeded their entitlement on a population basis (1 to 6),[3] it was still felt to be derisory by a people of whom a former Syrian President said that '50 per cent considered themselves national leaders, 25 per cent think that they are prophets and 10 per cent imagine that they are gods.'

To Syria's west the once profitable transit trade with the Lebanon had been disrupted. To her east, in the new Republic of Iraq, Brigadier Kassem, having quickly broken with his comrade-in-revolution, the Nasserite Colonel Aref, was pursuing an erratic course all his own, repressing Baathists and indeed all parties save the Communists, while attacking Nasser on the radio as the great Imperialist who plotted to enslave Iraq. That the lottery of an army *coup* should at this stage have thrown up a leader as mentally unstable as Abdel Karim Kassem was a major misfortune for the movement towards Arab Socialist unity.[4] Nor was it the only piece of bad luck. Nature herself played a major rôle in the undermining of the union with successive failures of the rains and Syrian harvests.

In August 1961, Nasser, in desperation, instructed the Syrian Ministers to come to Cairo and operate from there. But now even Colonel Abdul Hamid Serraj, the notorious Syrian Minister of the Interior whose heavy hand had both kept the union going and ensured its ultimate doom, revolted and resigned.

In 1954, among the innumerable party election posters plastered over the walls of Damascus was one which showed a valiant Syrian citizen, slashing out with a sword in either hand, at (1) a bear stamped with the hammer-and-sickle, (2) an octopus spattered with £ and $ signs, and (3) a viper bearing the Star of David. By 1961, most Syrians were ready to add a fourth malevolent assailant upon their virtue—a boa-constrictor with the head of a Pharaoh.

Only one member of the Syrian National Assembly in 1958 had voted against the union with Egypt; three-and-a-half years

---

[3] In the central U.A.R. Cabinet of 1961, out of thirty-nine Ministers, fourteen were Syrians (although Egyptian-picked Syrians).

[4] Cf. Ben Bella's comment on a visit to Kassem in 1962: 'It was almost impossible to have a consecutive conversation with him . . . he was consumed by an incredible feverish restlessness . . . the little I was able to grasp of his political beliefs horrified me.'

later none voted against its termination.[5] In September, another small group of officers, proclaiming yet another 'Revolutionary High Command,' put Abdel Hakim Amer on a plane and sent him back to Cairo. The moment of Arab Rebirth had again been postponed.

Yet when, in mid-1960, Nasser had compared the Egypt-Syrian union to 'a nuclear explosion, releasing formidable Arab energy' the metaphor had not been wholly empty. For if in Syria, at the end of 1961, there was once again the familiar cabinet of veteran politicians and bankers, supported now by a few Muslim Brethren, the revolution had nevertheless been both extended and deepened. In both Syria and Iraq land reforms, long promised but somehow always deferred, had actually been carried through on the plan successfully demonstrated in Egypt. New human claims had been for the first time unmistakably asserted in action. In Syria, villages had been rebuilt; social projects launched; merchant 'city-states' challenged by a wider view of national interest, embodied in a Plan. Even in the Lebanon, the oligarchy had shed just a little of its old cocksureness, and was re-insuring with a social security programme including, as it characteristically boasted, the highest minimum wage in the Middle East.

But the most important effect of the failed union was on the Egyptian Revolution itself. And if this derived in some part from Nasserism's brief and stormy liaison with the Baath, it owed much more to that natural enemy, the Syrian merchant class, which at last provided a counter-revolution worthy of it, and by so doing enabled it to complete itself.

In 1958, when the union with Syria was launched, Egypt's was still a capitalist economy. True, after Suez the public sector had moved forward, but the mixed public-private joint stock company was still common form, private capital still received a large part of total profits, and the future balance was undecided. In the National Bank and the Misr Bank, the new men, the 'officers and technocrats,' still sat beside the

[5] Again, there is the uncanny echo from history. In 1831, Mohamed Ali's son, Ibrahim, was rapturously greeted by Syrians as a liberator. But the Egyptians' modernising reforms 'were harshly applied and aroused sectarian opposition; several risings were with difficulty suppressed . . .' In 1840 Ibrahim left Syria in the face of revolt and execration.

representatives of that small, immensely wealthy and dominant Egyptian ruling class which Anwar Abdel Malek evocat-
ively calls *la grande bourgeoisie industrielle*.[6]

But as planning was professionally embraced, the new
régime sought more ways of directing the economy. In 1958
and 1959 it was still trying to do this by Industrial Organisation
Acts which gave the government power to control firms' out-
puts in basic or monopoly industries, limited dividends, directorial seats and remuneration, and so on. Inevitably, in the
Misr Bank and elsewhere, conflicts mounted. But the Egyptian
revolution was that contradiction in terms, a pragmatic revolution. In groping towards its large social goals, it worked out
both practice and theory as it went along. And here the Syrian
experience had some sharp lessons to impart. The mettlesome
resistance of the Syrian possessing classes to land reform, to
planning, to 'Arabisation' on the Egyptian model, demonstrated with a clarity hardly possible in the indulgent, tradi-
tion-ridden air of the Nile Valley that whatever co-operative
theory might say, the Oriental capitalist lion was unlikely to
lie down with the worker lamb, or remain passive while the
planners drew teeth and claws.

With the Syrian resistance now underlining experience in
Egypt, the point was taken. In February 1960 those 'commanding heights' of the Egyptian economy, the National Bank
of Egypt and the Misr Bank—with its constellation of modern
companies—were taken by the State. In May the nationalisation of the Press—'to prevent the domination of the information media by private capital'—showed the direction in which
the régime's thoughts were turning. At the end of 1960 the
break with Belgium over the Congo provided the opportunity
for the take-over of a number of important Belgian concerns
—the Cairo tramways, the Heliopolis *Métro*, the remaining
private cement concerns, further enlarging the public sector.

Even so, the future of the revolution was not determined.
As late as May 1961, Dr Kaissouni, the Minister for the
Economy, was reassuring Egyptian capitalists that 'guidance
does not imply domination.' The Egyptian wealthy class had
many ramifications, and in some areas 1957's 'Egyptianisation'
had actually strengthened its hold as it moved into positions

[6] *L'Egypte, Société Milititaire*, Paris, 1962.

vacated by foreigners.

But, once again, Egyptian experience in the 'Syrian Region' of the United Arab Republic underlined the danger to the revolution in excessive gradualism. In the Syrian elections to the National Union the predominant numbers of landowner and merchant family members elected offered a timely demonstration of the fact that in under-developed countries, with a vast gulf between a small, entrenched wealthy class and a poor and ignorant mass, 'parliamentary democracy,' the liberal approach, even when modified by a single political organisation, may be a bar, rather than a means, to social advance.

Thus, if an early effect of the union with Syria may have been to slow down the Egyptian revolution's development, a later effect was to stiffen its resolve and deepen it. The change was signalled on 9 July 1961 by a series of laws which attacked that central stronghold of Egyptian wealth, the Alexandria cotton trade. The cotton Bourse was shut down. Henceforth all purchases were to be made by the Egyptian Cotton Commission, under the Ministry of the Economy. The cotton export houses were required to accept 50 per cent Government participation, and the great Alexandria cotton-pressing warehouses were nationalised. To tighten control over foreign exchange and the export of capital, all import-export houses had to give up one-quarter of their share capital against Government bonds, thus bringing them under Ministry supervision.

But these were merely ranging shots; the main wave of nationalisation, transforming the balance of the Egyptian economy, came on 19 and 20 July. In both regions of the United Arab Republic all banks and insurance companies were nationalised. In Egypt, 44 companies in heavy and basic industry and transport were also nationalised; in a further 88 companies in manufacturing and commerce the public sector was henceforth to hold at least half of the share capital; and in another 147 companies all individual or company shareholdings in excess of £E10,000 were to be surrendered to the State against Government Bonds. Many of the companies were later to be nationalised completely.

The total effect was to bring the bulk of Egypt's manufacturing industry and external trade under public control. Politically, not the least significant change was the limitation on shareholding at £E10,000—for here compensation for excess shares was limited to the first £E15,000. Simultaneously, a steeply progressive income tax was instituted, together with a ceiling on director's salaries of £E5,000, which involved heavy cuts for some.

Again, it was Syria which provided the emphatic reaction. If it was the Syrian army which, in September, 1961, shattered the Union—as it had initiated it—it was the fury of the Syrian landowning and merchant classes which provided the impetus and explosive change. In so doing they confirmed the Egyptian revolution in its course, enabling that curiously reluctant revolution at last to accept its logic and necessities.

Certainly, for Gamal Abdel Nasser the collapse of the Syrian Union seems to have been a major point of departure. For a while at least the old vision of the regenerate nation, released from foreign domination, was paralleled by an almost Marxist revelation of class war. 'We fell victims to a dangerous illusion,' he told Egyptians on 16 October. 'We always refused to make peace with Imperialism, but we committed the error of coming to terms with reaction.' There had been insufficient effort to make the people conscious of their rights, and therefore willing to fight for them. They had tried to carry on the revolution through the old machinery of government. It needed renewal. The Syrian secession was the work of the financiers and industrialists of Damascus. They—and their counterparts in Egypt—must be 'neutralised' if the revolution were to be saved. It was the only way ahead—the only way if Egyptians were ever 'to achieve the society of equal opportunity.'

Six days later, on 22 October 1961, Vice-President and Minister of the Interior Zakaria Mohieddin directed the sequestration of the wealth of 147 of the wealthiest families in Egypt, including the régime's erstwhile collaborator, the multi-millionaire Ahmed Abboud. The sequestrations were accompanied by forty precautionary arrests. The object, Mohieddin explained, was 'to protect the hopes of the people . . . and its ability to ward off any stab in the back such as befell the social struggle of the Syrian people.' Further sequestrations continued until January when the total was a thousand. The sequestered persons were declared ineligible to serve as directors of firms, as administrators or legal advisers, or as officials of clubs and societies.

It remained a very Egyptian revolution. From February onwards many of the sequestrations and 'isolations' were lifted, and in 1964 it was ruled that those who remained under sequestration would each be allowed to keep property and shares up to £E30,000, plus any jewels or valuables that had been kept at home. Yet in this curiously malleable society the point had been made possibly more permanently and effectively than any guillotine could have made it. The revolution which had begun with the dethronement of the landed magnates in rural Egypt in 1952 had now at last demolished their alter egos, the magnates of the towns.

From the confusion and the tumult finally, and somewhat surprisingly, emerged the outlines of a new social and economic system capable of making a beginning on that task of rebuilding Egyptian society which had by this time been shown to be necessary. The decrees framing these changes, which came in an extraordinary rush in 1961, were promptly allocated their place in Egyptian history as 'the Socialist Laws' and undoubtedly merited their capital letters.

Contemplating the sweep and confidence of these structural changes, the student inevitably finds himself wondering how it came about that the Egyptian socialist system should thus suddenly emerge, fully fledged, from the tortuous developments which began with the conflict with Neguib and now ended with the exchange of insults with the Baath Socialists of Syria. Had the makers of the Egyptian Revolution really been as naïve as they appeared?

'I do not act, I react,' Nasser himself once told an interviewer, with that unpolitician-like frankness he sometimes displays. But was it frankness? Or, as some would argue, characteristic guile?

It is certainly true that for each major revolutionary departure it is possible to point to a major provocation from outside the Nile Valley—the Baghdad Pact, the Gaza attack, the abrupt refusal of the High Dam Loan by Dulles, the Suez Attack, the Eisenhower Doctrine, the Syrian 'counter-revolution'. . . . But were the dramatic sequels to these events truly 'reactions,' or were they rather the alert seizing of opportunities to move in a direction already determined? Did the man choose the moment—or the moment choose the man?

It is a question one often finds oneself asking about Nasser, and it is an indication of the nature of the man that so often the answer somehow has to accommodate both alternatives. After a lifetime moving about the Nile Valley villages, Father Henry Ayrout has observed of the Egyptian fellah that he has 'great adaptability . . . intelligence at the level of instinct.' Behaviour in the Arab East, adds another veteran Arabist, Jacques Berque, 'is almost always a matter of nerves and intuition, like riding a horse.' The possession of this peculiarly Arab faculty in a high degree enabled Nasser both to speak for the Arab millions and to see through the elaborate and frequently unreal formulations of Western diplomacy. Yet if intuition was the key element, in Nasser it was, in general, checked by reason. If tremendous risks were taken, they were calculated risks. If the calculation produced what to some might appear a startling result, this was perhaps because it gave due weight to such neglected and 'imponderable' factors as the play of mass opinion. In the autumn of 1955, referring to the development of nuclear weapons, Nasser told a London *Observer* interviewer: 'As I see it, war from now on will be different. It will be fought on internal fronts of all countries . . . it will use nationalism as a weapon . . .' Nor was it an accident that during the Canal nationalisation complex legal snares were avoided and the Egyptians kept so carefully within their rights: at the end of 1954, Colonel Younis and a committee had made a secret survey of the canal organisation.[7] According to Nasser's confidant, the journalist Mohamed Hassenein Heikal, before nationalising the Canal Nasser wrote, staff-officer style, two appreciations of the situation, one from the Egyptian, the other from the Western, point of view. He only went ahead when satisfied that the West could only act after a delay which would be fatal for its cause. Again, if on learning of the Syrian revolt his first reaction was to send para-

[7] The Canal concession in any event expired in 1968 and it was necessary to prepare for this. The highly complex situation of May/June 1967, leading to the Sinai confrontation and Egypt's defeat, does not really invalidate the point. Nasser's hand was then forced. Nevertheless, the calculations were made—and for a variety of reasons proved defective. See Chapter 26.

troops, his second—on sensing the true dimensions of the rebellion—was to call them back.

Such a precarious combination of circumspection and impulse, 'reactions' which were both calculated and authentic, represents a type of sophistication that does not correspond to anything in the West. For in the Nile Valley it is still possible to believe in historical evolution and to be intuitively aware of oneself as a participant in its continuing process. The history of the first Arab revolution, still present in most Arab minds, illuminates the theme. Earlier, in a famous passage, Nasser had spoken of a 'wandering rôle' in search of an actor. Now, in 1961, he cited the Koran on the evolution of the Muslim approach to strong drink:

> First . . . it pointed out that alcoholic drink was partly sinful, partly beneficial, but its disadvantages outweighed its advantages—which means that it was permissible. Next, later on, the Koran says: 'You shall not approach prayer while you are under the influence of alcohol.' That means that drinks are prohibited all day—until after evening prayer. But later again it states that drinking and gambling should be avoided because they are the works of Satan. This is a final and definite prohibition. But why did not the last verse come at the beginning of the Koran? . . . It gave the people a chance to proceed gradually from one stage to the next until the final stage was reached. . . . The people were convinced of the need for prohibition over their experience of twenty-three years during which the Koran was completed.

And thus after, not twenty-three years, but nine, the Egyptian Revolution, proceeding 'from one stage to the next,' had advanced from the vague reformism of 1952 to the Socialist Laws of 1961, and in November of that year Nasser set up a Preparatory Committee of 250 persons—professors, journalists, trade-union leaders, lawyers, sheikhs, engineers, co-operative officials, administrators, Ministers, army officers—to prepare 'the next stage,' the election of a 'National Congress of Popular Powers' which was to receive and consider a new basic document and statement of faith, a National Charter.

13

THE REVOLUTION WITHIN THE REVOLUTION

There is not, and cannot be, European, African, or any other kind of socialism. . . .
— *Kommunist* Magazine, U.S.S.R.

Social beliefs grow roots when they prove to be close to their advocates' hearts, minds and souls. A nation's heart is its aspirations; its mind is its present; its soul is its history.

—Gamal Abdel Nasser, interview in *Al Ahram*, February 1960

If the 'Socialist Laws' of 1961 in the main extended and consolidated existing trends, they did so in so thorough-going a fashion as almost to amount to a second revolution. It was as if the several sections of the jigsaw that had been gropingly assembled since 1952 had suddenly fallen into place to reveal the complete picture, carrying the 1952 revolution against rural 'feudalism' on into the city, and translating it into terms suited to an industrialising society.

Going back to the base of the revolution, the Socialist Laws instituted a second land reform in which the limit of individual ownership was halved—from the 200 feddans of 1952 to 100 feddans.[1] What was perhaps more important, no single family was now to rent over fifty feddans, nor as much as that if they already owned land: owned and rented land together must not exceed fifty feddans. The new laws cut the rate of repayments for both old and new land-reform holdings, extending them over forty years instead of thirty and halving the interest (likewise halved on the bonds given in compensation to former landowners).

By completing the nationalisation of most major industrial concerns the Socialist Laws brought three-quarters of all the investment under the Five Year Plan into the public sector.

[1] However, as under the 1952 Law, it remained legal for a farmer to register two further parcels of a hundred feddan each in the names of two of his children.

Until 1961 in order to husband the foreign exchange for the industrialisation plan imports had been licensed and selected necessities (like tea, fertilisers, wheat and some pharmaceuticals) government-imported and price-controlled. Now the Government went the whole hog, importing everything through public companies and extending its operations to exports. Those crucial sources of hard currency, the cotton export houses, were required by law to accept 50 per cent Government participation. In the event, they too became publicly-owned concerns while retaining their old names and identities, specialities and clientèle.

Besides placing the levers of control of the economy firmly in the hands of the Government, the Socialist Laws extended the process of income redistribution in urban, as well as in rural, Egypt. Income tax, which had only been introduced in 1939 (when it reached 50 per cent only on incomes of over £100,000), was again stepped up, reaching 90 per cent on incomes over £10,000.[2] A ceiling of £5,000 a year was set on company salaries, including those of managing directors. Taxes on the rental value of buildings, a major source of wealth in Egypt, were in some cases quadrupled. Rents were reduced by decree, putting money in tenants' pockets as it was siphoned from the landlords.

On the other side of the social balance, in order to enhance the position of the workers, both symbolically and materially, the Socialist Laws introduced the new departure of profit-sharing. 25 per cent of a company's profits were henceforth to be distributed to its workers—10 per cent directly (with a maximum of £E50 each), 5 per cent to local amenities and regional social services, and 10 per cent to central social services for workers, thus strengthening the outline of the welfare state sketched by social insurance legislation between 1955 and 1959. At the same time, hours in industry were cut from eight a day (1959 law) to seven (which in three-shift industries like textiles meant an effective rise in pay and, elsewhere, increased employment).

[2] In December 1965, Income Tax was further increased to 95 per cent on over £10,000, 40 per cent on £5,000-£6,000, 50 per cent on £6,000-£7,000, 60 per cent on £7,000-£8,000, 70 per cent on £8,000-£9,000, 80 per cent on £9,000-£10,000.

As the logical complement of the profit-sharing system, the Socialist Laws went on to provide for the election by the workers of two worker-directors (one shop-floor, one staff) to the board of directors of every company. Later the worker representation was to be increased to four, so that, on each statutory board of nine directors the elected directors made up half, with the company chairman in effect holding the casting vote. In such a country as Egypt this was a bold innovation indeed.

A year or so later, consolidating and clarifying the *fait accompli* of the Socialist Laws, the National Charter attempted to define, by division of sectors and function, the economic structure and balance in this new society. All the nation's heavy, medium, and mining industry was to be publicly owned, together with enough light industry to give the government an effective guiding rôle there. The import trade was to be wholly in public hands, as was three-quarters of the export trade.

But this, it was pointed out, was not public ownership for its own sake, but rather for the purpose of ensuring essential social control over the economy's development. It was considered a basic principle that the ownership of land and buildings should remain private—because, since the Land Reform, it had become possible to prevent exploitation in this area by such means as limitation of holdings, rent control, progressive taxation and low-cost public housing. Socialism is defined as 'Equality of opportunity plus an expanding base of wealth.' Once the planned framework of growth has been established through the public sector companies, 'national capitalists,' willing to work for a fair reward, have their place. 'By encouraging competition within the framework of planning the private sector is an invigorating element for the public sector,' ruled the Charter.

There will be a large field for the national capitalist in internal trade. Only a quarter of this was to be channelled through public concerns like the Co-operative Stores chain, which is seen as having the function of keeping down prices and raising the standard of mass consumption (which for a 'Westernised' country like Egypt has been grotesquely low). When does a 'good' capitalist become a 'bad' capitalist? The answer is, when he gets big enough to command political power or exact an over-high price. And this it seems is not in Egypt very big: the maximum permissible turnover for private builders and contractors was set at £E100,000. Above that, the undertakings were to be nationalised.[3]

Nehru's India, outlining 'the national objective . . . a socialist pattern of society,' in 1948 and again in 1956, had attempted to draw up a similar, if even vaguer, division between the spheres of public and private enterprise. But India, proceeding from theory to practice, was predictably sidetracked on the way, and the private sector continued to dominate. Egypt, muddling through from crisis-born action to theory, had perhaps taken a surer path for a society which needed to re-make itself.

The Socialist Laws of 1961 formed the economic basis of what was to be known as 'Arab Socialism,' an ideology and system which some British commentators, with the condescension reserved for things Egyptian, have called 'Arabised Tito-ism.' Egypt and Yugoslavia have, it is true, quite a lot of problems in common, and Egypt's design for workers' participation in management may well owe something to Tito's 'Law of Workers' Management' of 1950.[4] Nasser himself has said that he learned from Tito. But he also learned from many others; Egypt is nothing if not eclectic. 'National Capitalist' is a term of Chinese usage, the co-operative idea, basic in the agrarian revolution and a theme of the whole system, derives from British and Irish models—and so on.

But any attempt to interpret Arab Socialism purely in terms of economic structure, or as an assemblage of technical devices, must fall sadly short—because to do this is to see it through Western eyes. In the West today economics is sovereign; statistical 'growth' is the supreme, self-sufficient ideal, the means which somewhere along the way became the end. The East, however, has not yet attained this stage of development. Like the British Labour Party before it was overwhelmed by

[3] However, by a cell-like process of division and coalescence at which they are professionally adept, many contractors, otherwise suspect, were able to qualify as good 'national capitalists.'

[4] Both points were in fact incorporated in the Baath Socialist Party's 1951 Constitution.

the American Supermarket, Arab Socialism is concerned not only with the Gross National Product, but with social values, with the construction of a whole moral world. It is a faith as well as a programme, and a faith with a historic purpose. In this sense its vital source is religious, as once was British Socialism's. But the parallel here becomes inadequate, for in a truly Islamic country the overlap of political and religious worlds is very much more fundamental, and of a kind the Protestant countries of the West have long since forgotten.

In Europe the progression from church-community to nation-state took several centuries to complete; in Egypt it had to be telescoped into a few decades, its pace forced and evolution distorted by foreign intervention. Furthermore, there are a number of reasons why this transition must be more difficult and perilous in the Arab world than it was in Western Europe. It is the distinction of the Koran that its very words are sacred, and that its Truth is absolute and final: Mohamed's mission was to be 'the Seal of the Prophets.' Even the *Hadith*, the tradition of the sayings of the Prophet, had been scrutinised by learned doctors of Islam and finally codified and sanctified a thousand years before. Truth in the Islamic world was established. Nor was it merely established in the abstract; it was exceedingly particular, enshrined in a whole code of life and conduct woven into the law and into the very fabric of Muslim communities, and jealously protected in every detail by the swarming doctors of the Law.

One day in 1799 at the *Institut d'Égypte* which Bonaparte had recently founded in Cairo, a French zoologist rose to read a report on his researches into the varieties of fish in the Nile. After the first few sentences a learned sheikh stood up in the audience and interrupted the speaker to point out, kindly enough, that all his labours were unnecessary and indeed vain. For the matter had already been determined by God's revelation, through the Prophet, that he had created, in all, 30,000 species—10,000 on the land, and 20,000 inhabiting the water.

One hundred and fifty-three years later another army, this time Egypt's own, had embraced the gospel of Science and Progress. But the Arabic word for 'innovation' was still the same as the word for 'heresy.' The sheikh and the technocrat were still at odds. I recall discussing the subject of Islam with an Egyptian agriculturalist, a sincere and practising Muslim. Egyptians, he said, must stick by Islam's disciplines . . . for where, for instance, would the Egyptian fellahin have been, suffering the conditions they did, without the Koranic rules of life and health? And yet . . . and yet. . . . Then he told me of an occasion on which he had asked a high Muslim authority to introduce a monthly warning in the village mosques against the habit of urinating into the canals, an ingrained custom which is responsible for an appalling burden of disease. The authority replied that unfortunately this was not possible, because the dimensions of 'pure water' had been determined for all time by divine revelation, and were stated in the Koran, and it would be necessary to summon an Islamic Congress to consider the matter at length before any revision could be contemplated.

'That,' said the agriculturalist, 'is why I sometimes *hate* religion. I like religion—and yet I hate it.'

This dilemma, this deep and for the most part concealed conflict of loyalties and worlds, divorcing emotions from intellect, alienating people from state, subtly exacerbating the relations of Arab East and European West, is one of the fundamental sources of the disquiet of today's Arab world. And it is well thought of, certainly, in terms of a tangled affair of the heart: of people who, for three generations, have had increasing difficulty in living *with* the religion which so largely formed them, but who, equally, cannot live *without* it. This is, of course, a dilemma common in greater or lesser degree to most Eastern peoples coming under the impact of Western civilisation. But it is more acute and inescapable in Egypt for a number of reasons. The first derives from the closeness of the Levantine East-West encounter: it was a marriage of incompatibles perhaps, but marriage all the same. The second reason, an allied one, has to do with the common origins of Islam and Christianity (so-near-but-yet-so-far) which deny to the Egyptians the easy escape from Western intrusion possible for, say, the Indians who could retreat into the remote world of Hinduism. But the most important reason stems from the unique way in which Islam identified the Arabs, gave them their place in history, and a special relationship with the West.

If Egyptian nationalism was finally 'polished' in the salons of Paris, it had been born in the Nile Valley of the conjunction between a sense of outrage and the promise of Islam; if the names of Rousseau and Locke were later added to its texts, its true line of descent ran back to the Koran and the Crusades. The three men who were its founding fathers were all men rooted in the Islamic tradition. Colonel Arabi owed much of his early success with the fellahin to his ability to make dramatic use of the Koran's potent verses; and even Saad Zaghloul, though a westernised lawyer, was a graduate of El Azhar, former pupil and colleague of the reforming Sheikh Mohamed Abdu, and adept at deriving the case for constitutional reform from the precepts of Islam. Until yesterday, the only freely accepted authority in Egypt was that of the religious sheikhs, the only aristocracy that of descent from the Prophet. When Bonaparte invaded Egypt, he sought legitimisation from the sheikhs of El Azhar; when later the Turkish Governor was removed and Mohamed Ali acclaimed, it was again they who sanctified the transfer; and when, in 1956, Franco-British bombs were falling on Egypt, it was to the pulpit of El Azhar that Nasser went to rally the people. Throughout the years of the struggle for national independence, the 'Azharites' were passionately in the forefront. Whether by the stormy reaction of the Westernised intellectuals against its authority, or through the passionate devotion of its young sheikhs to their heritage, this venerable centre of Islamic learning, with its congeries of Koranic schools and institutes and student lodgings far from the smart boulevards of Cairo, remained the hidden heart of Egypt's life.

Yet if El Azhar still appeared the secret key to so much in Egypt, it was a key which would no longer fit the doors of either present or future. The nation-state, the joint-stock company, the assembly-line, were institutions unknown to the Koran—in whose sacred text interest is sinful 'usury,' and the rights of women those defined by the reforming laws of the Prophet in the 7th century. Within the mosque-university of El Azhar it was not merely verbally that 'innovation' and 'heresy' were identical terms; would-be Luthers hammered on these doors in vain. Even the Khedive Ismail, seeking to reintroduce secular subjects, had been forced to found a separate college. Islam is theoretically no more a religion of priest and prelate than Quakerism, and it is a cardinal principle in it that no intermediary should come between man and God. But for all that, the multiplying wearers of the sheikhly turban of El Azhar continued, in the present as the past, to hold the divine title-deeds of Egypt with an unction not exceeded by the great proprietors of the soil, and as an *ancien régime* they were a good deal more formidable.

Since Egypt, geographically placed as she was, could not withstand the advance of the modern world, what happened was that the Islamic institutions were simply by-passed. Neither that master company promoter, Ferdinand de Lesseps, nor the ubiquitous Greek grocer were much troubled by the views of the Koran on usury; and from the 1870s a civil code, based on the Code Napoléon, increasingly outflanked the old Islamic prohibitions—leaving, however, the Koranic family law to perpetuate the backward glance at the heart of society. Political ideas as well as institutions were inevitably imported, lock, stock and barrel, from the West. A new generation of liberal nationalists, mainly educated in the West, and unable to turn their backs on 'progress,' diligently strove to master the new idioms and play the parliamentary game in the best Western fashion. A small, well-off class, they thus cut themselves off yet further from the bulk of the people to whom these alien practices had little meaning; nor, in the 'forties, was the new generation of Marxist intelligentsia—despite its avowed intention of releasing the revolutionary energies of the masses—really in much better case.

A people already deeply divided by extremes of riches and poverty were thus further fissured by a head-on conflict of loyalties and values. In particular, the gulf between rural and urban Egypt was widened. Even now in the Egyptian villages the sheikhly turban is reverenced, and in provincial towns with El Azhar schools you will see in the photographers' shop-windows row after row of snapshots of 'young sheikhs,' each the apple of some family's eye. But in Cairo the anachronism is manifest. Here, the sheikhs, a vast superfluity, their minds cluttered attics of painfully acquired but irrelevant knowledge, have until recently eked out meagre livings as the lowliest employees of Government offices.

In 1952 the officers' régime had thus inherited two roads: the road of western-style parliamentarianism and materialistic progress, and the road of traditional Arab Islam; and despite earlier attempts to reconcile them, both continued to recede from each other. On the one hand, the Muslim Brethren had shown that they could tap the emotions of the masses; but they had no programme suited to the modern world. (On matters of property the Supreme Guide was more radical than official Islam which had issued a *fetwa* against land reform; yet the Supreme Guide's fundamentalism pointed to the seclusion of women, Koranic schools, the hand-chopping of thieves, the restoration of the Caliphate.) On the other road, the Communists offered a modern social programme; but with Marx's view of religion, they stood little chance of substituting their own sacred text for that long enshrined in the language and hearts of the people.

The events of 1956, clearing away the obscuring Levantine superstructure, had opened a site for new national foundations, simplifying the task of modernisation. Yet before any new structure could safely rise, the old dilemma stemming from the history and character of Islam and Egypt had to be resolved. Egypt had to find her own way to true modernisation, which would be true also to the character of land and people.

In Islam's first 'national revolution' in Turkey, Kemal Ataturk faced—in somewhat cruder form—a similar dilemma and sought to solve it by a wholesale onslaught on Muslim traditions and culture. He shut down the religious schools and the Ministry of Wakfs, closed the monasteries and sacred tombs, swept away Arabic script, replaced the *Sharia* by the Swiss legal code, and commanded the wearing of Western brimmed hats to hinder the performance of the five daily prayers. In 1923 he enacted a law making the exploitation of religion for political purposes high treason. Yet with all this, he failed. In Turkey the mosques still multiply and are crowded. And more than thirty years later—such is the durability of Islam—the Turkish Army considered it necessary to hang their Prime Minister, Adnan Menderes, for, amongst other things, offending against the law of 1923.

The approach of Nasser, a sincere but essentially modern-minded Muslim, was very different.[5] The army officers who made the revolution of 1952, were, of necessity, westernised, but not so westernised as to be cut off from their roots; in the army the two streams, the unchanging world and the world of ceaseless change, came together. It thus became possible to stand a little outside both, gaining a truer perspective. 'The national experience,' Nasser wrote in the Charter, 'passes through a stage akin to adolescence during which it needs all the intellectual sustenance it can get hold of.' Plainly, he was thinking of Egypt's eagerly eclectic, westernising, years. But he went on to insist: 'the real solutions cannot be imported from the experience of others.' They can only be worked out by a people itself, through its own history and experience, 'on its own soil.'

To work out these 'real solutions' from the national experience was the mission of Arab Socialism as Nasser conceived it; and if, to this end, its economic structure, founded on the Socialist Laws, was important, its political, spiritual and cultural concepts and institutions were certainly no less so. For only with their aid could mind and heart be re-united and the dichotomy of the 'secular' and the 'religious' which does violence to the personality of a Muslim nation be averted. A distinguished British professor, comparing the mongrel composition of Arab Socialism unfavourably with the intellectual purity of Communism, recently referred to it as 'a bazaar ideology.' In a somewhat different sense from the contemptuous one he implied Arab Socialism's future success may be measured by the extent to which it can become just that: a bazaar ideology.

In Egypt in the 'sixties, the vehicle of this major experiment in synthesis was the document of ten chapters and over a hundred pages called the National Charter.

[5] According to the Egyptian Marxist writer, Hassan Riad, Nasser himself was a Communist in his youth, but, being also deeply religious, was so shocked by the 'secular spirit' of Communism, that he abandoned it.

THE TECHNOCRATS

from top-left, clockwise

Sidky Suleiman, Minister for the High Dam, later Prime Minister.

Sayed Marei, pilot of the Land Reform.

Dr Abdel Moneim Kaissouny, London-educated economist, long the regime's chief financial adviser.

Mahmoud Yunis, the engineer officer who took over the Suez Canal and made a notable success of it.

Dr Kamal Ramzy Stino, the Copt who modernised food supply. developed state Co-op shops.

Dr Aziz Sidky, the American-educated university lecturer who became industrialiser-in-chief.

For more and more Egyptians every year, men and women alike, industry brings new ways of life. *Above* Car workers get lunch in the cafeteria of the Nasr Automotive Works, near Helwan. The cap-like objects are Arab bread. *Below:* Girls on the assembly line in a television set factory, south of Cairo.

PART FOUR

THE MATRIX

Backward societies are faced with problems much more critical than those which faced the old Europe. They *must* do things quickly. They *must* do things on a greater scale. The scale of their demographic growth impels them to quicker and greater capital accumulation. They have no 'empty' or 'undeveloped' lands to go to.

—Carlo Cipolla, *The Economic History of World Population*, 1962

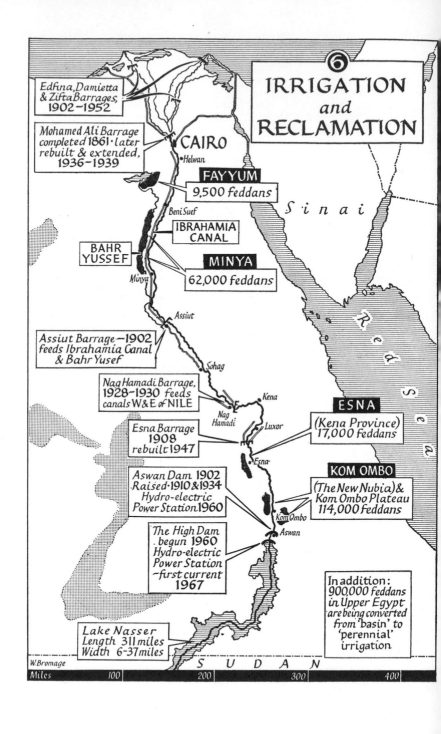

IRRIGATION and RECLAMATION

Edfina, Damietta & Zifta Barrages, 1902–1952

Mohamed Ali Barrage completed 1861· later rebuilt & extended, 1936–1939

CAIRO
•Helwan

S i n a i

FAYYUM
9,500 feddans

Beni Suef

IBRAHAMIA CANAL

BAHR YUSSEF

Minya

MINYA
62,000 feddans

Assiut

Assiut Barrage – 1902 feeds Ibrahamia Canal & Bahr Yusef

Sohag

Nag Hamadi Barrage, 1928–1930 feeds canals W & E of NILE

Kena

Nag Hamadi

Luxor

ESNA
(Kena Province) 17,000 feddans

Esna Barrage 1908 rebuilt 1947

•Esna

Aswan Dam 1902 ·Raised·1910 &1934 Hydro-electric Power Station 1960

KOM OMBO
(The New Nubia) & Kom Ombo Plateau 114,000 feddans

Kom Ombo

Aswan

The High Dam ·begun 1960 Hydro-electric Power Station – first current 1967

R e d   S e a

In addition: 900,000 feddans in Upper Egypt are being converted from 'basin' to 'perennial' irrigation

Lake Nasser Length 311 miles Width 6–37 miles

W. Bromage

S U D A N

Miles   100   200   300   400

14

'ARAB SOCIALISM' - A WORLD
REGAINED?

Sufficiency and Justice.
—Watchword of the Charter, 1962

You are like a person learning the alphabet, You are learning
the 'A' . . . socialism is the first letter, while 'B' is the beginning of Communism. . . .
—Khrushchev to Egyptian National Assembly Delegation in
Moscow

As he travelled about Egypt in the mid-'sixties, the enquiring
foreigner found himself listening to echoes from two works,
one 1,300 years old, the other composed only yesterday. In
the schools, the formal Koranic texts, stately gilt on traditional
green, are often joined by illuminated scrolls, executed by the
pupils, setting out aphorisms from the National Charter. Although the juxtaposition is accidental, it is not inappropriate.
For both Koran and Charter give an account of the pilgrimage
of a people, outline a social system and a code, indicate the
bounds of action and belief, and are eclectic, prolix and
repetitive narratives from which stand out short, sharp passages reflecting the insight born of experience. But here the
comparison—in any case blasphemous to any true Muslim—
ends, for whereas the Koran is God's final revelation, the
Charter is officially declared to be open to debate and revision
after the ten-year period of 'conversion to socialism.'

The manner in which the Charter emerged was itself an
interesting blending of East and West. It took Nasser, its
author, six hours on 21 May 1962 to read his draft to the
National Congress of Popular Powers, a 1,500-strong assembly
elected from the chief occupational groupings according to a
scheme devised by the Preparatory Committee of 250. The
discussions of both committee and congress were televised,

broadcast and reported in full in the newspapers.[1] Five thous-
and suggestions flowed in to the secretariat of the Congress,
1,500 of them from the trade unions. The debate was lively
enough, but inevitably diffuse, finding its focus in the Charter's author who, in all, made forty-three personal interventions. Some of these were quite trivial, others crucial. At
one moment we find Nasser answering a learned sheikh
from El Azhar who, *à propos* the clause on the Equality of
Women, suggested a regulation requiring young girls in offices
to wear long sleeves as prescribed for prayer in the Koran.
This, said Nasser, was a matter for families, not legislators. But
behind the learned sheikh's interventions lay the demand of
five thousand assembled delegates of the mosque-university of
El Azhar that Islam should be declared the religion of the state
and the guiding principle of its laws: the most explosive issue
to engage the Congress. At another moment, in reply to a Left-
wing writer, Nasser embarks on a justification of his position
on political detainees. 'We are not against Marxism . . . but
we are opposed to those taking instructions from foreign
countries. Should I leave them (the Communists), a reactionary party would emerge and receive instructions from imperialist countries—National elements would be lost between. I
don't want to get rid of anyone . . . on the contrary, I want
to gather together the sons of this country.' And then again,
like a firm but sympathetic master with an over-enthusiastic
Senior Class: 'I happen to have a very large number of definitions of socialism in my possession. . . . But we are not here
for pure theories. . . . Let each of us say what he has to say,
but let us all keep constantly in mind application and imple-
mentation. . . . A theory is nothing but a guide to action.'

In its earlier chapters, the Charter is essentially the sequel
of the *Philosophy of the Revolution*, continuing the narrative
of the revolution's progress. But contact with the intellectuals
of the Syrian Baath has done little for Nasser's prose, and the
naïve originality of the first testament is, in the second, often
obscured by clouds of crypto-Marxist jargon. Nevertheless, the

---

[1] The public debate and symposium was renewed in 1967 over the form
of the proposed Permanent Constitution to replace the provisional Constitution that followed the Charter. The public were invited to present their
suggestions, either in writing or personally to the Preparatory Committee.

message comes through with conviction. Chapter Six—'On the Inevitability of a Socialist Solution'—explains that in the conditions of the Nile Valley only comprehensive planning can tackle the necessary task of doubling the national income in a decade, while at the same time securing a more equitable distribution of income and employment. But, again in the conditions of the Nile Valley, comprehensive planning requires socialism. For Egyptian capitalists would (and did) inevitably become vassals of the vast capitalistic undertakings of the West.

If the economy outlined is a mixed economy, unlike most mixed economies it is compounded in unequivocally Socialist proportions. The rôle of the 'national capitalist' is firmly residual; for 'private' industrial endeavour a favoured form is the producers' co-operative, complementing the agricultural co-operative in the countryside. But the Charter deals with principle, not detail; its tone is humanist, rather than technical. While stressing the urgent necessity of investment, it insists that, unlike some countries, Egypt should not be prepared to sacrifice a generation for the sake of the future. Somehow, the New Egypt must both enable her people to live a little less miserably now, and, simultaneously, build the foundations for a better tomorrow.

But how? East and West meet again in the confident answer. By the fabulous powers of modern science and by that 'creative planning' which is 'not a mere process of working out the possible, but a process of achieving hope.' Throughout this long and diffuse document there is a continual re-avowal of this faith in science. But science is not *merely* seen as an Aladdin's Lamp—its essential qualities are understood:

In the life of a nation, as of an individual, the way to maturity and clarity of vision is through trial and error. . . . Science alone can ensure that trial and error in the national action will lead to development with guaranteed consequences.

We must put aside the idea that modern machines do not need large labour power and thus should not be used. . . . For modern machines enlarge the basis of production very quickly. This opens new horizons and so ultimately gives wider chances of labour.

We cannot waste a moment before entering the atomic age.

And a few other characteristic guide-lines from the Charter:

> The effectiveness of national armies lies in national, social and economic power . . . therefore . . . we must always bear in mind that the needs of defence should never have the upper hand over the needs of development.

> The family is the first call in a society and therefore must be afforded all means of protection.

> The universities are not ivory towers, but rather forerunners.

> The town has a moral responsibility towards the village.

> Peace cannot be stable on the brink of an abyss that separates the advanced nations from those upon whom under-development was imposed.

The idea of 'Science for Society' which runs through the Charter is counterpointed by another theme, also highly contemporary: the need for democratic control of both technocracy and bureaucracy as 'the greatest safeguard in great periods of change.' But the Syrian experience has deepened the conviction that, in the Arab East, only a completed social revolution can make parliamentary democracy other than a fraud. Nasser now acknowledges that it had been naïve of the Officers in 1952 to expect former landed magnates and capitalists closely allied with foreign interests to co-operate with the revolution. 'At this particular stage,' he told the Preparatory Committee, 'I have to ask myself: "Who are the people?"' Not certainly, these. These are manifestly 'the enemies of the people.' And when a member rejected this notably un-Egyptian phrase and suggested 'opponents,' Nasser insisted that 'opponents' was not enough. 'We are converting a state of reactionary "bourgeois dictatorship" into one of democracy of the whole people,' he reminded his audience.

Who then *are* the people? The people are all the rest—the mass of people outside the old oligarchy, whether peasants, workers, professionals, intellectuals or 'national capitalists.' And to ensure that they ('the popular powers') prevail and their revolution is not undermined, the 'reactionary' powers must be 'isolated,' i.e. deprived of the right to vote or hold office during the ten years of conversion to socialism. Thus bloody class collision can be averted. Five categories of those possessing vested interests in the *ancien régime* were defined.

But though the definitions were somewhat vague, in fact the revolution remained, by world standards, tolerantly Egyptian. Fewer than 7,000 individuals were 'isolated,' and many were permitted to go to appeal tribunals and 'work their passage' back if so minded.

Then comes a major constitutional innovation. To develop and strengthen the position of the hitherto neglected 'popular powers,' the Charter lays down that in the elected National Assembly, and other major elected bodies, one-half of the representatives must be 'farmers and workers.' A Congress member amended this to *at least* half, and another member, Dr Soleiman Husayan, then Rector of the new Assiut University, wrote a twenty-five feddan limit into the definition of farmer.[2]

The multi-party system is again rejected as, at Egypt's stage of reconstruction, dangerously divisive, liable to widen social breaches that need above all to be bridged. Nasser has said that for a time he considered allowing two rival socialist parties, but turned down the idea as wasteful of Egypt's limited resources of leadership. Instead, the Charter again establishes a nation-wide mass organisation (to which all Assembly candidates must belong), the Arab Socialist Union. Although this is a successor to the 'Libération Rally' and 'National Union' it appears that something has been learned from the earlier failures—there is emphasis now on the need to build patiently from the bottom upwards.

With around 5½ million two-piastre a year members, the Arab Socialist Union, in the event, includes the greater part of the active adult male population. In 1965 the two principal Egyptian Communist parties, both actually illegal, dissolved and declared that they, too, would enter its capacious embrace, formally closed only to expropriated magnates, convicted criminals, and, presumably, known Muslim Brethren. Four thousand A.S.U. 'basic units' in the villages are joined by a further three thousand in factories, offices, hospitals, educational institutions, and so on. Each basic unit must meet at

[2] In the nation-wide Arab Socialist Union elections of mid-1968 the land limit for a 'farmer' candidate was cut to ten feddans; also his sole livelihood had to be agriculture, and he had to live in the country. In fact, in 1965 only 1·2 per cent of all landowners owned over ten feddans.

least three times a year, and each elects a 20-man committee which elects a secretary and assistant-secretary and sends them, or other representatives, forward to the A.S.U. conference of town or district. Thence the structure pyramids to congresses at the level of the 25 governorates, and to a National Congress which meets every two years and is in theory the fountainhead of political authority, laying down the lines within which the National Assembly legislates.

The Western observer may find the Arab Socialist Union a somewhat baffling body. It is variously presented as the watchdog of the Revolution, as a school of democracy and nation-building, as a national forum, as an instrument of government and means of communication, both up and down, and, at the National Congress level, as the embodiment of the will of the people. As with most political parties, not all the prescribed roles are strictly compatible. 'Numbers,' the Secretary-General of the A.S.U., then the U.A.R. Vice-President Hussein el Shafei, remarked to me a little ruefully in 1965, 'are not always an advantage. That is why people are so hard to move . . .' By this time the A.S.U. chiefs were at work constructing an élitist core within the mass party, which now acquired a considerable apparatus of headquarters departments—farmers' affairs, trade unions, ideology, press and publishing, youth, women's affairs, and so on. At this time, key posts like governorate secretary were filled by appointment, and the National Congress had not met. But the declared plan was that election should prevail to the topmost levels, the National Congress forming the electoral college for the Higher Executive Committee, which would form, in effect, a sort of shadow Cabinet.

In mid-1968, in the process of renewal after military defeat, this 'coming stage' was initiated. Indirectly elected in three pyramiding levels from the base of 5½ million A.S.U. members, a 1,700-strong National Congress gathered under the dome of Cairo University on 23 July 1968, the sixteenth anniversary of the revolution. The A.S.U. then proceeded to elect its provincial secretaries, and also a Central Committee of the National Congress—150 members chosen on a territorial population basis. This Central Committee finally elected the 10-

man Higher Executive from twenty of its own number who proffered themselves.[3] It was decided that the '50-per-cent worker-and-farmer' rule should apply right to Central Committee level 'as a basic guarantee of the continuation of the process of socialist transformation.'

The society envisaged by the Charter is not formally monolithic. The Arab Socialist Union is very far from being the only representational body. In addition to trade-union and co-operative councils, the Charter requires, for instance, elected provincial councils. 'Local government,' it says, 'should gradually but resolutely transfer the authority of the State to the people; for they are in a better position to feel their own problems and find proper solutions.' It calls for criticism and self-criticism. 'Every citizen,' Nasser told the Congress of Popular Powers, 'will have the right to oppose any measure as not suitable for the country and to tell Gamal Abdel Nasser: "You have made a mistake."'

There is no reason to believe that Nasser was otherwise than sincere when he said this, but his view of democracy is not the Western one. 'Constructive' criticism is welcomed. But when opposition becomes *organised*, this is something different. To align on a *class* interest is anathema: workers must speak as individuals who are workers, but not as the proletariat. The Charter does admit a class struggle, but sees it as being conducted against the 'reactionary forces' that have been excluded, it does not take place within the collectivity. Of course, it is admitted that there will be differences between the various 'legitimate' sections of the nation—but these are seen as *family* differences, to be settled around the table, in family style. For the present, the Charter defines the broad limits of debate beyond which lies 'deviation.' For the Charter represents the consensus, 'the collectivity,' which at all levels is seen as the 'safeguard against the individual running loose.'

The puzzled Western observer may perhaps reflect that the

[3] The Central Committee, in fact, requested Nasser, as elected President of the Congress, to nominate the Executive, but he insisted on election. Votes cast for each candidate were made public. On the first ballot only eight candidates succeeded in getting the required minimum of more than half the electoral votes. Aly Sabri came first with 134 votes (out of 147 possible), Hussein El Shafei came second with 130.

more organic—and therefore potentially effective—an Arab
political system is, the less likely is it to be wholly intelligible
to those who hail from very different cultures. And if the
language of the Charter often seems crypto-Marxist, its underlying ideas are, in the broadest sense, Islamic. The Charter
slogan 'Sufficiency and Justice' has the ring of the desert and
of earlier chapters in the history of Islam; its author's tone,
often commonsensical, measured, pragmatic, as well as abstract
and cloudy, echoes the Prophet's. 'Reactionary Forces' and
'Popular Forces'—is not this the World of Unbelief and the
World of the True Believers, the Community of the Faithful,
Islam's only political form—implying brotherhood within and
jihad[4] without. Then the notion (which we sometimes are apt
to forget predates Communism) of the single, the absolute
Truth, the Code—the Line. 'Those in charge of great projects,'
rules the Charter, 'need to believe that over-expenditure, even
when no private profit is involved, is a kind of deviation.'
Experiment—but do not deviate. Criticise—but do not fall into
faction. All this becomes more intelligible when considered in
the perspective of a world where there has so often seemed
to be no halfway house between total brotherhood and total
anarchy—and where one can dissolve into the other with bewildering speed. All Arab history might indeed be considered a
warning against the dangers of 'the individual running loose.'

But adaptation to environment may run the risk of perpetu-
ating inability to make necessary change in it. Could the
Islamic qualities of the Charter be reconciled with its uphold-
ing of science as the key to the future? Or might the régime,
seeking this way out of the Arab Muslim dilemma, finally be
impaled upon it—or forced to proceed to more root-and-branch
remedies such as moving from Mr Khrushchev's 'A' to his 'B'?
On the main staircase of Cairo's Ministry of Wakfs, ever
thronged with sheikhs of all degree, hangs a framed quotation
from a speech of Nasser: 'God's word is a revolution in itself,
and it is the duty of religious teachers to show the truth behind the word.' If the first part of this proposition may be

---

[4] *Jihad* is Arabic for 'striving', i.e. striving for Islamic Truth and to win
over or subdue the Unbeliever, over-simplified and given a pejorative sense
in the Western Christian rendering of 'holy war.'

taken to represent orthodoxy, the authentic and unchangeable revolution of the 7th century, the second part quietly admits the revisionists. By the time the Charter was being debated, the 'revolution within the revolution' was in fact well under way.

In the autumn of 1955 Egypt had become the first Arab country to abolish the separate *Sharia*, or religious, courts governing matters of 'personal status.'[5] Family law remained Koranic, but would henceforth be interpreted by civil and religious judges sitting together. The following year women were given the vote, and in 1957 two women were actually elected to the National Assembly. In 1962 Nasser appointed the first woman Cabinet Minister in Egypt's history, the Minister of Social Affairs, Dr Hikmat Abu Zaid.

Such reforms, admitting the secular power into the inwardness of the Muslim home, struck at the heart of Islamic traditionalism. The great majority of sheikhs were flatly opposed to them. They obstructed as long as they could, although many now realised, that, as one regretfully remarked to me, 'the tide is too strong for us.' A few months before women were given the vote, the *ulema* of El Azhar issued an official ruling that 'the Sharia forbids women to exercise the legislative function, their inherently unstable nature' making them unfit to vote. Dr Abdel Rahman Tadj, then Rector of El Azhar, went on record in favour of polygamy as sanctioned by the Koran, and declared that the addition of lay faculties to the mosque-university would be a 'crime.' But in Egypt (as in Britain) the

---

[5] A number of other Arab countries were also considering their abolition, and indeed Tunisia later went further, and, perhaps perilously, faster. Bourguiba, educated in the French rationalist tradition, in 1956 not only abolished the Sharia courts, but also modernised the marriage law, abolishing polygamy sanctioned by the Koran. In 1960, he campaigned against the Great Fast of Ramadan, declaring that it endangered economic development, Tunisia's 'true jihad'. One result was a 24-hour riot in Kairouan when the mobs attacked the Governor's house, yelling 'Allah is great—he will not depart'; another was that 'natural disasters, floods, insufficient rains, a slight earthquake . . . were interpreted as signs of Allah's disapproval of Bourguiba's heresies' (Moore, *Tunisia since Independence*, 1965). Over-precipitate 'modernisation,' apart from causing deep moral confusion and alienating government from masses, is likely to be ineffective. 'Most Tunisians—probably in increasing numbers since 1960—continued to observe the fast,' writes Moore. In Egypt the road had long been prepared by the increasing codification of the law, and, as long ago as 1908, by the establishment of a government school for *Sharia* judges.

heads of the ecclesiastical establishment are ultimately appointed by the state (which also foots El Azhar's bills), and presently Dr Tadj found himself Ambassador to the Yemen, where the rigour of his interpretations was possibly more to local taste. And in 1959, a strong committee was set up under the Minister of Higher Education, Kamel eddin Hussein (a former 'Free Officer' and one-time Muslim Brother) to consider the modernisation of El Azhar.

In 1961, the year of the 'Socialist Laws,' the National Assembly approved an outline law for a reformed El Azhar based on this committee's report. 'Islam,' the report had pointed out, 'being in its true nature a social religion, makes no distinction between religious and secular science . . . it requires every Muslim to have his share of both religion and world interests . . . and since a Muslim needs no intercessors to bring him closer to God, it is fitting that religious scholars should learn other sciences, so that the standard of religion should not be reduced to a mere profession, a cause of idleness and social waste.'

From this unimpeachable—yet revolutionary—base, the Law proceeded to add to El Azhar's establishment faculties of medicine, engineering, agriculture and economics. While retaining the core of Koranic studies and the religious emphasis, it proposed to assimilate the mosque-university and its tributary secondary, intermediate and primary schools throughout Egypt to the national educational system—with common standards, certificates, and provision for transfer at various stages.

A saying of the Prophet much favoured in Government circles these days is one from the Hadith which runs: 'Study is better than worship. Go, seek knowledge far and wide—even unto China.' Even so the modernisers have by no means neglected the more formal aspects of religion. In late 1954 the régime set up a permanent scholarly Islamic Congress to promote the study and teaching of Islam, to finance scholarships for Koranic students from Africa and Asia, and so on. The Ministry of Wakfs has built 1,500 new mosques since the revolution, and has equipped many of the old ones with new libraries and Koranic recordings. It is gradually assuming financial responsibility for more of Egypt's total of 16,000 mosques (the bulk are private) raising the qualifications of the imams and also their often beggarly pay. At the same time, training courses have been devised, designed to widen the imam's knowledge of contemporary (rather than medieval) social issues. The radio now has a special channel given up to Koranic recitation, and there are television discussion programmes in which eminent sheikhs and leading personalities debate the moral problems of the hour.

But conceptions woven into the very texture of life are not changed overnight. Votes for women continued to co-exist with legal polygamy, and the Koranic law administered by the new civil courts still permitted a husband to divorce his wife virtually at will, while by no means extending the reciprocal privilege to a wife.[6] Liberal sheikhs existed, but were still a very small minority. In some ways the gulf between 'Eastern' and 'Western' worlds seemed almost as great as on the day when Bonaparte's armies arrived with their message of Science and Freedom. Could it indeed ever be bridged by a modernised Islam?

In 1908 Lord Cromer, although a patron of the great reforming sheikh, Mohamed Abdu, answered briskly: 'Let no practical politician think they have a plan capable of resuscitating a body . . . whose gradual decay cannot be arrested by any modern palliative, however skilfully applied. . . . Islam cannot be reformed; that is to say, reformed Islam is Islam no longer; it is something else; we cannot as yet tell what it will eventually be.'

Half a century later, Gamal Abdel Nasser replied, in effect, that it would be something not unlike Arab Socialism, as outlined in the Charter which the National Congress of Popular Powers duly resolved on 30 June 1962, 'to make the law of our lives and the rule of our conduct.' There was an Islamic echo in the very terms of that resolution—and it might indeed be claimed that the Egyptian revolution had not shattered a tradition but renewed one. Dr Montgomery Watt in his *Life of the Prophet* has described how the ethical code of Islam arose as a reassertion of the old tribal social values against the inroads made by the get-rich-quick merchant mono-

[6] For further developments in the reform of Family Law, see Chapter 22.

polists of Mecca. In *sura* 89, 'The Daybreak,' God speaking through the voice of the Prophet castigates the rich and self-absorbed Meccans:

> You respect not the orphan,
> Urge not to feed the destitute,
> Devour the heritage greedily,
> Love wealth with exceeding love.

It might equally well have been written (indeed it was written!) of the wealthy absentee pashas and monopolists of the Nile Valley in 1950.

Nasser has often claimed that the religion of Islam was the first to prescribe socialism; and the Charter can readily be presented as the translation of the Islamic social code into terms of contemporary life. Thus the Prophet's condemnation of usury and speculation becomes the insistence on a controlling public sector; Islam's stress on the brotherhood of man and on restraint in personal consumption translates into income-limitation and redistribution, not to mention worker-directors and profit-sharing; the Koranic duty of *zakat*, the charitable tithe, predicates social insurance and the welfare state; the emphasis on collectivity (as opposed to Christianity's preoccupation with individual salvation) suggests co-operatives and trade unions, replacing the Islamic craft guilds which under their sheikhs ruled Egyptian workshops until Western-model capitalism outlawed them.

It was the sort of synthesis which Christian Socialism and, more recently, and less wholeheartedly, the various post-war Catholic Christian Democratic parties had already attempted in the West—with notable lack of success. If Arab Socialism can achieve such a reunion of moral and economic worlds it would indeed be making a unique contribution to mid-twentieth-century history. But can it?

Islam, with its continuing vitality, its simplicity and practicality, certainly in some ways lends itself to such a process. But the effective social disciplines around which it has been built are increasingly threatened by the new patterns of life that technology, enthroned in the Charter, dictates.

  At the Misr textile mills at Kafr el Dawar, production drops 25-30 per cent during the fasting month of Ramadan; through this and the week-long feast that follows national output staggers; offices open late and close early and the European seeking to get something done needs a truly heroic patience. For this reason, Habib Bourguiba, the very Westernised President of Tunisia, has publicly condemned the 'excesses' of the Great Fast. No leader in the Arab East would go so far. The problem is acknowledged, but variously explained away. An Egyptian factory doctor assured me that production only fell because the workers thought they *ought* to be weak; intellectuals, their brains cleared, in fact, he said, produced their best work at this time. An eminent sheikh in the Ministry of Wakfs pointed out that the five daily prayers, seventeen *rakkas* or prostrations in all, took up only half an hour—and therefore need not interfere with work. And with characteristic commonsense Islam, by the doctrine of *qada* (or restitution), allows the duties of fasting or prayer which may be impossible at the moment prescribed to be carried out on some other occasion.

So far, the Iron and Steel Company at Helwan is one of the very few industrial concerns which ignore Ramadan, continuing to provide midday meals (which workers may, or may not, eat). Its Cairo offices are among the very few that will be found open at normal hours during the month. Continuous furnaces wait for no man, and rolling mills are even harder on the thirst than the desert. Sheikhs can agree with clear conscience that dispensation is due. Yet, if the dramatic, unifying disciplines of Islam are abandoned or 'postponed'—and if, additionally, the ringing revelation of the Koran is 'interpreted' in the light of science—one may wonder, with Cromer, how much will be left of the faith that shaped and still identifies the Arab people.

In the mid-'sixties the question gained point yearly as Egypt began to respond to the first stirrings of an industrial revolution that would penetrate the life of the Nile Valley from Mediterranean to First Cataract, changing the relationships between the classes, and between town and country, stimulating a widespread appetite for education and a voracious demand for technical skills, creating a new sort of family and a new rôle for the women within it which would be beyond the power of the most diehard sheikh to deny.

15

THE TOWN: THE TECHNOCRATS MAKE THE PACE

The fall in the death-rate does not occur as part of a balanced aggregate of changes but as the product of changes that matured elsewhere. For these countries there is one solution —to undergo the Industrial Revolution.

—Carlo Cipolla, *The Economic History of World Population* (1962)

What made Sweden Sweden—steel and electricity!

—Abdel Tawab el Mohandes, Principal, Higher Institute of Agriculture, Minya, to the author

On the pavement outside the Co-operative shop a big crowd jostled around a green mountain of new-season melons; inside a queue had formed to snap up the frozen, cellophane-wrapped American chickens which Dr Stino was importing to ease the meat shortage. The store, one of the more than two hundred such co-ops in Cairo, was well equipped and well stocked, with its stacks of Egyptian canned foods, its fresh tuna on ice (Russian-caught in the Indian Ocean), its assortment of cheeses, hard and soft local, Polish Gouda, Yugoslav, Hungarian Trappist. . . .

Yussef, the district manager, a former Lipton's man, watched the customers with satisfaction. 'You know,' he said, 'if you'd told me a few years ago that so much could be done in Egypt, so quickly, I'd never have believed you. The standard of living is rising all round. Why, you can get a fourteen-inch TV now for what it used to cost you to buy a radio! We are seeking "know-how" everywhere! We are learning much!'

It was a note often struck by Egyptians in conversation with a sympathetic foreigner up and down the Nile Valley in 1964 and 1965. And the Egyptians had, indeed, some excuse for giving rein to their natural ebullience. For years—as they now often complained—they had been instructed by their schoolbooks as a basic geographical fact that Egypt could never be a manufacturing nation. And now here was Dr Aziz Sidky, the Minister of Industry, conducting President Nasser around some newly opened factory almost, it seemed, every second day. Industrial investment had risen from £E7 millions in 1951—a good year—to £E105 millions in 1963/4; in the same period electric power generation (by kwh) had quintupled, industrial production more than doubled, reaching £E1,000 millions. Vast crowds packed the 1965 Cairo Industrial Exhibition night after night, queuing for hours to pay their entrance piastres. All Egypt was there: smartly dressed young 'employees,' village women in black *melayas* with babies sleeping on their shoulders, paterfamilias with their broods and plump wives, grave, turbanned sheikhs, sun-blackened fellahin in *galabiyas.* . . . They gazed upon the shiny Nasr cars in three sizes,[1] upon the railway trucks, the big steel pipes, the gleaming bicycles, the cables—all made for the first time in Egypt —upon the pink and yellow mountains of plastic goods and glasses and ceramics and the models of refineries and power plants with flashing lights and those twin symbols of Arab Man's resurgence, the *Kahira* rocket and the *Ideal* refrigerator, and they were filled with something of the same sense of wonder and opening horizons that the Great Exhibition of 1851 at London's Crystal Palace had called forth in the Victorians.

It was a new sort of popular festival, at once perfervidly Egyptian and insular, and yet also contemporary and international. For whereas the pioneer industrialiser Mohamed Ali, had perforce relied largely on France and Britain, and the impatient Ismail's cosmopolitanism had been that of the Bourse and banking house, Nasser's Egypt drew its 'know-how,' its new machinery and its finance with an extraordinary catholicity from the whole one-world of mid-twentieth-century technology. At Ezbet el Borg, where the Damietta branch of the Nile runs over the bar into the sea, the Japanese had lately completed a sardine-canning factory; with their newer talent, electronics, they had also piloted Egypt's first television-set plants. Eight hundred miles southward, at Edfu, Texans in wide-brimmed hats were crawling about a sophisticated apparatus of pipes for turning the waste bagasse of a sugar

[1] *Nasr* is Arabic for Victory, and is not a reference to the President.

factory into cellulose for paper-making: soon they would leave and the Egyptian chemists would take over. At Sohag, the Bulgarians had designed and equipped a large modern factory for the dehydration of export onions; at Aswan, the French had installed much of the fertiliser plant and were preparing to do the same at Assiut; in Sinai, a British firm was directing the opening-up of Egypt's first coal mine. If it was West Germany which furnished the new iron and steel works, it was East Germany that equipped textile mills; Czechoslovakia that provided the ceramics factories and much else; Hungary, canal bridges; Italy, a car and lorry plant; Spain, aid in aircraft construction. . . . Sometimes the deals were with governments, sometimes with private concerns; in either case they were generally accompanied by credits and tuition. And if this technological Tower of Babel was in part explained by foreign exchange stringencies, it also had certain manifest advantages. On the whole, Egyptians could afford to laugh at those Westerners who complained that there was nothing 'positive' about 'positive neutralism.'

In 1952 industrial income had amounted to 8 per cent of the total national income; by 1962-3 industrial income represented 28·8 per cent of the total, and in that year the value of Egypt's industrial production (including construction and electricity generation) for the first time passed the value of Egypt's agricultural production, which was itself expanding. This is a landmark in the growth of any nation and according to Dr Labib Showcair, then Egypt's Minister of Planning, it was accompanied by another: 'Between 1960 and 1964 the national income was increasing for the first time in our history at more than double the rate of population growth.'[2]

The question, of course, was: could it continue to do so? But whatever the answer, and however suspect statistics might be, there was in Egypt then no lack of visible evidence that modern industry, the Great Accelerator, the jinn which could disarm the old demon of diminishing returns, was beginning to take up the heroic rôle assigned to it. For miles around the industrial areas, agricultural labourers' wages rose to thirty-five piastres a day in the cotton and rice seasons as against the

[2] In an interview with the author. Between 1960 and 1964 the population grew by 11 per cent, the national income by 29 per cent, at constant prices.

legal minimum—by no means always paid earlier—of eighteen. In this notoriously 'overpopulated' land there was an actual shortage of labour in some activities, such as building work. Workers were choosing their jobs. As, with some assistance from 1961's seven-hour day, the total of industrial workers in workshops employing ten or more workers grew from 401,000 (1952) to 744,000 (end-1963) and the total wage packet more than doubled (with profit-sharing bonuses still to be added),[3] certain phenomena appeared which had a familiar ring to visitors from the industrialised West. City families anxiously discussed the servant problem: if a servant left now, it might be months before you could get another, even with 'exorbitant' pay. A director of a metal-working factory at Alexandria said to me: 'I'm going to make a survey to find out how many of our workers here have television sets. I'd say, well over half.' Domestic consumption of Butagaz (for the new Egyptian-made stoves), of kerosene, and of all sorts of clothing and furnishings soared. More and more women, both married and single, were going out to work in factories and offices to help maintain the rising standard of living.

But although increasing in both number and size, such islands of bourgeois aspirations still floated on a vast sea of poverty. A more than usually frank Egyptian confessed to me: 'We know that there are ten millions living decently and eighteen millions who are living miserably and the problems are terrible.' '*Malish!*' had no place in the vocabulary of the planners, but over large areas of Egypt it was still a very necessary word.

The industrialising plan took the classic, 'decolonialising,' form. It sought both to save foreign exchange and to provide work by manufacturing in Egypt all the ordinary consumer, and some durable, goods which had previously been imported, while processing as fully as practicable the local raw materials

[3] According to Dr Kaissouni, the professional economist, who has long been the régime's chief Economic Minister, during the first Five Year Plan the total of *all* workers rose from 6m. (1960) to 7·3m. (1965) and total wages from £E550m. to £E879m. According to the calculations of Professor Bent Hansen real disposable income grew by 80 per cent between 1952/3 and 1962/3.

traditionally exported in exchange for manufactures, or—as in the case of iron ore—neglected altogether. It would then employ the foreign exchange thus saved, supplemented by retained profits, foreign loans and internal saving, to lay the heavy foundations—metallurgical, power, chemical—necessary to a fully fledged industrial nation.

By 1965, the process of consumer-goods import-substitution (which had started long before the revolution) was almost complete. For if the street hawkers continued to do a brisk business with Glorious Pink Camay and similar pillars of modern living smuggled from Libya or the Gaza Strip, this testified to a cultural rather than a technological lag. Even in some highly developed countries the snobbism of the Imported flourishes; but in Egypt, with its Levantine heritage, 'baladi,' 'home-made'—'of the people'—has been a term of contempt. Yet no one could scorn the smart new transistor radios flooding the country from the new factory at Ismailia, or the Egyptian-made sulfa drugs, antibiotics, aspirins, and all the pharmaceuticals now being made in Egypt under Swiss and American licence, or the Nasr (Fiat) cars with their Egyptian 'Nisr' (Eagle) tyres and Egyptian-made batteries and springs— although for the cars the waiting list was two and a half years long and the black-market price heart-breaking.

Many of the new consumer industries had to import their raw materials, but some, like chinaware and the manufacture of particle-board from rice-straw and sugar-cane residues, found them ready to hand at home. But the most rapid gain was in the further processing of Egypt's outstanding raw material : her cotton. In 1951 the proportion of the cotton crop spun into yarn in Egypt had been one-seventh; by 1965 it exceeded òne-third—of a larger crop.[4] In the decade after the revolution the number of looms rose by 50 per cent, and of spindles from 50,000 to 1,300,000. At the same time, the manufacture of knitwear has more than quadrupled; jute fabric and yarn (from local flax) multiplied fifteen-fold; and in 1958 the extrusion, spinning and weaving of nylon was added to what was already the first rayon spinning and weav-

[4] Egypt now consumes almost all her medium-staple (Ashmouni) cotton, exporting the surplus of high-priced, extra-long staple for which she is famed.

ing plant in the Arab world. Cellophane sheet came in as a by-product and in 1965, at the Kafr el Dawar mill complex, a big extension of the cellophane plant was going up.

It is usual for textiles to form the leading sector of developing economies; but in Egypt, as shaped by the Misr Group on the twin foundations of economic nationalism and scientific management, they have been something more than this. The industry was the first to become sufficiently sophisticated and diversified to develop a generation of modern-type technical executives wholly trained in Egypt—in which task it is now assisted by the Textile Department established at Alexandria University in 1962. Spinning fine yarns up to 160-count (for parachute fabrics), the latest mills at Kafr el Dawar with their diffused lighting, spacious dust-free halls, and high-quality Swiss machinery are as advanced as any in the world. Quality control is pursued from the raw cotton (laboratory test-spun) stage onwards, and the modern design of Egyptian dress and furnishing fabrics would enable them to compete with success in American and European markets, were they not so often excluded by quotas or tariffs. In a style reminiscent of Britain in the 'forties, small red EXPORT tabs on looms and spinning frames, spur—or are supposed to spur—the patriotic zeal of the operatives. In 1967, textile exports reached a value of £E55,000,000, around a fifth of total visible exports, compared with textile exports valued at £E7 millions in 1952.

The rayon fibre is currently manufactured from imported wood pulp sheet, the nylon from German *caprolactum*. But with the High Dam power coming on tap the plan is to make the necessary wood cellulose from sugar-cane bagasse at Aswan; the nylon raw material will come from a new petrochemical plant at Alexandria.

Although Egypt opened the first working oilfield in the Middle East, in 1913, at the time of the revolution production was still inadequate to Egypt's own modest fuel needs. But by 1963, crude oil production had more than doubled—as had the value of petroleum products. As prospecting was pushed ahead oil began to come into view as an industrial raw material of increasing importance. The new Alexandria petrochemicals plant will produce, in addition to caprolactum, synthetic rubber and acrylonitrile (for synthetic wool fibres). At the

Suez refineries[5] a new delayed coking plant already produces material for detergents and another range of chemicals. Production of such basic chemicals as sulphuric acid, caustic soda, chlorine, has also been vastly expanded.

But although the chemical engineer can today do a good deal to build the foundations of industrialising nations, it is still the capacity to make steel that seems to most of them the indispensable symbol of arrival. And this is understandable enough, for not only is steel the fabric of modern civilisation and power, but for a primarily agricultural country an integrated modern steelworks such as Egypt projected at Helwan to utilise Egyptian ores offers a tremendous challenge on so many levels—physical, mental, organisational, scientific—that success may indeed be considered some sort of graduation.

The first blast furnace, of 400 tons daily capacity, was lit at Helwan in mid-1958, the second two years later. The early years were rough enough: heavy losses were sustained in under-capacity working. Coke had to be imported by sea, via Alexandria, at a cost of £E2 millions a year. Some of the difficulties met in establishing the first modern textile mills were repeated. Egyptian labourers, recruited from the surrounding villages, had neither the physique nor the stamina for this harsh world of blistering furnace heat and steel-mill roar. Labour turnover was disastrous.

Slowly these difficulties were tackled. On Nasser's orders, six very experienced German steel-men were brought in to advise their Egyptian colleagues through this teething period. Coke-ovens and sintering plant, installed by the Russians, made it possible to work from coal—using it was hoped some local ligneous coal from the newly opened Sinai mine (planned to work up to 300,000 tons a year in five years). The feeding of furnace slag and phosphates from the converters to the adjacent fertiliser plant helped reduce costs. Absenteeism was attacked by the now well-established method—a colony of model flat-blocks and clubs around the plant. At the same time, a system of targets and group bonuses was introduced; in 1964 bonuses earned added 40 per cent to wages.

[5] One of the two Suez refineries was very heavily damaged by Israeli artillery fire in October 1967.

By 1965, with production nearing capacity (based on 265,000 tons of pig iron a year), the plant's energetic production director, Dr Abu Bakr Mourad, claimed that losses had been turned into profits and that costs were now not too far from European levels. 'When we started, every nut and every bolt—everything—had to be imported. On the second stage, from 1960, the structure of our new buildings was fabricated from our own steel. Now we are making sheet. Next, it will be steel for simple machinery; then more complex machinery. . . . Step by step. You know, people are really proud to work here.' Passed first-class by Lloyds and the U.S. Navy, the Helwan plates were being used for shipbuilding in the Suez Canal Authority's yards, for railway wagons and petrol tanks. The new electric power pylons were of Helwan steel, likewise the railway sleepers and tram-lines, but not yet the railway lines.

Iron and steel production was allocated a substantial slice of the £E1,000 million to be invested under the third 'interim' industrialisation programme following the first Five Year Plan. By 1968, at a cost of £E65 millions, new hot and cold steel rolling mills, with galvanising and tinning sections, had been installed, with a capacity of 300,000 tons annually, extending to 500,000 tons within two years. In the same year the Russians agreed to finance the next major stage in the development of the Helwan complex, bringing its capacity up to 1,500,000 tons a year.[6]

If minuscule by the standards of the advanced industrial nations, this is still a useful beginning. In the form of ingots and bars much of Helwan's output has been going to Egypt's three existing steelworks for further processing, and these, too, are being enlarged. New steel plants have been planned at a sea-shore site in the Alexandria area and, again, in Aswan, the first a wide-plate mill, the second designed to use the High Dam's cheap power in electric furnaces to turn out 300,000 tons of special steels a year. The plan now is that the Aswan plant will use the Aswan ores (averaging 44 per cent iron) while Helwan will switch to richer ores to be brought in from the Bahariya Oasis in the Western Desert's 'New Valley.'

[6] The economic losses suffered in the Israeli-Arab war of June 1967 and its aftermath will no doubt affect the phasing of Egypt's industrial plans, but not their ultimate targets.

The overall aim, of course, is to ensure a controllable supply of the basic material on which metal-using industries can be built. Nasser has told Egyptians that in the 'next stage' Egypt will make machines for her own factories instead of having to buy them overseas—manifestly a critical point in the process of development into a self-sustaining industrial nation. When I raised this ambitious claim with Dr Aziz Sidky, the Minister for Industry, he pointed out that the military factories have already manufactured lathes and that the new industrialisation programme would create four large heavy engineering workshops in addition to fifteen new foundry projects. The idea, he said, was to manufacture heavy constructional machinery like bulldozers, then textile machinery, then machinery for the cement and sugar factories. 'First we shall make the looms for our own use; then for export. . . .'

When I remarked of the latter goal that there was already a great deal of heavy international competition in this area, Dr Sidky laughed sardonically. 'We have been told that so often before about so much. Difficulties? There are what I call the problems of synchronisation . . . and we are short of personnel at all levels. But we have been successful up to now. I have been watching the progress of several countries' plans —and I think we have done best. At least, we have been one of the most successful. We have been lucky. But *was* it luck?' —(that sardonic Egyptian laugh again)—'I don't think so!'

In any event, the 'luck' could hardly be said to have held out for Egypt's planners—whose 1960-65 Plan was the first half of a comprehensive design to double the national income in a decade. True, in terms of overall growth, the first Five Year Plan was 80 per cent successful; according to the independent assessment of Professor Bent Hansen the average annual growth rate achieved fell only 1-$1\frac{1}{2}$ per cent short of the 7·2 per cent target.[7] But whereas the Plan had anticipated a £E40 millions surplus on the balance of payments in the fifth year, in fact deficits persisted, mounting to £E136 million in 1963-4 and £E76 millions the year after, and giving rise to a foreign exchange crisis which exposed the Achilles' heel of

[7] Bent Hansen in *Egypt Since the Revolution* (London, 1968); also Hansen & Marzouk: *Development and Economic Policy in the U.A.R.* (Amsterdam, 1965).

the economy. Professor Hansen blames insufficient attention
to the speed of returns on investment projects and to their
true export potential. But there was bad luck, too. In 1961,
the cotton worm devastated the vital export crop, and, later,
the Congo troubles led to a sharp worsening in political relations with the West, particularly with the United States, a
key provider of credit through the 'surplus' wheat deals. The
assassination of John F. Kennedy in November 1963 removed
the first American President whom Nasser had felt capable of
sympathetic understanding of the Egyptian—and Arab—
revolution. The result, as Egyptian reserves dwindled, and the
American food shipments were placed in jeopardy by Con-
gressional action, was a severe credit squeeze. This brought a
decline in investment in the Plan's last year and a serious loss
of impetus. After several false starts the second Five Year
Plan was abandoned in favour of a stop-gap 1967-70 'Accom-
plishment Plan,' involving an investment of £E1,085 millions,
and stressing the completion of projects already under way.

For all that, the 1960-65 Plan is likely to appear, in retrospect, as a landmark in modern Egypt's history. In the National
Charter, Nasser, after commending planning, goes on to remark that it is not 'a mere process of working out the possible, but a process of achieving hope.' It is not a definition
that would occur to many modern economists (who may consider hope one imponderable too many), but in the circumstances of Egypt—where a psychological, as well as a material,
transformation was required—it went to the heart of things.
And by this definition, even if the hope were deferred, the
Plan was brilliantly successful. It opened up horizons. It
demonstrated, with conviction, and in a remarkably short space
of time, that Egyptians too could be the masters of their fate.
Old Egypt Hands, long inured to the bland rule of *Mafish!*
and *Malish!* ('There isn't any' and 'Not to worry'), and newcomers who had experienced the glazed affability (and im-
mobility) of the traditional Ministries, both found the whole
thing hard to credit. How *could* a people who consumed so
many thousands of hours daily merely trying to get their tele-
phones to work (on lines congested with *Insh'Allahs* and all
the lengthy prescribed rituals of Islamic piety and goodwill)

have got under way in a few years so ambitious and many-sided an industrial reconstruction?

The answer is worth seeking because it may well hold the key to the future of Egypt—and of the Arab world beyond. It is that behind the leisurely old hierarchy, behind the green baize doors of their Excellencies and the crowded divans of their minions, a new hierarchy and order, that of the techno-crats, had been quietly moving in. Egypt's new 'industrial revolution' was the work of just a few hundred energetic, modern-minded, technically equipped men who had certainly not destroyed the old bureaucracy, but who were outflanking it with increasing success, just as the 'new' ideological world of Arab Socialism was outflanking the old strongholds of Muslim obscurantism.

The sequestrations of 1956-7, followed by the nationalisa-tions of 1960-2, had rapidly brought into being a series of rami-fied industrial and financial corporations which dominated the economic life of the country. By 1963, a process of tidying-up had resulted in the emergence of nine major General Organi-sations—for Petroleum, Mining, Textile Industries, Chemicals, Foodstuffs Industries, Metallurgical Industries, Metal-using In-dustries, Building Materials and Ceramics, Small Industries and Co-operative Production. In 1964 the multitudinous banks were re-formed into a 'Big Five,' each looking after the financial needs of its allotted sector of the economy; in addition, there were the trading organisations.

These nation-wide organisations embrace a very wide range of mainly technical activity. Consider, for instance, the General Textile Organisation, which gathered under its wing forty-six companies, including those of the old Misr Group, covering cotton, wool, synthetics, ready-made clothing, carpets, jute manufacture. With a labour force of 200,000, a pay-roll of £E50 millions and an annual output of £E300 millions, the organisation had as its chairman a former Professor of Economics at Cairo University, Dr Mohamed Marzaban, pre-siding over some hundreds of technically qualified managers in the constituent concerns. At the supply end it deals with the Egyptian Cotton Commission, which buys the farmers' crops and sets prices according to world market conditions; through the General Cotton Organisation it is linked to the hundred-odd ginning mills up and down Egypt (now also nationalised); and through the General Cotton Pressing Organisation to the vast cotton blending, pressing and storing warehouses which occupy a vast area of Alexandria dockland and handle one million bales a year.

Thus the process already witnessed in the build-up of the Land Reform organisation at the revolution's outset was taken a long stage further; the technocrats of Egypt were at last entering into their kingdom. In the past such technocrats as existed had been subservient to the prestigious bureaucrats, just as they in their turn had been subservient to the pashas and dextrous lawyers who ran the political game. The Civil Service was the prey of a more or less open spoils system; the Wafd, whenever it returned to office, threw out incumbents to make room for its own. Professor Morroe Berger has pointed out that the problem of bureaucracy in the East is in some ways the converse of that in the West: there, in order to ensure continuous development one must somehow render the Civil Service 'less pliable in the hands of those in power.' It may be that the installation of this large stiffening of technocrats in Egypt will ultimately demonstrate at least one answer. They are, of course, under the ultimate orders of political chiefs. But their kingdoms are large and complex, and only they command the keys. In the face of the immediate economic challenge that Egypt has now taken up they are manifestly the men upon whom her survival depends. Since Egyptian planning is not yet tightly centralised on the Communist model, and the industrial corporations in fact enjoy a considerable degree of autonomy, their managers stand a good chance of developing an unoriental degree of effective independence, and perhaps ultimately, if they choose, of actual power.[8] And today there are more than forty General Organisations, controlling over 500 public enterprises, not to mention the fifteen older 'authorities' like the prestigious, and many-sided Suez Canal Authority, which itself controls seven manu-

[8] Patrick O'Brien, an economist who spent six months studying the Egyptian planning system from within, describes the productive organisation as 'standing between the command economies of Eastern Europe and the modified market systems of the West. Perhaps the term centralised market economy is roughly applicable to its unique amalgam of institutional forms and operational arrangements.'

facturing and shipbuilding companies.

In forwarding such developments the armed services officers who were the makers of Egypt's revolution are, on some levels at least, the technocrats' natural allies. W. W. Rostow has pointed out that the enlargement and modernisation of a country's armed forces can play the rôle of a leading sector in industrial 'take-off,' and was a factor in the take-offs of Russia, Japan and Germany.[9] For the modern services officer, the idea of rapid technical change, necessitating re-training at intervals, is now basic, and in recent years a rapid increase in the sophistication of weapons being used in the Middle East has underlined the challenge. In Egypt, as in the West, it is not uncommon for officers to be seconded to universities; many were sent on such courses in 1961 before moving into industry. A continuous survey of Egypt's top managers, covering 3,000 posts, by Cairo's National Institute of Management Development, shows that some 30 per cent are former army officers, 20 per cent drawn from the Civil Service, 36 per cent from private enterprise (generally taken over along with the concerns), 15 per cent from university staffs. (No fewer than 13 per cent are Ph.Ds.). And according to the head of the Institute of Management Development, Dr Fuad Cherif (a Chicago University graduate in Business Administration), 'the Army Engineering Corps could be considered the real breeding ground of our new management.' It supplied Sidky Suleiman to speed the High Dam, Mahmoud Younis to organise the Suez Canal Authority, and some scores of officers to tackle the epic—and crucial—task of desert reclamation from Liberation Province to the New Valley.

But if the army engineers were able to fill a gap, as the period of improvisation receded the survey of top management has shown ex-officers playing a smaller and smaller rôle. Technologies and technologists proliferate, and so do their kingdoms. The first course in chemical engineering in Egypt was started at Cairo University in 1943, yet already scores of its graduates hold vital posts in multiplying refineries, syn-

---

[9] The connection was strikingly demonstrated in France, where the National Convention in 1794 set up what later became the famed *Ecole Polytechnique*, largely for the training of the revolutionary army's engineers but now the Alma Mater of key French technocrats.

thetic plants, fertiliser plants and so on. Expenditure on scientific research shot up from £E200,000 in 1950 to £E5·6 millions in 1961, and the Ministry of Scientific Research (which includes an Atomic Energy Organisation) moved into a vast new white building near the centre of Cairo. By 1961 an estimated 58,000 Egyptians had graduated in technology and the natural sciences from Egyptian universities—10,000 of them engineers, 5,000 scientists. At the same time, management is being increasingly professionalised—by, for instance, so notably unoriental an institution as the American-inspired, state-owned National Institute for Management Development which operates both as a business school and a consultancy.

As yet only a few thousand strong, the New Men whom the industrialising plan was thus pushing into key position in Egyptian society were, in a number of ways, true—if non-political—revolutionaries. For whereas those earlier social arbiters, the religious sheikhs, and their successors, the westernised political lawyers, had fitted into the complacent insularity of the Nile Valley, the modern technologist is necessarily international in outlook. A steel-man is a steel-man, and an oil-man an oil-man, whatever the national tag. Not unusually, the Production Director of Helwan Steel, Dr Mourad, had studied metallurgy at Glasgow, where he took his Ph.D., as well as in Cairo, and had spent time in the steel plants of Germany, the U.S.S.R., France and Belgium. Many of the Egyptian technocrats are, in fact, deeply as well as widely travelled—and 'non-alignment' has usefully widened the scope of this experience. Even at the lower levels a good many technicians have now spent periods of training abroad in both Communist and non-Communist lands. For such men as these there is one insistent question, underlined by their travels: what *works* best now?

In the world of the 1960s it was a question which could never be closed, and in formulating it, and the novel ideas that derived from it, the new men were now sustained by a battery of new technological ministries—of Light Industry, of Heavy Industry, of Power Generation, of Petroleum and Mining, of the High Dam, of Land Reclamation—with technically qualified Ministers. The Ministers of Supply, of Economics and Finance, of Planning and Trade also were, during these forma-

tive years, all distinguished graduates of the economics departments of American, British and French universities.

Yet it is certain that many an Egyptian manager of the 1960s
must often have echoed in his heart of hearts Mohamed Ali's
remark to the British Consul, Bowring, in the 1820s: 'You
have numbers of intelligent persons to do your bidding; I can
find very few to understand me and do my bidding and I am
often deceived and know that I am deceived.' The technocrats
might have time on their side, but the Arab world was not yet
theirs. The obsequious and over-full divan advanced into the
ante-rooms of managerialism; the happy-go-lucky disorder of
the Egyptian village lapped at the feet of the conveyor-belt and
imperilled the life and limb of the Safety Manager himself.

Time-lags were inevitable and most serious in the educational system. University Arts faculties now became a swollen
sump for those who could not meet the more exacting standards of the science-technology side, aggravating the classic
problem of finding dignified employment for graduates. A
'Socialist Law' guaranteeing jobs to all graduates contributed
further to the distressing over-population of the Ministries.[10]
'How is it,' Nasser demanded in public one day, 'that we can
build the High Dam, but we cannot run the Kasr el Aini
Hospital?' The answer was not far to seek—the hospital, unlike the Dam, belonged to the old Eastern world. The remedy
was both politically and socially more difficult. Yet the enemies
were identified. In 1964, a presidential decree, abolishing the
old system by which officials were graded according to the
level of their university or school examinations, explained that
'it is the actual work rather than abstract qualifications which
counts.' *Bureaucrataya*, a word that had scarcely existed a few
years earlier, was to become a new pejorative only a little less
potent than *isti'mar*—or 'imperialism.'

---

[10] Lord Milner, Financial Under-Secretary in Egypt, 1889-92, described 'the
Government service in its lower orders' as 'a system of outdoor relief for
needy men of clerkly training'—and this is a tradition that dies hard.

16

THE TOWN: THE REACH AND THE GRASP

Egypt is a nation with limited resources and almost unlimited aspirations.
—Frederick Harbison & I. A. Ibrahim, *Human Resources for Egyptian Enterprise*, 1958

The spiritual tug-of-war between what is desired and what is possible. . . .
—Gamal Abdel Nasser, November 1965

Mohamed Ali built some of his pioneer 'European' factories and schools at Shubra, a few miles north of Cairo, driving a new road to link them to his capital. Four generations later the new industrialisers-in-a-hurry concentrated their major showpieces eight miles south of Cairo, at Helwan, formerly a genteel Nile-side spa, and drove their new Nile Corniche southwards to Helwan and northwards to a once again booming Shubra, past Cairo's phalanxes of new Nile-side hotels and the rotund mass of the TV Centre, past smartly suburban Maadi and the lingering mud villages and the serried workers' flat-blocks, along the twenty-mile axis of Africa's Megapolis, expanding, industrialising, drawing in more people year by year, though still hard-hemmed by desert.

At the south-eastern extremity of this monstrous urban oasis, the Nasr Automotive Plant occupies a bleak kilometre-square site beneath the harsh yellow cliff of the Mokattam Hills. From the wide avenue that links its six great hangars— a £E10 million workers' city is planned for the future—the visitor looks out over the desert to the furnace stacks of the iron and steel works, to the tall chimneys of the new foundry and the cement works, to the steel-pipe plant, the fertiliser factory and, emerging from the heat haze, the Step Pyramids of Sakkara, built by King Zoser's architect, Imhotep, in 2770 B.C.

The Nasr Automotive—by any standard a handsome plant.

clean and well laid-out, with a pay-roll of 5,500—was the New
Egypt's genuflection to the Assembly Line. The car side was
supplied by Fiat; the lorry and bus side uses a German Deutz
engine; the tractor's origin is Yugoslav. Capacity production is
an annual 18,000 cars and jeeps, plus 9,000 heavy vehicles and
tractors; but output in 1965 was only 20-23 cars and 20
lorries, buses, and tractors a day.

On the heavy-lorry line teams of four or five young men
bent over the growing lorries, bolting parts together labori-
ously with spanners. Others shaped steel tubes, welded girders
for the chassis. It was hard to keep the pace up, especially in
the hot weather, confessed the engineer in charge: in the villages in Egypt they were used to sleeping in the afternoons. I
asked him why they didn't use power hand-tools on the line:
'If we put in a lot of costly machinery we should make our
product too expensive—and we should not employ many
people.'

Here indeed is an inescapable dilemma for a country like
Egypt, travelling hopefully between centuries and worlds. And
it is a dilemma which becomes more acute as the capital-inten-
sive industries of the advanced industrial nations become more
automated and geared to overwhelming volume. What economic sense can a car plant—even with 'an Arab car' for the
'Arab Nation'—make in a poor, under-developed country, or
for that matter an integrated steelworks in a country without
a heavy industrial tradition which has to ship in most of the
necessary coal?

The Egyptians claim that the steelworks, with the completion of the first stage of the rolling mills in 1968, will save
over £E20 millions in foreign exchange annually. In any event
we might do well to remember that had industrial development
always waited on a suitable economic equation, much of the
world would be both very much poorer than it is today and
very different. By no means all the important functions of such
industrial show-places as those at Helwan can be demonstrated
statistically. They present an exciting visible goal. Their challenge and their stimulus are felt throughout the economy and
society. In them a nation goes to industrial school which is
much more than merely a school.

'We start with assembly. Then we make this part and that.

En route for the 'New Valley'. The tarmac road across the desert from Assiut winds down into the Kharga Oasis, the first of the long chain of Depressions that stretch towards the Mediterranean. *Below* 'Settling the Bedouin'—Bedouin children in school at the Kasr settlement near Mersa Matruh (Chapter 19)

New and Old in Upper Egy
Above Girls at a Teachers'
Training College in Kena be
each day by saluting the fla
and singing the Suez Hymr

Left Tarahiel, or migrant,
workers move down the
Valley in search of a new jc
carrying the tools of their
trade, the *fas* (mattock) an
earth-shifting basket. The
escarpment forms the easte
wall of the Valley. (Chapte

Then others. Thus we learn.' The lorry-line engineer echoed
the steel-man. Since a motor-car contains 20,000 components,
it is a considerable stimulator of light engineering versatility,
and Egypt's 1961 agreement with the Fiat Company of Italy
specified that Egyptians should themselves be manufacturing
96 per cent of the car by 1968. By 1965, they were making
over 2,000 parts, both in Nasr Automotive's own shops and
those of some two hundred sub-contractors, both public and
private, from the military factories (which make the radiators)
and the Nasr Spring Company to Mr Mohamed Sayed, a
'national capitalist' of Alexandria, who furnished silencers and
exhausts. The bodies were at this time being imported in
several sections and welded together at the start of the
assembly line, but when the big presses had been erected in
the new hall they would be stamped out on the spot from
imported sheet; later, when the Helwan strip-mill was operating, from local sheet.

That, at least, was the plan; events turned out somewhat
differently. The acute shortage of foreign exchange halted the
flow of car parts from Italy, and from the end of 1966 car
production was suspended. Indeed, perhaps the most useful
contribution of this showplace so far has been to serve as an
object-lesson illustrating the harsh clash which may exist between long-term goals and short-term necessities; the need,
in such a country, to reach, yet the high cost which may
attend the over-estimation of the grasp.

Nevertheless, Egyptians are unlikely to be too dismayed by
such initial mishaps. 'Step by step' as they love sententiously to
say. For people here often have an almost Victorian sense of pre-
ordained progression. At the steelworks, the Egyptian Training Director—rather bizarrely an English Literature graduate
of Exeter University—produced an enormous 3-sheet training
schedule, and when I enquired who in particular they were
training now, replied with enthusiasm: 'Everybody! Everybody—from the labourers to the chairman (another former
army engineer). The chairman? Oh, he's on a course at the
National Institute for Management. Then there's Dr Taher, another top executive—he's taking "Financial Analysis for Non-
Accountants." We have a surplus of labourers, so we're training some for various skilled vacancies—crane-operators,

drivers, lubricators. 171 are taking reading and writing classes —that's five days a week for four months. Then, we've got classes in German and Russian so that we can cope with our advisers. We have courses for foremen, office-boys, secretaries, storemen—and apprentices, naturally. There's a four-day induction course for the newcomers. In fact, this year over 3,000 of our 4,000 workers will be taking some course or other.'

Although Helwan Steel's zeal was no doubt exceptional, almost all the major industrial concerns run their own training departments to which, these days, hopeful young men come from all over Egypt. They work in conjunction with the craft-training centres the Ministry of Industry has established in the various regions. Almost everywhere in Egypt today, the young are learning to get on to terms with metal and machines. At Kharga Oasis, in the workshops of the General Desert Development Organisation, I watched the son of a local shopkeeper operating a crankshaft grinding machine, a smaller boy from a Nile Valley fellah family working a Chinese milling machine. At Aswan, the Egyptians have built and the Russians splendidly equipped with all manner of sectioned models, machines and visual aids, a very large training centre for fitters, welders, electricians, steel-erectors. The Principal was an ex-Chief Engineer of Cairo Transport, but most of the instructors were Russians, including a 'First Welder of the U.S.S.R.,' a burly blond figure whose welding goggles appeared to be almost welded to his forehead as he sat in the lunch-break reading a ten-day-old copy of *Komsomolskaya Pravda*.

I found Hassan Zaki Shaker, the centre's Principal—one of those supercharged, larger-than-life Egyptians with reverberant voice and staccato manner—studying with grudging admiration the filing work of a new class of orphans, sent up as an experiment by the Ministry of Social Affairs in Cairo. They were shaping well, he said. But the best trainees were still those who came from the families of craftsmen. It is Egypt's good fortune that she has a long enough industrial tradition to have such families. The bottleneck is not so much here as at a higher level, between graduate engineer and foreman. 'The technicians are still a largely absent class,' said the steelworks training director. 'At present engineers are often doing technicians' jobs as well as their own. . . .'

The Education Explosion

In so far as such jobs had formerly been done in Egypt, they had been done mainly by the foreign, although often local-born, minorities—Italians, Greeks, Maltese, Armenians.[1] Nor was this wholly a result of imperialist economic domination: a person who might get his hands dirty, who did things rather than ordered them to be done, did not rank high either in Ottoman or Bedouin estimation. And these Oriental attitudes had been largely confirmed by a narrow-based 'Western' system of higher education, discreetly designed to produce compliant bureaucrats and—where the fees were higher and the language of instruction foreign—'gentlemen.'

Industrialisation clearly required a transformation of the educational system and its values. And by the mid-'sixties it was possible to report that this was under way. It is the Egyptian custom to give first choice of university faculty to the students with highest marks in the secondary school terminal examination. Until recently, the first choice was Pharmacy and, after that, Medicine. For a pharmacy graduate could open a shop in some small town and, as one student put it, 'make £100 a month immediately.' The doctors did not get rich quite so quickly, but they got rich. Price controls, nationalised drug manufacture, free drugs in rural health centres,[2] with more and more 'health service' doctoring, have gravely reduced the commercial attractions of these two careers. Today Engineering comes easily first in students' choices; the Arts and Commerce receive the generous overflow, and Classics come last. Because of this new student bias, the Arts side in many secondary schools has become small, and sometimes non-existent. More than three-quarters of the students eligible for universities in 1968 graduated from the Science side of the secondary schools. At Cairo University, in 1965, even among girl students 17 per cent were reading Engineering.

---

[1] The tradition was old enough—Mohamed Ali's first spinning mill at Bulaq, Cairo in the 1820s was called 'Malta' because most of its workers were Maltese.

[2] In 1964, according to the Minister of Supply, Dr Stino, about 50 per cent of the drugs used in Egypt were issued free.

University laboratories are packed out, working on a shift system until late evening. When the new university of Assiut, the first in Upper Egypt, was opened in 1957, priority was given to engineering, science, agriculture, veterinary studies and medicine; the Arts will not be represented until later. The same emphasis appears in the modernisation of the mosque-university of El Azhar. Most rapid of all has been the expansion of the Higher Technical Institutes which have quadrupled in number between 1952 and 1965; and there is talk of linking them more closely to the universities, thus avoiding rigid stratification and opening paths to talent. Thus Egypt in her 'explosion' of higher education already echoes trends and philosophies in both the United States and Britain. Time and space are telescoped as both East and West come under the same twin pressures—of 'democratic' ambition and technological necessity.

University enrolment in Egypt has trebled since the revolution, reaching a total of 140,000 by 1966. Yet in the educational structure as a whole there are still crippling weaknesses. Egyptians can—and do—boast that half their secondary-school graduates go on to university—one of the highest proportions in the world. But what this statistic also points to is the narrowness of the area of recruitment: less than 10 per cent of primary-school children achieve high school; and the 1960 census showed that even in Cairo, 45 per cent of the people are illiterate—and a much higher proportion in rural Egypt.

Yet at this level, too, industrialisation forces the pace of change. The new industrial organisations are demanding literacy even in their labourers: safety, to look no further, demands an ability to read notices. All sorts of state organisations follow suit. At the same time, workers' and farmers' representation on the co-operatives, in the trade unions, on boards of directors, or in the National Assembly or Arab Socialist Union opens up many opportunities—for the literate. The result has been that fellahin who were formerly notoriously reluctant to spare their children from the fields are now actually *demanding* more and better schools, and both in the National Assembly and outside it educational opportunity has become one of the hottest—and most truly felt—topics of controversy.

'I used to be puzzled when I read in English history that arithmetic had to be taught to the people because of the Industrial Revolution,' said Yussef el Afifi, Director of Fundamental Education in Cairo. 'Now I understand! Education used to be something apart. Now it is being woven into the texture of life. You can't imagine the difference! Before the Revolution we had to make great efforts to get people to our literacy classes. Now, if we have a possibility of three classes, there will be applicants for six!'

By 1965, 75 per cent of the six-twelve year age-group were in primary school; and it is intended that all of it will be there by 1970. Moreover, in 1956—in what could well turn out to be the most far-reaching of all the educational reforms —the primary schools were for the first time integrated into the educational system, so that, very shakily, an 'educational ladder' reaches up towards the universities. University fees (1952: £E40 a term) have been progressively reduced almost to vanishing point, and annual grants are made to students gaining good grades.

The task remains formidable. Egypt is seeking to accomplish in a decade or two the educational revolution which in Britain took at least three generations between 1870 and the present day. Furthermore, a country in so tight an economic situation cannot afford supernumeraries; failure to tailor higher education to current national needs can be disastrous. Nor can such a country afford a lowering of academic standards: for the lowness of the existing average is already a grievous obstacle. At Cairo University, the premier university of Egypt, numbers have now reached 45,000 and 'one may sometimes find oneself teaching classes of 500.' Like most of his colleagues, the Vice-Rector, Professor Hussein Said, freely admitted to me that standards had fallen. 'Yet I think they are better than we were. They think better, are a lot sharper on the average, and if they had the proper care that my generation had, we could do wonders with them!'

Like so much else in the New Egypt, the educational programme is a vast gamble—or a major act of faith, according to one's philosophy. But if it is a gamble, like so much else in Egypt, it is a gamble that had to be taken, and a gamble which *has* to succeed.

The Economic Dilemma

But if in the world of education it is normal, even necessary, for the reach to exceed the grasp, in the economic field the international banker sooner or later rules a line and calls it bankruptcy.

The ten years ending in 1965 represented the revolution's euphoric phase, the external triumphs, the internal quickening, the quick social dividends in town and country. But revolutionary dawns are non-recurring. As industrialisation gathered pace and imports of raw materials and machinery mounted, the strain on the balance of payments grew formidable. Egypt was living from hand to mouth, allocating each bit of foreign exchange as soon as she received it. The burden was daunting. She had to service—and start to repay—her loans, import wheat and meat to sustain a soaring population (whose expectations were now rising), accumulate capital to finance her plan, and, with it all, sustain the momentum of her industrial expansion as she reached for take-off into self-sustaining growth.

It is one of the many ironies of the Arab world that Egypt, which possesses the people, the plan and the technical capacity to create a stable modern industrial state in the Middle East, is also among the Arab countries least endowed with the necessary natural resources. It is true that despite increased competition, she still grows half the world's extra-long-staple cotton. The winter sun and the Pharaohs still bring the world's tourists, and the Government has built many handsome new hotels to accommodate them. The country's geographical position is no mean asset, and the Suez Canal normally affords a third valuable source of foreign exchange. But raw cotton still provides over half of Egypt's visible exports, and cotton, rice, tourism and the Suez Canal plus textiles (both yarn and cloth) must provide the bulk of the country's foreign earnings for the next twenty years. By comparison with these, export contributions from Egypt's growing industries, other than textiles, have been small, but are now beginning to edge upwards.

The margin for error in the industrialising programme is

thus slender, and from time to time factories have been forced
to halt for lack of foreign exchange to purchase raw materials
or necessary machine parts. But after Pan-American Oil's
strike in the Gulf of Suez in 1965, hopes have risen of a wind-
fall from this now almost traditional source of Arab revenue.
With a further discovery near El Alamein in December 1965
and later strikes both in the Red Sea areas and the Western
Desert and much exploration under way, there was now a
near prospect of oil exports worth £30 millions, and, by the
early '70s, of an annual output of 30 million tons—a quarter
of Kuwait's. Meanwhile, natural gas discovered near Abu
Mady in Lower Egypt is reported to equal all the country's
current consumption of furnace fuel.

But if cotton—raw, spun and woven—underpinned the Plan
—and oil offered the prospect of eleventh-hour deliverance—
its keystone was still the High Dam. A High Dam, however,
that was no longer a vision but an undeniable fact, bringing
nearer each year not only its cheap power, but some easement
of the critical problem of feeding a country dependent on imports for most of its meat and bread-grains. If the cost of the
whole High Dam project was vast, so too would be its benefits:
according to the estimate agreed by the World Bank, the entire
cost will be recouped in the first two years.

Despite the obvious precariousness of the situation, Egyptian
planners are confident—and not wholly without reason. The
narrow, hard-edged confines of the Nile Valley where everything is sharply illuminated (though not necessarily *seen*) do
give them an immense advantage over their counterparts in,
say, India or Russia. As the High Dam project with its endless,
intricate interconnections over the entire country again demonstrates, the Nile Valley—for all its nightmare lapse into *laisser-
faire* under Ismail—has been natural planners' territory since
the days of the Pharaohs. 'Every day,' enthused Dr Labib Showcair, the then Minister of Planning, 'we develop new planning
techniques. We consider our mistake. We hide nothing. We
have studied every experience, both in other countries and
in Egypt.[3] Exports? Exports are really no problem. Take tex-

[3] An independent witness, the economist P. O'Brien, writes: '. . . compared with many poor countries the quantity and quality of information
about Egypt's economy is quite remarkable.' (1966).

tiles, fertilisers, cement, sugar, canned goods, tyres—we can double and treble our exports of all of them. We are turning orders down.'

The ability to manipulate export prices, of course, helps: at this time one-third of the rayon output was being exported at an 'international price' lower than that charged internally. And by 1965 the Egyptian planners, much more than their counterparts in mixed, but predominantly capitalist, economies did hold in their hands the means to render their decisions effective. They could fix a price so as to promote exports, or to accumulate capital, or to serve a social need, as the case and overall policy required. Profits in the public sector now became a more important source of capital formation than taxation, and the insurance companies, now wholly nationalised, also had a central rôle here. Since almost all financing was channelled through Governmental agencies, and private industrial projects required a Ministry of Industry licence, it was no longer difficult to direct investment into the areas of priority.

As so often, the real 'economic problem' is not so much economic as human and political.

On the governmental level, the price of keeping the revolutionary conscience of 'the Arab world has—particularly in more recent years—come high in terms of the dislocation of industrialising schedules and the interruption of technical aid and finance. The Arab break with West Germany in 1965 over her diplomatic recognition of Israel (preceded by the disclosure of a secret arms deal between Ben Gurion and Adenauer in 1960) was a conspicuous example. For West Germans were involved in many projects, including the plan for the hydroelectric utilisation of the Quattara Depression.

On the popular level, the heady promises of a political revolution and the hard slog of economic reconstruction do not always sit well together. If exports lag, it will not, probably, be so much because markets are lacking, as because the 'surplus' is being devoured at home. True, the plan projected increased internal consumption—both from humanitarian motives and to prime the economic pump and create a home market on which the import-saving industries could float. A minimum urban wage raised in 1961 to twenty-five piastres, successive decreases in land-reform farm repayments, cuts in urban rents, all the constructional activity, put more money into the pockets of the poorer people. Appetites denied for years were whetted. Consumption soared. To assuage the hunger for meat, the Ministry of Supply was driven to seek it around the world, even buying broilers from the U.S.A. Between 1961 and 1963 alone food imports doubled. For the skilled worker or 'employee' there was the Nasr TV or Ideal refrigerator, available on small monthly payments.

The result was that instead of increasing by the 25 per cent allowed for in the First Five Year Plan (1960-1965) consumption rose by 46 per cent. It was not surprising that inflation occurred; what was perhaps more surprising was that it was as professionally controlled as it was—by price limitations (with shops compelled to show tickets), subsidies on essentials (that on bread cost £25 million sterling a year), by the rationing of tea, sugar, kerosene, flour, vegetable oil, and, most interestingly, by the influence of the large chain of state-owned co-operative stores in the cities.

Through the critical years from 1956 to 1966, this vital area of supply was the domain of yet another American-educated technocrat, the ingenious Dr Kamel Ramzy Stino, Minister of Supply, a former professor of plant genetics and a specialist on vegetable cultivation, well-known in Egypt for his work on the use of the sweet potato in flour-making. With two hundred-odd co-operative food-shops in Cairo and a hundred in Alexandria, Stino, a Coptic Christian, challenged with Western methods of high turnover, display, machine-packaging and low prices, the old hole-in-the-wall grocer and baker working in the grand old Oriental tradition of adulteration and extortion. At the same time, by acting as wholesaler to private family grocers, the co-operative food organisation sought to establish price standards and discourage the black marketeer. It, too, suffered its share of peculating managers and staff, but when caught, they were prosecuted.

Since flour was so heavily subsidised, 90 per cent of the flour mills and 10 per cent of the bakeries were taken into public ownership and operated by an organisation under the Ministry of Supply. Another of that Ministry's organisations builds and operates silos to save some of the £8 million pounds-worth of grain estimated lost each year by the traditional method of storing it in mountainous piles in the open and paying a small boy to scare off the pigeons. New sources of home-produced food are being developed, such as beef cattle and broiler chickens which the Ministry of Agriculture's Animal Division is producing in a series of units around Cairo. There are fish-stocking and fish-canning schemes along the coasts of the Mediterranean and the Red Sea, inspired by the magnificently named 'Organisation for Aquatic Wealth.'

It remains true that if Egypt is to carry through her plan and become the first industrial nation in the Arab world, a great many Egyptians will have to rise from the table un-satisfied—and the better the spread, the more poignant the moment of departure. Grown for export on the newly re-claimed desert lands, the citrus crop cannot, for instance, go on being allowed to disappear before it reaches the ports. But perhaps the most graphic illustration of the cruelty of the dilemma is provided by the associated products, sugar and paper, basic pabulum for those twin voracious organs of developing nations, the stomach and the mind. The chairman of the El Nasr Sugar and Pulp organisation told me: 'In 1952 we were producing 160,000 tons of sugar in Egypt and we were exporting some of it. In 1963, we produced 380,000 tons —but we still had to import 100,000 tons. In 1970 we shall be producing one million tons—but consumption will still be rising faster. We still shan't have enough.' In the same period Egyptian production of paper and cardboard has quintupled, but is still short of local consumption—which in the mean-time has almost trebled. Yet the Plan requires Egypt to be ex-porting 350,000 tons of sugar by 1971, and to be self-sufficient (save for newsprint) in paper.

The difficulty is not merely that 'appetite comes with eat-ing' but that this appetite is augmented by 800,000 extra mouths a year. But if the régime at first tended to supplement the fellah's 'God will provide' with 'Science will provide,' the shock of the 1960 Census brought a change. The Charter de-scribes the high birth-rate as 'the most serious obstacle facing the Egyptian people in their drive to raise the standard of living.' The promotion of birth-control now began to receive a higher priority, and with 1965 came a belated switch in

emphasis from revolutionary rights to revolutionary obligations, from the Ministry of National Guidance's untiring re-
iteration of the Arabic version of 'you-never-had-it-so-good' to
exhortations on the need for saving, and even austerity.

Défendu la Viande: lundi, mardi, mercredi warned the
notices in the restaurants even of easy-going Alexandria as the
régime of weekly meatless days was introduced. In October
1965, prices were raised on a wide range of both luxuries and
essentials; and at the end of November, Nasser, addressing the
National Assembly, spoke gravely of what he called 'the spiritual tug-of-war between what is desired and what is possible.
. . . Our expectations have become greater than our incomes
or capabilities.' The political editor of a leading newspaper
house talked to me earnestly of the need to prepare the people
for the 'seven lean years' ahead.

Patience and capacity to endure the Egyptians have. But
they are not a provident people. With them, generosity is both
an instinct and a virtue. 'The Egyptians,' said the great Arab
historian, Ibn Khaldun, in the 14th century, 'act as if
there were to be no day of reckoning.' In the old world of
'malish!' discipline had been by hunger and the *kourbash*,
capital accumulation the pursuit and pleasure of the landlord
and the moneylender. Now it was proposed to substitute the
imperatives of the Plan, rationing, education, the appeal to
good citizenship via the Arab Socialist Union, the 'socialist
incentives' of profit-sharing, with prizes and office for the
worthy. The school of industry might have its excitements,
but some of its less publicised lessons were likely to prove
difficult to master.

17

THE VILLAGE: THE CO-OPERATIVES
TAKE OVER

It is not easy, not easy to convince them to adopt the co-operative principle—for every one wants to work for himself. But they find its way and they see its results and gradually they have confidence in their co-operative.

—Abdel Latif Mandour, Director-General of the
Agricultural Co-operative Organisation to author

The finished steel sections being transported from the steel mills at Helwan were carried on long carts, and I was delighted to observe that both steel and carts were liberally strewn with green berseem, the universal substance of rural Egypt—provender for the horses that hauled them. There was a touch of poetical appropriateness in that. For what the percipient Bonaparte had remarked in 1799 was still true: Egypt was still borne on the backs of the fellahin, even if what they supported now was factories and social welfare rather than pashas' palaces and Levantine opulence. Although it was the urban boom which made the headlines, the heart and sinews of Egypt still lay in the endless mud villages where 60 per cent of her people still lived. The revolution ultimately derived from them, and had first taken shape there in the Land Reform based on a peculiarly Egyptian pattern of agricultural co-operation. And it was upon sustaining—and extending—the agrarian revolution that the financing of the newly launched industrial revolution now depended.

In 1961, the second land reform (limiting individual ownership to one hundred feddans) together with sequestration of foreign-owned lands had raised the total of expropriated land to almost a million feddans, including land on which villages stood, and land too poor for use, or still unreclaimed. By June 1966 a total of 735,300 feddans had been distributed, and more than three hundred thousand families—1,500,000 people—had been settled on small holdings and organised in 500 land-reform co-operatives.

A great deal of faith, administrative effort and hard cash had been put into this form of rural organisation. How far had it proved justified? Was the performance of the land reform co-operatives living up to the promise?

It was threshing time again in the Delta, and outside the village of Robh Shandied the venerable *norag* (threshing throne) circled again over the golden floor of grain. But now it was being hauled not by a plodding ox, but by a tractor. The winnowing, though, was still done by a shovel and the wind: in rural Egypt it is important to spare the animals which yield milk and meat and calves, but men are super-abundant and over-fecund.[1]

Ten years after my first visit, I sat again with the co-operative committee of Robh Shandied, one of the thirteen village societies of the Land Reform Area of Etay el Baroud. They still met round the same trestle table in the small room in the old Royal stables, and there were still familiar faces. But the spry little secretary who had remained vividly in my memory through the intervening years was seventy now (and with another child, bringing his family to nine) and had retired, making way for a tall, immensely dignified young man with curling mustachios. With well over a thousand meetings—and nine bulging Minute Books—behind it, the committee was no longer a curious novelty but a well-tried institution and the heart of the village's life. It moved through the day's agenda with practised ease: the application for 400 sacks of nitrate for the rice land, the adjudication of a quarrel between two brothers over the succession to their father's land,[2] the £E10 grant from the social fund to a newly bereaved widow, the £E118 for the repair of the mosque. . . .

Yet if those nine Minute Books could have spoken, they

[1] Threshing machines have been tried in some places but have made little headway because the villagers complain that they cut the straw too short for cattle-feed—all-important to them in summer.

[2] A not infrequent necessity because under the Land Reform Law the holding may not be split and there can be only a single legatee. How the members of the family divide the income from the holding, however, is their own business—unless they can't agree, when the co-operative's conciliation committee may arbitrate.

would assuredly have revealed, behind the formal entries in
neat Arabic script, an intricate tale of conflict and struggle,
of setbacks and jealousies and human inadequacies as well as
of gradually consolidating achievement. Peasants as poor as
these face a hard test when offered loans. If they spend some
of the money on food or perhaps a dowry for the daughter,
they will certainly fall into default on their annual repayments
to the co-operative. If further loans are thereupon cut off, they
are plunged further into misery; if not, perhaps further into
debt. Some may seek a way out by selling on the black market
their co-operative-supplied fertiliser or animals. Or they may,
as it is rather quaintly put, 'embezzle' their own cotton crop
—that is, sneak some of it off for sale beyond the co-operative
creditor's eye. Because of the poverty of the Etay el Baroud
region, a fifth of all loans, according to one estimate, were at
first wrongly diverted, compared with a national Land Reform
average of 10-15 per cent.[3]

Again, although one of the objects of providing tractors was
to save the cattle for milk, the first response to the milk-col-
lecting centre, set up in 1957, had been meagre. Few peasants
can afford enough cotton-seed cake for the summer feeding of
their single cow, and, in any case, the idea dies hard in rural
Egypt that the peasant selling milk is somehow shamed—since
if a man has a respectable wife, she turns milk into cheese and
butter and *samna* (ghee). Another scheme which sought to
increase income by supplying farmers with five-month-old
calves to fatten for market—one man, one calf—had run into
bad trouble when disease swept through the cattle-sheds.

But a community so organised and supported can learn from
its mistakes. In Robh Shandied the calf-fattening scheme was
now going well, adding, they said, an average £E16 to each
participant's annual income. The champion calf fattener, one
Sheikh Hassenein, triumphantly claimed to have made £E22.
'He feeds that animal night and day,' someone said. All in all,
the members had every reason to be content. In 1955, the
society had hired its first tractor; now in the yard next door
were six tractors they fully owned, eight 'Bean' spraying engines, four movable pumps, twenty-seven portable crop-spray-
ers—and a mechanic and two helpers to look after them.

[3] Gabriel S. Saab, *The Egyptian Agrarian Reform, 1952-62* (Oxford, 1967).

Because of the successive cuts in 1961 and 1964 in the prices to be repaid for land-reform farms—first to one-half, then to one-quarter—most of the members were already freeholders, and the others soon would be.

Since 1961 all co-operative loans had been interest-free, and there had been two increases in the prices paid for cotton. Such governmental steps to improve the position of the fellah, plus the increasing yields they had achieved, had meant that at Robh Shandied the average net income had more than doubled, reaching £E4 and more a week for the 3-feddan family, without allowing for their subsistence from their land. The secretary of the society, the tall young man with the mustachios, reeled off his own personal 3-feddan farm accounts. From his cotton, wheat, rice, maize and berseem he now had a net income of £E228 a year—to which was to be added £E1 a week for the cheese, skim milk and butter from his two buffaloes, and thirty-forty piastres for eggs from his wife's twelve hens (although, he said, since the 'three meatless days a week' order he'd been eating some of those himself).

By Egyptian village standards this is affluence. Now, they said proudly, they ate meat twice a week. Before, they had eaten only maize; now they ate wheat and rice. But it was the meat that mattered. Its price was high and rising, but for them meat represented arrival, and they must have it, even if it cost two days' work or more.

But the village itself was changed hardly at all. They still lived, as ever, close to the earth, still sharing those heaped mud hovels with their families, donkey, cow and gamoose. But now, near the old stables, there was a concrete Club house, built from co-operatives' subscriptions, with electric light from a generator and a television set. Their favourite programme? *Nur al Nur*—'Light on Light,' the twice-weekly religious discussion in which sheikhs and various personalities debate the application of the precepts of the Koran to the problems of today.

The five artesian wells for Robh Shandied had been completed, making twenty-three for the Land Reform region as a whole. Ahmed Shaban, who had been so worried about this on my first visit, now had his rice, and so had the rest of them, 700 acres of fresh green shoots, rippling in the breeze. It was a notable contribution to the economy of the village, since one acre of rice brings in three times as much cash as an acre of wheat.

The cultivation of rice is part of a national policy aimed at diversifying crops and reducing Egypt's over-dependence on cotton. As more water from the reservoir rising behind the High Dam has come on tap, the rice allocation throughout the middle and lower Delta has been doubled, reaching over one million feddans in 1966. The high water-table and salinity of the soil in the Lower Delta, and in the land being reclaimed around the lagoons, makes salt-tolerant rice a suitable, as well as a valuable, crop. In Upper Egypt, by contrast, the extra water will go to extend sugar-cane cultivation, to be doubled in five years, again partly at the expense of cotton.

In these and other ways the rigid pattern of an agriculture wholly orientated to cotton is being modified. Fine Egyptian cotton is a lucrative crop, but horticulture, suited to Egypt's climate, soil and plentiful labour supply, can be more profitable still. Flax, citrus, grapes, mangoes (which sell to Sweden and Russia), vegetables and flower cultivation are being slowly extended. At the Land Reform area of Inchass, I found the chief agriculturalist excited about his acres of scarlet gladioli on newly reclaimed desert—1½ metre stems with thirty-six flowers, he said—to be air-freighted to European markets for Christmas, a two-month gain on the rest of North Africa. Fruit, also a high-yielding export, has been found ill-suited to the Land Reform pattern of 3-feddan holdings. The orchards either belong to the larger private farmers or are run by state agriculturalists for a specialised Fruit and Flower Organisation. In the next million acres to be reclaimed, the agricultural planners have allocated 15 per cent to fruit cultivation, as against 2½ per cent in the old lands of Egypt.

Such breaks in the traditional pattern are as yet small. Cotton remains the lifeblood of both the nation and the village, the crown of a remarkable agriculture. On the wall of many an agricultural office hangs a framed chart which shows the progression of the cotton crop, year-by-year, back to 1821 when it was 100,000 kantars.[4] In 1937, it reached over ten million kantar, and this remained the peak until 1965 which

[4] 1 kantar equals 99 lb (45 kilograms).

recorded the biggest crop ever. Egypt has, in general, the world's highest cotton yields, and in 1965 its highest yield of 7·58 kantars a feddan surpassed even that of tiny El Salvador, formerly the world champion.

Advances like these are striking evidence of the possibilities of plant-breeding and scientific culture, the application of whose lessons the Land Reform organisation has greatly facilitated. On the state experimental stations at Giza in Cairo and at Saka in the Delta, improved strains of cotton are always under development. Since 1959 the whole country has been zoned, with a single, tested variety of seed selected for each zone. Nationalisation made it possible to restrict each of the hundred-odd gins to a single variety of cotton, removing an old bane, the accidental mixing of seed. Tractor ploughing has encouraged early planting which is crucial in Egypt; if in a co-operative a member's seed is not in by the end of March, the co-operative committee can take over and do it for him. Avoidance of over-irrigation (a common fellah failing), better drainage (more pumps, as at Robh Shandied and, now, tiled drainage); big increases in fertiliser application, and a vast expenditure on pesticides (reaching £E16 million for the threatened cotton crop of 1966) have all had their continuing effect.

But an agriculture like this demands continuous care and vigilance—most particularly through those weeks of the early summer which the fellahin call 'the season of the pests.' No Egyptian agriculturalist is likely to forget the summer of 1961 when the cotton worm got hold, cut the crop by a third and threw the country's economic plan into confusion. Between 25 May and 16 July every plant has to be examined every three days—the eggs hatch in four. At Robh Shandied, forty boys and girls from the villages were out in the fields, two long lines, combing through the bushes, turning each over with a quick eye for the tell-tale dark specks on the undersides of the leaves. Behind them stood the *rayyis* (boss) with his long stick, and the small notebook in which were entered the names of the children, who receive ten piastres a day from the co-operative's funds.

For three months the villages of the Delta would live, eat and sleep cotton. Only forty-five days pass between the plant's flowering and the harvest, and then for six weeks the fields are a white blur as the women pick the cotton and it flows out, a white river, down to the Co-operative Organisation's stores and on to the ginning factories, where the bulging bales stand, a slowly diminishing mountain, through to the following April. Graded and stamped with their village of origin, the ginned bales move in endless lorry-loads down the Nile Valley to the vast pressing warehouses of Alexandria where the mixing rooms snow cotton as women blend the broken bales by hurling handfuls into the air in that unique Egyptian process known as *farfara*.

Egyptian long-staple cotton has continued to reward the care lavished upon it. At Robh Shandied the co-operative's books showed an annual advance in yield from 3·95 kantars per feddan in 1960 to 5·77 kantars in 1964, an average increase of 40 per cent over four years. But other crops besides cotton were now showing excellent yields. An American agriculturalist working in the country told me that Egyptian rice culture was now as good as any in the world; their groundnuts, planted on reclaimed desert, show yields second only to Japan's. At the Robh Shandied co-operative on my successive visits in 1955, 1964 and 1965, the agriculturalist produced his accounts which showed wide improvements in most of the main crops. Between 1955 and 1964, the average yield of wheat per feddan had grown from 3·5 to 7 ardebs, of rice from 1·5 to 2·8 dariba, of maize from 5 to 8·7 ardebs.[5] Possibly this was a good example, but increasing yields and incomes have been general in the Land Reform co-operatives.[6] The same factors, the increased application of capital to the land, and the 'scientific revolution' have, it is true, been producing similarly striking results in the developed countries. The quantity of fertiliser applied to the land in Egypt—to mention just one element— almost doubled between 1955 and 1963 and was then still

[5] 1 *dariba* of rice equals 935 kilograms approximately, 1 *ardeb* of wheat equals 150 kilograms approximately, 1 *ardeb* of maize equals 140 kilograms approximately.

[6] cf. United Nations Report, April, 1963, on 'Agrarian Reform': In the U.A.R. 'statistics show a remarkable development of agricultural crops, especially sugar and cotton. A comparison between 1952 and '59 shows an increase in the cotton crop of 45 per cent per feddan on Agrarian Reform lands.'

rising steeply. But however much of the credit should go to 'science' the figures suggest that in the Land Reform co-operatives Egyptians succeeded in devising a means by which the teachings of scientific agriculture can be brought down to grass-roots level and there combined with the virtues of peasant proprietorship.

Even when the Second Land Reform was completed, its co-operative form of organisation would cover only about one-seventh of the old (1952) area of Egyptian cultivation.[7] There were, in fact, now two distinct and sharply different rural Egypts: the one, egalitarian, an organised society of peasant proprietors, neither rich, nor—in Egyptian terms—very poor, and with the democratic machinery, funds and specialist aids of the co-operative organisation on tap; the other, several times larger, an older pattern in which owners of a hundred feddans (perhaps rented out) co-existed with *kulaks* of 20 feddans and with swarms of holders of three, two or some minute fraction of a feddan.

As a result of the successive agrarian reform laws, the pattern of land occupancy was now largely stabilised. The Land Bourse that had once been rural Egypt had ceased. But the pattern that was left was not a good pattern. Violent contrasts of riches and poverty remained. The law conferred security of tenure and limited rents, but, with the connivance of land-hungry peasants, the rent laws were evaded, and rent levels crept upwards. The effects of extreme pressure of population on the soil were in Egypt intensified by the Koranic law of inheritance which divides a father's land equally between all his sons (with half shares for his daughters), and in most villages this had produced a patchwork quilt of minute and widely scattered holdings bearing little relation to the complex irrigation and drainage networks. The resulting swarms of one, two or half-feddan tenants or owners conspicuously lacked the capital, knowledge or marketing strength needed if the land was to yield what it might.

[7] The total area transferred to smallholders was somewhat larger since it included parts of holdings in excess of the 1952 limit privately sold off by landlords and also 135,000 feddan of State Domain. Saab calculates that it amounted to over one-fifth of the 1952 cultivated area.

It was a situation which fatally barred the way to increased agricultural production. At the same time, the human problems involved in any reorganisation were obviously acute. But, again, the system of statutory co-operatives, proved in the Land Reform regions, seemed to suggest a way ahead. From about 1956 onwards, they were gradually being extended in a modified form to the rural Egypt outside the Land Reform areas. By 1965, there had come into being a network of 4,200 agricultural co-operatives, covering almost every village in the country. They differed from the Land Reform co-operatives in that the size of their members' holdings varied widely—as did their members' wealth. They differed also from the old, pre-revolutionary, co-operative societies in that they were comprehensive, provided with staff and specialist services, and directed to the needs of the small fellah—and to tenants as well as owners. Since they were the channel for the supply of tested seeds and fertiliser, not to mention interest-free loans, the bigger landholders were in practice obliged to join them; but the law insisted that four-fifths of the members of the elected committees of boards should be farmers of not more than five feddans. And from 1963 the co-operative offices had the duty of maintaining a register of land-ownership, tenancies, and rents—so that evasion of the various limitation laws became more difficult (if not impossible). Gradually, province by province, the purchase of the cotton crop was taken wholly out of the hands of local middlemen and moneylenders and confined to the Co-operative Organisation—and this, too, weakened the position of what revolutionary France knew as 'the *émigrés* of the Interior.'

But the greatest single benefit the extension of the co-operative network brought derived from its attack on the problem of land fragmentation. The solution devised had all the characteristic complexity of Egyptian agriculture—and politics. Voluntary, yet imposed and organised from above, the scheme involved the annual replanning of the land lay-out of each village in such a way as to combine the scores of tiny holdings into continuous patches under single crops—but without any change in permanent tenancy or ownership. The system was first tried out in a village near Tanta in 1955, and its progress was such that in 1960 it was decided to use the revitalised co-operatives to extend it by degrees all over Egypt.

In that year, for instance, the scheme was introduced into six widely separated villages in the province of Minya. But the task of persuading some hundreds of suspicious and illiterate fellahin to work together in this way remained a formidable one. 'We were cursed everywhere,' said one of the Minya agriculturalists who saw the thing through. 'They thought we were going towards Communism.' Nevertheless, by a mixture of bluff and persuasion, a beginning was made: in the first year in those six pioneer villages there was no patch of any crop less than twenty-five acres. And when the fellahin saw the effect on their incomes, they responded. By 1962, the average single-crop patch had been raised to fifty acres; two years later, it was ninety, with the odd patch running up to 400 acres.

Five years after the first wary introduction of the system into Minya, all the land in the province (outside the Land Reform's 100,000 acres) had been thus consolidated. In the Co-operative Organisation's provincial headquarters in El Minya town on the Nile's west bank are now filed hundreds of village land plans, totalling half a million acres, complicated jig-saws, painstakingly building up the countless fragments representing individual holdings into large patches, coloured pink and blue and brown. The pink stands for cotton, the blue for wheat, the brown for berseem. On the backs of the plans rows of thumb-prints, the signatures of the fellah representatives for each area of each co-operative, assent to the operational plan for the year. After that, under the law passed in 1963, the plan acquires legal force, and a member who plants outside it can be fined.[8]

There was some difficulty at first with the half-feddan tenants who found all their holding included within a single crop area. If it happened to be cotton, this meant that the farmer that year lacked the berseem he normally grew for his cow or gamoose: and this was serious, because for such minuscule holders—and there are a vast number of them—the gamoose is a life-saver. Bought from the co-operative for £E60 on instalments spread over seven years, she may well be worth £E150 two years after purchase, not to mention all her rich

---

[8] But fruit and vegetables, being export crops to be encouraged, are exempt from these restrictions.

milk and cheese. However, by a variety of stratagems, exchanges and compromises, such doubts were set at rest, or as nearly at rest as doubts ever will be in an Egyptian village. The grand design went ahead.

Saft el Leban ('the Hamlet of the Milk'), a village of 750 families, with thirty owners and the rest small tenants, was one of the first in Minya to experience the agonies of this 'consolidation' or 'unified rotation.' But by the time I visited it at the end of February 1965, the whole complicated annual operation, managed by the village co-operative and its resident agricultural engineer, had become routine. To one side of a mud road ran off a vast expanse of regular earth ridges and furrows, east to west to catch the sun all day, ready for the seeds of Ashmouni cotton, the variety for this part of the Nile Valley, and the oldest cultivated variety in the world. The land was ploughed with the co-operative's Fordson tractor, hauling three ploughs, and for this the farmers paid £E1 a feddan. But the principle of individual ownership and responsibility was still sedulously preserved—as could be seen on the other side of the road where the expanse of growing wheat was unbroken, but the different heights and conditions of the crop betrayed the boundaries of ownership. 'See,' laughed the agriculturalist, pointing to a particularly puny strip a few feet wide, 'that man can't sleep at night when he sees the wheat of his neighbours!'

The village could now be in no doubt that this complicated pattern of co-operation paid. For the more accurate irrigation, the deeper tractor ploughing, the timelier planting that consolidation made possible—together with tested seeds and more fertiliser and pesticides—had produced their usual results. At Saft el Leban the average cotton yield had risen by one third, and over the province as a whole the cotton yield reached its highest ever, an average of 7¼ kantar a feddan, though the wheat crop was little affected.

In the fields, a little way off the road, stood a new whitewashed building, enclosing a small courtyard. It was the village co-operative's store and office, one of 250 such centres erected in Minya in the last few years, which, with a further 100 projected, would shortly cover the entire province (as they were slowly covering the country).

CO-OPERATION, proclaimed a poster on the wall, WILL MOBILISE HUMAN EFFORT TO SOLVE THE PROBLEMS OF RURAL EGYPT. The fellahin had accepted the plan because it paid them, but the balance between the claims of the individual and those of the community which the co-operative ideal sought to maintain remained a precarious one. As I watched, a steady stream of fellahin with donkeys was arriving at the co-operative storehouse, each man intent on carrying off his allotment from the newly arrived sacks of fertiliser. They would not need it for six weeks, but until they had it inside their houses, with the cow and gamoose and the donkey, they did not, it seemed, feel secure.

However, they would certainly have approved unequivocally of another poster on the wall, a quotation from a speech of Nasser: 'We don't wish to build our society upon tenants. We would like every tenant to become an owner.' In this new rural pattern the absentee landlord, receiving his rents in Cairo —and he still existed, even if both his land and rents had been cut—was increasingly anomalous. In the Saft el Leban area one extended family, headed by a Supreme-Court Judge, still held in all 700 acres, divided between its various members. And then there was the vast number of absentee petty 'registered owners' of fragments of land whose rents, collectively, still formed a substantial tribute paid by the 'nation in *galabiyas*' of rural Egypt to the 'nation in trousers' in the towns. Yet by pursuing agrarian reconstruction with a Fabian gradualness the régime has been able to realise solid gains, both for the majority of fellahin and for the national economy.

By 1965 this process of co-operative consolidation had been applied to the cotton crop throughout Egypt, bringing an increase in output which the Minister of Agriculture, Dr Shafik el Keshin, put at 40 per cent. Such gains were of critical importance to the economy of a country struggling to finance its industrialising plan, and pointed to the need to push ahead with the further application of scientific agriculture. The Second Plan, running to 1970, allocated 22 per cent of its total investment to agriculture, compared with 8 per cent under the First Five Year Plan.

In the two provinces of Kafr el Sheikh in the Lower Delta,

and Beni Suef in the Nile Valley the logical next step was now being taken by bringing together the Land Reform co-operatives and the other village agricultural co-operatives to form a common modernising network embracing the entire province.

Kafr el Sheikh, with its northern shore on Lake Borollos and the sea, is one of the Delta's biggest, remotest, and hitherto most neglected, provinces. It is without industries and its million inhabitants are very poor even by Egyptian standards: many fellahin had only a *share* in a cow. It was therefore chosen as an experimental area in which, through a web of village co-operatives covering the entire province, the maximum intensity of agricultural services would be brought to bear. There would, for instance, be an agricultural assistant and a tractor allotted to every 750 acres, demonstration plots at frequent intervals, 150 local 'credit units' of the Co-operative Bank, five machine maintenance stations, seventy-five threshing machines, 10,000 hand sprayers and so on. Since the province varied very widely in the quality of its soils, a soil map was being prepared and deficiencies were being systematically made up. The whole operation was watched over by a large technical staff, ranging from a highly experienced and energetic Provincial Director to the agricultural assistants from the special agricultural secondary schools.

According to Dr Nashatar, chairman of the Agrarian Reform Authority, by 1965 £E2½ millions had been put into the scheme. But again the response had been dramatic: the province's agricultural income had, he claimed, increased by almost twice that amount. The provincial director in Kafr el Sheikh itself told me that the yield of cotton had increased over two years by 20 per cent, of wheat by 15 per cent, of beans by 35 per cent.

Intensive, scientific agriculture was hardly new in Egypt. With Mohamed Ali's large-scale cultivation of cotton as an export crop to be despatched to an industrialising Europe, Egypt might claim to have undergone a modern agricultural revolution long before any other Eastern country. What was new now was the motivation of the agricultural improvements and the character of the institutions devised to carry them through. The motive of the agrarian reform of 1953 had not been increased production, but social justice. But once distribution of the large estates had been determined on, technical—as well as social—needs dictated forms, and now following up the technical and social lessons of the first experiment had led (pragmatically as in the case of the industrial changes) to a many-sided agricultural revolution which embraced the greater part of the rural population.

By the mid-'sixties, the Egyptian co-operative system had been given a central place not only ideologically, in the Charter, but also in rural reality. It still sought to pursue social equity and democracy as well as agricultural efficiency. But they were not always the easiest of partners—and because of this the system was not without its critics. An American agriculturalist working in Egypt complained that the co-operative form did little to provide the fellah with what he called 'motivation'—that spirit of enterprise and self-help which, for historical reasons, he often notably lacks. It is true that there is a curious rigidity about the system which does not wholly stem from its dependence on cotton and centralised irrigation. The fellahin rarely seem to take even such initiatives as are allowed them. For instance, potatoes will yield two or three times the income of wheat and are exempted from the crop consolidation orders, but at Saft el Leban only one man was growing a strip of potatoes: seed potatoes are expensive and to the Egyptian fellah, who does not eat them, they appear an alien and suspect crop. Again, in a co-operative at Abis, one member, by purchasing other farmers' berseem, had managed to keep twelve cows; he had done so well that he had added a second storey to his house. But although additions to houses are not now uncommon, such departures from the Land Reform pattern of 'three-feddan-and-a-cow' (or two cows, or cow and gamoose) are relatively rare.

The last example is of particular significance in that, although a quarter of the land is given up to green fodder, milk-and-meat production has made relatively small progress. Yet it also illustrates the dilemma: that in a country so grossly over-populated, with so grave a legacy of neglect, one man's gain can all too easily become six men's loss, and the full unleashing of the purely personal profit motive could soon restore the old rural anarchy of exploitation and servitude. Ideally, the co-operative would form a frame capable of containing both private and community profit, a school both of technical and social values, well suited both to Egypt's present situation and to the character and religion of her people. Some co-operatives have tried to stimulate members' initiative by awarding prizes of cash or transistor radios for the best crop yields or most productive cattle. But for longer-term 'motivation' one must perhaps look to that development of community consciousness which the co-operatives are well placed to foster. In the Kulin Land Reform region of Kafr el Sheikh, for instance, the co-operatives, through their social fund, have built and equipped a new village school and health centre. Some provinces run co-operative training centres to which members and staff are sent to take courses and in general extend their horizons. In conjunction with the co-operative representational system with election to regional, provincial and national levels, this could lead, in time, to the discovery and development of much rural ability which has hitherto gone untapped.

In many revolutions the organisation of agriculture, the making over of backward peasant societies, the relationship of town and country, have proved the most serious of all stumbling blocks. The French Revolution created a peasantry, but failed to bring it into the national community; the agricultural difficulties of the Russians more than a generation after their revolutionary re-organisation of the countryside are notorious. The Egyptian revolution, which had the advantage of starting with an agriculture which was not *technically*—only humanly—backward, has made a promising beginning. But the real test will come later when the co-operatives are required to sustain and improve the level of production and effort, year after year. The reconciliation of co-operative democracy[9] and managerialism, complicated possibly by doctrinaire political 'guidance,' can never be easy. In 1968 the Arab Socialist Union and the National Assembly were busily surveying the state of the co-operatives, and it may well be that the co-operative system will still go through a variety of modifications before it finds its right balance and settles down.

[9] A refractory co-operative committee can be dismissed from Cairo; by 1965 this had happened to sixty or so out of 4,000, generally for some form of graft.

18

TOWN AND VILLAGE: THE GROWING FABRIC

Sometimes I hate myself that I was born in this transition
period. We are neither backward nor forward. Our heads go
round and around.

—Egyptian teacher to author

Egypt is unique in the Arab world in the density of its web
of towns, stretching over the Delta and far up into the Valley
—Mansoura, built between Nile and canal, a town with an
air, 'the city of victory' which held Louis IX for ransom in
the Seventh Crusade; Tanta, thronged with pilgrims to its
famous mosque and the potent tomb of its saint, Sayed Ahmed
el Badawi; Damietta, long famed for its craftsmen in furniture
and shoes and exotic sweetmeats; dusty old Damanhur, the
capital of Beheira, with its gins and mills; Mameluke Rosetta
with its red brick-and-palm-wood houses under a luminous sky,
and its startling museum tableau of the repulse of the British
Redcoats in 1807; Zagazig and Benha and Mehalla el-Kobra and
Shebin el Kom, and Beni Suef and Minya and Sohag, Fayyum
with its lake and Mataria beside its lagoon; Mallawi with its
tall churches, Pharaonic Akhmine with its silk and cotton
handloom weavers, 'Manchester before History,' as a board
outside quaintly puts it.

The Census list of towns runs to well over a hundred, and
if many of these are small and nondescript, others are substantial places. Nine—excluding Cairo and Alexandria—have
populations exceeding 100,000. Yet few tourists have even
heard of them, nor, in general, would they find anywhere to
stay if they had. One moves back half a century or more when
one enters their streets. It has been their fate to languish in
the long shadow of Cairo, the seat of authority and repository
of wealth and culture, into whose bloated tissues the lifeblood of the country has hitherto so largely drained. When an
Egyptian says he is going to *Masr* he means he is going to

Cairo—or that he is going to Egypt. The word is the same.

This is slowly beginning to change. It is true that the bulk of the new industry is concentrated around Cairo and Alexandria, and that in twenty years Cairo's population has doubled. But a good many of the provincial cities have grown as fast or faster. Not the least of the benefits of the agrarian reform lay in the way in which it forced Cairo bureaucrats out of the city to establish provincial offices and field units like the Combined Centres. When, in 1961, the twenty-four provinces were invited each to design and fly its own flag, this was not merely a decorative gesture but the symbol of a policy of decentralisation which had been stoutly proclaimed and was partially in being.

New textile factories, particularly spinning mills, are no longer being attached to the already large established complexes, but are spread about the country where they can generate work and perhaps even start an industrial tradition. Provinces were allocated industrialising funds under the Five Year Plan and 1960 saw the announcement of a programme for thirty-seven industrial centres. Thus Kafr el Sheikh, whose pre-revolution 'capital city' consisted of little but the royal palace, received £E1½ million for such projects as a rice-straw board plant, a dairy products factory, an oil-seed crushing establishment, and so on; Damietta—whose provincial flag now proudly displays a ship in sail—set out to restore its once famous, long-silted, Nile port; Port Said gained a sea-food factory which exports £E500,000 of frozen shrimps annually to the U.S.A. and elsewhere, a marine rope factory, a textile factory and an onion-drying plant. Small beer as all this may seem in the West, in Egypt's long-stagnant provinces it represents a mighty stirring, further encouraged by the profit-sharing law under which local industry often contributes (from the 'shared' total of 25 per cent) to local amenities. And the agricultural revolution added its quota of fruit-packing stations, new sugar factories, poultry hatcheries, co-op depots, date processing factories and so on. At the same time higher and technical education was being distributed more widely about the country. University education, not long ago a Cairo monopoly, spread its wings in Alexandria, Tanta, Mansoura and Assiut.

Local councils are far from being new in Egypt: the British
hopefully launched them long ago. But neither the old 'French'
bureaucratic tradition of centralisation, nor the lingering Ottoman style of autocratic *Mudirs* (governors) in the provinces
and *Omdas* in the villages favoured the growth of grass-roots
democracy. The local police chiefs acted as chairmen of the
village councils started in 1910 and it is hardly remarkable,
bearing in mind pre-revolutionary village conditions, that even
by 1952 there were still less than a hundred of them.

The National Charter ruled that 'local government should
gradually but resolutely transfer the authority of the State to
the people' and in 1960, a new Local Government Law had, in
fact, provided for a nation-wide network of provincial, town
and village councils with substantial elected majorities (and
ex-officio and nominated minorities). The councils were
allowed a wide field of action 'within the general policy of
the State,' including housing, health services, schools and training colleges, the promotion of local industries and running of
local labour exchanges, public utilities and so on. The local
proceeds of the land tax and buildings tax, formerly national
taxes, were transferred by law to the local councils and supplemented by various other 'common fund' taxes and grants-in-
aid from the central government. On paper at least it amounted
to quite a sophisticated structure of local popular government,
and in the following four years over a thousand new village
councils, covering the bulk of the country, were set up. At the
same time the administration of the Western Desert, formerly
military, was civilianised into 'the Province of Mersa Matruh,'
which since 1963 has had a council elected from the principal
Bedouin tribes.

The effects of this stimulation of provincial activity are to
be observed all over Egypt. But to anyone who has experienced
the bottomless lethargy of provincial Egypt it is not so much
the big things that impress—the new stadia, the palaces of
culture or Sohag's bright 'new town' on the other side of the
Nile—as the little things, here and there—a little green 'park'
with coloured lights, like the one in Akhmine, a bright municipal café in some long-somnolent town hitherto devoid of
amenity, new lamps beside the canal. . . . The old Egypt was
so supremely the land of 'private wealth and public squalor.'

In Minya, the pashas' palaces fronting on the Nile had looked over a waste of barren sand to the river; but now Minya, like Cairo, was building its Corniche with public gardens, stone seats, trees and cafés.

As I stood on Minya's incipient Corniche, watching King Farouk's old yacht, the *Khassed Keir*, tying up with its load of tourists at the Nile Bank, I got into conversation with another spectator, a middle-aged Egyptian. He was a clerk, a Catholic, whose father had been a labour-recruiter for the British in the war. He belonged to a class which had lost its favoured position and could not hope to regain it. He complained of the price of meat and the difficulty of supporting his mother and seven children on £E30 a month; he lamented his inability to get a suit of English worsted and the poorness of the Egyptian substitute; he complained of discrimination against Christians by 'those with bad hearts,' despite President Gamal's having said that the best man should get the job, whatever his religion. Yet he, too, like other Egyptians, quietly rejoiced in the sense of steady progress being made, the immense backlog of neglect being slowly overtaken. 'Yes,' he said, eyeing the newly planted saplings, 'little by little, all is done.'

Where the towns end, the villages begin: concrete and glass and tarmac give place abruptly to the mud-brick, the endless irrigation channels and that labyrinthine network of well-trodden paths on bunds which forms in a real sense the connective tissue of land and people. It is a connection, however, which has hitherto gone unavowed, for the villages formed a world apart, some thousands of islands, each living its own life, self-sufficient in its penury.

But this, too, is changing. Villages and towns—and few villages in Egypt are over thirty miles from a town—are being woven together in a growing fabric whose warp is formed by industry and transport and advancing social services, and whose weft is made from political organisation and education and visual and aural 'mass communications.' From the small village of Robh Shandied, sons and daughters of the land-reform farmers travel out to work in factories at Tanta, Damanhur, Mehalla el Kobra and Kafr el Dawar. The Delta—

which is a big world in a small compass—has a good network
of roads and bus-lines, today run by the General Organisation
for Transport. The multiplying factories demand regular
labour, and when, as happens, difficulty in reaching them from
the villages causes absenteeism, transport links have to be improved. In Kena, in Upper Egypt, one new factory solved its
labour problem by supplying workers from more distant villages with bicycles.

In the Land Reform area of Inchass there were only a few
children in primary schools before the revolution, and these
mainly the children of Royal Estate officials. Today, from a
total of 960 families, twelve students go to university in Cairo,
Alexandria and Assiut, and 145 younger boys and girls go to
technical and secondary schools in Cairo, Zagazig and Bilbeis.
Between them the undergraduates are studying Commerce,
Agriculture, Engineering and Medicine—the young man reading Medicine is the son of a four-feddan fellah with a family
of twelve. For the schoolchildren going into Cairo, the local
co-operatives combine to provide a mini-bus; for the university
students the co-operatives of the province have subscribed to
build a provincial hostel, Sharkiyah House, in Cairo. This is
perhaps a favourable example, but by no means an unusual
one: 'my' small village of Robh Shandied was sending six
students to Alexandria University; it had recently converted
another royal rest house into a second primary school, and
three-quarters of the children were continuing—beyond the
legal leaving-age of twelve—to intermediate or technical
schools.

There is nothing new in the sons of an Egyptian village
going either to town factory or university. What is new—and
critical—is the volume of the traffic and the fact that it is
now two-way. In 1892, Lord Milner reported, 'If the (village)
sheikh determines to give his son a regular schooling, the latter
ceases to be a sheikh and becomes an official. He loses his
familiarity with country life and his touch with the common
people.' Fifty years later this was still true, but seventy years
later things were changing. When a boy qualifies as a doctor,
he now has to spend his first two years in one of the village
health units or combined centres which now cover the country.
Of the three thousand graduates in Agriculture emerging an-

nually from the colleges, the majority will certainly get a little mud on their boots as they are posted to the nation-wide network of co-operatives. Even Arts graduates are badly needed in the countryside to staff the multiplying schools—while social science, a new vogue in Egypt, must seek its material in field studies.

Even if a student is not himself destined to work or live around the villages after graduation, he may well these days be drawn into the national 'Village Service' project. The idea is that the student, returning to his village in his vacation, should make a study of it, determine what it needs most, and then get together with fellow students—possibly from other universities or schools—to do something about it. The movement has been highly organised on a semi-official basis through the student unions. The volunteers attend preliminary lectures on tactics and methods ('First, create in the villagers a consciousness of need'); their projects may receive visits from their professors and awards are made for the most successful ventures. A project may be simply fixing oil-lamps in the village street, working in a health centre, teaching an illiteracy class, getting up a local band, organising wrestling matches or reviving an old ball-game, played with a palm-fibre ball, called 'Hoksha.' No money may be collected for the work, the idea being that materials readily to hand should be utilised.

The inevitable flavour of paternalism (professor to student, student to villager) may disconcert a Westerner, but it does not necessarily strike a false note with the people concerned. In the single university of Cairo in 1964, 1,500 students volunteered for vacation work in 250 villages. By chance, I met one young man who, with nineteen others, had spent part of his vacation in this way. From 7.30 to 9.30 in the mornings he taught in the village school; after that, the students organised a campaign to clean up the village; from 4.30 to 7.30 in the evening they ran their literacy classes for adults. He told me he had embarked on the venture in much doubt. 'I thought it would be hard to gather even a single class from the illiterate adults; but it was easy. I was very surprised. They were eager. We had 150 of them. I thought they wouldn't co-operate to clean the streets, either. But they did.'

There are many other strands in this growing fabric weaving together town and village, metropolis and province into something new in the Arab world, an edge-to-edge pattern, varied but articulated, the pattern of a modern nation. There is, for instance, the effect of service in a modern army, formed since the law of 1955 by universal conscription, not, as formerly, merely from the poorest. The new intake undergo medical observation for the first two months, and are given treatment if necessary; the illiterates are taught to read and write; if they do not exactly enjoy their army service (and the Egyptians are no more a martial nation than the English or the Americans), they can hardly fail to return to their villages with widened horizons. Like most villages, Robh Shandied had a soldier in the Yemen: on the radio the villagers listened to familiar voices on Forces' programmes sending messages home from the outer world.

In the villages, as in the towns, the political or constitutional strands in the web are of growing importance. On the gateposts of the former royal rest house at Etay el Baroud on my last visit there still lingered in blue paint the uncertain drawing of a clock-face, hands set at five past four. The same limp clock appeared on numerous walls about the place. It was not, it emerged, the work of some rustic disciple of Salvador Dali, but the symbol of a candidate in the last election for the Arab Socialist Union which, like the co-operative organisation, pyramids electorally from village to national level. For a 'military dictatorship,' Egypt indeed has a remarkable number of elections—generally actively contested—to the various councils of the co-operatives, of the Arab Socialist Union, to local government committees, to trade-union executives and branch committees, to company boards of directors (for workers' representatives), not to mention the General Elections for the National Assembly.

From a near famine at the grass-roots Egypt seemed to be moving to a plethora of popular representation. There is a positive orgy of 'discussion'—although, as in other countries, much of it turns out to be by the same people wearing different hats. But 'democratically' or otherwise, a common fabric is being woven: the villages begin to see themselves as part of an organised nation. Village Arab Socialist Union units may forward complaints about deficiencies to the Provincial Governor or to the Ministries, who may well send an official to 'discuss' them. They dutifully debate the national questions of the hour underlined by the President, and hear explanations of policy. The most intelligent of the A.S.U. higher leaders see this as a means of welding together the nation, while generating the will and discipline needed to carry it through the difficult years of transition. Their talk remotely echoes that of the more enlightened section of the British ruling class at the time of the second Reform Bill—'We must educate our masters'—although sometimes there is much the same implication that the process is likely to be a prolonged one.

And certainly in such a countryside, with its legacy of tyranny and obsequiousness, the task of establishing and sustaining reasonably uncorrupt local democratic government must be a formidable one. For the present, despite the everlasting 'discussion' and the elective majorities, the old name of 'governorate' probably still comes closer to political reality than the new name 'province.' The Governor, the agent of Cairo, is still the holder of the most important purse-strings, the inspector-general of the village and town councils' work, able, if necessary, to procure their dismissal by decree. He is a considerable personage, who enjoys the emoluments of a Minister, and in some places his comings and goings from his office are announced by trumpeter. Yet a Governor needs his council's approval for his Budget, and if he and his schemes are to thrive today, he must be able to claim the participation of 'the People' and their representatives with reasonable conviction. Thus the traditional autocracy of the *Mudir* is wedded to Arab Socialist 'democracy' as well as to up-and-coming Technocracy.

It may seem a precarious match, but as one eminent Egyptian observed to me hopefully : 'it will all boil down in five or six years.' The country is groping towards a balanced and effective governmental structure suited to new social patterns which are still in the process of emerging. And, inevitably, this process must generate friction between the up-and-coming of the new rural order and the survivors of the old one. For the most part the friction is hidden, but sometimes it comes into the open, as in the mid-1966 outcry against sporadic local evasions of the land laws, which led to the setting up of a high-level national committee for the 'Liquidation of Feudalism,' which purged some local councils and officials convicted of connivance in evasions.[1]

Enter Television

Even in 1965 vast numbers of villagers had never in their lives been to a cinema. But in that year the Egyptian Television, Cinema and Radio Organisation was opening new rural cinemas, often in village community centres, at the rate of four a week. In addition, travelling companies of actors toured the villages with popular comedies, folk operettas, and so on.

'We find,' said the head of the Organisation, 'that the young go to the new cinema first, then the women, then the men—and then the old. Of course, we have to choose proper films for them. Naturally we avoid films about fantastic town life, showing all the things they don't have . . .' He paused, then added thoughtfully, 'But, of course, we have to show a few such films—to raise the level of their expectations.'

It was already evident, however, that this nice balance might prove difficult to maintain—for in the field of mass-communications social revolutionaries more powerful than the cinema were now moving in. Launched in mid-1960, after a study mission's visits to the U.S.A., Britain, Italy, the two Germanies and Russia, Egyptian television established itself with remarkable speed and professionalism. By 1963 it had covered the Delta and the Valley as far south as Assiut (with a separate recorded programme for Aswan) and was operating programmes on three channels for a total of twenty-three hours a day. By 1965 there was an estimated audience of one and a half million, and TV sets were being fixed in public places, not only in the towns but also, increasingly, in the villages.

The medium exerted its usual hypnotic effect. The mayor of one small town told me that shortly after he put two tele-

[1] A 1968 law, making a major attack on graft, provides that everyone in the public service, in public sector companies, or holding office in co-operatives, trade unions, local councils, the Arab Socialist Union and National Assembly, from the President of the Republic downwards, must make a confidential declaration of his total wealth within three months of taking office, followed by declarations on leaving office, or at five-yearly intervals if still in it.

vision sets in the streets, he was visited by a deputation of café proprietors who complained that their clients had deserted the cafés to watch television. 'What can we do?' they wailed. 'We shall be ruined.' The Mayor replied: 'It's really very simple—put television sets in your cafés.' Seven did so. Most of the others, he said, bought radios.

And television is a medium which, in its nature, does not easily tolerate the old swaddling of traditionalism; it is eclectic, voracious, hob-nobbing, international. All the well established features of Western TV, quiz shows, discussions, interviews, on-the-spot news, situation comedies, series, music, drama and operetta (there are ten permanent TV theatre companies) were quickly reproduced on Egyptian TV in their Arabic versions. The fellahin of some mud village may find a girl announcer in the latest Western dress and hair-do gazing into their eyes from the small screen; they may attend a literacy class, or sit in on a debate in the National Assembly; listen to a sheikh expounding the Koran or watch an Arabic-dubbed Perry Mason or Sergeant Bilko; meet the President face-to-face, or watch a football match. The television service, of course, carries its share of unabashed political propaganda, and intervals tend to be endlessly filled by the celebrated baritone, Abdel Wahhab, belting out rousing 'Socialist' songs against a background of rising factories and onward-marching masses in the best early Soviet style. Yet a quarter of the television material is foreign, and that mainly American and British.

In the past the eclecticism of Cairo and Alexandria had been countered and nullified by the bed-rock traditionalism of village and valley. For the press, despite good production standards, remained a metropolitan and bourgeois institution with very little penetration of the larger Egypt. In 1965, although circulation trends were upwards, total daily newspaper sales did not exceed 500,000, and even the sensational weekly newspaper, *Akhbar El Yom*, with its 3-inch deep red banner headlines, only managed an Egyptian sale of 270,000 or so.[2]

[2] By 1968 the aggregate average daily sale of the Egyptian daily papers had topped 600,000; *Akhbar El Yom* had reached 380,000 and the 'special' Friday issue of *Al Ahram* with Mohamed Hassenein Heikal's weekly piece claimed a sale of half a million. But Japan, with a population a little more than three times as great, has a total daily newspaper sale of 35 millions; with a single paper selling 7 millions a day.

Furthermore, since the suspension of political parties, the newspapers have presented a problem which the régime, despite much worrying, has not known how to solve. They await full literacy and liberalisation to come into their own. Television, by contrast, at once offered a national forum—almost an electronic recreation of the clan council or Islamic *Umma* —where the debate could be both lively and 'around the table.' Audience participation (again from Western models) in such popular programmes as 'The People's Voice,' where a random assembly of members of the public questions Ministers and high officials, is well suited to Nasser's concept of the non-divisive, nation-building 'co-operative and socialist' democracy, and in the villages and towns alike such TV inquisitions can provide useful antidotes to old habits of cringing obsequiousness before the Powerful.

Television has also brought with it an innovation of great potential importance in such a society at so critical a stage— 'feedback' in the form of a systematic audience reaction survey, conducted by the National Institute of Social Research, founded in 1955. From the towns, the surveyors are now turning to the programme reactions of the fellahin. 'To reconcile and meet the needs of both town and village,' said a television executive, 'is a big problem. So far, the programmes have been mainly dictated by the tastes of the urban middle classes. But I believe that within ten years we shall have to change the map of the programmes completely.'

Meanwhile, in the villages—as everywhere in this antique land—the electronic society is heralded by the transistor radio. It tinkles incongruously from the deck of some great barge being poled down the Nile; it reverberates on the bund as the fellah plants out his rice; its everlasting Arabic song issues mysteriously from the pocket of a policeman on traffic duty; its chromium gleams in the dark interior of some mud hovel where the voice of the Cairo announcer reading the news mingles with the hoarse complaint of the family gamoose. The minarets of Islam radiating the call to prayer or to arms might be considered as one of the earliest forms of what we now call mass-communications. But now the muezzin on his minaret has a rival, though also an extension—for both in rural and in urban Egypt the sound that echoes from the transistors is often the voice of the sheikh intoning the familiar verses of the Koran.

Yet the remotest village today inhabits a world which far transcends the Islamic bounds. Since the emergence of Nasser on the world stage in 1955, and since the transistor brought its voices winging out of the air, one may find oneself in these primitive mud villages being asked questions by barely literate fellahin which betray a world view wider, and in some respects more real, than one would be likely to encounter in many an English or American small town.

And yet the dilemma of the film man who wished to kindle in the fellahin ambitions for a better life without raising too high their hopes of satisfaction is real. If urban and rural Egypt are today being woven into a common fabric, it is a fabric still full of holes. By the mid-'sixties, it is true, the spread of social and medical services had resulted in a lightening of the villagers' physical afflictions. Bilharzia no longer so frequently resulted in fatal complications, like cancer of the bladder. The awful legion of the one-eyed and the bleary-eyed gained few recruits. Between 1952 and 1962 infantile mortality fell from 136 to 105 per thousand; the male expectation of life increased by ten years, the female by seven. These were solid gains. But they were still being eroded by the burden the villagers imposed upon themselves. The Ministry of Social Affairs' posters and pennants displayed, beneath symbolic wings of aspiration, the 'Ideal Family'—man, wife, one boy and one girl. In the towns, among the middle classes, it was already a reality, but in Robh Shandied, and among the fellahin generally, the average number of children was still seven. They still bred like the nation's wild life up to the limits of territory and food supply.

In 1966, the Government allocated £E500,000 to a national birth-control campaign. The Prime Minister took the chairmanship of the Family Planning Supreme Committee; suddenly, 'family planning' became 'the line' of the day. 'In addition to their duties of combating crime,' said a newspaper, quaintly, 'the police should set a good example by forming family-planning committees among their own ranks.' Students marched the streets of Cairo chanting the slogan, 'Two healthy children are better than four ailing ones.' Doctors became frank and diagrammatic on radio and TV. Intra-uterine loops were distributed free and fitted in the health units and village midwives awarded a fifty piastre bonus for each 'obstinate client' brought over. The Pill was made available at a fifth of cost.

The Ministry of Social Affairs under its woman Minister, Dr Hikmat Abu Zaid, made a film in which the lot of the happy planned family was contrasted with the misery of the 'quiver-full.' Yet many thinking Egyptians were well aware that such a film underlined the intractability of the problem as much as it proposed a solution. As in the West, the small town family reflects a determination to hold an enhanced standard of living. In the mud villages the fellahin may be healthier, but they have little or no margin of income to provide more than the needs of the stomach—and the traditional Egyptian village would afford them small scope if they had. Beyond his land, the small fellah's family is his only real 'possession'; his wife may see a child a year as a guarantee against divorce. So both agree with the Psalmist.

This is the fundamental and most dangerous gulf between rural and urban Egypt. Here and there a few modest new houses now offer the fellahin the rudimentary foundations on which a better life might be built. In the Land Reform area of Inchass, the Co-operative organisation has built new homes on some of its members' holdings, at a price of £E250 for one storey, £E350 for two, half the price paid as deposit, and the rest in instalments. (Even so, the fellahin have difficulty in keeping up payments.) And in a few places advancing industrialisation, plus a new local government structure, is changing the environment. Toukh, a small town near the Delta Barrage, has been amalgamated with forty-six surrounding villages to form a single district under an energetic professional 'burgomeister'—and now 'economic' concrete flat-blocks rise alongside the old mud hovels. Toukh and its attendant villages are on their way.

But for most of the 17½ millions who inhabit the squalor of rural Egypt such elementary domestic amenities are as yet undreamed-of. Fortunately, perhaps, for it has been calculated that to rebuild the villages of Egypt to the simplest civilised standard would cost £2,740 millions; and a fact-finding mission sent around Europe reported that modern prefabrication would raise the cost even further.

Nevertheless, an experiment is being made, under U.N. auspices, with a 'Self-Build' scheme, using blocks of scientifically blended and stabilised clay, claimed to be superior to the traditional straw-and-clay brick of the Egyptian village which absorbs humidity and crumbles. Similar methods were successfully used in the late 'forties by the Egyptian architect, Hassan Fattih, in building the country's first new model village at Gourna, opposite Luxor, to accommodate—and rehabilitate— the former tomb-robbers of Thebes. With its arcaded streets, its simple mosque, school, market-place, its domed and vault-roof houses made by a process the architect copied from an excavation of the Third Dynasty, Gourna was cheap to erect, aesthetically pleasing and immeasurably superior to the usual Egyptian village.[3] (Unfortunately, the tomb-robbers preferred their caves, and the fellahin who took over blocked up windows, piled maize-stalks and other kindling on the roofs, and filled the streets with straw and cows and donkeys—so that the place took on the derelict air of the typical Egyptian village.)

Now Hassan Fattih has been brought back into the attack on rural squalor on a wider front. In his old house beneath Cairo's Citadel he plans the experimental redevelopment of a village in Giza Province, opening up the mud honeycomb to let in air and light, with vegetable gardens between the houses and a new village centre. The supply of mud and earth, he points out, is unlimited—and so is self-labour. Given a little expert help, he prophesies an upsurge of house-building activity among the fellahin.

One hopes he is right, but cannot help doubting. And yet the fellah's horizon is widening. His own children, returning from school in the towns, change his ideas. Instead of lusting after more land, which he can no longer readily get, he may set his hopes on his son's becoming a doctor, a dream now within reach. And behind the transistor and the battery tele-

---

[3] According to Hassan Fattih, the total cost—£300,000 with a thousand houses and public service buildings—was one-third of what it would have been using conventional methods.

vision set another major revolutionary is about to move in: electricity has already been taken to some villages; as the power grid from the High Dam extends all over Egypt, it will be taken to many more. Great hopes are pinned on this—and rightly—for the electric light switch can transform the lives of villages which are isolated in primeval darkness every day when the sun goes down.

Egypt's rural population has been estimated to exceed the needs of agriculture by as much as one-third. As the drift of the surplus to the towns continues, it is expected that by 1975 the proportion of the nation living in rural Egypt will have dropped from two-thirds to a little over a half. But by then, unfortunately, the total population could have reached forty millions. The Minister of Planning told me that he expects the birth-rate to begin to turn down after 1970. But it is inevitably a very long time before such changes work through to total population figures. So that although industry, and all the activities it stimulates, may ultimately take up the surplus,[4] during the years of transition the prospects for many Egyptians look bleak.

The official answer to this problem of rural over-population is a fairly familiar one—village crafts and self-generating small industry, scattered through the land. The Ministry of Social Affairs promotes a Gandhi-esque local handicrafts scheme called 'Productive Families,' mainly directed towards keeping the 'surplus' women and girls busy at home, adding, it is claimed, at least £E1 a week to their income. But much more substantial is the work of the 'C.P.O.'—the Co-operative Production and Small Industries Organisation, founded in 1960 under the aegis of the Ministry of Light Industry.

Individual craftsmen and two-or-three-man workshops already abound in Egypt. A million people are normally thus employed—more than the labour force of large-scale industry. But their techniques are outdated; equipment, finance and marketing facilities are largely lacking. The basic idea of the

[4] The projected 1970-1975 Plan anticipates that 1,660,000 workers will be employed for the first time bringing the total up to 11 million employed, as against 6,000,000 in 1959-60; 7,333,000 in 1965; and an estimated 9,356,000 for 1970.

C.P.O., working through its offices in each province of Egypt with the aid of a U.N. specialist mission, is to persuade these craftsmen to get together in co-operatives, to supply them with credit and raw materials, to modernise their designs and methods and organise the marketing of their products.

Simultaneously, more than two hundred craft-training units have been set up to teach groups of boys from villages where there is surplus labour, and, possibly, unused local raw materials. After two or three years these boys are sent to start up a new co-operative in their area with a fund formed from deductions from their wages. By 1965, fifty such new co-operatives had been founded and the C.P.O. had opened a Small Industries Institute near the Pyramids with demonstration workshops for training of foremen, a lecture room to teach accounting and costing, a design department and a research laboratory.

On the outskirts of Mansoura I visited a building where no fewer than thirteen small furniture workshops had been brought together into a co-operative. They'd started, the men said, in a big tent; but even now they didn't have enough space—because others wanted to come in. One big advantage of the new organisation, they said, was that the flow of work was now continuous, and they avoided cut-throat competition with each other: it was in a sense like a return to the old craft guilds.

In the centre of the town a large villa housed a shoemaking co-operative, formed from fifty separate workshops, totalling 115 workers. Formerly, each man had made the entire shoe. Now one of the U.N. experts had broken down the work into operations; a simple production line had been set up and a sales contract made with a store chain. The provincial C.P.O. chief was arranging to buy a bankrupt local tannery and re-float it as a co-operative to provide their leather.

By 1960 350 C.P.O. production co-operatives were at work, covering most parts of the country. There was a co-operative for working the salt-pans on the edge of Lake Manzala, a fishing co-operative of a thousand men and 300 boats at Ezbet el Bourg, three boat-building co-operatives, twenty-six for spinning and weaving, fourteen for palm-tree products, four for pottery, twenty-one for building work (with an output valued at £E3-4 millions a year), seventeen for carpets and rugs (which find markets in the U.S. and Central Europe), eleven for metal-industries, thirteen for ready-made clothes.

But if the range of activity was great and the prospects seemed promising, here again, as in agriculture, the co-operative form had been paternally insinuated from above. The state put up most of the capital, the members of most craft co-operatives being merely required to take out single £1 shares. But once within the fold they elected their own worker-directors and shared the profits, and, as in the agricultural structure, considerable prospects of self-improvement seemed open. Agriculture, however, unlike industry, imposes its own seasonal disciplines; and it remains to be seen whether the industrial co-operatives will be able to sustain the necessary managerial flexibility and drive.

In any event the Co-operative Production Organisation's activities are not confined to 'worker co-operatives'; they include the provision of shared common facilities for small private employers who subscribe, but do not merge their identities. And Egypt has its share of enterprising 'little men.' In Mansoura I watched one of them manufacturing spare tractor wheels in a workshop not much larger than a cupboard. He himself had constructed the juggernaut on which the strips of Helwan steel were bent and welded. A notice in Arabic hung upon this Heath Robinson contraption: DON'T BE ASTONISHED—IT IS THE WILL OF ALLAH. In an interstice between it and the wall another machine rattled away drilling slots in rice de-husking screens. One youth and two urchins danced attendance on both.

The proprietor's father had been a mechanic working on steam irrigation pumps; his grandfather a mechanic with a transport company; now he, after a year at secondary school, had set up for himself. The C.P.O. provincial chief had offered him accommodation on the 200-acre Industrial Estate the Organisation was developing at Mansoura; and, after a good deal of bargaining, he had accepted. He was, in the new political jargon, a 'national capitalist,' non-exploiting and, presumably, benign. But whether such mute, inglorious Fords are doomed to remain mute and inglorious, or whether their individualistic energies can be effectively harnessed under Egypt's socialist, co-operative and democratic system, remains one of the critical questions of the future.

19

THE OLD VALLEY - AND THE NEW

The Green Must Grow Bigger Every Day
Science is the Only Way to Freedom
Fool, 1 piastre; Cheese, 1 piastre; Vegetable Stew, 2 piastres,
Meat and Veg. 5½ piastres.
—Notices in Labourers' Canteen, Kharga, New Valley

In its task of nation-building, Nasserian Socialism had declared its intention to narrow the gaps between man and man, between class and class, between town and village; but there was another gap to be bridged, a venerable gap with six million people on the wrong side of it—the gulf between the Egypt of the Pharaohs and the Egypt of the Levant—between the Valley and the Delta. For although it is now about five thousand years since the Pharaohs united the two kingdoms, marrying the White Crown of the South to the Red Crown of the North in the Double Crown of all Egypt, then, and ever since, 'the Two Lands' of Upper and Lower Egypt have retained their separate identities. In our own times the Levantine excitements of the Delta passed Upper Egypt by; it remained a world apart; even today the civil servant despatched there draws large compensatory pay allowances like someone on onerous foreign service. But even a 30 per cent bonus will not stop the Cairene or Alexandrian in, say, Kena, from eating his heart out. For most educated Egyptians not themselves hailing from there, the Upper Nile Valley has appeared only a little less remote and alien than central Africa, a fabled land of fanaticism and jealously guarded women and the blood feud, a primitive world of abject poverty and brooding superstition and merciless heat.

But the single act of siting the High Dam at Aswan is now in process of doing what 5,000 years of history failed to do—uniting the country along the whole 750 miles or so of its length from First Cataract to Mediterranean. From Alexandria harbour great loads of equipment flow up the valley by river and rail, and back now come the daily shipments of crushed iron ore, the cargoes of fertiliser from Kima. They pass through an Upper Egypt which has been engaged in prodigies of reclamation and canal-building in preparation for the High Dam's water. In the single province of Sohag alone 20,000 labourers had been employed for three years (1962-65), digging hundreds of miles of new canals and distributaries. All over Upper Egypt endless banks of earth are thrown up as if a thousand regiments of moles had been at work. On the levelled tops of some of these, metalled roads have been laid, opening the valley to rapid road travel and to tourism. Edfu already has a magnificent new tourist hotel with a terrace on the Nile.

Agriculturally, Upper Egypt gets a double bonus from the Dam. For it makes possible not only the widening of the cultivated valley by reclamation, but the taking of three crops (by perennial irrigation) from a vast area of land, hitherto basin-irrigated, on which only one or two crops a year could formerly be grown. In the province of Kena, for instance, 17,000 new feddans were being won from the desert and 150,000 feddans 'converted'; in January, 1968, the Minister of Irrigation announced that in all Upper Egypt 782,000 feddans had been converted to perennial irrigation—with 150,000 feddans still to do. When it is remembered that the extra water also makes practicable crops much more profitable than the inferior variety of cotton cultivable in Upper Egypt and when the cumulative payments for canal-building and reclamation are added in, it can be seen that the result is an infusion of money into Upper Valley capable of transforming the situation of that long forgotten land.

And, little by little, the situation is indeed transformed.

Among Egyptians themselves the men of the Upper Valley have long been notorious for the fanatical strictness with which they protect the virtue of their women. Here the cause of female emancipation, long proclaimed in Cairo, might seem to sink to its nadir. Yet in Kena now every Monday evening is Ladies' Night in the Information Department's garden cinema, and for several hours rows of ghostly figures sit in the darkness watching interminable celluloid epics of the New Egypt, generously interspersed with song and dance. Most of the songs are love songs, but the motif of one, performed *con*

brio in a cotton field, was rendered to me as 'How very pleased
and amused I am to be picking cotton—and making good
money.' The ladies sat on, immobile and apparently absorbed,
perched on their seats like so many black crows—silently
rejoicing no doubt in the novelty of a night out.

Nor was this the end of Kena's daring. Half a mile from
the *al fresco* cinema stands a large Teachers' Training College
which draws girls from villages all over the province. Here at
8 a.m. every morning there is a ceremony of raising the flag
to the accompaniment of marching and counter-marching by
columns of young women with rifles on their shoulders. The
rifle drill is quite professional and as the flag is raised the three
appointed girls of the day bring their rifles to the salute and
the assembly breaks into the 'Suez Hymn'—*Allahu Akbar*[1]—
supported by a band of xylophones, drums and concertina, a
blessedly unmartial sound.

'And now,' said the English Language lecturer afterwards,
'she will show you where we put the bullets. . . .' As in the
secondary schools themselves, military instruction is now a
regular part of the curriculum; the girls, I was assured, actually
fired the rifles on a range. Just beyond a demure sewing class,
I was startled to notice, hanging on a corridor wall, a cross-
section diagram of a hand-grenade. 'It is necessary to protect
ourselves against Israel,' said the teacher stoutly, when I ques-
tioned whether this was really appropriate educational
material for Egypt's new female generation. The place was
indeed full of maps of Palestine Irredenta and poignant pictures
of Arab refugees, and here as elsewhere it appeared that the
Israel obsession was in danger of becoming the single lens
through which the rest of the world was viewed.

In the matter of female emancipation, 'fanatical' Upper
Egypt could be considered, in one respect, ahead of both Cairo
and Alexandria. There co-education beyond the primary stage
was unacceptable. But in Upper Egypt the shortage of both
schools and girl students has made it administratively un-
avoidable in the secondary schools also—and it has been
accepted. The girls, certainly, were scarcely 'co-eds,' but on

---

[1] 'God is great . . . God is above the malice of the Aggressor.' This rousing song, written in classical Arabic by Ahmed Shafi Kamel, became
enormously popular at the time of the Suez attack.

the fine modern campus of Upper Egypt's new University of Assiut, where eleven blocks of apartments for 4,000 male students look speculatively across to the five blocks for 1,500 girls, they might yet become so. In the 1964 election for the National Assembly in the Assiut, a woman candidate, Mrs Aziza Huzayan, came within a thousand votes of defeating a veteran male politician who had represented the region in parliament for many years.

The world pushes up into the Valley, and, more slowly, the Valley opens out towards the world. . . . TO GET YOUR OLD AGE PENSION WITHIN 72 HOURS . . . began a bold poster that caught my eye in the entrance hall of the Social Insurance Office in Sohag. It was flanked by others offering illustrated advice on how to apply for one's Unemployment Benefit, Industrial Injuries pay, Widow's Pension, Death Grant. . . . Beneath, a dozen women in the black robes of Upper Egypt patiently awaited interviews with one or another of the office's twenty-two officials.

The welfare state, like the transistor radio, now makes the whole world—and even all Egypt—kin. The first try at a social security system had been made in 1950 with a Government-financed scheme for payments to widows, the aged, the disabled, and orphans. This, however, proved ineffective and was allowed to lapse, and it had been left to the new régime to launch, in 1955, a contributory social insurance scheme covering industrial and commercial establishments with more than fifty workers, in Cairo and Alexandria. In 1959 this pilot scheme was extended to other towns, and in 1964 widened again to include unemployment insurance.

So far, said the Sohag director, only about a third of the workers eligible in his district were registered. To get the rest it would be necessary to send the inspectors out into the little workshops and into the bazaars—and that would be a formidable task. Ironically—but in such a country perhaps inevitably—such schemes tend first to reach the workers whose need is least. And, as usual, rural Egypt constituted a vast hiatus, although, in 1967, provision was made for contributory social insurance to include owner-cultivators of ten feddans and over. The spread of the village health units has also meant that a very large part of rural Egypt now has—what the towns still have not—a simple, largely free, health service.[2]

But if still sketchily filled in, the structure of social security was nevertheless boldly and practically outlined; the Social Insurance Organisation is now a solid institutional reality, its substantial Fund built into the structure of state finance (a useful source of capital formation), and its forms and regulations part of a new common fabric which now knits together the Valley and the Delta.[3]

Up here in Upper Egypt time is telescoped: the new and the archetypal lie cheek by jowl. A few hundred yards from the Sohag social security office, with the ladies preparing to fill in their forms, a crowd of *tarahiel* (migrant) labourers waited at the railway station, lying prone on the sacks which contained all their worldly goods. At their sides lay the tools of their trade, the *fass* (mattock), and the palm-woven baskets in which, ant-like, they carry away the earth they dig just as did their forebears in the days of the Pharaohs. As the corduroyed navvies, a special race of men, dug the foundations of industrial Britain, so from the days of Mohamed Ali to those of Gamal Abdel Nasser—and from the Suez Canal to the High Dam—these *tarahiel* workers of the Nile Valley have been in the most literal sense the makers of modern Egypt. One meets them marching along the road, *fass* over shoulder, basket swinging from it; or one passes them squatting on some newly dug earth bank, eating their frugal meal of Arab bread, and onions and *mish*, a sort of pickled and fermented cheese, the acrid relish of rural Egypt. A century earlier they were rounded up by the *corvée* and speeded by the hippopotamus-hide *kourbash*; now they are recruited by penury and quickened by the hope of piece-rate piastres. Fleets of earth-moving machines now roar around them. But Egypt never had more need of their muscle and sweat. They remain the Great Landless, the very bottom of this great pyramid of people, and for

---

[2] A pilot 'comprehensive health service' for the town was launched in Alexandria in 1965, moving the doctors out of the factories into clinics, where they became available to the families of insured workers as well as to the workers themselves.

[3] Total reserves of the Social Insurance Organisation in 1965/6 were stated to be £E201 millions; its income £E69 millions as against £E2,290,000 in 1957.

the same reason that so many of the navvies of Britain were Irish, very many of the *tarahiel* workers are sons of Upper Egypt. The race of labour contractors has grown rich upon them, transporting them hundreds of miles from their villages to sleep in ditches or in the corn-straw hovels still to be seen on the banks of canals under excavation. They do not protest : because to have work at all is good fortune. For three or six months of the year they may find none.

The *tarahiel* workers are the classic victims of the Malthusian vicious circle, the extruded 'surplus' of the Iron Law, men alone, disregarded, without property and—until 1965—without rights. They sum up in their persons the scale of Egypt's human problem, and it says a good deal for both the philosophy and the practice of the Egyptian Revolution that even at this basic level, there is constructive change.

On the railway station platform at Sohag I encountered an energetic young man in a brown suit who was followed by three porters bearing stacks of large leather-bound volumes. His name was Ezzat el Kerim, and he was Vice-President of the Land Workers' Union. I had last seen him in Cairo eight months before at the new union's inaugural delegate meeting. The large books were Minute Books, which he was in process of taking round to the new union's 274 village branches in the province of Sohag. So far, he said, they'd recruited 42,000 members out of a possible 100,000 or so. He himself was a foreman in the Civil Engineers' Department at Sohag and, having been to secondary school, was vastly better educated than most of the members.[4]

I vividly recalled that first meeting of the new union, held one hot July night in an empty school in a shabby Cairo sidestreet that was clamorous with the sounds of men and boys beating out crumpled cars. It was a remarkable occasion. Three hundred delegates from every part of Egypt jammed the stairs on their way to the lecture room where the election of the executive was to be held. There were statuesque giants from Upper Egypt, Nubians from the New Nubia, a Bedouin or two from Borg el Arab, wiry fellows from the labour gangs of Liberation Province and the reclamation projects on Lakes Borollos and Manzalah in the far north. What they had in

[4] This is a common pattern in Egyptian trade unionism. See Chapter 21.

common was their poverty. An old man in a white turban, from Minya, told me that, with five children in his family, his pay was twenty-five piastres a day. Work was still hard to find for two months in the winter; but before the revolution, he said, his pay had been eight piastres.

The delegates squeezed on to the tiered benches of the lecture room and sat there reading the new statutes of the union which they were being invited to pass. Lips moved painstakingly. It had not been possible to insist on the usual literacy requirements. To organise agricultural workers anywhere is difficult: to organise *tarahiel* labourers in a country like Egypt verges on the heroic. Several earlier attempts had failed, or resulted in little more than a union of Ministry of Agriculture employees. This time 4,000 committees had been formed covering all Egypt and it was these which had now sent forward their delegates.

As is the practice in Egypt, several Ministry of Labour Trade Union Department officials were present to supervise the election and see that legal requirements were met.

'Sometimes they are suspicious of each other,' their chief explained. 'With us here, they feel safe.'

But not, it appeared, quite safe enough—for within five minutes a faction fight had broken out which kept the room in an uproar for upwards of an hour. The volume of sound was truly formidable. Men climbed on tables, and chairs piled on tables, to gain a better vantage point for verbal fire. Accusing arms stabbed the air. After vainly pounding the table for ten minutes, the Ministry of Labour chief gave it up and walked out. 'They are *simplistes*,' he explained, tolerantly. 'They are ignorant. They like to make a noise.' They were insisting, it seemed, on voting immediately; they suspected that someone was trying to put something over on them.

The pandemonium subsided as swiftly as it had begun. The voting started. When a delegate was illiterate, a Ministry of Labour official sat beside him on the bench and quietly read down the list of seventy-one candidates (for twenty-one seats on the executive). As the voice read a favoured name, the man made his mark. They made their choice with great deliberation and earnestness. An Egyptian reporter asked me what I thought about it and I said it was a very moving sight, and I meant it.

And now, eight months later, the Land Workers' Union was an accomplished fact, an affiliate of the Trade Union Confederation of Egypt, and, with its three million members, by far the biggest trade union in the land. It was true that of this number, only half a million—the regular, year-round employees—could as yet afford to pay even the smallest subscription. But the casual and the *tarahiel* workers were registered and organised in the union's 4,000 branches, with their elected committees. For the first time it had become possible to plumb these lower depths—and not only plumb them, but build some sort of floor beneath. The union, for a start, was demanding proper tented camps and medical attention for the *tarahiel* workers; private contractors were to be abolished in favour of contracts negotiated through local union committees, backed by a special section of the Ministry of Labour, and plans were mooted for training centres to equip at least some 'surplus' labourers for jobs in industry or elsewhere.

One may modify a pattern, and yet remain imprisoned within it. Glimpsed, at one instant, as the new trade unionist, the *tarahiel* worker, at the next, dissolved in the fierce light of Upper Egypt into the little-changed descendant of the nameless hordes who built the Pyramids. Social insurance, at one moment the wave of the future, at the next seemed mocked by the swarming fecundity of this people. Yet, in such a country, if reach and grasp appear desperately at odds, it may be that the only answer is to reach yet further, seeking the response that will outface the challenge.

This has been done.

Four miles north of Assiut the break-out from the 7,000 year old pattern of the Valley becomes not merely metaphorical but actual; the early revolutionary theme of Liberation Province is picked up again as the valley road, running as ever alongside the water, divides and one branch strikes off across the desert towards what Nasser, in 1958, boldly announced as 'the New Valley.'

The road passes the usual police post, skirts the town's burial ground on the desert's edge and the domed and whitewashed tomb of some venerated sheikh, and runs off into the emptiness. It is an excellent tarmac road, but as it unrolled before one, black and smooth and endless across the featureless sand, it was difficult to feel much conviction that it had in fact a destination; even more difficult to link it, as history does, with the famous *Darb el Arba'in*, the Road of Forty Days, the old caravan route by which the Arab slave-traders ferried their black merchandise from the interior of Africa down to the Nile.

From time to time a gust of wind would pick up the sand and hang it, an opaque grey curtain, across the road. Then the wind would drop as suddenly as it had arisen and the curtain would fall and there would be the road, the black strip running on across the desert as far as the eye could see.

About a hundred miles from Assiut the road turned and abruptly descended, winding down on to a flat wide sandy floor, walled by shale escarpments hazily visible in the distance. We had entered 'the New Valley,' a chain of five major oases or depressions which, with a few breaks, extends diagonally for six hundred miles or so across the Libyan Desert from a level a little south of Aswan to the Qattara Depression near the Mediterranean.

It is a valley without a river, but not without water. In the more recent past, the cultivated parts of the oases have not been very extensive because their wells were unplanned and often ancient. But there is good reason to believe that the whole area, comprising more than eight million acres, is underlain by a vast reservoir of water, held in the many strata of Nubian sandstone—water which, over the centuries, has seeped down from the Nile, from the Ethiopian highlands or the equatorial rain belt of the Chad. Much of the soil is good and covered by only a thin layer of sand, and the ground is relatively flat. It has been estimated that one-fifth of the 'valley' can be readily claimed for cultivation and that in its five constituent oases—Kharga, Dakhla, Farafra, Bahariya and Siwa— it might support three million people.

The basic idea of the New Valley plan is not new. But again, it seems to have taken a revolution to stimulate action. In 1958, four or five officers of the Army Engineering Corps got together in a Desert Committee in order—as one of them put it—'to try to collect together the desert reclamation efforts of the various Ministries, to enlarge the possibilities and give it drive. We insisted on choosing our own men. We wanted to build out of our own experience, out of the difficulties of the project itself.'

The result was the Egyptian General Desert Development Organisation (EGDDO), the largest and most formidable of the numerous reclamation concerns now operating in Egypt. Established in 1959, the EGDDO was largely dominated by army engineers, but it was also fully staffed with civilian specialists: like the High Dam Authority, the Suez Canal Authority and the various industrial groups, it was another of those extensive, semi-autonomous technological kingdoms which are part of the fabric of modern Egypt. The EGDDO undertakes the staff work, the planning and experimentation, but for much of the execution it engages contractors, both public and private. Although it has projects east of the Nile, its main sphere of operation is the Western Desert and the coastal strip, its master-work the New Valley.

As the road from Assiut crosses the barren floor of the 'Valley,' the approach of El Kharga, its 'capital,' is announced, as it has been for centuries, by the appearance of palms and a minaret. One passes the Temple of Hebis, built by Darius I during the Persian Occupation in the 6th century B.C. and then the old village, which, with its date-groves and placid pools, its narrow serpentine streets and its often light-skinned Berberine people, has probably not changed much from that day to this. Abruptly, and briefly, the highway becomes a grand dual carriageway, alongside which rise the tall apartment blocks of the EGDDO technical staffs; there is a neon-lit cinema, a club, a power station, large army workshops for the fleets of lorries and earth-movers, laboratories, a big animal breeding station and an airport with a regular service of Comet Fours from the 'old' Valley and Delta. Six hundred technicians work for the Organisation in the area and live with their families in their own 'suburbs'; there are, in addition, 2,000 regular labourers.

The Kharga (or 'Outer') depression, is 115 miles long from North to South and between twelve and fifty miles wide. It is the largest oasis in Egypt, and at its north-western extremity goes on a further 113 miles to Mut, the chief place of Dakhla (or 'Inner') Oasis which stretches for thirty miles from east to west. The tarmac road which traverses the Kharga oasis goes on a further 113 miles to Mut, the chief place of Dakhla, and after that continues over the desert for another fifty miles or so towards the next oasis, Farafra. The plan—or the vision —is that the road will eventually go through from Farafra oasis to Bahariya and from Bahariya to Siwa oasis and from Siwa to the sea at the little summer resort of Mersa Matruh, which is also today the capital of the Western Desert Province.

For most of the journey the desert dominates the scene, its monotony sometimes relieved by strange-shaped hummocks of grey shale, chrome yellow sands, or purple streaks of iron. Then come the miles of green, growing crops on either side of the road, spreading out from new villages, a sight to lift the heart. Sometimes, one's progress will be abruptly halted by a mountain of sand athwart the road. Moving dunes are among the operation's many hazards: the direction of their movement is charted so that the new wells and fields can be kept out of their paths, but the road itself is too long to escape altogether.

By 1965, 40,000 acres had been reclaimed and put under cultivation in the first two oases; half a dozen villages were built and occupied, twenty more were on the drawing board. The New Valley emigrants are drawn from the landless of the Nile Valley from Beni Suef to Kena (those from Beni Suef northwards are theoretically destined for the new lands of Liberation Province on the Western Delta's edge); the individual villages eligible to participate are selected by the Ministry of Agriculture.

The first two hundred settler families from overcrowded villages in Sohag migrated from the Old Valley to the New in early 1963. The distance travelled was only 200 miles or so, but for all that it was a passage from one universe to another. Strange as Liberation Province might have been to its first settlers, the waters of the Nile ran in its canals. In the New Valley the break was total. From May onwards the temperature in the hours of sun is 110°F and over. Evaporation rules out the economic growing of cotton. The crops are winter wheat (which grows well), oil seeds, groundnuts, beans, hops, sweet potatoes and a seven-year variety of alfalfa, introduced from the United States to supply the basic feed for a projected New Valley cattle industry.[5] Dakhla Oasis had already acquired 10,000 head of cattle.

Strangest of all, perhaps, is the contrast between the close quarters and teeming landscape of the Old Valley and the wide empty spaces of the New. The new villages of the Kharga Depression, Nasser, Palestine, Algeria, Sana, are built on streets seventeen yards wide. The houses of whitewashed mud-brick are built in blocks of four, each with two rooms and its own sixteen-square yard walled courtyard. In general, the pattern pioneered in Liberation Province is repeated, though on a more meagre, cost-cutting scale. Each village has its own Club, its resident agricultural officer, its social worker and, of course, its smallholders' co-operative.

Young turkeys as well as Kharga-bred 'improved' Fayyumi chickens scratch about in the courtyards: the turkeys, a Dutch-American cross, are supplied by the Ministry of Agriculture's Kharga Turkey Farm, the largest in Egypt. A 100-acre state cattle farm sells the villagers cows and buys back the calves at six months for fattening. By such devices and from the crops on his four or five feddans, a New Valley settler achieves an income of around £E200 a year—in which easily the biggest single contribution comes from his 1½ feddans of perennial alfalfa. Many also work on the EGDDO's reclamation projects. By comparison with the £E30 a year many earned as landless labourers in the Nile Valley, the 'desert' offers riches indeed.

Not that the customs of the Nile Valley have been wholly discarded. Although separate cowsheds were provided, the villagers once again rejected them and built their own stalls for their animals in their house courtyards. And when a zealous social worker, eager to display the New Valley's modernity, incautiously flung open the door of the tube-closet at the end of a courtyard, he revealed the hole covered up by a stone and the place in the undisputed possession of a large red-wattled duck, which protested noisily at our intrusion. It must have been brought from the old village in the Nile Valley,

---

[5] According to the local agricultural chief, on this basis an acre in the New Valley would support two cows. A large state cattle-breeding station and farm have been established in Kharga.

the agricultural officer said ruefully. The breed was too large for the New Valley. He could not really approve of it. He hinted darkly at the dangers of miscegenation.

Despite its scale, the New Valley remains a pilot project, a vast and intricate experiment in which the elements are human beings, animals, soil and—above all—water. Its development calls for a high degree of scientific 'know-how,' and it has been intensely science-based from the start around 1960. A whole 'united nations' of experts—Americans, Russian, Yugoslav, Japanese, German, French, Italian, Iraqi, British—were enlisted. Aerial mapping was supplemented by various forms of geological, geophysical, chemical and hydrological survey. Egyptian hydro-geologists were sent to the United States to study the latest techniques of ground-water development. But the EGGDO's laboratories in Kharga still remain the real heart of the project. The soils laboratory prepares detailed soil-maps of the oases; for whereas the soil map of the Nile Valley would be largely of one colour only, representing its characteristic alluvium, the soil map of the New Valley is apt to be a crazy patchwork of blues and reds, violets, yellows and greys, representing widely varying qualities of soil. An average of 300 samples at various levels is taken from the area around each new well, determining the treatment required and the most suitable crops. A water chemistry laboratory analyses the content of the wells, which are often hot, possessing strongly corrosive ingredients. Most vital of all, a hydro-geological laboratory keeps continuous observation on 200 wells, logging the pressures and flow, analysing core samples, and building up a picture of the movement of water through the eight different aquifers in the Nubian sandstone below.

In the Dakhla oases the wells go down almost a mile before they reach the granite. Some authorities estimate that this water is 25,000 years old, the time taken for it to percolate through the sandstone at a rate of thirty metres a year from the Chad in Equatorial Africa. If it is used, will it be replaced? How *fast* will it be replaced? How can it be most economically exploited? These are some of the extremely complex questions which have to be answered and to speed the answers a model of the Western Desert, embodying the many variables involved, has been constructed at the University of Arizona for analysis by analog computer. Most of the wells are artesian and when first bored sometimes flow under pressures so fierce that they have to be stoppered down. But as time goes on the pressure falls off, and finally pumping will become necessary. The present plan is to settle 30,000 feddans in each oasis while the free flow lasts; then to treble that once pumps have been installed and the flow stepped up. Thus the directors of the project hope to learn as they go at minimum cost.

'But I do not think we can really say we have created a New Valley until we have reclaimed three million acres,' said one engineer officer frankly.

Will the water run to it? No one really knows for certain, although Mr Abdel Megid, the head of the New Valley project, a careful and honest man, says that all goes along very nicely. One Egyptian authority has estimated that there is enough water under the Kharga and Dakhla Depressions to provide 1,280 million cubic metres a year for 200 years; and a Russian hydrologist, Mr I. Pavlov, engaged by the United Nations, has suggested an annual infiltration of water into the underground reservoir at the rate of no less than seventeen million cubic metres a year.

The baffled non-specialist may have to content himself with the conclusion of the Kharga engineer already quoted, who is also a non-specialist. 'I believe myself that the water will continue . . . for, after all, life has gone on in these oases since 3000 B.C.'

At least no one can complain that the scale of the response in the New Valley does not match the scale of the challenge. Nor are the Valley's only potentialities agricultural: at Dahkla oasis there are phosphates; at Bahariya large deposits of phosphorus-free iron ore (55 per cent iron), which will be taken out by a railway line which is to be constructed to Helwan; a power line is to be taken from the High Dam grid to the oasis. And since the Libyan 'dome' extends into the Western Desert prospecting is under way for oil as well as water. Hopes on the former score have soared since the oil strike twenty-five miles south-west of El Alamein by the Phillips Petroleum Company of America, whose manager has described it as 'one of the most promising ventures in the company's history.' In

1967 another strike was reported just south of the Qattara Depression, and after promising seismic surveys by Russian prospecting teams in the Siwa Oasis, in the summer of 1968 drilling was under way there too.

At its southernmost extremity, the 'New Valley' abuts on the shores of Lake Nasser, now rising behind the High Dam. Soil surveys have suggested the productive use of the flood waters in surface cultivation of the shores—or, via spillways, to re-charge the subterranean reservoirs of the New Valley's oases. Meanwhile, in November 1968, Egypt and the Sudan announced an agreement to build a 630-mile road to link Cairo and Khartoum—through the New Valley.

'Settling the Bedouin'

Northwards from Siwa the route threading the oases of the New Valley enters the territory of the North-West division of the EGDDO, whose mission is to reclaim the coastal zone as far as the frontier at Sollum and to settle upon it the Bedouin whose world this is. The Bedouin are of two main tribes, the Ali Amer (Red) and the Ali Abeid (White), and since even here the rainfall is sparse and uncertain and mainly confined to the winter months, they often travel long distances in search of grazing for their flocks, moving across the frontier into Libya where their main body lives.[6]

In the twelve-mile-deep coastal zone, hundreds of windmills, powering wells, have been erected, small dams and dykes have been built to collect such rain as falls and ancient Roman cisterns rehabilitated. Tens of thousands of olive trees have been sold to the Bedouin through the co-operatives at two piastres a tree. Nearer Alexandria figs are planted, and almonds in the deeper valleys. Further back, catch-crops of barley are being grown, using fast tractor ploughing; and in the belt behind that again—as the rain grows ever sparser—pasture is being improved with special desert grasses sown from the air.

Such is the Desert Organisation's plan. But although many

[6] The sheep taken across the frontier are, however, branded and counted in order to prevent their being sold back to Egypt at enhanced prices as 'Libyan': a measure the Bedouin easily circumvent by taking across pregnant sheep. The Libyan Bedouin are permitted to travel into Egypt as far as Amarya, a few miles from Alexandria, but not beyond.

of their Bedouin clients have in fact long been semi-settled, in the tradition of their kind they seem to have given their EGDDO organisers a distinctly hard time. If two tribes were incorporated in a single co-operative society, civil war was apt to break out—so at first there had to be an inordinate number of co-operatives. One minuscule settlement had a co-operative for each family. But slowly fellahin obduracy wore down Bedou pride, and after four years, as the EGDDO Director put it, 'the collection was made': 160 tribal 'branch co-operatives' were amalgamated into fifty—still too small and too many, but progress. The stone houses multiplied around the windmills. The tents grew fewer. The lure of tractors and olive trees and subsidised United Nations cotton-seed cake to tide over the years of waiting for the trees to bear fruit proved more powerful than the 'freedom' of the desert. A fine mobile veterinary surgery toured the grazing areas, ministering to the sheep and camels. Schools multiplied. And now the Bedouin vote for their representatives both for the National Assembly and for the Council of the Provincial Governor at Mersa Matruh.

'Settling the Bedouin' is a universal preoccupation in the modern Arab world. The Western reader, brought up on Doughty and Lawrence, may find himself ruefully asking why. The educated Arab never asks; to him it is obvious. 'We want him to become a member of the community—a useful man in our nation,' said the EGDDO project's director. 'Actually,' said a young social scientist primly, 'it is very difficult to plan for people who have no fixed address.' But the provincial Governor—himself a Bedou on his mother's side—perhaps came nearest the root of the matter: 'In a year when there is no rain,' he said, 'they have a very bad time. . . .'

On the Provincial Council in Mersa Matruh the Bedouin elders sit on one side of the long council table and the Governor and his officials on the other, and it is said that the Bedouin representatives in the democratic process condescendingly refer to their official colleagues as 'the fellahin.' But if there was still the odd echo of the venerable struggle of the Desert and the Sown, of the noble warrior and his imperious camel against the ignoble 'turf-cutter' and the lowly cow, that classic conflict is at last almost over. As the Arab world slowly comes to rest, it can be seen that the new 'Arab revolution,' unlike the earlier ones, is the revolution of the fellahin and the sons of fellahin. The tractor and transistor have conquered where the mattock failed; the subversion of social welfare, of schools and health centres and co-operatives and old age pensions pervade Valley and Delta and Desert alike, and the Noble Bedouin's proud pennant of ancestral names has been fitted, with difficulty, on to the social worker's case-card.

PART FIVE

THE EMERGENT SOCIETY

Their countries have entered on a new historical era and
need Founding Fathers who know how to build stable authority and a consensus capable of achieving purposeful change.
— Manfred Halpern, *The Politics of Social Change
in the Middle East and North Africa* (1963)

Building factories is easy, building hospitals and schools is
possible, but building a nation of men is a hard and heavy task.
— Gamal Abdel Nasser, 22 July 1957

It took Europe a century of hard work from the 14th century
to the 15th century to build itself. The United States a hundred
or a hundred and fifty years ago started building itself. Who
did that? The people themselves built their own country. . . .
We are beginning from the starting point where they started.
— Gamal Abdel Nasser addressing Egyptian students
returned from study abroad, July 1966

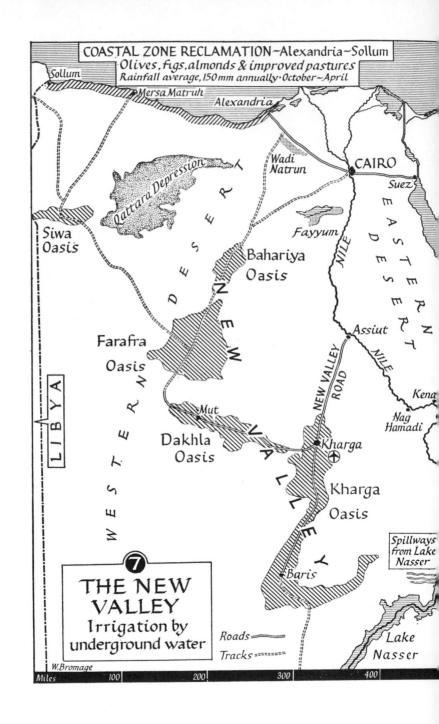

COASTAL ZONE RECLAMATION~Alexandria~Sollum
Olives, figs, almonds & improved pastures
Rainfall average, 150mm annually · October~April

Sollum

Mersa Matruh

Alexandria

CAIRO

Suez

Wadi Natrun

Qattara Depression

DESERT

Fayyum

Siwa Oasis

Bahariya Oasis

NEW

EASTERN

Farafra Oasis

WESTERN

LIBYA

Assiut

NEW VALLEY ROAD

NILE

Kena

Nag Hamadi

Mut

Dakhla Oasis

VALLEY

Kharga

Kharga Oasis

Spillways from Lake Nasser

⑦
THE NEW
VALLEY
Irrigation by
underground water

Baris

Roads ———
Tracks ========

Lake Nasser

W. Bromage

Miles   100   200   300   400

20

THE NEW MODEL

That there is a predisposition to autocratic government among
Muslim peoples is clear enough; that there is an inherent capacity for any other has yet to be proved.

—Professor Bernard Lewis, *The Middle East and the West*
(1963)

The sounds of slogan-chanting coming up from the courtyard
below penetrated the Minister's office and grew steadily louder.
An Under-Secretary doggedly pursued the subject of yields
from reclaimed lands. The noise grew nearer. Cries of 'Long
live Gamal!' appeared to be mounting the central stairs. Conversation was getting difficult. The immense racket, the rhyth-
mic chanting was in the corridor. Finally, deafeningly, it was
just behind the green baize doors. It gave no sign of
diminishing.

The Minister rose. 'Excuse me a moment. I'll just go and
have a word with them,' he said. Five minutes later he returned, smiling quietly, and resumed his seat. 'I told them to
go and read the President's speech,' he said.

This sort of thing had been going on for days. Between
Nasser's nomination for a new term as President, made by the
National Assembly in mid-January 1965, then the referendum,
then the inauguration in March, the bandwaggon had rolled
to much effect. There were the provincial rallies, the streams
of telegrams, the factory advertisements, the delegations from
Arab Socialist Union units all over Egypt, the lorryloads of
workers speeding excitedly into town, the chanting students
carrying their cheer-leaders on their backs like monkeys, the
processions of trade unionists with banners, the column from
this factory and—somewhat ragged—from that Ministry. . . .
It had been fine while it lasted, an occasion irresistibly com-
bining the display of patriotism, the joyous exercise of the
lungs and a free day out, in a manner that had the makings of
a new national feast. But now, as the huge newspaper head-

lines proclaimed, Nasser had been returned to the presidency with a 99·999 per cent majority[1] and, on the previous night, he had taken the oath of office before the National Assembly and the viewers on TV, and it was all over until next time, presumably in another six years.

Yet despite the echoes of an Oriental court (now wired for sound and vision) the enthusiasm was real and solidly based. Even those Egyptians who might entertain reservations about some policies pursued readily acknowledged this man as the author of Egypt's renaissance, this driving will as the source of all major modernising departures from the enfranchisement of women to the trade union organisation of landless labourers. A young man said to me before the referendum: 'He'll get 99 per cent. What's your opinion—what would you say to another Englishman? He's the only one—those around him are nothing. He's the only one through the whole Arab world.' A professor said: 'When he speaks, you feel he is speaking your thoughts, whether you are a professor or a peasant.' 'Yet,' said a factory doctor, 'this man was not known thirteen years ago. It was, as we say, hidden behind the curtain of God. We believe in God and we believe that if Gamal Abdel Nasser ends sometime—and everyone should have an end—there will be more and new men to carry on everything like Gamal.'

In such a situation the temptations to Mahdi-ism or to Bonapartism must be great. But if some other Afro-Asian leaders have succumbed, Nasser has appeared in relatively little peril. Since 1952, he has learned something of the demagogic arts, but it is inconceivable that he could declare, as did Bourguiba in 1959, 'The governor and the commissioner are an emanation of my person.' He had re-erected the mammoth statue of Rameses II outside Cairo Railway Station; but there were no statues of Nasser: de Lessep's plinth in Port Said harbour remained empty, likewise Ismail's in Tahrir Square. Offered the life presidency at the National Congress of Popular

---

[1] This figure was the percentage of 'Yes' votes of all valid votes. Expressed as a percentage of registered electors (7,055,564) the 'Yes' votes amounted to 98·51 per cent, which figure did not suffice for the enthusiasm of Egyptian editors. Sixty-five individualists voted 'No'; 4,890 papers were spoiled; and about 105,000 didn't vote. In Egyptian parliamentary elections voting is obligatory for males.

Powers in 1962, Nasser rejected it. And when in January 1965 the Speaker of the Assembly opened the lists for nominations for the President's office, it was not, perhaps, wholly a charade. Although his triumph in the referendum was predictable, Nasser nevertheless undertook a strenuous speech-making campaign throughout the country. It was explained that he wished to establish a precedent for future Presidential elections—and this did not seem improbable—for the domestic rôle into which Nasser had fallen was not that of Mahdi or Führer or *Osagyefo*,[2] but that of mentor, the gravely watchful Muslim elder brother, whose task in this instance was not protecting a family but building a nation.

This was a rôle well enough fitted to place and time. Thirteen years after the coup, although the *primus* of the Nasserian *primus inter pares* now carried capital letters, the theory and form of collective leadership was maintained. It was a collectivity which still owed more to Islam than to either Rousseau or Lenin; and its inner core was still constituted from the men of July 1952. It was true that the 'band of brothers' had thinned somewhat, both from natural and other causes. There had been precipitate and unexplained 'resignations' even of vice-presidents. For different reasons the leftward progress had alienated both the enterprising Wing-Commander Abdel Latif el Baghdady and the devout Kamel eddin Hussein. But every chief executive faces such hazards, and in the Middle East house arrest is hardly more than political routine. To a remarkable degree the inner group around Nasser remained in being. Nasser's crony of Military Academy days, Abdel Hakim Amer, now Commander-in-Chief (later to become a victim of Egypt's defeat in the Israeli-Arab war) was to remain for another two years yet the President's confidant and dependable go-between. Anwar el Sadat was Speaker of the National Assembly; the Mohieddin cousins were still active : Zakaria, the Free Officers' intelligence man from the early days, remained an effective shield against conspiracy, first as Home Minister and later (1965-6) as Prime Minister, while Khaled, now a newspaper editor, was in 1965 appointed chairman of the Press Council. The Sabri brothers, both former Air Force officers, moved be-

[2] The former President Nkrumah's title, meaning 'The Torch,' 'The Messiah.'

tween a number of key offices, including, for Ali, the Premiership; the dutiful Hussein el Shafei, for seven years Minister of Social Affairs, later Labour, was in 1961 made a Vice-President and set to organising the Arab Socialist Union; while Talaat Khairy was given the sensitive job of Minister of Youth.

Nasser's ability to command this nucleus of committed and now experienced former Free Officers, shuffling them according to technical and political needs of the moment, conferred on the technocratic government a sort of continuity and strength. But it was clearly a diminishing asset; and Nasser remained very much aware that the only lasting protection for the revolution must lie in broadening the whole base of government. For if Suez had consolidated the revolution and solved the problem of political support in general, it had not done so in particular. The economic and social reforms still had to be complemented by an effectively working, nation-wide political structure; and for a number of reasons this seemed likely to prove both the most difficult and most critical of all the immensely difficult task of reconstruction.

In the older Egypt participation in government and power had been on a narrow and cosily bourgeois basis. 'I used to come here,' a middle-aged Egyptian friend said one day in Groppi's, 'and I would know people at nine tables out of ten.' The expansion of higher education—and now industrialisation —was increasingly changing that. My friend, who had been brought up on *Tiger Tim's Weekly*, educated expensively by the French Catholic *Frères* (although a Muslim), and who still smoked English pipe-tobacco, added ruefully that now he knew hardly anyone. Here, as in Europe, the 'Society' of the old professions and good family was giving way to the incipient technological society of the expanding middle classes, trade unions, mass-communications and the rest.

The National Assembly of 1957, cut short by the union with Syria, had been made up one-third of lawyers and businessmen, almost another third of high civil servants, ex-ministers, former officers and landowners, one-tenth of village *omdas* and sheikhs. It had few small fellahin, and the merest handful of workers. The National Assembly that met in March 1964 looked very different. It was the first to be elected under the new draft Constitution with its clause reserving half the seats for elected 'farmers and workers.' It was in fact unlike any representative assembly ever seen in Egypt before.

Looking down from the gallery on the circular debating chamber with the National Assembly in session one was virtually looking down on a working model of Egypt's new society as sketched in Nasser's National Charter. Deployed on the green leather benches below in front of the big Republican eagle—the eagle of Saladin—are men and women of a great diversity of background, culture and fortune. Sun-browned fellahin in white *takias* and brown *galabiyas* sit beside smart-suited professional men; there are the sheikhly turbans of El Azhar and the crew-cuts of scientists and technologists trained in America or in godless Russia; there are men of wealth, and others for whom the member's salary of £E75 a month almost equals what they used to make in a year; there are 'with-it' young men and a couple of landowning elders from Upper Egypt for whom the red tarbushes under which they reclined seemed the only possible wear. Eight women members light-en a little the ponderousness inseparable from any formal assembly of Egyptian males. Down there is the handsome figure of Mulfira Abdel Rahman, a distinguished woman advocate; a little further on, the stocky figure of Fatma Diab, the member for the rural areas of Shebin el Kanater. Owner of a three-acre farm, affecting a black shawl, Fatma is something new in Egyptian feminism, a professional peasant. A graduate of Alex-andria University, she came up in politics through the co-operative organisation; her father is a teacher. Not far away sits a no less striking figure, wearing a small red 'Libyan' cap (*chechia*) and, over his shoulder, that toga-like fine white blanket which Libyans call the *barracan* and Egyptians the *jird*. He is one of the members for the Western Desert, and the last time I had seen him he was sitting in a back room of the filling station he part-owns in Mersa Matruh, listening to the com-plaints of his tribal constituents and preparing a question for the Minister about the state of the roads to the oases. His shiny Ford Fairlane waited in the unpaved street outside. A former *omda* and owner of olive-trees, he was elected in a nine-candidate contest together with another Bedou—the obligatory 'worker' member—a mechanic in the Desert Organisation's workshops. 'Bedouin,' he explained complacently, 'will only choose Bedouin. Egyptians try, but they haven't a chance.'

There were in fact six Bedouin in this Assembly. Other minorities did less well. Down on the right is to be seen the long, sad-merry face of Atheneos (better known as 'Tanashi') Randopoulo, of Greek parents but Egyptian birth and education,[3] an agricultural engineer from the Greek vineyards area in Beheira and one of the only two elected Christians in the House. The other Christian represents Coptic Assiut. This under-representation—for Christians make up somewhat less than 10 per cent of the population—is slightly corrected by the presence of ten Nominated Members, chosen by the President, among whom, in 1965, were eight Christians.[4]

To complete the new model, presiding as its Speaker, was that man of 1952, the once fiery, now saturnine, Anwar el Sadat, patiently guiding the members through their procedural paces, flanked by his Deputies, Sayed Marei, the executant of the Land Reform, and Ali Sayed Ali, the leader of the Petroleum Workers Union—one 'technocrat' and one 'worker.'

The general election which produced this Assembly was enthusiastically fought. The only requirements for candidates, in addition to being Egyptian, literate, and at least thirty years old, were one year's active membership of the Arab Socialist Union, and a £E20 deposit. Many of the two-member seats had ten or twelve rival contestants, spanning the social spectrum from wealthy merchants and old-régime lawyers to fellahin and manual workers. For Egyptians do not lack individual ambition and relish a public free-for-all. Dr Ahmed Khalifa, director of Egypt's Social Research Institute, told me that he considered this 'really the first free election in our history,' and if he had said 'the freest so far' (and the most representative) he could well have had a point. Dr Khalifa himself, although a newcomer to his own semi-rural constituency, and an intellectual at that, had been elected against the competition of the local *omda*'s two sons, and this he felt to be a significant victory over *assabya*—the binding obligations of clan and place, an old curse of Arab politics.

[3] In 1965 there were still 18,000 Greeks in Cairo with 2,000 children at Greek schools, which, however, have since 1954 taken Arabic courses.
[4] There is also the traditional Copt or two in the Cabinet.

Of the 350 elected members, 189 had stood as 'registered workers or peasants,' slightly over the statutory requirement. The method of ensuring this was slightly cumbersome. If in the first ballot neither 'peasant' nor 'worker' was elected in the two-member constituencies, the lower of the 'non-peasant-workers' was eliminated, and the highest polling 'worker-peasant' declared elected, or, if his vote fell below a minimum, a second ballot held.[5] But many voters took the hint and split their votes socially, picking, say, one professor and one peasant. It was, for all that, a much criticised provision. How, people asked, could ignorant fellahin understand the problems of state or approach their Excellencies, the Ministers? There is little doubt that to very many the idea appeared outlandish.

It probably appeared hardly less so to some of the 114 fellahin who duly took their seats on the green leather benches beneath the stately dome of Cairo's *Maglis el Umma*. Whether overawed or not, very many fell mute in that stately chamber —even though they might be vociferous enough, off-stage, in committee. Nevertheless, particularly through the Land Reform co-operatives—which contributed six members to the Assembly—a few potential fellah leaders had emerged.

One such is Abdel Hamid Ghazi, a typical Egyptian fellah of the better-off sort, with a strong oval face and a powerful figure, today the proprietor of 2½ acres in the land-reform village of Manshyet el Soghra where his father was a tenant on a large Lebanese estate—and his uncle owned the mill. Starting out as secretary of his village land-reform co-operative, Abdel Hamid Ghazi rose to the national Co-operative Board, taking in *en route* the Kafr el Sheikh Province Governor's Council. Although his formal education had halted at the village school level, experience had proved a rapid teacher. He found himself sitting in the National Congress of Popular Powers which debated the National Charter, and, in the 1964 Assembly elections, came top of the poll in a constituency contest which included two doctors, two lawyers, one large merchant, and seven other fellahin. He delivers his speeches in the classical Arab style, with accumulating, resonant

---

[5] A second ballot is held if the votes of the elected members fail to total at least half the electoral votes.

periods, their relentless onward march stressed with jabs of the arm.

His fellow Assembly members elected him a member of 'the Executive Committee of the Arab Socialist Union Parliamentary Group' (the latter being the National Assembly wearing its ideological hat), in fact an inner steering committee of forty persons including the Assembly's Speaker and Deputy Speakers. But his interests in politics remain almost wholly agricultural and he commutes busily between Cairo and his village in Kafr el Sheikh, where he now has a substantial brick bungalow, crowned with a TV aerial and surrounded by a neat grey wall topped by flower-pots in a manner reminiscent of the President's villa in a Cairo suburb. He sticks to the brown *galabiya* and skull cap of the fellah, but now permits himself a glimpse of cambric shirt sleeve and cuff-links.

Whereas the provisional Constitutional law gave a precise definition of a 'peasant' (not over twenty-five feddans), a 'worker' for election purposes was almost anyone employed for wage or salary—although, as one candidate observed, to put up as a worker when you are obviously an intellectual is a manœuvre that can misfire.[6] Nevertheless, of the seventy-five accredited workers in the 1964 Assembly, relatively few would be thought of as such in the class-conscious West. There was a bus-driver, a weaver or two, some foremen craftsmen; thirty-five trade unionists in all, a fifth of them from the textile union. But genuine manual workers seemed scarce. Partly this is because in the elections they put up in such numbers that they ruined each other's chances and the trade unions rarely organised support for any candidate. An exception was the resounding victory in the Ramleh suburb of Alexandria of Saad Eid, a foreman at the Egyptian Copper Works, an energetic trade unionist, backed by his trade union at the polls against fifteen other candidates. In the January, 1969, 'war-time' National

---

[6] In fact a 'worker' was required to be eligible for a trade union—in Egypt in 1964 a very elastic definition. In a May 1968 speech Nasser complained that the inadequate definitions had allowed many 'large farmers, landlords, national capitalists and employees' to get elected under the 50 per cent rule. He proposed that the 'worker' definition should bar graduates and those eligible for professional associations; and that a 'farmer' should live solely by agriculture, and not hold more than ten feddans. These closer definitions were adopted for the 1969 National Assembly elections.

Assembly elections, in which for the first time two-fifths of the candidates were given selective A.S.U. sponsorship, the number of 'workers' successful rose to 119—a third of the Assembly. The total of 'registered peasant' members fell to 64.)

In addition to the 'Peasants' and 'Workers,' the remaining 'sectors' of the 'popular powers' of Charter theory are the Army, the Intellectuals, and the National Capitalists. Serving officers are excluded from political candidature or involvement, but, in addition to its Speaker, the Assembly contains a sprinkling of officers who have resigned their commissions and moved on to wider fields. Down there, wearing the bold striped tie much favoured by Egyptian military men, is Magdy Hassenein, the pioneer of Liberation Province, now a businessman and Member for Cairo's central Kasr el Nil area; and, not far away, the rubicund features of a later man of the Desert, Ex-Brigadier Abdel Megid, Director of the New Valley project and Member for Kharga Oasis, a responsibility shared with a fellow-member who is a labourer on the water drilling rigs. There is also ex-Major Elwy Hafez, manager of the nationalised store chain, Gategno Magasins, known as a spirited performer at question time; and, in the rôle of free-lancing ideologist that suits him, bringing a touch of effervescence to this weighty assembly, Khaled Mohieddin, 'the Red Major' of 1952-4.

And the 'intellectuals' who have not claimed the shelter of 'worker' status? This first 'new model' National Assembly contained seven medical doctors (although one at least was a 'worker'), twenty journalists, a larger group of academics, a few Azharites, a number of technocrats, and the inevitable, indomitable lawyers—who, however, are no longer the professionals of politics they once were.

And those shadowy creatures the 'national capitalists?' It was a rôle which few Assembly members appeared over-anxious to claim, but one who had no hesitation was Sayed Galal, representing the poorest and most overcrowded district of Cairo, the Bab el Sharia quarter where he was born. One of the three members of the 1964 Assembly who also served in pre-Revolution Parliaments, Galal is a remarkable example of the hard-working, thrusting, tough, sardonic Egyptian individualist. His is the classic rags-to-riches story. At fourteen he was driving a horse and cart through the streets of Cairo; soon he was hiring other boys and had a fleet of carts. An office job (at 15) with a Greek shipping firm, gave him an insight into commerce, and he set up as a merchant, importing corn from Australia. By the 1930s he had built a large import-export business. He entered the Egyptian Parliament and promoted and got through a number of unusually tough and important laws: one (1946) to tax total incomes (and not merely merchant's profits—agricultural income being then exempt), another to curb corruption by requiring a declaration of total wealth; a third, in 1948, to shut down the licensed brothels which were concentrated in his constituency. He retains a sardonic Egyptian sense of humour. In his 1964 election campaign he neatly reversed the usual charges of vote-buying by announcing that all who voted for him must *pay* one piastre —towards welfare projects in the district.

Having retired from business once, he is now chairman of a thriving cardboard-box manufacturing company. In his view, the 'national capitalist,' whom he defines as 'one who sells a service without robbing people,' has a great chance now that 'feudalism is no longer pressing upon him' and he was demonstrating this faith by extending his factory (which has many small shareholders).

Clearly, Egypt could use the 'drive' of such individualists if it could be safely harnessed. It was one such, the engineer-contractor Osman Ahmed Osman, who got the first stage of the High Dam through on time.[7] Yet, despite Galal's optimism, the national capitalist seemed to remain an enigmatic figure, a beneficient Dr Jekyll who might, at any moment, dissolve into a hideous and exorbitant Hyde. In 1965 the last of the country cotton brokers were taken over by the state organisation; but in June 1966 Nasser was still complaining, at Damanhur, about the 'fabulous profits' being made by merchants 'building up the classes and building up capitalism' and promising that the Government would enlarge 'step by step and commodity by commodity' the public sector in wholesale

[7] The firm was duly nationalised under the 1961 Socialist Laws, but retained a rather special status, with 50 per cent private capital, and, in 1964, was de-nationalised in respect of its considerable foreign operations. Another demonstration that although the Egyptians love to theorise, they are not true doctrinaires!

trade.[8] At the same time he deplored the fact that 60 per cent of building and construction work was still going to private concerns, 'creating a new capitalism.' Here, too, the public share would be doubled over the next three years so that more of the profits on the £E200 million annually involved could be applied directly to investment.

In the vocabulary of Arab Socialism 'individualism' is normally a pejorative term. But this, in part, is dictated by reaction to the Levantine past and by the urgent imperatives of the 'present stage.' As the new national industrial structure takes shape and grows more complex, it may well be that the day of the 'national capitalist'—within the Assembly or outside it—will come. It is interesting that in May 1968, addressing a workers' rally at Kafr El Dawar, Nasser was again to be found presenting the Dr Jekyll face of the national capitalist, 'operating within the limits of the Charter and the public laws of society.' 'We want to encourage national capitalism, and not intimidate it,' he told the trade unionists. 'For given the opportunity, it will be able to play its role perfectly in society.'

If the new political vocabulary was properly 'revolutionary,' the Assembly itself was manifestly not. If its accredited peasants now saluted Socialism almost as often as they invoked Allah, their instincts remained the profoundly conservative instincts of peasants everywhere. And the rest of the members, whatever their category, remained overwhelmingly, if unaggressively, middle-class and aspiring.

Perhaps because this conferred some sort of coherence, the 'new model' Assembly lasted almost its full term, and was able to play an important steadying role through the months that followed the military débâcle of June 1967.[9] In its four-and-a half years in office the Assembly put through a great deal of solid, unspectacular work, and the 'new model' gave promise of establishing itself as the focus of the evolving political

---

[8] In December, 1967, the Minister of Supply announced that, in fulfilment of this promise, the public sector companies had already taken over the wholesale trade in rice, margarine, soap, tinned goods, sugar, tea, fish, imported dairy products, wheat, flour, sesame and spices.

[9] In accordance with the Constitution, the President dissolved the 1964 Assembly on 14 November 1968 and ordered new elections for 8 January 1969. The Assembly's full term ran to February 1969.

system of the new Egypt. Its authors claimed to be gratified by its progress. But how far could it justify the description 'democracy' which exuberant propagandists hastened to pin upon it?

Certainly the formal powers of the Assembly, under the Presidential Constitution, are considerable. It meets normally for a session of 'at least seven months' each November, but may be summoned at any time on the demand of a majority of its members. The Budget requires its ratification 'title by title.' Twenty members can demand a debate on a public issue. It can, after a delay, over-rule the Presidential veto, and it can dismiss a Government or any Minister therein by a vote withdrawing its confidence. Its agenda is determined by a committee elected from its members; another reviews members' proposals for Bills. Ministers must answer members' questions addressed to them in the half-hour or so of Question Time which, on the British model, opens the meetings—and this power alone, well used, must have a salutary effect.

Probably few assemblies anywhere are so much photographed, televised and generally publicised. 'It's an arena,' said one of its academic members. 'You can't hide yourself— your efficiencies and deficiencies. The Press are on the watch. So are the TV cameras. Some leaders have emerged from this, and, surprisingly, not always from the educated men. Others were simply a nullity. I suppose most of us were somewhere in between.'

Yet anyone watching the debates from the gallery must conclude that the outstanding characteristic of the Assembly is its docility. One feels a certain unreality, as if the whole thing were some complex, dogged and endless exercise. This, certainly, is in some degree the normal concomitant of the contemporary practice of democracy, but here there was perhaps a special reason for it, in addition to many members' inexperience. Great clouds of political theory still swirled around the new institutions. There is, for instance, the curious metaphysical relation of the National Assembly with its alter ego, the Arab Socialist Union. 'The National Assembly,' pronounces that body's statute, 'is the supreme authority in the state and implements, jointly with the trade unions and popular councils, the policy laid down by the Arab Socialist Union.' 'We know there are contradictions,' said Hussein el Shafei with disarming frankness. 'We are studying them. Sometimes, Mr Hopkins, our heads go round and around.'

In the midst of this head-turning constitution-making, the National Charter indicated the bounds of the permissible. Thus the Assembly committee to which members' proposals for Bills were submitted would throw out any found to transgress any principle or specific provision of the Charter. An attempt to reduce the individual land limit to ten feddans was rejected as contrary to the spirit of the Charter which endorses 'non-exploiting ownership.' But the frontiers of the Charter are reasonably wide—and extensible in the future—and despite political metaphysics, from time to time the Assembly's debates have sprung to life and the Government have been challenged—often, oddly enough, on issues that would rouse a Western assembly: higher education, housing and rents, or a tax on refrigerators. . . .

Western-style divisions, with totals of 'Ayes' and 'Noes' are relatively rare. Rather, as in a Quaker meeting, the search is for consensus ('after that,' as a Member put it, 'we argue some more'), in contrast to what an Egyptian sage, in a book on *Democracy in Islam*, published just before the revolution, called 'the sham democracy of weights and numbers.' Although the constitution does not indicate it, the Assembly's Speaker functions as a sort of buffer between it and the régime. When, on one occasion, it became clear that a Government proposal was about to be defeated, he adjourned the debate for the evening and came forward next day with a neatly packaged compromise, descending from the rostrum to present it in a persuasive speech to the Assembly. Face was saved all round, and the Press was able to acclaim a triumph for Democracy. It was, confided an Egyptian journalist, much 'nicer' to do it this way.

Thus, the Oriental art of reading between the lines is needed, and opposition tends to get expressed, if at all, in curious, and perhaps dangerously devious, ways. It was for this reason that Ataturk inaugurated a second party in Turkey in 1930. But he hastily shut it down again three months later, and few in Egypt in 1965 appeared eager to follow his example. Asked about their electoral campaigns, members tended to repeat that they made no promises ('We had too many of those in the past!') since in Egypt's situation all must be close-planned. Is that maturity—or timidity? Perhaps we need no longer set up Anglo-Saxon or Gallic forms as the sole criteria of political democracy. Certainly the Islamic aura of the New Egypt's still evolving political arrangements demands recognition. The Prophet, we are told, recommended *Shura* (or consultation between Ruler and People) in order to arrive at *Ijma* (or the consensus of the community): and from the beginning Nasser seems, in retrospect, to have been groping for some way out of the wilderness of an unlimited individualistic liberalism which was as unfitted as its obverse, 19th-century *laisser-faire* capitalism, to the needs of land and people. Here he is in *The Philosophy of the Revolution* describing the experiences of 1952-53:

> Every leader we came to wanted to assassinate his rival. Every idea we found aimed at the destruction of another. . . . If I were asked then what I required most, my instant answer would be: 'To hear but one Egyptian uttering a word of justice about another, to see but one Egyptian not devoting his time to wilfully criticising the ideas of another, to feel there was but one Egyptian willing to open his heart for forgiveness, indulgence and loving his brother Egyptians. . . . The word "I" was on every tongue. It was the magic solution to every difficulty. . . . Often did I meet men, referred to in the press as "great men" . . . from whom I sought the solution of a difficult problem. I could hear nothing from them save the word "I".'

To anyone who has had experience of Egyptians, this passage has the ring of truth. The whole history of modern Egyptian politics—and of Arab politics in general—bears it out. Despite the adoption of Western forms, the open, practical, 'call-it-a-day' compromises of Western secular democracy do not seem to have been possible. This is the world of all or nothing, of brotherhood or murder, of collectivity or chaos. In groping towards new political forms, Nasser and his friends, as much by instinct as by reason, were seeking to repair, adapt and renovate the Islamic collectivity. Here is Nasser addressing the National Assembly in 1965:

After Korban Bairam, God willing, I will have a meeting with

you. I will not speak at this meeting but will expect every one
of you to speak about what he has seen of the people's problems. The people's problems have to be solved, otherwise we
will have neglected the duties of leadership. . . .

Certainly this appears nearer to the Koranic 'consultation and
search for consensus' than to the language of a Western President or Prime Minister.

But at least as important as the debates in the Chamber has
been the members' participation on the many Assembly working committees which cover the whole of the national life.
The largest is the Committee for Agriculture, which has 118
members and numerous specialist sub-committees; the most
important is the Budget and Planning Committee. These committees continue to function outside the Assembly sessions.
Having been urged by Nasser to regard themselves as watch-
dogs, they form fact-finding parties to visit public-sector enterprises and so on. Again, in one seven-month session terminating
in June 1966, almost 14,000 petitions and complaints were
received from constituents and, according to the Speaker's report, about half of these drew replies from the appropriate
authorities to whom they were communicated by members.
In the same session, 212 questions were put to Ministers and
—to that date—168 answered.

A 'New Model' Press?

Not the least difficulty attending the effort to build a new
Egyptian political community on wider and deeper foundations
lay in the persistence of values and institutions from the old
one. The very Parliament Building which accommodated the
Nasserian 'new model' had been built in the nineteen-twenties
and some potent ghosts stalked through those Pharaonic-styled
halls. Egypt has by far the longest history of parliamentary institutions in the Arab world[10] and from the time that the

[10] For almost a generation Egypt was indeed the only place in the Middle
East where parliamentary institutions continued, since early constitutions
granted in Turkey (1876) and Tunisia were soon suspended. In 1834 Mohamed
Ali had set up a national council of sheikhs and merchants and also provincial councils; and Ismail's Consultative Assembly of 1866 marks the
beginning of the electoral process, although on a narrow base.

learned sheikh who led Mohamed Ali's first mission of students to Europe returned to Cairo and (in 1834) wrote a book about the experience, the inspiration had increasingly been the liberal tradition of the West. The equation 'A Constitution equals Liberty equals Progress' was nowhere more eagerly saluted than in Egypt. Nor had the matter stopped at parliaments. The learned sheikh's book had included commendation of 'printed sheets called newspapers.' By the end of the reign of the Khedive Ismail, Egypt had sixteen well-established newspapers, ten of them in Arabic, and was beginning to develop that flock of political pundits, *littérateurs* and columnists whose clamorous and competitive debate shattered the sleep of Islam. The young Nasser was certainly being no more than conventional when he wrote in his school magazine an article on 'Voltaire —Man of Freedom.'

If, by 1950, parliamentary democracy on the Western pattern was visibly bankrupt in Egypt, the liberal ideas it should have represented were still reflected in a varied and well-produced Press in which—through the hazards of censorship, fines, imprisonment, bribes and suspensions—several hundred increasingly professional journalists sustained a market in news and notions. One daily, *Al Ahram* ('The Pyramids') was over seventy years old; the distinguished magazine house, *Dar al Hilal* ('The Crescent') almost sixty. And if circulations were still small[11] and papers largely addressed to a small bourgeois class, the Amin brothers' 'Pulitzer' or 'Northcliffe' revolution of 1944, importing Western mass-sale techniques of sensationalism, comic strips, short sentences, 'human stories' in their highly successful *Akhbar el Yom* ('News of the Day'), had been felt throughout the field in a general brightening and simplification which drew new readers. There was also a range of attractive and well-produced magazines which took the world as their parish.

Thus by 1952 the Egyptian Press not only embodied the liberal idea of 'freedom of expression' (imperfectly achieved)

[11] Egyptian journalists bewail the fact that Egyptians are not natural newspaper addicts. They prefer their gossip live at the café table. In addition to illiteracy, Egypt's very low level of incomes is also a major obstacle to newspaper sales, and in particular has kept the sales of excellent magazines at derisory levels; e.g., the sale of *Aker Saa*, Egypt's well-produced *Life*-style illustrated magazine is only in the region of 75,000 an issue.

but had also become, like that of Britain and the United States, a substantial, prosperous and technically complex industry. Both these aspects inevitably presented serious difficulties for the revolution, and for a time the Press seemed likely to become Nasser's Achilles' heel, exposing the régime's schizophrenia in proclaiming the sovereignty of the People whom it dared not, it seemed, trust out of leading strings.

The Press Syndicate (which then included proprietors as well as journalists) had been purged in the struggles of 1954, and, after furious attacks on Nasser, the leading Wafdist newspaper, *Al Misri*, was shortly afterwards shut down. But Nasser, a great newspaper and magazine reader, continued to complain of the perversity and, perhaps worse, of the *frivolity* of the newspapers. The answer seemed to be for the Revolution to launch its own papers which it duly did, with *Al Shaab* ('The People'), *Al Goumhuriya* ('The Republic') and *Al Missa* ('The Evening'). *Al Shaab* soon failed, while the other two staggered dismally on under a long and rapid succession of officer-editors, starting with Anwar el Sadat and, at *Al Missa*, with Khaled Mohieddin. In 1964, Nasser thinking aloud about the problem of the Press before the National Assembly, complained rather bitterly that both were still losing money.

The attempt to provide an effective antidote to the capitalist Press having failed, the still worried Nasser had already turned, in 1960, to the nationalisation of the entire Egyptian Press on the—irrefutable—ground that it constituted an infraction of the basic Arab Socialist principle that private business wealth should not command political power.[12] 'The Press,' stated the new Press Law, 'must be a mission rather than a commodity or commercial goods . . . it is not only the right of the Press to criticise, but its duty to do so.'

The publishing houses did, in fact, retain separate identities, and the term 'nationalised' was indignantly rejected by one of Egypt's leading journalists, Mrs Amina Said, of *Dar al Hilal*,

---

[12] Nasser seems to have had something of the professional soldier's uneasiness about the Press. In 1956, he remarked that 'it would only require Bishara Takla of *Al Ahram*, the brothers Zaidan of *Dar al Hilal*, and the Amin brothers of *Akhbar el Yom* to combine in a campaign against the Government' for the public order to be imperilled. Of these proprietors of Egypt's major publishing enterprises, the first two were of Lebanese origin, a factor not making for accountability.

when I used it in 1964. 'I beg your pardon, but there is a big error there. We are not nationalised, but *socialised*. Under the Press Law, each group is owned, on paper, by the Arab Socialist Union. Of course, people can report us to them, but, in fact, this is nominal.' The groups were then run by Boards, consisting of five appointed journalist members and four elected from the rest of the staff; according to the law, the annual profit was split two ways, half for reinvestment in the business, half for distribution to the entire staff, journalistic, commercial, mechanical and so on. Since the profits of Mrs Said's group had been £250,000 in the previous year, this was highly satisfactory, particularly to the cleaners, tea-boys and so on, because the £E300 limit placed by the law upon the profit bonus meant that the worst paid were the most magnificently enriched.

Such a Press Law, confiding the running of a paper to its own staff, might seem an answer both to a journalist's prayer and also to the real political dilemma in a country such as Egypt. Unfortunately, the matter was not allowed to rest there. For the result was, as one young ASU zealot explained to me, that the Press was now in the hands of people who were not hostile to the régime, but equally were not actively supporting it. With the exception of *Al Ahram*, which had the good fortune to be edited by Nasser's disciple, Mohamed Hassenein Heikal, who equally had the good fortune to learn his craft before he became a politician, the journals were found to lack revolutionary spirit, failing to see life with the single eye of faith. In the autumn of 1964, the Press boards of directors were quietly dissolved, while Nasser installed as chairman of each house a convinced Socialist or Communist who might be relied upon to speed the work of regeneration: there was the perennial Judge Ahmed Fuad, the Communist missionary of the revolution's early days, at the house of *Rose el Yusef*; an able young Socialist journalist, Ahmed Bahaeddin at *Dar al Hilal*; and at the 'mass sale' house of *Akhbar el Yom*, the everfervent Khaled Mohieddin, who, in addition to being head of the Press section of the Arab Socialist Union, was now made Chairman of a council of these super-editors, presiding over the whole Press.

At night ablaze with light, the huge *Akhbar el Yom* building rides high above Cairo, its stern in the old working-class quarter of Bulaq, its prow turned towards Ismail's boulevards. A stream of donkeys and horse carts on their way to market push past the smart cars of the well-paid journalists parked around the building. Modern rotaries whine and rumble in the basement; on the ninth floor are the executive suites, furnished in international-Scandinavian style.

In the summer of 1965 the Chairman's large room, at the end of the curving corridor, was occupied by Khaled Mohieddin, the erstwhile 'Red Major,' returned to the fold and—as he explained in his newspaper column—to Islam, the mosque, and the keeping of Ramadan. 'Actually,' he explained, 'I was never an atheist. But of course I put God aside in order not to interfere with my study of scientific socialism. But I was too rigid. Experience of life has changed that. . . .' Yet he remained refreshingly boyish as with an almost priestly serenity he explained that the current aim was to reflect the same basic philosophy in all Egyptian newspapers, while preserving their individual styles and flavours. 'Socialism plus the very best journalistic techniques,' he summed up briskly.

'But suppose good journalists do not make good ideologues?'

'Yes, there is a difficulty, but it should be possible to create journalists who are animated by the true Socialist spirit.' And when the Arab Socialist Union had raised up such a race of newspapermen with a mission, it would be possible to insert them in key positions. 'You see, it's not only a question of support for the régime. We must make people ready to work hard, to accept sacrifices, to build Socialism. It's a tremendous task . . . a struggle. . . .'

When one suggests that it might perhaps be more effective to let the dissidents speak, and to defeat them in argument and performance, there is no patience with such liberal nonsense. 'They will tell lies about us. They will exploit people's ignorance. For instance, they will write about corruption in the co-operative stores. Well, as you know, there have been prosecutions there. But there was worse corruption before the revolution. . . .'

Further along the curving corridor of this executive floor were the doors of Ali and Mustafa Amin, the twin brothers—

sons of a former Ambassador to the U.S.A.—who had created this newspaper kingdom and who were now salaried employees within it. Their father had sent one, Mustafa, to England for education (in engineering, in Sheffield), the other, Ali, to America, and the improbable result had been the birth of Egyptian 'mass' journalism, an event deplored by many, yet an important step towards democratisation. Unlike the older school of journalists, they were politically uncommitted, without intellectual pretensions, zealous newspaper technicians of the modern Western type. Mustafa, in particular, an enormous, gently chuckling man, was a man for whom the expression 'the game of journalism' might have been invented; under him the House of Akhbar has schooled and given their chance to most of the leading Egyptian journalists of the 'sixties, including Nasser's favourite journalist, the celebrated editor of *Al Ahram*, Mohamed Hassenein Heikal.

The Egyptian Press was still able, within the scope of the Charter, to make factual criticisms, and sometimes its exposures of neglect in the factories or Ministries get results. In comment on such external events as the dismissal of Khrushchev or the India-Pakistan war, papers might take a variety of lines. But comment on Egyptian Government policy, although profuse and variously garnished, acquired in these years a total predictability. There was, indeed, only one licensed utterer of 'Opinions,' and the lengthy Friday lucubrations of Mohamed Hassenein Heikal have sent the circulation of *Al Ahram* soaring, as readers seek light from the source nearest the light. For a while, from 1964, a second prophet, Khaled Mohieddin, was licensed, but Heikal, the son of a small farmer and very much a self-made man, is an instinctive and professional journalist.[13] There are also scores of columnists, but though there is relatively little overt censorship of the hobnailed South African or Rhodesian variety, auto-censorship, refined by the normal instincts of self-preservation, is highly developed.

The installation of the Leftist commissars in 1964 was only

[13] Heikal met Nasser in Palestine, while reporting the 1948-9 war. Later he was editor of the picture magazine *Aker Saa* when it serialised Nasser's *Philosophy of the Revolution*, which Heikal is generally credited with having ghosted, but which certainly bears the imprint of Nasser's thinking.

one of the long series of baffled efforts to 'reform' the Press. Nor was it likely to be the last. Indeed by the end of 1965, Khaled Mohieddin (whose appointment was inferentially criticised in the National Assembly) had gone from his supervisory rôle at the House of Akhbar, and Heikal had taken over as head of the Socialist Union Press section. Below the surface, a subdued, long-drawn-out contest of wills and inclinations, journalists and soldiers, Western and Islamic influences, continued. The area remains critical. What will the outcome be? 'I think the Egyptian Press is too strong to be killed,' said Mustafa Amin. A few months later he was arrested on charges of currency smuggling and espionage, and subsequently sentenced to life imprisonment.[14] But about the Egyptian Press he may well have been right. In 1967, after the defeat by Israel, Heikal himself was publicly urging his colleagues to abandon their ingrained habits of self-censorship and speak out. And it appears that in some quarters, at least, the point was taken: in February 1968, 'greater Press freedom' was among the demands presented to the National Assembly by a student delegation.

The Intellectuals

Historically, the traditional professions have always provided secure bases from which a certain independence of view can grow. The professions in Egypt were, in their way, prerevolutionary pacemakers, and they still retain a good deal of the prestige which they once derived from their links with the West. Doctors, lawyers and architects are still among Egypt's biggest earners. And now the expansion of mass media has added actors, singers and writers, as well as journalists, to these well-paid ranks.

---

[14] He was accused of making regular secret reports on the Egyptian military and political situation to the C.I.A.'s man in Cairo. In the summer of 1966 he was sentenced to life imprisonment after trial in camera. He was found not guilty of divulging military secrets, but guilty of divulging political and economic secrets, and of illegally transferring capital abroad. After the arrest the Press Syndicate asked for details of the case as 'touching the dignity of the profession.' The prosecution thereupon provided a preview of the documentary and tape-recorded evidence at two six-hour meetings with Syndicate members.

Egyptian intellectuals—like American intellectuals—some-times complain that intellectuals do not have their 'proper place' in this new 'technocratic' society but it is also true that materially, many of them 'never had it so good.' Egypt has long had a tradition of drama, but since the revolution the theatres have been multiplied several times, covering a remark-able range of levels and tastes. A flock of writers is needed to feed them and the three television channels, and under the Egyptian socialist system their work is assessed by panels of their colleagues. An established playwright will get £E500 for a play—a small fellah's income for three years—and many columnists and journalists make £E200 a month. In addition to the private sector book-publishing houses, there are now four book-publishing companies under the state's General Or-ganisation for Literature, Information and Publishing. The Government has also put much new capital into the develop-ment of the Egyptian film industry, setting up a Film Institute for the training of directors, writers and technicians. Although there is no prohibition of private production, all the major studios are now state-owned and used by two public-sector production companies. One public-sector distribution company owns half Cairo's cinemas.

Should this be seen then as a programme for the subornation —rather than the encouragement—of Egyptian intellectuals? Must the quotation from the National Charter that appears on the National Theatre's programmes—'People should open their minds to new tendencies and free opinion'—be read ironically?

Such fears perhaps overlook the strength of Egypt's habits of eclecticism, deriving ultimately from her Mediterranean situation. Cairo is intellectually very much an international city, and though the influences may now come from rather more directions than they used to, they still wash up in pro-fusion. Modern plays and novels from abroad are produced in great variety in Arabic translation, and Egypt's own writers diligently ape, between them, most of the successive European voguish models. This may, or may not, be a good thing, but at least it does not make for doctrinal shibboleths. One is a long way from Soviet, and even more from Chinese, cultural line-toeing and heresy-hunting.

'Of course,' confessed a well-known film director, 'we cannot make a film *against* Socialism. In fact, of the sixty to eighty films we make a year we should probably make a quarter to show the fight *for* Socialism. . . . But the rest are international dramas, musicals, comedies, thrillers—just as yours.' The Egyptian cinema industry is in competition with American and British films in its home market. It must hold its audiences, as the newspapers must hold their readers, and ultimately return a profit, and in both cases this strengthens the position of the professionals and restrains propagandist zealots.

The composition of the 1964 National Assembly, with its range of professors, journalists, doctors and lawyers, fully acknowledged the Charter's ruling that 'Intellectuals are one of the five categories of the People'; and although some of them may feel stultified in the new society, through their associations, their prestige, their relatively good economic standing, they are certainly able to make their influence felt, should they choose to do so.

Consider, for example, the case of a body of professional people of the less pretentious sort—the teachers. The 120,000-strong Teachers' Union has its magnificent offices and club in the upper five floors of an eleven-storey tourist hotel in the middle of Cairo. It owns the building, and draws a handsome rent from the tenant hotel company. In a curious way it owes this good fortune to the revolution. When the union was formed in 1949, the Wafd, then in power, refused to recognise it. But its members doggedly continued to pay their subscriptions, with the result that by 1954, when the revolutionary régime amended the law and recognised the teachers' union, £E500,000 had accumulated. The teachers wisely used this to build the El Borg Hotel on the site of the old British El Alamein Club on the Nile bank; they also run three hospitals for teachers.

This is very nice. But as elsewhere, teachers in Egypt are not highly paid: a graduate starts at £E18 a month, rising annually by £2 increments. Is the union therefore pressing for higher pay, perhaps threatening strike action? 'I would rather say,' explained a spokesman mildly, 'that we have, as Vice-President, the Minister of Education—a former teacher—to fight for us.'

It was hardly the Western approach, but it might be a mistake to assume that quietism spelled surrender.

Thus, in one way or another, through the remodelled National Assembly, through the diversity of the mass media, through the professionals and intellectuals, the means existed for genuinely national public opinion to take shape and find expression. Certainly, the ultimate power of decision still lay off-stage, in the army, and Nasser himself has frankly admitted using its implicit threat—all the more effective for being so largely invisible and unspoken—to protect his evolving new model. Even so, perhaps the greatest obstacle to the new model's taking on organic life has lain elsewhere—in the incidence of that 'lack of moral courage' which the British journalist, Peter Mansfield, in *Nasser's Egypt*, discerns in the Egyptian Press. Islam possesses a religio-political doctrine known as *taqiya*, founded on a single verse of the Koran, whereby it becomes a virtue to dissemble one's opinion in unfavourable surroundings,[15] and Egypt's centuries of subjugation have ensured that it corresponds to a reality. Yet without an adequate base of independence of mind it must be hard to find a middle road between debilitating conformity and conspiracy and revolt.

This is something of which Nasser has long shown himself aware, but the political scope is narrowly limited by the precariousness of Egypt's economic situation. A Western liberal like Mr John S. Badeau, former U.S. Ambassador in Cairo, may call for a 'loyal Opposition' and an Egyptian Marxist intellectual like Anwar Abdel Malek may complain that 'monolithism smothers the dialectic.' But what if the opposition should prove both factious and disloyal, and the 'energising' dialectic should energise a bloody class conflict in which all Egypt's technocratic plans to break out of the vicious circle of poverty would be engulfed?

Egypt certainly will continue to grope—perhaps uneasily —towards some balance between the old individualistic liberalism and 'socialist' consensus; but whatever its shortcomings, it could be argued, in 1967, that Nasser's new-old model, based on 'family' dialogue and social equilibrium, offered the best hope of peaceful political evolution. For now, fifteen years

[15] R. Levy, *The Social Structure of Islam*, Cambridge, 1965; H. Kraemer, *World Cultures and World Religions*, London, 1960.

after the coup, there was within this society, dominated first by wealth, then by armed force, the beginnings of counter-vailing power and of a new social balance. If the ultimate sanction, as in most states in the modern world, lay with the army, increasingly, month-to-month power resided in the central body of technocrats, with their supporting phalanxes of managers, planners, specialists, technicians—the truly in-dispensable men.

The technocrats had their voice in the National Assembly along with the workers, peasants, intellectuals and national capitalists. But would this body continue to devote itself, as the Charter envisaged, to the search for consensus? The class war might be outlawed, but in so fissured a society, under severe economic strains, could it be avoided? Danger existed at either end of the social scale. The technocrats, for instance, had been allotted a prestigious rôle and a fairly high place on the national salary scale. This, however, in the interests of social justice, terminated for all at £E5,000 a year. Would they accept that—or seek to turn the levers of the economy into levers of personal profit and power?

The new model recognised the danger and provided a counterpoise. It was not certainly to be found in the ranks of the small fellahin represented in the National Assembly. They might provide useful ballast, but little more. Today, in Egypt as elsewhere, the future is made in the towns. The counter-poise recognised and employed by the régime from its earliest years had been organised labour. The expansion of the trade unions has been vigorously pushed ahead. The most fully developed in the Arab world, the unions have been strength-ened by the rapid growth of the industrial labour force and by the increasing number of large public-sector concerns in which a substantial, literate labour force confronts sophisti-cated management.

Confronts? Few Egyptian labour leaders would choose so crude a term, at least in public. It would tend to suggest in-correct thinking.

For in the 'new-model' factory, as in the new-model parlia-ment, all the tables are round.

21

'ALL WORKERS NOW'?

> Overbearance, or any form of haughtiness, must not be shown towards the working people . . .
> —Statute of the Arab Socialist Union, December 1962

> It must frankly be said that the advance of the U.A.R. towards socialism is not a simple one. The Egyptian revolution has entered its second stage which will be characterised by a clash between the workers and those who want to exploit them.
> —Nikita Khrushchev, May 1964

'But you must not judge Egypt by English standards. . . . We are a Socialist country now. The interests of the white-collar workers and the manual workers are the same. We don't have a class system any more . . . *Please* do not smile, Mr Hopkins!'

The speaker was an earnest young man at Egyptian Trade Union Federation headquarters; the subject, a recurring one, my inexplicable concern at the number of white-collar officials, supervisors, personnel department men and so on elected to office in industrial trade unions. Egyptian trade-union law provides that those who hire and fire shall be excluded, but short of this there is little acknowledgment of any clash of interests, the 'sides of industry.' At the Nasr Automotive Works I was shaken to find that the 'job evaluation' expert was a member of the union; but then the President of the works branch was the head of the Finance Department, an arrangement which the branch secretary, the Labour Culture Officer, explained was most useful since he was always able to explain to the members with fluency and conviction why they could not have their pay in advance, as so many wished to do.

Similarly, at national level, one was a little startled to discover that the elected Vice-President of the important Textile Union was a mill medical officer—in fact a valuable and dedicated man who explained that 'a doctor should not only be a medical man, but a social man' and who had, since 1953, been practising what he preached by pioneering the country's first workers' family medical service at the Mehalla textile complex.

The Egyptian manual worker's tendency to defer to his 'betters' was also strikingly revealed in the elections for the four worker-directors who today sit on the nine-man board of each plant. One did find the odd manual worker or two. The United Arab Airways board had a driver and a mechanic; the Kafr el Dawar cotton mills a spinner and a mechanic; Kima, at Aswan, an electrician. But there was a predominance of foremen, departmental managers, store-keepers, time-keepers, and again, very commonly, doctors. There were actually *two* doctors among the four elected members of the Helwan Steelworks Board, its other elected members being the chief strip-mill engineer and the steel-mill assistant-foreman—the latter being, additionally, a union official.

This does not happen because the elections are not properly conducted. There have been many worker candidates and often quite lively campaigns with posters and even lapel badges. At the Egyptian Copper Works in Alexandria, for instance, there were thirty-four candidates, of whom two-thirds were manual workers with enough spirit to 'have a go'; but only one was elected and he was a foreman. Class-consciousness is still weak, manual workers' prestige low, and the trade unions rarely concert support. Many workers solve the problem by voting for 'three managers and my pal.' Or, as one manager put it with unconscious irony: 'Well, our workers are somewhat advanced. When electing for the board, they want someone who can do the job well.' Doctors, like time-keepers, are elected because they are a source of favours (an Oriental reason), but also because the workers know them and trust them to speak on their behalf when once elected (a more modern reason).

All this betokens a stage rather than a destination. It would be premature to conclude that Egyptian trade unions or worker-participation on the boards of directors are merely hollow, window-dressing devices. For a labour movement can only develop on its own foundations, and in this poverty-stricken, over-populated land with a small and fragmented industrial labour force, the unions have inevitably depended on the buttressing of Governmental labour laws. In 'French' North Africa, Arab unionism was able to develop under the powerful wing of the French C.G.T., and its Arab leaders played a critical rôle both in the fight for independence and its immediate sequel.[1] In Egypt, by contrast, the unions, when they escaped the police, were *used* by rival politicians for their own ends, becoming victims of Egypt's endless party warfare. Without legal status until 1942, effective unionism was largely confined to those unions facing modern, foreign companies, like the petrol workers facing Shell, or the tram-workers of Cairo, the veterans of Egyptian unionism. A few genuine worker union leaders had emerged, but the essential step of confederation was still barred and further development had to await the revolution. In 1952, the organisation of agricultural workers—the great body of impoverished Egyptian workers—was legalised. The automatic 'check-off' of union dues from wages, given a certain minimum enrolment, was shortly afterwards instituted; a union could now only be dissolved by decree of a court of law; and in 1957 a Confederation came into being. But as important as these legal advances was the régime's—or at any rate, Nasser's—determination to give the unions status and to push forward their leaders on the national scene.

In 1967, the elected President of the Federation of Labour, the chief representative of the Egyptian workers, was Ahmed Fahim, a typically Egyptian figure, burly, with a wide ready smile and deep belly laugh, yet with a fundamental earnestness and plodding purpose. President of the highly organised Textile Workers, Fahim hails from a Nile-bank village in mid-Delta, learned to recite the Koran in the village *kuttab*, went on to the district primary school and, at thirteen, entered the training school which the new Misr Company had lately established at its Mehalla cotton mill in order to turn fellahin into millhands. Occupied in the trade school during the day, Fahim worked in the mill all night, and for this received a wage of three piastres a day. 'I didn't see the sun the whole year round and got hardly any sleep.' After two years in trade school he received that all-important Egyptian talisman, his 'diploma'

---

[1] Although at a later stage the unions lost this independence and were subordinated to the Bourguiba-bossed single party, the Neo-Destour, in Tunisia, and to a negative and repressed rôle in King Hassan's Morocco.

and henceforward, as a weaver, made from eight to twelve piastres a day, precariously, however, since textile companies were then in the habit of discharging young workers as soon as they qualified for adult pay.

Fahim joined the company union as soon as unions were legalised in 1942, and in 1955 he became a full-time textile union official, in this capacity visiting Britain and the United States. He is an obvious beneficiary of the régime, one of Egypt's 'new men.'

But despite the considerable experience of Fahim's union and one or two others, extensive Government midwifery was still needed before Egypt could achieve an effective, modern trade-union structure. In 1959 there were still 1,300 separate trade unions in Egypt. No fewer than 120 of these were in the textile industry—organised on a factory basis. As Ahmed Fahim put it to me: 'We went to the Government and we said: "This is no good" because the average membership of a union was 100, with an income of £10 a month. So then the 1959 law provided for national industrial unions. By the end of 1960 we had about sixty of them. But even these were small and too weak in resources—so in 1964 we consolidated into twenty-seven unions, which now cover the whole of industry, mining, transport, agriculture, the civil service. . . .'

To speed the process, Nasser in 1962 appointed a veteran trade-union leader, the President of the Petroleum Workers, Anwar Salama, as Minister of Labour, and a year later the second-in-command of the petrol workers' union, Ali Sayed Ali, was elected Deputy Speaker of the National Assembly. Ali Sayed Ali was a salesman, a former chief of Shell's internal marketing; but Salama, like Fahim, was a manual worker, a trade-school graduate, a fitter. A short, sallow man from Damanhur, needle-sharp both mentally and in dress, Salama did not permit his obvious delight in being a Minister to inhibit his skills (or, possibly, destroy his loyalties) as a trade-union leader. 'I come to you as one of you,' he would tell workers' meetings. 'You all know that my door at the Ministry is never closed to you.' Anyone who calls him a white-collar man does so at his peril. 'I worked with *these hands*'—holding out a well-manicured pair—'for twenty years. For twenty-one years I lay underneath lorries, while the oil dripped on my face eight hours a day. . . .'

Thus reinforced, the Ministry of Labour was able to put through the massive union consolidation scheme with remarkable dispatch. The sugar workers were briskly wedded to the food and beverage workers (themselves a 1959 marriage of nine unions); the petrol workers to the miners; the lorry and bus-drivers, the taxi-drivers, and, a little oddly, the car workers, were united in the road transport union. The amalgamation of the steel, engineering and metal industries' unions gave the workers in those key crafts an organisation which, through its ninety-one branches with their elected committees, could now offer representation in almost every part of Egypt.

At the same time, a national industrial pay structure with twelve grades (each with maximum and minimum rates), stretching from the adolescent apprentice (£E60 a year) to the departmental manager (£E1,800 a year) was worked out. A modern 'job evaluation' survey was carried out to determine the appropriate rating for each job in each public-sector industry. This had the effect of introducing into pay a logic rarely known in the West; it also had the ironic effect of reducing the pay of new entrants into the petroleum industry (where high profits and a strong union had led to pay far out of line with colleagues elsewhere).[2]

For such paternalism on one side and docility on the other there is inevitably a price, and a good many union officials appear complacent bureaucrats. 'The right to strike?' 'Well, of course, it is not specifically forbidden.[3] But why should we want to strike? All the problems of labour are solved by the laws we now have. We have the seven-hour day, profit-sharing, the best working conditions of any country and our social insurance is among the best in the world. We can't ask the Government for more than it can give—and we know exactly our resources. In five years' time we shall have more.'

[2] Existing workers continued at the old levels; the new 'national' scales were only to be applied to newcomers to the petroleum industry.

[3] By the 1964 Law, article 180, the Minister of Labour may request a court of law to dissolve the executive board of a union which 'incites to subversion, hatred or contempt of the established system of government or advocates doctrines aimed at changing the fundamental principles of the Constitution; or incites refusal to work by persons performing public functions, employed in public services or working to fulfil need'—pretty comprehensive, although action before a court of law is theoretically needed.

In many interviews with trade-union leaders of all degree I heard that speech, with minor variations, many times. A few, including the Minister of Labour, maintained that the right to strike existed; most would quickly brush aside so 'irrelevant' a topic. In fact, odd strikes do spasmodically occur—among the Alexandria dockers, the taxi-drivers, the workers at Helwan. . . . But they are kept quiet, smoothed over, and the strikers propitiated where possible: for unless directed against some reactionary 'non-national' capitalist, they would clearly seem contrary to 'the spirit of the Charter.'

Union attitudes, however, make more sense when one bears in mind the inevitable weakness of organised labour in a country of endemic overpopulation and under-employment. For the labour unions, the public-sector undertakings in fact function as pacemakers and underpinners; in being since the Second World War, statutory minimum wage rates did not become really effective until after the nationalisations of 1961. Half the industrial workers and 90 per cent of Trade workers are in private employment, mostly in minuscule establishments, next to impossible to organise or supervise. At the large garage in Cairo where I kept my car, there were four men whose indispensable function it was to push the cars about so that the maximum number could be fitted in. These men were paid no wage at all, but depended on the subventions of the car-owners who paid for extrication. In this socialist utopia, large numbers still live thus precariously; and if private employers now pay more than the public sector to attract skilled workers, they pay less for the unskilled.

But from 1965 the achievement of a nation-wide agricultural workers' union did begin to build some sort of floor under Egyptian labour; for the first time there was union organisation over the whole range of industry. The Textile Union, for instance, now had 200,000 members, a monthly subscription income of £E16,000, and a reserve fund of £E160,000 in the bank—minute figures by international standards but the beginning of solidity for Egyptian labour. The textile and paper industries claimed to be 75 per cent organised, the petroleum industry 100 per cent, steel and engineering 66 per cent, commerce 50 per cent. More important, perhaps, for the future, one more democratic structure had been erected, with a ladder of election from the hundreds of branch committees, through provincial union councils to the national councils and the twenty-one-member Federation Council at the summit.

I was present at the nuptial meeting when delegates of the Petroleum Workers' Union and of the Miners' Union came together to elect the first council of the combined union. I found it a serious and an impressive occasion. The 120 branch delegates of the two unions gathered under an immense *siwan* (a marquee with walls of colourfully embroidered cloth) on the roof of an old suburban house which was the Petroleum Union's Cairo Club. Even without a seating plan it wasn't hard to distinguish the lean, sunburned miners in their turbans and galabiyas, with the odd Bedouin from the manganese mines in Sinai among them, from the affluent petroleum men, often impeccably dressed and carrying shiny briefcases. But there were some horny-handed sons of toil on the petroleum side too —tanker drivers, a kerosene hand-cart seller from Upper Egypt, a driller from Ras Gharib on the Red Sea. . . .

The meeting lasted three hours. The delegates started a number of arguments—the alleged under-representation of the Miners (by the Miners), the inconvenience of shifting the Petrol HQ to Cairo, the unwisdom of the proposed cut in the union funeral grant, following the start of the state insurance grant system. But Ali Sayed Ali, the Petrol Workers' President, at his desk on the rostrum, nursing his microphone, fluent and persuasive, dominated the meeting, quelled each rebellion, smoothed down the contestants and moved on to next business. At the climax of the meeting, Anwar Salama, the Minister, appeared and called down the blessing of God upon the union. 'Try to live as friends. Try to live as colleagues. Try to live as brothers. Let there be neither Petroleum Workers nor Mine Workers, but only brothers in the Cause.' The meeting visibly basked in the warm glow of the Minister's love.

Yet despite the paternal flavour, the election was real enough. The voting for the twenty-one council members from a field of sixty-four candidates took place in a smaller, adjoining *siwan*, watched over by two scrutineers, one elected by the petrol workers and the other by the miners. The miners' man was a blue *galabiya*-clad foreman from the Aswan iron mines, with a brown skull-cap and seraphic smile; the petrol workers' choice was a young Cairo pump attendant in trousers and smart striped shirt. The poll and count was supervised by four officials from the Ministry of Labour's election section.

What with the worker elections to the boards of directors and to the new union councils, the Ministry men had been having a very busy time. 'The Banks voted yesterday,' one of them said. 'And we ourselves voted last week!'—for the council of the new Social Services Union to which their Ministry now belonged. Playing a rôle unfamiliar in the West but probably indispensable in the under-developed East, these men are also in their way professionals of the labour movement. Modern-minded, many have studied labour conditions and codes in the West; they look to the I.L.O. at Geneva as naturally as an earlier generation of Egyptians looked to Paris.

Thus a certain 'neutral' professionalism mingles with the old Islamic paternalism among the distinguishing flavours of Egypt's developing trade unionism. It is a tone likely to be increasingly reflected by the emerging labour leaders of the Federation of Labour, representing 1½ million organised workers. For their organisation is now harnessed to the larger purposes of the state, a built-in part of its socio-economic mechanism, and one of those legitimised major pressure groups which Egypt is now consciously bringing together to form the structure of the first modern industralised Arab society.

'Labour Culture'

'In Moscow,' explained Ali Sayed Ali, 'it's all "the proletariat". In the West, it's "workers versus capitalists"; but under our Egyptian Socialism there are no classes and all who work are "workers" and work together.'

Though a trade unionist from the West might find his head spinning, there is a good deal he would recognise through the abrupt switches of focus. In a rayon-works union branch club in Alexandria I found a workers' painting exhibition in one room (very reminiscent of London Transport's show), a class for illiterates going on in another, a dark room for camera-hobbyists next door. Half a mile away, in a Workers' Educational Association building in the Prophet Daniel street, a class of twenty 'worker-directors' on a five-week course were being lectured by an Alexandria University professor on the need for saving to 'protect the base of socialism and finance the new factories'; while a university colleague waited his turn to talk on costing and balance-sheets. Eighty factories in the area were sending their elected worker-directors to the course, sharing the cost with the unions. In Alexandria and Beheira Province alone there are twelve of these Workers' Educational Centres, giving a variety of courses for trades union leaders and ordinary workers.[4]

It is all a part of what is called 'Labour Culture.' Many factories have 'Labour Culture Officers,' one of whom became quite exasperated at my failure to appreciate instantly what Labour Culture was. It is, in brief, the pilotage of the new worker across several millenia from the world of the mud-village to the world of the time-clock. By no means a new function in Egyptian factories, it is now shared with the trade unions, and thus takes on a new dimension. 'Some,' said the Labour Culture officer, still trying to penetrate my strange opacity, 'do not treat their wives well. They sit all night in the cafés, spending their pay. We have a big problem of divorce here. . . .' An English Literature graduate of Cairo University, he was a harassed little man, as well he might be, torn between his 'cultural' duty to instil social discipline into the semi-literate workers and his 'labour' duty to represent their complaints with force to the Management. 'I must,' he said suddenly, 'really have some prizes.'

One of the lectures I heard at the W.E.A. Centre in Alexandria was on: 'How to Discuss.' In the theory of the new state, the unions in fact discuss only economic and industrial matters;[5] political affairs are supposed to be the preserve of the ASU, with its elected unit in every factory. But suppose

---

[4] The Workers Education Association is financed and managed by a board of trustees representing the unions, universities, the Ministries of Labour, Education, Industry and Culture, the Social Insurance Organisation and the Arab Socialist Union.

[5] A situation common to most 'new' or emergent states where cohesion is a first requirement. Thus, in Tunisia, after a crisis in 1956, the labour federation, the UGTT, was taken over by Bourguiba's Neo-Destour men, and its too independent and 'political' Secretary-General dismissed.

the two conflict, as seems highly likely? 'Yes, sometimes there is a clash. The ASU committee enquires about productivity, and the trade-union committee replies: "None of your business." But you see, we're all members of the ASU—so we all get together and discuss some more and decide.'

Was there ever, one wondered again, anywhere a society which 'discussed' so much—and, it seemed, disagreed so little?

Workers and Technocrats

I asked one of the three worker-directors in the Alexandria class what projects the worker-directors on his Board had been engaged in. He was a skilled craftsman, a turner, employed by the Stella Brewery. He mentioned a staff housing co-operative, a fund for helping newly-weds, a club for workers, and a re-arrangement of the works bonus distribution system. Repeated enquiries suggested that, as in other countries, it was mainly on this welfare level that worker-participation in management had so far taken place. As elsewhere, workers sometimes complained that managements, despite the injunctions of the Charter, still concealed from them essential facts and figures. In reality it appears that it is not too difficult for a chairman of an enterprise to by-pass the full board, except for the statutory meeting to pass the annual budget, and inevitably, it is upon the attitudes and necessities of the technocrats that the future of this rather Owenite 'Harmony Hall' conception of industry must depend.

One young engineer-manager, hard-pressed to maintain delivery quotas, complained in some exasperation that what with the elections in his factory, first for the trade union, then for the ASU, then for the Board, his workers had been put off their stroke for two months at least. Managers, he also observed, were currying favour with the workers to get votes in the elections, and this was bad for discipline. But few managers seemed to share his misgivings. Most of them have the same sort of social origins as the officers who made the revolution: they belong to that lower middle class, with its roots in the villages, which is the most solid social fact about Egypt. They are on the whole simple people, with few pretensions. As industrial managers they tend to the old paternal tradition, even though the younger ones no longer exclaim of their workers, as their elders sometimes do, 'I am their father and their brother.' One managing director, a chemist by profession, pronounced the worker-director system very useful '. . . because we are a family. Our relation is so strong with each other we want to know what the "brothers" are thinking; we want to know if someone has a complaint.' 'We discuss as long as we can,' said another of his own Board, 'and then we all come to one idea.'

On this modernised 'family' level, as a serviceable channel of communication with the people below, many managers are prepared to welcome the worker-directors. But beyond that, few seemed to think they had much to contribute. The worker-directors just did not know enough, they said—and some added the qualification 'yet.'

As in so many other areas of present-day Egypt an educational process is going on here which involves managers as well as workers. The old society might be said to have been dedicated to the concept of the Indignity of Labour. It is well to recall that the slave trade was not made illegal in Egypt until 1884 and, according to Lord Cromer, there were still slaves in Egyptian households in 1911: indeed, servants were treated like slaves until yesterday. But under the pressures mobilised by the revolution, a radical transformation of social values is under way. In the Alexandria cotton-pressing warehouses in 1965 one could still see wretched labourers leaping madly up and down from ropes into a pit of cotton, pressing it down into the baling press by their own weight and velocity, spurring themselves on with demoniacal cries. But, after a century or more of this, a machine called a 'trampler' was about to be installed. 'Because it's not human work, really,' apologised an engineer. 'You know we are progressing—but bit by bit, because it takes a lot of money.' This new social responsibility has led, for instance, to the appearance of safety officers, a novel idea in Egyptian industry. 'Now we have a new point of view. The workers are the source of production and so they are not cheap.' This particular man had a social-worker assistant, with a diploma in psychology, whose job it was to visit the injured in their homes, seeking to establish the root causes of the accidents which are very frequent in

Egyptian factories.

Technocrats like everybody else are affected by this changing social climate, and while the financial rewards they can
enjoy under Egyptian Socialism are limited, managerial per-
quisites such as low-rent factory villas and cars are considerable. Within Egypt's relative simplicity of life they do not
necessarily feel a compulsion to compete with each other in
gaining extravagant salaries, as in the West. An oil-refinery
manager, whose salary had been frozen because like other
petroleum salaries it was so far ahead of the national levels,
was ruefully prepared to agree that 'it is only just that there
should be no high salaries until the Government is able to
provide decent pay for all. After all, others are human beings
and have needs, besides oil-men.'

It is this widening sense of community, something that goes
much deeper than the old frenzied, frustrated nationalism,
which offers the best hope that the society now emerging will
work and endure. Workers and managers alike have been made
aware of the immensity of the challenge that Egypt is facing
and are conscious of participating in a critical moment both
in the history of Egypt and of the wider Arab world.

Roughly chalked on a wall behind a steel rolling mill I
noticed a worker's scribble in Arabic, and, thinking it might be
some rude remark about the foreman, asked for it to be translated. It ran: 'It is our duty to sweat for the sake of production and we should also shed blood for liberty.'

I said: 'I suppose the Arab Socialist Union sent somebody
along to write it up.'

'No, no. It is just some workmen or other. It is spontaneous.
That is how we all think.'

Brothers and Ph.Ds

Although the technocrats certainly have their quota both of
unredeemed *ancien régime* and of frustrated capitalists fret-
fully aware of the rewards available in the world outside, the
real threat to Egyptian socialism's design for an Arab industrial
democracy is deeper and quite impersonal. If the urgency of
the challenge calls for social unity, the longer-term technical
necessities of the response tend to new social division. Egypt

was now well on the way to becoming, under these pressures, the first full-fledged Arab meritocracy. And the more such a country aspires to egalitarian democracy the more firmly meritocracy is entrenched, because advancement by examination grades, diplomas, doctorates, awarded in open competition, repudiates the venerable Oriental institution of nepotism as nothing else can. One was often told in Egypt that 'even Nasser's daughter' had to go to a Higher Institute rather than University because her school-leaving examination marks were not high enough.

In central Cairo one morning, newspaper boys suddenly erupted on to the street with what looked like a Special Edition. Young men rushed up to buy copies. They stood on the pavement scanning the pages feverishly. Could it, one wondered, be some new national crisis? It was a crisis, certainly, a very personal one. The paper contained the final examination results of Cairo University and thus, to a large extent, the entire future life chances of the young men who dashed to buy it.

For the young Egyptian, life takes on a grimly competitive aspect. Certainly the old society of the Levant had its own limited, but bracing, mobility—of the favourite and clever slave who rose to be Grand Vizier; of the obscure individual who 'sold his wife's bangles' and progressed via usury to pashadom; of the proverbial Lebanese who arrived in Egypt with nothing but a carpet-bag full of scented soap and ended with a commercial empire; of the household electrician who first played with, then pimped for the King. But although it has been a relatively short progress from the poisoned cup to the Ph.D. thesis as an instrument of social mobility, the latter, less dramatic in the short term, sets on foot a process which transforms Oriental society, subjecting it to potentially explosive stresses.

In Egypt the meritocratic system is already beginning to break down the divisions of family and clan and village, opening up the national prospect. Yet, even as it does so, it threatens to open up new gulfs, less tolerable because so manifestly man-contrived. The New Egypt stratifies neatly into graduates of primary school, trade school, grammar school, higher institute and university, a division nicely reflected in the twelve grades of the national pay structure and in the terms of army conscripts' service. (The fellah conscript serves two or three years, the university student twelve to eighteen months—as an officer.)

And since there are only enough government secondary-school places to absorb a little over a quarter of those in primary schools, the competitive struggle extends downwards and Egyptian parents increasingly face the equivalent of that English family watershed, 'the eleven-plus' examination. For a few, as in England, private schools still offer a way out, but they are beyond the means of most.[6]

In under-developed nations, with their narrow range of occupations, the rigidities of meritocracy can breed a volume of frustration greater and more dangerous than in the affluent West. Egypt now 'guarantees' its graduates jobs, but the country seems full enough of disappointed young people in jobs they did not want. One may meet, for instance, an agricultural officer in some remote village who has no desire to be an agricultural officer and is one simply because his school-leaving marks would not admit him to an engineering course. It is fair, and seen to be fair, yet for such as he—and how much more for those who have failed to advance even so far —the 'classlessness' of the new Egyptian society may lack conviction.

It is significant that, with all its children not yet in primary school, Egypt has already experienced the full force of the contemporary democratic demand for 'university education for all.' Thus Nasser some time ago found it necessary to point out that:

Equal opportunity means that the student of industry (i.e. trade school or craft school, etc.) should have his chance as a student

[6] About 17 per cent of secondary schools are private schools. The good ones, the former British 'public schools' and French *lycées*, now Egyptian-ised and run by the Teachers' Syndicate (although still stressing foreign languages) are expensive enough to tend to be the preserve of businessmen, top managers and by no means inconsiderable *rentier* survivors of the old-wealthy class. So visibly undemocratic a survival certainly attests the régime's lack of doctrinal rigour—although a factor may be the prestige of these institutions which draw pupils from all over the Arab world. There is also an intermediate class of 'Government-supported' schools with lower fees.

of industry, and that a university student should have his chance
as a university student. But when a student of industry wants
to have the same opportunity as the university student, I say
to him—this is not the principle of equal opportunity in its
true light.

Within a decade of her revolution of the Common Man,
Egypt already faced the characteristic dilemma confronting
mid-twentieth-century social democracy: that technology,
which promises to liberate the Common Man, is ruthlessly
selective. Nasser, while sensing the distinction between equality and equality of opportunity, denies the conflict. Here he
is addressing an Arab Socialist Union Production Conference
in March 1967:

> Socialism consists rather in providing equal opportunities which
> eliminate class distinctions; but once this equality is assured,
> the road will be wide open to every individual to determine by
> himself and through his personal abilities the rôle he shall play
> in society, and what he should obtain from society.

To the West, this attempted marriage of 'brotherhood' and
'meritocracy' in Arab Socialism may seem to show that the
conflict between the soldier-technocrat and the ideologue-
socialist in Nasser is deeper than he realises. Yet Islam, almost
from the first, has displayed a persistent intermingling of the
aristocratic and the egalitarian themes, deriving, perhaps, from
the rough practical 'democracy' of clansmen who can respect
the dignity of each, yet bow to the superior wisdom of the
few. Certainly the feeling for the group, for that human
brotherhood outlined by Islam, militates against the hardening of industrial castes. 'You will see,' said the Rector of Assiut
University, showing me his growing campus, 'there are no
walls around these buildings. Anyone can walk in. That is to
make them feel that education is not to create a new class
and that professors also are only here to serve.' It is a good
doctrine. Yet to bring the egalitarianism of the Koran to the
industrial board-room table, to adapt the working democracy
of the clan to the exigencies of, say, chemical engineering or
steel production, is a formidable assignment.

The fundamental problem, which Egypt now shares with
advanced countries—and which industry reflects in common

with all human social and political organisations—is how to devise a satisfactory modern relationship between the individual and the group. Egypt, as an Islamic country, is strong on the group, but has been weak on individual responsibility. With her system of worker-participation, as with other devices, Egypt is groping towards her own solution as she struggles with the exacting demands of industrialisation.

'We need participation to develop management skills,' said Dr Fuad Cherif, director of Egypt's Management Development Agency. 'On the other hand, the enterprise manager must be responsible for the company. The thing is in a state of flux and it is very difficult to say what the ultimate form will be. But what is important is to maintain an experimental attitude. We should have experiment and flexibility—as in Yugoslavia. But we want a specifically Egyptian solution. We don't want to copy anyone.'

'Do you really think,' asked a young former-Communist journalist, 'that we can learn from your experience in the West and avoid the violence and cruelty of your industrial revolution in our own?'

It is a question to which it is still difficult to return any confident answer. Egypt's growing proletariat is now sketchily protected by minimum-wage and job-security laws, by trade-union organisation and welfare-state devices written into the Constitution. In the public sector, the spread between the lowest and highest paid is less than in Western industry[7]—but the lowest is on the margin of subsistence. Under such conditions the 'shotgun' marriage of the worker and his manager on the benches of the National Assembly and elsewhere would appear precarious. But the Egyptian instinct for group conformity and the rueful, all-embracing tolerance of *Malish!* may see them through.

In the Egyptian perspective, the 'Arab Socialist' model appears as a middle way between the twin extremes of the old Islamic theocracy on the one hand and the 'new' materialist

[7] Frcm £E5-7 per month for the non-adult, £E7-15 for the unskilled adult to £E80-150 for departmental chiefs such as production director, sales manager. In Nasr Automotive Works, for instance, an unskilled man got £E7½ per month, a skilled man £E15; chargehand £E20; foreman £E45 (1964).

Communism on the other. As such it is under risk of polarisation; for if the Egyptian Communists in 1965 threw in their lot with 'Arab Socialism,' they remained a recognisable element in the Press and elsewhere, offering a useful stalking-horse for the far more numerous extremists of the Right. In 1965, as on earlier and later occasions, there was a continuous under-current of agitation against the 'Communist menace'; and in the elections for the President of the Journalists' Syndicate a more or less open Left-Right fight took place—which the Right won. But in any such division in the nation at large, although the funds might be put up by 'capitalist' elements, the revival of Muslim Brethren conspiracy in 1965 suggests that the real emotional—and highly destructive—charge might come once again from Islamic atavism.

One is back again at the central dilemma of an Arab state in transition. But if the outcome is uncertain, the processes of modernisation are now moving very swiftly. In the centre of gravity of the New Egypt, the middle-class strata of towns, the fundamental cell of society, the family, is engulfed in a sea of change, extending to its fundamental relationship, the relationship between the sexes. Superficially, many of these changes and stresses mirror those already experienced in the West. But this is an area of the world, and an area of society, where appearance and reality are often strangers to each other.

22

THE INVISIBLE CAGE

Your wives are your field: go in, therefore, to your field as ye will; but do first some act for your soul's sake: and fear ye God, and know that you must meet Him. . . . And it is for the women to act as they (the husbands) act by them, in all fairness; but the men are a step above them. God is Mighty, Wise.

—The Koran, Sura II, The Cow

And if ye are apprehensive that ye shall not deal fairly with orphans, then, of other women who seem good in your eyes, marry but two, or three, or four; and if ye still fear that ye shall not act equitably, then one only. . . .

—The Koran, Sura IV, Women

But the Americans try to overthrow all traditions. We must have some tradition. . . .

—A leading sheikh of El Azhar to author

'These housewives are not good,' said the young medical student, earnestly. 'They make us many problems. When I marry I will marry a woman who works—to raise our economy. And when she has babes they will be better educated. All educated Egyptians now think like this.'

'But does your mother agree with these ideas?'

'Yes, because I have three sisters and one is at Tanta in first-year medical school and the others are teachers. But it is very difficult for us, even in Alexandria, even in the Medical Faculty. The girls sit in the same room with us, but speaking is limited—and we cannot walk with them on the street. We must separate when we leave the lecture room—for if she speaks she becomes refused [for marriage]. Here in Egypt, it is a shame.

'I encourage my sister to meet my friends. But they must meet inside the house, not outside—no! It is a terrible thing for us. We have little choice. I think myself that is the main reason for divorce. With us, divorce is a problem—the biggest after the population problem. Many men put away their wives for others and the children suffer much.'

It is now more than forty years since the celebrated Hoda Sharawi, the wife of a nationalist leader, returning from an international Women's Rights conference, symbolically dropped her veil into the Mediterranean to the scandal of the officials gathered at the Alexandria quayside to welcome her. The veil has long since virtually disappeared save in Upper Egypt.[1] Egyptian women of the middle classes follow European fashions, and there are many women doctors and journalists, and not a few engineers. One hundred thousand women work in Government offices, half a million in trade and industry. In 1965-66 almost a quarter of students at secondary schools, as at Cairo University, were girls.

Yet an invisible veil still exists between the sexes and is a barrier no less formidable and life-enclosing for being composed of nothing more than social inhibition. If the young now more often reject the marriage arranged by the families, it is only in the old 'café society' class that couples may meet in complete freedom and go out as they wish before betrothal. For the rest, there are many taboos to be observed and much tortuous, nerve-wracking contrivance. A superficially highly Westernised bank clerk told me the story of his marriage. It came, characteristically enough, after a severe disappointment in crypto-Western-style romantic love. 'It was a great shock. So I felt that I must have a wife at once. I saw a girl in the street whom I liked. I asked my friend about her and he said, she is a neighbour of theirs; she is of good family. So I went to her father and I asked for her. He agreed. She agreed. But it was very difficult for me to get accustomed. . . .'

This is the traditional pattern—and the modern dilemma. It is based on the view not only that every man is a rapist, but that the woman is a weak, defenceless creature, lost without her family's protection. A young man tries to talk to a girl on

[1] In Egypt the veil was a middle-class 'good family' institution. Village women of the Delta have customarily worked with their menfolk in the fields. But on coming to town or on the road, many still envelop themselves in a loose black *melaya* (sheet) which they hold half across the face. This, too, is decreasing.

an Alexandria beach. She replies: 'Why do you try to speak to me? You know where my father lives.' He takes the hint, goes to ask the father for the daughter's hand—and, according to my interlocutor, lives happily ever after. But every one can tell horrific tales, too: of, for instance, the father who insisted on Koranic grounds on the signing of the marriage contract between the families before the introduction, and then produced another sister, the ugly one, the young man going dutifully to his fate; this, it should be explained, was 'some years ago.' These days young love's opportunities visibly multiply yearly, but it is still considered 'nice' to ask the father before 'speaking to' the daughter, and it is still very easy for a girl careless of these forms to be 'ruined.' The love songs that throb endlessly from the radio, including those of that national heroine, Om Kolthoum, are vibrant with Injured Pride, the stabbings of Jealousy and the intolerable pangs of Unrequited Love, and if the matter-of-fact Englishman is sometimes put in mind of the romantic style of *Peg's Paper*, the confusions and frustrations engendered in the young Egyptian aspiring, like my medical student, to a 'modern' marriage, may be far from amusing.

Certainly this code of sex relationships and values is not peculiar to the world of Islam. Preoccupation with family honour vested in daughters' virginity is notoriously to be found around most of the South Mediterranean, often shot through with the lurid hues of original sin, a doctrine unknown to Islam.[2] But again Islam has been a uniquely effective social preservative. More than 1,300 years after the death of the Prophet, not only have such things as the detailed laws of inheritance, the prescriptions for the protection of married women's property (return of dowry on divorce, etc.), the rules for the custody of the children of divorce, the provisions for arbitration, survived into this very different world, but so also have such oddities as the Koranic ruling that only after the third divorcing has a couple exhausted the possibilities of

[2] Islam dominated Spain and Sicily under the Arabs and, via the Turks, the whole of the Balkans, and the profound social effects are still visible in these areas. But clearly, the share of Islam, of other religions, and of pre-Islamic or pre-Christian customs in the forming of present codes cannot be accurately assessed.

reconciliation—until, that is, the wife has married another man, whereupon she may divorce him and remarry the first.

Yet the movement for Women's Rights goes back to the early days of Egyptian nationalism. It was in 1899 that the famous nationalist lawyer, Kasim Amin, wrote his *Emancipation of Women* denouncing the 'animality' of polygamy and demanding primary education for girls. Two years later he replied to the uproar he had aroused with his challenging book, *The New Woman*. The weight of prejudice was great enough in Europe at this time; in the East, where the Koran had clearly indicated the inferior status of women, it was both overwhelming and sanctified. Although a man could divorce at will, it was not until 1920, as an incidental result of the war, that Egyptian women gained the right to go to the courts for divorce at all—on the grounds of desertion or impotence. In 1929 the grounds were expanded to include cruelty. But it was clearly understood that cruelty, although it might be physical or mental, was not to be confused with rightful chastisement, and this was ruled to depend on social class: while beating a middle-class wife might not be 'nice' and could even be 'cruel,' for a peasant woman the odd knock-down or two was considered more or less in the day's work.

Despite such judicial wisdom—or possibly with the aid of it—greater progress has been made in this critical area in the fifteen years since the revolution than in the entire half-century before it. The abolition of the *sharia* (religious) courts, which monopolised these matters, in 1955, was followed by the giving of the vote to women, and by the election in 1957 of the first two women members of Parliament in the Arab world. By 1964 the number of women M.P.s had risen to nine and there was a woman Minister to spur their efforts. Women were being officially encouraged to qualify themselves and to work in many occupations, including such male strongholds as engineering, and even village co-operative councils were known to have women members. At Inchass, the local midwife was a co-operative council member.

Yet, with all this, two unmistakable monuments to women's subjection remained intact: the legality of polygamy and the Muslim male's right to divorce his wife without giving any reason or going before a court. In the 'thirties, in the 'forties, and indeed earlier, strong attempts had been made to change these ludicrously anachronistic laws, responsible for glaring social evils. They were successfully blocked. In 1958 yet another committee was set up to consider reform of what is known as 'the law of Personal Status.' Significantly the committee, composed of suitably grave and elderly persons, had only one woman member, a distinguished lawyer. It deliberated for five years, but not until August 1966, after a number of postponements, was the new draft law published. It was, predictably, cautious and equivocal. Unlike the Tunisian law of 1956, it did not radically reinterpret the Koran by declaring polygamy illegal, but it did state that the taking of a second wife was to be considered 'an injury' to the first and a ground for divorce. Divorce for both parties was now to be through the courts, but courts meeting in private with the formal function of reconciliation. If that failed, they were to appoint two arbitrators from the parties' families,[3] or from outside them. If the husband was demanding divorce, and the arbitrators found the fault to be on his side, they might *suggest* in their report to the court that his request be denied. There were, in all, 400 Articles, of a similar bemusing complexity. Muslim divorce law automatically awards the custody of the children beyond an early age to the father; in the 1929 reform the age was raised for boys from seven to nine and for girls from nine to eleven; now it was raised to eleven and thirteen respectively— and might be cancelled if all access by the mother was denied.

Clearly a great deal depended on the spirit in which these provisions were applied (by male assessors in private). Equally clearly, they failed to make the sort of declaration the modernisers looked for. In April 1967, when the Bill was once again scheduled to be debated by the National Assembly, the important weekly *Al Mussawar* appeared with a big 'No!' across its cover, and an article described the proposed law as 'really astonishing and dangerous' and 'a catastrophe.'

But if, after two generations of rearguard action, the sheikhly guardians of orthodoxy massed in the mosque-university of El Azhar were now at their last ditch, it is a position

---

[3] 'If ye fear a breach between man and wife, then send a judge chosen from his family and a judge chosen from her family. . . .' Koran, Sura IV, verse 39.

to which they are accustomed and for which they are well equipped. In the sanctified halls of the Ministry of Wakfs, always abuzz with sheikhs, I sought enlightenment from a celebrated 'modern' authority, Sheikh Mohamed el Ghazaly, then Director of Mosques. He explained that it was not right that a husband should have to seek divorce in court, because such matters should not be exposed to public gaze: the privacy of the Muslim home must be inviolate. There should be an attempt at reconciliation, as specified in the Koran, but after that, even if the husband had no just reason for divorce, if he wished it, he must have it. In such a matter, between a man and his conscience, or a man and God, no one could intervene. This is the essential Muslim position.

It was a curious interview. For in order to guard against the infidel and ensure that each scholarly nuance was grasped, the sheikh had insisted that the questions be put in writing. Thus, three girl secretaries of the Ministry sat with us around a table, the one to translate the questions into Arabic for the sheikh, another to take his answers down in Arabic and a third to render them into English so that, as I insisted, each matter could be pursued.

I was much encouraged to observe that from time to time the girls rested their pencils to remonstrate mildly with the sheikh for his more outrageous observations. A young man— still in his 'thirties—of rocklike earnestness, immaculate in grey kaftan, rimless spectacles and the white turban of El Azhar, he remained, however, totally unmoved. On the question of female dress and the need to abolish the unhealthy, all-enveloping, black *melaya* he commented that the Koran clearly ruled that only woman's hands and feet should be publicly visible. He glanced around the table where the girls were wearing short-sleeved dresses with modest V-necks—for the summer was torrid. 'You and I,' he said, 'are the only ones here who are properly dressed.' One is glad to add that he laughed.

It is, of course, one of the ironies of history that the preachings of Mohamed, who did much to advance the status of women, should so long have been employed to perpetuate women's subjugation. But the more successful the revolution, the more rigid the 'anti-revisionists' and the more potent the vested interests. Liberal sheikhs bold enough to risk obloquy are few, and the laïty whose minds are not closed are a prey to ambivalent attitudes. Good Muslim families, one is repeatedly told, do not divorce—and to clinch the matter the *Hadith* is quoted: 'Of things lawful, the most hated in the sight of God is divorce.' Few, typically, feel any need to know the statistics of Muslims who do in fact divorce, although these are startling enough. In Egypt as a whole, 28 per cent of all marriages end in divorce—in Cairo very many more.[4] Similarly, one is continually told that polygamy is now so rare (2 per cent of marriages) that it is superfluous to legislate against it—and, in any case, it is a useful safeguard if a marriage is barren or produces only female children.[5]

For all the apparatus of modernity and the eager espousal of science, many are still troubled by the old uneasy sense of the secure, familiar world giving way beneath the feet. 'It is a dangerous law,' said a woman member of the National Assembly, Fatma Diab, explaining the delays over marriage law reform. 'It will change radically the life of the family. It is not easy to decide.'

Egyptian reformers long ago remarked that the traditional status of women constituted an inner fortress against social change of all sorts. The idea of the home, not merely as private, but as a family redoubt—or, more primitively, a tent with the flap down—undermines the perspectives of social responsibility which education and the new political institutions seek to open. The great Egyptian nationalist writer of the 'nineties, Ahmed Lutfi al Sayyid, vividly indicated the dangers facing a society in which girls were neglected—even despised—while boys were indulged. The woman, he said, was thus driven to exploit the only weapon she had: her man's

[4] Baer, *Population and Society in the Middle East* gives the 1950 figure for Cairo as 44 per cent (of all marriages), for Alexandria 38 per cent, Suez 36 per cent. But the figures are obscured by the Muslim division of the marriage ceremony into two halves *Katib el Kitab*, 'writing the book,' the legal formalities and, some months later, *El dukhla*, 'the entry' or consummation. According to Sheikh Mohamed el Ghazaly, of the 28 per cent divorces total, 10 per cent (of all marriages) refers to divorce between contract-signing and consummation (i.e. the Arab equivalent of a broken engagement), while 12 per cent were couples without children who 'constituted no problem.' Others, however, disputed these figures.
[5] According to Fatma Diab, in her own Delta village of 1,500 families there are 'not more than ninety' cases of polygamy.

sexual need; she 'perfected the art of tormenting her husband,' so that 'their relationship became one of subtle intrigue on her side, and abject submission on his.' The enslaved became the enslaver, to be duly confirmed in her tyranny as the Mother-in-Law who blinkered her son and ensured that his wife following exactly in her footsteps, enthroning ignorance and slamming the door on change.

Again, the segregation and family 'possession' of women incubates sexuality, which in turn necessitates segregation: in the autumn of 1966 the Governor of Cairo threatened to crop the hair of any further males caught pestering women in the city's streets and buses. The Westerner often forgets how profoundly male is that 'collectivity' which is the raw material of Arab politics: the speed with which brotherhood turns to fratricide may well have roots in sexual envy and dark family suspicion.

It is because so much is at stake that reform in this area has gone slowly; 'culture-shock' is no less real for being so well concealed. The prospect of having to abandon the intricate arabesques of the Ideal ('Good Muslim families never divorce') for the jaggedness of verified fact remains unnerving; and the nationalist compulsion to defend Islam against the aspersions of the West further confuses the issue and puts off the evil day.

New Patterns of Life

But if the dyke of dogma still somehow holds, its days are clearly numbered. It is being rapidly eroded from below. The sheikh of El Azhar who wished to return women to Koranic dress was likely to meet obstruction from his own daughter, studying Law at Cairo University; the three girl secretaries who took down his words did not turn for guidance to sheikhs or even, probably, to mothers-in-law; like most Cairenes they were addicts of American films, steady TV viewers, and dedicated students of the Egyptian woman's magazine *Hawa* (*Eve*). Not far from their Ministry, with the Arabic characters for the name of Allah rising from its roof, huge lurid cutouts outside a cinema announced *The Carpet-Baggers*. The Egyptian *Life*-style picture weekly *Aker Saa* carried a feature on the 'topless' dress only a week or two after that particular pseudo-event hit Europe: the 20th-century worlds of technology, tourism and fashion know few bounds. When, in 1959, the newly opened Hilton Hotel in Cairo engaged the first waitresses and chambermaids in Egypt, it seemed a reckless innovation, because for the ordinary Egyptian the girls' presence could have only one implication. Yet within a short time female hotel staff had become a commonplace, even in puritanical Upper Egypt.

Much of this, no doubt, is superficial, but the complex of changes following in the wake of developing industrialisation goes deeper—to the heart of the family itself. My bank clerk, having courted his wife in traditional style, then proceeded to install her in a 'nice apartment' in a middle-class suburb, from which in order 'to build our economy' (in the medical student's phrase) she, as well as the husband, went out to work, adding her monthly £E15 as a secretary to his £E30 as a clerk. Even so, with the instalments on the TV, the refrigerator and furniture, there was nothing left over, and any family would be small. Furthermore, in thus working, the wife was now not only demonstrating her modernity, but also patriotically responding to the Government's urgings. 'The State secures for female citizens the means for reconciling their family duties with their public responsibilities,' the 1957 Constitution had announced, hopefully. Prepacked, ready-washed potatoes had already appeared in the town co-operative shops for the benefit, it was explained, of working wives. These stores also reported a decline in the sales of flat, rubbery, Arab bread, which also serves as a spoon, and a rise in the demand for European-style loaves.

This sort of life is a long way from either of the two traditional styles—the conspicuous consumption—*Moda Luigi Khamastasher*[6]—of the pashas—and the earthy subsistence of the villagers, from whom my bank clerk was separated by a single generation. Yet once sampled, it is a mighty gatherer of recruits: a television set is less troublesome and possibly even more prestigious than an extra wife. It also carries within it an infinity of aspiration—wherein lies both political and

[6] This expression, an amalgam of Italian and Arabic to describe a French style—Louis Quinze—in itself eloquently sums up the values of the pre-1952 Levant.

economic peril and political and economic opportunity.

Already, under the pressures of this industrialising, 'techno-logical,' 'mass-communicating' society, Egyptian middle-class family life begins to reproduce with the sharpness of cari-cature much of the familiar pattern of the West—down to the complaints about the effects of 'TV violence' on the child-ren. Egypt's first mass-sale newspaper *Akhbar el Yom* rose to fame to a large extent by angling its stories for women; and today even the dignified *Al Ahram*—succumbing like the London *Times* in the 'fifties—carries its Woman's Page. Mean-while, the post-revolution boom of Egypt's biggest-selling magazine *Hawa* echoes, on that much smaller stage, the pub-lishing triumph of the *Ladies Home Journal* in the U.S. and, later, of *Woman* in Britain. It was, in fact, started in 1954 after two years' study of West European, British and Ameri-can models, and turning its seventy-odd pages, with their illustrated romantic fiction, beauty notes, advice on furnishing, knitting patterns, film gossip or complaints about holiday accommodation, one might think oneself in Europe. It is only when one reads further, turns for instance to the 'Problems of the Heart' page (*Send your problems to Eve*) that one realises the difference.

A 'Middle-aged Woman' writes to Eve with a problem in which new and old worlds meet. It seems that a man she met at the office where she works paid a visit to her home one afternoon and there encountered her daughter, a girl of twenty. He duly invited the woman's family to visit him and his family—his wife and nine children, the youngest aged one. So far, so good. But now a jarring voice from the old world breaks in on this modern scene. The other day the man returned to the woman reader's house and asked her for the hand of her daughter—as an additional wife. She was, she says, horrified. Fortunately, the daughter refused him. But the man persisted. The writer has tried hard to convince him that his ideas are outmoded. He refuses to be convinced. He is always around. He is rich—so she cannot stop him. What should she do?

The rep of Eve is brisk, if somewhat lengthy. There are men, she says, who after reaching middle-age, when the youth of their first wives is vanishing, believe that they have the right to marry a young girl, thinking that they will thus be rejuvenated. They are, however, in grievous error. 'You can explain all this to him clearly,' Eve concludes, 'and also tell him that he must not try the same thing with other families. If he still tries to speak to your daughter, you must refuse to know him any more and thank God that your daughter is wise enough to know her own interests and how to stop such a man.'

As every reader of *Hawa* is aware, such anachronistic males are likely to get short shrift as long as Mrs Amina Said is editor. In her features in the magazine, her columns elsewhere and on TV, she lays about the Islamic traditionalists and 'stiff-necked sheikhs who want to hold back the clock,' rallying her readers with such titles as THESE ARE OUR ENEMIES. The wife of a university lecturer, she looks back with true Feminist relish on the strides Egyptian women have made since the 'thirties when she herself was in the 'third group' of girls to 'force our way into Cairo University' (the first women entered in 1929). 'We were called every dirty name possible,' she recalls. 'Every day the yellow newspapers tried to humiliate us. If we were seen playing tennis, there was a rude cartoon. I myself always wanted to write. . . . But of course it was impossible for a woman to write to the papers. So I wrote under a male pseudonym. When my mother found out, the shock gave her a heart attack. She had not forgiven me when she died.'

Today she can point out with pride that of the thousand-odd members of the journalists' union, 250 are women. Women 'TV personalities' and announcers are a familiar part of life; Mrs Said's own sister, Kerima, is an Under-Secretary in the Ministry of Education, and the papers campaign—against stiff resistance—for the appointment of Egypt's first woman judge. Certainly, like many other aspects of modernisation, this is a development taking place over much of the Arab world. The first Muslim woman to enter a university (an Egyptian) did so at the American University of Beirut in 1924; women got the vote in Syria (at the hand of the military dictator, Zaim) in 1949, and in Lebanon in 1953, and the first woman Minister was appointed in Iraq in 1959. But Mrs Said justly claims that Egypt was the first to consolidate the paper concession of votes for women with the actual election of women to the National Assembly; and, in other ways, the emergence of women is now becoming a major social factor in Egypt. As editor of *Hawa* and a columnist, Mrs Amina Said receives thousands of letters from readers. Many are from men. Some are simply abusive, telling her to keep her nose out of male affairs. But many also are from men readers who are not a little bemused by the changes taking place and who are genuinely trying to understand these strange new ideas and ways.

Here, in fact, is a social and psychological revolution which is really only now getting under way. A survey in 1954 showed that of the mothers of today's Egyptian civil servants, 56 per cent were illiterate, and 20 per cent almost so. But only 13 per cent of the wives of these men were illiterate. It is now widely accepted that the education of girls is as necessary as that of their brothers—if for no better reason than that their marriage prospects now depend on it. A lower-middle-class father of six daughters told me, a little ruefully: 'Of course, we wanted a boy. But six is enough: now we have stopped. But the girls must not marry before they are highly graduated. That way they will be independent and can get good husbands. They will all go to university. *Insh'Allah!'*

Of course, the situation is full of paradoxes. The nine women members of the National Assembly, industrious speech-makers and champions of marriage-law reform that they are, were in fact largely elected by men. In the cities (which all save one represent) only 20 per cent of the eligible women cast their votes; in the rural areas less than 1 per cent. And in the National Assembly itself there are still 'old-fashioned' members who will change their seats in order to avoid sitting next to a woman colleague.

The fact remains that 'female emancipation' has ceased to be merely a noble cause and has become an awkward fragment of the jigsaw of the New Egypt which people fumblingly try to fit into the still vague but growing picture. The girls sit at their places in the already overcrowded Ministries, handbags on empty desktops, gazing decoratively at the ceiling, fulfilling their patriotic duty, occasionally twittering. If they type, their speed is likely to be ten words a minute. And if, inevitably, the purdah curtains have parted widely enough to admit an occasional 'office romance' (that subversive Western institution), the curtains, if invisible to the naked eye, are still very much there. A 'progressive' and travelled sheikh, the Head of the Islamic Research Institute, when invited to give his views on the propriety of waitresses in hotels, replied: 'Your question would be shrewder if you said private secretaries.' He cited his small son, aged ten, who had recently been asked whether, when he grew up, he would allow his wife to go out to work. The intelligent child had replied: 'Yes, but not as a private secretary.'

In the factories, the harem now gives way to that well-established Western phenomenon, the female assembly-line. Yet again the worlds fascinatingly overlap. The management of a TV factory had, perhaps unwisely, decided to start up with 'superior' girls from intermediate and secondary schools. They sat disdainfully at the conveyor-belt, complaining that the screwdrivers might damage their long nails. The line was frequently disrupted by individuals failing to arrive on time. When the distracted male management tried to discipline them, they despatched a letter to Nasser complaining: 'We are allowed to look neither to the right nor the left.'

Egypt's university 'co-eds,' numerous as they are, must like-wise straddle worlds. At Cairo University, a sixth of them were reading Engineering, yet at their closely guarded hostel on the campus they had to be in by 8 p.m., save for one evening a week when the time was extended to 9.30 p.m. Between 3 p.m. and 5 p.m. they could receive male visitors in the hostel. But the rule was that every boy must present his identity card, and the Warden was required to send his name to the girl's father. The Warden, a frank and sensible woman, chuckled as she told me this. It was necessary, she said, to give confidence to the parents, especially the 'very strict' parents of Upper Egypt, where a girl was not allowed to see even her own cousin without a chaperone. Naturally, she said, no boys called at the hostel; they met the girls outside—before 8 p.m. But the girls, she said, came to university to work, and they agreed with the 8 p.m. rule. I found that this was generally true, except for one very attractive student of agriculture in an

American-style blue denim dress who thought that it ought to be at least 9 p.m. The family is still a very tight unit, and it is common for mothers or fathers to come up to town to provide a safe home for their children during their higher education.

Not surprisingly, a male educationalist, perhaps momentarily stricken at the prospect of a growing female intake, confessed: 'Our girls are still not aware of real life.' They got angry when he addressed them as 'Girls' he said, because they thought it ought to be 'Ladies.' Dr Hikmat Abu Zaid, Egypt's first woman Minister, an M.A. of Glasgow University, summed up: 'In one way we are in the modern world; in another, in the traditional one. The mind is not clear. Psychological maturity will come later. It will not, I think, happen in this generation—which is in transition. But it will happen in the next.'

It would be a mistake to assume that the result will be merely a grateful acceptance of our own 'enlightened' Western patterns. For although Islamic laws of marriage and divorce may be outdated, in regarding this area of life as private and individual they may in some ways be more 'modern' and humane than the Anglo-American approach with its legalistic and theological preoccupations and frequent disregard of the actual failure or misery of the marriage. Despite the long-drawn campaign for women's rights, the true-blue feminist of the British or American variety is hardly conceivable in Egypt. Even that scourge of reactionary divines, the editor of *Hawa*, while upbraiding the woman 'peasant' Member of the Assembly, Fatma Diab, for wearing black headscarf and dress when she ought 'to be in the advance guard of civilisation,' confesses that she would not have cared for her own daughter to be out alone with a boy-friend. 'In Europe, women have experienced everything and are worn out before they are married. In Egypt, they are just embarking on their lives.'

Such ideas are widely shared. If the cage is now invisible, its security may still be enjoyed. Yet the fact remains that the bars *are* down, and therefore there is a groping towards new standards of behaviour, a growing debate on a 'new morality' distantly echoing that in the West. Television programmes re-enact contemporary family problems sent in by viewers, suggesting reasoned solutions. The rôle of that formidable Egyptian figure, the mother-in-law, is re-assessed. Sheikhs of El Azhar, journalists, writers, TV personalities, discuss interpretation of the Koranic prescriptions in the light of today. It is a debate which appears to have a good deal more reality for most people than the political debate and it may ultimately be more decisive for the future.

For if, as has been suggested, Egyptian society still stands on the brink where ours stood in the 'seventies, with the firm rock of the Book behind and the unplumbed depths of 'Darwinism' before, the difference is that whereas modern Egyptians espouse—and employ—Science, there are few indeed who renounce Belief. If the jagged edges of the technological society will not fit into the old pattern, the jigsaw may be modified, even reconstructed, but somehow its basic motifs must be preserved. This difficult and much deferred process is now at last under way. But is it really as difficult as conservatives, employing religion to protect private interests, have made it appear? To smooth the way for the 'new family' the Ministry of Social Affairs acquired an 'Islamic Consultant,' a progressive divine whose duty it would be, so to speak, to find new texts for old.[7] The Koran offers many, both admirable and relevant.

Whether one calls what is happening 'secularisation' or 'modernisation' is much a matter of one's personal bias. It has been suggested that another description might be 'reintegration.' The most obvious test-case seems likely to present itself in the massive reconstruction of the mosque-university of El Azhar, whose student numbers, in 1965 about 10,000, are in course of being doubled, mainly by adding 'lay' faculties of Commerce, Medicine, Agriculture and Engineering.

In the autumn of 1962 even this fortress of Islamic traditionalism acquired its Faculty of Women which, starting in several suburban villas, in 1966, moved into permanent new buildings in the Kubba Gardens. The woman chosen to head it was a brisk modern historian who took her Ph.D. degree at

[7] In late 1966 the question was underlined when the Ministry of Social Affairs and the Ministry of Wakfs were placed under a single Minister in the new Cabinet—a marriage of social science and religion inviting speculation as to which in the future may emerge as the dominant partner.

Liverpool University (with a thesis on Mohamed Ali's conquest of Cyprus). With an eye fixed on employment prospects for her girls, she planned a School of Translation (with shorthand and typing thrown in). When El Azhar orthodoxy objected, she retorted briskly that the Koran would never have gone around the world had it not been translated. She has designed two attractive uniforms for the girls—both without either headdress or veil. 'They can wear a scarf when they go out, if they like. Of course, they must not be *too* modern in their dress or behaviour. A girl must remember she has an Islamic tradition . . . and not be silly.'

Required to have a knowledge of the Koran as a condition of entry, and often from pious families, the girls spend two-thirds of their first year on Arabic and Islamic subjects, but these taper off as the four-year course continues. Sheikhs from El Azhar instruct them on morals. 'I don't know what the sheikhs teach them. But the girls are adult. They know from what they have seen what is best, and they will not be influenced even by the sheikhs if they don't agree.' El Azhar, however, will differ from the secular universities in that the sexes will be taught apart, and although the women medical students attend the same hospital as the men, a special operating theatre is set apart for them. In any case, concluded the Dean cheerfully, the women's college in Kubba Gardens will not be too far from the new El Azhar campus under construction at Nasr City.

23

THE WORD AND THE WORLD:
A PROBLEM OF IDENTITY

We cannot as yet predict with any degree of assurance the
moral, intellectual and political results likely to be obtained
by the transformation which is at present taking place in the
Egyptian character.

—Lord Cromer, *Modern Egypt* (1908)

The situation of the blind feeling the elephant is common to all
forms of culture in the present-day world.

—Mr Morihoro Matsuda, a Japanese businessman
advertising in *The Times*, 1966

All over Egypt, posters had gone up on the walls showing a
radiant New Egyptian worker manfully stepping into the
Future in the new 'national dress,' a denim suit of tunic and
trousers which the Minister of Labour, Mr Anwar Salama, had
announced was to replace the nightshirt-like *galabiya*. The
galabiya, the Minister told the Press, caught in the machinery.
It tangled with tractors. It was not suitable to a developed
society. The new suits, coming in six shades and four high-
quality materials from the Misr Company's mills, would
retail at around one Egyptian pound each and would serve the
needs of all citizens. There would be no compulsion, but
Egypt's present 'dress chaos' would gradually be eliminated.

These days, citizens of the emergent African nations proudly
flaunt their tribal costume on London pavements. The old
Harrovian, Nehru, wore the high-buttoned Indian *achan* and
its accompanying tight white trousers at international confer-
ences. Within the Arab world itself the Moroccan politician
or intellectual may still appear in the striped and hooded
jellaba of the Maghreb; the Libyan carries his *barracan* over
his shoulder with all the dignity of the Roman from whose
toga it may well derive; while in Damascus or the Gulf of
Arabia proper, wealthy merchants bring an extra dimension

to commerce with the functional but majestic Arab *keffiya*, *thobe* and *abba*. Yet one has the impression that most Egyptian middle-class citizens would be horribly embarrassed if invited to wear before the world the characteristic dress of the Egyptian masses. 'The *galabiya* is not our national dress,' a young Alexandrian protested. 'We really have no national dress—the Turks prevented us. The lounge suit is our national dress. The *galabiya*—I *hate* the *galabiya*!'

Certainly the *galabiya* often lacks style, being basically six yards of cloth made up into about the simplest possible covering for the human body. But it has a good many variants, and on some upstanding ten-feddan fellah of the Delta, with its long V-neck open to display the striped, many-buttoned vest beneath, it can be impressive; on a statuesque giant of Upper Egypt, now with broad blue stripes and generous sleeves, it seems to link the country's Past and Present with all the assurance of the Nile itself. And even in its less distinguished versions, the *galabiya*—in its naïveté, its insularity, its relaxed domesticity—excellently clothes the Egyptian character. Landscape, man and costume cohere. In the villages it is quickly slipped off for work in the fields; in the cities every boy soon masters the art of gripping the *galabiya* between the teeth while running for a bus.

Clearly it was going to take more than posters and exhortation to separate the Egyptians from this 'unsuitable' garment. Better results might perhaps have been obtained if the Minister of Labour and his Cabinet colleagues had taken a leaf from Chairman Mao's book and donned the tunic themselves. But Egyptian labour leaders are not horny-handed figures; when, in the individual Egyptian's social pilgrimage, the *galabiya* is discarded, it is promptly replaced by the smartest possible Western-style lounge suit. One evening in Cairo I found a group of lounge-suited youths gazing at a window-display of dummy 'New Egyptians' in the new 'national dress' with much the detached wonder with which they might have inspected men from the moon.

But if, as a contribution to the solution of the old Egyptian problem of identity, the new 'classless' dress was at least premature, it was a reminder of that problem's continuing presence and increasing complexity. Among themselves, in the

Nile Valley, in actual—or metaphoric—*galabiyas*, the Egyptians, high or low, had no doubt who they were; but in lounge-suits in, say, the Nile Hilton's coffee shop, with the Arab League building across the way and the world's tourists milling around, they were still not wholly sure. Within the space of a century they had been Ottoman gentlemen, upholders of Pan-Islam centred on the Sultan-Caliph, Muslim 'nationalists,' Western intellectuals orbiting on Paris, sons of the Pharaohs, Arabs—and now, Socialists and Workers. 'A dying Mecca and a still-born Rue de Rivoli,' General Sir William Butler had summed up Cairo in the 'nineties, dismissing the whole attempt at synthesis with soldierly briskness. But the Mecca, far from being dead, now drew eager pilgrims from half Africa, and the Rue de Rivoli, if faded, was only one of many modernising thoroughfares. The struggle towards synthesis—towards a national *persona* well-based and serviceable both at home and abroad, continued, mounting both in urgency and confusion.

Nor was the Japanese solution of two contrasted, alternating, styles really available. Unlike the Japanese, Egyptians could not put off the West with their city suits and regain assurance by re-entering the traditional world when they crossed their own threshold, because—as the sad tale of the *galabiya* hinted—they no longer possessed a confident inte-grated life-style or culture. Japan was not occupied by the West until 1945; Egypt was not delivered from her numerous occupations until 1955. In the Arab Far West that understand-ing Catholic, Marshal Lyautey, had tempered the clash of cul-tures by keeping apart the old Islamic cities and the new French cities built to complement them; in Ismailian Egypt the Levantine juggernaut had buried all beneath its golden wheels, further submerging and finally devaluing (as *baladi*) what local culture and style had survived earlier alien occupa-tions. And if in 1956 'Suez' had delivered the Egyptian revolu-tion from the economic Levantine over-burden, the cultural incubus, the archaic values, remained.

In the 'New Egypt' of the mid-1960s, this alleged classless community of workers, the Co-operative Organisation put on a show of its furniture at the Cairo Industrial Exhibition. For the European visitor, moving through it was rather like turn-ing back the pages of social history to the Second Empire and the heyday of the Rothschilds. Here were richly inlaid cabinets, dining tables of intimidating solidity and mirror-like gloss, wardrobes like monuments, majestic beds, carved and gilded, armchairs, damasked or tapestried, still awaiting, it seemed, the weight of some reigning *grande dame* or frock-coated pasha. A modest bedroom suite, it was whispered, cost one thousand pounds.

But the emotion affecting the Egyptians of all classes who packed the aisles was one of frank admiration. For this was the authentic, 'Good Family' thing—which it behoved every aspiring employee to attain to the limit of dowry or purse. And so in this Egypt of transistors, hire-purchase refrigerators and TV, the cabinet-makers of Damietta—in their co-operatives now —continued to ply carving tool and gilding brush in their old 'Greco-Roman' patterns. The 'Louis Quinze' thrones which they dispatched in their thousands about Egypt betrayed, in fact, a certain peasant sturdiness; but in the eyes of the purchasers their merit was quite otherwise. Their merit was that they were not *baladi*—'of the village,' that Levantine-Egyptian term of ultimate contempt.

It is true that, at last, the craft co-operatives are beginning to turn out what they call 'Popular' furniture—by which they mean the reasonably simple and functional. But the chosen adjective is still heavy with condescension; despite the revolution, it is not easy for most middle-class Egyptians to speak of the 'common man' (as distinct from the Muslim 'brother') without making it sound like an accusation.

In a strange way this Levantine legacy of pretension was compounded by the Arab legacy, at least by its all-important literary aspects. Classical Arabic, rooted in the language of the Prophet's clan, the Koreish of Mecca, had been a triumphant *lingua franca*; but by the 19th century it was the language only of the small educated élite. Its very richness, its archaic sophistication and structural complexities now ironically made it a barrier between the people it had so largely created and their heritage. There are obvious parallels with the decay of Latin; however, Arabic is not only the language of the sacred book, but, as the language of God's message delivered in the Koran, a manifestation of God himself, His 'uncreated word.' It was inevitable that it should fall into the hands of professional custodians, jealously preserving it against sacrilegious change.

Already, in the 14th century, the inroads being made into classical Arabic by local vernaculars were being deplored by the great Arab sociologist-historian, Ibn Khaldun, who urged the Arabs not to lose themselves in bastardised tongues but to stick to the language which God and History had given them. But by the late 19th century, it was painfully evident that, devoutly as such sentiments might be re-echoed, classical Arabic would not encompass the needs of modern times. The point was driven home as the new class of Paris-educated Egyptian *littérateurs* poured out a flood of translations of European works. For if the operas of Verdi, presented in Ismail's wooden Opera House, the drama of Racine and Molière and Hugo, the novels of Anatole France or Tolstoy, were exhilarating experiences, they also woefully showed up enormous gaps in Egypt's own culture—gaps which could not easily be filled, since the forms were unknown and often ill-adapted to a narrow and highly stylised Arabic literature.[1]

There was, however, one form in which the Arabs had excelled—and it was to this that, under the challenge of the West, the first 'new' Egyptian writers in Arabic turned. The revered Ahmed Shawky, who completed his studies at Montpellier University, founded his fame on odes, elegies and panegyrics in the classic manner of the Arab Golden Age, 'verses of great erudition which might have been written by some court poet of the 10th century.'[2]

But this was the 20th century. The neo-classicists were soon under attack from the rising generation of writers for their archaism, their preoccupation with stilted and elaborate rules, with form rather than content. A battle was joined which, literary in form, in fact went to the roots of Egyptian —and Islamic—society and continues to this day. The Arabist Jacques Berque has described it as the conflict of the Word and the World, of the Authentic and the Efficient.

To accommodate the 20th century, early Egyptian

---

[1] The first novel actually written in Arabic in Egypt was not produced until the 1920s, and even this had been started in French.

[2] The description of Professor A. J. Arberry.

writers and novelists next evolved modified forms of classical Arabic; and even the great Shawky forsook classical rigour to produce the first successful Arabic lyric drama. But the dilemma was not yet resolved; not only was the full impact of the West only just becoming felt, but in all the adaptations and compromises there lurked dark suspicions of surrender and betrayal.

The symbolic figure here is the celebrated Taha Hussein, now in his late 'seventies and the doyen of Egyptian writers. A blind youth, of humble village birth, Taha Hussein embarked on his career by the traditional route of the poor, clever boy, through the mosque-university of El Azhar. After studying six years there, he joined, in 1908, the newly opened secular university of Cairo, was awarded its first doctorate, and moved on to Paris and the Sorbonne. He thus passed, in a few years, from a climate of total dogma to one of rationalism, scepticism and even outright anti-clericalism. Returned to Egypt, Taha Hussein, like others, inevitably sought to break out of the verbal cage in which they now felt constricted. In 1926, in a book with the innocent-seeming title, *Pre-Islamic Poetry*, he deliberately flung himself against its bars, casting doubt, in the name of science, on the authenticity of the Arabic poetry of the time of the Prophet on which the learned sheikhs had for centuries relied in their interpretations of the Koran. It was a challenge 'from the West' which was characteristically Oriental in its obliquity. But its immediate effect seems to have been hardly less than that of Huxley's and Darwin's frontal assault on Genesis, Chapter 1. In the rising storm of protest, Taha Hussein's book was suppressed and he himself put on trial for attacking the religion of the state.

The trial is eloquent of the insecurity and divided personality of this generation. Testifying that he was a good Muslim, believing in Allah, his Angels, His Books, His Prophets, and the Day of Judgement, Taha Hussein explained to the court that it was possible for each person to find within himself two distinct personalities, one rational, the other 'sentient.' 'What is there, then, to prevent the first from being scholarly, inquisitive and critical, and the other from being a believing, assured person?'

But by the 1960s, such delicate attempts to live in two

e 'New Model' National
embly, inaugurated in 1964,
ession. A woman lawyer
n Alexandria has the floor: a
ner sits at her left, a
douin member from Mersa
truh behind her in the back
.

ht The theory of the new
p.c. worker-and-peasant'
y as seen by an Egyptian
toonist. (Chapter 20)

THE PILLARS OF THE NEW NATIONAL ASSEMBLY

The fellahin call the Nile 'El Bahr'—the Sea. Here, at Minya, village women board a boat to cross to the East bank. *Below* The weekly market in progress at a village in Sohag province.

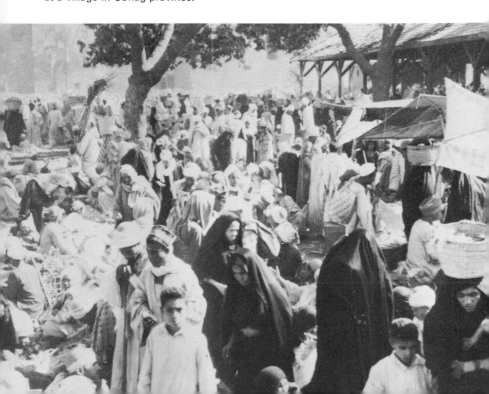

worlds, to reconcile preservationism and evolution, the Word
and the World, were becoming increasingly impracticable. For
as literacy widened and 'mass communications'—spoken as
well as written—moved in, this little galaxy of the clever,
French-educated *belletrists* was left behind. Mass-appeal newspapers, like *Akhbar el Yom*, developed an Arabic so basic
that it could be immediately grasped even by semi-illiterate
women. It was still correct Arabic, classical Arabic simplified,
but even that was not now safe—for, electronically unleashed,
the vulgar world was pressing in yet closer. Television and
radio use the newspaper's simplified classical Arabic for their
news; but for their popular programmes they perforce employ
colloquial. More and more novelists are now grasping the
nettle, too, and, permitting ordinary people to speak in their
books like ordinary people, following in this the example of
the most acclaimed novelist of the new generation, Neguib
Mafouz. They are duly berated by the one-time radicals, such
as Taha Hussein, for 'going too far,' and endangering their
Arab heritage.

And so the long *razzia* of the Word and the World continues, a uniquely inward and Arab conflict, although at times
it seems to echo the High Culture-Low Culture debate of the
contemporary Anglo-American world. Yet the engagements
grow closer, the retreats more difficult. The World presses in
upon the Word, as the élite is besieged by the 'sovereign' mass,
the 'Popular' chair dares to look the Louis Quinze throne in
the face, and in the new, industrialising Egypt the old quest
for identity is turned in directions far from those of either
Mecca or Paris.

One morning, while I was at breakfast in the café of a *baladi*
hotel in Sohag, laughingly called 'The Palace,' one of the
weirdest-looking individuals I have ever beheld abruptly
materialised from the street, drawing behind him a long and
serpentine trail of smoke. On his back he bore an ancient
British army haversack, a cylindrical tin hung around his neck
by a string, and from his right hand swung by a chain, like a
censer, a small pan of glowing charcoals. Long brown teeth
were bared in a grin at once villainous and ingratiating.

Watching us carefully, he cast a handful of seeds into the

charcoal, which crackled sharply and billowed forth a great cloud of aromatic smoke in which he was all but swallowed up. He was, it seemed, a member of one of Egypt's most ancient professions, a direct descendent of those 'magicians and sorcerers' of Pharaoh who were so unwise as to enter into competition with Moses and Jehovah. The cylindrical tin box on his back contained paper charms, numbered squares, passages from the Koran, the ninety-nine names of God and other well-recognised specifics against the Evil Eye.

However, the hour may have been a little early for casting a good spell, for the other patrons of the Palace continued to concentrate upon their *fool* and lentil broth, and the wizard, having announced his availability, vanished as swiftly as he had come, leaving only a slight acridity behind him.

'This man,' said the young petrol-pump mechanic at the next table, 'this man is very bad. Because in Egypt now there is work for all and there is no need for such superstitious things.' He shook his head, a modern technologist disapproving obsolete practice. 'He is *very* bad.'

Certainly most middle-class Egyptians would echo that disapproval. Such things clearly belong to the 'Age of Ignorance,' before the Koranic enlightenment, not to mention modern science. But at the local branch of the Ministry of Information and Culture I found a young man less censorious. For the wandering *gqla-gala* man (*gala-gala* being the Arabic equivalent of our abracadabra) might now clearly be accommodated under the general heading of folk lore—which had lately been given the Arab Socialist accolade. 'We now try to recover it and make it more clean and beautiful,' said the young man enthusiastically, expertly sketching for my benefit a lively Egyptian peasant trumpeter playing for a dancer at a village wedding.

In fact, no very great effort is required to 'revive' this popular culture of song, proverb and story because, although its roots often go back long before the advent of Islam, it is still very much alive.

In a grim Alexandria warehouse, a row of men bend low to roll up the raw cotton on the sorting floor for rebaling. As they reach the climax of their concerted push the leader suddenly sings out wildly, 'Ya Leil! Ya Ein!' ('Oh, night! Oh, eye!'). It is a line of poignant love song, centuries old.

At the melon market at the southern end of Cairo's Nile Corniche it is only a little after nine o'clock in the morning, but two 'trumpets' shrill, a drum beats and three men fall into a stick-dance. The crowd closes around, clapping hands to the rhythm.

By the Nile bank, at Minya, five sailors swab down the deck of a river steamer, timing their brush strokes to the vivid rhythm of a traditional Nile-boat work-song. There are many village work-songs, for raising water—by *sakia*, by *shaduf*, or by *tambour*—for ploughing or grinding the corn or picking the cotton. In these drab and dreary villages, the children wallowing in the dust breathe in with it a legacy of rustic poetry passed down the centuries.

The idea of drawing from this deep but unregarded well, of 'going to the people,' was not new in Egypt. In that earlier, frustrated, revolution of the early 'twenties, it had been boldly proclaimed by the great Alexandrian minstrel-writer, Sayed Darwish. Listening to the workers singing on their way home, Sayed Darwish asked an unprecedented question: 'What are *we* compared with them?' He answered it by spending his days moving about, recording the workers' snatches of song and cries, shaping them into melodies which offered a fleeting glimpse of a real—but hitherto unacknowledged—Egypt. He wrote—and inspired others to write—a series of folk operettas composed of traditional song and dance, stories, broad comedy and cross-talk, and these had a considerable vogue in the 'twenties.

But the moment passed. The revolution collapsed and 'folk art' had to wait for another revolution to be taken under that official patronage which may yet prove a graver threat to its continuing vitality than all Egypt's alien invaders. Encouraged by the example of Russian and Eastern bloc touring companies which now appeared in Cairo, university students recorded and performed the songs of the villages: with the help of radio and TV, some achieved wide popularity. A Folk Lore Institute and a Folk Lore magazine were started. The sensuous *Ya Leil! Ya Ein!* became a theme song in a pretty ballet, *The Bride of the Nile*, the story of a young peasant who falls in love with a water-sprite, which is now part of the repertory of the Reda

Folk Dance Troupe, while other theatre companies worked in the tradition of robust popular operetta and comedy, as native a Nile Valley vein as the Music Hall was an English one. The Television Organisation, which did much to promote these developments, also put on the TV screens much broad domestic comedy in which it was possible to be reasonably certain that the traditional cross-talk between the father-of-the-bride and prospective mother-in-law on the matter of the dowry was being received with almost as many guffaws in gilded bourgeois drawing rooms as before the village communal set.

In the artistic world, the village and the fellah are now 'in.' The prudent film director takes care to provide his quota of whining *sakias*, wallowing buffaloes, and women washing clothes at the canal bank. Saleh Abu Seif, one of Egypt's best directors, was much praised for his 'starkly realistic' film about the *tarahiel* (migrant) workers, starring Egypt's best actress, Faten Hamama, the wife of Omar Sharif. And the rising novelists and playwrights, too, are for the most part those who have embraced naturalism, social criticism or 'social realism.' Noman Ashur, a journalist formerly of the small Left-wing segment of the Wafd, rose to fame in 1954 with a play significantly entitled *The People Below*, about what the English would call 'the working class,' following this with another, *The People Above*, about the old ruling class, concluding the trilogy with *The Family of Straightness*, about the middle classes.

A good deal of this huge output is naïvely propagandist,[3] yet, at least since television, the market is popular as well as political and the play which does not hold its audience in a theatre will be taken off. The new drama, the colloquialising novelists, and the popular theatre, project a greatly widened and more realistic view of society, and all in all, Egypt has come a long way since the day when the Egyptian University despatched the newly graduated Taha Hussein to Paris with the advice that he study Latin and Greek and soak himself in classical culture so that his country might also, in its turn,

[3] In the film *Fagr el Yom Gedid* (Dawn of a New Day) the wife of an effete rich bourgeois, having tried ineffectually to work, parts from her student-technologist lover, off to Europe for training, with the words: 'I am the Past, you are the Future.'

enjoy the Renaissance which had come to Europe.

But although folk arts have been successfully employed in the regeneration of nations, in Egypt—with the cheap transistor radios now rattling off the assembly lines—it was a little late for all that. Cairo remains the great magnet and pacemaker, and a cynic, asked to locate the true cultural centre of Cairo, might not unreasonably reply : 'The Metro'—the 'super-cinema' (duly set fire to by the Muslim Brethren in 1952) into which for more than forty years Metro-Goldwyn-Mayer has been packing the great and ever-growing army of Hollywood's devotees.[4] The older 'Ismailian' eclecticism of the white wood-and-plaster Opera House, and the second-hand bookstalls beside it, exactly modelled on those beside the Seine in Paris, had been a limited and earnest tribute to European culture. But the new electronic eclecticism is boundless and vociferous. Egyptian folk opera and socialist song on the small screen is flanked by Perry Mason, Dr Kildare, Sergeant Bilko, and all. The Perry Mason novels are the best sellers of the publicly-owned National Book House's cheap translated reprints (challenged only by Agatha Christie's Poirot) and, according to a director of that concern, Perry Mason is even more widely known to the present Arab generation than Sherlock Holmes was to their fathers.

Egypt, in short, despite her rediscovered Arabism and her rediscovered fellahin, is now not only, as Ismail proudly claimed, 'a part of Europe,' but also—in Cairo at least—a 'part of the world,' an inveterate window-shopper in the global cultural supermarket of our times. The beautiful Arabic script still cuts off the Westerner from much; but if the first word he learns to recognise in Arabic calligraphy may well be 'Allah,' the second is very likely to be 'Coca-Cola.' One day, seeing, as I thought, an Egyptian football game on television, I asked a semi-literate Egyptian bystander the name of the team. He replied, as though it were the most natural thing in the world, 'Tot-en-*Ham*'—otherwise the famous London team of Tottenham Hotspur. (Football is a national passion, spanning the classes, Egyptian star players are as famed and fêted

---

[4] Among them was one Gamal Abdel Nasser. Russian films, by contrast, although they have frequently been shown, meet in general with a very tepid reception.

as their opposite numbers in Britain or the U.S., and if Britain really wishes to improve her image in Egypt, a tour by the veteran outside-right, Sir Stanley Matthews—whose name is widely known and honoured there—would do more than a hundred art exhibitions by the British Council.)

Meanwhile, the old vein of intellectual eclecticism is by no means worked out. At the bookstalls beside the Opera scores of young men grope nightly by the light of oil lamps among a fantastic assortment of volumes in French, English, German, Arabic, even Finnish. The names of Brecht, Sartre, Beckett, Arthur Miller, Ionescu, and so on, pepper the *causeries* of the numerous critics; and *Aida*, commissioned by the Khedive Ismail and first presented in Cairo in Italian in 1871, after three generations of seasons by Italian opera companies, now recurs in a repertoire which includes *La Traviata*, presented for the first time in Arabic in 1964, Egyptian folk operetta and Lehar's *Merry Widow*, also in Arabic.

The cultural gamut which modern Cairo spans, almost as a matter of course and as the natural result of its pivotal position, is amongst the widest in the world. It can take easily in its stride Verdi at the Opera, Tarzan at the Metro, Beckett at the Pocket Theatre, popular Egyptian comedy at the Rihani Theatre, a new social-realist play at the Ezbekiah, Perry Mason on TV, an expressionist experiment at the Hakim Theatre, and, if it should be the first Thursday of the month, the great Om Kolthoum vibrantly evoking the Arab Golden Age, not to mention Western classics from visiting companies and rival offerings from Yugoslavia, Poland, Russia or China.

Yet while all this may be evidence of a sort of vigour, it scarcely offers what the country needs: a firm place to stand, a national *persona* based on realities, and yet able to link the sacrosanct past and the technological future. How far indeed the search has still to go is suggested by the Egyptian cinema, which must perforce cater to a national, not a sectional, audience. The Egypt film industry has existed for a generation, has a large output, and a number of proficient directors and actors. Yet Egyptian films have quite failed to achieve the distinctive national style shown by some Japanese, Polish, Czechoslovak, French or Italian films. Most are sentimental melodramas, with involuted plots stretching down the years, villains of deepest dye (in Islam there is no last-reel redemption), whiter-than-white heroines and—although this is now no longer *absolutely* obligatory—pauses for traditional hip-wriggling dance and song.[5] For the rest, knockabout domestic comedy alternates with western-model *policiers* and suspense films.

It is ironic that in this would-be 'modern' and 'technological' society the serious, non-political voice that has the power to bridge all gulfs, to fuse the diverse social fragments into an emotional whole, is a voice essentially from the Arab past, the voice of the classical singer, Om Kolthoum. In Egypt, that voice is inescapable, welling from beneath the pedestrian surface of city life, as it embodies and celebrates the miracle of the Arabs and the faith that made them.

Today, Om Kolthoum is a woman in her middle-sixties, tall, composed, black-haired, modest. It is now more than half a century since she began her career as a poor village girl, singing in traditional style at weddings and family feasts; it was her custom at this time to perform dressed as a boy. She studied the Koran, becoming accomplished in its language. Her voice had a remarkable emotional range, and her fame spread through the countryside. In 1924 she moved to Cairo, and ten years later the voice of Om Kolthoum was heard on the radio for the first time.

Gradually she became a cult, her concerts a rite. Often they continue into the small hours; a single song, punctuated, decorated and echoed by the orchestra, may last two hours. And since it will be a collective celebration of the great Arab themes—nostalgia, memories of passion, languid or sweet, unrequited love, injured pride—there seems no reason why it should ever end. The audience remains rapt. This is the sphere of the Word, not the World, and the Word is given palpable substance by the human voice, sometimes husky and strained, at others touching cosmic depths, sometimes leaping with the pangs of love, at others producing those quivering tones which, according to one authority, 'blend grief and pleasure in intoxicating ambiguity,' but always rolling irresistibly on like the sea beating against the shore.

The position of Om Kolthoum, receiving £3,000 for a con-

[5] Two indicative titles: *Eternal Love* and *More precious than my Life.*

cert and £1,000 to make a recording, is anomalous in a socialist country where the maximum salary, attainable by very
few, has been set at £E5,000 a year. A few young socialist
critics have assailed such 'backwardness.' But both the position
and the rewards are in a tradition most Egyptians readily
honour.[6] Sitting near her in the theatre one day, I was struck
by the manner in which people came up to pay tribute. Not
only is she Egypt's unique possession but she keeps alive the
Islamic heritage. People are always telling one how 'respectable' she is: she wears correct, long-sleeved gowns of sober
hue; when she makes a film the most she will permit is for her
hand to be kissed. Today the phenomenal vitality of her singing, at the age of sixty-five, is a cause for added wonder and
it seems entirely appropriate that she should now have revealed herself as an authentic descendent of the Prophet.

If Om Kolthoum clings to the classical Arab world, the
poetry of the desert, Abdel Wahhab, the only other singer
inhabiting—although at some distance—the same sacrosanct
universe, is famed for his attempts, as a musician, to bring
about a marriage of East and West. Again there is the aura
of reverence, the unbroken gravity of mien which to a Westerner appears bizarre in an entertainer. Abdel Wahhab, the
son of a muezzin, was for some time a student at El Azhar, and
his much-discussed attempts at synthesis seem curiously self-
conscious and uneasy, as if reflecting Ibn Khaldun's warnings
of six centuries earlier against the insidious encroachments of
impure tongues.

Singers, the heirs of the poets, are heroes in the Arab world.
their glossy photographs appear beside those of the political
chiefs in the pantheon of the bazaar. They are garlanded in
wondering anecdote and gossip: one is told how the astonishingly youthful-looking Abdel Wahhab 'washes his hands in
cologne after he shakes hands and when he goes out keeps a
cloth over his mouth' lest ill befall the peerless throat. After
Abdel Wahhab, the best seller on records is Abdel Halim Hafez,

[6] Edward Lane, describing Egypt in 1835, wrote: 'The natives of Egypt
are generally enraptured with the performances' of their vocal and in-
strumental musicians . . . They are often very highly paid . . . so powerful is the effect of the singing of a very accomplished *al 'meh* (female
singer) that her audience, in the height of their excitement, often lavish
upon her sums which they can ill afford to lose.'

who sings very sweet, romantic Arab love-songs, followed by
El Kalaoui, an Egyptian who specialises in Bedouin songs, and
the Druse prince, Farid el Atrash (who has a Cairo skyscraper
named after him), who sings lyrically of the mountains, but is
at a disadvantage in Egypt on account of his Lebanese accent.

In the contemporary Arab world, says Jacques Berque, music
fulfils 'the rôle of a sort of mourner over social change.' But
social change, for all that, gathers pace and prepares to sap
this stronghold also. The traditional Arab orchestra, accompanying a singer, plays by ear, repeating or echoing lines or
refrains. Now the technical requirements of recording and
radio are causing the music to be written down. 'The musicians,' commented a recording manager, 'hate to work from
written music. But they are doing so.' It is, said an Egyptian
TV executive, the older generation which really rejoices in the
Om Kolthoum concerts. The younger people now like their
songs shorter—as in the West. The addition of full orchestration is leading to 'many variations.' 'Om Kolthoum,' he said,
'represents the zenith of the classical tradition. I believe that
when she dies, all will change.'

This world which has lived on nostalgia so long cannot do
so for ever. The professionally anguished tones of Om Kolthoum invite a more contemporary, less stylised, anguish.
What if Arab music is simply 'backward' as other aspects of
the Arab world are backward? What if the real truth is that
Arab music, unlike that of the West, failed to evolve beyond
its religious origins and the Middle Ages? And what if it is
now too late?

In the political sphere, the revolution had constructed between the Word and the World—and between East and West
—a bridge called 'Arab Socialism' which might, or might not,
carry the load. But in the wider world of the national character and culture, the 'folklorique' gala-gala man and the music
of Abdel Wahhab seemed to offer a shaky path indeed between Om Kolthoum and the Metro or Perry Mason.

For the present adult generation, adept at equivocation,
such questions could be left, as they have so long been left,
to hang in the air. But the next generation inheriting an Arab
world transformed by the Egyptian Revolution may face some
cruel choices.

24

NEXT GENERATION

In the front line created by the 1952 revolution succeeds in returning to civilian life, that will be the greatest victory of the revolution. Our generation has provided leaders for the transition period. What is necessary now is that other generations step forward to take their place in the government of the country.

—Gamal Abdel Nasser broadcasting to the nation,
23 July 1967

The Egyptian Revolution was conceived by men in their twenties, carried out by them in their mid-thirties. When the currents of change run so swift and deep, only those born into them have the skill or strength to breast them; in such a time and place, a nation is, in a sense, reborn with every generation.

The men who made the Egyptian revolution are now in or nearing their fifties. The new generation crowding the country's five universities have lived all their lives in an Egypt very different from that of their fathers. 'We grew up when the British were here,' Sayed Marei reminded me. '*We* thought we were a small, unimportant country. We thought we were inevitably poor. We didn't have, you know, very much hope.' For had not Lord Milner written: 'Such a race will not of itself develop great men or new ideas or take a leading part in the progress of mankind. But under proper guidance it is capable of much simple content'?

The older generation was often educated in the style of the French *lycée* or British public school; in its school history books, Egyptians, like other Africans and Asians, gratefully participated in walk-on parts in British and French Imperial history. Now the mould was turned inside out. This rendered it more appropriate, but no less ideological. Looking over the shoulder of a youth in a teachers' training college at Mersa Matruh I saw a school textbook of world history whose headings made a pejorative litany—'British Imperialism' . . . 'Russian Imperialism' . . . 'French Imperialism' . . . and whose main illustrations were of Gandhi, Nehru, Sukarno, Abdel Krim, King Mohamed V of Morocco—the pivots of history as seen from these latitudes.

And for this Egyptian generation, life—until 9 June 1967—had certainly lived up to the script. It had seen an Egyptian of humble birth become the hero of the Afro-Asian world. It had watched him presiding, it seemed, over the last rites, the Suez funeral pyre, of the French and British Empires. On the *Children's Paradise* programme on TV it had watched other twelve-year-olds romping through the High Dam Song while in a merry animated cartoon top-hatted imperialists, jealously tying up sacks of dollars, received their come-uppance.

Yet what it had really deduced from these experiences was hard to say. 'What we do not know,' confessed a newspaper editor, 'is what the young are really thinking.' The enigma was deepened by the large numbers of students who now come from the unsophisticated world of the villages. 'Those,' observed one middle-aged industrial executive, darkly, 'are the ones we are going to have trouble with.' Another, himself from a village, disagreed. 'When such a one goes back to the village, he will feel bitter—inside here (he covered his heart). But this will help the country later. At least he will say, I must have a bed—and then he will not wish to leave his mother also without a bed.' It is a social dynamic not unknown in Egypt's recent past; but when the old homoeopathic dosage is exceeded, it *could* become explosive.

Two thousand of these undergraduates from outside Cairo live on the Cairo University campus in small single or double rooms for which they pay £E5 a month, all meals included. A casual call at one apartment revealed a student of metallurgy from a village in Sharkiyah province, a fellah's son, one of a family of eight. His room-mate came from Mehalla, the textile town. A neighbour who was visiting them hailed from a village in Beheira. They were pleasant and unassuming young men, with an openness one rarely finds in the older generation. They were so eager to have an outsider's view upon Egypt that it was at first difficult to ask them anything. What did I think about Cairo? What did I think about Gamal Abdel Nasser? Not, one added, as a politician, but as a *man*. What did the English think about the Germans supplying arms to

Israel? (One is never far from Israel.)

On one wall there was a picture of Ahmed Arabi, flanked by pictures of El Afghani and Sheikh Mohammed Abdu—that trinity, spiritual and temporal, from which the 'New Egypt' may be said to derive. On the opposite wall was a framed poem of the great Shawky, a study time-table and another poem, handwritten, composed by a 'friend' to his girl. On the end wall, there was a picture of Nasser, a little larger than the others, and also one of Brigitte Bardot and an Egyptian film-star named Aziza.

Were there cinemas in England like the cinemas in Cairo, they asked naïvely. One of the students began to talk excitedly about the American and British films he had liked. I asked him whether he preferred American films to Egyptian films? He hesitated—but the truth won. The trouble was, Arabic films were always the same story, a love story. His friend chimed in, patriotically: 'Yes, but we have some great Egyptian writers. Neguib Mefuz is the greatest Egyptian writer. . . .'

The fathers of this generation, at university and high school, spent a vast amount of their time in political agitation, to the certain detriment of their studies, but the possible good of their souls. With the foreign occupier still in possession, rebellion could be the duty—as well as the pleasure—of youth. This generation is officially cast for the rôle of 'Guardians of the Revolution'—which may not prove so satisfying.

On paper at least the nation's youth is considerably organised. In 1963 the Higher Council of Youth, a joint agency of the Ministries concerned, the army, and the voluntary youth movements, blossomed into the Ministry of Youth. With that Pharaonic fondness for the grand organisational scheme which characterises Egyptians, the Ministry divided the youth of the nation into five sectors, spanning the years from the cradle to adulthood, and arranged to provide recreational facilities appropriate to each. Thus, in the district town of Toukh I found, arranged around a large games field, no fewer than five new and separate youth clubs, starting with a building for the 'toddlers,' and proceeding through those aged six to twelve, twelve to eighteen, and eighteen to twenty-two, with a final building for young adults. Each club had a full-time paid graduate leader in its office, a paid full-time secretary, and a wall newspaper. The plan is to cover Egypt with these youth clubs; at Toukh they had been built by the clubs' own members under the lead of a particularly zealous local government official.

But if the state caters for a youth which, outside a small favoured class, has certainly been grossly neglected in the past, it also exacts a return in loyalty. Many of the middle-class fathers of this generation looked upon army service as something strictly for the illiterate fellahin. Their sons are educated to accept it as a national duty. Since Suez students at secondary schools drill with the *Futuwa*, the military training corps run jointly by the Ministries of Education, Youth, and the Army. Each university forms an Arab Socialist Union 'basic unit' which elects a committee of ten (three students, four teaching staff, three 'others'), sending forward student delegates to the 1968 A.S.U. National Congress. There have been long-standing plans to merge the old Student Councils into the Socialist Youth Organisation, and after the student riots in Mansoura and Alexandria in November 1968 political control was tightened. The students can, one is told, 'debate anything —except the restoration of capitalism.' But the university libraries contain plenty of books assailing socialism (including, I noticed, Hayek's *Road to Serfdom*), much of the world's press is available, and one wonders how long even students as conformist, and now career-preoccupied, as the Egyptians will accept such leading strings. Between 1954 and 1968 the universities, like the country, enjoyed a longer period of political quiescence than they had ever known, a fact which enabled the country to make much progress. But revolutions cannot continue for ever in their heroic phase. When in the long and dismal aftermath of the Israeli victory of 1967, revolutionary reality fell conspicuously short of the revolutionary vision in which they had been nourished, they came on to the streets again. In the 'thirties the students had been inspired by the 'national socialist' movements in Europe, but the presence of the foreign Occupier had kept them in the mainstream of the common struggle: had not Zaghloul called the students his 'spearhead'? But now, in the late 'sixties the appearance of 'Student Power' in Europe offered a hardly less intoxicating idea in which the 'spearhead' could be turned against the adult order. Henceforth, my newspaper friend may no longer be in quite the same doubt as to what the young people are thinking. But it would hardly be remarkable if their thoughts were confused.

All the same, despite the frustrations of 1967-8, and the immense differences between the worlds in which sons and fathers have been raised, the gap between the generations appears narrower, much less felt, in Egypt than in the West. This is perhaps because the family remains a major reality, elders still receive deference, and, whether Muslim or Christian, parents and children still inhabit the same moral universe with its emphatic values. 'Juvenile delinquency' of the defiant, unreasoning kind so familiar in the West is still unusual. What impresses in Egypt, despite the scale of the change, political vicissitude, and the starkness of the choices that seem imminent, is still the sense of deep, underlying continuity, as assured as the flow of Nile.

The centrepiece of the new campus of El Azhar university now beginning to take shape on a 400-acre site in Nasr City, Cairo's overspill suburb on the desert's edge, will be a huge new mosque which will serve for student meetings, for prayer, and as a library—'multi-purpose' in the new town-planning jargon. But multi-purpose is what mosques in the old Arab world always have been, and a mile or two away, in the old Great Mosque of El Azhar, students are still to be seen sprawled on the carpets among that forest of venerable pillars, studying their books. A benign old sheikh sits at the foot of a pillar, as have his predecessors for centuries, expounding some subtle point of Koranic interpretation to an attentive group of students, including two Africans, who sit at his feet. Despite the university's enlargement and modernisation, it is intended that this still-living medieval tradition of teaching shall have its place. The ancient mosque becomes a 'Special Institute for Islamic Studies' awarding a diploma in Arabic and Islamic subjects from which it will be possible to go on into the larger university to take a degree.

In this setting, the 'secular' and the 'religious' do not indeed provide the antithesis that they do in the West. A stone's throw away from the old mosque, in an improvised classroom in the old El Azhar administration building, what the lecturer, an Egyptian architect and graduate of Durham university, describes as 'the first class in town-planning in the Middle East' is in progress. Students from Iraq and Kuwait and Jordan as well as young Egyptians—for the tradition of El Azhar transcends nationality—bend over drawing boards on which sketch-maps of Chandigarh, Stalingrad, and London take shape—a nice spread in time as well as ideology. One young Egyptian, labouring over a familiar residential area of London, told me that he came from the state secondary school at Tanta. Half the new 'Azharites' already enter from the old 'secular' state school system. I asked him what he felt about the four hours a week devoted here to religion. Did he enjoy this? 'Of course—it is my religion.' Yesterday, he added, they had had a lecture from Sheikh Hassan el Bakhouri, the Rector, on how to live the good life according to Islam. And the Koran? 'We must have a very exact knowledge.'

With all its faults of narrowness and pedantry, El Azhar has a long tradition of dedication to scholarship, and of aid generously held out to the poor village student, which it would certainly be a pity to lose. Despite assimilation into the modern national educational structure, it is intended that the Koranic entrance qualification shall be preserved, and that the 'lay' subjects will be studied in the light of Islam. But while to accommodate town-planning to Islam should present few difficulties, the task of Professor Lutfi el Essaoui, El Azhar's Professor of Business and Commerce, is far more worrying. The Faculty, he explains, is dedicated, amongst other things, to seeking a reconciliation between the needs of the Egyptian banks and insurance companies and the Koranic condemnation of usury (or interest). 'It will take some time, because the professors of economics don't know the Islamic religion. We must read and study much—we are studying business in Islamic times, as well as business today.' Pressed, he added that perhaps the co-operative form of association (which Egypt has made much of) might do the trick—because this involves merely shared profits, and what the Koran is against—although interpretations differ—is not profits, but rather the *fixed* element in interest—due whether it has, in fact, yielded fruit or not—in short, Shylock's 'pound of flesh.'

The Westerner, bemused at this notion of introducing moral considerations into the sacrosanct 'science' of economics, can scarce forbear to smile. Carlyle and Ruskin have been dead a long time. All the same, it will be interesting to see what the new generation of Azharite moralist-economists make of it.

There is another conspicuous respect in which Egypt's rising generation inhabits a world vastly different from that of its predecessor. The world of the fathers—and the range of choice —was orientated between Mecca, Paris and New York. For the sons there is a fourth point, Moscow—supported by Prague, East Berlin, Budapest and Sofia. At the High Dam, in the armed services, at the iron and steel works and various other technical projects, the Russians, like the French and the British before them, are a physical presence. The New Egypt's debt to Russia is obvious and huge. Twice at least, in stepping in to finance the High Dam in 1958 and in quickly rebuilding the Egyptian armed forces in 1967-8, the Russians have saved the situation, and, unlike the Americans under Dulles, they have not required political pre-payment.

Yet the psychological or cultural impact of Russia on the younger generation seems to have been slight. For Russia herself, like Egypt, is historically an Eastern country, western-ising; Mohamed Ali, that ruthless westerniser-in-a-hurry rebuilding Alexandria, curiously echoes Peter the Great, hewing 'his window on the West.' This may enable the Russians to understand Egyptian reactions in a way the West cannot, but it still leaves Egypt's face turned towards the West—whose technical superiority as well as cultural diversity has now been widely demonstrated on Egypt's own soil. The growing domin-ance of the English language, the language of instruction for science-technology—for the rising generation as commanding a theme as French culture was to their fathers—merely serves to strengthen an orientation which is deep-rooted in Egypt. It is interesting to note that, in 1954, Nasser himself told an interviewer that he could not play the part of an Ataturk as had been suggested, 'because we Egyptians are free *Western* people and not primitive barbarians, like the Turks.'[1] Few

[1] R. H. S. Crossman, *A Nation Reborn.*

Egyptians would now voice the sentiment so naïvely, but most would still utter a silent 'Amen.'

If much of the dross of the Levantine legacy has gone, a precious core remains. Geography ensures that Egypt will continue, as she has for centuries, to belong to the Mediterranean, the Greco-Roman, as well as to the Arab world. And religion reinforces geography. The religions of much of the Far East, other-worldly and metaphysical, effectively cut their peoples off from Europe. But Islam, Judaism, and Christianity, the religions of the Arab world, all born in the Levant, hold much in common. The long engagements of Crusaders and 'Saracens' have the peculiar bitterness of the feuds of sectaries; they bind as well as divide. The systematic vilification of Islam by generations of Christian divines testified to something deeper than theological interest; and the East has similarly betrayed an obsessive memory of its ancient encounters with the Christian west.

And in the old Levant, particularly in Egypt, 'East' and 'West,' the three religions with their common source in the faith of Abraham, the faithful of mosque and church and synagogue mingled in a well-worn, occasionally acrimonious, domesticity. Nowhere was the continuity of this close-woven pattern— which transcended both Nile Valley and the bounds of Islam —more manifest than in its Jewish strands. The Jews of Alexandria had played an honourable rôle there almost from the foundation of that city. In Cairo, the first vizier of the Fatamid dynasty was a Jew from Baghdad; the Egyptian Jewish community at this time 'had no real rival in the Eastern world.'[2] After the collapse of the Fatamids, the great Jewish philosopher, Moses Maimonides, was physician to the Sultan Salah ed-Din and his court, leader of the Cairo Jewish community, and the leading scholar in Egypt. In more recent times and right down to the mid-1950s, the many enterprises of the powerful and wealthy community of Egyptian Jews to a large extent furnished the country's economic dynamic. Writing of the days before the rise of political Zionism, the Jewish writer Louis Golding describes the relations of the Egyptian Jews and their Muslim neighbours as 'ideal.'[3] They were an essential

[2] James Parkes, *A History of the Jewish People* (1964).
[3] *The Jewish Problem* (London, 1938).

part of the rich Egyptian scene; the Grand Mufti, the Archbishop of the Coptic Church, the Chief Rabbi of Egypt formed the inevitable formal trinity of a people who had long lived together in this land and who were united at least in their worship of a single God.

Anti-Semitism, which produced political Zionism, and is its obverse, is not a Muslim or an Oriental phenomenon; its origins are firmly Christian and European. Yet if Zionism originated elsewhere, it was to the old Eastern world that it came, and it was the old Eastern world that it shattered with its insistence on making a single minority religion the basis of a modern territorial nation-state,[4] inevitably incubating in the process an intense and narrow nationalism, gathered around the prayer shawl that had become a flag—a national flag for which, as Herzl said, 'men live and die.'

And this is another—and a tragic—difference between the Egyptian ruling and the rising generation. The fathers were brought up in the old Eastern world with its complex and ancient harmonies—and occasional dissonances—largely intact. Nasser himself as a youth in Cairo was brought up with Jews as neighbours. The family's landlord was Jewish and a little synagogue, announced by the Star of David, lay a few steps away from the Nasser apartment. True, Zionism, with its assertive communalism and its territorial claims, was beginning to cast its long shadow; but it says much for the strength of old habits of mind and the old tolerance in Egypt that even after the creation of Israel and the Egyptian defeat in the first Jewish-Arab war the Jewish community was still able to live in Egypt, its members continuing to enjoy high positions in the professions and great commercial power.

Again, it was 1956 that was the watershed year. After the Israeli attack upon Egypt, in collusion with the British and the French, the religious shibboleth was harder to avoid. Zionism had turned a religion into a nationality and the new Egyptian generation passed its most impressionable years in an Egypt

----

[4] Zionism was fiercely opposed by many leading Egyptian Jews, as by many other Oriental Jews. According to Mr Gerold Frank, when in 1942 a Haganah agent called on Cattaui Pasha, the wealthy President of the Cairo Jewish Community, and asked him to finance Jewish immigration to Palestine, he threatened to set his dogs on her.

in which the Jews, who had been the neighbours, might become, tragically, the enemy, directly challenging the young as 'Arabs,' and, it seemed, invoking the support of the West against them.

None the less, baffled and bitter as it might be, the new generation would continue, like the old one, to direct its gaze westward. It had inherited enough of its fathers' world to know that Jews and Judaism could not really be the enemy—whatever temporary aberration might have seized them—and that the West was more than 'Imperialism.' There was hope in that.

PART SIX

THE WORLD'S DEBATE

Every Arab regrets and feels grieved to see the differences, quarrels, dissensions and altercations between Arab blood brothers. But who is to blame for this? In the past we used to blame colonialisation. But today when Arab countries have become free and responsible for the management of their own affairs, who is to blame? We must blame ourselves.

—King Feisal of Saudi Arabia, at Taif, September 1963

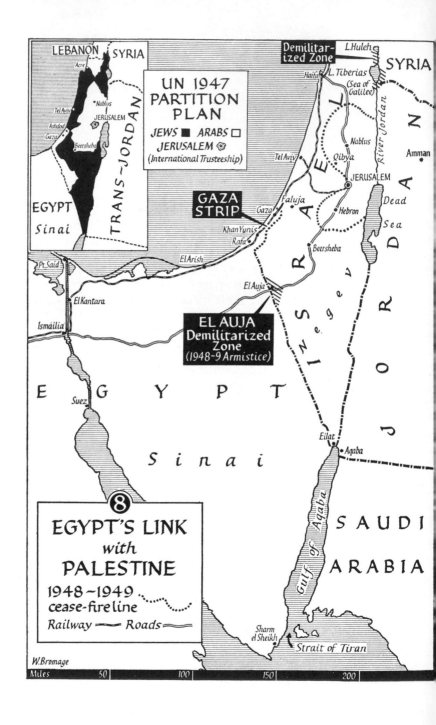

LEBANON SYRIA

Acre

UN 1947
PARTITION
PLAN
JEWS ■ ARABS □
JERUSALEM ⬡
(*International Trusteeship*)

Nablus

Tel Aviv

JERUSALEM

Ashdod
Gaza

Beersheba

TRANS~JORDAN

EGYPT

Sinai

Demilitar-
ized Zone

L.Huleh

Haifa L. Tiberias
(*Sea of
Galilee*)

SYRIA

Nablus

Tel Aviv

Qibya

JERUSALEM

Amman

River Jordan

J
O
R
D
A
N

GAZA
STRIP

Faluja

Gaza

Hebron

Dead

KhanYunis

Rafa

Beersheba

Sea

El Arish

El Auja

EL AUJA
Demilitarized
Zone
(*1948~9 Armistice*)

Pt.Said

El Kantara

Ismáilia

E G Y P T

Suez

S i n a i

N
e
g
e
v

I
S
R
A
E
L

Eilat

Aqaba

J
O
R
D
A
N

⑧
EGYPT'S LINK
with
PALESTINE
1948~1949
cease-fire line
Railway ━ Roads ━

SAUDI

ARABIA

Gulf of Aqaba

*Sharm
el Sheikh*

Strait of Tiran

W.Bromage

Miles   50   100   150   200

25

THE UNFINISHED REVOLUTION

In preparing an area for independence, it is our duty to see
that the sights are set on *our* target before we pull the trigger.
If, after leaving the muzzle, the bullet gets deflected and hits
quite a different target instead, that, alas, is something we can
no longer control. . . . What happens to all this after we go
is not our look-out. At least we have done our duty as we see
it.

—Sir Charles Johnston, High Commissioner Aden and South
   Arabian Protectorate, *The View from Steamer Point* (1964)

Sir Humphrey Trevelyan, High Commissioner for Aden and
South Arabia, left Aden for the last time—as a Marine band
played 'Puppet on a string' and 'Fings ain't what they used to
be.'

   —News Summary, *Financial Times*, 28 November 1967

The social revolution must start forthwith.

—Qahtan as-Shaabi, President of the People's Republic of
   South Yemen (formerly Aden & S. Arabian Protectorate),
   30 November 1967

At the end of a leafy street in the Cairo suburb of Dokki stands
a large villa, with a neat metal plate announcing 'The Arab
Petroleum Institute'—otherwise the residential college maintained by the Arab Federation of Petroleum Workers. Inside,
twenty-one young men sit decorously around a horse-shoe
table, notebooks open before them, listening to a lecture on
'How to express oneself effectively' by a gentleman from the
personnel department of Misr (ex-Shell) Petroleum. It is the
final section ('How to be a Trade Union Leader') of a three-
week course, and the young men around the table—who
have by this time just about got used to each other's 'odd'
Arabic—have travelled from Morocco, Syria, Iraq, Jordan,
Libya, the Sudan, the sheikhdom of Qatar, and Aden. They
draw £2 a week pocket-money besides being provided with

rooms and their keep at the Institute, and they were sent here by the constituent national petroleum unions in their own countries—all, that is, except the Libyan, whose government harbours such suspicions of Cairo that he has been obliged to sneak in as a tourist and may well, he hints, be arrested on his return. It seems more than possible, for when by way of an exercise each of the young men is invited to give a short address, the Libyan observes that although the presidents and monarchs signed an agreement at the 1964 Arab 'Summit' conference, true agreement can only be based on the unity of the workers all over the Arab world—which Kings and Feudalists seek to prevent. One must unify the workers before one can unify the Arabs.

There is no dissent from the young men around the horse-shoe table, mild-mannered but modern-minded. They are mostly clerkly types, some supervisors of administration sections, a few technicians. They belong neither to the world of the fellahin nor to the world of the old bourgeois nationalists. With them the Louis Quinze throne and the salon decisively give way to the office and metal stacking chairs; it is they who occupy the other side of the managerial table. They stand at the confluence of two great interacting forces which will shape the Arab world of tomorrow—the dynamic and logic of a technology based on massive oil wealth and oil-financed industry, and the 'revolution of the Common Man.'

For these young men, as for thousands like them, there was a certain inevitability about the journey to Cairo. It was, in fact, a pilgrimage; they had travelled there much as an older generation might have journeyed to Mecca. For as a source of revolutionary energy in the Arab world, Cairo from 1955 echoed Paris in 1792, with the Convention scattering its Honorary Citizenships about Europe and offering 'fraternity and aid to all peoples who wish to recover their liberty.' And Cairo's call embraced the Arab West as well as East. In the Cairo *Maghreb* Office Allal al-Fassi, leader of the Moroccan Istiqlal, Salah ben Yousseff, Secretary-General of Bourguiba's Neo-Destour, Ben Bella, the ex-sergeant in the French army, and Mohamed Khider, the ex-Algiers trolley-bus conductor, worked together, securing Egyptian aid in money and arms for the liberation and making over of their countries. In Cairo as nowhere else, the young oil workers around the trade union table could feel themselves in the mainstream of history, at the very hub of the new Arab revolution which was transforming the Arab world before their eyes.

In this emotional judgment it seems at least likely that they will be confirmed by history. Before the Egyptian revolution, systematic and radical land- or income-redistribution was almost inconceivable in the Arab countries. By an irony familiar enough in the history of religions, Islam, the creed of brotherhood and social justice, had petrified into the sanctification of property as God-given. This institutionalised attitude had reached the point of caricature in the Yemen, but, in greater or lesser degree, it prevailed everywhere in the Arab world. The Free Officers with their initial land reform had broken through this log-jam that blocked the social evolution of even such Arab countries as had then become independent. Land reforms followed in Syria, in Iraq, in Tunisia, later in Iran and Turkey. The Egyptians went on to shape the hitherto conveniently inscrutable Divine Will to social ends with the aid of an investment plan, and, from 1957, the nationalisation of key sectors of the economy. Wage, taxation and labour legislation unmistakably asserted the claims of the ordinary man and sought to institutionalise them in forms more effective than those offered either by the council of tribal elders or by mock western-model parliamentarianism. At last the Arab world was moving; the endless palace revolutions gave way to true social revolution; words were clothed in action. Long before Suez there were few corners of the Arab world which remained unaffected.

On Bahrein island in 1954 appeared the nucleus of the first political party in the primitive world of the Gulf, the so-called 'Higher Executive Committee' (of four local Shias, four Sunnis[1]), challenging the autocracy of the Ruler's family and the oil company. It called for island elections,[2] the legalisation of

---

[1] The two wings of Islam which emerged after the split following the assassination of the Fourth Caliph, the Prophet's son-in-law, Ali. The Sunnis are 'orthodox'; the Shias (Partisans) uphold the claims of Ali, and are numerous in Iraq and dominant in Persia.

[2] Owing to the 'liberal' influence of the Ruler's Adviser, Sir Charles Belgrave, there had been elections in Bahrein for years, but only for the two

trade unions, a court of appeal and a modern legal code (all judges were members of the Ruler's Family). Again, in the Aden of the 1940s the British had provided for trade unions as part of the new progressive colonial package. Yet, up to the year of the Egyptian Revolution, only a single trade union had been formed there. 'Then, suddenly,' to quote Sir Tom Hickin-botham, the Governor, 'trade unions became fashionable and everyone wanted to have these new toys with the result that by March 1956 twenty-five unions had been registered. . . . The leaders were mostly young men.' The Aden Trades Union Congress soon became a revolutionary force, turning what had not long before been merely a remote Crown Colony and bunkering station into one of the focal points of a new Arab world-in-the-making.

Such movements inevitably looked across the old colonial— and often meaningless—frontiers to the larger Arab world. In Aden, a National United Front brought together the rapidly multiplying nationalists, progressives, and some 'Free Yemenis,' to demand independence and the union of Aden, the Aden Protectorate, Yemen and the Sultanate of Muscat and Oman in a 'democratic republican' state of 'South Arabia.' Both in Bahrein and Aden these movements found ardent support amongst the young coming from the new schools, among the clerks, school teachers, minor technicians, that growing lower middle class ('half-baked intelligentsia') between the wealthy merchant class and the Ruling Families.

Spreading outwards from the Nile Valley, the winds of change travelled down the Red Sea as well as the Gulf and, reaching across the Arabian peninsula's vast desert spaces, were felt even in Riyadh where the heirs of the great Ibn Saud were madly squandering the oil millions which they still re-garded as their private property. The events in Egypt strength-ened the hands of the westernising Crown Prince Feisal against his obscurantist elder brother, King Saud. In 1954 the reform-ing Feisal became President of the Council of Ministers; four years later—as the revolution gathered pace in the wider Arab world—the Family prudently pushed King Saud into semi-

municipalities, and only half the municipal council was elected. The Ruler's Family supplied the chairman, and, given the power situation on the island, the Ruler's autocracy was little disturbed.

retirement, giving Feisal executive powers. Annual budgets were now instituted, with a separate—though huge—privy purse, and six new ministries were set up, most notably a Ministry of Health and a Ministry of Education. Meanwhile, in the fastnesses of the Yemen, the Imam faced a mounting 'Free Yemeni' movement financed by Yemeni merchants from Aden, and the attempted coups of 1948, 1953, 1955 and 1959 increasingly mingled ideology with their normal content of fratricidal jealousy and private ambition.

The foreign intervention at Suez had its classic result in deepening and speeding the course of revolution. There followed the attempted coup and successful counter-coup in Jordan, the overthrow of the conservative Hashemite régime in Iraq, and another—frustrated—attempt at revolution in the Yemen. Even Bourguiba in Tunisia, assailed by the more radical, pan-Arabist supporters of Salah ben Yousseff, his Neo-Destour's former Secretary-General, shed a little of his studied moderation and declared that if his policy was not Nasserian neutralism, it was nevertheless 'non-engagement'—which, by 1961, had turned into the bloody battle with the French for the possession of Bizerta. On Bahrein island, the Higher Executive Committee's candidates in the first elections swept the board, and, since the Ruler still refused to surrender complete Family control, were duly, after strikes and anti-British riots, sentenced to fourteen years' imprisonment and exiled to St Helena.[3] Further south, in Aden, seven 'so-called Nationalists' —to quote the Governor, Sir Tom Hickinbotham, again—had been elected to the Municipal Council; and in the neighbouring Protectorate state of Lahej, Britain had in 1958 'withdrawn recognition' from the Sultan for 'forbidden political contacts' and failing to co-operate with the Governor of Aden in arresting his pro-Egyptian nationalist Ministers and friends. In Aden itself the Trade Union Congress prepared to boycott the first elections for a Legislative Council with an elective majority.

[3] The elections were for the health and education councils. Even so, only half the members were to be elected, the rest being nominated by the Sultan, with a member of the Family as chairman. In the notable absence of any 'modern' democratic approach or conciliatory spirit in the nominated and Family members, this amounted to a recipe for revolution and it was hardly surprising that the elected members declined to take their seats.

For all its great spaces and its immense differences in development, the Arab world, with its sensitive nervous system—now electronically extended—formed to an extraordinary degree in these years a psychological unity in which change in one part was quickly felt in every other. In 1960 the conflict of the Egyptian planners from Cairo and the wily Damascus merchants in the 'Northern Region of the United Arab Republic' led to a deepening of Egypt's own revolution, with, at last, the full-blooded espousal of Socialism. A thousand miles away in the sheikhdom of Kuwait, the ruling Sabah, a shrewd and prudent man, reading the signs of the times, called a sharp halt to the Family's great palace-building spree (fifty in ten years averaging £1m. each), cancelled his own order for a yacht, instructed his eldest son to turn his new £4½m. palace into a Government Guest House, and his brother and Deputy, Abdullah Mubarak to halt work on his new palace at Basra. By 1961, the 'Supreme Council' of ten Sabahs, which until then had governed Kuwait, had been enlarged into a 'Joint Council' with ten merchants added. From there it was a quick step to giving the vote to all literate adult Kuwaitis, and the Constituent Assembly of twenty, elected in 1962, began its proceedings in what was no doubt judged proper democratic form by proposing a vote of censure on the Ruler and Family (who could perhaps afford it since they nevertheless retained eleven Ministries out of fourteen).

In Saudi Arabia the 'modernising' Crown Prince Feisal clove to Nasserian neutralism—the doctrine of the revolution—while his brother King Saud supported the Eisenhower Doctrine. And in August 1962 there was the remarkable spectacle of another royal brother, Tallal, giving a Press conference at the St George's Hotel, Beirut, in which he complained that Saudi Arabia lacked a Constitution and civil liberties, and went on to commend the British and Scandinavian types of socialism. Saudi Arabia, the Prince said, required a moderate socialism, suited to her environment and history, but leading to social equality with a redistribution of wealth. He said that although the Government was naturally against him, many important Saudis agreed, and he named four princes accompanying him.

King Saud withdrew the princes' passports; but by September 1962 the long-rehearsed revolution in Yemen had occurred, and less than two months later Feisal had been placed firmly in control in Saudi Arabia. He produced a ten-point programme of reform, which although vaguely phrased, proposed a basic law setting out the powers and organisation of the state and the rights of private citizens. There was to be a modernising Ministry of Justice, a system of local government, social security (with 'free medicine'), road and water development, an industrial and agricultural bank and a General Petroleum and Minerals Agency to exploit the country's raw material wealth. 'With the help of God,' Feisal proclaimed, 'Saudi Arabia will soon become an industrial country. . . .'

There were, furthermore, to be 'innocent means of recreation for all classes.' The phrase was carefully chosen: it had to be in this fatherland of Wahhabi puritanism,[4] where, among other stern restraints on conduct, Saudi visits to Aramco's 'impious' cinemas were forbidden. (The impiety of TV—which began to operate in 1966—was still under discussion.) As a curtain-raiser to the welfare state, slavery was to be abolished, with 'compensation for all those who prove deserving of compensation.'

By the mid-'sixties there had thus begun to appear in all the Arab countries, however far apart in their degrees of development, a certain common pattern of aspiration, which might sometimes be superficial, but which testified to the compulsive power of the ideas which inspired it. In their name Time was ruthlessly telescoped. Sophisticated notions of social security marched with the settling of the Bedouin. 'Nomadism,' proclaimed Article 43 of the Baath Party Constitution severely, 'is a primitive social state. It decreases the national output . . . and makes an important part of the nation a paralysed member.' Inferentially at least, pride, pedigree, custom, the old Arab values of the desert, were discarded; education, industrialisation and planning were installed as the obligatory new watchwords. And planning seemed to imply a public sector—

---

[4] The ultra-austere and fanatic warrior brotherhood of Koranic fundamentalists, founded in Arabia by Abdul Wahhab in the 18th century, and harnessed to tribal conquest by the House of Saud. In our own times, Ibn Saud revived the Wahhabis to rebuild his fallen family fortunes and create the 'Kingdom of Saudi Arabia.'

whether this carried its full ideological overtones as in Egypt, Algeria, and, after the nationalising waves of 1963-65, Syria and Iraq, or was mainly seen as an instrument of development —as in Bourguiba's Tunisia. Even Saudi Arabia now had its state General Organisation for Petroleum and Minerals (with a 75 per cent interest in the refinery planned for Jiddah and control of a steel rolling mill and fertiliser factory). All needed foreign capital; equally, all wished it firmly under control.

In Egypt, the co-operatives had been the product of much planning and technical expertise. In Algeria, 'worker-management'—*autogestion*—both on farms and in factories, began as a stop-gap after the flight of foreign managements. But almost everywhere the co-operative seemed a form which had much to offer.

The pattern emerging testified not only to the penetrative power of the ideas, but also to the common elements in the Islamic societies on which the ideas acted. In one form or another, the single political organisation sought—through its internal struggle, intrigue and debate—to achieve the consensus necessary to nation-building. In less evolved areas like Saudi Arabia, the Ruling Family with its various collaterals— and Ibn Saud married 300 times—amounted in a sense to a single political party in itself; in the future it might take in non-Family members—or be taken over by them. In the few remaining countries like Morocco and Jordan which had persisted with it, the Western multi-party parliamentary system had again broken down. Lebanon remained an exception. Its peculiar combination of archaic religious sectarianism and modern financial sleight of hand held together a parliamentary system of infinite complexity. Yet—despite the boasted 88 per cent gold cover for the Lebanese pound—its stability was the stability of a spinning top. And as elsewhere, it depended ultimately (as was seen in 1958) on the army's holding the ring.

'Neutralism' was now part of the basic grammar of the whole region. Even Feisal was at pains to point out that the airfield the U.S. rented at Dahran merely gave her rights of passage. And if, according to the Korans of some, Communism was the root of all impiety, outside Saudi Arabia remarkably little of it appeared to have rubbed off on the Russians, who were now almost as widely accepted in the Arab world as the British once had been. Announced in the spring of 1966, Russia's contract to finance and construct Syria's huge Euphrates Dam, designed to irrigate 1½ million acres and generate 600,000 kilowatt-hours of electricity, clearly echoed the Egyptian High Dam. In the same year King Hassan of Morocco signed a cultural, scientific and economic agreement with the Russians, and Sheikh Jabir, the Finance Minister of Kuwait, sent trade missions to Moscow and Peking 'to broaden,' as he explained, 'our horizons.' In Morocco the Russians had agreed to build a dam on the Draa River, followed by a Casablanca metallurgical plant, and a power station in Eastern Morocco, with aid in lead-silver-zinc mining in the Atlas.

If the themes—and sometimes the actual models—of the Nasserian revolution emerge clearly from this new Arab pattern, it was by no means their sole source. Syria had been incubating its highly infectious form of 'Arab Socialism' a decade before Nasser's version achieved expression; Algeria, because of contacts with the French Left through the trade unions and the destruction of the long war, might well have turned to socialism anyhow. Old Ibn Saud had pioneered rudimentary agricultural colonies for the Bedouin in the 'twenties, and by 1927 had more than a hundred Ikhwan (religious brotherhood) settlements spread through Arabia. In Tunisia Bourguiba had built in the Neo-Destour a highly effective 'one-nation' peasant-and-worker political organisation well before Nasser falteringly attempted it in Egypt; for that matter, the old Imam of Yemen had anticipated 'positive neutralism' by turning for help to the Italians in 1926, and to the Russians (with whom he concluded a Treaty of Friendship) in 1927.[5] As for the public sector, Lyautey in Morocco had confided the exploitation of the country's rich phosphate deposits to a state organisation as long ago as 1920. State ownership of industry had also been a central feature of Ataturk's New Turkey.

Nevertheless, the rôle of the Egyptian Revolution in the jelling of the new Arab pattern had been crucial. The earlier

[5] In the event, the Imam's dislike of outsiders in general proved stronger than his fear of a particular outsider, the British in Aden Protectorate, and the Italian experts, having arrived, were ignored and their aircraft left to rust.

changes had been partial, and for that reason ineffective; the Egyptian revolution had continued until a new pattern— political, social, economic—was complete and had been dramatically projected. In particular, the Arab world had been delivered in 1955 and 1956 from its debilitating old psychological dependence on the Western Powers; and from 1961 onwards, the word 'Socialism' had been projected across the Arab skies, a bright new star of great portent.

In 1961 even in Saudi Arabia—to quote Feisal—'our Press started discussing socialism . . . some writers were in favour, others against. When the discussion grew into what we feared might compromise certain governments or leaders, we advised our friends of the Press to avoid discussing this subject.' Elsewhere the debate was not to be so easily silenced. In newly independent Algeria, Ben Bella, consciously modelling himself on Nasser, in March 1963 nationalised the big landed estates, preventing an Algerian owning class taking over in the room of the French. Next door, in Tunisia, where in the late 'thirties the radical nationalist 'mass' Neo-Destour had taken over from the traditionalist nationalist 'Good Family' Destour (Constitution) party, Habib Bourguiba, who had always boasted his pragmatism, in 1964 ordered another change of title—to the Neo-Destour *Socialist* Party.

This 'Arab Socialism,' it is true, was often little more than an ardent humanism, a claim on behalf of the Arab common man a good deal less specific than that of Victorian Chartism which it perhaps emotionally resembled. *Le socialisme, c'est libérer l'homme! Le socialisme, c'est la route barrée aux speculateurs!* cried the Algerian hoardings. But for all the vagueness, a new order of social priorities was being proclaimed; the dominant public sector erected in Egypt between 1956 and 1962 had demonstrated the possibility of enforcing it; and as events unfolded, 'socialism' was to become a serviceable shibboleth, separating the serious 'modernisers' from the camouflaging traditionalists, or in Koranic terms, the True Believers from the 'Hypocrites'[6] who, out of prudence, were

---

[6] The Hypocrites, who figure in the Koran, were those Medinans who nominally declared for Islam while covertly opposing Mohamed. 'They have taken their oaths for a protection. . . . They resemble pieces of timber set up against a wall. They imagine every shout to be against them. . . .' (Koran, Sura 63).

Left, then clockwise
Mohamed Hassenein
Heikal, Editor of *Al Ahram*.
Ali Sayed Ali, Petroleum
Workers' union leader.
Ahmed Fahim, President,
Federation of Labour
and Deputy Speaker,
National Assembly.
Dr Hikmat Abu Zaid,
Egypt's first woman
Cabinet Minister.
Anwar Salama, the ex-
Shell fitter Nasser made
Minister of Labour.
Khaled Mohieddin, once
'the Red Major', then
editor and columnist.

The most famous Egyptian after Nasser—the classic Arab singer, Om Kolthoum, here seen giving a recital in the Lebanon in 1968. *Below* Scene from the Cairo production of 'The Tree Climber', a surrealistic play (1962) by the veteran Egyptian writer, Tewfik El Hakim, the leading dramatist of the Arab world. (Chapter 23)

merely riding the tide.

This process, at its most rudimentary, was visible between 1955 and 1962 in the Yemen.

Confrontation in the Yemen

In the year 631 the Prophet himself sent his son-in-law Ali to establish order in the newly converted Yemen, whose merchants were familiar visitors in Mecca. Ali succeeded imperfectly; the year after his arrival the tribes rose in 'the first apostasy.' Since then this mountain kingdom on the fringe of the classic Arab heartland had known only its peculiarly local —and vibrant—version of the 'Islamic Peace' under the absolute rule of its Zeidi (Shia) Imam-caliphs, the supposed descendants of Ali and the Prophet. It was a curious system of 'managed anarchy,' based on the exclusion of foreigners, the Imamate's monopoly of trade and sanctity, and the manipulation of the proud and warlike tribes by cash, by hostage-taking,[7] and by unstinted exemplary public beheadings. By these means the Imam was able to sustain into the Jet Age his absolute rule over this vast, largely roadless but fertile land, about half of whose inhabitants—those dwelling mainly in the plains and foothills—are of the rival Shafei (Sunni) sect of Islam and thus reluctant to acknowledge his profitable sanctity.

For the Imam, the fly in the ointment lay in the fact that around 1948 the British in Aden had rediscovered their civilising mission and resolved to carry it to that vast, undemarcated tribal hinterland which the Imam had long regarded as within his own, God-given realm. They announced an intention to take 'sound administration' and 'progressive self-government,' through British Advisers and political officers, to those numerous quarrelsome chiefs with whom Britain had in the last century concluded treaties (better described as 'deals') which both provided the chiefs with tribe-buying income, and furnished them with protection against rival masters like the Turks or ambitious neighbours.

[7] Under this remarkable, but no doubt effective, system, the Imam in the 'thirties is estimated to have been holding no fewer than 4,000 hostages—sons of chiefs and so on—as security for the good behaviour of the tribes.

When in pursuance of this new policy there was unveiled in Aden in 1954 a plan for a Federation of the Protectorate Rulers' territories 'leading ultimately' to the blessings of Dominion Status, the darkest suspicions of the Imam were confirmed. In the desultory 'frontier' war that followed between the Imam's tribal pensionaries and the British-paid native levies of the so-called states of the Protectorate, the Imam turned for support to Nasser's Egypt in much the same way as before the war he had briefly turned to Italy and Russia.

But this time there could be no retreat: in the Arab world of the 'fifties isolation was no longer possible, even in such mountain fastnesses as the Yemen. This time the Russians, recalled, actually constructed a new deep-water port near Hodeida; the Chinese built an all-weather road from there to the capital of Sana; the Egyptians trained the army and advised on agriculture and education. After the union between Egypt and Syria in 1958, the Imam applied to join the United Arab Republic, but when Nasser pointed out that union was not really appropriate, he had to content himself with membership of the 'United Arab States.'

The motive of the Imam Ahmed in embracing the Egyptians was clearly the usual one of preserving the integrity of his kingdom against, as he saw it, the British 'threat' from the coast. But his heir, Saif al-Islam al-Badr, whether from conviction or youthful ambition, seems to have espoused the message of the Egyptian Revolution as ardently as the Saudi princes in Beirut. He travelled to Cairo, to the East European capitals and to China; and as Crown Prince, he appointed an Egyptian Director of Public Security. It was scarcely remarkable that by 1959 clandestine leaflets signed 'The Free Officers of the Yemen Army' had made their appearance in Taif or that the usual attempts to overthrow the Imam's tyranny began to reflect the republican-socialist idiom made familiar by Cairo radio.

After putting down another attempted coup with the usual bloodbath, Imam Ahmed was plainly having second thoughts about his invitation to the Egyptians. In 1961, he broadcast on Sana Radio a poem condemning socialism as a deviation from the Sharia of Islam, and condemning such impious 'innovations' as the 'taking away of the property of people who have rightfully earned it on the pretext of nationalisation and equalisation.'

Alas, it was too late, both for Ahmed and for the Crown Prince. In 1962, the tanks with which the Russians had equipped the Yemeni army were employed by Colonel Abdullah Sallal to demolish the Palace in Sana with the newly acceded Imam, the 'liberal' Saif al-Islam al-Badr, inside it. And this time, with the aid of the almost immediate military support from the Egyptians, the coup—at least the sixth attempt since 1945 —succeeded.

The newest Arab revolution was acclaimed.

But if the Egyptians had inevitably promoted the Yemen revolution by their mere presence, and if Arab Socialism had provided a shibboleth powerful enough to reveal the contradictions inherent in an egalitarian Imamate, it would be altogether absurd to credit the Egyptians alone. As early as 1947 a 'Free Yemeni' Press was calling for a Constitution and an end to theocratic autocracy, and the coup's immediate author, Abdullah Sallal, was a true Zeidi Yemeni who for at least half of his forty years had been in the mainstream of the Arab revolutionary movement. The son of a Sana blacksmith, he had been one of the very few Yemenis sent abroad for education under a treaty with Iraq; the Imam had sent him for three years to the Military College at Baghdad. Three years had been enough. Soon after returning to serve as an officer in the Yemeni Army he was gaoled for subversion. Possibly he had been fired by news from his late comrades of the Raschid Ali revolt against the British and Hashemites in Iraq—in any event he was to spend eleven years in the Imam's gaols. Whether or not he studied Nasser's *Philosophy of the Revolution* there (as some claim), he can hardly have needed much assistance in acquiring a distaste for Yemen's medieval Imamate—a distaste shared by most educated Yemenis from self-imposed exile in Aden, Cairo and elsewhere. Sallal, in fact, got to know a number of the leading Yemeni 'liberals' in gaol.

General Carl von Horn, the Swedish commander of the U.N. mission in the Yemen, has described how he 'became convinced that Sallal was patently sincere and genuinely devoted to what he believed the best interests of his people.' He goes on to add '. . . I had the feeling that, however convinced he was of the rightness of his cause, he remained dubious of its chances of success.'

And well indeed he might be. For if revolution in the Yemen was by now inevitable, so too was that revolution's failure. The materials for more than a 'palace revolution' simply did not exist in this vast and primitive land whose only social structure, beyond its 'royal' Family was a maze of shifting alliances of widely separated tribes and their restless, feuding chieftains. President Sallal's solution—his substitute for the missing revolutionary base—was to fall back upon the Egyptian army.

Everything suggests that the Egyptians had no idea of the immensity of the task to which they had thus committed themselves in the Yemen, and Nasser has since frankly admitted as much, describing the whole astonishing affair as 'a miscalculation.'[8] It was, however, a miscalculation which was to keep a large part of the Egyptian Army, a rotating body rising to 70,000 men, in the wilds of the Yemen, more than a thousand miles from home, for five years.

But if the Egyptian army possessed no magical formula for turning hordes of illiterate tribesmen into dedicated social revolutionaries, its massive presence here, on the edge of the old Arab heartland, as inevitably diffused the ideas of the Egyptian revolution as the French armies in Italy did those of the French revolution. For five years it protected and projected Yemen's symbolic revolution incorporating the new socialist shibboleths. It is fascinating to note, for instance, that the first Constitution of the Yemen Republic, in 1964, while it did not provide for an elected assembly, ritualistically states 'the formation of trade unions is a guaranteed right.'

The urgency of trade unions in a country which had only just then acquired its first technical school may seem doubtful. But the message was received and understood in the larger Arab world. And as events to the south, in Aden, demonstrated, trade unions could indeed form the natural vehicle of the young, modern-minded and aspiring of the dawning Arab world, the clerks, the teachers, the students, the well-paid oil workers, the skilled operatives, the technicians, the potential

---

[8] Interview with Mr William Attwood, *Look* magazine, March 1968.

beneficiaries of a social and political revolution which they were thus enabled to make their own. Nasser, when he plotted the Egyptian revolution, had been a junior army officer, son of a minor postal official; Abdullah al Asnag, the leader of the Aden TUC, who carried the banner of Arab Socialism into South Arabia, was an airline clerk, in his twenties, son of a local health inspector. Mohsin Al Aini, a Yemen Republican Prime Minister, was a teacher, ex-Secretary-General of the Aden Teachers' Trade Union. Bringing together the 'lower middle class,' the 'employees' and the labourers, to form a broader social base, the unions were an organised body which in the power to withhold labour possessed a weapon less potent only than the guns of the army.[9]

The point was taken, to the north, in Riyadh. King Feisal now began to succour and supply with arms the 'Royalist' tribal forces of the Imam. The Yemen became the theatre of a confrontation of the forces (and ideas) of Arab tradition and the forces (and ideas) of the new Arab revolution such as had not been seen since that old vizier, Nuri, confronted the young Nasser over the symbol of the Baghdad Pact. On that occasion the Western Powers had drawn much of the fire; now they had dropped into the background, to figure largely as a sinister, off-stage presence, 'the forces of Imperialism.' The confrontation in Arabia was a confrontation between Arabs—and all the more clarifying for that.

Monarchists and Republicans

Henceforward the theme of the two hostile political camps of 'monarchists' and 'republicans,' of the confrontation of the 'feudalists' and the 'socialists,' 'the reactionaries' and the 'revolutionaries' (or from the other side of the street, of the 'good Muslims' versus the 'impious betrayers of Islam') was to form a counterpoint, sometimes muted, sometimes shrill or thunderous, to the old, richly orchestrated *motif* of 'Arab Unity.'

Most Western observers were in the habit of attaching the

[9] Notably demonstrated during and after the Israeli attack of 1967 when the trade unions of the port workers and oil workers, etc., took the lead, sometimes in defiance of their own governments, in stopping the oil flow and banning U.K., U.S. and German shipping.

adjective 'so-called' at least to the progressive camp's description of the position—for nothing in the Arab world is ever quite that simple. But though it might be rare indeed to find its undiluted essence, the issue was by no means spurious. On the contrary, it was real and central, both in terms of the Islamic past and of the modernising future.

The formal titles to loyalty of the Arab monarchs of Morocco, Jordan, Libya and Saudi Arabia rest on traditional Islamic grounds: those of Kings Hassan and Hussein on membership of a religious nobility deriving from the family of the Prophet, those of King Idris and King Feisal on their rôle as leaders of Islamic brotherhoods, the Senussi and Wahhabi. 'If they consider monarchy a thing to be decried,' said Feisal at Riyadh in 1963, answering Egyptian attacks, 'we consider it only an imported title. We are not kings, emperors, and despots, but preachers of the Book of God, and the Code of the Prophet.'

As Feisal's remark suggests, the Western concept of hereditary monarchy, introduced to the Middle East after the First World War, could only with difficulty be fitted into the Arab scheme. '*Mulk*—royal power,' rules the Encyclopedia of Islam, 'belongs to God alone; He has no associates therein.' And if the struggle between the principle of election and the fact of nepotism and dynastic power had been lost quite early in the history of the Caliphate, its echoes continued. Thus when, in 1805, the Egyptians deposed their Turkish Governor in favour of Mohamed Ali, the sheikhs of El Azhar were able to claim that they did so 'according to established usage and the rules of the Sharia which permits the people to choose their rulers, and to depose them if they deviate from the paths of justice.' In this they merely re-stated a classic doctrine which saw the Caliph as ruling by virtue of a contract between him and the people, 'a contract which lapses should he prove to be wicked and evil-doing.' And in point of fact, in so far as they have succeeded in carrying their people with them, the Arab monarchs of today have done so not by virtue of their 'blood,' but as nationalist leaders in their own right: Hassan and Hussein by reason of their youthful and masterful vigour (Hassan being greatly helped by his father, Mohamed V's, fight against the French); old Idris by his saintliness and his record of undeviating resistance to the Italians.

Nevertheless, it was the religious ground which Feisal chose in his riposte to Nasser, aligning himself with the monarchs of Morocco, Jordan, and Iran in a proposed 'Islamic Pact,' a Holy Alliance against 'atheist' revolution. In the eyes of most educated Arabs, he thereby accepted the 'reactionary traditionalist' rôle that had been allotted to him; and despite the 'modern' patterns which Saudi Arabia, in common with other Arab states, had at least superficially adopted, there were still many respects in which it and its proposed allies dismally failed to meet the new shibboleths. In Saudi Arabia, where trade unions were effectively repressed,[10] and where a Constitution had been promised as long ago as 1932, the 'liberal' Feisal continued to repeat that the only needful Constitution was the Sharia; in Morocco, King Hassan, ruling in person, repressed the large, radical, trade-union-backed UNFP (*Union Nationale de Forces Populaires*) whose outstanding leader, the former teacher, Mehdi ben Barka, was mysteriously murdered; while in Jordan King Hussein had repeatedly turned to his Bedouin troops to buttress his personal rule against the politically-conscious Palestinians.

The day had gone by when—as in an earlier schism in Islam—a Cause could be won in the Arab world by going into battle with the Koran held out on the point of one's lance.[11] In the sheikhdom of Kuwait the Constituent Assembly now demanded and got the right to *elect* the next Ruler, with the proviso that he need not be a member of the Sabah Family. A rough-and-ready spiritual egalitarianism is a persistent feature

---

[10] An instructive eye-witness account of Saudi methods of dealing with strikes and labour demonstrations has been given by King Saud's former Swiss Chief Steward, José Arnold, in his book *Golden Swords and Pots and Pans*. The labour demonstration in question took place in 1956 and was met by flogging ten 'agitators' in public—seven to death—and gaoling 200, with subsequent banishment for all 'in any previous political trouble' and the promise of death if ever found again in the Eastern (oil) province.

[11] In the battle of Siffin on the Euphrates, where in A.D. 657 in the civil war over the succession to the Caliphate, the army of the fourth Caliph, Ali, fresh from victories in Iraq, was defeated by the forces of the Omayyed Governor of Damascus, Muawiya, which advanced into battle with Korans tied to their lances. This appeal to the sanctity of the Koran was so effective that Ali's cause was lost, and four years later, Muawiya became Caliph, bringing about the transfer of the centre of Islamic power to Damascus, and the end of the elective Caliphate.

of Islam, and it now readily joined hands both with 'socialist' egalitarianism and with that older vein of 'French' Republicanism, enshrined in the Tunisian Constitution, which pronounces the republican form of government to be 'the best guarantee of human rights and the establishment of equality.' 'Could it be God's will that the King of Saudi Arabia should get an annual salary of £20 millions? Could it be God's will that the present monarch of Saudi Arabia should buy the abdication of ex-King Saud at a yearly salary of £20 millions?' asked Mohamed Hassenein Heikal in *Al Ahram in* 1966. It is unlikely that many members of Heikal's large Arab audience had much difficulty in supplying an answer.

And so 'the Voice of the Arabs' from Cairo contended with the 'Voice of Islam' from Riyadh, and every Arab capital added its urgent protestations to—in Gibbon's phrase—'the long quarrel of the East,' an interminable debate which in the Yemen and South Arabia now again received its customary punctuation by bullet and bomb, the terror and counter-terror of zealot and hired hand.

To the West it was apt to appear merely as a struggle for power. That it certainly was, but it was also much more than that. The men who struggled stood for ideas, social forms—even eras. It was the Great Debate of the West, transplanted on the Mediterranean's other shore, where the cry for equality between 'natives' and Westerners had proceeded logically to the demand for equality between natives. In the West, this long debate between 'genealogy and demography' had now been cushioned and blurred by a new abundance, and truncated by the dictates of the technology that produced it. In the East—though in Egypt technology was already tightening its grip on the argument—the whetting of appetites was still accompanied by an emptiness of stomachs and could be relied upon to keep the edge on the debate.

Oil Remakes a World

Another major revolutionary force was about to be unleashed over the Arab world. Oil and the Middle East have so long been linked in the public mind that it tends to escape attention that until the threshold of the 'fifties the impact of oil was in fact peripheral. Even Iraq, which had been producing oil commercially since 1927, had by 1951 reached a royalty income of only £13,700,000 a year. Saudi Arabia did not make its first oil shipment until 1938 and by 1950 had only worked up to an oil income of £20 million a year, in which year Kuwait reached £5 millions. But two years later, Kuwait's oil income was £60 million a year, and by 1954 the newly succeeded King Saud was receiving oil payments of over one million pounds a week. By 1961-2 both figures had trebled and were still rising.

Nor was the golden flow any longer confined to the Arab East. Visiting Libya in 1955, I found the numerous foreign experts preoccupied with the problem of how this new 'nation' ('deficitary to an extraordinary degree,' observed a United Nations report drily) with an almost wholly illiterate population of 1½ millions spread over a vast wilderness, could possibly support the apparatus of a modern state. Ten years later I found another set of experts hardly less preoccupied with the equal and opposite problem—of how to spend an enormous and rocketing oil income without totally disrupting the country in the process. In 1961, oil had begun to flow from the great Zelten field: a national budget of £4 millions had become one of £187 millions. And again there was a great deal more to come.

Westwards, the discovery of two rich oilfields and a natural gas field in the Sahara in 1956 had opened new horizons for Algeria, and by 1964 two pipelines were carrying the oil to the Mediterranean at Bougie and Skirra (Tunisia) and a third delivering natural gas to the £30 million CAMEL liquefaction plant at the small port of Arzew, east of Oran. By January, 1968, the first 100 million tons of Sahara crude had flowed down the pipelines to the Mediterranean and a second natural gas field had been discovered in the Sahara: that year oil revenues would amount to one-fifth of Algeria's total receipts.

More spectacularly yet, the great oil bonanza was moving from Kuwait (oil revenues over £200 million in 1964) down the Gulf. By 1962, the oil income of the sheikhdom of Qatar, a desert peninsula with a population of 40,000, had reached £20 million a year, and the Sheikh had duly offered a lifetime grant of £350 monthly to all members of the ruling tribe siring a male child. But the Sheikh of Qatar was soon to be left behind by the Sheikh of Abu Dhabi, and in 1964 oil was struck in Muscat and Oman. Meanwhile, with over 60 per cent of the world's known oil reserves already lying under Arab lands, prospecting goes ahead in the Gulf, in the Aden Protectorate, in Saudi Arabia, in Libya, in Egypt, in the Yemen, even in the Empty Quarter of the Great Central Desert of Arabia. The potential is still great; according to an I.M.F. estimate, Saudi production alone will double between 1963 and 1973, but already, in the single year 1967, the Saudi Arabian oilfields yielded the Saudi government an oil revenue of over £300 millions without taking into account the company's large local disbursements for services and wages.

The economic, social and political effects of this massive introduction both of capital and of an international science-based industry in a vast area of the Arab world are multiple, and only just beginning. As a creator of revolutionary situations, today's Arab oil flood in some respects leaves the coal-mines and mills of Engel's early Victorian Lancashire far behind.

In the classic case of Saudi Arabia, in the very heartland of Islam, the oil industry provided the country's first modern education and its first glimpse of Western standards of living. In a country in which 'son of an artisan' was an insult, Aramco had to find its first Saudi workers among the so-called 'ignoble tribes' (who, lacking pedigree, performed the menial tasks), while perforce relying mainly on imported labour. Yet by 1960 two-thirds of Aramco skilled and semi-skilled workers were Saudis. In a single generation individuals were moving from tribal nomadism to a very different and very new sort of Arab nomadism, the internationalism of oil workers. The reversal of values involved would probably take a generation to work through; but there could be no going back. And if no Saudi oil-workers' leader, valuing life and limb, yet judged it expedient to appear openly round the petroleum union table in Cairo, it is certain that many were already there in the spirit.

For if, from the 1920s onwards, the first effect of the appearance of oil in the Middle East was to hasten the drawing of frontiers, bringing the restless old Arab world to a halt, a much later effect—still gathering force in the 1960s—has been to

transcend those frontiers and set the Arab world—a transformed Arab world—once again in motion.

It was the smell of oil[12] as well as the British desire to protect the new kingdoms of Iraq and Transjordan against the
'holy' ferocity of Ibn Saud's Wahhabi warriors that had led to
the remarkable meeting called by Sir Percy Cox, British High
Commissioner at Baghdad, at Oqair on the Persian Gulf in
1922, and attended by Ibn Saud, a delegation of Iraqis, and a
representative of the sheikhdom of Kuwait. The meeting's
announced purpose was the delimitation of the frontiers of these
new neighbouring Arab 'states.' The Iraqi delegates asserted
that 'since God created the world' Iraq's boundaries had
stretched to within twelve miles of Riyadh, running down the
Red Sea coast as far as Medina and down the west coast of
the Gulf as far as Bahrein. Ibn Saud asserted that from the
days of Abraham, his ancestor, the boundaries of his Bedouin
had extended to Aleppo and included all the lands to the west
of the Euphrates down to Basra and the Gulf. The Sheikh of
Kuwait claimed a large part of the Hasa (Gulf west coast), but
since he had abandoned his foreign relations to the British
political agent, his claims were not advanced with the eloquence he could have desired.

After seven days of deadlock in the camp on the Gulf shore,
Sir Percy Cox seized a red pencil and traced a frontier line
westwards across the head of the Arabian peninsula, a thousand miles to Transjordan, including, as a sop to Arab obstin-
acy, two small neutral zones (which still exist) in which the
flocks of 'Iraqis' and 'Saudis' and 'Saudis' and 'Kuwaitis' could
enjoy equal sovereignty. Since the British were the paymasters
of all the parties, the Arabs acquiesced. But they did not
accept. For in the old Arab world of limitless space and movement and self-fulfilling grandiloquence, their claims appeared
to them not only just but self-evident.

There was, however, a fifth, uninvited, but by no means un-
noticed, representative at the conference at Oqair, a New
Zealander named Major Frank Holmes. Purportedly collecting
rare butterflies, Major Holmes was in fact intent on netting

[12] It had already resulted in the successful claim for a British 'sphere of
influence' in Central Persia.

oil concessions in a region where, as the seepages noted in the Kuwait desert and Bahrein suggested, they could well prove profitable. The frontier lines which the British had insisted on ruling across the empty desert were to acquire considerable significance for at least some of the Arabs present at Oqair.

But if the accountancy of oil played its part in the bizarre process of state-making in the Arab East, the technology and commercial logic and financial pressures of oil was later to thrust powerfully against those largely arbitrary boundaries. If the new frontiers—and the R.A.F.—halted the movements of flocks and raiders, the oilfields, now constituting the Arab world's biggest, most omnipresent and most modern industry, brought new Arab migrations—of teachers, and doctors and mechanics and oilfield workers and technicians and clerks, young educated Palestinians, Egyptians, Iraqis, Syrians, who transcended both the old tribal bounds and the new Western-made frontiers and also now possessed a common fund of experience and 'modern' 'democratic' ideas which loosely coincided with those expressed by the Egyptian Revolution.

The 'Kuwait Effect'

The explosive possibilities are well enough demonstrated in the 'model' oil state of Kuwait, roughly a hundred square miles of largely waterless desert, with a frontier line ruled around it and a fifth of the world's oil reserves beneath. As late as 1946 Kuwait was little more than a dhow port at the head of the Gulf and a meagre tribal camping ground with a local-born population that had dwindled to 37,000. Its sheikh had preserved his independence by signing in 1899 a treaty with the British, who undertook to protect him from the suzerain Turks and others in return for a large measure of control.

Since 'coming into oil,' the number of native-born Kuwaiti citizens has risen to 220,000 (1965). By paying out hundreds of millions in 'compensation' for land or property purchased for 'Kuwait development' (at prices reaching in the usual oil-spiral to £50 a square foot), the Ruling Family prudently turned many poor Kuwaitis into rich ones. Some penurious citizens transformed their fortunes by simply sticking markers in a patch of unclaimed desert, registering ownership at the land office, and selling out a few days later to the beneficent sheikhly government. Understandably, it was soon being estimated that there were more people enjoying million-dollar yearly incomes in Kuwait than in the U.S.A. Ultra-low-rent housing, sinecures, free schooling with clothes and pocket money thrown in, free well-equipped hospitals, together with the continual opportunity (confined to Kuwaitis) to rush out and buy shares in booming Kuwaiti companies, preserve the less rich from excessive envy.

The same can hardly be said of the relatively sophisticated non-Kuwaiti immigrants, mainly from other Arab countries, who make up more than half the population and provide the larger part of the essential skills and labour. (In 1967, for instance, there were still only a handful of Kuwaiti doctors working in Kuwait.) Well-paid these may be, but the Kuwaiti authorities leave little doubt as to who is the master and owner and who is the servant. Naturalisation for an Arab requires a minimum of ten years' residence, and by an Act of 1966, another twenty years must pass before the new citizen can vote! Meanwhile, 'Arab brothers' providing indispensable skills to Kuwait, find prospects of advancement barred by 'figurehead' Kuwaitis set over them, and they remain liable to deportation at three months' notice. At the same time the judicious naturalisation of visiting Bedouin tribesmen notoriously provides the government with a ready means of ensuring that, despite the existence of a vociferous 'Nasserite' Press and following, elections do not 'go wrong.'

In Kuwait oil has thus given a grotesque twist to the old Arab melodrama of riches and poverty, pashas and fellahin, but it has scarcely diminished its force. However Kuwait's super-welfare state may appear to Kuwaitis, to their Arab employees of all degree, who may come from Arab worlds of fathomless poverty, the enormously costly schools and colleges not fully utilised by the small (60 per cent illiterate) native population, with free study abroad available to all but the most backward Kuwaitis (from which only a small proportion appear to graduate), all this grandiose provision can hardly appear the best use of those 'Arab oil' resources which, by a freak of nature, happen to lie within the lines which Sir Percy Cox ruled across the desert forty-odd years ago.

The ruling Sabahs' answer has been both adroit and politically prudent. The Fund for Arab Economic Development, launched in 1962, has by now lent many millions to constructive projects in most Arab lands. But this, though an effective gesture, suggesting a way in which a rational Arab world might solve the problems created by Nature's caprice, still falls far short either as a measure of inter-Arab equity or of the planned employment of Arab resources in overall Arab development. After being doubled in 1966, the Fund for Arab Development totalled £200 millions. But in 1967 the cumulative total of Kuwait's oil wealth was £2,300 million and, according to an estimate by a London *Times* financial specialist, private Kuwaitis may well hold as much as £750 million in foreign investments. While the undeveloped world cries out for capital, a vast proportion of Arab oil money drains away to the West, where it can earn most in dividends and capital gains for its owners. Meanwhile, Kuwait contracted out of the Arab Common Market (for which it might have been the banker). Almost wholly untaxed, its fabulously rich get fabulously richer, the aura of the Welfare State competes, somewhat unequally, with that of the stockjobbing partnership; and into the great golden sump of Beirut drains the flight capital of old pasha and new oil sheikh alike, seeking the comforting anonymity of the numbered bank account and refuge from past, present and projected revolution.

But if Kuwait appears to be the *reductio ad absurdum* in the process of endowing various largely arbitrary areas with the apparatus of 20th-century national sovereignty, by the 1960s it was clear that it was not to be the ultimate one. Further south on the western shore of the Gulf lies the once negligible desertic Trucial sheikhdom of Abu Dhabi, whose 20,000 primitive inhabitants now enjoy (statistically) a *per capita* oil income even exceeding that of the citizens of Kuwait. In 1958, a great deal of oil was discovered off its desert shore; other rich fields have since been found, and by 1968 the 'state's' oil income had reached around £40 millions a year.

However, the ruling sheikh of Abu Dhabi, a simple soul, a poet, obstinately retained his sense of proportion. Remarking that 'few people bothered to visit me when I was poor,' he continued to sleep on the floor of his palace fortress and—plainly a trial to his British political officer—declined to invest his money abroad. By the spring of 1966 he had only succeeded in spending the pitiful sum of £2 millions. By August he had been neatly deposed and replaced by his younger brother Zaid, newly returned from a three-month grooming period at a Beaconsfield stately home, with shopping trips to British firms and a visit to the Royal Enclosure at Ascot where, according to a reporter, he appeared 'dressed in white robes set off with a jewelled dagger and brown Chelsea boots.'

Soon the contracts were being signed for a 'new capital' in the sand, with ring-roads, hospitals, schools, an electrification scheme, and the single hotel was packed with Lebanese businessmen paying £20 a night for their accommodation in hope of gaining an audience with the new Sheikh. Not having spent his weeks in Beaconsfield in vain, the Sheikh had engaged the services of a London public relations firm.[13]

Nor was this likely to be the end of what by now may surely be called 'the Kuwait Effect.' In 1966, oil strikes were reported in two more Trucial sheikhdoms, while further south, in the Sultanate of Muscat and Oman, oil, found in the interior in 1964, was brought into production in 1967. Oman has long had a formidable reputation as a wild and primitive land, closed to Europeans and torn by fanatic tribal feuding. This, however, did not deter the new 'Oil Sultan' from announcing that experts had been retained to prepare a plan for his twin coastal 'capitals' of Muscat (pop. 5,000) and Matrah (pop. 14,000) with public buildings, hospitals, schools, 'recreation areas and neighbourhood centres.' Perhaps he had retained a public relations man too.

But if this is comedy, it is tragi-comedy. For it has long been evident that the harnessing of these vast amounts of capital to an overall development plan for the Arab world, matching needs, capital, potential and existing capacities, could transform its situation and create a real instead of merely meta-

---

[13] A director of the firm concerned was the son of the Sir Charles Belgrave who, in 1926, was supplied by the India Office as Adviser to the Sheikh of Bahrein, continuing to serve the island until after the 'Belgrave Must Go!' troubles of 1956. Thus public relations man succeeds Adviser—an interesting and possibly suggestive footnote to the history of imperialism in decline.

physical Arab solidarity. Such an approach has not, however, been promoted by those Western Powers which, when not seeing the region wholly in terms of national strategic advantage (equated, despite all evidence to the contrary, with 'stability') have been unable to rise above a huckster's view of it as a Heaven-sent opportunity for quick sales of air-conditioned palaces, jet-fighters and banking services to whichever petty sheikh wakes up in the morning to discover that he has been sleeping on a fortune.

In default of such a broad approach, the effects of the oil rush are likely to be the more subversive in that the largest oil discoveries have unfailingly been made in the most primitive areas, least equipped to put the vast revenues to socially productive use. In the case of Abu Dhabi the point needs no labouring. But even within the vast wastes of Libya, the major oil finds so far have occurred in tribal Cyrenaica rather than in the relatively sophisticated 'Maghrebian' or Italianate Tripolitania, and it must surely be accounted one of the cruder jokes of history that the great bonanzas of both Libya and Saudi Arabia erupted in countries whose governments were founded on Islamic religious brotherhoods—the Senussi and the Wahhabi Orders—which make a central virtue of asceticism.[14]

It is true that in Libya, thanks to the presence under UN auspices of a large body of foreign advisers from the start, the country's first *nouveau riche* steps have been sensibly guided. On the 1950 Anglo-Iraqi model, 70 per cent of the oil royalties are placed at the disposal of a Development Council. Large sums have been allocated, in particular, to roads and public works. But, as Lord Salter warned ten years earlier in Iraq, however many millions are expended, there are strict limits to what engineers can do. In Libya, the sudden influx of money intensified rather than solved the country's immediate—basically human—problems. To turn the country's nomadic or semi-nomadic herdsmen into farmers (on the old

---

[14] The styles differed, however—since the founder of the one was a scholarly and cosmopolitan Algerian, personally revered as the 'Grand Senussi,' and of the other, a fierce and narrow Koranic fundamentalist. Both were missionary orders, but the one aggressive, plebeian and iconoclast, the other more educational, philosophic and faintly aristocratic.

Italian settlements and elsewhere) was even in 1955 a formidable task; after the oil boom, with so much easy money being
made in the towns, it became an almost impossible one. The
roseate hopes of the infant state of 1955 were drowned in the
great glut of the post-oil years. In 1955 there had been excited
talk of beating all comers with early vegetables for the
European markets; ten years later, the country was expensively
importing nearly all its vegetables and fruit (from Italy) and
much of its barley and other foods, although in fact capable
of both self-sufficiency and export. Up on the Barce plateau
of the fertile *Jebel Akhdar* (Green Mountain) sheep and goats
still nibbled away at still unfenced crops; but the sheep too
were threatened now, not by advancing agriculture but by oil
as the herdsmen and country people flooded into the town.
Oil, however, could only employ a small number (perhaps
20,000), and if building and much else cried out for labour,
the labour required was skilled—or at least the hard and steady
work for which near-Bedouins have small appetite. A lean
herdsman, moving with his tribe in search of sparse grazing,
is one thing; an unemployed—or strictly unemployable—individual going hungry and homeless in town as prices and wages
soar suffers deprivation of a very different—and more dangerous—order.

The thrusting foreign companies inevitably outbid whatever
the services of the nascent Libyan state can offer, and the university students—desperately needed as teachers—rush off to
highly paid work in the oil companies as soon as they graduate. As millions (in addition to the royalty payments) are
poured out by the oil companies yearly on local services and
materials, a few Libyans become immensely rich, and generally (though not always) these are those who were well-placed
to start with. And, as in pre-revolutionary Egypt, the rich show
little inclination to invest productively in industry. The joke
goes that the Senussi family has become a business: a brotherhood, a plutocracy.

No one says that sort of thing of *the* Senussi, King Idris himself, and it is perhaps due to the steady, if invisible, influence
of this scholarly and ascetic old man that, though Libyan
politics are inevitably the politics of money, the scandals
do not quite reach the heights of those in Saudi Arabia,

where, from 1950 onwards, the oil millions were poured into
an even more primitive and inadequate social structure—with
the result, as David Howarth remarks in his recent study of
Ibn Saud, that 'men who stole a sheep were mutilated, while
those who stole hundreds of thousands of pounds went free.'

Whose Oil?

In the decade and a half following the Egyptian revolution
the social and political pressures generated by the Oil Boom
were further multiplied by major changes of approach and
structure within the international oil industry itself. It was,
in short, transformed in the Arab world from the old 'imperialist' form in which it had been confined to a few great 'mono-
polistic' companies to a free-for-all with competing bidders of
many nationalities.

In the earlier days, the subversive world of oil could be
segregated in some wired-off enclave. Ensconced within this
'state-within-a-state' such a pioneer concern as the Iraq
Petroleum Company, although in fact a consortium of companies of four nations, was able to sustain an attitude of lofty
statesmanship, and even to act, with some conviction, the
rôle of Benefactor of the Arabs. But in 1951, the Arabian-
American Oil Company (Aramco) made its 50/50 profit-sharing
agreement with Saudi Arabia. Undertaken at a critical juncture
in the post-war history of the Middle East—in the year of the
British retreat from the Persian oilfields, the year before the
Egyptian revolution—this was possibly the most important
action taken by America in this area before the advent of John
Foster Dulles (and it was taken, ostensibly, not by the Government but by a commercial concern). It broke the front maintained by the big oil companies in a world which still looked
back, as point of reference, to the classic 16 per cent agreement of the D'Arcy (Anglo-Iranian) oil concession of 1909
(revised upwards after Persian resort to the League of Nations
in 1933).

By the time Nasser (after studying a Chicago University
treatise) was writing the pregnant couple of pages on the
unique cheapness and quantity of Arab petroleum in his
Philosophy of the Revolution, that commodity was leaving the

world of old-style economic imperialism and preparing to enter that of open market bargaining—an exercise at which Arabs are not without experience. No fewer than forty-six oil companies competed in bidding for oil concessions in Libya in 1966. The rigs and installations of a dozen nations are scattered about the Arab world—and they now include those of state-controlled concerns as well as of an Asian nation, Japan (in the Gulf and Benghazi). Now even Iraq has broken from the IPC's grip to start its own national oil company and to admit the oil-men of Russia and France, and Saudi Arabia, so long the domain of Aramco, in 1967, through the State concern Petromin, concluded a far-reaching partnership agreement with the Italian state oil concern, Agip, and Phillips.

The effect is both to enhance the position of the Arab nations vis-à-vis the West, and also to enhance the position of technocrat and technician within the Arab nations. For, increasingly, in this 'liberated' oil world, the Arab nations' own petroleum organisations have infiltrated the field, whether in the form of supervising ministries, national companies—increasingly an Arab status symbol—with varying percentages of Government shareholding, joint exploration agreements, or Government-planned and financed petro-chemical complexes.

And this is the world—of technology and politics—of the young petroleum trade unionists gathered around the table in Cairo's Arab Petroleum Institute. It may be a grandiloquent name for a converted suburban villa, yet the idea it represents is not small. For these young men, all oil workers in one way or another, gathered together in Cairo from over the vast expanse of the Arab world between Rabat and Baghdad, Aleppo and Aden, represent perhaps the most contemporary form of 'Arab Unity,' and one which could yet prove the most far-reaching. It might be true that the larger part of the £E1,000 million or so paid out in that year 1965 to the Arab countries in oil dues had found its way into the pockets of what the young men would undoubtedly call 'feudal' sheikhs, ruling families and their eager clients. It might also be true that, in alliance with international capitalism and international oil companies, operating through 'joint' national organisations, these anachronistic rulers might be capable of formidable renovation. Yet the fact remained that since this was, by general insistence, an Arab world, it was the Arab oil workers' world and not the sheikhs', because only they could operate it and they would not remain content for ever with a sort of chromium-plated slavery without political rights.

The Kuwaitis, for instance, might seek to keep their vast oil wealth for themselves and lucrative foreign investment. But Kuwait could not continue without the Arab outsiders who made up two-thirds of her labour force, and the more she developed, the more dependent she would become.[15] Libya was likewise chronically frustrated by a shortage of suitable labour. She could find it readily 'next door,' in overcrowded Egypt. But because of fears of political contamination, the Senussi régime narrowly controlled the numbers of Egyptians admitted. Again, it was evident that sooner or later either the social and political price of 'industrialisation' would have to be paid—or the flood of oil money, not productively employed, would corrupt and destroy the state as surely as the much smaller cotton booms corrupted and destroyed Egypt between Ismail and Farouk.

If technocracy backed by political organisation and trade unions might yield an adequate social frame for the new Arab states, technocracy backed merely by tribal loyalty would not. Technology demanded sophisticated education; science imported sceptical and radical attitudes of mind, and the students who returned from abroad were scornful of traditional authority. The relative political quiescence of the 'traditionalist' countries has so far owed much to their vast spaces and sparse population. Yet this too is a diminishing asset as, via the oilfields and in other ways, 'modernisation' intrudes. In Saudi Arabia Feisal had at first relied on enlarging and motorising the *Jaish al Abayda* (the White Army), a 30,000-strong national guard drawn from the tribes, and 'notable for its extraordinary mobility and the great respect which its appearance in various parts of the country can generate in local populations which might contemplate resistance to public authority.'[16] But a modern state requires regular armed forces, and these, with their educated officers, notoriously lack the

[15] See Report of Mission of Bank of International Reconstruction, 1965.
[16] *Saudi Arabia*, by G. A. Lipsky and others, HRAF Press, New Haven, 1959, a survey sponsored by Yale and sixteen other U.S. universities.

'political reliability' of tribesmen—as some officers of the Saudi Air Force have already demonstrated.[17] The sophisticated jet fighters, radar defences, surface-to-air missiles which Feisal, stimulated by the revolution in the Yemen, was in 1966 purchasing from Britain and America might yet prove a greater threat internally than all the external 'revolutionary' enemies against whom they were deployed. The more the country was opened up the more it must be exposed to this contagion; roads have a central place in the Saudi development plan, but they are roads that lead out of Saudi Arabia as well as across it.

But unfortunately for the young Libyan oil worker who wished to achieve Arab Unity by bringing together the Arab workers and overthrowing the Arab 'feudalists,' discontinuities in the Arab world rarely favour so simple an approach. The debate is cut about by so many cross-currents that to many in the East, as well as in the West, its outlines are inevitably blurred. The simple confrontation of family and people, reaction and revolution, modernity and tradition, is at one point cut across by the feuding of Baath Socialists and Nasser Socialists, dating from 1958, and, at the next—as in the Yemen or Iraq—by the muted antagonisms of Shia and Sunni dating from A.D. 654. And in Beirut the debate comes under verbal cross-winds from leader-writers of no fewer than thirty daily newspapers, subsidised by a dozen or more busy embassies, offering almost as many versions of the transcendental truth. Here the trade unions—the only 'free' ones in the Arab world according to one proud American-Lebanese—belong, according to persuasion, to no fewer than three rival international federations—the (pan-Arab) Arab Trade Union Federation, the (communist-controlled) WFTU, the ('Free World') ICFTU. (The Lebanese hotel and restaurant workers, for instance, are split between two separate hotel unions, one affiliated to the ICFTU, the other to the WFTU.)

As Beirut bears witness, much of the Middle East's chronic

---

[17] During the 'Republicans v. Royalists' war in the Yemen, backed by Egypt on one side and Saudi Arabia on the other, some Saudi Arabian Air Force pilots went on strike, and others flew their arms cargoes straight to Cairo, according to the U.N. Commander in the Yemen, General Carl von Horn, *Soldiering for Peace* (1966).

confusion still derives from far beyond its bounds. Although missionary ardour has flagged somewhat since the days of Mr Dulles, the rival churches of Washington and Moscow still contribute their missile-underlined dogmas to enrich the older —merely gun-toting—contentions of Maronite Christian, Druse, and Sunni Muslim. Even reduced as it was, the British presence in Aden and the Gulf, the British and American bases in Libya, the Russian backing for Syria and Egypt, and the American backing for Saudi Arabia and Jordan, did much to sustain the debate at fever pitch. Behind the 'feudalist' the young Arab trade unionist still discerned the 'imperialist' and, behind the imperialists, their agents the Zionists, now powerfully entrenched in the Arab world and buttressed by a ceaseless flow of American dollars.

And here the character of the debate might change abruptly. For in the face of the Zionist challenge class solidarity was apt to be swallowed up in the solidarity of all Arabs, and the darkest feudalist to be transformed into an Arab Patriot and Brother. Nevertheless, in the autumn of 1967 a swift sequence of events on the southern periphery of the Arab world suggested that the theme of the 'unfinished revolution,' if much overlaid, was in little danger of being abandoned.

Aden Becomes South Yemen

In November 1903, Lord Curzon, then Viceroy of India, paid a state visit to the Trucial Coast sheikhdoms and Kuwait and there delivered a speech. There were, he said, persons who had been asking why Great Britain should continue to exercise the powers that she did in the Gulf. He himself had not a moment's doubt of the answer. 'We were here before any other power, in modern times, had shown its face in these waters. We found strife and we have created order. . . . We saved you from extinction at the hands of your neighbours. . . . We opened these seas to the ships of all nations and enabled their flags to fly in peace. . . . The peace of these waters must be maintained . . . the influence of the British Government must remain supreme. . . . We shall not wipe out the most unselfish page in history.'

By November 1967, there were, alas, many more who asked

the question which had called forth Lord Curzon's eloquence, but there were now few indeed who could return Lord Curzon's ringing answer. Britain's 'Lawrentian' policy of building up members of the Islamic 'nobility' or tribal sheikhs into national Kings and Rulers had long outlived its usefulness. But possibly because it made a deep appeal to the romantic conservatism of so many Britons, it had been doggedly persisted in—with the result that, by the 'sixties, the British arrangements in the Gulf and around the southern shores of the Arabian peninsula for the preservation of numerous petty sheikhs (frequently representing no one but their own families) inevitably appeared to educated Arabs at best anachronistic, at worst, evidence of neo-colonialist conspiracy. (Either way, it promoted in the Arab world the polarisation towards the extremes of Right and Left.)

In the mid-'fifties, it is true, the classic British approach was a little modified. By mingling, in the federal council of a South Arabian Federation, inaugurated in 1962, elected representatives of Aden Town and the sheikhs (or 'sultans') of the twenty-three up-country 'states,' it was hoped that the sheikhs would ballast Adeni 'extremism' while the Adeni merchants would educate the frequently somewhat primitive sheikhs, thus achieving the twin desiderata of stability and progress. Alas, other interpretations of these arrangements were possible and the young men of Adan swiftly arrived at them. The familiar colonial tragedy of 'too-little-and-too-late' was now played out again at a hectic pace. By the time the representatives of the Crown had come round to the view that some 'subversive' merchant nationalist was, in fact, in the new Arab perspective a conservative, if not a reactionary, leadership would have passed to more radical elements. As the British conscientiously sought to ensure order and an effective Constitution preparatory to their departure, scheduled for 1968, the political battle shifted to the streets, and was fought with bullets and bombs as well as words.

In the spring of 1967, with the aid of a United Nations mission, Britain at last determined to recognise current political realities in at least this portion of the Arab world. But almost to the end she was negotiating with the Protectorate's sheikhs on the size of the British armed forces which they considered necessary to protect them before they could safely accede to the new Federal constitution. Then, suddenly, the sheikhs were dropped, and, several weeks in advance of the announced date, Britain had gone from Aden.

She left behind her no agreed, working constitution. She had capitulated to the power of one more National Liberation Front, the names of whose leaders were hardly known. It might be said—as many Adenis would certainly have said—that Britain had in effect, capitulated to the Arab Revolution. Portraits of President Nasser floated over the wildly rejoicing crowds who gathered in Aden on 26 November 1967 to celebrate the birth of a new Arab state, the People's Republic of South Yemen. In fact, the Egyptians had supported, not the NLF but its bitter rival-in-revolution, the Front for the Liberation of Occupied South Yemen. Nevertheless there can have been few present that day to whom the symbolic presence of Gamal Abdel Nasser did not seem both just and necessary. The ideas and pattern of the 'South Yemen' revolution were in the main those that had emerged in Egypt. The leaders of the new republic were from neither the merchant nor the sheikhly class. They tended to be, in the inadequate British terms, 'lower-middle-class,' middling civil servants, teachers, technicians, officers, men mainly in their 'thirties, well educated, but of relatively humble up-country origins. Somewhat older than the rest, the new President, Qahtan as-Shaabi, had gone to an Islamic school in a small sheikhdom, later graduating from the Agricultural Faculty of Khartoum University, and serving as an agricultural officer in Lahej state which bordered on Aden.

The new government, which made 'collective leadership' a watchword, proceeded to confiscate the property of thirteen sultans, thirteen sheikhs, fifty emirs, and other members of the *ancien régime*, setting up a committee to administer it. It promised a social revolution, and, as an earnest of this, renamed the old federal capital *Medina as-Shaab*, 'the People's City.' It announced its intention to pursue 'positive neutralism' in foreign policy, and presumably to establish this point, opened negotiations for aid 'without strings' with both Britain and Russia. Elsewhere, said Qahtan as-Shaabi, the new régime was committed to the general aims of the Arab Revolution of which they were a part.

It proclaimed the 'natural unity of the Yemen,' proffered aid to the 'North Yemen,' and in January 1968 claimed that its army was fighting alongside the Yemen republican forces 'against the "common enemy" sultanic and feudalistic elements.' By November 1967 the Egyptian army had withdrawn from the Yemen, but so had the British from Aden, and, looking well ahead, it might be said that the emergence of republican South Yemen at last promised to supply the precarious Yemen revolution with its missing revolutionary class. 'South Yemen' possessed no oil so far and only the slenderest of resources, but geographically the new republic enjoyed a notable position, with the only good harbour on the whole vast length of Arabia's southern shore, an asset now underlined by the British transfer of the islands of Kamaran and Perim, the latter commanding the narrow straits at the entrance to the Red Sea.

In the vast Arabian peninsula the confrontation of conservative and revolutionary, of 'monarchist' and 'republican'— of Sacred Past and Boundless Future—continued. Yet here, too, in the perspective of history these years may appear as a watershed. For in its impact on the Yemen in the reign of the 66th Imam Egypt's five-year-long occupation echoed the rude awakening brought by the Napoleonic occupation to Egypt itself. The Egyptian Army, like the French, took along its mission of 'savants'—doctors, agriculturalists, engineers, 225 teachers, 100 scholars of El Azhar. Many Yemenis gained their first experience of modern medicine. Hundreds of primary schools appeared in the villages; three vocational and three secondary schools in the towns. Two thousand young Yemenis were sent abroad to study. The country got its first daily newspaper, a 14 hours a day radio service, and a national bank. The administration ceased to be the monopoly of the religious aristocracy. A regular 7,000-strong army was brought into being. The Americans gave the town of Taiz the first pure piped water supply in the country; the Chinese provided a textile factory; and Chinese, Russians and Americans built a series of roads opening up the interior to the coasts, and bringing the tribesmen swinging down out of the mountains into town.[18] In 1967 the Egyptians evacuated Yemen, as in 1961 they had

[18] Dana Adams Smith : Yemen—the Unknown War, London, 1968.

evacuated Syria; but upon the Arabian peninsula, as upon Syria and Iraq, the Egyptian revolution had left its ineffaceable mark.

For the camp of the Arab traditionalists, further shocks were to come. Withdrawing from Aden to new bases in the Gulf, Britain now announced the firm intention to vacate these also by the end of 1971. In this transformed world, the best safeguard of 'our oil supplies' was now seen to lie in the Arab countries need to sell them.

A great deal of very empty space separates the Gulf oil sheikhdoms from the revolutionary centres of the Arab world. But it no longer insulates them. Certainly the British announcement of withdrawal seems to have clarified the minds of the Gulf sheikhs with remarkable speed. Jealous rivals who had for years resisted British attempts to induce them to come together in larger territorial units now suddenly discovered the overwhelming attractions of federation. After the sheikh of Abu Dhabi's initial offer to pay for the continued presence of the British army out of the oil money had met with a pained reception in Whitehall, the seven Trucial Coast sheikhs and the sheikhs of Qatar and Bahrein held a meeting and resolved to form a union. The sheikh of Bahrein also announced a plan to build a causeway joining his island to Saudi Arabia. But, although his proposal met with no support, it seems possible that the greatest foresight of all was displayed by the Ruler of the small—and still oil-less—'state' of Ras al Khaimah, who suggested that the new federation of sheikhdoms—already being enthusiastically hailed in the Cairo Press as 'the fifteenth Arab State'—should be a Republic.

26

AN EXCESS OF MANIFEST DESTINY

'I wish my Arabic was as good as yours,' said Joseph. 'What
was the old sheikh explaining so solemnly?'
'He explained that every nation has a right to live according
to its fashion, right or wrong, without outside interference.
He explained that money corrupts, that fertiliser stinks, and
tractors make a noise, all of which he dislikes.'
'And what did you answer?'
'Nothing.'
'But you saw his point of view?'
Bauman looked at him steadily: 'We cannot afford to see the
other man's point of view.'

—Arthur Koestler, *Thieves in the Night: the Chronicle of an
Experiment*, 1948

This was indeed the whole problem of Palestine: it was inhabited.

—Christopher Sykes, *Crossroads to Israel*, 1963

Dr Chaim Weizmann, who combined in his person in an extraordinary way the Oriental feeling for continuity and tradition and the brisk radicalism of Western science, liked to think
of his reborn Zion as a sort of pilot-plant of a revivified, industrialising, democratising, science-backed Middle East, a yeast
which, as in one of his own more momentous experiments,
would inaugurate long and intricate processes of molecular re-
arrangement, progressive and world-changing.

In a sense, something of this has happened, although not at
all, one imagines, in the way that Weizmann—a humane man
—visualised. We cannot, of course, know what the Arab East
would look like today had the political Zionists accepted—as
their founder, the Viennese-Hungarian journalist Herzl, proposed that they should—the British offer made in 1903 of
Uganda as a Jewish haven, or had Weizmann failed to secure

in 1917 the Balfour Declaration promising a 'national home' in Palestine. It is an interesting speculation, but wholly academic. For probably the most important historical process in the Middle East since the passing in 1918 of the Ottoman Empire has been the process then installed at the geographical heart of the Arab East in which a rising Arabism has been ground and honed over the years against a hardening Zionism. For this ardent interaction of two branches of the Semitic 'race' possessed an inwardness and a continuity which the struggle against French and British imperialisms lacked; and it has persisted after they have failed.

In 1920, when Palestine was a barren and somnolent relic of the Ottoman empire, such Arab nationalism as existed was, in the main, either of the romantic-apocalyptic type or the older, fiercer, Muslim xenophobic variety. Egyptian nationalism, if more mature, was insular. But already, in 1921, after the Arab-Jewish riots in Jaffa—stimulated by Zionist claims and by an early bout of Jewish illegal immigration and arms-smuggling[1]—the new High Commissioner for Palestine, Sir Herbert Samuel, was noting a growing political consciousness among the Arabs. This he and succeeding High Commissioners, and a great host of politically sophisticated Zionist immigrants, were to extend in many ways—for the Jaffa Riots were merely the beginning of an interminable series of conflicts between Arab and Jew in Palestine which would continue over the next quarter of a century.

Arab resistance, in turn, strengthened Zionist extremism. By 1929, the Zionist Congress at Zurich was listening to unequivocal calls for a National State with a Jewish majority, while in the Old City of Jerusalem Jewish youths unfurled the 'national' flag at the Wailing Wall. Two years later, as the Zionist threat brought together Christians and Muslims, transcending both the old social and the new national frontiers, Arab Palestine got its first modern political party, the pan-Arab Istiqlal. In Egypt the Palestine Cause became the leading motif of Hassan el Banna, leader of the Muslim Brethren, enabling his movement to spread rapidly, and to strike deep.

The great strength of the Jewish immigrants was that they

---

[1] Christopher Sykes, *Crossroads to Israel* (London, 1965).

had already experienced, in Europe, the social revolution the Arabs still lacked. But when Arab landlords sold out to the Zionists for high prices, and left their peasant tenants and herdsmen to be cleared off their lands, they demonstrated the need for a social, as well as a nationalist, revolution in the Arab world as well. The Arab Palestine rebellion of 1936 (set off by increased Jewish immigration) began with strikes which much alarmed Arab traditionalists; and when the belated social revolution did arrive in the Arab world, in Egypt in the 1950s, it was, as we have seen, speeded and deepened by each major crisis in the Arab-Israeli conflict—by the Arab débâcle of 1948-9, the Gaza Raid of 1955, the Israeli 'preventive' assault of 1956. The Anglo-French backing of Israel in 1956 was the last straw which finally broke up the old Anglo-Arab world.

In yet another way the Zionist presence in Palestine forced the pace of Arab development. The terms of the British Mandate mirrored the basic requirement of the Balfour Declaration that nothing should be done 'which may prejudice the civil and religious rights' of the non-Jewish communities. Since the Jews had refused to co-operate in common Palestinian schools, the British Mandatory Government felt obliged to seek to match for the Arabs the ardent Jewish-financed efforts in education and agriculture. The result, assisted by Arab service with the Mandatory administration, was the creation of a substantial body of educated, progressive Arab Palestinians—another significant East-West human synthesis to supplement the French-educated Syrians, the mercantile Lebanese, and the British and French-schooled Egyptians. Uprooted by the 1948-9 war, those notably un-feudal and often enterprising Palestinians were to become, as the Diaspora of the oilfields and elsewhere, natural carriers of the gospel of social revolution and Nasserism. (Over five thousand of them were being employed as teachers in Saudi Arabia in 1969.)

But the price of this process has been high and may prove ruinous. If the development of the Arab East was stimulated by the Zionist intrusion, it was also violently distorted. First because of Arab boycott, then because of Jewish boycott (until a Jewish majority should be available), a generation of Arab Palestinians at this critical point in time and place was deprived of the constructive potentialities of repre-

sentative government.[2] After the emergence, in war, of the
enlarged state of Israel in 1948-9, the Middle East was once
again clamped in the iron jacket of the *status quo* which had
cramped its development ever since a moribund Turkey had
begun to be bolstered by the Western Powers. A festering
sense of injustice was implanted in vast numbers of Arabs,
educated and primitive alike. A conviction of betrayal and a
deepening despair fed the more negative aspects of the Arab
character. Most disastrously of all, the Arabs—both Muslim
and Christian now—were again alienated from the West, and
East and West locked in a vicious circle of mutual ignorance,
misrepresentation and distrust.

To the Westerner, the notion of the creation and expansion
of Israel as presenting evidence of 'Anglo-American imperialist
conspiracy' appears grotesque.[3] But anyone who will take the
trouble to examine objectively the long, sustained, and finally
exultant, course of deception—conscious and unconscious—
to which the Arab inhabitants of Palestine and Syria were sub-
jected over the years, will see that, to an Arab, it may well
appear the only feasible explanation of the extraordinary
course of events in the half century since the Balfour Note.

'Examine Mr Balfour's careful words,' Winston Churchill,
then Colonial Secretary, told protesting Palestine Arab leaders
in 1921, 'Palestine is to be "a national home" (for the Jews)
not "the national home"—a great difference in meaning. The
establishment of a national home does not mean a Jewish
Government to dominate the Arabs.' It was the first of how
many such assurances, right down to 1946, when the Anglo-
American Committee on Palestine—even as it broke the undertakings of the White Paper of 1939 by favouring the immediate admission of the 100,000 Jews—promised that 'Jews shall

---

[2] In 1935 the British Mandatory Government offered a Legislative Council
of eleven Muslims, seven Jews, three Christians, two commercial representatives, and a non-Palestinian chairman. But although their representation
exceeded the proportion their numbers indicated, the Zionists rejected the
offer. Only a Jewish majority would now suffice.

[3] In point of fact, there is plenty of evidence that the idea that a Jewish
colony in Palestine would provide a politically reliable base for Britain
in the Middle East was a factor in securing the Balfour Note: in 1947
Congressman Sol Bloom, chairman of the U.S. Senate Foreign Relations
Committee, advised President Truman to recognise Israel in order to keep
Palestine and the Near East from Soviet domination.

not dominate Arabs and Arabs shall not dominate Jews in a Palestine which shall be neither a Jewish State nor an Arab State.'

By 1947 it was as if all these solemn, multiple undertakings had never been. Weakened by the war, battered by the fury of the Zionists, now inextricably entangled in the vast web of equivocation spun from the original Balfourian verbal duplicity, Britain in Palestine was morally and physically bankrupt. In April, she threw her Mandate back into the lap of the United Nations. But even before that President Truman, although unwilling to commit 'a single American soldier' to the task of peace-making in Palestine, had in effect taken over. Totally unburdened by Britain's pledges to the Arabs, he cheerfully over-rode both his State and his Defence Departments to press the claims of the Jews to immediate and massive entry into the Holy Land. The fate of Palestine now became a counter in the American political contest, and the Arabs could look on from afar as the American party leaders bid against each other for the Jewish vote and for the Jewish campaign contributions. To a group of perturbed American diplomats gathered from the Middle East, the President explained his difficulties: 'I am sorry, gentlemen, but I have to answer to hundreds of thousands who are anxious for the success of Zionism. I do not have hundreds of thousands of Arabs among my constituents.'[4] Economically, the new state of Israel was, and remained, dependent on the United States, its build-up and vast immigration programme sustained from afar, year after year, by massive, tax-free subventions from American Jewry.

The plight of the Jewish survivors from the Nazi concentration camps rightly aroused the compassion of the world. But the Arabs were unable to see why it should be they who should be elected to suffer—and to lose one's land and home is to suffer—to purge Europe's guilt, particularly since at this time America's own immigration laws still very narrowly restricted the entry of Jewish refugees into that vast, rich country;[5] and

[4] Col W. F. Eddy, former U.S. Ambassador to Saudi Arabia: *FDR Meets Ibn Saud* (1954). There is ample documentation indicating the critical importance of the Jewish vote in these matters. Cf., for instance, the *Forrestal Diaries* (1952) and the references to 'top Jewish leaders putting all sorts of pressure on me', etc., in *The Truman Memoirs* (1956).

particularly since in 1950, Israel took Zionism to its logical conclusion by enacting the Law of Return, enshrining the
fundamental doctrine of the Ingathering and conferring on all
the 12½-million or so Jews in the world the right to 'return'
to Palestine. By 1964 the population of Israel had reached 2½
millions, 88 per cent Jewish. While the new Jewish immigrants, financed by German reparation payments and American funds, moved onto abandoned Arab property ('one of the
greatest contributions to making Israel a viable state,' writes
Mr Don Peretz) a million or so Palestinian refugees, barred
from their land, languished in tents and mud hovels.

'Israel, for the Jews,' Mr Walter Eytan, her Ambassador in
Paris, has said, 'represents the stored-up anguish of two
thousand years.' But by 1967 that small area of land represented a good deal of stored-up anguish for the Arabs also.
What was worse, the wall of distrust between Arab and Jew
had become a wall between East and West also.

When in 1945 the Arab world was confronted by the
American-backed Zionist demand for the immediate entry into
Palestine of 100,000 Jews, the Egyptian Secretary-General of
the Arab League, Abdur Rahman Azzam, warned the Western
nations that by supporting it they would launch a 'new
Crusaders' war.' And inflated as this description might seem,
it was not inapt. For the Arabs remembered, if the West had
forgotten, that the Arab-Zionist struggle for Palestine was not
a unique event, but merely one more chapter in the long, often
violent, curiously obsessional dialogue between East and West
that Gibbon called the 'World's Debate.'

Sir Steven Runciman has related how the protracted strain
of containing, then repelling, the Crusaders shattered the old
relaxed and tolerant Islamic world beyond repair, and how,
as the main seats of civilisation shifted from Constantinople
and Cairo to the West, 'the Muslims enclosed themselves

---

[5] It was not true that the Jewish refugees had 'no other place to go' than
Palestine. But the Zionist movement strenuously obstructed efforts to provide alternative homes. See A. M. Lilienthal: *What Price Israel?* (Chicago,
1953) for an instructive account, via the New York lawyer, Morris Ernst,
of how Roosevelt's project for settling 150,000 refugees in the U.S. as part
of a world resettlement scheme was torpedoed by U.S. Zionist pressures.

behind the curtain of their faith.'

Once again, a wave of invaders out of the West shattered the relaxed tolerance of the old Levantine world, and once again, the Arab world, feeling betrayed and humiliated, withdrew within itself. Yet the parallel was ·of limited validity. The new militant pilgrims from the West came seeking not the Holy Places of Christendom, but the relics of Solomon's Temple; they were already of the East, using a language of the East, although owing much of their strength to their long sojourn in the West, and conspicuously possessed of that 'peculiar energy of character . . . active and imitative spirit unknown to their more polished rivals in the Islamic East' which Gibbon (whose words these are) singles out as the reason for the rise of the West and the long ragged decline of the East that followed the Crusades.

Ironically, Zionism, which rejected assimilation, was able to achieve the progress it did because of the success of Jewish assimilation in the West. No movement in history ever had such a world-wide network of powerful agents, wealthy backers, well-placed, sophisticated propagandists, or influential friends. The Arabs, looking on, were able to observe how on almost every critical occasion the Zionist cause was able to command the support of a key Western figure—Balfour, the British Foreign Minister, the 'ardent Zionist' (his own description) of 1917; Churchill in 1921, and again in 1940, when he supported the idea of a Jewish Army which eventually emerged as the Jewish Brigade; Wingate, who, with his 'Special Night Squads' gave the Jews an effective military method and tradition; above all, President Truman.

But if the Jews, returning to Palestine, drew vital sustenance from their widespread branches in the West, these years were to show that their roots in the East were still deep and alive. When it came to the point it was found that there ran in the most sophisticated and assimilated of Jews the same electric communion with the *Yishuv*, the Jewish People, as linked all Muslims, under challenge, to the Muslim *Omma*; with its different idiom, the Jewish apocalyptic notion of the Ingathering, now enshrined in Zionism, echoed the Muslim obsession with 'Arab Unity' or a 'return' to the lost 'Arab Nation.' Jews and Arabs alike remained uniquely 'People of the Book,' as the

Muslims say, made and identified by it, its revealed texts woven into the fabric of their cultures, conforming to its social and moral laws—Talmud for Sharia, Torah for Koran—re-enacting the heroic story of their people's mission in such still vital and central observances as the Feast of the Passover and the Fast of Ramadan. That 'nostalgia, hope and precariousness' which Jacques Berque identifies as the dimensions of Arab life might be detected in Jewish life too. And for both the nostalgia is, or has been, a cherished, an indispensable, a ritual nostalgia— for Jerusalem before its destruction, or for the Golden Age of the Ommayyeds.

Such affinities are hardly to be wondered at, for if the dialogue of Arab and Jew has now become a part of the long debate of East and West, its beginnings long preceded it. In its very emergence, Islam was deeply involved with those Jewish clans of Arabia, and, in particular, of Medina, which although reduced to the status of clients of the Arabs, were set apart by their possession of a Scripture and a Law. Mohamed had at first insisted that his Koranic revelation rehearsed and reinforced the messages of Moses and Jesus, and until A.D. 624 the Muslims, when they prayed, turned towards Jerusalem. But when the Jewish rabbis scorned the would-be new prophet, derided his revelation and (according to the Koran, Surah II, verse 94) continued to assert that Paradise was reserved for Jews, the uneasy alliance broke up. The Muslims, when they prayed, now turned to Mecca, but still towards the Kaaba which was reputed to be Abraham's Temple; and the Prophet charged the Jews with 'deviation,' with 'altering and concealing' the truth about the 'religion of Abraham' of which the Koran was henceforth to be considered the only uncorrupted version.

But if 'the people of Allah' and 'the people of Jehovah' now took their separate ways, both retained in a high degree the consciousness of unique, God-given appointments with Destiny: of having been unalterably Chosen. And 1,500 years later, Arabism and Zionism were still in a curious and complex way opposite faces of the same coin, still rival proprietors of a single indivisible Truth, as fatally interlocked as Israel and Jordan when the 1949 armistice frontier wound its way through the Judaean hills, slicing through ancient Jordanian villages and their lands. If Zionism stimulated Arab development, it was hardly less true that Arabism in its turn powerfully served Zionism. Ben Gurion has explained how it was Arab hostility that really forced the pace of Jewish agricultural expansion and—for instance—the development of the new city of Tel Aviv instead of Haifa; without it, he says, Israel might have become 'merely a Jewish Carthage' with 'weak roots.'

Although it seems that both parties would die rather than admit it, there is, in fact, a striking parallelism not only between the problems of Israel and those of Egypt, but also, since the Nasserian revolution, between the policies and philosophies adopted to meet them. Both countries face a formidable demographic challenge, Israel from immigration, Egypt from natural growth, and both have found in it a central dynamic, responding with heroic, Nature-transforming measures. Both offer an ardent popular nationalism, with an ancient religious base, which their theorists have endeavoured to transfigure by a somewhat Messianic socialism and by the strenuous tasks of nation-building. For both, favoured instruments have been institutionalised trade unions (closely linked with government), equalitarian incomes policies, co-operatives and collectives, public ownership (with an attempt at workers' participation). Sometimes the parallels are very close; Israel, for instance, has at Tel Aviv a university whose special mission—'the integration of the wisdom of the Torah and modern knowledge'—almost exactly corresponds to the mission of the new El Azhar. Both Israel and Egypt proclaim faith in science, faith in God, and a mission to 'build the nation' and erase past humiliations by such feats as conquering the desert. Both states face problems of cultural assimilation (complicated in Israel by language); both are heavily dependent on capital loans and gifts, look to the future for solvency and in the present face chronic problems of inflation. In both the army has had a central rôle. And in both, behind the high Utopian flights, lurks an instinctive pragmatism.

Israel has enjoyed the unique advantage that, until 1930, at least, her citizens were, in the main, eager volunteers; the Egyptian reformers, by contrast, confronted an age-old prudential apathy which required endless effort to dispel. Yet, as with the Jewish leaders, the belief that human society *could* be changed for the better was central in them. If social democracy, an aspiration of the new Arab leaders, was nearer to realisation with the Israelis, this was because the Jews had already undergone, in Europe, that social revolution which in the Arab world was now in full, tumultuous course. Again, if the timing differs, the parallelism is striking. Dr Weizmann himself has pointed out that the founding Zionists were mainly East European Jews of the lower middle class who were making their revolt against their own rich 'Oriental' notables and religious obscurantists. Some sought their just new world in Zionism; others, turning to purely secular Socialism and Communism, played their considerable part in the Russian Revolution.

And yet, in founding the modern state of Israel, the Jews had not escaped the central dilemma springing from their Eastern origins, but had rather impaled themselves upon it. Like the Muslims seeking modern political forms, they had somehow to adapt what was basically a historic religious community to the needs of the nation-state and the political nationalism that sustained it; and they had to do so without loss of the religious values and traditions from which both derived their energies and identity. As Theodor Herzl had written—much in the vein of Nasser's Charter—'If faith keeps us united, science makes us free.'

This task of fascinating complexity and doubtful feasibility —this need to reconcile the Word and the World—is again common ground between Egypt and Israel. In 1949, Dr Weizmann, Israel's first President, was warning his people of the need to curb Jewish religious zealots who would exploit religion for political ends; this exactly parallels the warnings given in the Arab progressive camp. Weizmann foresaw 'a great struggle . . . a *kultur-kampf*'—just such indeed as Nasser and his fellow Free Officers launched in 1954 when they broke with the Muslim Brotherhood, and such as they continued to fight through their reforms of later years. Ironically, in the 1950s and '60s, it was 'Oriental' Egypt which was able to advance furthest towards *formal* modernisation and secularisation, since Ben Gurion dared not abolish the Jewish religious courts, monopolising the law of marriage, divorce and 'personal status,[6] whereas Nasser swept away Egypt's separate Sharia court system (if not all its Koranic laws) in 1955; likewise, Israel's total withdrawal of public transport on the Sabbath shows a religious rigour hard to conceive in urban Egypt. In fact, for modernising Israelis the dilemma goes deeper than it does for modernising Arabs because Zionism's central purpose in the creation of Israel was the perpetuation of Jewishness, and for the religious authorities to surrender the control of marriages, making possible mixed marriage, might imperil that basic purpose. In his book *Israel Without Zionism*, the Israeli editor and Knesset member, Uri Avnery, remarks that 'not one of the big Zionist parties' advocate the separation of church and state: 'All of them declare state and religion, nation and religion, to be one in the unique case of the Jews.'

For the rest, Ben Gurion's professed aim 'to build a model society, based on social, economic and political equality' almost exactly echoes Gamal Abdel Nasser's, and was enunciated with a like passion and faith in the human future, drawn from the wells of a great, still vital religious faith and culture. Both men, superlatively, embodied, lived—and made—their people's history. On their behalf both had, in a sense, 'appointments with destiny.' And therein peril lay—for there remained another—and possibly a fatal—similarity between the Arabs and the Jews. The Semitic devotion to absolutes and rejection of compromise, the peculiar arrogance of two chosen peoples, had been given a renewed edge by the long conflict in Palestine. The result was a dual intransigence which was perhaps basically 'tribal' in psychology and origin, but which popular 'democratic' nationalism had certainly done nothing to soften. The Arabs who had quite legitimately, if perhaps unwisely, begun their frontal assault on political Zionism in 1920, forty-five years later were still steadfastly refusing to recognise the fact of their defeat and Israel's existence. Their position of 1947, rejecting outright the

---

[6] Under the rabbinical law administered by these courts, marriage of Jews and non-Jews is forbidden, and any children of such a marriage are illegitimate—although children of Jewish parents born out of wedlock are legitimate. Similarly Israeli freethinkers or atheists (not unnumerous) cannot secure a divorce in Israel, because there is no civil court before which they could go.

vote of the United Nations' General Assembly in favour of partition, remained formally, unanimously, and bleakly unchanged. Even in so 'moderate' a country as Libya, the very name of Israel was scratched from school-children's atlases. Yet, if the Arabs' insistence on a continuing, if largely inactive, state of war was frustrating and dangerous, it is equally clear that the victorious Israelis, in spite of their large gains in the 1948-9 war over the area allotted in the U.N. Plan, appeared unwilling to make any real concessions to secure peace,[7] and, subsequently, systematically pushed their rights under the Armistice Agreements to the very hilt—and indeed sometimes beyond it. By 1956, after ten years of intensive Jewish immigration into Israel, stimulated by powerful Zionist drives, Moshe Shertok, the Israeli Foreign Minister, was making repeated speeches stating that Israel would now never repatriate the Arab refugees.

The return—even the token return—of the refugees has been a rock against which successive peace-making efforts, from Count Bernadotte's in 1948 to President Kennedy's in 1961, have all shattered. Describing the Cabinet meeting that followed Bernadotte's proposals, Ben Gurion's authorised biographer, Michel Bar-Zohar, writes: 'As for the Arab refugees, he was quite emphatic: "We must do everything to ensure that they do not return." ' Through all the proposals that hopeful peacemakers put to him, Ben Gurion never wavered from this line, although it was the indispensable point for the Arabs, whose pride required at least acknowledgment of the grave wrong done. Certainly there were practical difficulties: some refugees were 'unreliable'; the old lands were no longer vacant. But the true reason for the unyielding Israeli stand lies elsewhere—in the potent mystique of Zionism. The Arabs could not be admitted because they would dilute the Jewishness of Israel. They would bring with them, however distantly, the threat of assimilation.

While Israeli politicians often speak of their desire for peace and co-operation with the Arabs, true partnership, 'bi-nation-

[7] In his book, *The First Ten Years*, Walter Eytan, the then Director-General of the Israeli Foreign Office, plainly regards the suggestion of the U.N. Mediator, Count Bernadotte, that they should compromise over their hard-won gains as quite extraordinary.

alism,' has never found favour with more than a small minority—and in later years these have often been fiercely
denounced as traitors to their people. 'It is not unfair to say,'
reported the Anglo-American Committee on Palestine in 1946,
'that the Jewish community in Palestine has never, as a community, faced the problem of co-operation with the Arabs.'
The Committee counselled change; but the essential Zionist
attitude towards the Arabs remained that of the progressive
colonial power towards a 'backward' native race. Within Israel
itself, wrote tht U.S. Consul-General in Jerusalem, Hedley V.
Cooke (and recent Jewish social surveys bear him out), 'true
friendships between Jews and Arabs are practically non-
existent. . . . The Jews are the mentors forever, the Arabs
the eternal protégés.'[8] Marriage between Jews and Arabs is, in
effect, prohibited. Arab citizens of Israel may participate in
Jewish political parties where they form a minute minority,
but when, in 1958, they tried to form an Arab party, this was
crushed under—magnificent irony—an old Ottoman law
against sectarian organisations. Hundreds of Arabs were dismissed from Government Service to make way for immigrant
Jews just as hundreds were turned off their lands for the same
purpose. The greater part of the country's good land, much
of it Arab property in 1948, is now held by the Jewish National
Fund, a historic Zionist institution dedicated to preserving it
'as the perpetual and inalienable possession of the Jewish
people.'[9]

Certainly, by 1967, the Arabs of Israel, almost 12 per cent
of the population, had succeeded in occupying 2 per cent of
the government administrative posts. But however sincerely
Israelis seek to remove discrimination—which does not exist
in their political theory—it is difficult to understand how they
can convincingly do so in a state in fact founded upon it, whose
very name, flag, anthem, institutions, passionately proclaim
its *raison d'être*—its Jewishness.

In its 3,500 years of history, Jerusalem has changed hands

[8] H. V. Cooke : *Israel—A Blessing and a Curse* (London, 1960).
[9] In 1959-60, 1/47th of all the irrigated land in Israel was cultivated by
the 'national minorities' (Muslim Arab, Christian and Druse), who are mainly
agricultural and constituted about 1/9th of the total population. Georges
Friedman, *The End of the Jewish People*, London, 1967.

twenty-five times, and sometimes bloodily. But probably only the 20th century could have devised for the Eternal City of the East a fate so neatly and sustainedly heartless or so ironic as that which befell it between 1948 and 1967. From Suleiman the Magnificent's great walls around the Old City— or from the upper floors of houses beside a new wall erected against stray bullets—the Arab citizens of Jerusalem could look out across the barbed wire and rank grass of the narrow strip of no-man's-land to the houses and shops on the other side, in which they had lived for years and often had owned. On their side, in that Israel which, in the vision of Dr Weizmann, was to regenerate the Middle East, the Jews could look across to the Dome of the Rock, indicating the position of the Wailing Wall, the relic of the Temple on which their people's yearnings for more than a thousand years had been centred. But they could not visit it. In this city sacred to both faiths and to a third, the breach between these kindred peoples, who had lived here for centuries cheek by jowl, was total.

If, in Jerusalem, the Israeli victory of 1967 removed the physical breach, the spiritual breach remained, and—here and elsewhere—was deepened. Once again the great stream of Arab refugees, fleeing before the war and its aftermath, were effectively denied the right to return to their homes; once again the vacated Arab lands were being planted with new Jewish colonies, while Israel objected to the United Nations' concerning itself with her future frontiers, insisting on her right to redraw the map of this critical area of the world in 'direct negotiation' with the defeated Arabs.

Under the U.N. Partition plan of 1947, the sole legal warrant of Israel's existence, other than the so-called rights of conquest, Jerusalem was to have been internationalised. Although Israel had nevertheless claimed the city as, in Ben Gurion's words, 'Israel's Eternal Capital,' her unilateral action had never been recognised, and almost all the major powers had kept their embassies in Tel Aviv. Now, in July 1967, Israel by a special decree annexed the Old City of Jerusalem which had lain in the Jordanian sector and proceeded with its 'integration into Israel' in the face of a 99-0 vote by the United Nations General Assembly, backed by the Security Council, instructing her to desist from this course. U Thant's personal representative, despatched to the spot on the Assembly's instructions, was told by the Israeli authorities that the annexaion was 'irreversible and not negotiable'; Jerusalem was Jewish. To clarify the point, by early 1968, 800 acres of Arab land strategically placed in the Arab sector of Jerusalem had been expropriated and were being developed for a Jewish residential area. For refusing to co-operate in this 'integration,' the elected Arab mayor of the Arab sector had been expelled. In February, the Jewish Mayor of Jerusalem complained with some bitterness that the Israeli Government's attempt to 'integrate' the Arab citizens had been a 'total failure.'

'Palestine,' wrote the Anglo-American Committee of Inquiry of 1945, 'is a Holy Land sacred to Christian, to Jew and to Muslim alike, and, because it is a Holy Land, Palestine is not, and can never become, a land which any race or religion can justly claim as its very own. . . . [Its history] is dedicated to the principles and practice of the brotherhood of man.'

Bitterly as this now reads, it remains essentially true. The very stones of Jerusalem—annexed or unannexed—testify to the interdependence of the worlds and peoples and religions that have for centuries met here. The Wailing Wall of the Jews encloses the *Haram el Sherif*, the 'Noble Sanctuary' of the Muslims, and the mosque within, the 'Dome of the Rock,' the earliest extant monument of Muslim architecture, is plainly inspired by Christian churches and was probably executed by Byzantine craftsmen. It stands over the rock from which the Prophet made his legendary night flight to Heaven on his winged steed, El Baruk—and on which, somewhat earlier, and still in evidence, stood David's Altar of the Burnt Offering.

And the intricately inter-woven fabric of Jerusalem merely reflects the organic unity of the region as a whole. The offence of the exclusive 'religious-racial' state of Israel in Arab eyes has been that, small as it was, its intrusion did intolerable violence to this unity. Israel was minute—as a speck in the eye is minute. Like some re-fortified Crusader castle, it stands athwart the natural land bridge between the East and the West of the Arab world over which people and armies had passed for millennia from the Nile Valley to Western Asia. With its creation, the Arab world's old Palestinian window on the West slammed shut; and the region's major—and potentially most fertile—geographical reality, the unity of Syria, was destroyed.[10] This was a unity which was generous and assured enough to accommodate the quintessential diversity of the Levant. Here had flourished and mingled an extraordinary range of major traditions and cultures, Egyptian, Greek, Roman, Jewish—and when Islam came, it prevailed by the readiness with which it received within its capacious embrace races and cultures other than Arab, and made them 'Arab' or part-Arab; and those whom it did not absorb or convert it tolerated.

It was not only in Egypt that the Jews had an ancient, and even honoured, place in this old Islamic world. In North Africa the advance of the Arab Muslim armies in the 7th century came just in time to save the ancient Jewish communities from persecutions and forced conversion by the Christian Byzantines;[11] and this was a service which, more than twelve centuries later, Mohamed V renewed when he sheltered Morocco's numerous Jews from the Nazi anti-Semitic laws brought in by the Vichy Government. Many prosperous merchants of the great Arab city of Fez are, or were, of Jewish origin; Tunisia had an ancient and prosperous Jewish community; and in the Yemen the Jews provided all the artisan services. In Baghdad in 1948, there was a historic Jewish community of 125,000 in sixty synagogues which had been there, continuously, since Nebuchadnezzar led them there in 986 B.C. after the destruction of the first kingdom of Judah. In 1946 they told the Anglo-American Committee of Inquiry of their fears of what Zionism would do to their world. The Chief Rabbi of Iraq issued a statement saying that in Iraq 'Jews and Arabs have enjoyed the same rights and privileges for a thousand years.'

In that part of the Levant which lies between the eastern shore of the Mediterranean and the desert this capacity of the old Islamic world to accommodate diversity was strengthened

[10] Graphically expressed in a telegram of protest in 1917 from the Syrians in Cairo to Lord Balfour after the publication of the Balfour Declaration: 'Palestine is to Syria as the heart is to the body.' (Quoted by Monroe in *Britain's Moment in the Middle East*, London, 1963).

[11] Cecil Roth, 'The Jews' in *Encyclopedia Britannica*, 1967.

by what the geographer, Professor W. B. Fisher[12] calls 'a fundamental unity both from the physical and human standpoints.' Recalling that 'for centuries before the Versailles settlement the name "Syria" was held to apply to the whole of the coastal region between Asia Minor and the Sinai desert,' Fisher goes on to remind us—'as an indication of the essential unity of the Levant'—'that only when the region was organised as a single unit did periods of greatest advance and prosperity occur.'

Since 1920 all attempts to allow this 'essential unity' to re-emerge have been frustrated. But Syria has, nevertheless, remained a region of the mind. In 1919, the American King-Crane Commission, sent to the Middle East by Woodrow Wilson, reported that an 'overwhelming majority' of the people wanted a United Syria which they took to include Palestine and Lebanon. In the event partition was piled on partition, but the idea of Syria continued to run like a theme through the tempestuous orchestration of pan-Arab politics. King Abdullah, carving out of the desert his kingdom of Transjordan, adding many years later the West Bank of war-divided Palestine, dreamed all the time of recreating Syria. From Baghdad, looking westward as Abdullah looked east, the other branch of the Hashemites dreamed the same dream.

Today, no less than in the past, this world behind the Eastern and Southern shores of the Mediterranean, home of so many minorities, essentially a place of movement—of both ideas and people—and sacred to three great world religions, demands a structure and form of government which can accommodate its rich diversity and allow its processes of cross-fertilisation to continue. The Ottoman Empire, with all its vices and occasional savagery, offered some such frame. When this 'old' Levant collapsed with the eclipse of the Sultan-Caliph, it was succeeded in the Nile Valley by the new-old Levant of the Khedive and de Lesseps, of pashas and Greeks and Jewish bankers which, with its broad money-based tolerance and its endless commercial trafficking, was also able, after its fashion, to maintain the indivisibility of this world.

Before the Middle East can achieve the peace and progress of which it is capable a new Levant will have to be called

[12] W. B. Fisher : *The Middle East* (5th edition, London, 1953).

into being. It will be very different from the old one, yet like it, must reject the balkanisation of narrow nationalism, and reject, above all, any suggestion of *apartheid*. It is possible to see that the Arabs, a people of ninety millions, with their new oil wealth and technology, with their modernising ideas, and their comprehensive vision of Arab Unity based not on sectarianism but on loyalty to a region of the world, might yet be able to build such a new Levant. But it is hard to see how political Zionism can fit into it.

But what of the Arabs' own intransigence? In a televised interview immediately before the outbreak of the Israel-Arab war of June 1967, President Nasser was asked whether he thought the Arabs should rule Palestine. He replied: 'Well, the Arabs—Christians, Muslims and Jews . . . but not a State based on Judaism.' This is the universal modern Arab position and it is capable of development into a framework of government which could restore harmony to the Middle East.

Let us compare an address given in New York in 1952 by that very practised Israeli spokesman, currently Israel's Foreign Minister, Abba Eban:

'. . . while paying all honour to the potentiality of the Arab tradition, we came to Israel with the purpose of reviving and maintaining the Hebrew tradition. Moreover Israel possesses unique interests, the paramount one of which is the connection with the Jewish world in all the countries of the Dispersion. We should not therefore look upon the separateness of Israel as a transient phenomenon imposed by Arab boycott; it is imposed by the desire and the aspiration of Israel herself. The idea should not be one of integration. Quite the contrary. . . . One of the great apprehensions which afflict us . . . is the danger lest the predominance of immigrants of Oriental origin force Israel to equalise its cultural level with that of the neighbouring world. So far from regarding our immigrants from Oriental countries as a bridge towards our integration with the Arabic-speaking world, our object should be to infuse them with an Occidental spirit. . . . The slogan should be . . . not Israel as an organic part of the Middle East, but Israel as a separate and unique entity living at peace with the Middle East.'

This view—if not always so frankly stated—appears as characteristically Zionist as the view expressed by Nasser is characteristically 'modern Arab.'

The Zionists, like the Arabs, have their difficulties in accommodating the Word to the World.

'Co-operation between the Jews and the Arabs,' Mr Ben Gurion has written, 'can turn the Middle East into one of the great cultural centres of the world, as it once was. And only they can achieve it. No outside powers, however strong, whether from the East or the West, can do what the Arabs and Jews can do for each other.'

Yet the veteran Ben Gurion, no less than Abba Eban, has expressed great fear that Israel may become 'Levantised.' Ben Gurion himself appeared on the Middle Eastern scene in the days of the Ottoman Levant (after studying in Constantinople) and it is possible to understand his fears. Yet the Zionists resolutely shut their eyes to the social revolution which has since occurred in the Arab world (and to which Zionism, admittedly, has contributed). While Ben Gurion has, on occasion in his writings, recognised Nasser's stature as leader of that revolution, the Israeli propaganda machine has been tireless in building up a grotesque picture of Nasser as an anti-Semitic Middle Eastern Hitler—and the Arabs are by no means the only people in the Middle East who become victims of their own propaganda.

There is the deeper reason for this dread of 'Levantisation' which goes to the heart of Zionism and reveals its dilemma. The Jewish message, Ben Gurion has insisted, is not limited to the Jewish people, but is a message 'of peace, righteousness and equality' for all peoples. But the Jews, historically, have been more concerned with the preservation of their message than with its diffusion and, as Eban points out, Zionism's purpose was to ensure this preservation in 'modern' national form. Since the Jews, unlike Christians and Muslims, no longer seek converts, they necessarily remain the sole proprietors of their message. Hence derive those Zionist claims which must strike a non-Jew as disingenuous: such as the claim advanced to the British Commission of Enquiry in 1920 that the Jews in Palestine must predominate, but did not intend to dominate; or the parallel modern claim to accord 'Equal rights to all citizens.' Hence, too, Ben Gurion's desire for 'co-

operation between Arab and Jew,' sincere, but seen as a somewhat special sort of co-operation in which the Jews do all the
giving (thus remaining un-Levantised) and the Arabs are the
perpetual receivers; or his passionate insistence on the precept
of the Torah to 'Love thy neighbour as thyself'—with the
apparently implicit proviso that those Arab neighbours who
failed to appreciate their rôle and thus became refugees should
be re-settled elsewhere.

But if this Messianic single-mindedness has enabled the
Zionists—assisted at a critical stage by the rise of Hitler—to
re-shape the map of the Middle East, it may be that the geography of the Middle East is now about to take its revenge
by embarking on the re-shaping of Zionism. By 1963, 69 per
cent of Israel's Jewish citizens were Jews of Asian and
African origin, the greater part of them from old Arabic-
speaking communities in the Arab lands whence the upheavals
Zionism brought had forced them. It is estimated that by 1980
the proportion of 'Oriental' Jews in Israel's Jewish population
will be 80 per cent. As a consequence, the late Prime Minister,
Levi Eshkol, said that he had come to see the assimilation of all Israel's immigrants to the common (European
Zionist) Israeli pattern as 'a long process and a matter of
generations.'[13] Meanwhile, by another of those extraordinary
ironies in which Middle Eastern history is so rich, these Oriental Jewish refugees, merely 'Jews' in their former homes,
become 'dark' Jews, 'Yemenites,' 'Iraqis' or 'Moroccans' on
reaching Israel. The Government and bureaucracy remains, of
course, 'European,' and if the army is a *sabra* (native born)
institution, 'the *sabra* stereotype is decidedly European,' and
'higher education is nearly a European monopoly.'[14] It is well
known that the Oriental Jews are far from content with their
status[15] and although the gigantic task of assimilation and re-

[13] Thus, a large part of the 80 per cent would be Israeli-born—but Israeli-
born 'Orientals.'
[14] Dr Alex Weingrod, *Group Relations in Israel* (London, 1965). Dr Weingrod was until 1962 Research Director of the Settlement Department of the
Jewish Agency in Israel.
[15] 'The feeling of being unfairly treated, of being discriminated against,
is widespread among the Jews from North Africa'—Georges Friedman,
The End of the Jewish People? (London, 1967). The commission appointed

orientation may be tackled by the Israeli establishment with the old single-mindedness, the moat of Israel's Crusader castle no longer looks so deep as it did.

Dr Chaim Weizmann long ago begged the more ardent— and remotely located—of his fellow Zionists to bear in mind that 'whatever the Jewish National Home will ultimately become, even if it absorbs millions of Jews . . . it will nevertheless remain an island in an Arab sea.' In the aftermath of the third of Israeli's victorious wars against her Arab neighbours the wisdom of that warning in Baltimore in 1923 is more than ever evident.

On the one hand, the Israeli military challenge has forced the pace of Arab modernisation, and since the end of 1967 'revolutionary' Arab states occupy not one, but both, ends of the Red Sea. On the other hand, Israel herself has come to the end of an era. Her extraordinary dynamism, the Zionist expansion from the toehold of 1921 to the conquered land of 1967 embracing the whole of the old Palestine plus the Sinai peninsula and a piece of Syria, has been based on the influx not only of arms and money, but, above all, of people—in the later years, a mighty tide. But since the six million Jews of the United States have resolutely refused to be ingathered, since the Jews of Russia are not permitted to leave, and the supply of Jews from the Afro-Asian world is largely exhausted, this source of impetus is approaching its end. In 1966, more Jews left Israel than entered. In addition, if Israel were to retain the areas she occupied in 1967, she would add a further million Arabs to the 300,000 already living in Israel (whose Jewish population is 2,365,000). The Arab birth-rate in Israel is more than twice that of the Jewish; not to mention the large gap between the birth-rate of the prolific Oriental Jews and the 'Europeans.'

Determinedly as Zionism may reject 'Levantisation,' the Levant is still able to claim its own. Yet it is already a new Levant—one which Arabs as well as Jews have played their part in making. The new Arab revolution and Zionist socialism alike were both reactions against the decadence of the old

by the Knesset to investigate the 'White/Black' Jewish riots in Haifa and Tel Aviv, 1959, regretted that 'numerous and various sections of the settled Israeli public still have many prejudices.'

Levant in which Arabs and Jews were both, in a sense, submerged peoples. Moving back several centuries in the long racial memory, both were also reactions against the barbaric presumption of the Christian West which humiliated both. The Crusaders on their way to pillage the Muslim East paused in city after city as they crossed Europe to rob and murder the Jews in Christ's name, inaugurating the habit of pogrom. For both Arabs and Jews their national revolutions may be seen as a necessary phase of renewal; but when this has been so substantially accomplished, it seems ironic that they must continue to react, now against each other; tragic if they cannot work together in the creation of the New Levant which must surely come into being.

To do so, both Arabs and Jews will need to make large adjustments; but the Jews who, by returning to the East, inaugurated this process which now approaches a new phase, will need to change the most. Old-style exclusive nationalism, based on the proprietorship of Truth, can have small future in today's world, and if such a nationalism ('My country, right or wrong')—in the Middle East, above all—should be globally supported by the citizens of other countries in a sort of proxy patriotism, its disruptive potentialities are multiplied indeed. Plainly, it will become necessary for Israel to be 'of' the whole region as well as merely 'in' it : and in fairness it must be said that in recent years she has been given little chance to acquire any such habit of mind. She will need to see the millions of Arabs who surround her not as 'landscape' but as people, not as 'the natives' to be enlightened and organised, but as equal partners; and she will have to acknowledge that the human claims of the Arab refugees are no less valid than those of Jewish refugees and that a great wrong has been done. A young Israeli named Shimon Tzabar, who fought in the three Arab-Jewish wars of 1948, 1956, and 1967, recently wrote that the really relevant question is not 'Has Israel a right to exist?' but 'What *sort* of Israel has a right to exist?' He added: 'We are all people living in Israel or Palestine, whichever you like to call it.'

This simple, humanist creed—amalgamating destinies—is the essential condition of peace in the Middle East. But for the Old-line Zionist such an attitude calls for a reorientation hardly less extensive and disturbing than that confronting the 'traditional' Arab adapting to the modern world. But Israel is today a land full of great unresolved issues, a nation in flux, and here, as in Egypt, a new generation, born into a world totally different from that of the present holders of power, is knocking at the door. The word *sabra* which characterises this Israel-born generation, is an Arabic word (for 'prickly pear'); Judaism, unlike Zionism, is a religion which belongs to the world; and, to one who is neither Jew nor Arab, but who recalls that Arabs and Jews once shared a Golden Age, the distance between the greetings *'shalom aleichem'* and *'assalaamu aleikum'* would not appear unbridgeable.

If it cannot be bridged this is no longer a parochial affair in which Arab is at loggerheads with Jew; it is the East which is alienated from the West, to the infinite loss of both. In a real sense, the destinies of all of us now lie in the Levant.

27

THE ECHO AND THE DREAM

The Egyptians act as if there would be no day of reckoning.
—Ibn Khaldun, the *Muquaddimah*, 1380

The only road ahead of us is the road of work. Through work we shall build. This road is not new to us. It is our road and will remain so for ever. In the past we used to work and sacrifice for nothing. But now we work and sacrifice as owners of our wealth and returns. We own this wealth for ourselves, our children and our grandchildren, as well as for the future of our country for ever.
—Gamal Abdel Nasser, speech March 1967

You can't breed all meat; there must be some bone.
—Egyptian saying, quoted to author

By one of those 'traditions' in which revolutions are so fecund, July 23, 'Revolution Day,' had become in Egypt by the 1960s the established climax of the national year. It was the day on which workers officially moved into their new 'popular' flat-blocks, on which peasants in many parts of the country took over lands reclaimed from the desert, or received the title-deeds of holdings in new Land Reform areas; on which the President delivered his 'State of the Nation' speech to the rejoicing—and holidaying—masses, on which Egypt's military resurgence was paraded and Youth displayed its eagerness and dedication.

And each year since the resounding moral triumph of 'Suez' in 1956, so perfect and potent in its global symbolism, there had been much to celebrate. A daunting challenge had been boldly taken up, and, visibly, 'step by step,' was being met; each year industrial output mounted, each year old lands yielded more abundantly and new land yielded for the first time, there was more social justice and education and training, and Egypt's fellahin and workers were drawn into the national community as they had never been before. People were better clothed and healthier and better fed; but the most important aspect of the social revolution was not measurable statistically, for it was psychological. For the first time ordinary people began to feel that it was possible for Egypt to break out of the vicious circle of impoverishment which had so long gripped her.

23 July 1967, the fifteenth anniversary of the Free Officers' coup, should have set the seal on the revolution's first decade and a half of solid achievement. For the date had long been appointed for the ceremonial starting-up of the first generators powered by the High Dam, which from the outset had formed so powerful and symbolic a theme in this story. In the previous August, the Nile boat carrying the first of the huge turbines from the Leningrad Electrosila factory had been joyfully greeted on its way up the Nile, and many Cairenes had gone aboard to take snapshots or write messages of gratitude on the 130-ton monster's sides. The gratitude to the Russians was genuine, but the pride was, deservedly, Egyptian. From Aswan, on both sides of the Nile, the high pylons strode off across the desert, and on Revolution Day, 1967, the first flow of the coming flood of cheap power, coursing out over the length and breadth of the country, should have triumphantly signalled the 'opening of a new chapter' in the building of the New Egypt.

In the event, July 1967 found the Egyptian people and their leader and teacher facing the humiliation of total defeat after a five-day Israeli *Blitzkrieg* which had laid low the Arab armed forces under Egyptian leadership. The boasted air force had been destroyed on the ground, the omnipotent rockets had proved ineffective, the massed heavy tanks, deprived of air cover, littered the wastes of Sinai, and the Palestinian refugees were once again in flight, both from their homes and their old camps on the West Bank. The Israelis were at the Canal. And unlike Egypt's setbacks in Syria in 1961 and in the Yemen, this abject defeat was not easily explainable in terms of 'counter-revolution' or treachery. Israel had been publicly challenged, and she had taken up the challenge with devastating promptitude. Accepting 'the entire responsibility' for the 'grave setback,' Nasser in a broadcast to the nation announced his intention 'to give up completely and finally every official post and return to the ranks of the public.'

The catastrophe was the more bewildering in that it had been brought about by a force so largely irrelevant to Egypt's long and arduous national struggle—almost, it seemed, as if by the intervention of some malevolent *deus ex machina*. And yet, from her off-stage position, Israel had somehow, for more than twenty years, commanded the course of the drama at critical junctures in just this way. In this latest episode, all the familiar actors appeared, playing their rôles with an extraordinary consistency, yet now, it seemed, with a sort of sleepwalking unreality. The Arabs were wronged, betrayed, conspired against. They asked only for Justice. The Israelis asked only to be left to live in peace, while packing with all the God-given assurance of David the sling-shot that would fell Goliath. The Russians played their customary British 19th-century rôle of champion of nations 'struggling to be free.' The British and Americans appealed to both sides to be reasonable and compromise like good Anglo-Saxons. And the actors on the stage addressed not each other, but the audience—and themselves.

President Nasser again brought to bear with dramatic effect his characteristic, highly charged mixture of moral force sharpened by the threat of physical force. But since Egypt had advanced since 1956, the physical element was now larger, more complex and more explicit. And once again the immediate starting point of the train of events lay outside Egypt—in that jangling nerve-centre of the Arab East, Damascus.

At the end of February 1966, a coup within the ruling Baath Socialist party overthrew the 'moderate' wing reflecting the party's somewhat academic founder, Michel Aflaq, and his partner, Saleh Bitar, and installed the more Marxist, 'revolutionary' leaders of the so-called 'international Baath.' The apocalyptic view of history, always latent in Damascus, now took command, and the new leaders' concept of 'a people's war' led to an increase in the small hit-and-run raids over the Israeli border by Palestinian terror organisations, to support for the so-called Palestine Liberation Army, led by the former Saudi Arabia U.N. representative, Ahmed Shukairy, and to threats against the 'reactionary' King Hussein.

The numbers of Israelis killed in these irregular raids—which had never wholly ceased since 1948—was small (twelve in October 1966—a very bad month). But the strain they occasioned must nevertheless have been great. And, as on many other occasions, an Israeli complaint against Syria to the Security Council was blocked by the Soviet veto. On 13 November, after three Israeli soldiers had been killed by a land mine, the Israeli army replied with one of their reprisal actions. It was directed in brigade strength against the Jordanian village of Samu which was alleged to have harboured the terrorists, and 125 houses, a school and a clinic were destroyed. Eighteen Jordanians were killed and fifty-four wounded (U.N. figures). Unlike earlier Israeli reprisal actions this was conducted openly in broad daylight. It was characterised by Lord Caradon, the British representative at the United Nations, as 'calculated, admitted, and wholly disproportionate' and was condemned by the Security Council, as had been Israel's earlier reprisal attacks over the preceding twelve years.

In the same month, in a *rapprochement* with the Baath in part dictated by the hardening line-up between 'revolutionary' and 'reactionary' in the Arab world, Nasser had concluded a Defence Pact with Syria which pledged Egypt to go to her aid if she were attacked. As ever, the Israeli reprisal had heightened the Arab fever; in November and December there was rioting on Jordan's West Bank and Ahmed Shukairy and his Palestine Liberation Army now openly called for the overthrow of the 'reactionary' Hussein. In mid-February 1967, the United Nations Israel-Syria border tension talks were broken off indefinitely.

In early April there were the usual incidents over spring ploughing in the demilitarised zone between Israel and Syria. But they were fiercer than usual. In a substantial air attack over Syrian territory near Lake Tiberias on 7 April, the Israeli Air Force shot down six Syrian MiG fighters. It was another step-up—the use of aircraft in reprisal raids. The 'reactionary' Hussein was again to be heard upbraiding the 'revolutionary' Nasser for failing to go to the aid of Syria as he had earlier failed to go to the aid of Jordan. Hussein did not omit to point out that Nasser lay safe behind the screen of the United Nations Emergency Force, while others took the brunt of the Zionist-Imperialist assault. From Riyadh, Feisal's radio enquired sardonically what the Egyptian army was waiting for.

This accusation struck home; it was, for an Arab, unanswerable. On 11 May a high Israeli officer was reported by international news-agencies to have threatened military action to overthrow the Syrian régime and occupy Damascus if the El Fatah raids did not cease. The Israeli Prime Minister, Levi Eshkol, echoed this masterful statement in a Tel Aviv speech suggesting that 'in view of fourteen incidents in the last month alone' Israel might 'have to adopt measures no less drastic than those of 7 April' (when Israeli jets had appeared over Damascus). If they received little or no attention in the British Press, these —and various other—Israeli threats about this time seemed so inflammatory in the Middle Eastern context that both the U.S. State Department and the United Nations Secretary-General officially voiced their concern. Despite the tension, on 15 May Eshkol was obliged by Israeli public opinion to revert to the practice of holding the anniversary military parade in Jerusalem, inevitably under the eyes of the Arabs— an old, much condemned, source of avoidable provocation like the Israeli insistence on pushing canals and cultivation to the furthest limit in the demilitarised zones.[1] This time Eshkol did however keep out tanks and artillery, so that the parade conformed to the letter, if not to the spirit, of the Armistice Agreement. The Arabs merely concluded that the tanks and guns were absent because they were being deployed elsewhere: as U Thant reported to the U.N. 'persistent rumours of troop movements and concentrations, particularly on the Israeli side of the Syrian border, had been causing anxiety.'

Nasser has said that the Syrians informed him that eighteen Israeli brigades were massing on their frontier; the Egyptians checked and found thirteen. An Egyptian parliamentary delegation visiting Moscow was told that information reaching the Russians indicated that Israel was planning a surprise attack on Syria for the end of May. The information about troop concentrations was, in fact, wrong. But it is not difficult to see

---

[1] On both these subjects, indicative of a consistent Israeli attitude, the detailed accounts given by the chief of the U.N. Truce Supervision Organisation, General Carl von Horn in *Soldiering for Peace* (1966) will be found instructive.

why it was readily believed. 'Suez' was still fresh in Arab minds—the full truth about the three-power collusion then having only recently come to light. Surprise, feints, deceptions were boasted features of Israeli army tactics; both in 1955 and 1956 Israeli leaders had said one thing and done its opposite. Moreover, in 1967, suspicions of Western intentions in Cairo were peculiarly intense. That May, King Feisal, who was supporting the 'royalists' in the Yemen against the 'republicans' and their Egyptian backers, was welcomed on a State visit to Britain—with whom U.A.R. relations had been severed since November in accordance with the OAU Addis Ababa resolution on Rhodesia's 'white' revolt. The United States was supplying Feisal with modern armaments; but for eleven months Egypt's request for the usual—and vital—wheat aid (paid for in local currency) had been held up. Most of the Arab States had broken off relations with West Germany in 1965 after the revelation of her secret (1960) arms deal with Israel, which had been followed by German formal 'recognition' of Israel.

The American *Chargé d'Affaires* in Cairo (who has since resigned from the diplomatic service), David G. Nes, has said that, although he advised the Egyptian Foreign Ministry that there was no truth in the reports of Israeli troop concentrations, 'Egyptian distrust of American credibility was at such a point that the Egyptians were convinced we were covering up for Israel.' This lack of communication with the West was, in a sense, the root cause of the disastrous sequence of events that followed. Nes went on: 'If we had been able to persuade Nasser that we were not hostile . . . we might have been able to prevent the conflict. . . . We warned Washington from Cairo . . . but no one in Washington was willing to take the political risk involved in doing anything for Egypt. Nobody wanted to be accused of helping Nasser. This was true at all levels—the State Department, Congress, the White House.'[2]

At a press conference, President Johnson dismissed Nes's views as 'parochial.' It is an interesting choice of words, but one wonders who it was who was truly 'parochial'?

Two years earlier, in 1965, another American who knows the Middle East well, and who also happens to be Jewish, Alfred M.

[2] Interview, reported by the Associated Press, from Washington, 8 February 1968.

Lilienthal, had written: 'If the White House will do nothing to reverse the "Israel First" edict of the politicians, it will simply be a question of time before our policy of "impartial but pro-Israel" will drive Nasser and the nationalist Arab countries to a fixed counter-position of "neutral but pro-Soviet." '[3]

It is clear that in May 1967—much as in 1958 on the eve of the union with Syria—Nasser had, in fact, little choice. With Israel openly threatening further, stepped-up, reprisals, with the air full of rumours of doom, and the communication line to the West largely cut, he had to act or abdicate. But if his hand was forced, he nevertheless played it with the old panache. On 16 May Egypt requested the withdrawal of the United Nations Emergency Force from Sinai where it had constituted a screen between Israel and Egypt since November 1956. On 22 May, Nasser declared the Straits of Tiran closed to Israeli shipping and to stragetic goods destined for Israel. 'Our sovereignty over the Gulf is indisputable. If Israel threatens us with war, we will reply "Go ahead then." '

Criticism of Egypt's demand for the withdrawal of the United Nations Emergency Force from Sinai was impugned by the fact that, although Egypt, the victims in 1956, had voluntarily accepted this force on her own soil, Israel, the condemned aggressor, had flatly refused to have United Nations patrols on her side of the frontier (as the U.N. resolution required) 'under any circumstances.' When U Thant in 1967 suggested to Israel that the U.N. screening force might simply be moved to her side of the border (which would almost certainly have prevented the war), the U.N. representative was again informed that this was 'completely unacceptable.'

Again, the Gulf of Aqaba was an excellent theatre for demonstrating both the geographical realities of this world and the West's built-in bias. Effectively less than three miles wide at its mouth, surrounded for centuries by Arab lands, and since the 'twenties by four Arab states, this hitherto obscure appendix of the Red Sea could claim the title of 'international waterway' only by virtue of the very small Israeli port of Eilat, being developed from what in 1949 had

[3] A. M. Lilienthal: *The Other Side of the Coin*, New York, 1965.

been the Palestine police post of Um Rash Rash. It was also noteworthy that Eilat had been seized by an Israeli force after, and in direct contravention of, the U.N. Egypt-Israel Armistice Agreement of 1949. And if it was true that the U.N. Partition Plan of 1947 had given the Negev to the Jews, it was also true that after the large Israeli gains in the 1948 war the 'Bernadotte Line' proposed by the United Nations' mediator had allotted the southern Negev to the Arabs to provide a land bridge between Egypt and the Arab East; for this Count Folke Bernadotte had been murdered by Jewish terrorists. Of captured Eilat, Ben Gurion had boasted : '. . . for the first time in its history the sovereign Jewish nation borders two seas.' But for 1965-6 cargo through Eilat totalled 260,000 tons compared with 4·4 millions for all Israeli ports, and 3·8 millions for Haifa. Its main importance lay in its rôle in the Israeli vision of the future.

Until 1956, Egypt had in fact excluded Israeli shipping from the Gulf of Aqaba, and Nasser told U Thant that he did not intend war but merely wished to restore Egypt's position to what it had been before the Israeli-British-French invasion, including a restoration of the 1948-9 armistice agreement between Israel and Egypt. Both legalistically and morally, assuming a world no longer ruled by the rights of conquest, this was not a wholly unreasonable position. Had Egyptian control of the Gulf of Aqaba in conjunction with the other Arab riparian states been tested in the International Court, the outcome would have been far from certain.[4] But the drama as Nasser had staged it was never permitted to reach even the first Act—an 'Anglo-American imperialist' test of the blockade. And in truth, even in terms of the old Nasserian morality play of Right versus Might, the plot had now become a little confused. For the confrontation of tanks and aircraft across the Sinai desert was manifestly not primarily a moral confrontation. Yet Nasser, still endeavouring to make it so, had pledged himself not to strike the first blow. In so doing he had lost the war, because as Pearl Harbour demonstrated, in the

[4] Even the Dulles Note of February 1957 'guaranteeing' the Israeli Government right of free passage in the Gulf af Aqaba contained the proviso 'In the absence of some over-riding decision to the contrary, as by the International Court of Justice . . .'

conditions of modern war the first blow is of surpassing importance, and delivered with sufficient surprise, pre-planning
and relentlessness, may almost immediately determine the
issue.

Nasser, in fact, in the Arab military build-up of May and
June 1967 was moving out of his proper ground. For although
sections of the British Press, even in 1967, still persisted in
calling him 'Colonel,' he is, essentially, the intuitive politician
who became a soldier, rather than the soldier who turns to
politics. It is true that in the *Philosophy of the Revolution*,
he writes: 'Power is not merely shouting aloud. Power is
to act positively with all the components of power.' But the
components he then goes on to name are Arab culture and
moral unity, Arab petroleum resources, and geographical position at the 'crossroads and the military corridor of the world.'

These are all political factors, and, in the long run, the
determinants of the future of this Middle Eastern world. But
in the short run, skill in the use of modern armaments, backed
by a faith like Zionism capable of generating a fanatical singleness of purpose, can over-rule them. While Gamal Abdel
Nasser had, since 1948, been marshalling words and ideas with
dramatic effect, the Israelis, embattled since the 'thirties, had
been quietly perfecting their plans for 'the next round.' Under
the code name *Shin-Tav-Shin* the nucleus of such a plan had
indeed existed since 1949 when King Abdullah of Jordan's
suing for peace had caused the Israeli advance to be reluctantly
halted; according to the Zionist writer, Jon Kimche, this 'unfinished battle' that would take Israel to the Jordan had
'haunted the Palestine situation ever since.' In 1967, the Israeli
Air Force Chief, General Hodd, claimed that 'sixteen years of
planning' had gone into the Israeli Air Force's onslaught upon
the airfields of her Arab neighbours.

On 26 May, and again on 1 June, the Egyptian Ambassador
in Washington was warned, at the instance of President Johnson, that 'very serious consequences' would follow any attack
upon Israel. As the American Sixth Fleet was then in position
in the Eastern Mediterranean, this was no idle warning: it
is clear that Nasser had every reason for his expressed belief
that the United States would have intervened in the event of a
successful Egyptian attack upon Israel. What was not so clear

was what the United States would do if Israel attacked Egypt. It was assumed that the Israeli Foreign Minister in Washington on 27 May had, like the Egyptians, given a pledge not to attack first. But it is also evident from what followed that the nuances, if no more, of President Johnson's words to Eban were different from those of his words to Nasser.

'Most diplomatists stationed in Washington,' reported the Washington correspondent of the London *Times* on 12 June, 'are persuaded that the United States was in collusion with Israel last week, and perhaps before . . . clearly some assurances were given to the Israelis before the hostilities began. The more faint-hearted in Jerusalem could rest assured that an Israel defeat would never be allowed. General Moshe Dayan must have been fairly sure of about ninety-six hours in which to achieve his objectives before the Security Council could call a halt.'

It appears that when Foreign Minister Abba Eban reached Washington on 25 May, President Johnson asked Israel to hold her hand—for two weeks or so, a somewhat remarkable allowance of time in which to ease the complex tensions of the Middle East. Eban was further assured that the Pentagon's information indicated that the Israeli forces could readily handle all the Arab states combined—a confidence which Israel's military chiefs fully shared.

In fact, Israel waited not fourteen days, but nine. Diplomatic activity between Egypt and the U.S. was in progress when she struck. The emissary President Johnson had sent to Cairo had reached a preliminary agreement with the Egyptian Foreign Minister. Egypt was ready to submit the Gulf of Aqaba issue to the World Court. Meanwhile, she would allow through the straits all ships not flying the Israeli flag, and would probably not extend the embargo on strategic goods to oil. It was not much, perhaps, but it was a beginning. And it had been arranged that the Egyptian Vice-President, Zakaria Moheiddin, would visit Washington on 7 June to continue the negotiations with President Johnson in person, while the U.S. Vice-President Hubert Humphrey would visit Cairo.[5]

[5] Maxime Rodinson: *Israel and the Arabs*, (1968); David Kimche and Dan Bawly: *The Sandstorm*, (1968); Walter Laqueur: *The Road to War, 1967*, (1968).

On 3 June, General Moshe Dayan, newly appointed Minister of Defence, was, in fact, telling a Press conference that 'now diplomacy must be given a chance.' Less than two days later, at 7.45 a.m. on 5 June, the Israeli Air Force launched its pre-emptive strike. Half an hour after that—the enemy having been totally deprived of air cover and therefore, in the conditions of desert warfare, of any prospect of victory—the Israeli army launched its attack into Egyptian territory.

The military advantages of the chosen hour have since been fully expounded by Israeli Generals; but there was another advantage, not wholly military: at this time it would be impossible to get the U.N. Security Council together.[6] As it was, at 3.10 a.m., New York time, Gideon Raphael, the Israeli representative, informed the President of the Security Council that the Egyptian forces had launched an attack against Israel. The Egyptian representative—without the possibility of fore-knowledge—did not arrive until twenty minutes later. Later that day, at the emergency meeting of the Security Council, Mr Raphael gravely informed members that 'huge Egyptian armies had launched a "holy war" for the conquest of Palestine.'

In the Security Council, Russia immediately proposed a call for a cease-fire and a return to the positions occupied before the fighting started—a routine enough measure, one might have thought. The United States, which got the backing of Britain, proposed a simple cease-fire with no further addition. The resolution bogged down in talks over wording, and a cease-fire resolution with a time-limit was not passed until 7 June. It is impossible to believe that this could have happened had the United States' primary purpose been to halt the war. 'Washington,' reported the London *Times* correspondent, 'began to press Jerusalem to accept the cease-fire resolutions only when the victory of Israel arms was assured. Mr Arthur Goldberg was heard to say after one period of negotiation with his Russian opposite number: "Take your time." . . . Really heavy pressure to stop the fighting was not applied before Friday (9 June) when Israel began to move into Syria.'

[6] An American General, attached as an observer with the Israeli Army, stated in an American TV programme on the war that he *knew* that this was an important factor in the precise timing.

Meanwhile, the Israelis now quietly admitted that it was they who, despite undertaking to seek a diplomatic solution, had launched this Middle Eastern war in which perhaps 20,000 Arabs had been killed, many consumed by napalm rained from the air,[7] vast numbers rendered homeless, and the seeds of yet more bitter harvests sown. But by this time it hardly mattered. A large part of the Western world was lost in admiration at the 'brilliance' of the Israeli pre-emptive strike and subsequent ground attack. Much indignation was expended over the Nasser-Hussein allegation that American and British aircraft had supported Israel—a mistake which, in all the circumstances, was readily explicable. Not a word was heard about the Israeli deception at the United Nations. On the contrary, the Israeli success was hailed in some quarters as a triumph for Western civilised values. Abder Rahman Azzam had been right, it seemed: we were, indeed, back again in the days of the Crusades.

In 1956, with the nationalisation of the Suez Canal, Nasser had set out to expose the pretensions of the Western powers who sought to dictate to the Arab nations and he had succeeded brilliantly. In 1967, by resuming Egyptian control of the Gulf of Aqaba, he sought to expose the pretensions of the Israelis and he had failed disastrously.

The reasons for the sharply differing results are perhaps instructive. The ability to marshal and dramatically focus public opinion was one of Nasser's gifts. But the Israelis, enclosed within their own Truth, were—unlike the British at Suez— largely impervious to the pressures of world opinion. In any case, come what might, they were assured of massive emotional, financial and political support in the United States. In 1956, when the case appeared that of the old 'colonialist' Gunboat Goliaths anachronistically beating down an Egyptian David, American and British liberals alike had recognised a situation they understood and they had rallied to the Egyptian side. But few knew anything of the Arab world, and in 1967

[7] According to General John Glubb, former commander of the Jordan army, 'the greater part of the Jordan army was destroyed by napalm . . . many soldiers say their units were destroyed by fire without their ever seeing a single Israeli soldier.' *The Middle East Crisis* (London, 1967).

the rôles appeared to be reversed—the valiant little Israeli David against the rocket-clad, Russian-backed, bullying Goliath of massing Arab power. It was a travesty of the true situation, but it was probably what most people saw. The whirling Arab words, the threats blood-curdlingly amplified by the Arab mass-media, built up this picture. Thus the Israeli Foreign Minister found a ready audience for such disingenuous arguments as that 'there is no difference in civil law between murdering a man by slow strangulation and killing him by a short head' and that, therefore, after the announced blockade of the Straits of Tiran, 'the question of who started the war was irrelevant.' The blockade of the tiny port of Eilat was not, in fact, threatening Israel with strangulation, slow or otherwise. But it did involve a serious moral defeat, as it was meant to. As a *casus belli*, particularly before the blockade had even been tested or diplomatic measures seriously instituted, it was wholly inadequate. In fact the true cause, if not justification, of the Israel decision to attack was—in 1967 as in October 1956—the defence pact between Jordan and Egypt, concluded on this occasion on May 30. For in 1967, as in 1956, Israel's relations with the Arabs were still such that she could not tolerate any but a weak buffer state on her most vulnerable frontier.

'By posing the threat to our frontier,' writes the Israeli editor, Uri Avnery, 'Nasser rang the bell hidden in the unconscious mind of every Israeli, a signal which turns Israel, within the minute, from a peaceful country into an armed camp.' And certainly it is in this sphere of morale, communal emotion, psychological necessities, that the true causes of the 1967 war must be sought. For despite the blundering partisanship of the Super-Powers, and the large incidence of mischance, what happened here was merely a continuation of the classic process of escalation and confrontation that had been developing and hardening for more than a generation. Zionism had sought to concentrate and unify World Jewry on the soil of Palestine, bodily if possible, financially, politically, spiritually, if not, and when this produced, as in the historical circumstances of the Middle East it was bound to, a parallel closing of ranks and retreat into isolation by the Arabs, tensions rose until an explosion was detonated. Then *jihad* confronted *jihad*.

When the Israeli military chiefs learned of the 'closing' of the Straits of Tiran by Nasser on 23 May, they wished to attack at once. They did not favour international action, even less the normal use of vessels going into Eilat not flying the Israeli flag. For that would have been to concede a moral victory to the Arabs, and henceforth the military 'deterrent' upon which Israel was founded would have lost its power. The Generals were overruled. But their logic was impeccable. They had to wait only eleven days to demonstrate this fact again.

Professor Maxime Rodinson, French Jewish specialist on Middle Eastern affairs, sums up succinctly the reasoning of the key Israeli military and activist element: 'The possible gains to be had from diplomacy did not seem to them worth the human and strategic sacrifices it would mean for Israel. Some at least thought less in terms of defence than of attack. It was an ideal point at which to strike a heavy blow and administer the promised "good lesson" to the Arabs. After that the diplomats could have free rein.'

The political drama of Nasser had been defeated by the *realpolitik* of the Ben Gurion school. In the conditions of 1956 ideas had indeed proved 'stronger than armies'; but in 1967 it was superior armed power that prevailed. And yet, on both sides, it had been a battle of faiths and of wills, a confrontation of Absolutes of Old Testament or Koranic grandeur. And this battle was neither won, nor over. For the Israeli victory proved hollow—because it evoked, more insistently than ever, the question: what now? And in Zionist terms there was no answer, except a continuing progress towards Armageddon. There might, Mr Ben Gurion said in a BBC interview on 1 May 1968, be a fourth, a fifth, and a sixth Arab-Israeli war 'without an end.' Israel's major need, he stressed, was immigration.

But the bleak negativism of the Arab response also stood revealed. In the changed Arab world of 1967 Nasser was to some degree captive of the forces he himself had evoked. It was often mistakenly assumed in the West that Nasser was free to act as he chose. But in fact that very community of instinct and emotion which had enabled him to communicate so compellingly with the Arabs constituted a limitation when dealing with the outside world. In the dismal aftermath of the 'six-day war,' with Sinai littered with abandoned Egyptian tanks, with the Canal—which for eleven years had justifiably been Egypt's pride and chief foreign currency-earner—again closed by block-ships, and relations with much of the West severed, Nasser himself seemed guilty of having fallen into the belief against which he had warned fellow Arabs—the belief 'that power is merely shouting aloud.' For there had been, in the tank-to-tank confrontation in Sinai, in the dramatic Arab troop movements and military pledges and exultant rallying to the Cause, a strong echo of the old Arab *razzia*, in which the battle cries, the proud confrontation itself, the stirring-up of dust, could satisfy honour, without the necessity of much actual bloodshed. The Arabs exterminated Israel many times over with bitter tongues and, sometimes, privately, killed a few Israelis with mines or booby-traps, and the West expressed its repugnance and horror. The Israelis, with a better grasp of the realities of Western war, restrained their words and when they struck, struck hard, killed thousands, and much of the West cheered as if it were watching a football match.

And there, perhaps, was the Arabs' fundamental failure— their failure in communication. The odds were heavily stacked against them in presenting their case to the West. But at bottom their failure was due to pride, hurt pride, which, as a result, was hurt again. Nasser's revolution had intensified both the pride and the hurt. But it had also changed their nature. The dialogue with the West—'the World's Debate'— was shifting, slowly, on to a different plane.

In his 9 June broadcast to the nation Nasser described Egypt's crushing military defeat as a 'grave setback.' To the Western reader it seemed an odd choice of nouns. Yet it may well prove to have been the right one. Certainly the chapter which concluded with the six-day war was nearer the beginning than the end of the book.

A Catalyst Still

In 1967, as on earlier occasions, the Israeli challenge accelerated the pace of development in the Arab world.

In 1966, in a BBC programme to mark the tenth anniversary of the Suez action, Mr Abba Eban, the Israeli Foreign Minister, referring to the disarray of the Arab world at that time—the civil war in the Yemen, the split into 'revolutionary' and 'traditionalist' camps, and the many lesser feuds—spoke with some assurance of 'the postponement of a Dream, and perhaps its relinquishment.'

The dream in question was not the dream of Zion, but the dream of Arab Unity, of a resurgent, modern and powerful 'Arab Nation' which the strange genius of Gamal Abdel Nasser had so potently renewed. Yet, in less than a year, all the lines of force in the Arab world had again swung round, like the iron filings under a magnet's pull, to point towards Cairo, and from Rabat to Kuwait the Arab world spoke with one voice and pledged itself to united action.

The single cause of this extraordinary transformation was Israel, her threats of action against Syria, and Nasser's dramatic response. Nor were the Arab nations' pledges empty. Despite poor co-ordination—and Israel hardly left time for overmuch of this—the level of common action, both military and economic, was more complete than it had ever been before. Algeria, Iraq, the Sudan, and Kuwait dispatched troops; Kuwait, Saudi Arabia and Libya sent money; Bourguiba hastened to patch up his feud with Cairo; and even in Lebanon and in 'royalist' Libya and Morocco, the Arab trade unions ensured the stoppage of oil shipments and boycotting of 'suspect' shipping.

What was more extraordinary, and wholly Arab, was that Egypt's humiliating defeat, and Nasser's resignation, instantaneously gave rise to acclamation and a demand for his return, with renewed pledges of brotherhood and support from all over the Arab world. For Nasser represented Arab pride and self-respect, and this could not be abandoned. In the Yemen, the leaders of the two most powerful tribes, the Hashed and Bakil, who for ten months had been in rebellion against the Egyptian-backed régime, marched into Sana and pledged themselves to follow the lead of President Nasser in the Arab struggle for justice. In Libya, the withdrawal of the U.S. and British bases was speeded; in Aden there was a mutiny of 'Federal Government' Arab troops and police; again, as at Suez, the course of revolution was speeded and broadened. At the Khartoum summit conference in September, the major

Arab oil states agreed to pay £95 millions a year to Egypt to replace the lost Suez Canal dues and £40 millions annually to Jordan, a precedent which could prove of historic importance.

Certainly, this rediscovered 'unity' might well prove no less transitory than on former occasions. But then, was not the very persistence and instinctive character of this urge, this extraordinary electricity that almost instantaneously brought together Arabs of all sorts over so vast an area, even if only temporarily, in itself a phenomenon of which the world should take note?

Despite the failure of the Syrian union in 1961, Egypt had retained the name 'United Arab Republic'; and on two occasions since there had been tentative moves towards closer ties, including 'federation,' with both Syria and Iraq. The constitutions of many Arab countries referred to their being a 'part of the Arab Nation' and 'Arab Unity' remained an unfailing theme of Arab perorations.[8]

In face of the frequently displayed *disunity* of the Arab nations, could this concept of an 'Arab nation' have any real meaning? The answer is of more than academic importance because on it must turn in large degree our interpretation of the tumultuous developments in the Arab world in recent years. If, for instance, it does have substance, Nasser's widely condemned 'adventurism' or 'imperialism' in the Yemen and elsewhere outside the Nile Valley may become, even if still ill-judged, the acceptance of an Arab responsibility, an involvement to be expected of the largest and most advanced Arab nation.

'The Arab Nation' is rhetoric certainly, but it is a good deal more than that—as the whole course of the new Arab revolution indicates. 'Arabism' is at least as real—and more obsessional—than was pan-Germanism in 19th-century Europe, and the bickering of the Arab states is not notably greater than was that of the former petty states of Germany. Nor is the difference between a Moroccan and an Egyptian greater than between, say, an East Prussian and a Bavarian.

[8] In March 1967, members of the Egyptian preparatory committee for the Permanent Constitution rejected a proposal to change the country's name to the 'Egyptian Arab Republic.' The Constitutions of Morocco, Algeria and Tunisia specify 'the Greater Maghreb'; those of Lebanon and Libya (the latter a U.N. product) are discreetly silent.

Because of its vast spaces, and that lack of natural frontiers which facilitated the original spread of Islam, the Arab world is woven into an intricate web of relationships, of family, clan, and sect, which really does stretch, in the words of the Baath Party Constitution, 'from the Taurus Mountains to the Atlantic.' Even so apparently remote a land as the Yemen is of this fabric. It is said that the army with which General Amr captured Cairo for Islam in 640 was largely composed of Yemenis; the founder of the Zeidi Imamate migrated to the Yemen from Iraq, and paid homage to the Fatamid Caliphs in Cairo, who had originated in 'Algeria' and Syria; later the Kurd Saladin conquered the Yemen, and in the 14th century, it became an Egyptian (Mameluke) colony.

This intermixing has remained normal at all levels, military, political, and simply domestic, to the present day. Lawrence in his campaign in the desert had with him not only Hejazis, Syrians, Iraqis, but also Algerians-in-exile; the father of Egyptian nationalism, Ahmed Arabi, claimed to be of Bedouin origin; the great King Ibn Saud's first Foreign Minister was a Lebanese, his first Education Minister, and long-time London Ambassador, an Egyptian. On a less exalted level, Stewart Perowne[9] tells of a 'typical foothill village in Palestine' one half of whose 300 families was descended from an ancestor who came from Libya, the other half from soldiers who came with Ibrahim Pasha's Egyptian army in 1831. And even in the relative insularity of the Nile Valley personal links with the Arab world outside are many. The great crowds of Egyptians who yearly made pilgrimage to the tomb of Sheikh Ahmed el Badawi in Tanta are honouring a saint who hailed from Fez in distant Morocco.

Islam, the culture in which these inter-relationships were developed and preserved, has also given a close family resemblance to all the widely separated Arab nationalist movements; for it was Islam that enabled the peoples to hold together under alien domination, and, later, to summon the strength to break out of it. The French in Algeria faced a *jihad* within a few weeks of landing in 1830. Here they set out to undermine Islam, dividing Berbers from Arabs, teaching little or no Arabic in their schools, finally offering French citizenship at the price

[9] S. Perowne: *The One Remains*, London, 1954.

of surrender of status under Muslim law. But though they found, as usual, many eager students, they found few who would surrender their Muslim identity, and in the 1930s it was an association of Muslim religious teachers who set the nationalist pace, starting 'free' schools for the teaching of Arabic. In Morocco it was a scholar of the University of Karouane at Fez, Allal al-Fassi, who, beginning with clubs to reform Islam, ended by founding the Independence Party which in the 1950s linked with the Algerian F.L.N. to expel the French from North Africa and bring down the Fourth Republic.

Most of the Algerian nationalists received their real education in France or in the French army where they met the full force of French secularism and scepticism. Yet if the Arabic of its leaders was sometimes fragmentary, the FLN was soon displaying a truly Islamic Puritanism in action, and when it became a government, 'Arabisation'—involving a heavy burden of bilingual teaching in primary schools—became a shibboleth. 'Algerians,' wrote Ben Bella, 'experience . . . a deep disquiet when they try to give expression to their ideas in French while they "feel" in Arabic. A state of perpetual divorce is thus established in us between the head and the heart.' So in a country by Arab standards far from devout or even religious, new mosques were being erected everywhere. Only thus, it was felt, could a national identity be firmly based, and Algerians become more than second-class Frenchmen. Nor was it, perhaps, against the logic of events that the *lycée*-educated Ben Bella, holder of the French *Médaille Militaire*, although himself more 'Arab' than such earlier 'assimilated' leaders as Ferhat Abbas, was in due course displaced by the aboriginally Muslim graduate of El Azhar, Houari Boumedienne.

Thus, in the present as in the past, in the Maghreb as in the East, the foundations of Arabism were reinforced; and in the mid-20th century, major political, or more accurately, religio-political, movements like the Muslim Brotherhood, Baath Socialism, and 'Nasserism' were able quickly to transcend their frontiers of origin to swell and deepen the currents flowing across the Arab world as a whole.

It was an organic unity of a sort, not of the body, but of the emotions and the nervous system, and the very swiftness and frequency of those abrupt transitions which so bewilder the Westerner testify to its reality. 'A nation,' wrote Renan, 'is a soul, a spiritual principle. . . . To share the common glories of the past, to have a common will in the present, to have done great things together, to want to go on doing them, such are the essential conditions of being a people. . . .'

It is hardly remarkable, perhaps, that Arab writers quote Renan.

'The Arab Nation——'

The West was much misled in these matters by the neat maps of the Arab world it had prepared and by its habit of reading into them the same sort of significance it would have attached to such areas and frontiers north of the Mediterranean. It subconsciously assumed 'edge-to-edge' nations with an integrated government and social fabric, and an importance in some way proportionate to the area taken up on the map.

But reality was otherwise. For instance, 'Yemen' is the Arabic for 'Right'—south of Mecca, it is on the right hand of an Arab facing East towards Mecca. And, as far as coherence, firm frontiers, and governmental structure goes, 'the land to the South,' occupied by shifting alliances of tribes, is about all the Yemen still is, even though it contains something like half the population of the whole Arabian peninsula. But what, for that matter, is 'Saudi Arabia' beyond a great deal of empty desert, a great deal of oil money, and the Family of old Ibn Saud, inter-married and interlocked with the Sheikh Family, the descendants of the first Mohamed Ibn Abdel Wahab, with the aid of whose Islamic fanaticism Ibn Saud built and cemented his kingdom? Although proclaimed 'The United Kingdom' in 1932, Saudi Arabia has so far failed to reach its natural physical limits on the Gulf, and since 95 per cent of its inhabitants are illiterate, 60 per cent nomadic or semi-nomadic, occupying a vast and arid emptiness, the failure is hardly remarkable.

Thus while the 'Arab Nation' may lack physical substance, it has greater reality than a good many so-called 'Arab nations': and for many of the modern citizens of these, the magic of Gamal Abdel Nasser lay in his ability to project and

symbolise in contemporary form a real—if rather metaphysical
—'Arab Nation' to which they could owe allegiance.

——and the Arab Nations

Yet the nuances of this potent old idea of 'Arab Unity' were
in fact changing rapidly as modern communications developed
and independent Arab governments grew up within the
frontiers the West had drawn. A laden camel travels at 2½
miles an hour, a lorry at fifty or more, and an airliner at 400:
a world of space and movement was now giving place to a
world of uncomfortably near neighbours. Thanks in the main
to the road-building energies of the French and the Italians, it
is today a simple matter to traverse the 5,000 miles or so of
the 'Arab Fatherland . . . from the Atlantic to the Taurus
Mountains' at speed by ordinary motor-car. Apart from the
break occasioned by 'unrecognised' Israel, the only obstruc-
tions which impede the rapid progress of such a traveller are
the frontiers between brother Arab nations. 'Artificial' these
frontiers may be, but their customs-and-immigration barriers
are all too real; and anyone making such a journey must be
at least as much impressed by the sharp differences as by the
underlying similarities it reveals.

They are differences etched by geographical circumstance,
by historical experience, by cultural and 'racial' inter-mixture;
and often they go deep. In spite of the nearness of Europe and
the skyscrapers of Casablanca, on entering the Arab world via
Morocco one still has a sense of entering a complex, still intact,
civilisation from the Islamic past, such as one finds in no other
part of this world. The Turks never pushed so far West, the
French did not begin to penetrate Morocco until 1907, and
its vast universe of great mountains and upland plains was not
'pacified' until 1934. The present King, Hassan II, stands nineteenth in a line that goes back to the 17th century, and the
country, despite fluctuating frontiers and intervals of anarchy,
has been ruled by its own Berber and Arab dynasties since the
9th century.

Morocco's first Arab neighbour, Algeria, shares with her the
vast mountain ranges and uplands, and the large, imperfectly

'Arabised,' Berber (Kabyle) population that still lives there.[10] 'We accepted the Koran,' one Kabyle intellectual explained, 'but the Arab *ésprit* did not *'pénétrer l'âme.'* Nor had it, to hear his views on Ben Bella, penetrated that particular Kabyle soul even yet. The language and idiom pointed to another major source of inter-Arab division: Algeria was joined to France for over a century. Contacts with French administrators, newspapers, culture over such a length of time, above all, ready access to France herself via Marseilles, have given many Algerians habits of thought—even ways of standing and moving—as ostensibly French as the neat squares and box-trees and *mairies* of the towns of the Algerian coastal plain. There is a mental spark here, a readiness for the cut-and-thrust of dialectic, which elsewhere in the Arab world would seem impious or embarrassing. The Algerians have received much aid from their Egyptian 'brothers'; but propinquity with, for instance, the many Egyptian teachers can bring a clash of temperament that puts brotherhood in some peril. 'I don't care for Nasser,' said a young Algerian *garagiste*, a former FLN sergeant. 'Not because he has not done much for his people— he has. But because the Algerians and Egyptians are *different*. *Les Egyptiens sont égoistes.'* It is a question of style; but, as the reactions of Syrians, Yemenis, and Sudanese to the Egyptian brothers have in their time demonstrated, in the Arab world style can be very important.

However, fervent—and necessary—Algeria's 'Arabisation' policy, the pull of France—economic as well as cultural—is likely to remain powerful. 'We must,' wrote Ben Bella, 'preserve that breadth of mind which the French language has given us.' Of the six newspapers published in Algiers, five are in French and one, the weakest, in Arabic; it is not surprising, then, that when they reach the secondary-school stage, students are still inclined to opt for French. For as one judiciously observed to me, 'Arabic is not an international language' —and educated young Algerians consider themselves very much citizens of the world. They are also emphatic nationalists, but their nationalism is Algerian first, and Arab, if at all. some considerable way after. *'Arabe?'* pronounced a young

[10] It is estimated that 40 per cent of the population of Morocco speaks both Arabic and one or other of the Berber dialects.

man in Bône fiercely. *'Cela ne fait rien! Berber? Cela ne fait rien! Nous sommes Algériens! Algériens!'*

There spoke, perhaps, eight years of civil war in which a million died and thousands of villages were destroyed.

The mountains, the cork trees, the olives, the vines continue over the frontier into Tunisia. But then the memory of those wrecked Kabyle mountain villages, bravely rebuilding, recedes —for Tunis belongs to an older, mellower, Mediterranean world. Here, in this small headland, with the hot breath of the vast Eastern desert at the gates, the fusion of Berber and Arab is complete, and Tunisians, who can claim a tradition of urban life going back to the time of Carthage, take a quiet pride in their rôle as the holders of the Arab world's bridgehead to Europe. (Sicily is 120 miles away.) Islam in its great tidal movements paused here twice, once on its way westward when it entrenched itself in the fortress-mosque of Kairouan, the second time, seven or eight centuries later, on the return journey—no longer primitive, but endowed now with the sophistication of Andalusia. Tunisians are justly famed for an urbanity.

Three hundred miles south and east of Tunis, the Libyan frontier brings not only new languages—Italian and English— but one of the vast hiatuses of the Arab world—more than a thousand miles of desert, relieved only by a brief coastal strip and the two hundred scrubby miles of Jebel Akhdar, the Green Mountain. This phantom—if now oil-rich—country serves to link the Arab West and the Arab East, but amid the faded splendours of Mussolini's 'Fourth Shore' and the oil-company hustle, the Libyans remain elusive. Generations devoted to watching sheep, and to little else, seem to have endowed them with a bottomless inertia. Even now in Cyrenaica most do not move outside their clan: a young man in charge of the Benghazi tourist office had not even been to Tripolitania, and when it was decided to mark white traffic lines on the Benghazi streets it was necessary to send for Tripoli sophisticates to do it. An Arabist with considerable experience said in puzzled tones: 'They are the *quietest* Arabs I know.' A contractor, with experience in twelve eastern countries, observed less kindly that the Libyan 'workers' were the most hopeless he'd ever encountered.

King Idris, head of the Senussi mystic missionary brotherhood, who has *been* 'Libya' to all intents and purposes for the last twenty years, is now a frail old man who spends most of his time in retreat in his 'palace' at Tobruk on the eastern extremity of his vast, empty domain. But if otherwise hard to grasp, the country is at least well provided with 'capitals.' In addition to the rival metropolises of Tripoli and Benghazi, separated by 800 miles of sand, Libya—a unitary state since 1963—now has yet another, even further east, built at a cost of £6,000,000 in the remote Jebel Akhdar. A 'city' of portentous Ministerial buildings, and a vast domed Parliament, its site was selected by the King personally because it was the birthplace of the Senussi cult in Cyrenaica, the site of the *Zawilya el-Beida* (the White Monastery), built by his grandfather, the Grand Senussi, and the spot where the Prophet's standard-bearer died. All in all, the $1\frac{1}{2}$ million Libyans, inhabiting a country bigger than all Western Europe, remain a shadowy presence in the councils of the 'Arab Nation.'

The Egyptian frontier at Sollum marks no real break in this desert world: the tribes and flocks move over it. Yet a certain cheerful professionalism in the Egyptian officials indicates that one has indeed crossed a frontier and reached a nation; and strange as it may seem to those who have suffered in the toils of Egyptian bureaucracy, this first impression of plodding, workaday professionalism is correct. This again is something that derives from history, and marks the Egyptian off from his fellow Arabs.

'Fellow Arabs?' Even now, within the Nile Valley itself, the ascription seems a little odd, and Egyptians themselves sometimes betray a certain ambivalence in their approach to the 'Arab' shibboleth. Yet the diversity of the Arab world is certainly wide enough to accommodate them—for even within the Arabian peninsula itself, whose ten million inhabitants might reasonably claim to be the only unequivocally *Arab* Arabs, much more than physical distance separates the little mountain warriors of the Yemen from the princely merchants of the Gulf, or from the isolated tribal sheikhs of the desert oases. Travel through the Arab world is illustrative of nothing so much as that 'the Arab Nation' belongs to the realm of ideas (and is nonetheless potent for that).

Arabia's ocean of sand sweeps on eastwards for more than a thousand miles into the Syrian Desert. With Syria, the Arab world is bathed again in Mediterranean light, yet a light that is different from either the Nile Delta's or North Africa's. A touch of the radiance of old Byzantium, perhaps, fused with Arab romanticism, French intellectualism, archaic sectarianism, and, now, Marxist-Lenism—a volatile blend. Then, as one crosses the green wall of anti-Lebanon and Lebanon and comes down from the Mountain, the Arab apocalypse, while no less imminent, changes its nature and—in weeks when there are not too many bank failures—its golden glint may be clearly discerned from the baroque apartment blocks that soar from Ras Beirut.

The Christian Lebanese, who are Lebanon's raison d'être, like to cast their country as 'Phoenicia' to Tunisia's 'Carthage,' and they have a point; yet in its small compass this country spans the gamut of the Arab East. The shiny Mercedes cars and taxis that screech up and down the road over the Mountain can transport one in a matter of minutes from the world of the slick financial operators and the American filling-station-and-supermarket gloss ('20,000 Hamburgers sold so far' boasts a proud 'Pizzeria' window) to simple Maronite Christian villages with their sturdily independent life or to the meagre world of the Muslim helots of the 'feudal' lords of the Bekaa. Sometimes indeed the Lebanese miracle contrives to encompass half these contradictory worlds in a single individual—like the celebrated Lebanese Socialist leader, Kemal Jumblatt, a Druse clan chief, chairman of a crypto-Communist Labour Liberation Front, who in the last resort owes his political position to the support of his mettlesome Druse private army.

Some Arab frontiers correspond to realities; others are figments: the Arab world's process of adjustment, its quest for stable and meaningful modern organisation, has only just begun. Travelling across it with the continuity which modern transport makes possible, one becomes aware of both the strength and the complexity of the forces at work. Everywhere, 'the Arab Nation' remains a master theme, but now it is counterpointed by the particularist nationalism of some rising Arab nations. 'Algeria' might have been, in origin, a French artefact, yet from the furnace of the FLN's war may emerge a true Algerian nation. And if Tunisia also faces problems created by French cultural domination, a homogeneity and continuity equalled in the Arab world propably only by Egypt should enable her to surmount them. Even the Lebanon, that strange relic of the Crusader Kingdom, its present frontiers the product of French gerrymandering, may claim to be a functional nation by reason of the flair which it brings to its rôle as the Arab world's conning tower, balance mechanism, and safety valve. If the Lebanese did not exist, it would probably be necessary to invent them.

Yet, despite the confident labels on the maps, the Arab world is full of 'non-nations' too, with archaic social and governmental structures and formidable natural obstacles to cohesion and modernisation. The Yemen, Saudi Arabia, Libya, Jordan, Kuwait, the Gulf Sheikhdoms, and now 'South Arabia' are elusive entities which have come into being through a variety of historical accidents and have been maintained by inertia, the *status quo*, and narrowly vested interests. Here the idea of 'Arab Unity' may still be a potent force both for disruption and cohesion.

The Arab World of Tomorrow

But the modern approach to 'Arab Unity,' bringing a demand that the idea be embodied in practical political and economic terms, clearly presents a challenge absent from the older style, which amounted to a sort of Arab epic poem of self-sufficient validity. Among the first results of freedom in the Arab West were bitter frontier disputes between Morocco and Algeria and between Tunisia and Algeria (with mineral prizes at stake). In the Arab East also, despite a somewhat longer experience of independence, and successive efforts towards closer ties, the passions of the politicians have generally proved stronger than the logic of the still outnumbered technocrats. Poem and reality, Word and world, still overlap confusingly. Signed in 1962 under Arab League auspices, the Economic Unity Agreement provided for 'The Arab State' which was to have 'a unified, integrated, proportionate, Arab economy, guided by a single economic policy for all component parts.'

In fact, what was, precariously, shaping was a mechanism of co-ordination for the Arab West and Arab East separately. In November 1964 the Economic Ministers of Morocco, Algeria, Tunisia, and Libya set up a permanent secretariat at Tunis to co-ordinate their agricultural exports. Economic ties are strengthened for the three countries of the Maghreb by their common links with France, with whom Algeria, for instance, does more than three-quarters of her trade.

In the Arab East, a progressive Common Market agreement between Egypt, Jordan, Syria and Iraq came into operation in 1965, implying inter-member tariff reductions of 10 per cent annually for ten years, providing for regional planning, and for various pan-Arab enterprises such as an Arab tanker company and world shipping lines. But the 'Market's' style was badly cramped by the absence of the 'banker' countries— Lebanon, Saudi Arabia, and Kuwait.[11] The crux of the matter lay in the willingness or lack of willingness, in the oil-rich Arab countries, to finance development in those Arab areas where investment would most effectively build up the region as a whole. So far a very large part of the oil money has flowed out to the West, has been sunk in Beirut apartment blocks, or simply used to import floods of consumer goods which could have been made in the Arab lands. In 1964, intra-regional trade was estimated at only 10 per cent of the region's total trade.[12]

But tremendous outside pressures upon the Arab world— 'Suez' in 1956, the Arab-Israeli war of 1967—force the pace of pan-Arab development. Then, for instance, the 'Western' oil industry in the Arab countries appears more than ever a challenge, an indictment of Arab 'backwardness' which can only be met by joint action. 'Suez' first demonstrated the possibilities vividly, if crudely; and in 1959 the first Arab Petroleum Congress met in Cairo, followed by the formation of the

[11] These countries, it is true, contribute to the Arab Development Bank, but the capital of this remains puny beside Kuwait's own Arab Fund. Kuwait at first signed the Common Market agreement, then on a vote of its Assembly withdrew.
[12] A. J. Meyer in *The United States and the Middle East* (Prentice Hall, 1964). Professor Meyer estimates that between 1953 and the mid-'sixties, capital movements from the Arab oil countries westwards totalled well over £800 millions.

Organisation of Petroleum Exporting Countries in Baghdad in 1960. And although OPEC was not wholly Arab, the rich rewards it won from the oil companies by its expertise and its common front underlined the value of the pan-Arab technocratic approach to the Arab world's needs.

But however dismal the gap between promise and performance, the picture of a disintegrating, fanatical Arab world which is often all that comes through to the West is remote from reality. As one moves through the Arab world today there is one sight one sees everywhere—in the remote countryside as well as in the towns, in the mountains as well as the desert: the sight of bright-eyed, decently clad young children, plodding along the roads with their plastic satchels on their way to school. Tunisia, Egypt, Lebanon and Syria are already moving quickly towards universal primary education. But even in Cyrenaica, with more than 90 per cent illiteracy, you will see small Bedouin *girls* with tattooed faces, wearing attractive bright blue smocks with golden bands around the waist on their way to school.

In education and social welfare, in modern communications, in industrialisation, and even in the age-old occupations of agriculture, the people of the Arab world are rushing forward into modern times. In the West, Tunisia's new steel complex at Bizerta, built by the Anglo-French-Swiss consortium, echoes Algeria's iron and steel plant to be provided by Russia at Bône; Algeria's planned petrochemical plant at the end of the natural-gas line for the Sahara, at Arzew, mirrors Morocco's modern heavy chemicals complex at Safi on the Atlantic coast, based on that country's rich phosphate deposits. In the Arab East, Iraq has doubled her *per capita* income since 1950, and Jordan was at last within sight of economic viability when she entered the Arab-Israeli war at the call of her attacked ally, Egypt. Even Syria—through her endless political turmoil since 1948—has vastly expanded her cotton growing, increased her industry, and created a new grain-growing area in the north-east, multiplying the number of tractors in use by at least ten times. Roads have been pushed ahead, in many places large irrigation and land-improvement schemes are in progress, and now Syria is embarking, with Russian aid, on the great Euphrates Dam.

All over the Arab world, roads are being pushed out: into the wilds of the Hadramaut, from Kuwait to Basra in Iraq (completed in 1961), along the Libyan coast and down into Africa. The Saudi Road Plan provides for metalled roads to continue from both the Red Sea and Gulf coasts a thousand miles or so into Jordan. The Arab world is slowly knitting together in spite of itself. In 1964 Kuwait finally brought herself to sign an agreement to take water by pipeline from the Shatt el Arab sixty miles away in Iraq, a measure previously avoided at fabulous cost out of fear of placing herself at her neighbour's mercy.

The old maps of the Arab world were basically maps of rainfall, rivers, sects, and foreign occupations or spheres of influence. The new maps are maps of raw materials (including oil), industrial installations and projects, technological skills and training capacity. Over the years, these maps will finally merge to form the map of a new Arab world which one can imagine polarising around its industrial complexes—Rabat—Casablanca, Oran-Algiers, Helwan-Alexandria, and, assuming that the breach which has energised so much of this development can ever be healed, Tel Aviv—Beirut. Aden, historically 'the Eye of the Yemen,' with its refinery, its shipping and its lively mixed population, might become a major centre[13] of the South, backed by the vast, fertile hinterland of a literate and developed Yemen—the *Arabia Felix* of the ancients.

Yet anyone speculating on the future shape of the Arab world who neglects the socio-political maps does so at his peril, for it is these which in the long run will prove decisive. Modern armaments may be purchased but are of little avail without the skills and, even more, the will to use them; oil wealth can finance modern industrial plants, but it cannot create the social cohesion and participation indispensable to a modern industrialising society. A true modernity cannot be created overnight or even in a single generation—a point which those who favour the building up of Saudi Arabia as a counterweight to 'Nasser' would do well to bear in mind.

When, in 1964, the 'modernising' Feisal took over in Saudi

[13] An Egyptian agricultural expert of high repute, who had just returned from a survey of Yemen, told me that there were 10 million acres of good soil of which only 2 million are at present cultivated.

Arabia, Saud's deposition and his own installation was decreed by the Council of Royal Princes and *Ulema*, or Wahhabi divines, who were thus confirmed as the twin sources of supreme—and almost sole—power. But the Saudi *Ulema* have fought every change; in the 'thirties they protested against the teaching of geography, foreign languages and drawing; there are those who still contest the spherical earth.[14] It is true the *Ulema* are now in retreat before television, and have even been brought (under protest) to agree that Micky Mouse on the TV screen may put an arm around Minnie. But even with steel mills on the Gulf, quintupled education, colleges of petroleum and engineering technology, and a 950-mile metalled road, completed in 1968, across the country from Gulf to Red Sea, it is not easy to see how this vast and torrid void can contain the makings of a modern nation.

On both the old 'geographical' and the new socio-political and technological maps, Egypt, however, occupies a truly pivotal position. Egypt is the hinge of the Arab world: her population of almost 30 millions roughly equals that of all the Arab countries to her east, and again of all the Arab countries to her west and south. Numbers are not necessarily an advantage in a country with few natural resources, but in Egypt they are accompanied not only by a homogeneity rare in the Arab world—and likely to become more effective as village clannishness breaks down—but by a proportionately greater predominance in the skills, techniques and knowledge necessary to a modern, industrialising society. Whereas the Saudi Arabian government established a technical and craft training school in 1964, Mohamed Ali, in Egypt, established his in 1821. Iraq did not acquire a Ministry of Agriculture until 1952; Kitchener set one up in Egypt in 1911 and by 1952 Egypt had at least a generation of trained agriculturalists. By 1961, more than 100,000 Egyptians had graduated from the Egyptian universities, 58,000 of them in the natural sciences and technology, forming a reasonably solid base on which the rapid expansion of higher education in the last few years could be built. By contrast, Morocco was still very largely dependent on the

[14] For a full account of this unusual obstacle to educational advance, see *Arabian Days*, by Sheikh Hafiz Wahba, the first Minister of Education.

French; Algeria, where 90 per cent of trade and industry was in European hands, and the top civil service was only 5 per cent Algerian, was brought almost to a standstill by the *colons'* departure, and it was 1955 before Tunisia got a teachers' training college. Lebanon boasts the highest literacy rate (85 per cent) in the Arab world, but has only vestigial industry and only 2¼ million people. 'Egypt alone among the Arab states,' considers Professor Polk,[15] 'has the potential for industrialisation on a large scale.' In 1964, Egypt's Gross National Product was estimated to equal half the total of those of all the other Arab states put together.

It was thus inevitable that it should fall to Egypt to provide the teachers and various sorts of specialists for a large part of the Arab world. Nearly all Libya's judges and teachers were at first Egyptian, and for some time at least the Egyptian teacher became a figure only a little less ubiquitous than once was the Greek grocer. At the same time, students from other Arab countries travel in large numbers to Egypt's numerous educational establishments. Of 839 Kuwaitis studying abroad in 1965, nearly 500 were in Egypt. Ten per cent of the places in Egyptian universities are reserved for foreign students, mainly from other Arab lands.

And to these must now be added trainees in such contemporary art-sciences as TV, the cinema, and other forms of those 'mass communications' which constitute the vital fluid of a modern nation. 'Cairo Radio' is a name of ill-omen in the West, but its potency is due not only to its vehemence, but also to the professionalism which has made its three Arabic programmes, among the many put out into the Arab ether, listened to so widely. Egyptian television and the Egyptian cinema are also both by far the biggest in the Arab world; Egyptian films draw half their revenue from audiences in other Arab or Arabic-speaking countries. But Egyptian predominance is perhaps most striking in print. The great bulk of Arabic novels are by Egyptian writers, and the circulations of Egyptian newspapers and magazines are incomparably greater than those of their Arabic counterparts in other Arab countries. Cairo's *Al Ahram* and the weekly *Akhbar el Yom*,

[15] Lately Assistant Professor of Semitic Languages and History at Harvard, *Foreign Affairs Quarterly Review*, October 1965.

sell around 400,000 each; the biggest-selling newspaper in Beirut sells less than 30,000.

Firmly based in geography, history and demography, the inevitability of Egypt's central rôle in the developing Arab world is underlined as the old imperial powers withdraw from their last positions, leaving behind them a confusion which they can no longer hope to remedy. Egypt can no more retire into the Nile Valley now than the United States can return to isolationism (although both Egyptians and Americans by inclination might like to).

Yet in an Arab world so vast, so full of discontinuities, and torn by sectarian, tribal, and personal feuds—enlarged and built upon by Great Power rivalries—progress must inevitably be patchy and erratic. Egyptian bombs dropped on rebel Yemenis in the 1960s did not notably differ from the R.A.F. bombs of the earlier 'civilising mission,' except in their more 'up-to-date' composition. Nor was execution by firing squad, from the point of view of the recipients, much of an advance on execution by the headsman's sword in the main square.

Patience is not an Arab virtue and Egyptians, discarding over-suddenly their Nile Valley insularism, have perhaps been too precipitate in their zeal to assist the Arab World towards its Manifest Destiny. The more ardent pan-Arab 'revolutionaries' might, at this stage, do well to consider in the context of other Arab nations than their own a principle enunciated by Nasser himself in his 'Charter': 'the real solutions for the problems of a people cannot be imported from the experiences of others.'

But so, equally, might the Great Powers who, having sought in vain to impose their own favoured forms, must now surely at last see that 'stability' in the Arab world is something which can only grow from within.

The View from Alexandria

This is a region of the world where perspectives are both uniquely long and preposterously short. In the summer of 1967, it was possible in Egypt vividly to experience both varieties. In the North, the Egyptian army looked across the Canal to Israeli troops on the East bank and knew once again the bitterness of defeat. But 700 miles to the south, behind the rock-and-sand mountain of the High Dam, the water was still rising in that vast and sombre granite basin. It would rise steeply to 1970, thereafter more slowly, to reach its peak, perhaps, about 1980. And in the land below the Dam, from the white villages of Nubia to the citrus orchards of Liberation Province, thousands of miles of new channels, a vast new capillary system, carried the fertilising water over new fields. By 1967/8 a total of 825,000 feddans had been added to Egypt's cultivated area. The green of the Valley was pushing outwards; the Delta was almost visibly widening. To the east, half a million marshy acres, carrying the Delta up to the Canal's edge, were now to be reclaimed. To the West, a dozen big reclamation schemes were beginning to knit together; the vision of Liberation Province was on its way to realisation, in substance, if not in name and detail. Beneath the Desert Road from Cairo to Alexandria now flowed the new Hurreya (Independence) Canal in which the 'used' saline water from a Delta main exit drain, instead of being pumped into the lakes and the sea, was mixed, in scientific proportion, with the 'new' water of the Nile and thus made to serve its turn again—an ultimate in organic economy. To the Delta's north-west, cultivation was being pushed back from the rain-touched coast by means of wells and cisterns; and the New Valley, linking the western oases, held out its speculator's promise of a break-out from the old valley's seven millenia of close confinement.

And while, as population still soared, this was a Sisyphean labour, the harnessing of science, electric power, and industry symbolised by the High Dam now offered ultimate deliverance. Land-per-head was no longer the sole, dominating statistic. By 1969, the High Dam's turbines would be twelve, and by 1970 the annual output would have reached 12,000 million kilowatt-hours, doubling the country's power supply. Nor was that the end. In its journey from Aswan to the sea, the Nile falls seventy-five metres and this, with its great water flow, means that its potency is far from exhausted. Four new hydro-electric stations on present barrages have been envisaged, seven new barrages could be constructed. Beyond that, there is a fifteen-year project for harnessing the Nile further south, where half its flow is lost in the vast swamps of the Sudd in the Sudan. And beyond that there is the Qattara Depression hydro-electric generation scheme, seawater desalination by atomic power, both already prospected, not to mention the growing hopes of oil.

These were the vistas that had been opened up—and given an edge of reality by actual achievements—by the Egyptian revolution since 1952, and no pre-emptive air strike by Israel could close them now. In his speech of resignation on the evening of that military disaster in early June 1967, Nasser spoke of his continuing pride in 'the contribution of this generation of revolutionaries.' It had, he said, 'brought about a profound change in the Arab way of life.' It had 'defined Egypt's Arab character, fought the policy of zones of influence in the Arab world, led the socialist revolution.' It had 'affirmed the people's control over their resources, recovered the Suez Canal, laid down the bases of industrial build-up . . . placed the workers in the leadership of political action. . . .'

These were just claims and it was a proper pride. It might also be noted in passing that Nasser's resignation was discussed and rejected by an elected National Assembly. The army's humiliating defeat—and the subsequent unsuccessful plot by dismissed officers and the sacked Minister of War to reinstate themselves and the former Commander-in-Chief, Abdel Hakim Amer—had the salutary effect of moving the military further back on the national stage. The details of this somewhat half-baked conspiracy, which ended in the suicide of Nasser's old friend and right-hand man, Abdel Hakim Amer, were revealed in the lengthy public trial of the officers involved—a course adopted, Nasser told a meeting of Arab journalists in February 1968, 'so that the alert people may know . . . that the process is a political and social process and that there was a military class which considered itself the legitimate heir to power. Thank God all that is over, and the Armed Forces have been put in their proper place.'

Some may find this a somewhat too timely afterthought, yet it is, in fact, the continuation of a theme—the need for renewal from the people—which Nasser took up some years before the war. In 1956, the régime had taken the first step back towards constitutionalism when its officer ministers resigned from the army and a large civilian element was taken

into the Cabinet. The process of 'civilianisation' and 'democratisation' was a continuing one, and Nasser was saying
nothing new when, on Revolution Day 1967, he called on the
'old guard' to step back to make way for the new generation
of leaders produced by its revolution. In the spring of 1968,
following the student demonstrations which appear in some
ways almost as an orchestration of this theme, the Egyptian
Cabinet was reconstituted to admit another influx of 'new
faces,' mainly university professors and technocrats. By 1968,
the army's crucial political and technological rôle in the making of the New Egypt was over. It may be that in the perspective of history, the tragic death of Abdel Hakim Amer will be
seen to mark the end of a phase in Egypt's revolution.

The deficiencies of the armed forces—this time brought
home—illuminated the deficiencies in the nation—and usefully
showed how much further the revolution still had to go.
'Emergent' or under-developed countries such as Egypt inevitably suffer from an extreme unevenness of capacity in their
citizens: the best are first-rate, the worst are terrible, the average is unreliable. In many fields the good are able to carry
the mediocre. But an organisation as large as a national
army, in operations where there are rarely second chances,
exposes these inherent weaknesses: then the chain is as strong
as its weakest link. It exposes, too, the social fissures—the
crippling legacy of the 'Bey-to-fellah' relationship—which pre-
vents the necessary rapport between officers and men.

In the 1880s, in a moment of despair, Mohamed Abdu once
wrote that Egypt would only 'reawaken to the touch of a just
dictator.' For fifteen years (he wrote) this man, possessed of
that will and tenacity his people notably lacked, would labour
to rebuild a corrupted society on wider, cleaner, popular
foundations, restoring to the fellah, in the process, his sense
of dignity and self-respect. At the end of this necessary—but
transitional—régime of fifteen years, the 'just dictator' would
'muster a great multitude who will support reform.'

In July 1967 Gamal Abdel Nasser and the small group of
'Free Officers' around him had presided over the destinies of
Egypt for fifteen years. By their command of the army, both
as a multi-purpose instrument of policy, and as a symbol of
authority, they had been able in this short space of time, and

with uniquely little bloodshed, to bring about a deep transformation of Egyptian society.

The old small wealthy ruling class, with its Levantine and
foreign ramifications, had passed into history. In its place, as
the army elements moved back, had increasingly emerged a
widening range of middle-class managers and technocrats,
holders of the keys of the large technological kingdoms of the
expanding public sector, which, in a limited sense, had replaced the great estates. But, unlike the pashas, these men were
part of a complex and growing structure; they were bound by
professional standards of global validity, and politically balanced by the organised rural smallholders and the increasing
numbers of organised workers.

The old Egyptian state had rested on a narrowly-based Cairo
bureaucracy, shuffled by a party spoils system. The new state
rested on a widening, increasingly technical and meritocratic
network which, through public sector trade and industry,
through the agricultural and co-operative system, through the
labour, education, health and welfare systems, now extended
to the furthermost corners of the country. And, increasingly,
this state was brought into focus, its elements geared together,
by the process and mystique of Planning, which the revolution
had installed at its hub. 'Targets' publicised by the mass media,
programmes for 'the next stage,' dramatised the challenge of
Egypt's situation, and used it to define a common frame and
purpose. The urgent accountancy of 'growth-rates' confined
politial choices.

After fifteen years of severely testing experience, this
modern structure was increasingly self-sustaining, the invisible
support of a revolution which was, in many respects, irreversible. Yet, as Nasser himself repeatedly stressed, political renewal was indispensable. Had the promised 'great multitude
who will support reform' appeared?

The 'new model' National Assembly had successfully
absorbed the shock of military defeat; the system of 'worker-
and-fellah' reserved seats was continued in the new elections
of 1969. The wider debate had been renewed. In the summer
of 1968 the nation-wide Arab Socialist Union had elected its
1,700-strong National Congress, its provincial officials, its
Central Committee of 150, its Higher Executive Committee.

The discussions of the 1,700-strong National Congress were televised and broadcast live. The relations between the Arab Socialist Union and other representative and institutional bodies—the Press, the trade unions, the co-operative organisation, the professional associations—remained unclear. The political system was still evolving.

What could hardly be doubted was the effort to spread responsibility and participation. Nasser still worried away at the old problem of how to widen the dialogue without disrupting it, groping now for some Egyptian path between the old 'liberalism' and the new 'socialism.' His March 1968 Manifesto, accepted by the nation in a referendum, looked to the future after the war emergency should be over. The 'programme' stressed the need for the Rule of Law as a safeguard of personal freedoms, and of freedom of expression and the Press. Nasser himself now talked of the 'open society,' although, characteristically he later explained that this meant 'open revolutionism,' not the liberal multi-party society of the West. He spoke, too, of the need to get rid of the 'fear complex' which caused people to keep silent about abuses by the powerful. Heikal, in *Al Ahram* in November 1968, analysed British and Russian political systems, enlarging on the need to develop, through the various social institutions, a multi-lateral debate.

The debate continues—as it has, intermittently and often muffled, ever since the revolution. Will Egyptian socialism survive it? Can the revolution indeed renew itself? I believe it can—if the Super-Powers will allow Egypt to find her own way. For the diagnosis of Nasser's Charter was written by Egyptian experience and history. In the conditions of the Nile Valley only a socialist system can provide the necessary capital accumulation and close direction necessary to meet the immense challenge of the people's poverty. This was a new sort of revolution, the revolution of the technologist and social engineer which forestalls a bloodier revolution. It still does so. Yet in Egypt it has also grown from the central nationalist tradition; the people are not cut off from their roots. It is a bourgeois revolution, but now 'Left-wing bourgeois'—and thus borne along on that prevailing, rose-tinted wind of change that blows over the Arab lands and so much of the Third World. Further to the Left a grittily secular Communism, 'the dictatorship of the proletariat,' poses small threat; and to the Right, Muslim fundamentalism, while still capable of trouble-making, has no practical programme to offer.

Meanwhile, the military disaster of June 1967, following on the easy—yet psychologically valuable—'victories' of the previous decade, will prove timely if it brings Egypt to a more self-critical approach. Complacency, a certain native smugness, has long appeared the country's greatest danger, and the shock of the Sinai débâcle is likely to be more effective than all Nasser's injunctions to self-criticism. Nor will Nasser himself any longer be treated as infallible and superhuman—as he never, in truth, asked to be. And that marks a new stage too.

With the Israelis on the Canal and in Sinai, Egypt was utterly dependent on Russia for the restoration of her shattered military forces. From that source re-equipment and training was promptly forthcoming. Did that imply, as some suggested, the failure of what had once been proudly hailed as 'positive neutralism'? Or could it, rather, still be counted among its fruits?

In the crisis of 1967, the Great Powers had not followed the pattern of action that they had in the earlier Middle East crisis of 1958. Then, the British and American forces had intervened in person in Lebanon and Jordan; in 1967, both they and the Russians remained on the sidelines. Washington and Moscow merely talked on the hot line. The celebrated 'vacuum in the Middle East' still sucked in large armaments and American and British and Russian instructors—but no longer, it seemed, external armies. And the difference, while precarious, was not merely nominal: it was an aspect of the new psychological, economic and social realities the Egyptian revolution had created in the Middle East.

In 1950, the region—whatever its nominal status—was still firmly under the 'management' of the Great Powers. For Britain, the Middle East was still mainly a matter of Imperial communications: the famous 'jugular' which, in 1945, Ernest Bevin complained that Russia, in Persia, was 'getting across.' Eighteen years later, Britain was preparing to withdraw from her last remaining outposts in the Arab world, and, following the example set somewhat earlier by France, seeking to substitute the bonds of trade for those of armed power. After

150 years in which the West strove unremittingly to block her, Russia was in the Mediterranean, both navally, and through a variety of industrial projects around its Arab shores. This, too, was one of the fruits of 'positive neutralism'—and of Mr John Foster Dulles's reaction to it.

Since Odessa is less than 500 miles from the Dardenelles and Soviet Russia possesses a large merchant marine, this long-dreaded appearance might perhaps now be considered un-remarkable. It remains, nevertheless, a fact of great significance for the future growth of the Arab world. For if the United States can accept with calm the new geopolitical realities—including that of a rising Arab world which wishes, above all, to be nobody's slave—and if Russia, likewise, can refrain from a too ardent application to the old Middle Eastern chess-game, this region of the world can become a solid bridge across which East and West—in every sense of those words—can come to terms. If, on the other hand, the Super-Powers prefer the weapons of brute power to trade and aid, and, if in pursuit of 'unparochial' interests, each seeks to establish its captive client states, they will not only prolong the ordeal of the Arabs, but may render it also the ordeal of the world.

The Arabs are a people for whom too much of history has been aftermath; and in the summer of 1967 history seemed aftermath still. For if, from Aswan, from the steps of the Kalabsha temple above the High Dam, there still opened up a brave vista of an expanding Arab future, 800 miles to the north, on the Mediterranean shore, Iskanderia, the city of Alexandria, seemed to echo the words of Gibbon, describing the Islamic East in the wake of the Crusades . . . 'and a mournful and solitary silence prevailed along the coast which has so long resounded with the world's debate.'

'Alexandria,' sighed an Alexandrian, a Muslim, 'used to be the most cosmopolitan city in the Mediterranean. But not now!' Three wars of Zionists and Arabs have taken their deadly toll. Alexandria's Greeks and Jews, who contributed much to Egypt's life and progress in the past, have largely departed. Outside the faded splendours of the Athenios café, that pillared hall of the Five o'Clock Tea, an old sheikh in the turban of El Azhar sits endlessly at a pavement table, gazing with his single bleary eye at the opposite wall.

Once again, in the aftermath of the 1967 war, as when Gibbon wrote, communication between the Mediterranean's Arab and European shores seemed totally severed. Inhabiting lands littered with the remains of Greece and Rome, the ninety million people of the Arab world appeared to the British newspaper reader almost as distant and as alien as the Chinese. But the silence will not last; and the Debate—which could be rewarding—will be resumed. For the Egyptians are a tolerant and a kindly people and they would not have had it thus. The Egyptians love Cairo, but they also love Alexandria and what it represents. They will surrender neither love. Nor, equally, can the West and America afford exclusion from this crossroads of continents which Napoleon once called 'the most important country in the world.' Geography, in a sense the master-theme of this study, remains so to the end.

SOURCES AND BIBLIOGRAPHY

The view of this book and much of its material spring from personal observation and investigation in Egypt and other Arab countries in 1952, 1955, 1964 and 1965. In the latter year I travelled overland to the Nile Valley in my own car, not only to assist the process of seeing Egypt in the perspective of the Arab world to its west and east, but also to be able to move freely about the country with the minimum of official guidance. I did in fact cover it from end to end and side to side, stopping where I chose. Not that the Egyptian authorities were unco-operative in meeting my many requests over a long period: on the contrary I became much indebted to a large number of people in all parts of Egypt, official and non-official alike, for their willing help and friendship. Since they are too numerous to list and to select would be invidious, I must ask them to accept this assurance that they are remembered with gratitude.

Although a good deal has been written about the 1952 coup and the political background of the Free Officers' movement, and also about the international aspects of 'Nasserism,' books on the extensive agrarian, economic and socio-political reforms in Egypt are relatively few. On the Egyptian revolution's 19th- and 20th-century antecedents, from the arrival of Bonaparte to the rise and fall of the Wafd, there is a large and often curious literature, although that astonishing character, Mohamed Ali, is still inadequately covered. Much of this is, of course, highly ethnocentric, and the British perspective in particular is greatly coloured by the impressive flow of pro-consular memoirs, including the classic works of Cromer, Milner and Lloyd. Lately this source has become an interesting index of changing attitudes. Thus Sir Tom Hickinbotham, Governor of Aden in 1956, in his memoirs of 1958, and Sir Charles Belgrave, the veteran Adviser of the Sheikh of Bahrein, in his memoirs of 1960, still maintain an essentially Cromerian stance, but by 1963 Mr Harold Ingrams, Adviser, Aden Protectorate, is ready to concede that 'boys will be boys,' and a year later with the memoirs of Sir Charles Johnston, late Ambassador to Jordan, then High Commissioner Aden and Protectorate, we arrive at the breezy, hobnobbing Head, a Mountbatten of the Arabian peninsula, whose mission is the decent transfer of power.

Since the Second World War, however, this restricted and over-political angle of vision, whether nationalist or 'imperialist,' has been increasingly overtaken by the sociological approach to the Arab world developed in the multiplying centres of Middle Eastern studies in the United States. While this approach may sometimes give rise to a certain bland unreality, it nevertheless offers emancipation from the fearful incubus of political and religious prejudice that has bedevilled the subject. Unfortunately it is less easily applied to the Arab-Israeli conflict. Sir Ronald Storrs long ago wrote: 'Two hours of Arab grievances drive me into the Synagogue, while after an intensive course of Zionist propaganda I am prepared to embrace Islam' and any student of the literature in this field will still recognise the feeling. Many books are so single-eyed that it is necessary to fit a book from one 'side' into a book from the other like a jigsaw puzzle before cause can be married to its effect. For this reason, 'crossbench' testimony is essential —such as that of Storrs himself from the earlier days of the Mandate; of Albert Hyamson, Jewish, but also a Mandate civil servant and head of the vital Immigration Department; of Christopher Sykes, a recent surveyor; of the United Nations 'Palestine' truce supervisors like Generals Burns, Carl von Horn and Commander E. H. Hutchison; of Walter Schwarz, a journalist investigating the true situation of the Arabs in Israel; or of Alfred M. Lilienthal, as a non-Zionist Jewish-American. The recent biography of Ben Gurion by Michel Bar-Zohar, who was given access to Ben Gurion's private diaries and papers, is more than usually frank and instructive, and so, on a more informal level, is the first-hand account of the Israeli journalist and Knesset member, Uri Avnery, *Israel Without Zionists*.

The books somewhat arbitrarily classified below have been used in the preparation of this one. I have, I hope with due caution, drawn on the reports of Government Departments, on various official compilations of statistics, such publications as the UAR Year Book, the annual volumes of the speeches of

Gamal Abdel Nasser, and the Arab Political Encyclopedia, a periodical compendium of decrees, treaties, contracts, Ministerial statements, the proceedings of the National Assembly and Arab Socialist Union, and so on. In addition, there is the embarrassing profusion of the newspaper and periodical Press, not only of Egypt, but of the surrounding Arab countries. The books listed below are published in London unless otherwise stated.

EGYPT: THE HISTORICAL SETTING

ANCIENT

J. H. Breasted: *A History of Egypt to the Persian Conquest* (1905)
W. B. Emery: *Archaic Egypt* (1961)
E. M. Forster: *Alexandria* (3rd edition, New York, 1961)
S. R. K. Glanville: *The Legacy of Egypt* (Oxford, 1942)
H. Wood Jarvis: *Pharaoh to Farouk* (1955)
H. Kees: *Ancient Egypt, a Cultural Topography* (1955)
Herodotus: *The Histories* (trans. A. de Selincourt, 1954)
M. A. Murray: *The Splendour that was Egypt* (1949)
Karl A. Wittfogel: *Oriental Despotism* (Yale, 1957)

THE 'AWAKENING,' MOHAMED ALI AND THE 'NEW LEVANT'

John Barker: *Syria and Egypt under the Last Five Sultans* (1876)
Charles Beatty: *Ferdinand de Lesseps* (1956)
D. A. Cameron: *Egypt in the Nineteenth Century* (1896)
H. Dodwell: *Mohamed Ali, Founder of Modern Egypt* (Cambridge, 1931)
Shafik Ghurbal: *The Beginnings of the Egyptian Question and the Rise of Mohamed Ali* (1928)
J. Christopher Herold: *Bonaparte in Egypt* (1963)
David S. Landes: *Bankers and Pashas* (1958)
Edward Lane: *The Manners and Customs of Modern Egyptians* (1936: Everyman 1954 Edition)
John Marlowe: *The Making of the Suez Canal* (1964)
Mustafa Sabri. *L'Empire Egyptién sous Mohamed Ali* (1930)

Augustus Wild: *Mixed Grill in Cairo* (1952)

BRITISH RULE AND THE RISE OF EGYPTIAN NATIONALISM

J. M. Ahmed: *The Intellectual Origins of Egyptian Nationalism* (Oxford, 1960)
W. S. Blunt: *My Secret Diaries* (1919)
Valentine Chirol: *The Egyptian Problem* (1921)
Lord Cromer: *Modern Egypt* (1908)
George A. Lloyd: *Egypt Since Cromer* (1933)
Viscount Milner: *England in Egypt* (1892)
Mary Rowlatt: *Founders of Modern Egypt* (1959)
Nadav Safran: *Egypt in Search of Political Community* (Harvard, 1961)
H. J. Schonfield: *The Suez Canal* (1939)
Sir George Young: *Egypt* (1927)
(for aspects overlapping with pan-Arab nationalism, see below)

EGYPT: THE REVOLUTION AND AFTER, 1952-67

POLITICAL AND GENERAL

M. Samir Ahmed: *Nasser's Arab Socialism* (Harvard, 1966)
Rasched el Barawi: *The Military Coup in Egypt* (Cairo, 1952)
P. Calvocoressi (ed.): *Suez, Ten Years After* (1967)
Erskine Childers: *The Road to Suez* (1962)
J. Heyworth Dunne: *Religious and Political Trends in Modern Egypt* (Washington, 1950)
Abul Fath: *L'Affaire Nasser* (Paris, 1962)
Sayegh Fayez: 'The Structure of Nasser's Socialism' in No, 4, *Middle Eastern Affairs* (Oxford, 1963)
Joachim Joesten: *Nasser, the Rise to Power* (1960)
Jean and Simonne Lacouture: *Egypt in Transition* (1958)
Tom Little: *Egypt* (1960)
Tom Little: *Modern Egypt* (1967)
Barrie St Clair McBride: *Farouk of Egypt* (1967)
Anouar Abdel Malek: *Egypte, société militaire* (Paris, 1962)
P. Mansfield: *Nasser's Egypt* (1965)
Gamal Abdel Nasser: *The Philosophy of the Revolution* (Cairo, 1954)

General Mohamed Neguib: *Egypt's Destiny* (1953)

Anthony Nutting: *No End of a Lesson—the Story of Suez* (1967)

Hassan Riad: *Egypte Nasserienne* (Paris 1964)

Robert St John: *The Boss* (1961)

Michael Stern: *Farouk* (New York, 1965)

Desmond Stewart: *Young Egypt* (1958)

Keith Wheeler: *Nasser's New Egypt* (New York, 1960)

Anwar el Sadat: *Revolt on the Nile* (1957)

G. C. Stevens: *Egypt, Yesterday and Today* (New York, 1963)

R. J. Vatikiotis: *The Egyptian Army in Politics* (Indiana University Press, 1961)

R. J. Vatikiotis ed.: *Egypt Since the Revolution* (1968)

Georges Vaucher: *Gamal Abdel Nasser et son équipe* (Paris, 1954)

OFFICIAL PUBLICATIONS

The Goals of the Revolution (1954); *The Charter* (1961); *The Constitution, Basic Law and Rules of Procedure of the National Assembly* (1964); *The Statute of the Arab Socialist Union* (1962).

AGRICULTURE, AGRARIAN REFORM, IRRIGATION, RECLAMATION

H. Addison: *Sun and Shadow at Aswan* (1959)

H. H. Ayrout: *The Egyptian Peasant* (Boston, 1963)

Gabriel Baer: *Land Ownership in Modern Egypt* (Oxford, 1962)

C. H. Brown: *Egyptian Cotton* (1953)

G. R. Gliddon: *A Memoir of Cotton in Egypt* (1841)

Leslie Greener: *High Dam over Nubia* (1962)

H. E. Hurst: *The Nile* (1952)

C. S. Jarvis: *Three Deserts* (1931)

Ivan Komzin: *The High Dam* (Moscow)

Tom Little: *High Dam at Aswan* (1965)

Liverpool Raw Cotton Annual special number 1963

H. W. Marden: *A Geography of Egypt and the Sudan* (1906)

Sayed Marei: *Agrarian Reform in Egypt* (Cairo, 1957)

Sayed Marei: *UAR Agriculture Enters a New Age* (Cairo, 1960)

Gabriel Saab: *The Egyptian Agrarian Reform, 1952-62* (Oxford, 1962)

Doreen Warriner: *Land Reform and Development in the Middle East* (Oxford, 1962)

OFFICIAL PUBLICATIONS

Dr Hassan Abussoud, *Land Reform in Egypt* (Cairo, 1954); *Agrarian Reform and Land Reclamation* (1952-63); *Irrigation and Drainage in Egypt* (1962); Y. M. Simaika, *Alternative Sources of Water Supply in the UAR*; Mohsin al Didi, *The Hundredth Anniversary of Ashmouni Cotton*; Idris Hussein, *Hydrological Investigations in the Egyptian Deserts*.

ECONOMIC AND INDUSTRIAL

Board of Trade: *Egypt, Monthly Economic Reports* (1950-1956)

A. E. Crouchley: *The Economic Development of Modern Egypt* (1938)

B. Hansen & G. A. Marzouk: *Development and Economic Policy in the U.A.R.* (Amsterdam, 1965)

F. Harbison and A. Ibrahim: *Human Resources for Egyptian Enterprise* (New York, 1958)

Charles Issawi: *Egypt, an Economic and Social Analysis* (Oxford, 1947)

Charles Issawi: *Egypt in Mid-Century* (Oxford, 1954)

Charles Issawi: *Egypt in Revolution* (Oxford, 1963)

P. O'Brien: *The Revolution in Egypt's Economic System* (Oxford 1966)

OFFICIAL PUBLICATIONS

Permanent Council for the Development of National Production Report (1954); *General Frame of the Five Year Plan* (1960); *Twelve Years of Industrial Development in the UAR* (1952-64); *Co-operative Production and Small Industries Report* (1962); *National Institute of Management Development Case Studies*; *National Bank of Egypt Quarterly Bulletin*.

SOCIAL

R. Ainslie: *The Press in Africa* (1966)

Rhoda Gordon Amin: *Seven Years in the Sun* (1959)

Morroe Berger: *Bureaucracy and Government in Modern Egypt* (Princeton, 1957)

Ion Davies: *African Trade Unions* (1966)

Dr Ahmed Hussein: *Rural Social Centres in Egypt* (Cairo, 1961)

Abdel Moneim Ismail: *Drama and Society in Contemporary Egypt* (Cairo, 1967)

C. S. Jarvis: *Desert and Delta* (1938)

Simonne Lacouture: *Egypt* (1963)

Emine Foat Tugay: *Three Centuries, a Family Chronicle of Turkey and Egypt* (Oxford, 1963)

OFFICIAL PUBLICATIONS

UAR Trade Union Federation: *Labour Legislation, Past and Present*; *Trade Unions in the UAR*. Arab Socialist Union: *L'organisation de la Jeunesse Socialiste* (1966); Dr El-Said Mustafa El-Said, *L'Expansion de l'Enseignement Supérieure dans la RAU*, 1960; Dr Alsayed Mahmoud Zaki, *An Outline of the Local Government System in the UAR* (1963); Law No 103, 1961, for Reorganising El Azhar and its Affiliated Institutions.

THE ARAB WORLD

GENERAL

A. J. Arberry: *Aspects of Islamic Civilisation* (1964)

Edward Atiyah: *The Arabs* (1955)

Morroe Berger: *The Arab World Today* (1962)

Morroe Berger: *The New Metropolis in the Arab World* (1963)

Jacques Berque: *The Arabs, their History and Future* (1964)

Alfred Guillaume: *Islam* (1954)

Charles D. Cremeans: *The Arabs and the World* (New York, 1963)

Sylvia Haim (ed.): *Arab Nationalism, an Anthology* (Berkeley, 1964)

Manfred Halpern: *The Politics of Social Change in the Middle East and North Africa* (Princeton, 1963)

David Hirst: *Oil and Public Opinion in the Middle East* (1966)

Taha Hussein: *An Egyptian Childhood, an Autobiography* (1932)

The Koran: translations and commentaries of M. M. Pickthall, (1953), J. M. Rodwell (1861), George Sale (1734)

Rom Landau: *Islam and the Arabs* (1958)

T. E. Lawrence: *The Seven Pillars of Wisdom* (1935)

Reuben Levy: *The Social Structure of Islam* (1965)

Bernard Lewis: *The Arabs in History* (1954)

R. W. Macdonald: *The League of Arab States* (Princeton, 1965)

Anthony Nutting: *The Arabs* (1964)

Steven Runciman: *A History of the Crusades* (1954)

J. J. Saunders, *Aspects of the Crusades* (Canterbury, N.Z., 1962)

Hisham B. Sharabi: *Nationalism and Revolution in the Arab World* (Princeton, 1966)

Benjamin Shwadran: *The Middle East, Oil and the Great Powers* (New York, 1959)

Wilfred C. Smith: *Islam in Modern History* (Princeton, 1957)

Wayne S. Vucinich: *The Ottoman Empire, its Record and Legacy* (Princeton, 1965)

W. Montgomery Watt: *Muhammad, Prophet and Statesman* (Oxford, 1961)

Peter Worsley: *The Third World* (1964)

THE ARAB EAST

Gabriel Baer: *Population and Society in the Arab East* (1964)

Gertrude Bell: *Selected Letters* (1955)

Lord Birdwood: *Nuri es Said* (1959)

Alfred Bonné: *State and Economics in the Middle East* (Revised edition, 1955)

Emile Bustani, *March Arabesque* (1961)

Caractacus: *Revolution in Iraq* (1959)

Robin Feddan: *Syria and Lebanon* (1956)

S. N. Fisher: *The Middle East in History* (New York, 1959)

W. B. Fisher: *The Middle East* (Fifth edition, 1963)

Gerald de Gaury: *Three Kings in Baghdad, 1921-58* (1961)

Sir John Glubb: *A Soldier with the Arabs* (1957)

George L. Harris: *Jordan, its People, its Society, its History* (New York, 1968)

Michael Ionides: *Divide and Rule* (1960)

Malcolm Kerr: *The Arab Cold War, 1958-64* (Oxford, 1955)

R. C. Kingsbury and N. J. G. Pounds: *An Atlas of Middle Eastern Affairs* (1964)

G. E. Kirk: *Contemporary Arab Politics* (1961)

Walter Z. Laqueur: *Communism and Nationalism in the Middle East* (Third edition, 1961)

Daniel Lerner: *The Passing of Traditional Society: the Modernisation of the Middle East* (New York, 1958)

Bernard Lewis: *The Middle East and the West* (1963)

S. Longrigg: *The Middle East, a Social Geography* (1963)

Elizabeth Monroe: *Britain's Moment in the Middle East, 1914-56* (1963)

James Morris: *The Hashemite Kings* (1959)

Kermit Roosevelt: *Arabs, Oil and History* (1949)

Royal Institute of International Affairs: *The Middle East, a Political and Economic Survey* (1951)

Patrick Seale: *The Struggle for Syria* (Oxford, 1965)

G. C. Stevens (ed.): *The United States and the Middle East* (Columbia University, 1964)

Desmond Stewart: *The New Babylon, a Portrait of Iraq* (1956)

Desmond Stewart: *Orphan with a Hoop, the life of Emile Bustani* (1967)

Peter Young: *Bedouin Command* (1956)

ARABIA AND THE GULF

José Arnold: *Golden Swords and Pots and Pans* (1964)

H. C. Armstrong: *Lord of Arabia* (1924)

Charles Belgrave: *Personal Column* (1960)

Wahba Hafiz: *Arabian Days* (1964)

Gerald de Gaury: *Faisal, King of Saudi Arabia* (1964)

Hans Helfritz: *The Yemen* (1958)

Sir Tom Hickinbotham: *Aden* (1958)
Ralph Hewins: *A Golden Dream* (1963)
David Howarth: *The Desert King* (1964)
Harold Ingrams: *The Yemen* (1963)
Charles Johnston: *The View from Steamer Point* (1964)
The Economic Development of Kuwait (The Johns Hopkins Press, Baltimore, 1965)
G. A. Lipsky and others: *Saudi Arabia, its People, Society and Culture* (New Haven, 1958)
John Marlowe: *The Persian Gulf in the Twentieth Century* (1962)
H. St John Philby: *My Forty Years in the Wilderness* (1957)
Wendell Phillips: *Unknown Oman* (1966)
Dana Adams Smith: *Yemen, the Forgotten War* (1968)
Walter Thesinger: *Arabian Sands* (1959)
John Tunstall: *Vanishing Kingdoms* (1966)

THE ARAB WEST

Nevill Barbour: *Morocco* (1965)
Jacques Baulin: *The Arab Rôle in Africa* (1962)
Edward Behr: *The Algerian Problem* (1961)
Richard M. Brace: *Morocco, Algeria, Tunisia* (New Jersey, 1964)
Richard and Joan Brace: *Ordeal in Algeria* (Princeton, 1960)
Nina Epton: *The Libyan Story* (1952)
Daniel Guérin: *L'Algérie que se cherche* (Paris, 1964)
André Maurois: *Lyautey* (1931)
Robert Merle: *Ben Bella* (1967)
C. A. Micaud: *Tunisia, the Politics of Moderation* (1964)

THE ARAB-ISRAELI CONFLICT

Uri Avnery: *Israel Without Zionism* (1968)
Michel Bar-Zohar: *The Armed Prophet* (1967)
D. Bawly and D. Kimche: *The Sandstorm* (1967)
David Ben Gurion: *The Rebirth and Destiny of Israel* (1949)
David Ben Gurion: *The Years of Challenge* (1964)
Norman Bentwich: *Mandate Memories* (1965)
General E. L. M. Burns: *Between Arab and Jew* (1962)
R. S. and W. S. Churchill: *The Six Day War* (1967)

H. V. Cooke: *Israel, a Blessing or a Curse?* (1960)

R. H. S. Crossman: *A Nation Reborn* (1960)

Moshe Dayan: *Diary of the Sinai Campaign* (1966)

Abba Eban: *The Voice of Israel* (1958)

Maurice Edelman: *Ben Gurion* (1964)

Walter Eytan: *The First Ten Years* (1958)

James Forrestal: *The Forrestal Diaries* (1952)

Gerold Frank: *The Deed* (New York, 1963)

Georges Friedmann: *The End of the Jewish People?* (1967)

Sir John Glubb: *The Middle East Crisis* (1967)

Louis Golding: *The Jewish Problem* (1938)

General Carl von Horn: *Soldiering for Peace* (1966)

E. H. Hutchison: *Violent Truce* (1956)

A. M. Hyamson: *Palestine under the Mandate* (1950)

Jon and David Kimche: *Both Sides of the Hill* (1960)

Arthur Koestler: *Thieves in the Night* (1946)

Walter Laqueur: *The Road to War, 1967* (1968)

A. M. Lilienthal: *The Other Side of the Coin* (New York, 1965)

A. M. Lilienthal: *What Price Israel?* (Chicago, 1953)

Roderick Macleish: *The Sun Stood Still* (1967)

James Parkes: *A History of the Jewish People* (1962)

Moshe Pearlman: *Ben Gurion Looks Back* (1965)

Stewart Perowne: *The One Remains* (1954)

Maxime Rodinson: *Israel and the Arabs* (1968)

Walter Schwarz: *The Arabs in Israel* (1959)

Ahmed Shukairy: *Liberation, not Negotiation* (Beirut, 1966)

Sir Ronald Storrs: *Orientations* (1943)

Christopher Sykes: *Crossroads to Israel* (1962)

Alex Weingrod: *Israel, Group Relations in a New Society* (1965)

Chaim Weizmann: *Trial and Error* (1949)

INDEX

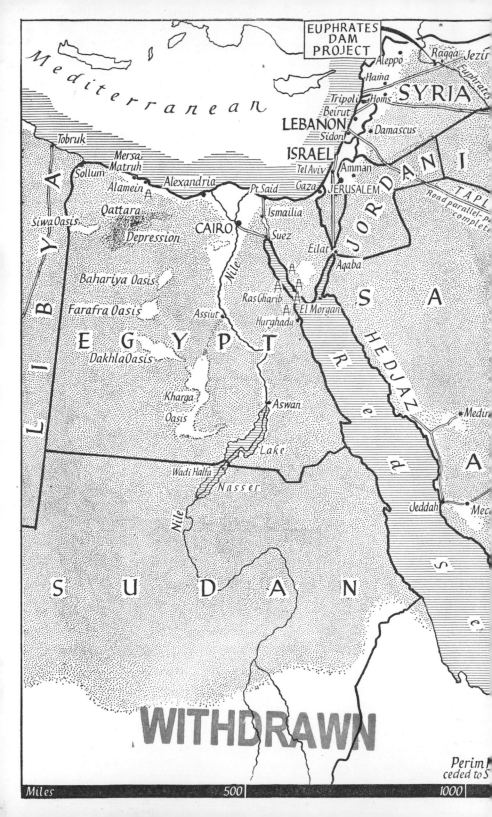

EUPHRATES
DAM
PROJECT

Mediterranean

Cyprus

Tobruk

Mersa
Matruh

Sollum

Alamein

Qattara
Depression

Siwa Oasis

Alexandria

CAIRO

Ismailia

Suez

Pt. Said

Tel Aviv
Gaza

ISRAEL

JERUSALEM

LEBANON
Beirut
Sidon

Tripoli
Homs
Hama

Aleppo

Raqqa
Jezir

Euphrates

SYRIA

Damascus

Amman

JORDAN

TAPL
Road parallel...
complete

Eilat
Aqaba

L   I   B   Y   A

Bahariya Oasis

Farafra Oasis

Assiut

E   G   Y   P   T

Dakhla Oasis

Kharga
Oasis

Ras Gharib

Hurghada

El Morgan

R

e

d

H   E   D   J   A   Z

S

A

Medir

Aswan

Lake

Nasser

Wadi Halfa

Nile

S   U   D   A   N

S   e

Jeddah

Mec

A

WITHDRAWN

Perim
ceded to S

| Miles | 500 | 1000 |